DATA STRUCTURES USING C++

SECOND EDITION

D.S. MALIK

COURSE TECHNOLOGY
CENGAGE Learning

Australia • Brazil • Japan • Korea • Mexico • Singapore • Spain • United Kingdom • United States

COURSE TECHNOLOGY
CENGAGE Learning

Data Structures Using C++, Second Edition
D.S. Malik

Executive Editor: Marie Lee
Acquisitions Editor: Amy Jollymore
Senior Product Manager: Alyssa Pratt
Editorial Assistant: Zina Kresin
Marketing Manager: Bryant Chrzan
Content Project Manager: Heather Furrow
Art Director: Faith Brosnan
Image credit: © Fancy Photography/Veer
   (Royalty Free)
Cover Designer: Roycroft Design
Compositor: Integra

For product information and technology assistance, contact us at
Cengage Learning Customer & Sales Support, 1-800-354-9706
For permission to use material from this text or product, submit all requests online at **cengage.com/permissions**

Further permissions questions can be emailed to
permissionrequest@cengage.com

ISBN-13: 978-0-324-78201-1
ISBN-10: 0-324-78201-2

Course Technology
20 Channel Center Street
Boston, MA 02210
USA

Cengage Learning is a leading provider of customized learning solutions with office locations around the globe, including Singapore, the United Kingdom, Australia, Mexico, Brazil, and Japan. Locate your local office at: **international.cengage.com/region**

Cengage Learning products are represented in Canada by Nelson Education, Ltd.

For your lifelong learning solutions, visit
www.cengage.com/coursetechnology

Purchase any of our products at your local college store or at our preferred online store **www.ichapters.com**

Printed in the United States of America
1 2 3 4 5 6 7 15 14 13 12 11 10 09

TO

My Parents

BRIEF CONTENTS

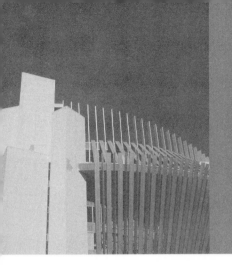

TABLE OF CONTENTS

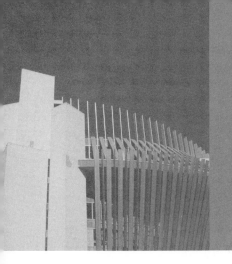

PREFACE TO SECOND EDITION

Welcome to *Data Structures Using C++, Second Edition*. Designed for the CS2 C++ course, this text will provide a breath of fresh air to you and your students. The CS2 course typically completes the programming requirements of the Computer Science curriculum. This text is a culmination and development of my classroom notes throughout more than 50 semesters of teaching successful programming and data structures to computer science students.

This book is a continuation of the work started to write the CS1 book *C++ Programming: From Problem Analysis to Program Design, Fourth Edition*. The approach taken in this book to present the material is similar to the one used in the CS1 book and therefore driven by the students' demand for clarity and readability. The material was written and rewritten until students felt comfortable with it. Most of the examples in this book resulted from student interaction in the classroom.

This book assumes that you are familiar with the basic elements of C++ such as data types, control structures, functions and parameters, and arrays. However, if you need to review these concepts or you have taken Java as a first program language, you will find the relevant material in Appendix G. If you need to quickly review CS1 topics in more details than given in Appendix G, you are referred to the C++ programming book by the author listed in the preceding paragraph and also to Appendix H. In addition, some adequate mathematics background such as college algebra is required.

Changes in the Second Edition

In the second edition, the following changes have been implemented:

- In Chapter 1, the discussion of algorithm analysis is expanded with additional examples.

- In Chapter 3, a section on creating and manipulating dynamic two-dimensional arrays, a section on virtual functions, and a section on abstract classes is included.

- To create generic code to process data in linked lists, Chapter 5 uses the concept of abstract classes to capture the basic properties of linked lists and then derive two separate classes to process unordered and ordered lists.

- In Chapter 6, a new section on how to use recursion and backtracking to solve sudoku problems is added.

- Chapters 7 and 8 use the concept of abstract classes to capture the basic properties of stacks and queues and then discuss various implementations of stacks and queues.

- In Chapter 9, the discussion of hashing is expanded with additional examples illustrating how to resolve collisions.

- In Chapter 10, we have added the Shellsort algorithm.

- Chapter 11 contains a new section on B-trees.

- Chapter 12, on graphs, contains a new section on how to find Euler circuits in a graph.

- Appendix F provides a detailed discussion of the analysis of insertion sort and quicksort algorithms.

- Throughout the book, new exercises and programming exercises have been added.

These changes were implemented based on comments from the reviewers of the second proposal and readers of the first edition.

Approach

Intended as a second course in computer programming, this book focuses on the data structure part as well as OOD. The programming examples given in this book effectively use OOD techniques to solve and program a particular problem.

Chapter 1 introduces the software engineering principles. After describing the life cycle of a software, this chapter discusses why algorithm analysis is important and introduces the Big-O notation used in algorithm analysis. There are three basic principles of OOD—encapsulation, inheritance, and polymorphism. Encapsulation in C++ is achieved via the use of classes. The second half of this chapter discusses user-defined classes. If you are familiar with how to create and use your own classes, you can skip this section. This chapter also discusses a basic OOD technique to solve a particular problem.

Chapter 2 continues with the principles of OOD and discusses inheritance and two types of polymorphism. If you are familiar with how inheritance, operator overloading, and templates work in C++, then you can skip this chapter.

The three basic data types in C++ are simple, structured, and pointers. The book assumes that you are familiar with the simple data types as well as arrays (a structured data type). The structured data type class is introduced in Chapter 1. Chapter 3 discusses in detail how the pointer data type works in C++. This chapter also discusses the relationship between pointers and classes. Taking advantages of pointers and templates, this chapter explains and develops a generic code to implement lists using dynamic arrays. Chapter 3 also discusses virtual functions and abstract classes.

C++ is equipped with the Standard Template Library (STL). Among other things, the STL provides code to process lists (contiguous or linked), stacks, and queues. Chapter 4 discusses some of the STL's important features and shows how to use certain tools provided by the STL in a program. In particular, this chapter discusses the sequence containers **vector** and `deque`. The ensuing chapters explain how to develop your own code to implement and manipulate data, as well as how to use professionally written code.

Chapter 5 discusses linked lists in detail, by first discussing the basic properties of linked lists such as item insertion and deletion and how to construct a linked list. This chapter then develops a generic code to process data in a single linked list. Doubly linked lists are also discussed in some detail. Linked lists with header and trailer nodes and circular linked lists are also introduced. This chapter also discusses the STL class `list`.

Chapter 6 introduces recursion and gives various examples to show how to use recursion to solve a problem, as well as think in terms of recursion.

Chapters 7 and 8 discuss stacks and queues in detail. In addition to showing how to develop your own generic codes to implement stacks and queues, these chapters also explain how the STL classes `stack` and `queue` work. The programming code developed in these chapters is generic.

Chapter 9 is concerned with the searching algorithms. After analyzing the sequential search algorithm, it discusses the binary search algorithm and provides a brief analysis of this algorithm. After giving a lower bound on comparisons-based search algorithms, this chapter discusses hashing in detail.

Sorting algorithms such as selection sort, insertion sort, Shellsort, quicksort, mergesort, and heapsort are introduced and discussed in Chapter 10. Chapter 11 introduces and discusses binary trees and B-trees. Chapter 12 introduces graphs and discusses graph algorithms such as shortest path, minimum spanning tree, topological sorting, and how to find Euler circuits in a graph.

Chapter 13 continues with the discussion of STL started in Chapter 4. In particular, it introduces the STL associative containers and algorithms.

Appendix A lists the reserved words in C++. Appendix B shows the precedence and associativity of the C++ operators. Appendix C lists the ASCII (American Standard Code for Information Interchange) and EBCDIC (Extended Binary Code Decimal Interchange) character sets. Appendix D lists the C++ operators that can be overloaded. Appendix E discusses some of the most widely used library routines. Appendix F contains the detailed analysis of the insertion sort and quicksort algorithms. Appendix G has two objectives. One of its objectives is to provide a quick review of the basic elements of C++. The other objective of Appendix G is, while giving a review of the basic elements of C++, to compare the basic concepts such as data types, control structures, functions and parameters, and arrays of the languages C++ and Java. Therefore, if you have taken Java as a first programming language, Appendix G helps familiarize you with these basic elements of C++. Appendix H provides a list of references for further study and to find additional C++ topics not reviewed in Appendix G. Appendix I gives the answers to odd-numbered exercises in the text.

How to Use This Book

The main objective of this book is to teach data structure topics using C++ as well as to use OOD to solve a particular problem. To do so, the book discusses data structures such as linked lists, stacks, queues, and binary trees. C++'s Standard Template Library (STL) also provides the necessary code to implement these data structures. However, our emphasis is to teach you how to develop your own code. At the same time, we also want you to learn how to use professionally written code. Chapter 4 of this book introduces STL. In the subsequent chapters, after explaining how to develop your own code, we also illustrate how to use the existing STL code. The book can, therefore, be used in various ways. If you are not interested in STL, say in the first reading, then you can skip Chapter 4 and in the subsequent chapters, whenever we discuss a particular STL component, you can skip that section.

Chapter 6 discusses recursion. However, Chapter 6 is not a prerequisite for Chapters 7 and 8. If you read Chapter 6 after these chapters, then you can skip the section "Removing Recursion" in Chapter 7, and read this section after reading Chapter 6. Even though Chapter 6 is not required to study Chapter 9, ideally, Chapters 9 and 10 should be studied in sequence. Therefore, we recommend that you should study Chapter 6 before Chapter 9. The following diagram illustrates the dependency of chapters.

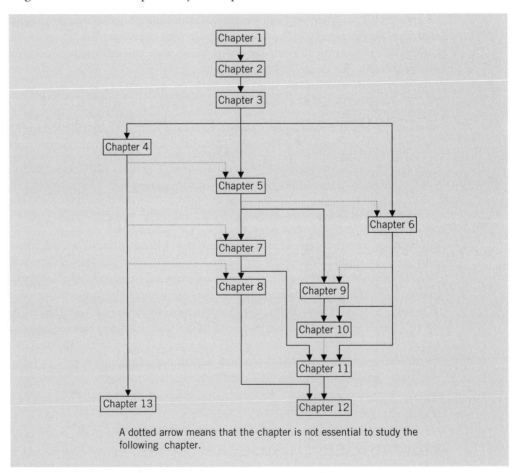

A dotted arrow means that the chapter is not essential to study the following chapter.

FIGURE 1   Chapter dependency diagram

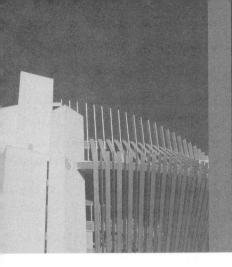

FEATURES OF THE BOOK

The features of this book are conducive to independent learning. From beginning to end, the concepts are introduced at an appropriate pace. The presentation enables students to learn the material in comfort and with confidence. The writing style of this book is simple and straightforward. It parallels the teaching style of a classroom. Here is a brief summary of the various pedagogical features in each chapter:

- *Learning objectives* offer an outline of C++ programming concepts that will be discussed in detail within the chapter.

- *Notes* highlight important facts regarding the concepts introduced in the chapter.

- Visual diagrams, both extensive and exhaustive, illustrate difficult concepts. The book contains over 295 figures.

- Numbered *Examples* within each chapter illustrate the key concepts with relevant code.

- *Programming Examples* are programs featured at the end of each chapter. These examples contain the accurate, concrete stages of Input, Output, Problem Analysis and Algorithm Design, and a Program Listing. Moreover, the problems in these programming examples are solved and programmed using OOD.

- *Quick Review* offers a summary of the concepts covered within the chapter.

- *Exercises* further reinforce learning and ensure that students have, in fact, learned the material.

- *Programming Exercises* challenge students to write C++ programs with a specified outcome.

The writing style of this book is simple and straightforward. Before introducing a key concept, we explain why certain elements are necessary. The concepts introduced are then explained using examples and small programs.

Each chapter contains two types of programs. First, small programs called out as numbered Examples are used to explain key concepts. Each line of the programming code in these examples is numbered. The program, illustrated through a sample run, is then explained line-by-line. The rationale behind each line is discussed in detail.

As mentioned above, the book also features numerous case studies called Programming Examples. These Programming Examples form the backbone of the book. The programs are designed to be methodical and user-friendly. Beginning with Problem Analysis, the Programming Example is then followed by Algorithm Design. Every step of the algorithm is then coded in C++. In addition to teaching problem-solving techniques, these detailed programs show the user how to implement concepts in an actual C++ program. I strongly recommend that students study the Programming Examples very carefully in order to learn C++ effectively.

Quick Review sections at the end of each chapter reinforce learning. After reading the chapter, readers can quickly walk through the highlights of the chapter and then test themselves using the ensuing Exercises. Many readers refer to the Quick Review as a way to quickly review the chapter before an exam.

All source code and solutions have been written, compiled, and quality assurance tested. Programs can be compiled with various compilers such as Microsoft Visual C++ 2008.

SUPPLEMENTAL RESOURCES

The following supplemental materials are available when this book is used in a classroom setting. All of the teaching tools available with this book are provided to the instructor on a single CD-ROM.

Electronic Instructor's Manual

The Instructor's Manual that accompanies this textbook includes:

- Additional instructional material to assist in class preparation, including suggestions for lecture topics
- Solutions to all the end-of-chapter materials, including the Programming Exercises

ExamView®

This textbook is accompanied by ExamView, a powerful testing software package that allows instructors to create and administer printed, computer (LAN-based), and Internet exams. ExamView includes hundreds of questions that correspond to the topics covered in this text, enabling students to generate detailed study guides that include page references for further review. These computer-based and Internet testing components allow students to take exams at their computers, and save the instructor time because each exam is graded automatically.

PowerPoint Presentations

This book comes with Microsoft PowerPoint slides for each chapter. These are included as a teaching aid either to make available to students on the network for chapter review, or to be used during classroom presentations. Instructors can modify slides or add their own slides to tailor their presentations.

Distance Learning

Cengage Learning is proud to offer online courses in WebCT and Blackboard. For more information on how to bring distance learning to your course, contact your local Cengage Learning sales representative.

Source Code

The source code is available at *www.cengage.com/coursetechnology*, and also is available on the Instructor Resources CD-ROM. If an input file is needed to run a program, it is included with the source code.

Solution Files

The solution files for all programming exercises are available at *www.cengage.com/coursetechnology* and are available on the Instructor Resources CD-ROM. If an input file is needed to run a programming exercise, it is included with the solution file.

ACKNOWLEDGEMENTS

I owe a great deal to the following reviewers who patiently read each page of every chapter of the current version and made critical comments to improve on the book: Stefano Basagni, Northeastern University and Roman Tankelevich, Colorado School of Mines. Additionally, I express thanks to the reviewers of the proposal package: Ted Krovetz, California State University; Kenneth Lambert, Washington and Lee University; Stephen Scott, University of Nebraska; and Deborah Silver, Rutgers, The State University of New Jersey. The reviewers will recognize that their criticisms have not been overlooked, adding meaningfully to the quality of the finished book. Next, I express thanks to Amy Jollymore, Acquisitions Editor, for recognizing the importance and uniqueness of this project. All this would not have been possible without the careful planning of Product Manager Alyssa Pratt. I extend my sincere thanks to Alyssa, as well as to Content Project Manager Heather Furrow. I also thank Tintu Thomas of Integra Software Services for assisting us in keeping the project on schedule. I would like to thank Chris Scriver and Serge Palladino of QA department of Cengage Learning for patiently and carefully proofreading the text, testing the code, and discovering typos and errors.

I am thankful to my parents, to whom this book is dedicated, for their blessings. Finally, I would like to thank my wife Sadhana and my daughter Shelly. They cheered me up whenever I was overwhelmed during the writing of this book.

I welcome any comments concerning the text. Comments may be forwarded to the following e-mail address: *malik@creighton.edu*.

D.S. Malik

CHAPTER 1

SOFTWARE ENGINEERING PRINCIPLES AND C++ CLASSES

IN THIS CHAPTER, YOU WILL:

- Learn about software engineering principles

- Discover what an algorithm is and explore problem-solving techniques

- Become aware of structured design and object-oriented design programming methodologies

- Learn about classes

- Become aware of **private**, **protected**, and **public** members of a class

- Explore how classes are implemented

- Become aware of Unified Modeling Language (UML) notation

- Examine constructors and destructors

- Become aware of abstract data type (ADT)

- Explore how classes are used to implement ADT

Most everyone working with computers is familiar with the term *software*. Software are computer programs designed to accomplish a specific task. For example, word processing software is a program that enables you to write term papers, create impressive-looking résumés, and even write a book. This book, for example, was created with the help of a word processor. Students no longer type their papers on typewriters or write them by hand. Instead, they use word processing software to complete their term papers. Many people maintain and balance their checkbooks on computers.

Powerful, yet easy-to-use software has drastically changed the way we live and communicate. Terms such as *the Internet*, which was unfamiliar just a decade ago, are very common today. With the help of computers and the software running on them, you can send letters to, and receive letters from, loved ones within seconds. You no longer need to send a résumé by mail to apply for a job; in many cases, you can simply submit your job application via the Internet. You can watch how stocks perform in real time, and instantly buy and sell them.

Without software a computer is of no use. It is the software that enables you to do things that were, perhaps, fiction a few years ago. However, software is not created overnight. From the time a software program is conceived until it is delivered, it goes through several phases. There is a branch of computer science, called software engineering, which specializes in this area. Most colleges and universities offer a course in software engineering. This book is not concerned with the teaching of software engineering principles. However, this chapter briefly describes some of the basic software engineering principles that can simplify program design.

Software Life Cycle

A program goes through many phases from the time it is first conceived until the time it is retired, called the *life cycle* of the program. The three fundamental stages through which a program goes are *development*, *use*, and *maintenance*. Usually a program is initially conceived by a software developer because a customer has some problem that needs to be solved and the customer is willing to pay money to have it solved. The new program is created in the *software development* stage. The next section describes this stage in some detail.

Once the program is considered complete, it is released for the user to use. Once users start using the program, they most certainly discover problems or have suggestions to improve it. The problems and/or ideas for improvements are conveyed to the software developer, and the program goes through the maintenance phase.

In the *software maintenance* process, the program is modified to fix the (identified) problems and/or to enhance it. If there are serious/numerous changes, typically, a new version of the program is created and released for use.

When a program is considered too expensive to maintain, the developer might decide to *retire* the program and no new version of the program will be released.

The software development phase is the first and perhaps most important phase of the software life cycle. A program that is well developed will be easy and less expensive to maintain. The next section describes this phase.

Software Development Phase

Software engineers typically break the software development process into the following four phases:

- Analysis
- Design
- Implementation
- Testing and debugging

The next few sections describe these four phases in some detail.

Analysis

Analyzing the problem is the first and most important step. This step requires you to do the following:

- Thoroughly understand the problem.
- Understand the problem requirements. Requirements can include whether the program requires interaction with the user, whether it manipulates data, whether it produces output, and what the output looks like.

  Suppose that you need to develop a program to make an automated teller machine (ATM) operational. In the analysis phase, you determine the functionality of the machine. Here, you determine the necessary operations performed by the machine, such as withdraw money, deposit money, transfer money, check account balance, and so on. During this phase, you also talk to potential customers who would use the machine. To make it user-friendly, you must understand their requirements and add any necessary operations.

  If the program manipulates data, the programmer must know what the data is and how it is represented. That is, you need to look at sample data. If the program produces output, you should know how the results should be generated and formatted.

- If the problem is complex, divide the problem into subproblems, analyze each subproblem, and understand each subproblem's requirements.

Design

After you carefully analyze the problem, the next step is to design an algorithm to solve the problem. If you broke the problem into subproblems, you need to design an algorithm for each subproblem.

Algorithm: A step-by-step problem-solving process in which a solution is arrived at in a finite amount of time.

STRUCTURED DESIGN

Dividing a problem into smaller subproblems is called **structured design**. The structured design approach is also known as **top-down design**, **stepwise refinement**, and **modular programming**. In structured design, the problem is divided into smaller problems. Each subproblem is then analyzed, and a solution is obtained to solve the subproblem. The solutions of all the subproblems are then combined to solve the overall problem. This process of implementing a structured design is called **structured programming**.

OBJECT-ORIENTED DESIGN

In object-oriented design (OOD), the first step in the problem-solving process is to identify the components called objects, which form the basis of the solution, and determine how these objects interact with one another. For example, suppose you want to write a program that automates the video rental process for a local video store. The two main objects in this problem are the video and the customer.

After identifying the objects, the next step is to specify for each object the relevant data and possible operations to be performed on that data. For example, for a video object, the data might include the movie name, starring actors, producer, production company, number of copies in stock, and so on. Some of the operations on a video object might include checking the name of the movie, reducing the number of copies in stock by one after a copy is rented, and incrementing the number of copies in stock by one after a customer returns a particular video.

This illustrates that each object consists of data and operations on that data. An object combines data and operations on the data into a single unit. In OOD, the final program is a collection of interacting objects. A programming language that implements OOD is called an **object-oriented programming (OOP)** language. You will learn about the many advantages of OOD in later chapters.

OOD has the following three basic principles:

- **Encapsulation**—The ability to combine data and operations in a single unit
- **Inheritance**—The ability to create new (data) types from existing (data) types
- **Polymorphism**—The ability to use the same expression to denote different operations

In C++, encapsulation is accomplished via the use of data types called classes. How classes are implemented in C++ is described later in this chapter. Chapter 2 discusses inheritance and polymorphism.

In object-oriented design, you decide what classes you need and their relevant data members and member functions. You then describe how classes interact with each other.

Implementation

In the *implementation* phase, you write and compile programming code to implement the classes and functions that were discovered in the design phase.

This book uses the OOD technique (in conjunction with structured programming) to solve a particular problem. It contains many case studies—called Programming Examples—to solve real-world problems.

The final program consists of several functions, each accomplishing a specific goal. Some functions are part of the main program; others are used to implement various operations on objects. Clearly, functions interact with each other, taking advantage of each other's capabilities. To use a function, the user needs to know only how to use the function and what the function does. The user should not be concerned with the details of the function, that is, how the function is written. Let us illustrate this with the help of the following example.

Suppose that you want to write a function that converts a measurement given in inches into equivalent centimeters. The conversion formula is 1 inch = 2.54 centimeters. The following function accomplishes the job:

```
double inchesToCentimeters(double inches)
{
    if (inches < 0)
    {
        cerr << "The given measurement must be nonnegative." << endl;
        return -1.0;
    }
    else
        return 2.54 * inches;
}
```

> **NOTE** The object `cerr` corresponds to the unbuffered standard error stream. Unlike the object `cout` (whose output first goes to the buffer), the output of `cerr` is immediately sent to the standard error stream, which is usually the screen.

If you look at the body of the function, you can recognize that if the value of inches is less than 0, that is, negative, the function returns −1.0; otherwise, the function returns the equivalent length in centimeters. The user of this function does not need to know the specific details of how the algorithm that finds the equivalent length in centimeters is implemented. However, the user must know that in order to get the valid answer, the input must be a nonnegative number. If the input to this function is a negative number, the program returns −1.0. This information can be provided as part of the documentation of this function using specific statements, called preconditions and postconditions.

Precondition: A statement specifying the condition(s) that must be true before the function is called.

Postcondition: A statement specifying what is true after the function call is completed.

The precondition and postcondition for the function `inchesToCentimeters` can be specified as follows:

```
//Precondition: The value of inches must be nonnegative.
//Postcondition: If the value of inches is < 0, the function
//    returns -1.0; otherwise, the function returns the
//    equivalent length in centimeters.
double inchesToCentimeters(double inches)
{
    if (inches < 0)
    {
        cerr << "The given measurement must be nonnegative." << endl;
        return -1.0;
    }
    else
        return 2.54 * inches;
}
```

In certain situations, you could use C++'s `assert` statement to validate the input. For example, the preceding function can be written as follows:

```
//Precondition: The value of inches must be nonnegative.
//Postcondition: If the value of inches is < 0, the function
//    terminates; otherwise, the function returns the
//    equivalent length in centimeters.
double inchesToCentimeters(double inches)
{
    assert(inches >= 0);
    return 2.54 * inches;
}
```

However, if the `assert` statement fails, the entire program will terminate, which might be appropriate if the remainder of the program depends on the execution of the function. On the other hand, the user can check the value returned by the function, determine if the returned value is appropriate, and proceed accordingly. To use the `assert` function, you need to include the header file `cassert` in your program.

 NOTE To turn off the `assert` statements in a program, use the preprocessor directive `#define NDEBUG`. This directive must be placed before the statement `#include <cassert>`.

As you can see, the same function can be implemented differently by different programmers. Because the user of a function need not be concerned with the details of the function, the preconditions and postconditions are specified with the function prototype. That is, the user is given the following information:

```
double inchesToCentimeters(double inches);
   //Precondition: The value of inches must be nonnegative.
   //Postcondition: If the value of inches is < 0, the function
   //    returns -1.0; otherwise, the function returns the
   //    equivalent length in centimeters.
```

As another example, to use a function that searches a list for a specific item, the list must exist before the function is called. After the search is complete, the function returns `true` or `false` depending on whether the search was successful.

```
bool search(int list[], int listLength, int searchItem);
   //Precondition: The list must exist.
   //Postcondition: The function returns true if searchItem is in
   //    list; otherwise, the function return false.
```

Testing and Debugging

The term *testing* refers to testing the correctness of the program; that is, making sure that the program does what it is supposed to do. The term *debugging* refers to finding and fixing the errors, if they exist.

Once a function and/or an algorithm is written, the next step is to verify that it works properly. However, in a large and complex program, errors almost certainly exist. Therefore, to increase the reliability of the program, errors must be discovered and fixed before the program is released to the user.

You can certainly prove this by using some (perhaps mathematical) analysis of the correctness of a program. However, for large and complex programs, this technique alone might not be enough because errors can be made in the proof. Therefore, we also rely on testing to determine the quality of the program. The program is run through a series of specific tests, called test cases, in an attempt to find problems.

A test case consists of a set of inputs, user actions, or other initial conditions, and the expected output. Because a test case can be repeated several times, it must be properly documented. Typically a program manipulates a large set of data. It is, therefore, impractical (although possible) to create test cases for all possible inputs. For example, suppose that a program manipulates integers. Clearly, it is not possible to create a test case for each integer. You can categorize test cases into separate categories, called equivalence categories. An equivalence category is a set of input values that are likely to produce the same output. For example, suppose that you have a function that takes an integer as input and returns `true` if the integer is nonnegative, and `false` otherwise. In this case, you can form two equivalence categories—one consisting of negative numbers and the other consisting of nonnegative numbers.

There are two types of testing—*black-box* testing and *white-box* testing. In black-box testing, you do not know the internal working of the algorithm or function. You know only what the function does. Black-box testing is based on inputs and outputs. The test cases for black-box testing are usually selected by creating equivalence categories. If a function works for one input in the equivalence category, it is expected to work for other inputs in the same category.

Suppose that the function isWithInRange returns a value true if an integer is greater than or equal to 0 and less than or equal to 100. In black-box testing, the function is tested on values that surround and fall on the boundaries, called **boundary values**, as well as general values from the equivalence categories. For the function isWithInRange, in black-box testing, the boundary values might be: -1, 0, 1, 99, 100, and 101; and so the test values might be -500, -1, 0, 1, 50, 99, 100, 101, and 500.

White-box testing relies on the internal structure and implementation of a function or algorithm. The objective is to ensure that every part of the function or algorithm is executed at least once. Suppose that you want to ensure whether an if statement works properly. The test cases must consist of at least one input for which the if statement evaluates to true and at least one case for which it evaluates to false. Loops and other structures can be tested similarly.

Algorithm Analysis: The Big-O Notation

Just as a problem is analyzed before writing the algorithm and the computer program, after an algorithm is designed it should also be analyzed. Usually, there are various ways to design a particular algorithm. Certain algorithms take very little computer time to execute, whereas others take a considerable amount of time.

Let us consider the following problem. The holiday season is approaching and a gift shop is expecting sales to be double or even triple the regular amount. They have hired extra delivery people to deliver the packages on time. The company calculates the shortest distance from the shop to a particular destination and hands the route to the driver. Suppose that 50 packages are to be delivered to 50 different houses. The shop, while making the route, finds that the 50 houses are one mile apart and are in the same area. (See Figure 1-1, in which each dot represents a house and the distance between houses is 1 mile.)

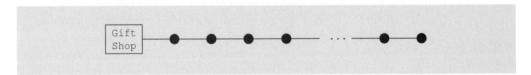

FIGURE 1-1 Gift shop and each dot representing a house

To deliver 50 packages to their destinations, one of the drivers picks up all 50 packages, drives one mile to the first house and delivers the first package. Then he drives another mile and delivers the second package, drives another mile and delivers the third package, and so on. Figure 1-2 illustrates this delivery scheme.

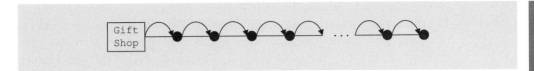

FIGURE 1-2 Package delivering scheme

It now follows that using this scheme, the distance driven by the driver to deliver the packages is:

$1 + 1 + 1 + \ldots + 1 = 50$ miles

Therefore, the total distance traveled by the driver to deliver the packages and then getting back to the shop is:

$50 + 50 = 100$ miles

Another driver has a similar route to deliver another set of 50 packages. The driver looks at the route and delivers the packages as follows: The driver picks up the first package, drives one mile to the first house, delivers the package, and then comes back to the shop. Next, the driver picks up the second package, drives 2 miles, delivers the second package, and then returns to the shop. The driver then picks up the third package, drives 3 miles, delivers the package, and comes back to the shop. Figure 1-3 illustrates this delivery scheme.

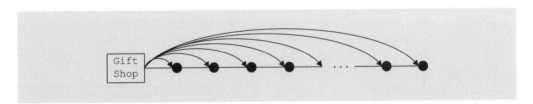

FIGURE 1-3 Another package delivery scheme

The driver delivers only one package at a time. After delivering a package, the driver comes back to the shop to pick up and deliver the second package. Using this scheme, the total distance traveled by this driver to deliver the packages and then getting back to the store is:

$2 \cdot (1 + 2 + 3 + \ldots + 50) = 2550$ miles

Now suppose that there are n packages to be delivered to n houses, and each house is one mile apart from each other, as shown in Figure 1-1. If the packages are delivered using the first scheme, the following equation gives the total distance traveled:

$$1 + 1 + \ldots + 1 + n = 2n \qquad (1\text{--}1)$$

If the packages are delivered using the second method, the distance traveled is:

$$2 \cdot (1 + 2 + 3 + \ldots + n) = 2 \cdot (n(n+1)/2) = n^2 + n \qquad (1\text{--}2)$$

In Equation (1-1), we say that the distance traveled is a function of n. Let us consider Equation (1-2). In this equation, for large values of n, we will find that the term consisting of n^2 will become the dominant term and the term containing n will be negligible. In this case, we say that the distance traveled is a function of n^2. Table 1-1 evaluates Equations (1-1) and (1-2) for certain values of n. (The table also shows the value of n^2.)

TABLE 1-1   Various values of n, $2n$, n^2, and $n^2 + n$

n	$2n$	n^2	$n^2 + n$
1	2	1	2
10	20	100	110
100	200	10,000	10,100
1000	2000	1,000,000	1,001,000
10,000	20,000	100,000,000	100,010,000

While analyzing a particular algorithm, we usually count the number of operations performed by the algorithm. We focus on the number of operations, not on the actual computer time to execute the algorithm. This is because a particular algorithm can be implemented on a variety of computers and the speed of the computer can affect the execution time. However, the number of operations performed by the algorithm would be the same on each computer. Let us consider the following examples.

EXAMPLE 1-1

Consider the following algorithm. (Assume that all variables are properly declared.)

```
cout << "Enter two numbers";                          //Line 1

cin >> num1 >> num2;                                  //Line 2

if (num1 >= num2)                                     //Line 3
    max = num1;                                       //Line 4
else                                                  //Line 5
    max = num2;                                       //Line 6

cout << "The maximum number is: " << max << endl;     //Line 7
```

Line 1 has one operation, <<; Line 2 has two operations; Line 3 has one operation, >=; Line 4 has one operation, =; Line 6 has one operation; and Line 7 has three operations. Either Line 4 or Line 6 executes. Therefore, the total number of operations executed in the preceding code is $1 + 2 + 1 + 1 + 3 = 8$. In this algorithm, the number of operations executed is fixed.

EXAMPLE 1-2

Consider the following algorithm:

```
cout << "Enter positive integers ending with -1" << endl;   //Line 1

count = 0;                                                   //Line 2
sum = 0;                                                     //Line 3

cin >> num;                                                  //Line 4

while (num != -1)                                            //Line 5
{
    sum = sum + num;                                         //Line 6
    count++;                                                 //Line 7
    cin >> num;                                              //Line 8
}

cout << "The sum of the numbers is: " << sum << endl;        //Line 9

if (count != 0)                                              //Line 10
    average = sum / count;                                   //Line 11
else                                                         //Line 12
    average = 0;                                             //Line 13

cout << "The average is: " << average << endl;               //Line 14
```

This algorithm has five operations (Lines 1 through 4) before the while loop. Similarly, there are nine or eight operations after the while loop, depending on whether Line 11 or Line 13 executes.

Line 5 has one operation, and four operations within the while loop (Lines 6 through 8). Thus, Lines 5 through 8 have five operations. If the while loop executes 10 times, these five operations execute 10 times. One extra operation is also executed at Line 5 to terminate the loop. Therefore, the number of operations executed is 51 from Lines 5 through 8.

If the while loop executes 10 times, the total number of operations executed is:

$10 \cdot 5 + 1 + 5 + 9$ or $10 \cdot 5 + 1 + 5 + 8$

that is,

$10 \cdot 5 + 15$ or $10 \cdot 5 + 14$

We can generalize it to the case when the while loop executes n times. If the while loop executes n times, the number of operations executed is:

$5n + 15$ or $5n + 14$

In these expressions, for very large values of n, the term $5n$ becomes the dominating term and the terms 15 and 14 become negligible.

Usually, in an algorithm, certain operations are dominant. For example, in the preceding algorithm, to add numbers, the dominant operation is in Line 6. Similarly, in a search algorithm, because the search item is compared with the items in the list, the dominant operations would be comparison, that is, the relational operation. Therefore, in the case of a search algorithm, we count the number of comparisons. For another example, suppose that we write a program to multiply matrices. The multiplication of matrices involves addition and multiplication. Because multiplication takes more computer time to execute, to analyze a matrix multiplication algorithm, we count the number of multiplications.

In addition to developing algorithms, we also provide a reasonable analysis of each algorithm. If there are various algorithms to accomplish a particular task, the algorithm analysis allows the programmer to choose between various options.

Suppose that an algorithm performs $f(n)$ basic operations to accomplish a task, where n is the size of the problem. Suppose that you want to determine whether an item is in a list. Moreover, suppose that the size of the list is n. To determine whether the item is in the list, there are various algorithms, as you will see in Chapter 9. However, the basic method is to compare the item with the items in the list. Therefore, the performance of the algorithm depends on the number of comparisons.

Thus, in the case of a search, n is the size of the list and $f(n)$ becomes the count function, that is, $f(n)$ gives the number of comparisons done by the search algorithm. Suppose that, on a particular computer, it takes c units of computer time to execute one operation. Thus, the computer time it would take to execute $f(n)$ operations is $cf(n)$. Clearly, the constant c depends on the speed of the computer and, therefore, varies from computer to computer. However, $f(n)$, the number of basic operations, is the same on each computer. If we know how the function $f(n)$ grows as the size of the problem grows, we can determine the efficiency of the algorithm. Consider Table 1-2.

TABLE 1-2 Growth rates of various functions

n	$\log_2 n$	$n \log_2 n$	n^2	2^n
1	0	0	1	2
2	1	2	2	4
4	2	8	16	16
8	3	24	64	256
16	4	64	256	65,536
32	5	160	1024	4,294,967,296

Table 1-2 shows how certain functions grow as the parameter n, that is, the problem size, grows. Suppose that the problem size is doubled. From Table 1-2, it follows that if the number of basic operations is a function of $f(n) = n^2$, the number of basic operations is quadrupled. If the number of basic operations is a function of $f(n) = 2^n$, the number of basic operations is squared. However, if the number of operations is a function of $f(n) = \log_2 n$, the change in the number of basic operations is insignificant.

Suppose that a computer can execute 1 billion basic operations per second. Table 1-3 shows the time that the computer takes to execute $f(n)$ basic operations.

TABLE 1-3 Time for $f(n)$ instructions on a computer that executes 1 billion instructions per second

n	$f(n) = n$	$f(n) = \log_2 n$	$f(n) = n\log_2 n$	$f(n) = n^2$	$f(n) = 2^n$
10	0.01μs	0.003μs	0.033μs	0.1μs	1μs
20	0.02μs	0.004μs	0.086μs	0.4μs	1ms
30	0.03μs	0.005μs	0.147μs	0.9μs	1s
40	0.04μs	0.005μs	0.213μs	1.6μs	18.3min
50	0.05μs	0.006μs	0.282μs	2.5μs	13 days
100	0.10μs	0.007μs	0.664μs	10μs	4×10^{13} years
1000	1.00μs	0.010μs	9.966μs	1ms	
10,000	10μs	0.013μs	130μs	100ms	
100,000	0.10ms	0.017μs	1.67ms	10s	
1,000,000	1 ms	0.020μs	19.93ms	16.7m	
10,000,000	0.01s	0.023μs	0.23s	1.16 days	
100,000,000	0.10s	0.027μs	2.66s	115.7 days	

In Table 1-3, $1\mu s = 10^{-6}$ seconds and $1ms = 10^{-3}$ seconds.

Figure 1-4 shows the growth rate of functions in Table 1-3.

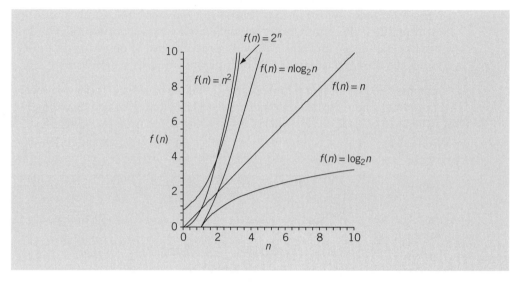

FIGURE 1-4 Growth rate of various functions

The remainder of this section develops a notation that shows how a function $f(n)$ grows as n increases without bound. That is, we develop a notation that is useful in describing the behavior of the algorithm, which gives us the most useful information about the algorithm. First, we define the term *asymptotic*.

Let f be a function of n. By the term **asymptotic**, we mean the study of the function f as n becomes larger and larger without bound.

Consider the functions $g(n) = n^2$ and $f(n) = n^2 + 4n + 20$. Clearly, the function g does not contain any linear term, that is, the coefficient of n in g is zero. Consider Table 1-4.

TABLE 1-4 Growth rate of n^2 and $n^2 + 4n + 20$

n	$g(n) = n^2$	$f(n) = n^2 + 4n + 20$
10	100	160
50	2500	2720
100	10,000	10,420
1000	1,000,000	1,004,020
10,000	100,000,000	100,040,020

Clearly, as n becomes larger and larger the term $4n + 20$ in $f(n)$ becomes insignificant, and the term n^2 becomes the dominant term. For large values of n, we can predict the behavior of $f(n)$ by looking at the behavior of $g(n)$. In algorithm analysis, if the complexity of a function can be described by the complexity of a quadratic function without the linear term, we say that the function is of $O(n^2)$, called Big-O of n^2.

Let f and g be real-valued functions. Assume that f and g are nonnegative, that is, for all real numbers n, $f(n) \geq 0$ and $g(n) \geq 0$.

Definition: We say that $f(n)$ is **Big-O** of $g(n)$, written $f(n) = O(g(n))$, if there exists positive constants c and n_0 such that $f(n) \leq cg(n)$ for all $n \geq n_0$.

EXAMPLE 1-3

Let $f(n) = a$, where a is a nonnegative real number and $n \geq 0$. Note that f is a constant function. Now

$f(n) = a \leq a \cdot 1$ for all $n \geq a$.

Let $c = a$, $n_0 = a$, and $g(n) = 1$. Then $f(n) \leq cg(n)$ for all $n \geq n_0$. It now follows that $f(n) = O(g(n)) = O(1)$.

From Example 1-3, it follows that if f is a nonnegative constant function, then f is $O(1)$.

EXAMPLE 1-4

Let $f(n) = 2n + 5$, $n \geq 0$. Note that

$f(n) = 2n + 5 \leq 2n + n = 3n$ for all $n \geq 5$.

Let $c = 3$, $n_0 = 5$, and $g(n) = n$. Then $f(n) \leq cg(n)$ for all $n \geq 5$. It now follows that $f(n) = O(g(n)) = O(n)$.

EXAMPLE 1-5

Let $f(n) = n^2 + 3n + 2$, $g(n) = n^2$, $n \geq 0$. Note that $3n + 2 \leq n^2$ for all $n \geq 4$. This implies that

$f(n) = n^2 + 3n + 2 \leq n^2 + n^2 \leq 2n^2 = 2g(n)$ for all $n \geq 4$.

Let $c = 2$ and $n_0 = 4$. Then $f(n) \leq cg(n)$ for all $n \geq 4$. It now follows that $f(n) = O(g(n)) = O(n^2)$.

In general, we can prove the following theorem. Here we state the theorem without proof.

Theorem: Let $f(n)$ be a nonnegative real-valued function such that

$$f(n) = a_m n^m + a_{m-1} n^{m-1} + \cdots + a_1 n + a_0,$$

where a_i's are real numbers, $a_m \neq 0$, $n \geq 0$, and m is a nonnegative integer. Then $f(n) = O(n^m)$.

In Example 1-6, we use the preceding theorem to establish the Big-O of certain functions.

EXAMPLE 1-6

In the following, $f(n)$ is a nonnegative real-valued function.

Function	Big-O
$f(n) = an + b$, where a and b are real numbers and a is nonzero.	$f(n) = O(n)$
$f(n) = n^2 + 5n + 1$	$f(n) = O(n^2)$
$f(n) = 4n^6 + 3n^3 + 1$	$f(n) = O(n^6)$
$f(n) = 10n^7 + 23$	$f(n) = O(n^7)$
$f(n) = 6n^{15}$	$f(n) = O(n^{15})$

EXAMPLE 1-7

Suppose that $f(n) = 2\log_2 n + a$, where a is a real number. It can be shown that $f(n) = O(\log_2 n)$.

EXAMPLE 1-8

Consider the following code, where m and n are int variables and their values are nonnegative:

```
for (int i = 0; i < m; i++)          //Line 1
    for (int j = 0; j < n; j++)      //Line 2
        cout << i * j << endl;       //Line 3
```

This code contains nested for loops. The outer for loop, at Line 1, executes m times. For each iteration of the outer loop, the inner loop, at Line 2, executes n times. For each iteration of the inner loop, the output statement in Line 3 executes. It follows that the total number of iterations of the nested for loop is mn. So the number of times the statement in Line 3 executes is mn. Therefore, this algorithm is $O(mn)$. Note that if $m = n$, then this algorithm is $O(n^2)$.

Table 1-5 shows some common Big-O functions that appear in the algorithm analysis. Let $f(n) = O(g(n))$ where n is the problem size.

TABLE 1-5 Some Big-O functions that appear in algorithm analysis

Function $g(n)$	Growth rate of $f(n)$
$g(n) = 1$	The growth rate is constant and so does not depend on n, the size of the problem.
$g(n) = \log_2 n$	The growth rate is a function of $\log_2 n$. Because a logarithm function grows slowly, the growth rate of the function f is also slow.
$g(n) = n$	The growth rate is linear. The growth rate of f is directly proportional to the size of the problem.
$g(n) = n\log_2 n$	The growth rate is faster than the linear algorithm.
$g(n) = n^2$	The growth rate of such functions increases rapidly with the size of the problem. The growth rate is quadrupled when the problem size is doubled.
$g(n) = 2^n$	The growth rate is exponential. The growth rate is squared when the problem size is doubled.

NOTE It can be shown that

$$O(1) \leq O(\log_2 n) \leq O(n) \leq O(n\log_2 n) \leq O(n^2) \leq O(2^n).$$

Classes

In this section, we review C++ classes. If you are familiar with how classes are implemented in C++, you can skip this section.

Recall that in OOD, the first step is to identify the components called objects; an object combines data and the operations on that data in a single unit, called *encapsulation*. In C++, the mechanism that allows you to combine data and the operations on that data in a single unit is called a class. A **class** is a collection of a fixed number of components. The components of a class are called the **members** of the class.

The general syntax for defining a class is

```
class classIdentifier
{
    class members list
};
```

where **class members list** consists of variable declarations and/or functions. That is, a member of a class can be either a variable (to store data) or a function.

- If a member of a class is a variable, you declare it just like any other variable. Furthermore, in the definition of the class, you cannot initialize a variable when you declare it.

- If a member of a class is a function, you typically use the function prototype to define that member.

- If a member of a class is a function, it can (directly) access any member of the class—data members and function members. That is, when you write the definition of the member function, you can directly access any data member of the class without passing it as a parameter. The only obvious condition is that you must declare an identifier before you can use it.

In C++, **class** is a reserved word, and it defines only a data type; no memory is allocated. It announces the declaration of a class. Moreover, note the semicolon (;) after the right brace. The semicolon is part of the syntax. A missing semicolon, therefore, will result in a syntax error.

The members of a **class** are classified into three categories: **private**, **public**, and **protected**, called member **access specifiers**. This chapter mainly discusses the first two types—that is, **private** and **public**.

Following are some facts about **private** and **public** members of a class:

- By default, all members of a class are **private**.
- If a member of a class is **private**, you cannot access it outside the class.
- A **public** member is accessible outside the class.
- To make a member of a class **public**, you use the member access specifier **public** with a colon.

In C++, **private**, **protected**, and **public** are reserved words.

EXAMPLE 1-9

Suppose that we want to define a **class**, **clockType**, to implement the time of day in a program. Furthermore, suppose that the time is represented as a set of three integers: one to represent the hours, one to represent the minutes, and one to represent the seconds. We also want to perform the following operations on the time:

1. Set the time.
2. Return the time.
3. Print the time.
4. Increment the time by one second.
5. Increment the time by one minute.
6. Increment the time by one hour.
7. Compare two times for equality.

From this discussion, it is clear that the class clockType has 10 members: three data members and seven function members.

Some members of the class clockType will be private; others will be public. Deciding which member to make private and which to make public depends on the nature of the member. The general rule is that any member that needs to be accessed outside the class is declared public; any member that should not be accessed directly by the user should be declared private. For example, the user should be able to set the time and print the time. Therefore, the members that set the time and print the time should be declared public.

Similarly, the members to increment the time and compare the time for equality should be declared public. On the other hand, to control the *direct* manipulation of the data members hr, min, and sec, we will declare these data members private. Furthermore, note that if the user has direct access to the data members, member functions such as setTime are not needed.

The following statements define the class clockType:

```
class clockType
{
public:
    void setTime(int hours, int minutes, int seconds);
      //Function to set the time
      //The time is set according to the parameters
      //Postcondition: hr = hours; min = minutes; sec = seconds
      //    The function checks whether the values of hours,
      //    minutes, and seconds are valid. If a value is invalid,
      //    the default value 0 is assigned.

    void getTime(int& hours, int& minutes, int& seconds) const;
      //Function to return the time
      //Postcondition: hours = hr; minutes = min; seconds = sec

    void printTime() const;
      //Function to print the time
      //Postcondition: Time is printed in the form hh:mm:ss.

    void incrementSeconds();
      //Function to increment the time by one second
      //Postcondition: The time is incremented by one second.
      //    If the before-increment time is 23:59:59, the time
      //    is reset to 00:00:00.

    void incrementMinutes();
      //Function to increment the time by one minute
      //Postcondition: The time is incremented by one minute.
      //    If the before-increment time is 23:59:53, the time
      //    is reset to 00:00:53.
```

```
        void incrementHours();
          //Function to increment the time by one hour
          //Postcondition: The time is incremented by one hour.
          //    If the before-increment time is 23:45:53, the time
          //    is reset to 00:45:53.

        bool equalTime(const clockType& otherClock) const;
          //Function to compare the two times
          //Postcondition: Returns true if this time is equal to
          //    otherClock; otherwise, returns false

private:
    int hr;  //stores the hours
    int min; //store the minutes
    int sec; //store the seconds
};
```

We note the following in the definition of the class clockType:

- The class clockType has seven function members: setTime, getTime, printTime, incrementSeconds, incrementMinutes, incrementHours, and equalTime. It has three data members: hr, min, and sec.

- The three data members—hr, min, and sec—are private to the class and cannot be accessed outside the class.

- The seven function members—setTime, getTime, printTime, incrementSeconds, incrementMinutes, incrementHours, and equalTime—can directly access the data members (hr, min, and sec). In other words, we do not pass data members as parameters to member functions.

- In the function equalTime, the parameter otherClock is a constant reference parameter. That is, in a call to the function equalTime, the parameter otherClock receives the address of the actual parameter, but otherClock cannot modify the value of the actual parameter. You could have declared otherClock as a value parameter, but that would require otherClock to copy the value of the actual parameter, which could result in poor performance. (For an explanation, see the section, "Reference Parameters and Class Objects (Variables)" located later in this chapter.)

- The word const at the end of the member functions getTime, printTime, and equalTime specifies that these functions cannot modify the data members of a variable of type clockType.

NOTE (Order of public and private members of a class) C++ has no fixed order in which you declare public and private members; you can declare them in any order. The only thing you need to remember is that, by default, all members of a class are private. You must use the public label to make a member available for public access. If you decide to declare the private members after the public members (as is done in the case of clockType), you must use the private label to begin the declaration of the private members.

Note that we have not yet written the definitions of the function members of the `class clockType`. You will learn how to write them shortly.

The function `setTime` sets the three data members—`hr`, `min`, and `sec`—to a given value. The given values are passed as parameters to the function `setTime`. The function `printTime` prints the time, that is, the values of `hr`, `min`, and `sec`. The function `incrementSeconds` increments the time by one second, the function `incrementMinutes` increments the time by one minute, the function `incrementHours` increments the time by one hour, and the function `equalTime` compares the two times for equality.

Constructors

C++ does not automatically initialize variables when they are declared. Therefore, when an object is instantiated, there is no guarantee that the data members of the object will be initialized. To guarantee that the instance variables of a class are initialized, you use constructors. There are two types of constructors: with parameters and without parameters. The constructor without parameters is called the **default constructor**.

Constructors have the following properties:

- The name of a constructor is the same as the name of the class.
- A constructor, even though it is a function, has no type. That is, it is neither a value-returning function nor a **void** function.
- A class can have more than one constructor. However, all constructors of a class have the same name.
- If a class has more than one constructor, the constructors must have different formal parameter lists. That is, either they have a different number of formal parameters or, if the number of formal parameters is the same, the data type of the formal parameters, in the order you list, must differ in at least one position.
- Constructors execute automatically when a class object enters its scope. Because they have no types, they cannot be called like other functions.
- Which constructor executes depends on the types of values passed to the class object when the class object is declared.

Let us extend the definition of the `class clockType` by including two constructors:

```
class clockType
{
public:
    //Place the function prototypes of the functions setTime,
    //getTime, printTime, incrementSeconds, incrementMinutes,
    //incrementHours, and equalTime as described earlier, here.

    clockType(int hours, int minutes, int seconds);
    //Constructor with parameters
    //The time is set according to the parameters.
    //Postconditions: hr = hours; min = minutes; sec = seconds
    //    The constructor checks whether the values of hours,
    //    minutes, and seconds are valid. If a value is invalid,
    //    the default value 0 is assigned.

    clockType();
    //Default constructor with parameters
    //The time is set to 00:00:00.
    //Postcondition: hr = 0; min = 0; sec = 0

private:
    int hr;  //stores the hours
    int min; //store the minutes
    int sec; //store the seconds
};
```

Unified Modeling Language Diagrams

A class and its members can be described graphically using a notation known as **Unified Modeling Language (UML)** notation. For example, Figure 1-5 shows the UML class diagram of the `class clockType`.

```
                    clockType
-hr: int
-min: int
-sec: int
+setTime(int, int, int): void
+getTime(int&, int&, int&) const: void
+printTime() const: void
+incrementSeconds(): int
+incrementMinutes(): int
+incrementHours(): int
+equalTime(clockType) const: bool
+clockType(int, int, int)
+clockType()
```

FIGURE 1-5 UML class diagram of the **class** clockType

The top box contains the name of the class. The middle box contains the data members and their data types. The last box contains the member function name, parameter list, and the return type of the function. A + (plus) sign in front of a member indicates that this member is a **public** member; a – (minus) sign indicates that this is a **private** member. The symbol # before the member name indicates that the member is a **protected** member.

Variable (Object) Declaration

Once a class is defined, you can declare variables of that type. In C++ terminology, a class variable is called a **class object** or **class instance**. To help you become familiar with this terminology, from now on we will use the term class object, or simply **object**, for a class variable.

A class can have both types of constructors—default constructor and constructors with parameters. Therefore, when you declare a class object, either the default constructor executes or the constructor with parameters executes. The general syntax for declaring a class object that invokes the default constructor is:

```
className classObjectName;
```

For example, the statement

```
clockType myClock;
```

declares `myClock` to be an object of type `clockType`. In this case, the default constructor executes and the instance variables of `myClock` are initialized to 0.

 NOTE   If you declare an object and want the default constructor to be executed, the empty parentheses after the object name are not required in the object declaration statement. In fact, if you accidentally include the empty parentheses, the compiler generates a syntax error message. For example, the following statement to declare the object `myClock` is illegal:

```
clockType myClock();   //illegal object declaration
```

The general syntax for declaring a class object that invokes a constructor with a parameter is

```
className classObjectName(argument1, argument2, ...);
```

where each of `argument1`, `argument2`, and so on is either a variable or an expression. Note the following:

- The number of arguments and their type should match the formal parameters (in the order given) of one of the constructors.
- If the type of the arguments does not match the formal parameters of any constructor (in the order given), C++ uses type conversion and looks for the best match. For example, an integer value might be converted to a floating-point value with a zero decimal part. Any ambiguity will result in a compile-time error.

Consider the following statement:

```
clockType myClock(5, 12, 40);
```

This statement declares the object `myClock` of type `clockType`. Here, we are passing three values of type `int`, which matches the type of the formal parameters of the constructor with a parameter. Therefore, the constructor with parameters of the `class` `clockType` executes and the three instance variables of the object `myClock` are set to 5, 12, and 40.

Consider the following statements that declare two objects of type `clockType`:

```
clockType myClock(8, 12, 30);
clockType yourClock(12, 35, 45);
```

Each object has 10 members: seven member functions and three instance variables. Each object has separate memory allocated for `hr`, `min`, and `sec`.

In actuality, memory is allocated only for the instance variables of each class object. The C++ compiler generates only one physical copy of a member function of a class, and each class object executes the same copy of the member function.

Accessing Class Members

Once an object of a class is declared, it can access the members of the class. The general syntax for an object to access a member of a class is:

```
classObjectName.memberName
```

In C++, the dot, . (period), is an operator called the **member access operator**.

The class members that a class object can access depend on where the object is declared.

- If the object is declared in the definition of a member function of the class, the object can access both the `public` and `private` members. (We will elaborate on this when we write the definition of the member function `equalTime` of the `class clockType` in the section "Implementation of Member Functions," later in this chapter.)
- If the object is declared elsewhere (for example, in a user's program), the object can access *only* the `public` members of the class.

Example 1-10 illustrates how to access the members of a class.

EXAMPLE 1-10

Suppose we have the following declaration (say, in a user's program):

```
clockType myClock;
clockType yourClock;
```

Consider the following statements:

```
myClock.setTime(5, 2, 30);
myClock.printTime();

if (myClock.equalTime(yourClock))
.
.
.
```

These statements are legal; that is, they are syntactically correct.

In the first statement, `myClock.setTime(5, 2, 30);`, the member function `setTime` is executed. The values 5, 2, and 30 are passed as parameters to the function `setTime`, and the function uses these values to set the values of the three instance variables `hr`, `min`, and `sec` of `myClock` to 5, 2, and 30, respectively. Similarly, the second statement executes the member function `printTime` and outputs the contents of the three instance variables of `myClock`.

In the third statement, the member function `equalTime` executes and compares the three instance variables of `myClock` to the corresponding instance variables of `yourClock`. Because in this statement `equalTime` is a member of the object `myClock`, it has direct access to the three instance variables of `myClock`. So it needs one more object, which in this case is `yourClock`, to compare. This explains why the function `equalTime` has only one parameter.

The objects `myClock` and `yourClock` can access only `public` members of the class. Thus, the following statements are illegal because `hr` and `min` are declared as `private` members of the `class clockType` and, therefore, cannot be accessed by the objects `myClock` and `yourClock`:

```
myClock.hr = 10;              //illegal
myClock.min = yourClock.min;  //illegal
```

Implementation of Member Functions

When we defined the `class clockType`, we included only the function prototype for the member functions. For these functions to work properly, we must write the related algorithms. One way to implement these functions is to provide the function definition rather than the function prototype in the class itself. Unfortunately, the class definition would then be long and difficult to comprehend. Another reason for providing function prototypes instead of function definitions relates to information hiding; that is, we want to hide the details of the operations on the data.

Next, let us write the definitions of the member functions of the `class clockType`. That is, we will write the definitions of the functions `setTime`, `getTime`, `printTime`, `incrementSeconds`, `equalTime`, and so on. Because the identifiers `setTime`, `printTime`, and so forth are local to the class, we cannot reference them (directly) outside the class. To reference these identifiers, we use the **scope resolution operator**, :: (double colon). In the function definition's heading, the name of the function is the name of the class, followed by the scope resolution operator, followed by the function name. For example, the definition of the function setTime is as follows:

```
void clockType::setTime(int hours, int minutes, int seconds)
{
    if (0 <= hours && hours < 24)
        hr = hours;
    else
        hr = 0;

    if (0 <= minutes && minutes < 60)
        min = minutes;
    else
        min = 0;

    if (0 <= seconds && seconds < 60)
        sec = seconds;
    else
        sec = 0;
}
```

Note that the definition of the function setTime checks for the valid values of hours, minutes, and seconds. If these values are out of range, the instance variables hr, min, and sec are initialized to 0.

Suppose that myClock is an object of type clockType (as declared previously). The object myClock has three instance variables. Consider the following statement:

myClock.setTime(3, 48, 52);

In the statement myClock.setTime(3, 48, 52);, setTime is accessed by the object myClock. Therefore, the three variables—hr, min, and sec—to which the body of the function setTime refers, are the three instance variables of myClock. Thus, the values 3, 48, and 52, which are passed as parameters in the preceding statement, are assigned to the three instance variables of myClock by the function setTime (see the body of the function setTime). After the previous statement executes, the object myClock is as shown in Figure 1-6.

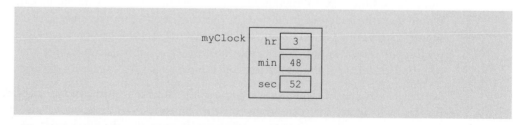

FIGURE 1-6 Object myClock after the statement myClock.setTime(3, 48, 52); executes

Next, let us give the definitions of the other member functions of the `class clockType`. The definitions of these functions are simple and easy to follow.

```cpp
void clockType::getTime(int& hours, int& minutes, int& seconds) const
{
    hours = hr;
    minutes = min;
    seconds = sec;
}

void clockType::printTime() const
{
    if (hr < 10)
        cout << "0";
    cout << hr << ":";

    if (min < 10)
        cout << "0";
    cout << min << ":";

    if (sec < 10)
        cout << "0";
    cout << sec;
}

void clockType::incrementHours()
{
    hr++;
    if (hr > 23)
        hr = 0;
}

void clockType::incrementMinutes()
{
    min++;
    if (min > 59)
    {
        min = 0;
        incrementHours(); //increment hours
    }
}

void clockType::incrementSeconds()
{
    sec++;

    if (sec > 59)
    {
        sec = 0;
        incrementMinutes(); //increment minutes
    }
}
```

From the definitions of the functions `incrementMinutes` and `incrementSeconds`, it is clear that a member function of a class can call other member functions of the class.

The function `equalTime` has the following definition:

```
bool clockType::equalTime(const clockType& otherClock) const
{
    return (hr == otherClock.hr
            && min == otherClock.min
            && sec == otherClock.sec);
}
```

Let us see how the member function `equalTime` works.

Suppose that `myClock` and `yourClock` are objects of type `clockType`, as declared previously. Further suppose that we have `myClock` and `yourClock`, as shown in Figure 1-7.

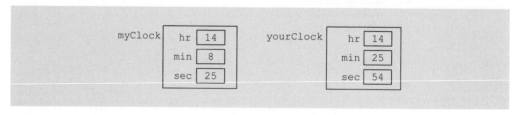

FIGURE 1-7 Objects `myClock` and `yourClock`

Consider the following statement:

```
if (myClock.equalTime(yourClock))
.
.
.
```

In the expression

```
myClock.equalTime(yourClock)
```

the object `myClock` accesses the member function `equalTime`. Because `otherClock` is a reference parameter, the address of the actual parameter `yourClock` is passed to the formal parameter `otherClock`, as shown in Figure 1-8.

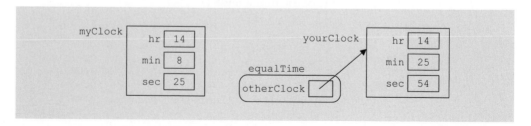

FIGURE 1-8 Object `myClock` and parameter `otherClock`

The instance variables hr, min, and sec of otherClock have the values 14, 25, and 54, respectively. In other words, when the body of the function equalTime executes, the value of otherClock.hr is 14, the value of otherClock.min is 25, and the value of otherClock.sec is 54. The function equalTime is a member of myClock. When the function equalTime executes, the variables hr, min, and sec in the body of the function equalTime are the instance variables of the variable myClock. Therefore, the member hr of myClock is compared with otherClock.hr, the member min of myClock is compared with otherClock.min, and the member sec of myClock is compared with otherClock.sec.

Once again, from the definition of the function equalTime, it is clear why this function has only one parameter.

Let us again look at the definition of the function equalTime. Notice that within the definition of this function, the object otherClock accesses the instance variables hr, min, and sec. However, these instance variables are private. So is there any violation? The answer is no. The function equalTime is a member of the class clockType and hr, min, and sec are the instance variables. Moreover, otherClock is an object of type clockType. Therefore, the object otherClock can access its private instance variables within the definition of the function equalTime.

The same is true for any member function of a class. In general, when you write the definition of a member function, say dummyFunction, of a class, say dummyClass, and the function uses an object, dummyObject of the class dummyClass, then within the definition of dummyFunction, the object dummyObject can access its private instance variables (in fact, any private member of the class).

This definition of the class clockType includes two constructors: one with three parameters and one without any parameters. Let us now write the definitions of these constructors.

```
clockType::clockType()   //default constructor
{
    hr = 0;
    min = 0;
    sec = 0;
}

clockType::clockType(int hours, int minutes, int seconds)
{
    if (0 <= hours && hours < 24)
        hr = hours;
    else
        hr = 0;

    if (0 <= minutes && minutes < 60)
        min = minutes;
    else
        min = 0;
```

```
        if (0 <= seconds && seconds < 60)
            sec = seconds;
        else
            sec = 0;
}
```

From the definitions of these constructors, it follows that the default constructor sets the three instance variables—hr, min, and sec—to 0. Also, the constructor with parameters sets the instance variables to whatever values are assigned to the formal parameters. Moreover, we can write the definition of the constructor with parameters by calling the function setTime, as follows:

```
clockType::clockType(int hours, int minutes, int seconds)
{
    setTime(hours, minutes, seconds);
}
```

Once a class is properly defined and implemented, it can be used in a program. A program or software that uses and manipulates the objects of a class is called a **client** of that class.

When you declare objects of the **class clockType**, every object has its own copy of the instance variables hr, min, and sec. In object-oriented terminology, variables such as hr, min, and sec are called **instance variables** of the class because every object has its own instance of the data.

Reference Parameters and Class Objects (Variables)

Recall that when a variable is passed by value, the formal parameter copies the value of the actual parameter. That is, memory to copy the value of the actual parameter is allocated for the formal parameter. As a parameter, a class object can be passed by value.

Suppose that a class has several instance variables requiring a large amount of memory to store data, and you need to pass a variable by value. The corresponding formal parameter then receives a copy of the data of the variable. That is, the compiler must allocate memory for the formal parameter, so as to copy the value of the instance variables of the actual parameter. This operation might require, in addition to a large amount of storage space, a considerable amount of computer time to copy the value of the actual parameter into the formal parameter.

On the other hand, if a variable is passed by reference, the formal parameter receives only the address of the actual parameter. Therefore, an efficient way to pass a variable as a parameter is by reference. If a variable is passed by reference, then when the formal parameter changes, the actual parameter also changes. Sometimes, however, you do not want the function to be able to change the values of the instance variables. In C++, you can pass a variable by reference and still prevent the function from changing its value by using the keyword const in the formal parameter declaration. As an example, consider the following function definition:

```
void testTime(const clockType& otherClock)
{
    clockType dClock;
       .
       .
       .
}
```

The function `testTime` contains a reference parameter, `otherClock`. The parameter `otherClock` is declared using the keyword `const`. Thus, in a call to the function `testTime`, the formal parameter `otherClock` receives the address of the actual parameter, but `otherClock` cannot modify the contents of the actual parameter. For example, after the following statement executes, the value of `myClock` will not be altered:

```
testTime(myClock);
```

Generally, if you want to declare a class object as a value parameter, you declare it as a reference parameter using the keyword `const`, as described previously.

Recall that if a formal parameter is a value parameter, within the function definition you can change the value of the formal parameter. That is, you can use an assignment statement to change the value of the formal parameter (which, of course, would have no effect on the actual parameter). However, if a formal parameter is a constant reference parameter, you cannot use an assignment statement to change its value within the function, nor can you use any other function to change its value. Therefore, within the definition of the function `testTime`, you cannot alter the value of `otherClock`. For example, the following would be illegal in the definition of the function `testTime`:

```
otherClock.setTime(5, 34, 56); //illegal
otherClock = dClock;           //illegal
```

BUILT-IN OPERATIONS ON CLASSES

The two built-in operations that are defined for class objects are member access (.) and assignment (=). You have seen how to access an individual member of a class by using the name of the class object, then a dot, and then the member name.

We now show how an assignment statement works with the help of an example.

Assignment Operator and Classes

Suppose that `myClock` and `yourClock` are variables of type `clockType` as defined previously. The statement

```
myClock = yourClock;          //Line 1
```

copies the value of `yourClock` into `myClock`. That is, the value of `yourClock.hr` is copied into `myClock.hr`; the value of `yourClock.min` is copied into `myClock.min`; and the value of `yourClock.sec` is copied into `myClock.sec`. In other words, the values of the three instance variables of `yourClock` are copied into the corresponding instance variables of `myClock`. Therefore, an assignment statement performs a memberwise copy.

Class Scope

A **class** object can be either automatic (that is, created each time the control reaches its declaration, and destroyed when the control exits the surrounding block) or static (that is, created once, when the control reaches its declaration, and destroyed when the program terminates). Also, you can declare an array of **class** objects. A **class** object has the same scope as other variables. A member of a **class** is local to the **class**. You access a (**public**) **class** member outside the **class** by using the **class** object name and the member access operator (.).

Functions and Classes

The following rules describe the relationship between functions and classes:

- Class objects can be passed as parameters to functions and returned as function values.

- As parameters to functions, class objects can be passed either by value or by reference.

- If a class object is passed by value, the contents of the instance variables of the actual parameter are copied into the corresponding instance variables of the formal parameter.

Constructors and Default Parameters

A constructor can also have default parameters. In such a case, the rules for declaring formal parameters are the same as those for declaring default formal parameters in a function. Moreover, actual parameters to a constructor with default parameters are passed according to the rules for functions with default parameters. Using the rules for defining default parameters, in the definition of the class clockType, you can replace both constructors using the following statement. (Notice that in the function prototype, the name of a formal parameter is optional.)

```
clockType clockType(int = 0, int = 0, int = 0); //Line 1
```

In the implementation file, the definition of this constructor is the same as the definition of the constructor with parameters.

If you replace the constructors of the class clockType with the constructor in Line 1, (the constructor with the default parameters), you can declare clockType objects with 0, 1, 2, or 3 arguments as follows:

```
clockType clock1;             //Line 2
clockType clock2(5);          //Line 3
clockType clock3(12, 30);     //Line 4
clockType clock4(7, 34, 18);  //Line 5
```

The data members of clock1 are initialized to 0. The data member hr of clock2 is initialized to 5, and the data members min and sec of clock2 are initialized to 0. The

1

data member `hr` of `clock3` is initialized to `12`, the data member `min` of `clock3` is initialized to `30`, and the data member `sec` of `clock3` is initialized to `0`. The data member `hr` of `clock4` is initialized to `7`, the data member `min` of `clock4` is initialized to `34`, and the data member `sec` of `clock4` is initialized to `18`.

Using these conventions, we can say that a constructor that has no parameters, or has all default parameters, is called the **default constructor**.

Destructors

Like constructors, destructors are also functions. Moreover, like constructors, a destructor does not have a type. That is, it is neither a value-returning function nor a `void` function. However, a class can have only one destructor, and the destructor has no parameters. The name of a destructor is the *tilde* character (`~`), followed by the name of the class. For example, the name of the destructor for the `class clockType` is:

```
~clockType();
```

The destructor automatically executes when the class object goes out of scope.

Structs

Structs are a special type of classes. By default, all members of a `class` are `private`, whereas by default all members of a `struct` are `public`. In C++, you define structs by using the reserved word `struct`. If all members of a class are `public`, C++ programmers prefer to use a `struct` to group the members, as we will do in this book. A `struct` is defined just like a `class`.

Data Abstraction, Classes, and Abstract Data Types

For the car that we drive, most of us want to know how to start the car and drive it. Most people are not concerned with the complexity of how the engine works. By separating the design details of a car's engine from its use, the manufacturer helps the driver focus on how to drive the car. Our daily life has other similar examples. For the most part, we are concerned only with how to use certain items, rather than with how they work.

Separating the design details (that is, how the car's engine works) from its use is called **abstraction**. In other words, abstraction focuses on what the engine does and not on how it works. Thus, abstraction is the process of separating the logical properties from the implementation details. Driving the car is a logical property; the construction of the engine constitutes the implementation details. We have an abstract view of what the engine does, but are not interested in the engine's actual implementation.

Abstraction can also be applied to data. Earlier sections of this chapter defined a data type `clockType`. The data type `clockType` has three instance variables and the following basic operations:

1. Set the time.
2. Return the time.
3. Print the time.
4. Increment the time by one second.
5. Increment the time by one minute.
6. Increment the time by one hour.
7. Compare two times to see whether they are equal.

The actual implementation of the operations, that is, the definitions of the member functions of the class, `clockType` was postponed.

Data abstraction is defined as a process of separating the logical properties of the data from its implementation. The definition of `clockType` and its basic operations are the logical properties; storing `clockType` objects in the computer, and the algorithms to perform these operations, are the implementation details of `clockType`.

Abstract data type (ADT): A data type that separates the logical properties from the implementation details.

Like any other data type, an ADT has three things associated with it: the name of the ADT, called the **type name**; the set of values belonging to the ADT, called the **domain**; and the set of **operations** on the data. Following these conventions, we can define the `clockType` ADT as follows:

```
dataTypeName
    clockType

domain
    Each clockType value is a time of day in the form of hours,
    minutes, and seconds.

operations
    Set the time.
    Return the time.
    Print the time.
    Increment the time by one second.
    Increment the time by one minute.
    Increment the time by one hour.
    Compare the two times to see whether they are equal.
```

To implement an ADT, you must represent the data and write algorithms to perform the operations.

The previous section used classes to group data and functions together. Furthermore, our definition of a class consisted only of the specifications of the operations; functions to implement the operations were written separately. Thus, we see that classes are a convenient way to implement an ADT. In fact, in C++, classes were specifically designed to handle ADTs.

EXAMPLE 1-11

A list is defined as a set of values of the same type. Because all values in a list are of the same type, a convenient way to represent and process a list is to use an array. You can define a list as an ADT as follows:

```
typeName
   listType
domain
   Every element of listType is a set of, say at most 1000 numbers.
operations
   Check to see whether the list is empty.
   Check to see whether the list is full.
   Search the list for a given item.
   Delete an item from the list.
   Insert an item in the list.
   Sort the list.
   Print the list.
```

The following class implements the ADT list. To be specific, suppose that the list is a set of elements of the type int.

```
class intListType
{
public:
    bool isEmpty();
      //Function to determine whether the list is empty.
      //Precondition: The list must exist.
      //Postcondition: Returns true if the list is empty,
      //    false otherwise.
    bool isFull();
      //Function to determine whether the list is full.
      //Precondition: The list must exist.
      //Postcondition: Returns true if the list is full,
      //    false otherwise.
    int search(int searchItem);
      //Function to determine whether searchItem is in the list.
      //Postcondition: If searchItem is in the list, returns its
      //    index, that is, its position in the list;
      //    otherwise, it returns -1.
    void insert(int newItem);
      //Function to insert newItem in the list.
      //Precondition: The list must exist and must not be full.
      //Postcondition: newItem is inserted in the list and
      //    length is incremented by one.
```

```
    void remove(int removeItem);
      //Function to delete removeItem from the list.
      //Precondition: The list must exist and must not be empty
      //Postcondition: If found, removeItem is deleted from the
      //    list and the length is decremented by one;
      //    otherwise, an appropriate message is printed.
    void printList();
      //Function to output the elements of the list.
      //Precondition: The list must exist.
      //Postcondition: The elements of the list are
      //    printed on the standard output device.
    intListType();
      //Default constructor
      //Postcondition: length = 0

private:
    int list[1000];
    int length;
};
```

The class personType that is designed in Example 1-12 is quite useful; we will use this class in subsequent chapters.

EXAMPLE 1-12

The most common attributes of a person are the person's first name and last name. The typical operations on a person's name are to set the name and print the name. The following statements define a class with these properties.

```
//************************************************************
// Author: D.S. Malik
//
// class personType
// This class specifies the members to implement a name.
//************************************************************

#include <string>

using namespace std;

class personType
{
public:
    void print() const;
      //Function to output the first name and last name
      //in the form firstName lastName.

    void setName(string first, string last);
      //Function to set firstName and lastName according to the
      //parameters.
      //Postcondition: firstName = first; lastName = last
```

```
    string getFirstName() const;
      //Function to return the first name.
      //Postcondition: The value of firstName is returned.

    string getLastName() const;
      //Function to return the last name.
      //Postcondition: The value of lastName is returned.

    personType();
      //Default constructor
      //Sets firstName and lastName to null strings.
      //Postcondition: firstName = ""; lastName = "";

    personType(string first, string last);
      //Constructor with parameters.
      //Sets firstName and lastName according to the parameters.
      //Postcondition: firstName = first; lastName = last;

private:
    string firstName; //variable to store the first name
    string lastName;  //variable to store the last name
};
```

Figure 1-9 shows the UML class diagram of the class personType.

```
┌─────────────────────────────────────────┐
│                personType                │
├─────────────────────────────────────────┤
│ -firstName: string                       │
│ -lastName: string                        │
├─────────────────────────────────────────┤
│ +print(): void                           │
│ +setName(string, string): void           │
│ +getFirstName() const: string            │
│ +getLastName() const: string             │
│ +personType()                            │
│ +personType(string, string)              │
└─────────────────────────────────────────┘
```

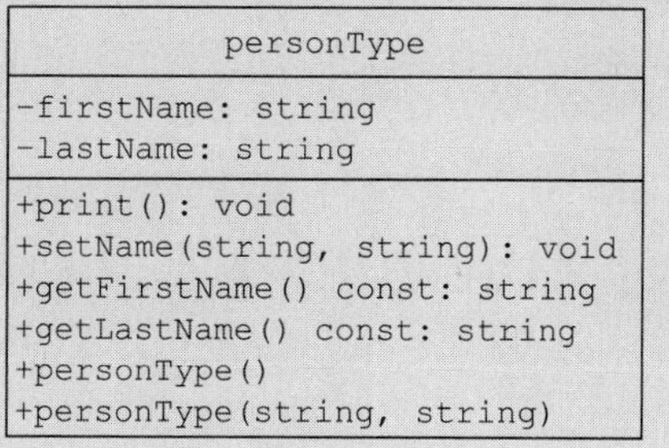

FIGURE 1-9 UML class diagram of the **class** personType

We now give the definitions of the member functions of the class personType.

```
void personType::print() const
{
    cout << firstName << " " << lastName;
}

void personType::setName(string first, string last)
{
    firstName = first;
    lastName = last;
}
```

```
string personType::getFirstName() const
{
    return firstName;
}

string personType::getLastName() const
{
    return lastName;
}

    //Default constructor
personType::personType()
{
    firstName = "";
    lastName = "";
}

    //Constructor with parameters
personType::personType(string first, string last)
{
    firstName = first;
    lastName = last;
}
```

PROGRAMMING EXAMPLE: Fruit Juice Machine

A new fruit juice machine has been purchased for the cafeteria, and a program is needed to make the machine function properly. The machine dispenses apple juice, orange juice, mango lassi, and fruit punch in recyclable containers. In this programming example, we write a program for the fruit juice machine so that it can be put into operation.

The program should do the following:

1. Show the customer the different products sold by the juice machine.
2. Let the customer make the selection.
3. Show the customer the cost of the item selected.
4. Accept money from the customer.
5. Release the item.

Input The item selection and the cost of the item.

Output The selected item.

PROBLEM
ANALYSIS AND
ALGORITHM
DESIGN

A juice machine has two main components: a built-in cash register and several dispensers to hold and release the products.

Cash
Register

Let us first discuss the properties of a cash register. The cash register has some cash on hand, it accepts the amount from the customer, and if the amount deposited is more than the cost of the item, then—if possible—the cash register returns the change. For simplicity, we assume that the user deposits at least the amount of money for the product. The cash register should also be able to show the juice machine's owner the amount of money in the register at any given time. The following class defines the properties of a cash register.

```
//***********************************************************************
// Author: D.S. Malik
//
// class cashRegister
// This class specifies the members to implement a cash register.
//***********************************************************************

class cashRegister
{
public:
    int getCurrentBalance() const;
      //Function to show the current amount in the cash register.
      //Postcondition: The value of cashOnHand is returned.

    void acceptAmount(int amountIn);
      //Function to receive the amount deposited by
      //the customer and update the amount in the register.
      //Postcondition: cashOnHand = cashOnHand + amountIn;

    cashRegister();
      //Default constructor
      //Sets the cash in the register to 500 cents.
      //Postcondition: cashOnHand = 500.

    cashRegister(int cashIn);
      //Constructor with a parameter.
      //Sets the cash in the register to a specific amount.
      //Postcondition: cashOnHand = cashIn;

private:
    int cashOnHand; //variable to store the cash in the register
};
```

Figure 1-10 shows the UML class diagram of the **class cashRegister**.

cashRegister
-cashOnHand: int
+getCurrentBalance const(): int +acceptAmount(int): void +cashRegister() +cashRegister(int)

FIGURE 1-10 UML class diagram of the **class** cashRegister

Next, we give the definitions of the functions to implement the operations of the class **cashRegister**. The definitions of these functions are simple and easy to follow.

The function **getCurrentBalance** shows the current amount in the cash register. It returns the value of the instance variable **cashOnHand**. So, its definition is the following:

```
int cashRegister::getCurrentBalance() const
{
    return cashOnHand;
}
```

The definitions of the remaining function(s) and constructors are as follows:

```
void cashRegister::acceptAmount(int amountIn)
{
    cashOnHand = cashOnHand + amountIn;
}

cashRegister::cashRegister()
{
    cashOnHand = 500;
}

cashRegister::cashRegister(int cashIn)
{
    if (cashIn >= 0)
        cashOnHand = cashIn;
    else
        cashOnHand = 500;
}
```

Dispenser The dispenser releases the selected item if it is not empty. The dispenser should show the number of items in the dispenser and the cost of the item. The following class defines the properties of a dispenser. Let us call this `class dispenserType`.

```
//*************************************************************
// Author: D.S. Malik
//
// class dispenserType
// This class specifies the members to implement a dispenser.
//*************************************************************

class dispenserType
{
public:
    int getNoOfItems() const;
        //Function to show the number of items in the machine.
        //Postcondition: The value of numberOfItems is returned.

    int getCost() const;
        //Function to show the cost of the item.
        //Postcondition: The value of cost is returned.

    void makeSale();
        //Function to reduce the number of items by 1.
        //Postcondition: numberOfItems--;

    dispenserType();
        //Default constructor
        //Sets the cost and number of items in the dispenser to 50.
        //Postcondition: numberOfItems = 50; cost = 50;

    dispenserType(int setNoOfItems, int setCost);
        //Constructor with parameters
        //Sets the cost and number of items in the dispenser
        //to the values specified by the user.
        //Postcondition: numberOfItems = setNoOfItems;
        //    cost = setCost;

private:
    int numberOfItems;    //variable to store the number of
                          //items in the dispenser
    int cost;  //variable to store the cost of an item
};
```

Figure 1-11 shows the UML class diagram of the **class dispenserType**.

```
dispenserType
-numberOfItems: int
-cost: int
+getNoOfItems() const: int
+getCost() const: int
+makeSale(): void
+dispenserType()
+dispenserType(int, int)
```

FIGURE 1-11 UML class diagram of the **class** dispenserType

Because the juice machine sells four types of items, we shall declare four objects of type `dispenserType`. For example, the statement

```
dispenserType appleJuice(100, 50);
```

declares `appleJuice` to be an object of type `dispenserType`, and sets the number of apple juice cans in the dispenser to `100` and the cost of each can to `50` cents.

Following the definitions of the **class dispenserType**, the definitions of the member functions and constructors are as follows:

```
int dispenserType::getNoOfItems() const
{
    return numberOfItems;
}

int dispenserType::getCost() const
{
    return cost;
}

void dispenserType::makeSale()
{
    numberOfItems--;
}

dispenserType::dispenserType()
{
    numberOfItems = 50;
    cost = 50;
}
```

```
dispenserType::dispenserType(int setNoOfItems, int setCost)
{
    if (setNoOfItems >= 0)
        numberOfItems = setNoOfItems;
    else
        numberOfItems = 50;

    if (setCost >= 0)
        cost = setCost;
    else
        cost = 50;
}
```

MAIN
PROGRAM

When the program executes, it must do the following:

1. Show the different products sold by the juice machine.
2. Show how to select a particular product.
3. Show how to terminate the program.

Furthermore, these instructions must be displayed after processing each selection (except exiting the program), so that the user need not remember what to do if he or she wants to buy two or more items. Once the user has made the appropriate selection, the juice machine must act accordingly. If the user has opted to buy a product and if that product is available, the juice machine should show the cost of the product and ask the user to deposit the money. If the amount deposited is at least the cost of the item, the juice machine should sell the item and display an appropriate message.

This discussion translates into the following algorithm:

1. Show the selection to the customer.
2. Get the selection.
3. If the selection is valid and the dispenser corresponding to the selection is not empty, sell the product.

We divide this program into three functions—showSelection, sellProduct, and main.

showSelection This function displays the information necessary to help the user select and buy a product. The definition of this function is:

```
void showSelection()
{
    cout << "*** Welcome to Shelly's Fruit Juice Shop ***" << endl;
    cout << "To select an item, enter " << endl;
    cout << "1 for apple juice" << endl;
    cout << "2 for orange juice" << endl;
    cout << "3 for mango lassi" << endl;
    cout << "4 for fruit punch" << endl;
    cout << "9 to exit" << endl;
}//end showSelection
```

sellProduct   This function attempts to sell the product selected by the customer. Therefore, it must have access to the dispenser holding the product. The first thing that this function does is check whether the dispenser holding the product is empty. If the dispenser is empty, the function informs the customer that this product is sold out. If the dispenser is not empty, it tells the user to deposit the necessary amount to buy the product.

If the user does not deposit enough money to buy the product, sellProduct tells the user how much additional money must be deposited. If the user fails to deposit enough money, in two tries, to buy the product, the function simply returns the money. (Programming Exercise 5, at the end of this chapter, asks you to revise the definition of the function sellProduct so that it keeps asking the user to enter the additional amount as long as the user has not entered enough money to buy the product.) If the amount deposited by the user is sufficient, it accepts the money and sells the product. Selling the product means to decrement the number of items in the dispenser by 1, and to update the money in the cash register by adding the cost of the product. (We also assume that this program does not return the extra money deposited by the customer. So the cash register is updated by adding the money entered by the user.)

From this discussion, it is clear that the function sellProduct must have access to the dispenser holding the product (to decrement the number of items in the dispenser by 1 and to show the cost of the item) as well as the cash register (to update the cash). Therefore, this function has two parameters: one corresponding to the dispenser and the other corresponding to the cash register. Furthermore, both parameters must be referenced.

In pseudocode, the algorithm for this function is:

1. If the dispenser is not empty

   a. Show and prompt the customer to enter the cost of the item.

   b. Get the amount entered by the customer.

   c. If the amount entered by the customer is less than the cost of the product,

      i. Show and prompt the customer to enter the additional amount.

      ii. Calculate the total amount entered by the customer.

   d. If the amount entered by the customer is at least the cost of the product,

      i. Update the amount in the cash register.

      ii. Sell the product—that is, decrement the number of items in the dispenser by 1.

      iii. Display an appropriate message.

   e. If the amount entered by the user is less than the cost of the item, return the amount.

2. If the dispenser is empty, tell the user that this product is sold out.

The definition of the function `sellProduct` is:

```cpp
void sellProduct(dispenserType& product, cashRegister& pCounter)
{
    int amount;  //variable to hold the amount entered
    int amount2; //variable to hold the extra amount needed

    if (product.getNoOfItems() > 0) //if the dispenser is not empty
    {
        cout << "Please deposit " << product.getCost()
             << " cents" << endl;
        cin >> amount;

        if (amount < product.getCost())
        {
            cout << "Please deposit another "
                 << product.getCost()- amount << " cents" << endl;
            cin >> amount2;
            amount = amount + amount2;
        }

        if (amount >= product.getCost())
        {
            pCounter.acceptAmount(amount);
            product.makeSale();
            cout << "Collect your item at the bottom and enjoy."
                 << endl;
        }
        else
            cout << "The amount is not enough. "
                 << "Collect what you deposited." << endl;

        cout << "*-*-*-*-*-*-*-*-*-*-*-*-*-*-*-*-*-*-*"
             << endl << endl;
    }
    else
        cout << "Sorry, this item is sold out." << endl;
}//end sellProduct
```

main   The algorithm for the function `main` is as follows:

1. Create the cash register—that is, declare a variable of type `cashRegister`.

2. Create four dispensers—that is, declare four objects of type `dispenserType` and initialize these objects. For example, the statement

   `dispenserType mangoLassi(75, 45);`

   creates a dispenser object, `mangoLassi`, to hold the juice cans. The number of items in the dispenser is 75, and the cost of an item is 45 cents.

3. Declare additional variables as necessary.

4. Show the selection; call the function showSelection.

5. Get the selection.

6. While not done (a selection of 9 exits the program),

   a. Sell the product; call the function sellProduct.

   b. Show the selection; call the function showSelection.

   c. Get the selection.

The definition of the function main is as follows:

```cpp
int main()
{
    cashRegister counter;
    dispenserType appleJuice(100, 50);
    dispenserType orangeJuice(100, 65);
    dispenserType mangoLassi(75, 45);
    dispenserType fruitPunch(100, 85);

    int choice;   //variable to hold the selection

    showSelection();
    cin >> choice;

    while (choice != 9)
    {
        switch (choice)
        {
        case 1:
            sellProduct(appleJuice, counter);
            break;

        case 2:
            sellProduct(orangeJuice, counter);
            break;

        case 3:
            sellProduct(mangoLassi, counter);
            break;

        case 4:
            sellProduct(fruitPunch, counter);
            break;

        default:
            cout << "Invalid selection." << endl;
        }//end switch
```

```
            showSelection();
            cin >> choice;
        }//end while

        return 0;
    }//end main
```

PROGRAM LISTING

```
//******************************************************************
// Author: D.S. Malik
//
// This program uses the classes cashRegister and dispenserType
// to implement a fruit juice machine.
// ******************************************************************

#include <iostream>
#include "cashRegister.h"
#include "dispenserType.h"

using namespace std;

void showSelection();
void sellProduct(dispenserType& product, cashRegister& pCounter);

//Place the definitions of the functions main, showSelection, and
//sellProduct here.
```

Sample Run: In this sample run, the user input is shaded.

```
*** Welcome to Shelly's Fruit Juice Shop ***
To select an item, enter
1 for apple juice
2 for orange juice
3 for mango lassi
4 for fruit punch
9 to exit
1
Please deposit 50 cents
50
Collect your item at the bottom and enjoy.
* _* _* _* _* _* _* _* _* _* _* _* _* _* _* _* _* _*
```

```
*** Welcome to Shelly's Fruit Juice Shop ***
To select an item, enter
1 for apple juice
2 for orange juice
3 for mango lassi
4 for fruit punch
9 to exit
9
```

The complete definitions of the classes `cashRegister`, `dispenserType`, the implementation files, and the `main` program is available at the Web site accompanying this book.

Identifying Classes, Objects, and Operations

The hardest part of OOD is to identify the classes and objects. This section describes a common and simple technique to identify classes and objects.

We begin with a description of the problem and then identify all of the nouns and verbs. From the list of nouns we choose our classes, and from the list of verbs we choose our operations.

For example, suppose that we want to write a program that calculates and prints the volume and surface area of a cylinder. We can state this problem as follows:

Write a **program** to *input* the **dimensions** of a **cylinder** and *calculate* and *print* its **surface area** and **volume**.

In this statement, the nouns are bold and the verbs are italic. From the list of nouns—**program**, **dimensions**, **cylinder**, **surface area**, and **volume**—we can easily visualize **cylinder** to be a class—say, `cylinderType`—from which we can create many cylinder objects of various dimensions. The nouns—**dimensions**, **surface area**, and **volume**—are characteristics of a **cylinder** and, thus, can hardly be considered classes.

After we identify a class, the next step is to determine three pieces of information:

- Operations that an object of that class type can perform
- Operations that can be performed on an object of that class type
- Information that an object of that class type must maintain

From the list of verbs identified in the problem description, we choose a list of possible operations that an object of that class can perform, or has performed, on itself. For example, from the list of verbs for the cylinder problem description—*write*, *input*, *calculate*, and *print*—the possible operations for a cylinder object are *input*, *calculate*, and *print*.

For the `cylinderType` class, the dimensions represent the data. The `center` of the base, `radius` of the base, and `height` of the cylinder are the characteristics of the dimensions. You can input data to the object either by a constructor or by a function.

The verb *calculate* applies to determining the volume and the surface area. From this, you can deduce the operations: `cylinderVolume` and `cylinderSurfaceArea`. Similarly, the verb *print* applies to the display of the volume and the surface area on an output device.

Identifying classes via the nouns and verbs from the descriptions to the problem is not the only technique possible. There are several other OOD techniques in the literature. However, this technique is sufficient for the programming exercises in this book.

QUICK REVIEW

1. Software are programs run by the computer.
2. A program goes through many phases from the time it is first conceived until the time it is retired, called the life cycle of the program.
3. The three fundamental stages through which a program goes are development, use, and maintenance.
4. The new program is created in the software development stage.
5. In the software maintenance process, the program is modified to fix the (identified) problems and/or to enhance it.
6. A program is retired if no new version of the program will be released.
7. The software development phases are analysis, design, implementation, and testing and debugging.
8. During the design phase, algorithms are designed to solve the problem.
9. An algorithm is a step-by-step problem-solving process in which a solution is arrived at in a finite amount of time.
10. Two well-known design techniques are structured-design and object-oriented design.
11. In structured design, a problem is divided into smaller subproblems. Each subproblem is solved, and the solutions of all the subproblems are then combined to solve the problem.
12. In object-oriented design (OOD), a program is a collection of interacting objects.
13. An object consists of data and operations on those data.
14. The three basic principles of OOD are encapsulation, inheritance, and polymorphism.
15. In the implementation phase, you write and compile programming code to implement the classes and functions that were discovered in the design phase.
16. A precondition is a statement specifying the condition(s) that must be true before the function is called.
17. A postcondition is a statement specifying what is true after the function call is completed.

18. During the testing phase, the program is tested for its correctness; that is, for making sure that the program does what it is supposed to do.

19. Debugging refers to finding and fixing the errors, if they exist.

20. To find problems in a program, it is run through a series of test cases.

21. A test case consists of a set of inputs, user actions, or other initial conditions, and the expected output.

22. There are two types of testing—black-box testing and white-box testing.

23. While analyzing a particular algorithm, we usually count the number of operations performed by the algorithm.

24. Let f be a function of n. The term asymptotic refers to the study of the function f as n becomes larger and larger without bound.

25. A class is a collection of a fixed number of components.

26. Components of a class are called the members of the class.

27. Members of a class are accessed by name.

28. In C++, **class** is a reserved word.

29. Members of a class are classified into one of three categories: **private**, **protected**, and **public**.

30. The **private** members of a class are not accessible outside the class.

31. The **public** members of a class are accessible outside the class.

32. By default, all members of a class are **private**.

33. The **public** members are declared using the member access specifier **public**.

34. The **private** members are declared using the member access specifier **private**.

35. A member of a class can be a function or a variable (that is, data).

36. If any member of a class is a function, you usually use the function prototype to declare it.

37. If any member of a class is a variable, it is declared like any other variable.

38. In the definition of the class, you cannot initialize a variable when you declare it.

39. In the Unified Modeling language (UML) diagram of a class, the top box contains the name of the class. The middle box contains the data members and their data types. The last box contains the member function name, parameter list, and the return type of the function. A + (plus) sign in front of a member indicates that this member is a **public** member; a − (minus) sign indicates that this is a **private** member. The symbol # before the member name indicates that the member is a **protected** member.

40. In C++, a **class** is a definition. No memory is allocated; memory is allocated for the class variables when you declare them.

41. In C++, class variables are called class objects or simply objects.

42. A class member is accessed using the class variable name, followed by the dot operator (.), followed by the member name.

43. The only built-in operations on classes are the assignment and member selection.

44. Class objects can be passed as parameters to functions and returned as function values.

45. As parameters to functions, classes can be passed either by value or by reference.

46. Constructors guarantee that the data members are initialized when an object is declared.

47. The name of a constructor is the same as the name of the class.

48. A class can have more than one constructor.

49. A constructor without parameters is called the default constructor.

50. Constructors automatically execute when a **class** object enters its scope.

51. Destructors automatically execute when a **class** object goes out of scope.

52. A class can have only one destructor with no parameters.

53. The name of a destructor is the tilde (~), followed by the class name (no spaces in between).

54. Constructors and destructors are functions without any type; that is, they are neither value-returning nor **void**. As a result, they cannot be called like other functions.

55. A data type that specifies the logical properties without the implementation details is called an abstract data type (ADT).

56. An easy way to identify classes, objects, and operations is to describe the problem in English and then identify all of the nouns and verbs. Choose your classes (objects) from the list of nouns and operations from the list of verbs.

EXERCISES

1. Mark the following statements as true or false.

   a. The life cycle of software refers to the phases from the point the software was conceived until it is retired.

   b. The three fundamental stages of software are development, use, and discard.

   c. The expression $4n + 2n^2 + 5$ is $O(n)$.

    d.   The instance variables of a class must be of the same type.

    e.   The function members of a class must be **public**.

    f.   A class can have more than one constructor.

    g.   A class can have more than one destructor.

    h.   Both constructors and destructors can have parameters.

2.   What is black-box testing?

3.   What is white-box testing?

4.   Consider the following function prototype, which returns the square root of a real number:

```
double sqrt(double x);
```

What should be the pre- and postconditions for this function?

5.   Each of the following expressions represents the number of operations for certain algorithms. What is the order of each of these expressions?

    a. $n^2 + 6n + 4$

    b. $5n^3 + 2n + 8$

    c. $(n^2 + 1)(3n + 5)$

    d. $5(6n + 4)$

    e. $n + 2\log_2 n - 6$

    f. $4n \log_2 n + 3n + 8$

6.   Consider the following function:

```
void funcExercise6(int x, int y)
{
    int z;

    z = x + y;
    x = y;
    y = z;
    z = x;
    cout << "x = " << x << ", y = " << y << ", z = " << z << endl;
}
```

Find the exact number of operations executed by the function funcExercise6.

7.   Consider the following function:

```
int funcExercise7(int list[], int size)
{
    int sum = 0;

    for (int index = 0; index < size; index++)
        sum = sum + list[index];

    return sum;
}
```

    a.   Find the number of operations executed by the function `funcExercise7` if the value of `size` is 10.

    b.   Find the number of operations executed by the function `funcExercise7` if the value of `size` is n.

    c.   What is the order of the function `funcExercise7`?

8.   Consider the following function prototype:

```
int funcExercise8(int x);
```

The function `funcExercise8` returns the value as follows: If $0 <= x <= 50$, it returns 2x; if $-50 <= x < 0$, it returns x^2; otherwise it returns −999. What are the reasonable boundary values for the function `funcExercise8`?

9.   Write a function that uses a loop to find the sum of the squares of all integers between 1 and n. What is the order of your function?

10. Characterize the following algorithm in terms of Big-O notation. Also find the exact number of additions executed by the loop. (Assume that all variables are properly declared.)

```
for (int i = 1; i <= n; i++)
    sum = sum + i * (i + 1);
```

11. Characterize the following algorithm in terms of Big-O notation. Also find the exact number of additions, subtractions, and multiplications executed by the loop. (Assume that all variables are properly declared.)

```
for (int i = 5; i <= 2 * n; i++)
    cout << 2 * n + i - 1 << endl;
```

12. Characterize the following algorithm in terms of Big-O notation.

```
for (int i = 1; i <= 2 * n; i++)
    for (int j = 1; j <= n; j++)
        cout << 2 * i + j;
cout << endl;
```

13. Characterize the following algorithm in terms of Big-O notation.

```
for (int i = 1; i <= n; i++)
    for (int j = 1; j <= n; j++)
        for (int k = 1; k <= n; k++)
            cout << i + j + k;
```

14. Find the syntax errors in the definitions of the following classes:

    a.
```
class AA
{
public:
    void print();
    int sum();
    AA();
    int AA(int, int);
private:
    int x;
    int y;
};
```

b.
```
class BB
{
    int one ;
    int two;
public:
    bool equal ();
    print ();
    BB(int, int);
}
```

c.
```
class CC
{
public;
    void set(int, int);
    void print();
    CC();
    CC(int, int);
    bool CC(int, int);
private:
    int u;
    int v;
};
```

15. Consider the following declarations:

```
class xClass
{
public:
    void func();
    void print() const;
    xClass ();
    xClass (int, double);
private:
    int u;
    double w;
};

xClass x;
```

a. How many members does class xClass have?

b. How many private members does class xClass have?

c. How many constructors does class xClass have?

d. Write the definition of the member function func so that u is set to 10 and w is set to 15.3.

e. Write the definition of the member function print that prints the contents of u and w.

f. Write the definition of the default constructor of the class xClass so that the private data members are initialized to 0.

g. Write a C++ statement that prints the values of the data members of the object x.

h. Write a C++ statement that declares an object t of the type xClass, and initializes the data members of t to 20 and 35.0, respectively.

16. Consider the definition of the following class:

```
class CC
{
public:
    CC();                    //Line 1
    CC(int);                 //Line 2
    CC(int, int);            //Line 3
    CC(double, int);         //Line 4
    .
    .
    .
private:
    int u;
    double v;
};
```

a. Give the line number containing the constructor that is executed in each of the following declarations:

    i.   CC one;

    ii. CC two(5, 6);

    iii. CC three(3.5, 8);

b. Write the definition of the constructor in Line 1 so that the **private** data members are initialized to 0.

c. Write the definition of the constructor in Line 2 so that the **private** data member u is initialized according to the value of the parameter, and the **private** data member v is initialized to 0.

d. Write the definition of the constructors in Lines 3 and 4 so that the **private** data members are initialized according to the values of the parameters.

17. Given the definition of the class clockType with constructors (as described in this chapter), what is the output of the following C++ code?

```
clockType clock1;
clockType clock2(23, 13, 75);

clock1.printTime();
cout << endl;
clock2.printTime();
cout << endl;

clock1.setTime(6, 59, 39);
clock1.printTime();
cout << endl;
```

```
clock1.incrementMinutes();
clock1.printTime();
cout << endl;

clock1.setTime(0, 13, 0);

if (clock1.equalTime(clock2))
    cout << "Clock1 time is the same as clock2 time." << endl;
else
    cout << "The two times are different." << endl;
```

18. Write the definition of a class that has the following properties:

    a. The name of the class is secretType.

    b. The class secretType has four instance variables: name of type string, age and weight of type int, and height of type double.

    c. The class secretType has the following member functions:

       print—Outputs the data stored in the instance variables with the appropriate titles

       setName—Function to set the name

       setAge—Function to set the age

       setWeight—Function to set the weight

       setHeight—Function to set the height

       getName—Value-returning function to return the name

       getAge—Value-returning function to return the age

       getWeight—Value-returning function to return the weight

       getHeight—Value-returning function to return the height

       Default constructor—Sets name to the empty string and age, weight, and height to 0

       Constructor with parameter—Sets the values of the instance variables to the values specified by the user

    d. Write the definition of the member functions of the class secretType as described in Part c.

19. Assume the definition of the class personType as given in this chapter.

    a. Write a C++ statement that declares student to be a personType object, and initialize its first name to "Buddy" and last name to "Arora".

    b. Write a C++ statement that outputs the data stored in the object student.

    c. Write C++ statements that change the first name of student to "Susan" and the last name to "Miller".

PROGRAMMING EXERCISES

1.   Write a program that converts a number entered in Roman numerals to decimal form. Your program should consist of a `class`, say `romanType`. An object of `romanType` should do the following:

   a.   Store the number as a Roman numeral.

   b.   Convert and store the number into decimal form.

   c.   Print the number as a Roman numeral or decimal number as requested by the user. (Write two separate functions—one to print the number as a Roman numeral and the other to print the number as a decimal number.)

   The decimal values of the Roman numerals are:

```
M    1000
D     500
C     100
L      50
X      10
V       5
I       1
```

   Remember, a larger numeral preceding a smaller numeral means addition, so `LX` is 60. A smaller numeral preceding a larger numeral means subtraction, so `XL` is 40. Any place in a decimal number, such as the 1s place, the 10s place, and so on, requires from zero to four Roman numerals.

   d.   Test your program using the following Roman numerals: `MCXIV`, `CCCLIX`, and `MDCLXVI`.

2.   Write the definition of the `class dayType` that implements the day of the week in a program. The `class dayType` should store the day, such as `Sunday` for Sunday. The program should be able to perform the following operations on an object of type `dayType`:

   a.   Set the day.

   b.   Print the day.

   c.   Return the day.

   d.   Return the next day.

   e.   Return the previous day.

   f.   Calculate and return the day by adding certain days to the current day. For example, if the current day is Monday and we add 4 days, the day to be returned is Friday. Similarly, if today is Tuesday and we add 13 days, the day to be returned is Monday.

   g.   Add the appropriate constructors.

3.   Write the definitions of the functions to implement the operations for the `class dayType` as defined in Programming Exercise 2. Also, write a program to test various operations on this class.

4. Example 1-12 defined a `class personType` to store the name of a person. The member functions that we included merely print the name and set the name of a person. Redefine the `class personType` so that, in addition to what the existing class does, you also can do the following:

   a. Set the first name only.

   b. Set the last name only.

   c. Store and set the middle name.

   d. Check whether a given first name is the same as the first name of this person.

   e. Check whether a given last name is the same as the last name of this person.

   Write the definitions of the member functions to implement the operations for this class. Also, write a program to test various operations on this class.

5. The function `sellProduct` of the Fruit Juice Machine programming example gives the user only two chances to enter enough money to buy the product. Rewrite the definition of the function `sellProduct` so that it keeps prompting the user to enter more money as long as the user has not entered enough money to buy the product. Also, write a program to test your function.

6. The equation of a line in standard form is $ax + by = c$, where a and b both cannot be zero, and a, b, and c are real numbers. If $b \neq 0$, then $-a\,/\,b$ is the slope of the line. If $a = 0$, then it is a horizontal line, and if $b = 0$, then it is a vertical line. The slope of a vertical line is undefined. Two lines are parallel if they have the same slope or both are vertical lines. Two lines are perpendicular if either one of the lines is horizontal and another is vertical, or if the product of their slopes is -1. Design the `class lineType` to store a line. To store a line, you need to store the values of a (coefficient of x), b (coefficient of y), and c. Your class must contain the following operations:

   a. If a line is nonvertical, then determine its slope.

   b. Determine if two lines are equal. (Two lines $a_1x + b_1y = c_1$ and $a_2x + b_2y = c_2$ are equal if either $a_1 = a_2$, $b_1 = b_2$, and $c_1 = c_2$ or $a_1 = ka_2$, $b_1 = kb_2$, and $c_1 = kc_2$ for some real number k.)

   c. Determine if two lines are parallel.

   d. Determine if two lines are perpendicular.

   e. If two lines are not parallel, then find the point of intersection.

      Add appropriate constructors to initialize variables of `lineType`. Also write a program to test your class.

7. **(Tic-Tac-Toe)** Write a program that allows two players to play the tic-tac-toe game. Your program must contain the `class ticTacToe` to implement a `ticTacToe` object. Include a 3 by 3 two-dimensional array, as a `private` instance variable, to create the board. If needed, include additional member variables. Some of the operations on a `ticTacToe` object are printing the current board, getting a move, checking if a move is valid, and determining the winner after each move. Add additional operations as needed.

CHAPTER 2

OBJECT-ORIENTED DESIGN (OOD) AND C++

IN THIS CHAPTER, YOU WILL:

- Learn about inheritance
- Learn about derived and base classes
- Explore how to redefine the member functions of a base class
- Examine how the constructors of base and derived classes work
- Learn how to construct the header file of a derived class
- Explore three types of inheritance: `public`, `protected`, and `private`
- Learn about composition
- Become familiar with the three basic principles of object-oriented design
- Learn about overloading
- Become aware of the restrictions on operator overloading
- Examine the pointer `this`
- Learn about `friend` functions
- Explore the members and nonmembers of a class
- Discover how to overload various operators
- Learn about templates
- Explore how to construct function templates and class templates

Chapter 1 introduced classes, abstract data types (ADT), and ways to implement ADT in C++. By using classes, you can combine data and operations in a single unit. An object, therefore, becomes a self-contained entity. Operations can directly access the data, but the internal state of an object cannot be manipulated directly.

In addition to implementing ADT, classes have other features. For instance, you can create new classes from existing classes. This important feature encourages code reuse.

Inheritance

Suppose that you want to design a class, partTimeEmployee, to implement and process the characteristics of a part-time employee. The main features associated with a part-time employee are the name, pay rate, and number of hours worked. In Example 1-12 (in Chapter 1), we designed a class to implement a person's name. Every part-time employee is a person. Therefore, rather than design the class partTimeEmployee from scratch, we want to be able to extend the definition of the class personType (from Example 1-12) by adding additional members (data and/or functions).

Of course, we do not want to make the necessary changes directly to the class personType—that is, edit the class personType, and add and/or delete members. In fact, we want to create the class partTimeEmployee without making any physical changes to the class personType, by adding only the members that are necessary. For example, because the class personType already has data members to store the first name and last name, we will not include any such members in the class partTimeEmployee. In fact, these data members will be inherited from the class personType. (We will design such a class in Example 2-2.)

In Chapter 1, we extensively studied and designed the class clockType to implement the time of day in a program. The class clockType has three data members to store hours, minutes, and seconds. Certain applications—in addition to hours, minutes, and seconds—might also require us to store the time zone. In this case, we would likely extend the definition of the class clockType and create a class, extClockType, to accommodate this new information. That is, we want to derive the class extClockType by adding a data member—say, timeZone—and the necessary function members to manipulate the time (see Programming Exercise 1 at the end of this chapter). In C++, the mechanism that allows us to accomplish this task is the principle of inheritance. Inheritance is an "is-a" relationship; for instance, "every employee is a person."

Inheritance lets us create new classes from existing classes. The existing classes are called the **base classes**; the new class that we create from the existing classes is called the **derived class**. The derived class inherits the properties of the base classes. So rather than create completely new classes from scratch, we can take advantage of inheritance and reduce software complexity.

Each derived class, in turn, becomes a base class for a future derived class. Inheritance can be either a **single inheritance** or a **multiple inheritance**. In a single inheritance, the derived class is derived from a single base class; in a multiple inheritance, the derived class is derived from more than one base class. This chapter concentrates on single inheritance.

Inheritance can be viewed as a treelike, or hierarchical, structure wherein a base class is shown with its derived classes. Consider the tree diagram shown in Figure 2-1.

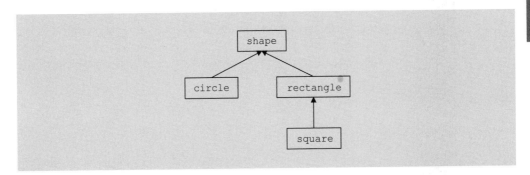

FIGURE 2-1 Inheritance hierarchy

In this diagram, `shape` is the base class. The `classes circle` and `rectangle` are derived from `shape`, and the `class square` is derived from `rectangle`. Every `circle` and every `rectangle` is a `shape`. Every `square` is a `rectangle`.

The general syntax of a derived class is:

```
class className: memberAccessSpecifier baseClassName
{
     member list
};
```

where `memberAccessSpecifier` is **public**, **protected**, or **private**. When no `memberAccessSpecifier` is specified, it is assumed to be a **private** inheritance. (We discuss **protected** inheritance later in this chapter.)

EXAMPLE 2-1

Suppose that we have defined a class called `shape`. The following statements specify that the `class circle` is derived from `shape`, and it is a **public** inheritance:

```
class circle: public shape
{
    .
    .
    .
};
```

On the other hand, consider the following definition of the `class circle`:

```
class circle: private shape
{
    .
    .
    .
};
```

This is a `private` inheritance. In this definition, the `public` members of `shape` become `private` members of the `class circle`. So any object of type `circle` cannot directly access these members. The previous definition of `circle` is equivalent to the following:

```
class circle: shape
{
    .
    .
    .
};
```

That is, if we do not use either the `memberAccessSpecifier` `public` or `private`, the `public` members of a base class are inherited as `private` members.

The following facts about the base and the derived classes should be kept in mind.

1. The `private` members of a base class are `private` to the base class; hence, the members of the derived class cannot directly access them. In other words, when you write the definitions of the member functions of the derived class, you cannot directly access the `private` members of the base class.

2. The `public` members of a base class can be inherited either as `public` members or as `private` members by the derived class. That is, the `public` members of the base class can become either `public` or `private` members of the derived class.

3. The derived class can include additional members—data and/or functions.

4. The derived class can redefine the `public` member functions of the base class. That is, in the derived class, you can have a member function with the same name, number, and types of parameters as a function in the base class. However, this redefinition applies only to the objects of the derived class, not to the objects of the base class.

5. All member variables of the base class are also member variables of the derived class. Similarly, the member functions of the base class (unless redefined) are also member functions of the derived class. (Remember Rule 1 when accessing a member of the base class in the derived class.)

The next sections describe two important issues related to inheritance. The first issue is the redefinition of the member functions of the base class in the derived class. While discussing this issue, we also address how to access the `private` (data) members of the base class in the derived class. The second key inheritance issue is related to the constructor. The constructor of a derived class cannot *directly* access the `private` member variables of the base class. Thus, we need to ensure that the `private` member variables that are inherited from the base class are initialized when a constructor of the derived class executes.

Redefining (Overriding) Member Functions of the Base Class

Suppose that a `class derivedClass` is derived from the `class baseClass`. Further assume that both `derivedClass` and `baseClass` have some member variables. It then follows that the member variables of the `class derivedClass` are its own member variables, together with the member variables of `baseClass`. Suppose that `baseClass` contains a function, `print`, that prints the values of the member variables of `baseClass`. Now `derivedClass` contains member variables in addition to the member variables inherited from `baseClass`. Suppose that you want to include a function that prints the member variables of `derivedClass`. You can give any name to this function. However, in the `class derivedClass`, you can also name this function as `print` (the same name used by `baseClass`). This is called redefining (or overriding) the member function of the base class. Next, we illustrate how to redefine the member functions of a base class with the help of an example.

NOTE To redefine a `public` member function of a base class in the derived class, the corresponding function in the derived class must have the same name, number, and types of parameters. In other words, the name of the function being redefined in the derived class must have the same name and the same set of parameters. If the corresponding functions in the base class and the derived class have the same name but different sets of parameters, this is function overloading in the derived class, which is also allowed.

Consider the definition of the following class:

```
//**********************************************************
// Author: D.S. Malik
//
// class rectangleType
// This class specifies the members to implement the properties
// of a rectangle.
//**********************************************************

class rectangleType
{
public:
    void setDimension(double l, double w);
      //Function to set the length and width of the rectangle.
      //Postcondition: length = l; width = w;

    double getLength() const;
      //Function to return the length of the rectangle.
      //Postcondition: The value of length is returned.
```

```
    double getWidth() const;
        //Function to return the width of the rectangle.
        //Postcondition: The value of width is returned.

    double area() const;
        //Function to return the area of the rectangle.
        //Postcondition: The area of the rectangle is calculated
        //    and returned.

    double perimeter() const;
        //Function to return the perimeter of the rectangle.
        //Postcondition: The perimeter of the rectangle is
        //    calculated and returned.

    void print() const;
        //Function to output the length and width of the rectangle.

    rectangleType();
        //default constructor
        //Postcondition: length = 0; width = 0;

    rectangleType(double l, double w);
        //constructor with parameters
        //Postcondition: length = l; width = w;

private:
    double length;
    double width;
};
```

Figure 2-2 shows the UML class diagram of the class rectangleType.

```
                rectangleType
-length: double
-width: double

+setDimension(double, double): void
+getLength() const: double
+getWidth() const: double
+area() const: double
+perimeter() const: double
+print() const: void
+rectangleType()
+rectangleType(double, double)
```

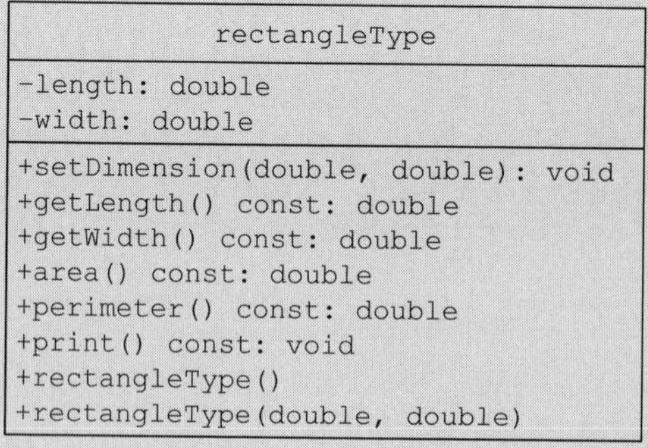

FIGURE 2-2 UML class diagram of the class rectangleType

Suppose that the definitions of the member functions of the class `rectangleType` are as follows:

```cpp
void rectangleType::setDimension(double l, double w)
{
    if (l >= 0)
        length = l;
    else
        length = 0;

    if (w >= 0)
        width = w;
    else
        width = 0;
}

double rectangleType::getLength() const
{
    return length;
}

double rectangleType::getWidth() const
{
    return width;
}

double rectangleType::area() const
{
    return length * width;
}

double rectangleType::perimeter() const
{
    return 2 * (length + width);
}

void rectangleType::print() const
{
    cout << "Length = " << length
         << "; Width = " << width;
}

rectangleType::rectangleType(double l, double w)
{
    setDimension(l, w);
}

rectangleType::rectangleType()
{
    length = 0;
    width = 0;
}
```

Now consider the definition of the following class boxType, derived from the class rectangleType:

```
//****************************************************************
// Author: D.S. Malik
//
// class boxType
// This class is derived from the class rectangleType and it
// specifies the members to implement the properties of a box.
//****************************************************************

class boxType: public rectangleType
{
public:
    void setDimension(double l, double w, double h);
      //Function to set the length, width, and height of the box.
      //Postcondition: length = l; width = w; height = h;

    double getHeight() const;
      //Function to return the height of the box.
      //Postcondition: The value of height is returned.

    double area() const;
      //Function to return the surface area of the box.
      //Postcondition: The surface area of the box is
      //    calculated and returned.

    double volume() const;
      //Function to return the volume of the box.
      //Postcondition: The volume of the box is calculated and
      //    returned.

    void print() const;
      //Function to output the length, width, and height of a box.

    boxType();
      //Default constructor
      //Postcondition: length = 0; width = 0; height = 0;

    boxType(double l, double w, double h);
      //Constructor with parameters
      //Postcondition: length = l; width = w; height = h;

private:
    double height;
};
```

Figure 2-3 shows the UML class diagram of the `class boxType` and the inheritance hierarchy.

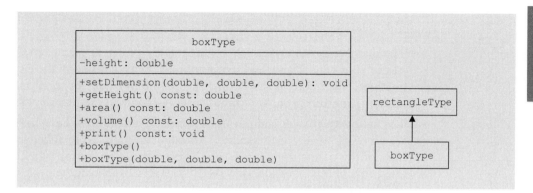

FIGURE 2-3 UML class diagram of the `class boxType` and the inheritance hierarchy

From the definition of the `class boxType`, it is clear that the `class boxType` is derived from the `class rectangleType`, and that it is a `public` inheritance. Therefore, all `public` members of the `class rectangleType` are `public` members of the `class boxType`. The `class boxType` also overrides (redefines) the functions `print` and `area`.

In general, while writing the definitions of the member functions of a derived class to specify a call to a `public` member function of the base class, we do the following:

- If the derived class overrides a `public` member function of the base class, then to specify a call to that `public` member function of the base class, you use the name of the base class, followed by the scope resolution operator, `::`, followed by the function name with the appropriate parameter list.

- If the derived class does not override a `public` member function of the base class, you may specify a call to that `public` member function by using the name of the function and the appropriate parameter list. (See the following note for member functions of the base class that are overloaded in the derived class.)

NOTE   If a derived class *overloads* a `public` member function of the base class, then while writing the definition of a member function of the derived class, to specify a call to that (overloaded) member function of the base class, you might need (depending on the compiler) to use the name of the base class followed by the scope resolution operator, `::`, followed by the function name with the appropriate parameter list. For example, the `class boxType` overloads the member function `setDimension` of the `class rectangleType`. (See the definition of the function `setDimension` of the `class boxType` given later in this section.)

Next, let us write the definition of the member function `print` of the `class boxType`. The `class boxType` has three member variables: `length`, `width`, and `height`. The member function `print` of the `class boxType` prints the values of these member variables. To write the definition of the function `print` of the `class boxType`, keep in mind the following:

- The member variables `length` and `width` are `private` members of the `class rectangleType`, and so cannot be directly accessed in the `class boxType`. Therefore, when writing the definition of the function `print` of the `class boxType`, we cannot access `length` and `width` directly.

- The member variables `length` and `width` of the `class rectangleType` are accessible in the `class boxType` through the `public` member functions of the `class rectangleType`. Therefore, when writing the definition of the member function `print` of the `class boxType`, we first call the member function `print` of the `class rectangleType` to print the values of `length` and `width`. After printing the values of `length` and `width`, we output the values of `height`.

To call the member function `print` of `rectangleType` in the definition of the member function `print` of `boxType`, we must use the following statement:

```
rectangleType::print();
```

This statement ensures that we call the member function `print` of the base `class rectangleType`, not of the `class boxType`.

The definition of the member function `print` of the `class boxType` is:

```
void boxType::print() const
{
    rectangleType::print();
    cout << "; Height = " << height;
}
```

Let us write the definitions of the remaining member functions of the `class boxType`.

The definition of the function `setDimension` is as follows:

```
void boxType::setDimension(double l, double w, double h)
{
    rectangleType::setDimension(l, w);

    if (h >= 0)
        height = h;
    else
        height = 0;
}
```

Notice that in the preceding definition of the function `setDimension`, a call to the member function `setDimension` of the `class rectangleType` is preceded by the name of the class and the scope resolution operator, even though the `class boxType` overloads—not overrides—the function `setDimension`.

The definition of the function `getHeight` is as follows:

```
double boxType::getHeight() const
{
    return height;
}
```

The member function `area` of the `class boxType` determines the surface area of a box. To determine the surface area of a box, we need to access the length and width of the box, which are declared as `private` members of the `class rectangleType`. Therefore, we use the member functions `getLength` and `getWidth` of the `class rectangleType` to retrieve the length and width, respectively. Because the `class boxType` does not contain any member functions that have the names `getLength` or `getWidth`, we call these member functions of the `class rectangleType` without using the name of the base class.

```
double boxType::area() const
{
    return 2 * (getLength() * getWidth()
                + getLength() * height
                + getWidth() * height);
}
```

The member function `volume` of the `class boxType` determines the volume of a box. To determine the volume of a box, you multiply the length, width, and height of the box, or multiply the area of the base of the box by its height. Let us write the definition of the member function `volume` by using the second alternative. To do this, you can use the member function `area` of the `class rectangleType` to determine the area of the base. Because the `class boxType` overrides the member function `area`, to specify a call to the member function `area` of the `class rectangleType`, we use the name of the base class and the scope resolution operator, as shown in the following definition:

```
double boxType::volume() const
{
    return rectangleType::area() * height;
}
```

In the next section, we discuss how to specify a call to the constructor of the base class when writing the definition of a constructor of the derived class.

Constructors of Derived and Base Classes

A derived class can have its own `private` member variables, and so a derived class can explicitly include its own constructors. A constructor typically serves to initialize the member variables. When we declare a derived class object, this object inherits the members of the base class, but the derived class object cannot directly access the `private` (data) members of the base class. The same is true for the member functions of a derived class. That is, the member functions of a derived class cannot directly access the `private` members of the base class.

As a consequence, the constructors of a derived class can (directly) initialize only the (public data) members inherited from the base class of the derived class. Thus, when a derived class object is declared, it must also automatically execute one of the constructors of the base class. Because constructors cannot be called like other functions, the execution of a derived class constructor must trigger the execution of one of the base class constructors. This is, in fact, what happens. To make this explicit, a call to the base class constructor is specified in the *heading of the definition* of a derived class constructor.

In the preceding section, we defined the class `rectangleType` and derived the class `boxType` from it. Moreover, we illustrated how to override a member function of the class `rectangleType`. Let us now discuss how to write the definitions of the constructors of the class `boxType`.

The class `rectangleType` has two constructors and two member variables. The class `boxType` has three member variables: `length`, `width`, and `height`. The member variables `length` and `width` are inherited from the class `rectangleType`.

First, let us write the definition of the default constructor of the class `boxType`. Recall that, if a class contains the default constructor and no values are specified when the object is declared, the default constructor executes and initializes the object. Because the class `rectangleType` contains the default constructor, when writing the definition of the default constructor of the class `boxType`, we do not specify any constructor of the base class.

```
boxType::boxType()
{
    height = 0.0;
}
```

Next, we discuss how to write the definitions of constructors with parameters. To trigger the execution of a constructor (with parameters) of the base class, you specify the name of a constructor of the base class with the parameters in the heading of the definition of the constructor of the derived class.

Consider the following definition of the constructor with parameters of the class `boxType`:

```
boxType::boxType(double l, double w, double h)
        : rectangleType(l, w)
{
    if (h >= 0)
        height = h;
    else
        height = 0;
}
```

In this definition, we specify the constructor of `rectangleType` with two parameters. When this constructor of `boxType` executes, it triggers the execution of the constructor with two parameters of type `double` of the class `rectangleType`.

Consider the following statements:

```
rectangleType myRectangle(5.0, 3.0);   //Line 1
boxType myBox(6.0, 5.0, 4.0);          //Line 2
```

The statement in Line 1 creates the `rectangleType` object `myRectangle`. Thus, the object `myRectangle` has two member variables: `length` and `width`. The statement in Line 2 creates the `boxType` object `myBox`. Thus, the object `myBox` has three member variables: `length`, `width`, and `height`. See Figure 2-4.

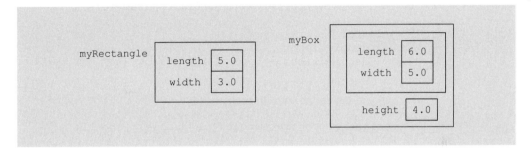

FIGURE 2-4 Objects `myRectangle` and `myBox`

Consider the following statements:

```
myRectangle.print();    //Line 3
cout << endl;           //Line 4
myBox.print();          //Line 5
cout << endl;           //Line 6
```

In the statement in Line 3, the member function `print` of the `class rectangleType` is executed. In the statement in Line 5, the function `print` associated with the `class boxType` is executed. Recall that, if a derived class overrides a member function of the base class, the redefinition applies only to the objects of the derived class. Thus, the output of the statement in Line 3 is:

```
Length = 5.0; Width = 3.0
```

The output of the statement in Line 5 is:

```
Length = 6.0; Width = 5.0; Height = 4.0
```

 NOTE **(Constructors with default parameters and the inheritance hierarchy)** Recall that a class can have a constructor with default parameters. Therefore, a derived class can also have a constructor with default parameters. For example, suppose that the definition of the `class rectangleType` is as given next. (To save space, these definitions have no documentation.)

```
class rectangleType
{
public:
    void setDimension(double l, double w);
    double getLength() const;
    double getWidth() const;
    double area() const;
    double perimeter() const;
    void print() const;
    rectangleType(double l = 0, double w = 0);
      //Constructor with default parameters

private:
    double length;
    double width;
};
```

Suppose the definition of the constructor is:

```
rectangleType::rectangleType(double l, double w)
{
    setDimension(l, w);
}
```

Now suppose that the definition of the class boxType is as follows:

```
class boxType: public rectangleType
{
public:
    void setDimension(double l, double w, double h);
    double getHeight() const;
    double area() const;
    double volume() const;
    void print() const;
    boxType(double l = 0, double w = 0, double h = 0);
      //Constructor with default parameters

private:
    double height;
};
```

You can write the definition of the constructor of the class boxType as follows:

```
boxType::boxType(double l, double w, double h)
        : rectangleType(l, w)
{
    if (h >= 0)
        height = h;
    else
        height = 0;
}
```

Notice that this definition also takes care of the default constructor of the class boxType.

> **NOTE**
>
> Suppose that a base class, baseClass, has private member variables and constructors. Further suppose that the class derivedClass is derived from baseClass, and derivedClass has no member variables. Therefore, the member variables of derivedClass are the ones inherited from baseClass. A constructor cannot be called like other functions, and the member variables of baseClass cannot be directly accessed by the member functions of derivedClass. To guarantee the initialization of the inherited member variables of an object of type derivedClass, even though derivedClass has no member variables, it must have the appropriate constructors. A constructor (with parameters) of derivedClass merely issues a call to a constructor (with parameters) of baseClass. Therefore, when you write the definition of the constructor (with parameters) of derivedClass, the heading of the definition of the constructor contains a call to an appropriate constructor (with parameters) of baseClass, and the body of the constructor is empty—that is, it contains only the opening and closing braces.

EXAMPLE 2-2

Suppose that you want to define a class to group the attributes of an employee. There are both full-time employees and part-time employees. Part-time employees are paid based on the number of hours worked and an hourly rate. Suppose that you want to define a class to keep track of a part-time employee's information such as name, pay rate, and hours worked. You can then print the employee's name together with his or her wages. Because every employee is a person, and Example 1-12 (Chapter 1) defined the class personType to store the first name and the last name together with the necessary operations on name, we can define a class partTimeEmployee based on the class personType. You can also redefine the print function to print the appropriate information.

```
//**************************************************************
// Author: D.S. Malik
//
// class partTimeEmployee
// This class is derived from the class personType and it
// specifies the members to implement the properties of a
// part-time employee.
//**************************************************************

class partTimeEmployee: public personType
{
public:
    void print() const;
      //Function to output the first name, last name, and
      //the wages.
      //Postcondition: Outputs: firstName lastName wages are $$$$.$$
```

```
    double calculatePay() const;
      //Function to calculate and return the wages.
      //Postcondition: Pay is calculated and returned.

    void setNameRateHours(string first, string last,
                          double rate, double hours);
      //Function to set the first name, last name, payRate,
      //and hoursWorked according to the parameters.
      //Postcondition: firstName = first; lastName = last;
      //    payRate = rate; hoursWorked = hours

    partTimeEmployee(string first = "", string last = "",
                     double rate = 0, double hours = 0);
      //Constructor with parameters
      //Sets the first name, last name, payRate, and hoursWorked
      //according to the parameters. If no value is specified,
      //the default values are assumed.
      //Postcondition: firstName = first; lastName = last;
      //    payRate = rate; hoursWorked = hours

private:
    double payRate;      //variable to store the pay rate
    double hoursWorked;  //variable to store the hours worked
};
```

Figure 2-5 shows the UML class diagram of the class partTimeEmployee and the inheritance hierarchy.

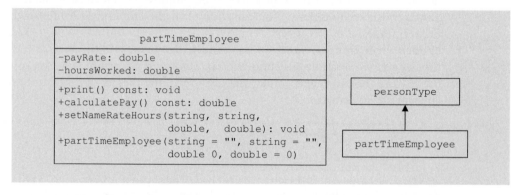

FIGURE 2-5 UML class diagram of the class partTimeEmployee and inheritance hierarchy

The definitions of the member functions of the class partTimeEmployee are as follows:

```
void partTimeEmployee::print() const
{
    personType::print();  //print the name of the employee
    cout << "'s wages are: $" << calculatePay() << endl;
}
```

```
double partTimeEmployee::calculatePay() const
{
    return (payRate * hoursWorked);
}

void partTimeEmployee::setNameRateHours(string first,
                      string last, double rate, double hours)
{
    personType::setName(first, last);
    payRate = rate;
    hoursWorked = hours;
}

    //Constructor
partTimeEmployee::partTimeEmployee(string first, string last,
                          double rate, double hours)
      : personType(first, last)
{
    payRate = rate;
    hoursWorked = hours;
}
```

Header File of a Derived Class

The previous section explained how to derive new classes from previously defined classes. To define new classes, you create new header files. The base classes are already defined, and header files contain their definitions. Thus, to create new classes based on the previously defined classes, the header files of the new classes contain commands that tell the computer where to look for the definitions of the base classes.

Suppose that the definition of the class personType is placed in the header file personType.h. To create the definition of the class partTimeEmployee, the header file—say, partTimeEmployee.h—must contain the preprocessor directive:

```
#include "personType.h"
```

before the definition of the class partTimeEmployee. To be specific, the header file partTimeEmployee.h is as follows:

```
//Header file partTimeEmployee

#include "personType.h"

//*****************************************************************
// Author: D.S. Malik
//
// class partTimeEmployee
// This class is derived from the class personType and it
// specifies the members to implement the properties of a
// part-time employee.
//*****************************************************************
```

```
class partTimeEmployee: public personType
{
public:
    void print() const;
        //Function to output the first name, last name, and
        //the wages.
        //Postcondition: Outputs: firstName lastName wages are $$$$.$$

    double calculatePay() const;
        //Function to calculate and return the wages.
        //Postcondition: Pay is calculated and returned.

    void setNameRateHours(string first, string last,
                          double rate, double hours);
        //Function to set the first name, last name, payRate,
        //and hoursWorked according to the parameters.
        //Postcondition: firstName = first; lastName = last;
        //     payRate = rate; hoursWorked = hours

    partTimeEmployee(string first = "", string last = "",
                     double rate = 0, double hours = 0);
        //Constructor with parameters
        //Sets the first name, last name, payRate, and hoursWorked
        //according to the parameters. If no value is specified,
        //the default values are assumed.
        //Postcondition: firstName = first; lastName = last;
        //     payRate = rate; hoursWorked = hours

private:
    double payRate;      //variable to store the pay rate
    double hoursWorked;  //variable to store the hours worked
};
```

The definitions of the member functions can be placed in a separate file (whose extension is .cpp). Recall that to include a system-provided header file, such as iostream, in a user program, you enclose the header file between angular brackets; to include a user-defined header file in a program, you enclose the header file between double quotation marks.

Multiple Inclusions of a Header File

The previous section discussed how to create the header file of a derived class. To include a header file in a program, you use the preprocessor command include. Recall that before a program is compiled, the preprocessor first processes the program. Consider the following header file:

```
//Header file test.h

const int ONE = 1;
const int TWO = 2;
```

2

Suppose that the header file `testA.h` includes the file `test.h` to use the identifiers `ONE` and `TWO`. To be specific, suppose that the header file `testA.h` looks like:

```
//Header file testA.h

#include "test.h"
.
.
.
```

Now consider the following program code:

```
//Program headerTest.cpp

#include "test.h"
#include "testA.h"
.
.
.
```

When the program `headerTest.cpp` is compiled, it is first processed by the preprocessor. The preprocessor includes first the header file `test.h` and then the header file `testA.h`. When the header file `testA.h` is included, because it contains the preprocessor directive `#include "test.h"`, the header file `test.h` is included twice in the program. The second inclusion of the header file `test.h` results in compile-time errors, such as the identifier `ONE` already being declared. This problem occurs because the first inclusion of the header file `test.h` has already defined the variables `ONE` and `TWO`. To avoid multiple inclusion of a file in a program, we use certain preprocessor commands in the header file. Let us first rewrite the header file `test.h` using these preprocessor commands, and then explain the meaning of these commands.

```
//Header file test.h

#ifndef H_test
#define H_test
const int ONE = 1;
const int TWO = 2;
#endif
```

    a.   `#ifndef H_test` means "if not defined `H_test`"
    b.   `#define H_test` means "define `H_test`"
    c.   `#endif` means "end if"

Here `H_test` is a preprocessor identifier.

The effect of these commands is as follows: If the identifier `H_test` is not defined, we must define the identifier `H_test` and let the remaining statements between `#define` and `#endif` pass through the compiler. If the header file `test.h` is included the second time in the program, the statement `#ifndef` fails and all the statements until `#endif` are skipped. In fact, all header files are written using similar preprocessor commands.

Protected Members of a Class

The private members of a class are private to the class and cannot be directly accessed outside the class. Only member functions of that class can access the private members. As discussed previously, the derived class cannot access private members of a class. However, it is sometimes necessary for a derived class to access a private member of a base class. If you make a private member become public, anyone can access that member. Recall that the members of a class are classified into three categories: public, private, and protected. So, for a base class to give access to a member to its derived class and still prevent its direct access outside the class, you must declare that member under the member access specifier **protected**. Thus, the accessibility of a **protected** member of a class is in between **public** and **private**. A derived class can directly access the **protected** member of a base class.

To summarize, if a derived class needs to access a member of a base class, that member of the base class should be declared under the member access specifier **protected**.

Inheritance as public, protected, or private

Suppose class B is derived from class A. Then B cannot directly access the private members of A. That is, the private members of A are hidden to B. What about the public and protected members of A? This section gives the rules that generally apply when accessing the members of a base class.

Consider the following statement:

```
class B: memberAccessSpecifier A
{
    .
    .
    .
};
```

In this statement, memberAccessSpecifier is either public, protected, or private.

1. If memberAccessSpecifier is public—that is, the inheritance is public—then

   a. The public members of A are public members of B. They can be directly accessed in class B.

   b. The protected members of A are protected members of B. They can be directly accessed by the member functions (and friend functions) of B.

   c. The private members of A are hidden to B. They can be accessed by the member functions (and friend functions) of B through the public or protected members of A.

2. If `memberAccessSpecifier` is `protected`—that is, the inheritance is `protected`—then

   a. The `public` members of `A` are `protected` members of `B`. They can be accessed by the member functions (and `friend` functions) of `B`.

   b. The `protected` members of `A` are `protected` members of `B`. They can be accessed by the member functions (and `friend` functions) of `B`.

   c. The `private` members of `A` are hidden to `B`. They can be accessed by the member functions (and `friend` functions) of `B` through the `public` or `protected` members of `A`.

3. If `memberAccessSpecifier` is `private`—that is, the inheritance is `private`—then

   a. The `public` members of `A` are `private` members of `B`. They can be accessed by the member functions (and `friend` functions) of `B`.

   b. The `protected` members of `A` are `private` members of `B`. They can be accessed by the member functions (and `friend` functions) of `B`.

   c. The `private` members of `A` are hidden to `B`. They can be accessed by the member functions (and `friend` functions) of `B` through the `public` or `protected` members of `A`.

NOTE
The section, "`friend` Functions of Classes" (located later in this chapter) describes the `friend` functions.

Composition

Composition is another way to relate two classes. In composition, one or more members of a class are objects of another class type. Composition is a "has-a" relationship; for example, "every person has a date of birth."

Example 1-12, in Chapter 1, defined a class called `personType`. The `class personType` stores a person's first name and last name. Suppose we want to keep track of additional information for a person, such as a personal ID (for example, a Social Security number) and a date of birth. Because every person has a personal ID and a date of birth, we can define a new class, called `personalInfoType`, in which one of the members is an object of type `personType`. We can declare additional members to store the personal ID and date of birth for the `class personalInfoType`.

First, we define another `class`, `dateType`, to store only a person's date of birth, and then construct the `class personalInfoType` from the classes `personType` and `dateType`. This way, we can demonstrate how to define a new class using two classes.

To define the class dateType, we need three data members to store the month, day number, and year. Some of the operations that need to be performed on a date are to set the date and to print the date. The following statements define the class dateType:

```
//************************************************************
// Author: D.S. Malik
//
// class dateType
// This class specifies the members to implement a date.
//************************************************************

class dateType
{
public:
    void setDate(int month, int day, int year);
        //Function to set the date.
        //The member variables dMonth, dDay, and dYear are set
        //according to the parameters.
        //Postcondition: dMonth = month; dDay = day; dYear = year

    int getDay() const;
        //Function to return the day.
        //Postcondition: The value of dDay is returned.

    int getMonth() const;
        //Function to return the month.
        //Postcondition: The value of dMonth is returned.

    int getYear() const;
        //Function to return the year.
        //Postcondition: The value of dYear is returned.

    void printDate() const;
        //Function to output the date in the form mm-dd-yyyy.

    dateType(int month = 1, int day = 1, int year = 1900);
        //Constructor to set the date
        //The member variables dMonth, dDay, and dYear are set
        //according to the parameters.
        //Postcondition: dMonth = month; dDay = day; dYear = year. If
        //    no values are specified, the default values are used to
        //    initialize the member variables.

private:
    int dMonth; //variable to store the month
    int dDay;   //variable to store the day
    int dYear;  //variable to store the year
};
```

Figure 2-6 shows the UML class diagram of the class dateType.

```
                    dateType
    -dMonth: int
    -dDay: int
    -dYear: int
    +setDate(int, int, int): void
    +getDay() const: int
    +getMonth() const: int
    +getYear() const: int
    +printDate() const: void
    +dateType(int = 1, int = 1, int = 1900)
```

FIGURE 2-6   UML class diagram of the class dateType

The definitions of the member functions of the class dateType are as follows:

```
void dateType::setDate(int month, int day, int year)
{
    dMonth = month;
    dDay = day;
    dYear = year;
}
```

The definition of the function setDate, before storing the date into the data members, does not check whether the date is valid. That is, it does not confirm whether month is between 1 and 12, year is greater than 0, and day is valid (for example, for January, day should be between 1 and 31). In Programming Exercise 2 at the end of this chapter, you are asked to rewrite the definition of the function setDate so that the date is validated before storing it in the data members.

The definitions of the remaining member functions are as follows:

```
int dateType::getDay() const
{
    return dDay;
}

int dateType::getMonth() const
{
    return dMonth;
}

int dateType::getYear() const
{
    return dYear;
}
```

```
void dateType::printDate() const
{
    cout << dMonth << "-" << dDay << "-" << dYear;
}


    //Constructor with parameters
dateType::dateType(int month, int day, int year)
{
    setDate(month, day, year);
}
```

Because the constructor uses the function setDate before storing the date into the data members, the constructor also does not check whether the date is valid. In Programming Exercise 2 at the end of this chapter, when you rewrite the definition of the function setDate to validate the date, and the constructor uses the function setDate, the date set by the constructor will also be validated.

Next, we give the definition of the class personalInfoType:

```
//**********************************************************
// Author: D.S. Malik
//
// class personalInfo
// This class specifies the members to implement a person's
// personal information.
//**********************************************************

class personalInfoType
{
public:
    void setPersonalInfo(string first, string last, int month,
                         int day, int year, int ID);
        //Function to set the personal information.
        //The member variables are set according to the
        //parameters.
        //Postcondition: firstName = first; lastName = last;
        //    dMonth = month; dDay = day; dYear = year;
        //    personID = ID;

    void printPersonalInfo () const;
        //Function to print the personal information.

    personalInfoType(string first = "", string last = "",
                     int month = 1, int day = 1, int year = 1900,
                     int ID = 0);
        //Constructor
        //The member variables are set according to the parameters.
        //Postcondition: firstName = first; lastName = last;
        //    dMonth = month; dDay = day; dYear = year;
        //    personID = ID;
        //    If no values are specified, the default values are
        //    used to initialize the member variables.
```

```
private:
    personType name;
    dateType bDay;
    int personID;
};
```

Figure 2-7 shows the UML class diagram of the class personalInfoType and composition (aggregation).

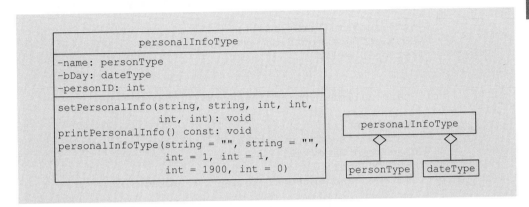

FIGURE 2-7   UML class diagram of the class personalInfoType and composition (aggregation)

Before we give the definition of the member functions of the class personalInfoType, let us discuss how the constructors of the objects bDay and name are invoked.

Recall that a class constructor is automatically executed when a class object enters its scope. Suppose that we have the following statement:

```
personalInfoType student;
```

When the object student enters its scope, the objects bDay and name, which are members of student, also enter their scopes; as a result, one of their constructors is executed. We therefore need to know how to pass arguments to the constructors of the member objects (that is, bDay and name). Recall that constructors do not have a type and so cannot be called like other functions. The arguments to the constructor of a member object (such as bDay) are specified in the heading part of the definition of the constructor of the class. The following statements illustrate how to pass arguments to the constructors of the member objects:

```
personalInfoType::personalInfoType(string first, string last, int month,
                        int day, int year, int ID)
        : name(first, last), bDay(month, day, year)
    {
        .
        .
        .
    }
```

Member objects of a class are constructed (that is, initialized) in the order they are declared (not in the order they are listed in the constructor's member initialization list) and before the enclosing class objects are constructed. Thus, in our case, the object `name` is initialized first, then `bDay`, and, finally, `student`.

The definitions of the member functions of the `class personalInfoType` are as follows:

```cpp
void personalInfoType::setPersonalInfo(string first, string last,
                          int month, int day, int year, int ID)
{
    name.setName(first,last);
    bDay.setDate(month,day,year);
    personID = ID;
}

void personalInfoType::printPersonalInfo() const
{
    name.print();
    cout << "'s date of birth is ";
    bDay.printDate();
    cout << endl;
    cout << "and personal ID is " << personID;
}

personalInfoType::personalInfoType(string first, string last,
                          int month, int day, int year, int ID)
        : name(first, last), bDay(month, day, year)
{
    personID = ID;
}
```

In the case of inheritance, use the class name to invoke the base class's constructor. In the case of composition, use the member object name to invoke its own constructor.

Polymorphism: Operator and Function Overloading

In Chapter 1, you learned how classes in C++ are used to combine data and operations on that data in a single entity. The ability to combine data and operations is called **encapsulation**. It is the first principle of object-oriented design (OOD). Chapter 1 defined the abstract data type (ADT) and described how classes in C++ implement ADTs. The first section of this chapter discussed how new classes can be derived from existing classes through the mechanism of inheritance. Inheritance, the second principle of OOD, encourages code reuse.

The remainder of this chapter discusses the third principle of OOD—polymorphism. First we discuss polymorphism via **operator overloading**, and then via **templates**. Templates enable the programmer to write generic codes for related functions and classes. We will simplify function overloading through the use of templates, called **function templates**.

Operator Overloading

This section describes how operators are loaded in C++. But first let us see why you would want to overload operators.

Why Operator Overloading Is Needed

Chapter 1 defined and implemented the `class clockType`. It also showed how you can use the `class clockType` to represent the time of day in a program. Let us review some of the characteristics of the `class clockType`.

Consider the following statements:

```
clockType myClock(8,23,34);
clockType yourClock(4,5,30);
```

The first statement declares `myClock` to be an object of type `clockType` and initializes the data members `hr`, `min`, and `sec` of `myClock` to 8, 23, and 34, respectively. The second statement declares `yourClock` to be an object of type `clockType` and initializes the data members `hr`, `min`, and `sec` of `yourClock` to 4, 5, and 30, respectively.

Now consider the following statements:

```
myClock.printTime();
myClock.incrementSeconds();
if (myClock.equalTime(yourClock))
    .
    .
    .
```

The first statement prints the value of `myClock` in the form `hr:min:sec`. The second statement increments the value of `myClock` by one second. The third statement checks whether the value of `myClock` is the same as the value of `yourClock`.

These statements do their job. However, if we can use the insertion operator `<<` to output the value of `myClock`, the increment operator `++` to increment the value of `myClock` by one second, and relational operators for comparison, we can enhance the flexibility of C++ considerably and can improve code readability. More specifically, we prefer to use the following statements instead of the previous ones:

```
cout << myClock;
myClock++;
if (myClock == yourClock)
    .
    .
    .
```

Recall that the only built-in operations on classes are the assignment operator and the member selection operator. Therefore, other operators cannot be directly applied to class objects. However, C++ allows the programmer to extend the definitions of most of the operators so that operators such as relational operators, arithmetic operators, insertion operators for data output, and extraction operators for data input can be applied to classes. In C++ terminology, this is called **operator overloading**. In addition to operator overloading, this chapter discusses function overloading.

Operator Overloading

Recall how the arithmetic operator / works. If both operands of / are integers, the result is an integer; otherwise, the result is a floating-point number. Similarly, the stream insertion operator, <<, and the stream extraction operator, >>, are overloaded. The operator << is used as both a stream insertion operator and a left shift operator. The operator >> is used as both a stream extraction operator and a right shift operator. These are examples of operator overloading.

Other examples of overloaded operators are + and −. The results of + and − are different for integer arithmetic, floating-point arithmetic, and pointer arithmetic.

C++ allows the user to overload most of the operators so that the operators can work effectively in a specific application. It does not allow the user to create new operators. Most of the existing operators can be overloaded to manipulate class objects.

To overload an operator, you must write functions (that is, the header and body). The name of the function that overloads an operator is the reserved word `operator` followed by the operator to be overloaded. For example, the name of the function to overload the operator >= is

```
operator>=
```

Operator function: The function that overloads an operator.

Syntax for Operator Functions

The result of an operation is a value; therefore, the operator function is a value-returning function.

The syntax of the heading for an operator function is as follows:

```
returnType operator operatorSymbol(arguments)
```

In C++, `operator` is a reserved word.

Operator overloading provides the same concise expressions for user-defined data types as it does for built-in data types. To overload an operator for a class, you do the following:

1. Include the statement to declare the function to overload the operator (that is, the operator function) in the definition of the class.
2. Write the definition of the operator function.

Certain rules must be followed when you include an operator function in a class definition. These rules are described in the section "Operator Functions as Member Functions and Nonmember Functions," later in this chapter.

Overloading an Operator: Some Restrictions

When overloading an operator, keep the following in mind:

- You cannot change the precedence of an operator.
- The associativity cannot be changed. (For example, the associativity of the arithmetic operator + is from left to right and it cannot be changed.)
- You cannot use default arguments with an overloaded operator.
- You cannot change the number of arguments that an operator takes.
- You cannot create new operators. Only existing operators can be overloaded. The operators that cannot be overloaded are

    .   .*   ::   ?:   sizeof
- The meaning of how an operator works with built-in types, such as int, remains the same.
- Operators can be overloaded either for objects of the user-defined type, or for a combination of objects of the user-defined type and objects of the built-in type.

The Pointer this

A member function of a class can (directly) access the data members of that class for a given object. Sometimes it is necessary for a function member to refer to the object as a whole, rather than the object's individual data members. How do you refer to the object as a whole (that is, as a single unit) in the definition of the member function, especially when the object is not passed as a parameter? Every object of a class maintains a (hidden) pointer to itself, and the name of this pointer is **this**. In C++, **this** is a reserved word. The pointer **this** is available for you to use. When an object invokes a member function, the member function references the pointer **this** of the object. For example, suppose that test is a class and has a member function called funcOne. Further suppose that the definition of funcOne looks like the following:

```
test test::funcOne()
{
    .
    .
    .
    return *this;
}
```

If **x** and **y** are objects of type test, the statement

```
y = x.funcOne();
```

copies the value of the object **x** into the object **y**; that is, the data members of **x** are copied into the corresponding data members of **y**. When the object **x** invokes the function funcOne, the pointer this in the definition of the member function funcOne refers to the object **x**, and so this means the address of **x** and * **this** means the value of **x**.

The following example illustrates how the pointer **this** works.

EXAMPLE 2-3

In Example 1-12 (in Chapter 1), we designed a class to implement a person's name in a program. Here we extend the definition of the **class** personType to individually set a person's first name and last name, and then return the entire object. The extended definition of the **class** personType is as follows:

```
//**********************************************************
// Author: D.S. Malik
//
// class personType
// This class specifies the members to implement a name.
//**********************************************************

class personType
{
public:
    void print() const;
        //Function to output the first name and last name in
        //the form firstName lastName

    void setName(string first, string last);
        //Function to set firstName and lastName according to the
        //parameters.
        //Postcondition: firstName = first; lastName = last

    personType& setFirstName(string first);
        //Function to set the first name.
        //Postcondition: firstName = first
        //      After setting the first name, a reference to the
        //      object, that is, the address of the object, is
        //      returned.

    personType& setLastName(string last);
        //Function to set the last name.
        //Postcondition: lastName = last
        //      After setting the last name, a reference to the object,
        //      that is, the address of the object, is returned.

    string getFirstName() const;
        //Function to return the first name.
        //Postcondition: The value of firstName is returned.

    string getLastName() const;
        //Function to return the last name.
        //Postcondition: The value of lastName is returned.

    personType(string first = "", string last = "");
        //Constructor
        //Sets firstName and lastName according to the parameters.
        //Postcondition: firstName = first; lastName = last
```

```
private:
    string firstName; //variable to store the first name
    string lastName;  //variable to store the last name
};
```

Notice that in this definition of the class personType, we replace the default constructor and the constructor with parameters by one constructor with default parameters.

The definitions of the functions print, setTime, getFirstName, getLastName, and
the constructor is the same as before (see Example 1-12). The definitions of the functions
setFirstName and setLastName are as follows:

```
personType& personType::setLastName(string last)
{
    lastName = last;

    return *this;
}

personType& personType::setFirstName(string first)
{
    firstName = first;

    return *this;
}
```

The following program shows how to use the **class** personType. (We assume that the
definition of the **class** personType is in the file personType.h.)

```
//****************************************************************
// Author: D.S. Malik
// Test Program: class personType
//****************************************************************

#include <iostream>                                          //Line 1
#include <string>                                            //Line 2
#include "personType.h"                                      //Line 3

using namespace std;                                         //Line 4

int main()                                                   //Line 5
{                                                            //Line 6
    personType student1("Lisa", "Smith");                    //Line 7
    personType student2;                                     //Line 8
    personType student3;                                     //Line 9

    cout << "Line 10 -- Student 1: ";                        //Line 10
    student1.print();                                        //Line 11
    cout << endl;                                            //Line 12

    student2.setFirstName("Shelly").setLastName("Malik");    //Line 13

    cout << "Line 14 -- Student 2: ";                        //Line 14
    student2.print();                                        //Line 15
    cout << endl;                                            //Line 16
```

```
    student3.setFirstName("Cindy");                          //Line 17

    cout << "Line 18 -- Student 3: ";                        //Line 18
    student3.print();                                        //Line 19
    cout << endl;                                            //Line 20

    student3.setLastName("Tomek");                           //Line 21

    cout << "Line 22 -- Student 3: ";                        //Line 22
    student3.print();                                        //Line 23
    cout << endl;                                            //Line 24

    return 0;                                                //Line 25
}                                                            //Line 26
```

Sample Run:

```
Line 10 -- Student 1: Lisa Smith
Line 14 -- Student 2: Shelly Malik
Line 18 -- Student 3: Cindy
Line 22 -- Student 3: Cindy Tomek
```

The statements in Lines 7, 8, and 9 declare and initialize the objects `student1`, `student2`, and `student3`, respectively. The objects `student2` and `student3` are initialized to empty strings. The statement in Line 11 outputs the value of `student1` (see Line 10 in the sample run, which contains the output of Lines 10, 11, and 12). The statement in Line 13 works as follows. In the statement

```
student2.setFirstName("Shelly").setLastName("Malik");
```

first the expression

```
student2.setFirstName("Shelly")
```

is executed because the associativity of the dot operator is from left to right. This expression sets the first name to `"Shelly"` and returns a reference to the object, which is `student2`. Thus, the next expression executed is

```
student2.setLastName("Malik")
```

which sets the last name of `student2` to `"Malik"`. The statement in Line 15 outputs the value of `student2`. The statement in Line 17 sets the first name of the object `student3` to `"Cindy"`, and ignores the value returned. The statement in Line 19 outputs the value of `student3`. Notice the output in Line 18. The output shows only the first name, not the last name, because we have not yet set the last name of `student3`. The last name of `student3` is still empty, which was set by the statement in Line 9 when `student3` was declared. Next, the statement in Line 21 sets the last name of `student3`, and the statement in Line 23 outputs the value of `student3`.

Friend Functions of Classes

A **friend function** of a class is a nonmember function of the class, but has access to all the members (public or non-public) of the class. To make a function as a friend of a class, the reserved word `friend` precedes the function prototype (in the class definition). The word `friend` appears only in the function prototype in the class definition, not in the definition of the friend function.

Consider the following statements:

```
class classIllusFriend
{
    friend void two(/*parameters*/);
    .
    .
    .
};
```

In the definition of the `class classIllusFriend`, `two` is declared as a `friend` of the `class classIllusFriend`. That is, it is a nonmember function of the `class classIllusFriend`. When you write the definition of the function `two`, any object of type `classIllusFriend`—which is either a local variable of `two` or a formal parameter of `two`—can access its `private` members within the definition of the function `two`. (Example 2-4 illustrates this concept.) Moreover, because a `friend` function is not a member of a class, its declaration can be placed within the `private`, `protected`, or `public` part of the class. However, they are typically placed before any member function declaration.

DEFINITION OF A `friend` FUNCTION

When writing the definition of a `friend` function, the name of the class and the scope resolution operator do not precede the name of the `friend` function in the function heading. Also, recall that the word `friend` does not appear in the heading of the `friend` function's definition. Thus, the definition of the function `two` in the previous `class classIllusFriend` is as follows:

```
void friendFunc(/*parameters*/)
{
    .
    .
    .
}
```

Of course, we will place the definition of the `friend` function in the implementation file.

The next section illustrates the difference between a member function and a nonmember function (`friend` function), when we overload some of the operators for a specific class.

The following example shows how a `friend` function accesses the `private` members of a class.

EXAMPLE 2-4

Consider the following class:

```
class classIllusFriend
{
    friend void friendFunc(classIllusFriend cIFObject);

public:
    void print();
    void setx(int a);

private:
    int x;
};
```

In the definition of the class classIllusFriend, friendFunc is declared as a friend function. Suppose that the definitions of the member functions of the class classIllusFriend are as follows:

```
void classIllusFriend::print()
{
    cout << "In class classIllusFriend: x = " << x << endl;
}

void classIllusFriend::setx(int a)
{
    x = a;
}
```

Consider the following definition of the function friendFunc:

```
void friendFunc(classIllusFriend cIFObject)           //Line 1
{                                                     //Line 2
    classIllusFriend localTwoObject;                  //Line 3

    localTwoObject.x = 45;                            //Line 4

    localTwoObject.print();                           //Line 5

    cout << "Line 6: In friendFunc accessing "
         << "private member variable " << "x = "
         << localTwoObject.x
         << endl;                                     //Line 6

    cIFObject.x = 88;                                 //Line 7

    cIFObject.print();                                //Line 8

    cout << "Line 9: In friendFunc accessing "
         << "private member variable " << "x = "
         << cIFObject.x << endl;                      //Line 9
}                                                     //Line 10
```

The function `friendFunc` contains a formal parameter `cIFObject` and a local variable `localTwoObject`, both of type `classIllusFriend`. In the statement in Line 4, the object `localTwoObject` accesses its `private` member variable `x` and sets its value to 45. If `friendFunc` is not declared as a `friend` function of the `class classIllusFriend`, this statement would result in a syntax error because an object cannot directly access its `private` members. Similarly, in the statement in Line 7, the formal parameter `cIFObject` accesses its `private` member variable `x` and sets its value to 88. Once again, this statement would result in a syntax error if `friendFunc` is not declared a `friend` function of the `class classIllusFriend`. The statement in Line 6 outputs the value of the `private` member variable `x` of `localTwoObject` by directly accessing `x`. Similarly, the statement in Line 9 outputs the value of `x` of `cIFObject` by directly accessing it. The function `friendFunc` also prints the value of `x` by using the function `print` (see the statements in Lines 6 and 9).

Now consider the definition of the following function `main`:

```
int main()                                              //Line 11
{                                                       //Line 12
    classIllusFriend aObject;                           //Line 13

    aObject.setx(32);                                   //Line 14

    cout << "Line 15: aObject.x: ";                     //Line 15
    aObject.print();                                    //Line 16
    cout << endl;                                       //Line 17

    cout << "*~*~*~* Testing friendFunc *~*~*~*"
         << endl << endl;                               //Line 18

    friendFunc(aObject);                                //Line 19

    return 0;                                           //Line 20
}                                                       //Line 21
```

Sample Run:

```
Line 15: aObject.x: In class classIllusFriend: x = 32

*~*~*~* Testing friendFunc *~*~*~*

In class classIllusFriend: x = 45
Line 6: In friendFunc accessing private member variable x = 45
In class classIllusFriend: x = 88
Line 9: In friendFunc accessing private member variable x = 88
```

For the most part, the output is self-explanatory. The statement in Line 19 calls the function `friendFunc` (a friend function of the `class classIllusFriend`) and passes the object `aObject` as an actual parameter. Notice that the function `friendFunc` generates the four lines of output.

Operator Functions as Member Functions and Nonmember Functions

Earlier in this chapter we stated that certain rules must be followed when you include an operator function in the definition of a class. This section describes these rules.

Most operator functions can be either member functions or nonmember functions—that is, `friend` functions of a class. To make an operator function be a member or non-member function of a class, keep the following in mind:

1. The function that overloads any of the operators `()`, `[]`, `->`, or `=` for a class must be declared as a member of the class.

2. Suppose that an operator `op` is overloaded for a class—say, `opOverClass`. (Here, `op` stands for an operator that can be overloaded, such as `+` or `>>`.)

    a. If the leftmost operand of `op` is an object of a different type (that is, not of type `opOverClass`), the function that overloads the operator `op` for `opOverClass` must be a nonmember—that is, a friend of the class `opOverClass`.

    b. If the operator function that overloads the operator `op` for the class `opOverClass` is a member of the class `opOverClass`, then when applying `op` on objects of type `opOverClass`, the leftmost operand of `op` must be of type `opOverClass`.

You must follow these rules when including an operator function in a class definition.

You will see later in this chapter that functions that overload the insertion operator, `<<`, and the extraction operator, `>>`, for a class must be nonmembers—that is, they must be `friend` functions of the class.

Except for certain operators noted previously, operators can be overloaded either as member functions or as nonmember functions. The following discussion shows the difference between these two types of functions.

To facilitate our discussion of operator overloading, we will use the class `rectangleType`, defined earlier in this chapter. Also, suppose that you have the following statements:

```
rectangleType myRectangle;
rectangleType yourRectangle;
rectangleType tempRect;
```

That is, `myRectangle`, `yourRectangle`, and `tempRect` are objects of type `rectangleType`.

C++ consists of both binary and unary operators. It also has a ternary operator, which *cannot* be overloaded. The next few sections discuss how to overload various binary and unary operators.

Overloading Binary Operators

Suppose that # represents a binary operator (arithmetic, such as +; or relational, such as ==) that is to be overloaded for the class rectangleType. This operator can be overloaded as either a member function of the class or as a **friend** function. We describe both ways to overload this operator.

OVERLOADING THE BINARY OPERATORS AS MEMBER FUNCTIONS

Suppose that # is overloaded as a member function of the class rectangleType. The name of the function to overload # for the class rectangleType is

```
operator#
```

Because myRectangle and yourRectangle are objects of type rectangleType, you can perform the following operation:

```
myRectangle # yourRectangle
```

The compiler translates this expression into the following expression:

```
myRectangle.operator#(yourRectangle)
```

This expression clearly shows that the function operator# has only one parameter, which is yourRectangle.

Because operator# is a member of the class rectangleType and myRectangle is an object of type rectangleType, in the previous statement, operator# has direct access to the private members of the object myRectangle. Thus, the first parameter of operator# is the object that is invoking the function operator#, and the second parameter is passed as a parameter to this function.

GENERAL SYNTAX TO OVERLOAD THE BINARY (ARITHMETIC OR RELATIONAL) OPERATORS AS MEMBER FUNCTIONS

This section describes the general form of the functions to overload the binary operators as member functions of a class.

Function Prototype (to be included in the definition of the class):

```
returnType operator#(const className&) const;
```

where # stands for the binary operator, arithmetic or relational, to be overloaded; returnType is the type of value returned by the function; and className is the name of the class for which the operator is being overloaded.

Function Definition:

```
returnType className::operator#
                    (const className& otherObject) const
{
    //algorithm to perform the operation

    return value;
}
```

NOTE The return type of the function that overloads a relational operator is **bool**.

EXAMPLE 2-5

Let us overload +, *, ==, and != for the class rectangleType. These operators are overloaded as member functions.

```
class rectangleType
{
public:
    void setDimension(double l, double w);
    double getLength() const;
    double getWidth() const;
    double area() const;
    double perimeter() const;
    void print() const;

    rectangleType operator+(const rectangleType&) const;
        //Overload the operator +
    rectangleType operator*(const rectangleType&) const;
        //Overload the operator *

    bool operator==(const rectangleType&) const;
        //Overload the operator ==
    bool operator!=(const rectangleType&) const;
        //Overload the operator !=

    rectangleType();
    rectangleType(double l, double w);

private:
    double length;
    double width;
};
```

The definition of the function operator+ is as follows:

```
rectangleType rectangleType::operator+
                        (const rectangleType& rectangle) const
{
    rectangleType tempRect;

    tempRect.length = length + rectangle.length;
    tempRect.width = width + rectangle.width;

    return tempRect;
}
```

Notice that `operator+` adds the corresponding lengths and widths of the two rectangles. The definition of the function `operator*` is as follows:

```
rectangleType rectangleType::operator*
                        (const rectangleType& rectangle) const
{
    rectangleType tempRect;

    tempRect.length = length * rectangle.length;
    tempRect.width = width * rectangle.width;

    return tempRect;
}
```

Notice that `operator*` multiplies the corresponding lengths and widths of the two rectangles.

Two rectangles are equal if their lengths and widths are equal. Therefore, the definition of the function to overload the operator == is as follows:

```
bool rectangleType::operator==
                        (const rectangleType& rectangle) const
{
    return (length == rectangle.length &&
            width == rectangle.width);
}
```

Two rectangles are not equal if either their lengths are not equal or their widths are not equal. Therefore, the definition of the function to overload the operator != is as follows:

```
bool rectangleType::operator!=
                        (const rectangleType& rectangle) const
{
    return (length != rectangle.length ||
            width != rectangle.width);
}
```

OVERLOADING THE BINARY OPERATORS (ARITHMETIC OR RELATIONAL) AS NONMEMBER FUNCTIONS

Suppose that # represents the binary operator (arithmetic or relational) that is to be overloaded as a *nonmember* function of the `class rectangleType`.

Further suppose that the following operation is to be performed:

`myRectangle # yourRectangle`

In this case, the expression is compiled as follows:

`operator#(myRectangle, yourRectangle)`

Here, we see that the function `operator#` has two parameters. This expression also clearly shows that the function `operator#` is neither a member of the object `myRectangle` nor a member of the object `yourRectangle`. Both the objects, `myRectangle` and `yourRectangle`, are passed as parameters to the function `operator#`.

To include the operator function `operator#` as a nonmember function of the class in the definition of the class, the reserved word `friend` must appear before the function heading. Also, the function `operator#` must have two parameters.

GENERAL SYNTAX TO OVERLOAD THE BINARY (ARITHMETIC OR RELATIONAL) OPERATORS AS NONMEMBER FUNCTIONS

This section describes the general form of the functions that overload binary operators as nonmember functions of a class.

Function Prototype (to be included in the definition of the class):

```
friend returnType operator#(const className&, const className&);
```

where # stands for the binary operator to be overloaded, `returnType` is the type of value returned by the function, and `className` is the name of the class for which the operator is being overloaded.

Function Definition:

```
returnType operator#(const className& firstObject,
                     const className& secondObject)
{
    //algorithm to perform the operation

    return value;
}
```

Overloading the Stream Insertion (<<) and Extraction (>>) Operators

The operator function that overloads the insertion operator, <<, or the extraction operator, >>, for a class must be a nonmember function of that class for the following reason.

Consider the following expression:

```
cout << myRectangle;
```

In this expression, the leftmost operand of << (that is, `cout`) is an `ostream` object, not an object of type `rectangleType`. Because the leftmost operand of << is not an object of type `rectangleType`, the operator function that overloads the insertion operator for `rectangleType` must be a nonmember function of the `class rectangleType`.

Similarly, the operator function that overloads the stream extraction operator for `rectangleType` must be a nonmember function of the `class rectangleType`.

OVERLOADING THE STREAM INSERTION OPERATOR (<<)

The general syntax to overload the stream insertion operator, <<, for a class is described next.

Function Prototype (to be included in the definition of the class):

```
friend ostream& operator<<(ostream&, const className&);
```

Function Definition:

```
ostream& operator<<(ostream& osObject, const className& cObject)
{
      //local declaration, if any
      //Output the members of cObject.
      //osObject << . . .

      //Return the stream object.
   return osObject;
}
```

In this function definition:

- Both parameters are reference parameters.
- The first parameter—that is, osObject—is a reference to an ostream object.
- The second parameter is a const reference to a particular class.
- The function return type is a reference to an ostream object.

OVERLOADING THE STREAM EXTRACTION OPERATOR (>>)

The general syntax to overload the stream extraction operator, >>, for a class is described next.

Function Prototype (to be included in the definition of the class):

```
friend istream& operator>>(istream&, className&);
```

Function Definition:

```
istream& operator>>(istream& isObject, className& cObject)
{
      //local declaration, if any
      //Read the data into cObject.
      //isObject >> . . .

      //Return the stream object.
   return isObject;
}
```

We note the following in this function definition.

- Both parameters are reference parameters.
- The first parameter—that is, isObject—is a reference to an istream object.

- The second parameter is usually a reference to a particular class. The data read will be stored in the object.
- The function return type is a reference to an `istream` object.

Example 2-6 shows how the stream insertion and extraction operators are overloaded for the `class rectangleType`. We also show how to overload arithmetic and relational operators as member functions of the class.

EXAMPLE 2-6

The definition of the `class rectangleType` and the definitions of the operator functions are as follows:

```
#include <iostream>

using namespace std;

class rectangleType
{
        //Overload the stream insertion and extraction operators
    friend ostream& operator<< (ostream&, const rectangleType &);
    friend istream& operator>> (istream&, rectangleType &);

public:
    void setDimension(double l, double w);
    double getLength() const;
    double getWidth() const;
    double area() const;
    double perimeter() const;
    void print() const;

    rectangleType operator+(const rectangleType&) const;
      //Overload the operator +
    rectangleType operator*(const rectangleType&) const;
      //Overload the operator *

    bool operator==(const rectangleType&) const;
      //Overload the operator ==
    bool operator!=(const rectangleType&) const;
      //Overload the operator !=

    rectangleType();
    rectangleType(double l, double w);

private:
    double length;
    double width;
};

//The definitions of the functions operator+, operator*, operator==,
//operator!=, and the constructor are the same as in Example 2-5.
```

```
ostream& operator<< (ostream& osObject,
                     const rectangleType& rectangle)
{
    osObject << "Length = "  << rectangle.length
            << "; Width = " << rectangle.width;

    return osObject;
}

istream& operator>> (istream& isObject,
                     rectangleType& rectangle)
{
    isObject >> rectangle.length >> rectangle.width;

    return isObject;
}
```

Consider the following program. (We assume that the definition of the `class` `rectangleType` is in the header file `rectangleType.h`.)

```
//*****************************************************************
// Author: D.S. Malik
//
// This program shows how to use the modified class rectangleType.
//*****************************************************************

#include <iostream>                                      //Line 1

#include "rectangleType.h"                               //Line 2

using namespace std;                                     //Line 3

int main()                                               //Line 4
{                                                        //Line 5
    rectangleType myRectangle(23, 45);                   //Line 6
    rectangleType yourRectangle;                         //Line 7

    cout << "Line 8: myRectangle: " << myRectangle
         << endl;                                        //Line 8

    cout << "Line 9: Enter the length and width "
         << "of a rectangle: ";                          //Line 9
    cin >> yourRectangle;                                //Line 10
    cout << endl;                                        //Line 11

    cout << "Line 12: yourRectangle: "
         << yourRectangle << endl;                       //Line 12

    cout << "Line 13: myRectangle + yourRectangle: "
         << myRectangle + yourRectangle << endl;         //Line 13
    cout << "Line 14: myRectangle * yourRectangle: "
         << myRectangle * yourRectangle << endl;         //Line 14

    return 0;                                            //Line 15
}                                                        //Line 16
```

Sample Run: In this sample run, the user input is shaded.

```
Line 8: myRectangle: Length = 23; Width = 45
Line 9: Enter the length and width of a rectangle: 32 15

Line 12: yourRectangle: Length = 32; Width = 15
Line 13: myRectangle + yourRectangle: Length = 55; Width = 60
Line 14: myRectangle * yourRectangle: Length = 736; Width = 675
```

The statements in Lines 6 and 7 declare and initialize `myRectangle` and `yourRectangle` to be objects of type `rectangleType`. The statement in Line 8 outputs the value of `myRectangle` using `cout` and the insertion operator. The statement in Line 10 inputs the data into `yourRectangle` using `cin` and the extraction operator. The statement in Line 12 outputs the value of `yourRectangle` using `cout` and the insertion operator. The `cout` statement in Line 13 adds the lengths and widths of `myRectangle` and `yourRectangle` and outputs the result. Similarly, the `cout` statement in Line 14 multiplies the lengths and widths of `myRectangle` and `yourRectangle` and outputs the result. The output shows that both the stream insertion and stream extraction operators were overloaded successfully.

OVERLOADING UNARY OPERATORS

The process of overloading unary operators is similar to the process of overloading binary operators. The only difference is that in the case of unary operators, the operator has only one argument; in the case of binary operators, the operator has two operands. Therefore, to overload a unary operator for a class we do the following.

- If the operator function is a member of the class, it has no parameters.
- If the operator function is a nonmember—that is, a `friend` function of the class—it has one parameter.

Operator Overloading: Member Versus Nonmember

The preceding sections discussed and illustrated how to overload operators. Certain operators must be overloaded as member functions of the class, and some must be overloaded as nonmember (`friend`) functions. What about the ones that can be overloaded as either member functions or nonmember functions? For example, the binary arithmetic operator + can be overloaded as a member function or a nonmember function. If you overload + as a member function, the operator + has direct access to the data members of one of the objects, and you need to pass only one object as a parameter. On the other hand, if you overload + as a nonmember function, you must pass both objects as parameters. Therefore, overloading + as a nonmember could require additional memory and computer time to make a local copy of the data. Thus, for efficiency purposes, wherever possible, you should overload operators as member functions.

PROGRAMMING EXAMPLE: Complex Numbers

A number of the form $a + ib$, where $i^2 = -1$, and a and b are real numbers, is called a complex number. We call a the real part and b the imaginary part of $a + ib$. Complex numbers can also be represented as ordered pairs (a, b). The addition and multiplication of complex numbers is defined by the following rules:

$$(a + ib) + (c + id) = (a + c) + i(b + d)$$

$$(a + ib) \star (c + id) = (ac - bd) + i(ad + bc)$$

Using the ordered pair notation, these rules are written as follows:

$$(a, b) + (c, d) = ((a + c), (b + d))$$

$$(a, b) \star (c, d) = ((ac - bd), (ad + bc))$$

C++ has no built-in data type that allows us to manipulate complex numbers. In this example, we will construct a data type, `complexType`, that can be used to process complex numbers. We will overload the stream insertion and stream extraction operators for easy input and output. We will also overload the operators + and * to perform addition and multiplication of complex numbers. If x and y are complex numbers, we can evaluate expressions such as $x + y$ and $x \star y$.

```
#ifndef H_complexNumber
#define H_complexNumber

//**********************************************************
// Author: D.S. Malik
// class complexType.h
// This class specifies the members to implement a complex number.
//**********************************************************

#include <iostream>
using namespace std;

class complexType
{
        //Overload the stream insertion and extraction operators
    friend ostream& operator<<(ostream&, const complexType&);
    friend istream& operator>>(istream&, complexType&);

public:
    void setComplex(const double& real, const double& imag);
        //Function to set the complex numbers according to
        //the parameters.
        //Postcondition: realPart = real; imaginaryPart = imag;

    void getComplex(double& real, double& imag) const;
        //Function to retrieve the complex number.
        //Postcondition: real = realPart; imag = imaginaryPart;
```

```
      complexType(double real = 0, double imag = 0);
        //Constructor
        //Initializes the complex number according to the parameters.
        //Postcondition: realPart = real; imaginaryPart = imag;

      complexType operator+
                      (const complexType& otherComplex) const;
        //Overload the operator +

      complexType operator*
                      (const complexType& otherComplex) const;
        //Overload the operator *

      bool operator== (const complexType& otherComplex) const;
        //Overload the operator ==

private:
    double realPart;       //variable to store the real part
    double imaginaryPart;  //variable to store the imaginary part
};
```

```
#endif
```

Next, we write the definitions of the functions to implement various operations of the class complexType.

The definitions of most of these functions are straightforward. We discuss only the definitions of the functions to overload the stream insertion operator, <<, and the stream extraction operator, >>.

To output a complex number in the form:

(a, b)

where a is the real part and b is the imaginary part, clearly the algorithm is as follows:

    a.   Output the left parenthesis, (.

    b.   Output the real part.

    c.   Output the comma.

    d.   Output the imaginary part.

    e.   Output the right parenthesis,).

Therefore, the definition of the function operator<< is as follows:

```
ostream& operator<<(ostream& osObject, const complexType& complex)
{
    osObject << "(";                        //Step a
    osObject << complex.realPart;           //Step b
    osObject << ", ";                       //Step c
    osObject << complex.imaginaryPart;      //Step d
    osObject << ")";                        //Step e

    return osObject;      //return the ostream object
}
```

Next, we discuss the definition of the function to overload the stream extraction operator, >>.

The input is of the form:

(3, 5)

In this input, the real part of the complex number is 3 and the imaginary part is 5. Clearly, the algorithm to read this complex number is as follows:

    a.   Read and discard the left parenthesis.

    b.   Read and store the real part.

    c.   Read and discard the comma.

    d.   Read and store the imaginary part.

    e.   Read and discard the right parenthesis.

Following these steps, the definition of the function operator>> is as follows:

```
istream& operator>>(istream& isObject, complexType& complex)
{
    char ch;

    isObject >> ch;                         //Step a
    isObject >> complex.realPart;           //Step b
    isObject >> ch;                         //Step c
    isObject >> complex.imaginaryPart;      //Step d
    isObject >> ch;                         //Step e

    return isObject;      //return the istream object
}
```

The definitions of the other functions are as follows:

```
bool complexType::operator==
                (const complexType& otherComplex) const
{
    return (realPart == otherComplex.realPart &&
          imaginaryPart == otherComplex.imaginaryPart);
}
```

```cpp
    //Constructor
complexType::complexType(double real, double imag)
{
    realPart = real;
    imaginaryPart = imag;
}


    //Function to set the complex number after the object
    //has been declared.
void complexType::setComplex(const double& real,
                                  const double& imag)
{
    realPart = real;
    imaginaryPart = imag;
}

void complexType::getComplex(double& real, double& imag) const
{
    real = realPart;
    imag = imaginaryPart;
}


        //overload the operator +
complexType complexType::operator+
                         (const complexType& otherComplex) const
{
    complexType temp;

    temp.realPart = realPart + otherComplex.realPart;
    temp.imaginaryPart = imaginaryPart
                            + otherComplex.imaginaryPart;

        return temp;
}

    //overload the operator *
complexType complexType::operator*
                            (const complexType& otherComplex) const
{
    complexType temp;

    temp.realPart = (realPart * otherComplex.realPart) -
                  (imaginaryPart * otherComplex.imaginaryPart);
    temp.imaginaryPart = (realPart * otherComplex.imaginaryPart)
                      + (imaginaryPart * otherComplex.realPart);
    return temp;
}
```

The following program illustrates the use of the `class complexType`:

```cpp
//**********************************************************
// Author: D.S. Malik
//
// This program shows how to use the class complexType.
//**********************************************************

#include <iostream>                              //Line 1
#include "complexType.h"                         //Line 2

using namespace std;                             //Line 3

int main()                                       //Line 4
{                                                //Line 5
    complexType num1(23, 34);                    //Line 6
    complexType num2;                            //Line 7
    complexType num3;                            //Line 8

    cout << "Line 9: Num1 = " << num1 << endl;   //Line 9
    cout << "Line 10: Num2 = " << num2 << endl;  //Line 10

    cout << "Line 11: Enter the complex number "
         << "in the form (a, b): ";              //Line 11
    cin >> num2;                                 //Line 12
    cout << endl;                                //Line 13

    cout << "Line 14: New value of num2 = "
         << num2 << endl;                        //Line 14

    num3 = num1 + num2;                          //Line 15

    cout << "Line 16: Num3 = " << num3 << endl;  //Line 16

    cout << "Line 17: " << num1 << " + " << num2
         << " = " << num1 + num2 << endl;        //Line 17

    cout << "Line 18: " << num1 << " * " << num2
         << " = " << num1 * num2 << endl;        //Line 18

    return 0;                                    //Line 19
}                                                //Line 20
```

Sample Run: In this sample run, the user input is shaded.

```
Line 9: Num1 = (23, 34)
Line 10: Num2 = (0, 0)
Line 11: Enter the complex number in the form (a, b): (3, 4)

Line 14: New value of num2 = (3, 4)
Line 16: Num3 = (26, 38)
Line 17: (23, 34) + (3, 4) = (26, 38)
Line 18: (23, 34) * (3, 4) = (-67, 194)
```

2

Function Overloading

The previous section discussed operator overloading. Operator overloading provides the programmer with the same concise notation for user-defined data types as the operator has with built-in types. The types of arguments used with an operator determine the action to take.

Similar to operator overloading, C++ allows the programmer to overload a function name. Recall that a class can have more than one constructor, but all constructors of a class have the same name, which is the name of the class. This case is an example of overloading a function.

Overloading a function refers to the creation of several functions with the same name. However, if several functions have the same name, every function must have a different set of parameters. The types of parameters determine which function to execute.

Suppose you need to write a function that determines the larger of two items. Both items can be integers, floating-point numbers, characters, or strings. You could write several functions as follows:

```
int largerInt(int x, int y);
char largerChar(char first, char second);
double largerDouble(double u, double v);
string largerString(string first, string second);
```

The function `largerInt` determines the larger of the two integers, the function `largerChar` determines the larger of the two characters, and so on. These functions all perform similar operations. Instead of giving different names to these functions, you can use the same name—say, `larger`—for each function; that is, you can overload the function `larger`. Thus, you can write the previous function prototypes simply as

```
int larger(int x, int y);
char larger(char first, char second);
double larger(double u, double v);
string larger(string first, string second);
```

If the call is `larger(5,3)`, for example, the first function executes. If the call is `larger('A', '9')`, the second function executes, and so on.

For function overloading to work, we must give the definition of each function. The next section teaches you how to overload functions with a single code segment and leave the job of generating code for separate functions to the compiler.

Templates

Templates are very powerful features of C++. By using templates, you can write a single code segment for a set of related functions, called a **function template**, and for related classes, called a **class template**. The syntax we use for templates is as follows:

```
template <class Type>
declaration;
```

where `Type` is the type of data, and `declaration` is either a function declaration or a class declaration. In C++, `template` is a reserved word. The word `class` in the heading refers to any user-defined type or built-in type. `Type` is referred to as a formal parameter to the template.

Just as variables are parameters to functions, types (that is, data types) are parameters to templates.

Function Templates

In the section, "Function Overloading" (located earlier in this chapter), when we introduced function overloading, the function `larger` was overloaded to find the larger of two integers, characters, floating-point numbers, or strings. To implement the function `larger`, we need to write four function definitions for the data type: one for `int`, one for `char`, one for `double`, and one for `string`. However, the body of each function is similar. C++ simplifies the process of overloading functions by providing function templates.

The syntax of the function template is as follows:

```
template <class Type>
function definition;
```

where `Type` is referred to as a formal parameter of the template. It is used to specify the type of parameters to the function and the return type of the function, and to declare variables within the function.

The statements

```
template <class Type>
Type larger(Type x, Type y)
{
    if (x >= y)
        return x;
    else
        return y;
}
```

define a function template `larger`, which returns the larger of two items. In the function heading, the type of the formal parameters `x` and `y` is `Type`, which will be specified by the type of the actual parameters when the function is called. The statement

```
cout << larger(5, 6) << endl;
```

is a call to the function template `larger`. Because 5 and 6 are of type `int`, the data type `int` is substituted for `Type` and the compiler generates the appropriate code.

If we omit the body of the function in the function template definition, the function template, as usual, is the prototype.

The following example illustrates the use of function templates.

EXAMPLE 2-7

This example uses the function template `larger` to determine the larger of the two items.

```
//**************************************************************
// Author: D.S. Malik
//
// This program illustrates how to write and use a template in a
// program.
//**************************************************************

#include <iostream>                                      //Line 1
#include <string>                                        //Line 2

using namespace std;                                     //Line 3

template <class Type>                                     //Line 4
Type larger(Type x, Type y);                             //Line 5

int main()                                               //Line 6
{                                                        //Line 7
    cout << "Line 8: Larger of 5 and 6 = "
         << larger(5, 6) << endl;                        //Line 8

    cout << "Line 9: Larger of A and B = "
         << larger('A','B') << endl;                     //Line 9

    cout << "Line 10: Larger of 5.6 and 3.2 = "
         << larger(5.6, 3.2) << endl;                    //Line 10

    string str1 = "Hello";                               //Line 11
    string str2 = "Happy";                               //Line 12

    cout << "Line 13: Larger of " << str1 << " and "
         << str2 << " = " << larger(str1, str2) << endl; //Line 13

    return 0;                                            //Line 14
}                                                        //Line 15

template <class Type>
Type larger(Type x, Type y)
{
    if (x >= y)
        return x;
    else
        return y;
}
```

Output

```
Line 8: Larger of 5 and 6 = 6
Line 9: Larger of A and B = B
Line 10: Larger of 5.6 and 3.2 = 5.6
Line 13: Larger of Hello and Happy = Hello
```

2

Class Templates

Like function templates, class templates are used to write a single code segment for a set of related classes. For example, in Chapter 1, we defined a list as an ADT; our list element type there was **int**. If the list element type changes from **int** to, say, **char**, **double**, or **string**, we need to write separate classes for each element type. For the most part, the operations on the list and the algorithms to implement those operations remain the same. Using class templates, we can create a generic **class** listType, and the compiler can generate the appropriate source code for a specific implementation.

The syntax we use for a class template is as follows:

```
template <class Type>
class declaration
```

Class templates are called **parameterized types** because, based on the parameter type, a specific class is generated. For example, if the template parameter type is **int**, we can generate a list to process integers; if the parameter type is **string**, we can generate a list to process strings.

A class template for the ADT listType is defined as follows:

```
template <class elemType>
class listType
{
public:
    bool isEmpty();
    bool isFull();
    void search(const elemType& searchItem, bool& found);
    void insert(const elemType& newElement);
    void remove(const elemType& removeElement);
    void destroyList();
    void printList();

    listType();

private:
    elemType list[100];   //array to hold the list elements
    int length;           //variable to store the number
                          //of elements in the list
};
```

This definition of the class template `listType` is a generic definition and includes only the basic operations on a list. To derive a specific list from this list and to add or rewrite the operations, we declare the array containing the list elements and the length of the list as **protected**.

Next, we describe a specific list. Suppose that you want to create a list to process integer data. The statement

```
listType<int> intList;              //Line 1
```

declares `intList` to be a list of 100 components, with each component being of type **int**. Similarly, the statement

```
listType<string> stringList;        //Line 2
```

declares `stringList` to be a list of 100 components, with each component being of type `string`.

In the statements in Lines 1 and 2, `listType<int>` and `listType<string>` are referred to as **template instantiations** or **instantiations** of the class template `listType<elemType>`, where `elemType` is the class parameter in the template header. A template instantiation can be created with either a built-in or user-defined type.

The function members of a class template are considered function templates. Thus, when giving the definitions of function members of a class template, we must follow the definition of the function template. For example, the definition of the member `insert` of the **class** `listType` is as follows:

```
template<class elemType>
void listType<elemType>::insert(const elemType& newElement)
{
    .
    .
    .
}
```

In the heading of the member function's definition, `elemType` specifies the data type of the list elements.

Header File and Implementation File of a Class Template

Until now, we have placed the definition of the class (in the specification file) and the definition of the member functions (in the implementation file) in separate files. The object code was generated from the implementation file (independently of any client code) and linked with the client code. This strategy does not work with class templates. Passing parameters to a function has an effect at run time, whereas passing a parameter to a class template has an effect at compile time. Because the actual parameter to a class is specified in the client code, and because the compiler cannot instantiate a function template without the actual parameter to the template, we can no longer compile the implementation file independently of the client code.

This problem has several possible solutions. We could put the class definition and the definitions of the function templates directly in the client code, or we could put the class definition and the definitions of the function templates together in the same header file. Another alternative is to put the class definition and the definitions of the functions in separate files (as usual), but include a directive to the implementation file at the end of the header file (that is, the specification file). In either case, the function definitions and the client code are compiled together. For illustrative purposes, we will put the class definition and the function definitions in the same header file.

QUICK REVIEW

1. Inheritance and composition are meaningful ways to relate two or more classes.
2. Inheritance is an "is a" relationship.
3. Composition is a "has a" relationship.
4. In single inheritance, the derived class is derived from only one existing class, called the base class.
5. In multiple inheritance, a derived class is derived from more than one base class.
6. The `private` members of a base class are `private` to the base class. The derived class cannot directly access them.
7. The `public` members of a base class can be inherited either as `public`, `protected`, or `private` by the derived class.
8. A derived class can redefine the function members of a base class, but this redefinition applies only to the objects of the derived class.
9. A call to a base class's constructor is specified in the heading of the definition of the derived class's constructor.
10. When initializing the object of a derived class, the constructor of the base class is executed first.
11. Review the inheritance rules given in this chapter.
12. In composition, a member of a class is an object of another class.
13. In composition, a call to the constructor of the member objects is specified in the heading of the definition of the class's constructor.
14. The three basic principles of OOD are encapsulation, inheritance, and polymorphism.
15. An operator that has different meanings with different data types is said to be overloaded.
16. In C++, << is used as a stream insertion operator and as a left shift operator. Similarly, >> is used as a stream extraction operator and as a right shift operator. Both are examples of operator overloading.

17. The function that overloads an operator is called an operator function.

18. The syntax of the heading of the operator function is

    `returnType operator operatorSymbol(parameters)`

19. In C++, `operator` is a reserved word.

20. Operator functions are value-returning functions.

21. Except for the assignment operator and the member selection operator, to use an operator on class objects, that operator must be overloaded.

22. Operator overloading provides the same concise notation for user-defined data types as is available with built-in data types.

23. When an operator is overloaded, its precedence cannot be changed, its associativity cannot be changed, default arguments cannot be used, the number of arguments that the operator takes cannot be changed, and the meaning of how an operator works with built-in data types remains the same.

24. It is not possible to create new operators. Only existing operators can be overloaded.

25. Most C++ operators can be overloaded.

26. The operators that cannot be overloaded are ., .*, ::, ?:, and `sizeof`.

27. The pointer `this` refers to the object as a whole.

28. The operator function that overloads the operators (), [], ->, or = must be a member of a class.

29. A `friend` function is a nonmember of a class.

30. The heading of a `friend` function is preceded by the word `friend`.

31. In C++, **friend** is a reserved word.

32. If an operator function is a member of a class, the leftmost operand of the operator must be a class object (or a reference to a class object) of that operator's class.

33. The binary operator function as a member of a class has only one parameter; as a nonmember of a class, it has two parameters.

34. The operator functions that overload the stream insertion operator, <<, and the stream extraction operator, >>, for a class must be `friend` functions of that class.

35. In C++, a function name can be overloaded.

36. Every instance of an overloaded function has different sets of parameters.

37. In C++, `template` is a reserved word.

38. Using templates, you can write a single code segment for a set of related functions—called the function template.

39. Using templates, you can write a single code segment for a set of related classes—called the class template.

40. A syntax of a template is

    ```
    template <class elemType>
    declaration;
    ```

    where `elemType` is a user-defined identifier, which is used to pass types (that is, data types) as parameters, and `declaration` is either a function or a class. The word `class` in the heading refers to any user-defined data type or built-in data type.

41. Class templates are called parameterized types.

42. In a class template, the parameter `elemType` specifies how a generic class template is to be customized to form a specific class.

43. Suppose `cType` is a class template and `func` is a member function of `cType`. The heading of the function definition of `func` is

    ```
    template <class elemType >
    funcType cType<elemType>::func(formal parameters)
    ```

    where `funcType` is the type of the function, such as `void`.

44. Suppose `cType` is a class template, which can take `int` as a parameter. The statement

    ```
    cType<int> x;
    ```

    declares `x` to be an object of type `cType`, and the type passed to the `class` `cType` is `int`.

EXERCISES

1. Mark the following statements as true or false.

   a. The constructor of a derived class specifies a call to the constructor of the base class in the heading of the function definition.

   b. The constructor of a derived class specifies a call to the constructor of the base class using the name of the class.

   c. Suppose that `x` and `y` are classes, one of the data members of `x` is an object of type `y`, and both classes have constructors. The constructor of `x` specifies a call to the constructor of `y` by using the object name of type `y`.

   d. A derived class must have a constructor.

   e. In C++, all operators can be overloaded for user-defined data types.

   f. In C++, operators cannot be redefined for built-in types.

   g. The function that overloads an operator is called the operator function.

   h. C++ allows users to create their own operators.

   i. The precedence of an operator cannot be changed, but its associativity can be changed.

j. Every instance of an overloaded function has the same number of parameters.

k. It is not necessary to overload relational operators for classes that have only int data members.

l. The member function of a class template is a function template.

m. When writing the definition of a friend function, the keyword friend must appear in the function heading.

n. The function heading of the operator function to overload the pre-increment operator (++) and the postincrement operator (++) is the same because both operators have the same symbols.

2. Draw a class hierarchy in which several classes are derived from a single base class.

3. Suppose that a **class** employeeType is derived from the **class** personType (see Example 1-12, in Chapter 1). Give examples of data and function members that can be added to the **class** employeeType.

4. Explain the difference between the **private** and **protected** members of a class.

5. Consider the following class definition:

```
class aClass
{
public:
      void print() const;
      void set(int, int);
      aClass();
      aClass(int, int);

private:
      int u;
      int v;
};
```

What is wrong with the following class definitions?

a.
```
class bClass public aClass
   {
   public:
         void print();
         void set(int, int, int);
   private:
         int z;
   };
```

b.
```
class cClass: public aClass
   {
   public:
         void print();
         int sum();
         cClass();
         cClass(int);
   }
```

6. Consider the following statements:

```
class yClass
{
public:
    void one();
    void two(int, int);
    yClass();
private:
    int a;
    int b;
};

class xClass: public yClass
{
public:
    void one();
    xClass();
private:
    int z;
};

yClass y;
xClass x;
```

a. The **private** members of yClass are **public** members of xClass. True or False?

b. Mark the following statements as valid or invalid. If a statement is invalid, explain why.

   i.
```
void yClass::one()
{
    cout << a + b << endl;
}
```

   ii.
```
y.a = 15;
x.b = 30;
```

   iii.
```
void xClass::one()
{
    a = 10;
    b = 15;
    z = 30;
    cout << a + b + z << endl;
}
```

   iv. `cout << y.a << " " << y.b << " " << x.z << endl;`

7. Assume the declaration of Exercise 6.

   a. Write the definition of the default constructor of yClass so that the **private** data members of yClass are initialized to 0.

   b. Write the definition of the default constructor of xClass so that the **private** data members of xClass are initialized to 0.

c. Write the definition of the member function two of yClass so that the **private** data member a is initialized to the value of the first parameter of two, and the **private** data member b is initialized to the value of the second parameter of two.

8. What is wrong with the following code?

```
class classA
{
protected:
    void setX(int a);              //Line 1
        //Postcondition: x = a;     //Line 2
private:                           //Line 3
    int x;                         //Line 4
};
.
.
.
int main()
{
    classA aObject;                //Line 5

    aObject.setX(4);               //Line 6
    return 0;                      //Line 7
}
```

9. Consider the following code:

```
class one
{
public:
    void print() const;
        //Outputs the values of x and y
protected:
    void setData(int u, int v);
        //Postcondition: x = u; y = v;
private:
    int x;
    int y;
};

class two: public one
{
public:
    void setData(int a, int b, int c);
        //Postcondition: x = a; y = b; z = c;
    void print() const;
        //Outputs the values of x, y, and z
private:
    int z;
};
```

a. Write the definition of the function setData of the class two.

b. Write the definition of the function print of the class two.

10. What is the output of the following C++ program?

```cpp
#include <iostream>
#include <string>

using namespace std;

class baseClass
{
public:
    void print() const;

    baseClass(string s = " ", int a = 0);
      //Postcondition: str = s; x = a
protected:
    int x;

private:
    string str;
};

class derivedClass: public baseClass
{
public:
    void print() const;

    derivedClass(string s = "", int a = 0, int b = 0);
      //Postcondition: str = s; x = a; y = b

private:
    int y;
};

int main()
{
    baseClass baseObject("This is base class", 2);
    derivedClass derivedObject("DDDDDD", 3, 7);

    baseObject.print();
    derivedObject.print();

    return 0;
}

void baseClass::print() const
{
    cout << x << " " << str << endl;
}

baseClass::baseClass(string s, int a)
{
    str = s;
    x = a;
}
```

```
void derivedClass::print() const
{
    cout << "Derived class: " << y << endl;
    baseClass::print();
}

derivedClass::derivedClass(string s, int a, int b)
            :baseClass("Hello Base", a + b)
{
    y = b;
}
```

11. What is the output of the following program?

```
#include <iostream>

using namespace std;

class baseClass
{
public:
    void print() const;

    int getX();

    baseClass(int a = 0);

protected:
    int x;
};

class derivedClass: public baseClass
{
public:
    void print() const;

    int getResult();

    derivedClass(int a = 0, int b = 0);

private:
    int y;
};


int main()
{
    baseClass baseObject(7);
    derivedClass derivedObject(3,8);

    baseObject.print();
    derivedObject.print();
```

```
        cout << "**** " << baseObject.getX() << endl;
        cout << "#### " << derivedObject.getResult() << endl;

        return 0;
}

void baseClass::print() const
{
        cout << "In base: x = " << x << endl;
}

baseClass::baseClass(int a)
{
        x = a;
}

int baseClass::getX()
{
        return x;
}

void derivedClass::print() const
{
        cout << "In derived: x = " << x << ", y = " << y
             << ", x + y = " << x + y << endl;
}

int derivedClass::getResult()
{
        return x + y;
}

derivedClass::derivedClass(int a, int b)
              :baseClass(a)
{
        y = b;
}
```

12. What is a `friend` function?

13. Suppose that the operator `<<` is to be overloaded for a user-defined **class** `mystery`. Why must `<<` be overloaded as a `friend` function?

14. Suppose that the binary operator + is overloaded as a member function for a class `strange`. How many parameters does the function **operator**+ have?

15. Consider the following declaration:

```
class strange
{
.
.
.
};
```

a. Write a statement that shows the declaration in the `class strange` to overload the operator `>>`.

b. Write a statement that shows the declaration in the `class strange` to overload the binary operator `+` as a member function.

c. Write a statement that shows the declaration in the `class strange` to overload the operator `==` as a member function.

d. Write a statement that shows the declaration in the `class strange` to overload the postincrement operator `++` as a member function.

16. Assume the declaration of Exercise 15.

a. Write a statement that shows the declaration in the `class strange` to overload the binary operator `+` as a **friend** function.

b. Write a statement that shows the declaration in the `class strange` to overload the operator `==` as a **friend** function.

c. Write a statement that shows the declaration in the `class strange` to overload the postincrement operator `++` as a **friend** function.

17. Find the error(s) in the following code:

```
class mystery                            //Line 1
{
    ...
    bool operator <= (mystery);          //Line 2
    ...
};

bool mystery::<=(mystery rightObj)       //Line 3
{
    ...
}
```

18. Find the error(s) in the following code:

```
class mystery                                //Line 1
{
    ...
    bool operator <= (mystery, mystery);     //Line 2
    ...
};
```

19. Find the error(s) in the following code:

```
class mystery                            //Line 1
{
    ...
    friend operator+ (mystery);          //Line 2
        //Overload the binary operator +
    ...
};
```

20. How many parameters are required to overload the preincrement operator for a class as a member function?

21. How many parameters are required to overload the preincrement operator for a class as a **friend** function?

22. How many parameters are required to overload the postincrement operator for a class as a member function?

23. How many parameters are required to overload the postincrement operator for a class as a **friend** function?

24. Find the error(s) in the following code:

```
template <class type>      //Line 1
class strange              //Line 2
{
    ...
};

strange<int> s1;           //Line 3
strange<type> s2;          //Line 4
```

25. Consider the following declaration:

```
template <class type>
class strange
{
    ...
private:
    Type a;
    Type b;
};
```

a. Write a statement that declares sObj to be an object of type strange such that the private data members a and b are of type int.

b. Write a statement that shows the declaration in the class strange to overload the operator == as a member function.

c. Assume that two objects of type strange are equal if their corresponding data members are equal. Write the definition of the function operator== for the class strange, which is overloaded as a member function.

26. Consider the definition of the following function template:

```
template <class Type>
Type surprise(Type x, Type y)
{
    return x + y ;
}
```

What is the output of the following statements?

a. `cout << surprise(5, 7) << endl;`

b. ```
string str1 = "Sunny";
string str2 = " Day";
cout << surprise(str1, str2) << endl;
```
```

27. Consider the definition of the following function template:

```
Template <class Type>
Type funcExp(Type list[], int size)
{
    Type x = list[0];
    Type y = list[size - 1];

    for (int j = 1; j < (size - 1)/2; j++)
    {
        if (x < list[j])
            x = list[j];
        if (y > list[size - 1 -j])
            y = list[size - 1 -j];
    }

    return x + y;
}
```

Further suppose that you have the following declarations:

```
int list[10] = {5,3,2,10,4,19,45,13,61,11};
string strList[] = {"One", "Hello", "Four", "Three", "How", "Six"};
```

What is the output of the following statements?

a. `cout << funcExp(list, 10) << endl;`

b. `cout << funcExp(strList, 6) << endl;`

28. Write the definition of the function template that swaps the contents of two variables.

PROGRAMMING EXERCISES

1. In Chapter 1, the class `clockType` was designed to implement the time of day in a program. Certain applications, in addition to hours, minutes, and seconds, might require you to store the time zone. Derive the **class extClockType** from the class `clockType` by adding a data member to store the time zone. Add the necessary member functions and constructors to make the class functional. Also, write the definitions of the member functions and the constructors. Finally, write a test program to test your class.

2. In this chapter, the class `dateType` was designed to implement the date in a program, but the member function `setDate` and the constructor do not check whether the date is valid before storing the date in the data members. Rewrite the definitions of the function `setDate` and the constructor so that the values for the month, day, and year are checked before storing the date into the data members. Add a function member, `isLeapYear`, to check whether a year is a leap year. Moreover, write a test program to test your class.

3. A point in the x-y plane is represented by its x-coordinate and y-coordinate. Design a class, `pointType`, that can store and process a point in the x-y plane. You should then perform operations on the point, such as showing the point, setting the coordinates of the point, printing the coordinates of the point, returning the x-coordinate, and returning the y-coordinate. Also, write a test program to test the various operations on the point.

4. Every circle has a center and a radius. Given the radius, we can determine the circle's area and circumference. Given the center, we can determine its position in the x-y plane. The center of a circle is a point in the x-y plane. Design a class, `circleType`, that can store the radius and center of the circle. Because the center is a point in the x-y plane and you designed the class to capture the properties of a point in Programming Exercise 3, you must derive the **class** `circleType` from the `class` `pointType`. You should be able to perform the usual operations on a circle, such as setting the radius, printing the radius, calculating and printing the area and circumference, and carrying out the usual operations on the center.

5. Every cylinder has a base and height, where the base is a circle. Design a class, `cylinderType`, that can capture the properties of a cylinder and perform the usual operations on a cylinder. Derive this class from the `class circleType` designed in Programming Exercise 4. Some of the operations that can be performed on a cylinder are as follows: Calculate and print the volume, calculate and print the surface area, set the height, set the radius of the base, and set the center of the base.

6. In Programming Exercise 2, the `class dateType` was designed and implemented to keep track of a date, but it has very limited operations. Redefine the `class dateType` so that it can perform the following operations on a date in addition to the operations already defined:

   a. Set the month.

   b. Set the day.

   c. Set the year.

   d. Return the month.

   e. Return the day.

   f. Return the year.

   g. Test whether the year is a leap year.

   h. Return the number of days in the month. For example, if the date is 3-12-2011, the number of days to be returned is 31 because there are 31 days in March.

   i. Return the number of days passed in the year. For example, if the date is 3-18-2011, the number of days passed in the year is 77. Note that the number of days returned also includes the current day.

j. Return the number of days remaining in the year. For example, if the date is 3-18-2011, the number of days remaining in the year is 288.

k. Calculate the new date by adding a fixed number of days to the date. For example, if the date is 3-18-2011 and the days to be added are 25, the new date is 4-12-2011.

7. Write the definitions of the functions to implement the operations defined for the class dateType in Programming Exercise 6.

8. The **class** dateType defined in Programming Exercise 6 prints the date in numerical form. Some applications might require the date to be printed in another form, such as March 24, 2003. Derive the class extDateType so that the date can be printed in either form.

Add a data member to the class extDateType so that the month can also be stored in string form. Add a function member to output the month in the string format followed by the year—for example, in the form March 2003.

Write the definitions of the functions to implement the operations for the **class** extDateType.

9. Using the classes extDateType (Programming Exercise 8) and dayType (Chapter 1, Programming Exercise 2), design the class calendarType so that, given the month and the year, we can print the calendar for that month. To print a monthly calendar, you must know the first day of the month and the number of days in that month. Thus, you must store the first day of the month, which is of the form dayType, and the month and the year of the calendar. Clearly, the month and the year can be stored in an object of the form extDateType by setting the day component of the date to 1, and the month and year as specified by the user. Thus, the **class** calendarType has two data members: an object of type dayType and an object of type extDateType.

Design the class calendarType so that the program can print a calendar for any month starting January 1, 1500. Note that the day for January 1 of the year 1500 is a Monday. To calculate the first day of a month, you can add the appropriate days to Monday of January 1, 1500.

For the **class** calendarType, include the following operations:

a. Determine the first day of the month for which the calendar will be printed. Call this operation firstDayOfMonth.

b. Set the month.

c. Set the year.

d. Return the month.

e. Return the year.

f. Print the calendar for the particular month.

g. Add the appropriate constructors to initialize the data members.

10. a. Write the definitions of the member functions of the class calendarType (designed in Programming Exercise 8) to implement the operations of the class calendarType.

   b. Write a test program to print the calendar for either a particular month or a particular year. For example, the calendar for September 2011 is as follows:

```
                      September 2011
   Sun     Mon     Tue     Wed     Thu     Fri     Sat
                                    1       2       3
    4       5       6       7       8       9      10
   11      12      13      14      15      16      17
   18      19      20      21      22      23      24
   25      26      27      28      29      30
```

11. In Chapter 1, the class clockType was designed and implemented to implement the time of day in a program. This chapter discussed how to overload various operators. Redesign the class clockType by overloading the following operators: the stream insertion << and stream extraction >> operators for input and output, the pre- and postincrement increment operators to increment the time by one second, and the relational operators to compare the two times. Also write a test program to test various operations of the **class** clockType.

12. a. Extend the definition of the class complexType so that it performs the subtraction and division operations. Overload the operators subtraction and division for this class as member functions.

   If (a, b) and (c, d) are complex numbers,

   $(a, b) - (c, d) = (a - c, b - d)$,

   If (c, d) is nonzero,

   $(a, b) / (c, d) = ((ac + bd) / (c^2 + d^2), (-ad + bc) / (c^2 + d^2))$

   b. Write the definitions of the functions to overload the operators − and / as defined in part a.

   c. Write a test program that tests the various operations on the class complexType. Format your answer with two decimal places.

13. a. Rewrite the definition of the class complexType so that the arithmetic and relational operators are overloaded as nonmember functions.

   b. Write the definitions of the member functions of the class complexType as designed in part a.

   c. Write a test program that tests the various operations on the class complexType as designed in parts a and b. Format your answer with two decimal places.

14. Let $a + ib$ be a complex number. The conjugate of $a + ib$ is $a - ib$ and the absolute value of $a + ib$ is $\sqrt{a^2 + b^2}$. Extend the definition of the `class` `complexType` of the Programming Example, Complex Numbers by overloading the operators $\sim$ and ! as member functions so that $\sim$ returns the conjugate of a complex number and ! returns the absolute value. Write the definitions of these operator functions.

15. Redo Programming Exercise 13 so that the operators $\sim$ and ! are overloaded as nonmember functions.

16. In C++, the largest `int` value is `2147483647`. So an integer larger than this cannot be stored and processed as an integer. Similarly, if the sum or product of two positive integers is greater than `2147483647`, the result will be incorrect. One way to store and manipulate large integers is to store each individual digit of the number in an array. Design the `class largeIntegers` so that an object of this class can store an integer up to 100 digits long. Overload the operators + and − to add and subtract, respectively, the values of two objects of this class. (In the Programming Exercises in Chapter 3, we will overload the multiplication operator.) Overload the assignment operator to copy the value of a large integer into another large integer. Overload the stream extraction and insertion operators for easy input and output. Your program must contain appropriate constructors to initialize objects of the `class largeIntegers`. (*Hint:* Read numbers as strings and store the digits of the number in the reverse order. Add instance variables to store the number of digits and the sign of the number.)

17. The roots of the quadratic equation $ax^2 + bx + c = 0$, $a \neq 0$ are given by the following formula:

$$\frac{-b \pm \sqrt{b^2 - 4ac}}{2a}$$

In this formula, the term $b^2 - 4ac$ is called the **discriminant**. If $b^2 - 4ac = 0$, the equation has a single (repeated) root. If $b^2 - 4ac > 0$, the equation has two real roots. If $b^2 - 4ac < 0$, the equation has two complex roots. Design and implement the `class quadraticEq` so that an object of this class can store the coefficients of a quadratic equation. Overload the operators + and − to add and subtract, respectively, the corresponding coefficients of two quadratic equations. Overload the relational operators == and != to determine if two quadratic equations are the same. Add appropriate constructors to initialize objects. Overload the stream extraction and insertion operator for easy input and output. Also, include function members to determine and output the type and the roots of the equation. Write a program to test your class.

18. Programming Exercise 6 in Chapter 1 describes how to design the `class lineType` to implement a line. Redo this programming exercise so that the `class lineType`:

a. Overloads the stream insertion operator, <<, for easy output.

b. Overloads the stream extraction operator, >>, for easy input. (The line $ax + by = c$ is input as (a, b, c).

c. Overloads the assignment operator to copy a line into another line.

d. Overloads the unary operator + as a member function, so that it returns true if a line is vertical; false otherwise.

e. Overloads the unary operator – as a member function, so that it returns **true** if a line is horizontal; false otherwise.

f. Overloads the operator == as a member function, so that it returns true if two lines are equal; false otherwise.

g. Overloads the operator || as a member function, so that it returns true if two lines are parallel; false otherwise.

h. Overloads the operator && as a member function, so that it returns true if two lines are perpendicular; false otherwise.

Write a program to test your class.

19. Rational fractions are of the form a / b, where a and b are integers and $b \neq 0$. In this exercise, by "fractions" we mean rational fractions. Suppose a / b and c / d are fractions. Arithmetic operations on fractions are defined by the following rules:

$a / b + c / d = (ad + bc) / bd$

$a / b - c / d = (ad - bc)/bd$

$a / b \times c / d = ac / bd$

$(a / b) / (c / d) = ad / bc$, where $c / d \neq 0$.

Fractions are compared as follows: a / b op c / d if ad op bc, where *op* is any of the relational operations. For example, $a / b < c / d$ if $ad < bc$.

Design a class—say, fractionType—that performs the arithmetic and relational operations on fractions. Overload the arithmetic and relational operators so that the appropriate symbols can be used to perform the operation. Also, overload the stream insertion and stream extraction operators for easy input and output.

a. Write a C++ program that, using the class fractionType, performs operations on fractions.

b. Among other things, test the following: Suppose x, y, and z are objects of type fractionType. If the input is 2/3, the statement

```
cin >> x;
```

should store 2/3 in x. The statement

```
cout << x + y << endl;
```

should output the value of **x** + **y** in fraction form. The statement

```
z = x + y;
```

should store the sum of **x** and **y** in **z** in fraction form. Your answer need not be in the lowest terms.

20.   a.   In Programming Exercise 1 in Chapter 1, we defined a **class romanType** to implement Roman numerals in a program. In that exercise, we also implemented a function, **romanToDecimal**, to convert a Roman numeral into its equivalent decimal number.

Modify the definition of the **class romanType** so that the data members are declared as **protected**. Use the **class string** to manipulate the strings. Furthermore, overload the stream insertion and stream extraction operators for easy input and output. The stream insertion operator outputs the Roman numeral in the Roman format.

Also, include a member function, **decimalToRoman**, that converts the decimal number (the decimal number must be a positive integer) to an equivalent Roman numeral format. Write the definition of the member function **decimalToRoman**.

For simplicity, we assume that only the letter I can appear in front of another letter and that it appears only in front of the letters V and X. For example, 4 is represented as **IV**, 9 is represented as **IX**, 39 is represented as **XXXIX**, and 49 is represented as **XXXXIX**. Also, 40 will be represented as **XXXX**, 190 will be represented as **CLXXXX**, and so on.

   b.   Derive a **class extRomanType** from the **class romanType** to do the following. In the **class extRomanType**, overload the arithmetic operators +, -, *, and / so that arithmetic operations can be performed on Roman numerals. Also, overload the pre- and postincrement and decrement operators as member functions of the **class extRomanType**.

To add (subtract, multiply, or divide) Roman numerals, add (subtract, multiply, or divide, respectively) their decimal representations and then convert the result to the Roman numeral format. For subtraction, if the first number is smaller than the second number, output a message saying that, "**Because the first number is smaller than the second, the numbers cannot be subtracted**". Similarly, for division, the numerator must be larger than the denominator. Use similar conventions for the increment and decrement operators.

   c.   Write the definitions of the functions to overload the operators described in part b.

   d.   Write a program to test your **class extRomanType**.

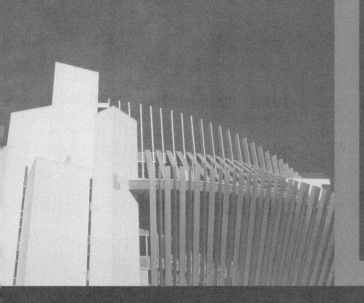

CHAPTER 3

POINTERS AND ARRAY-BASED LISTS

IN THIS CHAPTER, YOU WILL:

- · Learn about the pointer data type and pointer variables
- · Explore how to declare and manipulate pointer variables
- · Learn about the address of operator and dereferencing operator
- · Discover dynamic variables
- · Examine how to use the `new` and `delete` operators to manipulate dynamic variables
- · Learn about pointer arithmetic
- · Discover dynamic arrays
- · Become aware of the shallow and deep copies of data
- · Discover the peculiarities of classes with pointer data members
- · Explore how dynamic arrays are used to process lists
- · Learn about virtual functions
- · Become aware of abstract classes

The data types in C++ are classified into three categories: simple, structured, and pointers. Until now, you have worked with only the first two data types. This chapter discusses the third data type: the pointer data type. You first learn how to declare pointer variables (or pointers, for short) and manipulate the data to which they point. Later, you use these concepts when you study dynamic arrays and linked lists. Linked lists are discussed in Chapter 5.

The Pointer Data Type and Pointer Variables

The values belonging to pointer data types are the memory addresses of your computer. However, there is no name associated with the pointer data type in C++. Because the domain, (that is, the values of a pointer data type), consists of addresses (memory locations), a pointer variable is a variable whose content is an address, that is, a memory location.

Pointer variable: A variable whose content is an address (that is, a memory address).

Declaring Pointer Variables

The value of a pointer variable is an address. That is, the value refers to another memory space. The data is typically stored in this memory space. Therefore, when you declare a pointer variable, you also specify the data type of the value to be stored in the memory location to which the pointer variable points.

In C++, you declare a pointer variable by using the asterisk symbol (*) between the data type and the variable name. The general syntax to declare a pointer variable is as follows:

```
dataType *identifier;
```

As an example, consider the following statements:

```
int *p;
char *ch;
```

In these statements, both p and ch are pointer variables. The content of p (when properly assigned) points to a memory location of type int, and the content of ch points to a memory location of type char. Usually p is called a pointer variable of type int, and ch is called a pointer variable of type char.

Before discussing how pointers work, let us make the following observations. The following statements that declare p to be a pointer variable of type int are equivalent:

```
int *p;
int* p;
int * p;
```

Thus, the character * can appear anywhere between the data type name and the variable name.

Now consider the following statement:

```
int* p, q;
```

In this statement, only p is a pointer variable, not q. Here q is an **int** variable. To avoid confusion, we prefer to attach the character * to the variable name. So the preceding statement is written as follows:

```
int *p, q;
```

Of course, the statement

```
int *p, *q;
```

declares both p and q to be pointer variables of type **int**.

Now that you know how to declare pointers, next we discuss how to make a pointer point to a memory space and how to manipulate the data stored in these memory locations.

Because the value of a pointer is a memory address, a pointer can store the address of a memory space of the designated type. For example, if p is a pointer of type int, p can store the address of any memory space of type **int**. C++ provides two operators—the address of operator (&) and the dereferencing operator (*)—to work with pointers. The next two sections describe these operators.

Address of Operator (&)

In C++, the ampersand, &, called the **address of operator**, is a unary operator that returns the address of its operand. For example, given the statements

```
int x;
int *p;
```

the statement

```
p = &x;
```

assigns the address of x to p. That is, x and the value of p refer to the same memory location.

Dereferencing Operator (*)

The previous chapters used the asterisk character, *, as the binary multiplication operator. C++ also uses * as a unary operator. When *, commonly referred to as the **dereferencing operator** or **indirection operator**, is used as a unary operator, * refers to the object to which the operand of the * (that is, the pointer) points. For example, given the statements

```
int x = 25;
int *p;
p = &x;    //store the address of x in p
```

the statement

```
cout << *p << endl;
```

prints the value stored in the memory space to which p points, which is the value of x. Also, the statement

```
*p = 55;
```

stores 55 in the memory location to which p points—that is, 55 is stored in x.

Example 3-1 shows how a pointer variable works.

EXAMPLE 3-1

Let us consider the following statements:

```
int *p;
int num;
```

In these statements, p is a pointer variable of type **int** and num is a variable of type **int**. Let us assume that memory location 1200 is allocated for p and memory location 1800 is allocated for num. (See Figure 3-1.)

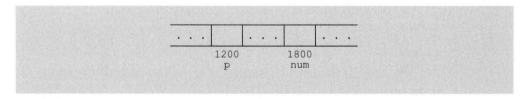

FIGURE 3-1 Variables p and num

Consider the following statements:

1. num = 78;
2. p = #
3. *p = 24;

The following shows the values of the variables after the execution of each statement.

After statement	Values of the variables	Explanation
1	. . . [ ] . . . [78] . . . 　　1200　　　　1800 　　　p　　　　　num	The statement num = 78; stores 78 into num.
2	. . . [1800] . . . [78] . . . 　　1200　　　　1800 　　　p　　　　　num	The statement p = # stores the address of num, which is 1800, into p.
3	. . . [1800] . . . [24] . . . 　　1200　　　　1800 　　　p　　　　　num	The statement *p = 24; stores 24 into the memory location to which p points. Because the value of p is 1800, statement 3 stores 24 into memory location 1800. Note that the value of num is also changed.

Let us summarize the preceding discussion.

1. A declaration such as **int** *p; allocates memory for p only, not for *p. Later, you learn how to allocate memory for *p.
2. The content of p points only to a memory location of type **int**.
3. &p, p, and *p all have different meanings.
4. &p means the address of p—that is, 1200 (as shown in Figure 3-1).
5. p means the content of p, which is 1800, after the statement p = # executes.
6. *p means the content of the memory location to which p points. Note that the value of *p is 78 after the statement p = # executes; the value of *p is 24 after the statement *p = 24; executes.

The program in Example 3-2 further illustrates how a pointer variable works.

EXAMPLE 3-2

```
//*************************************************************
// Author: D.S. Malik
//
// This program illustrates how a pointer variable works.
//*************************************************************

#include <iostream>                                    //Line 1

using namespace std;                                    //Line 2
```

```
int main()                                          //Line 3
{                                                   //Line 4
    int *p;                                         //Line 5
    int num1 = 5;                                   //Line 6
    int num2 = 8;                                   //Line 7

    p = &num1; //store the address of num1 into p; Line 8

    cout << "Line 9: &num1 = " << &num1
         << ", p = " << p << endl;                  //Line 9
    cout << "Line 10: num1 = " << num1
         << ", *p = " << *p << endl;                //Line 10

    *p = 10;                                        //Line 11
    cout << "Line 12: num1 = " << num1
         << ", *p = " << *p << endl << endl;        //Line 12

    p = &num2; //store the address of num2 into p; Line 13

    cout << "Line 14: &num2 = " << &num2
         << ", p = " << p << endl;                  //Line 14
    cout << "Line 15: num2 = " << num2
         << ", *p = " << *p << endl;                //Line 15

    *p = 2 * (*p);                                  //Line 16
    cout << "Line 17: num2 = " << num2
         << ", *p = " << *p << endl;                //Line 17

    return 0;                                       //Line 18
}                                                   //Line 19
```

Sample Run:

```
Line 9: &num1 = 0012FF54, p = 0012FF54
Line 10: num1 = 5, *p = 5
Line 12: num1 = 10, *p = 10

Line 14: &num2 = 0012FF48, p = 0012FF48
Line 15: num2 = 8, *p = 8
Line 17: num2 = 16, *p = 16
```

For the most part, the preceding output is straightforward. Let us look at some of these statements. The statement in Line 8 stores the address of num1 into p. The statement in Line 9 outputs the value of &num1, the address of num1, and the value of p. (Note that the values output by Line 9 are machine dependent. When you execute this program on your computer, you are likely to get different values of &num1 and p.) The statement in Line 10 outputs the value of num1 and *p. Because p points to the memory location of num1, *p outputs the value of this memory location, that is, of num1. The statement in Line 11 changes the value of *p to 10. Because p points to the memory location num1, the value of num1 is also changed. The statement in Line 12 outputs the value of num1 and *p.

The statement in Line 13 stores the address of num2 into p. So after the execution of this statement, p points to num2. So, any change that *p makes immediately changes the value of num2. The statement in Line 14 outputs the address of num2 and the value of p. This statement in Line 16 multiplies the value of *p, which is the value of num2, by 2 and stores the new value into *p. This statement also changes the value of num2. The statement in Line 17 outputs the value of num2 and *p.

Pointers and Classes

Consider the following statements:

```
string *str;
str = new string;
*str = "Sunny Day";
```

The first statement declares str to be a pointer variable of type string. The second statement allocates memory of type string and stores the address of the allocated memory in str. The third statement stores the string "Sunny Day" in the memory to which str points. Now suppose that you want to use the string function length to find the length of the string "Sunny Day". The statement (*str).length() returns the length of the string. Note the parentheses around *str. The expression (*str).length() is a mixture of pointer dereferencing and the class component selection. In C++, the dot operator, ., has a higher precedence than the dereferencing operator, *. Let us elaborate on this a little more. In the expression (*str).length(), the operator * evaluates first, so the expression *str evaluates first. Because str is a pointer variable of type string, *str refers to a memory space of type string. Therefore, in the expression (*str).length(), the function length of the **class** string executes. Now consider the expression *str.length(). Let us see how this expression gets evaluated. Because . has a higher precedence than *, the expression str.length() evaluates first. The expression str.length() would result in a syntax error because str is *not* a string object, so it cannot use the function length of the class string.

As you can see, in the expression (*str).length(), the parentheses around *str are important. However, typos are unavoidable. Therefore, to simplify the accessing of class or struct components via a pointer, C++ provides another operator, called the **member access operator arrow**, ->. The operator -> consists of two consecutive symbols: a hyphen and the "greater than" symbol.

The syntax for accessing a class (struct) member using the operator -> is as follows:

```
pointerVariableName->classMemberName
```

Thus, the expression

```
(*str).length()
```

is equivalent to the expression

```
str->length()
```

Accessing class (struct) components via pointers using the operator -> thus eliminates the use both of the parentheses and of the dereferencing operator. Because typos are unavoidable and missing parentheses can result in either an abnormal program termination or erroneous results, when accessing class (struct) components via pointers, this book uses the arrow notation.

Initializing Pointer Variables

Because C++ does not automatically initialize variables, pointer variables must be initialized if you do not want them to point to anything. Pointer variables are initialized using the constant value 0, called the **null pointer**. Thus, the statement p = 0; stores the null pointer in p; that is, p points to nothing. Some programmers use the named constant NULL to initialize pointer variables. The following two statements are equivalent:

```
p = NULL;
p = 0;
```

The number 0 is the only number that can be directly assigned to a pointer variable.

Dynamic Variables

In the previous sections, you learned how to declare pointer variables, how to store the address of a variable into a pointer variable of the same type as the variable, and how to manipulate data using pointers. However, you learned how to use pointers to manipulate data only into memory spaces that were created using other variables. In other words, the pointers manipulated data into existing memory spaces. So what is the benefit to using pointers? You can access these memory spaces by working with the variables that were used to create them. In this section, you learn about the power behind pointers. In particular, you learn how to allocate and deallocate memory during program execution using pointers.

Variables that are created during program execution are called **dynamic variables**. With the help of pointers, C++ creates dynamic variables. C++ provides two operators, new and **delete**, to create and destroy dynamic variables, respectively. When a program requires a new variable, the operator new is used. When a program no longer needs a dynamic variable, the operator delete is used.

In C++, **new** and **delete** are reserved words.

Operator new

The operator **new** has two forms: one to allocate a single variable, and another to allocate an array of variables. The syntax to use the operator **new** is as follows:

```
new dataType;          //to allocate a single variable
new dataType[intExp];  //to allocate an array of variables
```

where intExp is any expression evaluating to a positive integer.

The operator new allocates memory (a variable) of the designated type and returns a pointer to it—that is, the address of this allocated memory. Moreover, the allocated memory is uninitialized.

Consider the following declaration:

```
int *p;
char *q;
int x;
```

The statement

```
p = &x;
```

stores the address of x in p. However, no new memory is allocated. On the other hand, consider the following statement:

```
p = new int;
```

This statement creates a variable during program execution somewhere in memory, and stores the address of the allocated memory in p. The allocated memory is accessed via pointer dereferencing—namely, *p. Similarly, the statement

```
q = new char[16];
```

creates an array of 16 components of type char and stores the base address of the array in q.

Because a dynamic variable is unnamed, it cannot be accessed directly. It is accessed indirectly by the pointer returned by new. The following statements illustrate this concept:

```
int *p;    //p is a pointer of type int

p = new int;   //allocates memory of type int and stores the address
               //of the allocated memory in p
*p = 28;       //stores 28 in the allocated memory
```

 NOTE The operator **new** allocates memory space of a specific type and returns the (starting) address of the allocated memory space. However, if the operator **new** is unable to allocate the required memory space (for example, there is not enough memory space), the program might terminate with an error message.

Operator `delete`

Suppose you have the following declaration:

```
int *p;
```

This statement declares p to be a pointer variable of type **int**. Next, consider the following statements:

```
p = new int;    //Line 1
*p = 54;        //Line 2
p = new int;    //Line 3
*p = 73;        //Line 4
```

Let us see the effect of these statements. The statement in Line 1 allocates memory space of type **int** and stores the address of the allocated memory space into p. Suppose that the address of allocated memory space is 1500. Then, the value of p after the execution of this statement is 1500. (See Figure 3-2.)

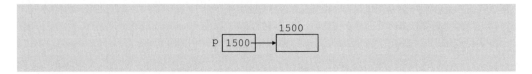

FIGURE 3-2   p after the execution of p = new int;

In Figure 3-2, the number 1500 on top of the box indicates the address of the memory space. The statement in Line 2 stores 54 into the memory space to which p points, which is 1500. In other words, after execution of the statement in Line 2, the value stored into memory space at location 1500 is 54. (See Figure 3-3.)

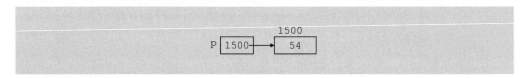

FIGURE 3-3   p and * p after the execution of * p = 54;

Next, the statement in Line 3 executes, which allocates a memory space of type **int** and stores the address of the allocated memory space into p. Suppose the address of this allocated memory space is 1800. It follows that the value of p is now 1800. (See Figure 3-4.)

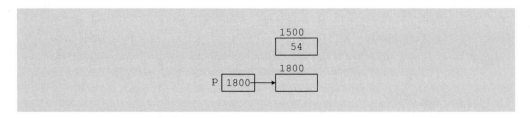

FIGURE 3-4   p after the execution of p = new int;

The statement in Line 4 stores 73 into the memory space to which p points, which is 1800. In other words, after execution of the statement in Line 4, the value stored into the memory space at location 1800 is 73. (See Figure 3-5.)

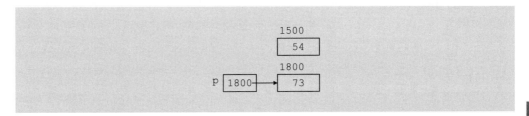

FIGURE 3-5 p after the execution of $*p = 73$;

Now the obvious question is, what happened to the memory space 1500, to which p was pointing, before the execution of the statement in Line 3? After execution of the statement in Line 3, p points to the new memory space at location 1800. The previous memory space at location 1500 is now inaccessible. In addition, the memory space 1500 remains marked as allocated. In other words, it cannot be reallocated. This is called **memory leak**. That is, there is an unused memory space that cannot be allocated.

Imagine what would happen if you execute statements such as Line 1 a few thousand times, or a few million times. There will be a good amount of memory leak. The program might then run out of memory space for data manipulation, and eventually result in an abnormal termination of the program.

The question at hand is how to *avoid* memory leak. When a dynamic variable is no longer needed, it can be destroyed; that is, its memory can be deallocated. The C++ operator delete is used to destroy dynamic variables, so that its memory space can be allocated again when needed. The syntax to use the operator delete has the following two forms:

```
delete pointerVariable; //to deallocate a single dynamic variable
delete [] pointerVariable; //to deallocate a dynamic array
```

Thus, given the declarations of the previous section, the statements

```
delete p;
delete str;
```

deallocate the memory spaces to which the pointers p and str point.

Suppose p is a pointer variable, as declared previously. Note that an expression such as

```
delete p;
```

only marks as deallocated the memory spaces to which these pointer variables point. Depending on a particular system, after these statements execute, these pointer variables might still contain the addresses of the deallocated memory spaces. In this case, we say that these pointers are **dangling**. Therefore, if you later access the memory spaces via these pointers without properly initializing them, depending on a particular system, either the program will access a wrong memory space, which might result in corrupting data, or the program will terminate with an error message. One way to avoid this pitfall is to set these pointers to NULL after the **delete** operation.

The program in the following example illustrates how to allocate dynamic memory and how to manipulate data into that dynamic memory.

EXAMPLE 3-3

```
//************************************************************
// Author: D.S. Malik
//
// This program illustrates how to allocate dynamic memory
// using a pointer variable and how to manipulate data into
// that memory location.
//************************************************************

#include <iostream>                                    //Line 1

using namespace std;                                   //Line 2

int main()                                             //Line 3
{                                                      //Line 4
    int *p;                                            //Line 5
    int *q;                                            //Line 6

    p = new int;                                       //Line 7
    *p = 34;                                           //Line 8
    cout << "Line 9: p = " << p
         << ", *p = " << *p << endl;                   //Line 9

    q = p;                                             //Line 10
    cout << "Line 11: q = " << q
         << ", *q = " << *q << endl;                   //Line 11

    *q = 45;                                           //Line 12
    cout << "Line 13: p = " << p
         << ", *p = " << *p << endl;                   //Line 13
    cout << "Line 14: q = " << q
         << ", *q = " << *q << endl;                   //Line 14

    p = new int;                                       //Line 15
    *p = 18;                                           //Line 16
    cout << "Line 17: p = " << p
         << ", *p = " << *p << endl;                   //Line 17
    cout << "Line 18: q = " << q
         << ", *q = " << *q << endl;                   //Line 18

    delete q;                                          //Line 19
    q = NULL;                                          //Line 20
    q = new int;                                       //Line 21
    *q = 62;                                           //Line 22
    cout << "Line 23: p = " << p
         << ", *p = " << *p << endl;                   //Line 23
    cout << "Line 24: q = " << q
         << ", *q = " << *q << endl;                   //Line 24

    return 0;                                          //Line 25
}                                                      //Line 26
```

Sample Run:

```
Line 9: p = 00355620, *p = 34
Line 11: q = 00355620, *q = 34
Line 13: p = 00355620, *p = 45
Line 14: q = 00355620, *q = 45
Line 17: p = 003556C8, *p = 18
Line 18: q = 00355620, *q = 45
Line 23: p = 003556C8, *p = 18
Line 24: q = 00355620, *q = 62
```

The statements in Lines 5 and 6 declare p and q to be pointer variables of type **int**. The statement in Line 7 allocates memory of type **int** and stores the address of the allocated memory into p. (See Figure 3-6.)

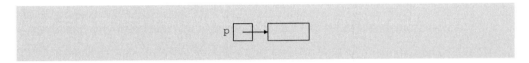

FIGURE 3-6   Pointer p and the memory space to which it points

The box indicates the allocated memory (in this case, of type **int**), and p together with the arrow indicates that p points to the allocated memory. The statement in Line 8 stores 34 into the memory location to which p points. (See Figure 3-7.)

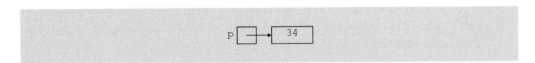

FIGURE 3-7   Pointer p and the value of the memory location to which p points

The statement in Line 9 outputs the value of p and *p. (Note that the values of p and q shown in the sample run are machine dependent. When you execute this program, you are likely to get different values of p and q.)

The statement in Line 10 copies the value of p into q. (See Figure 3-8.)

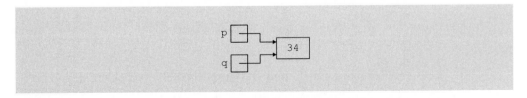

FIGURE 3-8   Pointers p and q and the memory space to which they point after the execution of the statement in Line 10

After the execution of the statement in Line 10, p and q both point to the same memory location. So any changes made into that memory location by q immediately change the value of *p. The statement in Line 11 outputs the value of q and *q. The statement in Line 12 stores 45 into the memory location to which q points. (See Figure 3-9.)

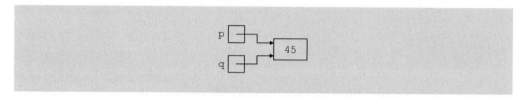

FIGURE 3-9 Pointers p and q and the memory space to which they point after the execution of the statement in Line 12

The statements in Lines 13 and 14 output the values of p, *p, q, and *q.

The statement in Line 15 allocates memory space of type **int** and stores the address of that memory into p. (See Figure 3-10.)

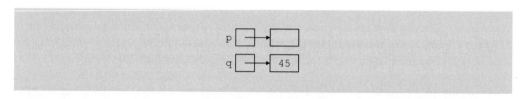

FIGURE 3-10 Pointers p and q and the memory space to which they point after the execution of the statement in Line 15

The statement in Line 16 stores 18 into the memory location to which p points. (See Figure 3-11.)

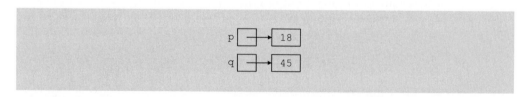

FIGURE 3-11 Pointers p and q and the memory space to which they point after the execution of the statement in Line 16

The statements in Lines 17 and 18 output the values of p, *p, q, and *q.

The statement in Line 19 deallocates the memory space to which q points and the statement in Line 20 sets the value of q to NULL. After the execution of the statement in Line 20, q does not point to any memory location. (See Figure 3-12.)

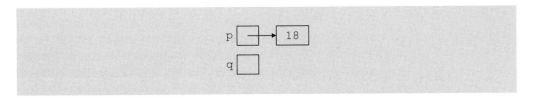

FIGURE 3-12 Pointers p and q and the memory space to which they point after the execution of the statement in Line 20

The statement in Line 21 allocates a memory space of type **int** and stores the address of that memory space into q. The statement in Line 22 stores 62 in the memory space to which q points. (See Figure 3-13.)

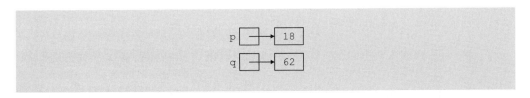

FIGURE 3-13 Pointers p and q and the memory space to which they point after the execution of the statement in Line 22

The statements in Lines 23 and 24 output the values of p, *p, q, and *q.

In the preceding program, omit statements in Lines 19 and 20, rerun the program, and note how the last output statements change.

Operations on Pointer Variables

The operations that are allowed on pointer variables are the assignment and relational operations and some limited arithmetic operations. The value of one pointer variable can be assigned to another pointer variable of the same type. Two pointer variables of the same type can be compared for equality, and so on. Integer values can be added and subtracted from a pointer variable. The value of one pointer variable can be subtracted from another pointer variable.

For example, suppose that we have the following statements:

```
int *p, *q;
```

The statement

```
p = q;
```

copies the value of q into p. After this statement executes, both p and q point to the same memory location. Any changes made to *p automatically change the value of *q, and vice versa.

The expression

```
p == q
```

evaluates to **true** if p and q have the same value—that is, if they point to the same memory location. Similarly, the expression

```
p != q
```

evaluates to true if p and q point to different memory locations.

The arithmetic operations that are allowed differ from the arithmetic operations on numbers. First, let us use the following statements to explain the increment and decrement operations on pointer variables:

```
int *p;
double *q;
char *chPtr;
```

Suppose that the size of the memory allocated for an int variable is 4 bytes, a double variable is 8 bytes, and a char variable is 1 byte.

The statement

```
p++;  or p = p + 1;
```

increments the value of p by 4 bytes because p is a pointer of type **int**. Similarly, the statements

```
q++;
chPtr++;
```

increment the value of q by 8 bytes and the value of chPtr by 1 byte, respectively.

The increment operator increments the value of a pointer variable by the size of the memory to which it is pointing. Similarly, the decrement operator decrements the value of a pointer variable by the size of the memory to which it is pointing.

Moreover, the statement

```
p = p + 2;
```

increments the value of p by 8 bytes.

Thus, when an integer is added to a pointer variable, the value of the pointer variable is incremented by the integer times the size of the memory to which the pointer is pointing. Similarly, when an integer is subtracted from a pointer variable, the value of the pointer variable is decremented by the integer times the size of the memory to which the pointer is pointing.

 NOTE Pointer arithmetic can be quite dangerous. Using pointer arithmetic, the program can accidentally access the memory locations of other variables and change their content without warning. The programmer is then left to try to find out what went wrong. If a pointer variable tries to access either the memory spaces of other variables or an illegal memory space, some systems might terminate the program with an appropriate error message. Always exercise extra care when doing pointer arithmetic.

Dynamic Arrays

The arrays used earlier are called static arrays because their size was fixed at compile time. One of the limitations of a static array is that every time you execute the program, the size of the array is fixed, so it might not be possible to use the same array to process different data sets of the same type. One way to handle this limitation is to declare an array that is large enough to process a variety of data sets. However, if the array is big and the data set is small, such a declaration would result in memory waste. On the other hand, it would be helpful if, during program execution, you could prompt the user to enter the size of the array and then create an array of the appropriate size. This approach is especially helpful if you cannot even guess the array size. In this section, you learn how to create arrays during program execution and how to process such arrays.

An array created during the execution of a program is called a **dynamic array**. To create a dynamic array, we use the second form of the **new** operator.

The statement

```
int *p;
```

declares p to be a pointer variable of type **int**. The statement

```
p = new int[10];
```

allocates 10 contiguous memory locations, each of type **int**, and stores the address of the first memory location into p. In other words, the operator **new** creates an array of 10 components of type **int**, it returns the base address of the array, and the assignment operator stores the base address of the array into p. Thus, the statement

```
*p = 25;
```

stores 25 into the first memory location, and the statements

```
p++;        //p points to the next array component
*p = 35;
```

store 35 into the second memory location. Thus, by using the increment and decrement operations, you can access the components of the array. Of course, after performing a few increment operations, it is possible to lose track of the first array component. C++ allows us to use array notation to access these memory locations. For example, the statements

```
p[0] = 25;
p[1] = 35;
```

store 25 and 35 into the first and second array components, respectively. That is, p[0] refers to the first array component, p[1] refers to the second array component, and so on. In general, p[i] refers to the (i + 1)th array component. After the preceding statements execute, p still points to the first array component.

The following **for** loop initializes each array component to 0:

```
for (int j = 0; j < 10; j++)
    p[j] = 0;
```

When the array notation is used to process the array to which p points, p stays fixed at the first memory location. Note that p is a dynamic array, created during program execution.

EXAMPLE 3-4

The following program segment illustrates how to obtain a user's response to get the array size and create a dynamic array during program execution. Consider the following statements:

```
int *intList;                       //Line 1
int arraySize;                      //Line 2

cout << "Enter array size: ";       //Line 3
cin >> arraySize;                   //Line 4
cout << endl;                       //Line 5

intList = new int[arraySize];       //Line 6
```

The statement in Line 1 declares intList to be a pointer of type int, and the statement in Line 2 declares arraySize to be an int variable. The statement in Line 3 prompts the user to enter the size of the array, and the statement in Line 4 inputs the array size into the variable arraySize. The statement in Line 6 creates an array of the size specified by arraySize, and the base address of the array is stored in intList. From this point on, you can treat intList just like any other array. For example, you can use the array notation to process the elements of intList and pass intList as a parameter to the function.

Array Name: A Constant Pointer

The statement

```
int list[5];
```

declares list to be an array of five components. Recall that list itself is a variable and the value stored in list is the base address of the array—that is, it is the address of the first array component. Suppose the address of the first array component is 1000. Figure 3-14 shows list and the array list.

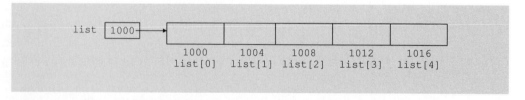

FIGURE 3-14 list and array list

Because the value of list, which is 1000, is a memory address, list is a pointer variable. However, the value stored in list, which is 1000, *cannot be altered during program execution.* That is, the value of list is *constant.* Therefore, the increment and decrement operations cannot be applied to list. In fact, any attempt to use the increment or decrement operations on list results in a compile-time error.

Notice that here we are *only* saying that the value of list cannot be changed. However, the data in the array list can be manipulated as usual. For example, the statement list[0] = 25; stores 25 into the first array component. Similarly, the statement list[2] = 78; stores 78 into the third component of list. (See Figure 3-15.)

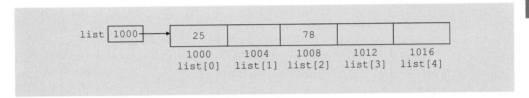

FIGURE 3-15   Array list after the execution of the statements list[0] = 25; and list[2] = 78;

If p is a pointer variable of type **int**, then the statement

```
p = list;
```

copies the value of list, which is 1000, the base address of the array, into p. We are allowed to perform increment and decrement operations on p.

An *array name* is a *constant pointer.*

Functions and Pointers

A pointer variable can be passed as a parameter to a function either by value or by reference. To declare a pointer as a value parameter in a function heading, you use the same mechanism as you use to declare a variable. To make a formal parameter be a reference parameter, you use & when you declare the formal parameter in the function heading. Therefore, to declare a formal parameter as a reference parameter, you must use &. Between the data type name and the identifier name, you must include * to make the identifier a pointer and & to make it a reference parameter. The obvious question is: In what order should & and * appear between the data type name and the identifier to declare a pointer as a reference parameter? In C++, to make a pointer a reference parameter in a function heading, * appears before the & between the data type name and the identifier. The following example illustrates this concept:

```
void example(int* &p, double *q)
{
    .
    .
    .
}
```

In this example, both p and q are pointers. The parameter p is a reference parameter; the parameter q is a value parameter.

Pointers and Function Return Values

In C++, the return type of a function can be a pointer. For example, the return type of the function

```
int* testExp(...)
{
    .
    .
    .
}
```

is a pointer of type int.

Dynamic Two-Dimensional Arrays

The beginning of this section discussed how to create dynamic one-dimensional arrays. You can also create dynamic multidimensional arrays. In this section, we discuss how to create dynamic two-dimensional arrays. Dynamic multidimensional arrays are created similarly.

There are various ways you can create dynamic two-dimensional arrays. One way is as follows. Consider the statement:

```
int *board[4];
```

This statement declares board to be an array of four pointers wherein each pointer is of type **int**. Because board[0], board[1], board[2], and board[3] are pointers, you can now use these pointers to create the rows of board. Suppose that each row of board has six columns. Then the following for loop creates the rows of board.

```
for (int row = 0; row < 4; row++)
    board[row] = new int[6];
```

Note that the expression new int[6] creates an array of six components of type int and returns the base address of the array. The assignment statement then stores the returned address into board[row]. It follows that after the execution of the previous for loop, board is a two-dimensional array of 4 rows and 6 columns.

In the previous for loop, if you replace the number 6 with the number 10, the loop will create a two-dimensional array of 4 rows and 10 columns. In other words, the number of columns of board can be specified during execution. However, the way board is declared, the number of rows is fixed. So in reality, board is not a true dynamic two-dimensional array.

Next, consider the following statement:

```
int **board;
```

This statement declares board to be a pointer to a pointer. In other words, board and *board are pointers. Now board can store the address of a pointer or an array of pointers of type int, and *board can store the address of an int memory space or an array of int values.

Suppose that you want `board` to be an array of 10 rows and 15 columns. To accomplish this, first we create an array of 10 pointers of type `int` and assign the address of that array to `board`. The following statement accomplishes this:

```
board = new int* [10];
```

Next we create the columns of `board`. The following `for` loop accomplishes this:

```
for (int row = 0; row < 10; row++)
    board[row] = new int[15];
```

To access the components of `board`, you can use the array subscripting notation. For example, see the next example. Note that the number of rows and the number of columns of `board` can be specified during program execution. The program in Example 3-5 further explains how to create two-dimensional arrays.

EXAMPLE 3-5

```cpp
//**********************************************************
// Author: D.S. Malik
//
// This program illustrates how to use two-dimensional dynamic
// arrays.
//**********************************************************

#include <iostream>                                      //Line 1
#include <iomanip>                                       //Line 2

using namespace std;                                     //Line 3

void fill(int **p, int rowSize, int columnSize);         //Line 4
void print(int **p, int rowSize, int columnSize);        //Line 5

int main()                                               //Line 6
{                                                        //Line 7
    int **board;                                         //Line 8

    int rows;                                            //Line 9
    int columns;                                         //Line 10

    cout << "Line 11: Enter the number of rows "
         <<"and columns: ";                              //Line 11
    cin >> rows >> columns;                              //Line 12
    cout << endl;                                        //Line 13

        //Create the rows of board
    board = new int* [rows];                             //Line 14

        //Create the columns of board
    for (int row = 0; row < rows; row++)                 //Line 15
        board[row] = new int[columns];                   //Line 16
```

```
        //Insert elements into board
    fill(board, rows, columns);                         //Line 17

    cout << "Line 18: Board:" << endl;                  //Line 18

        //Output the elements of board
    print(board, rows, columns);                        //Line 19

    return 0;                                           //Line 20
}                                                       //Line 21

void fill(int **p, int rowSize, int columnSize)
{
    for (int row = 0; row < rowSize; row++)
    {
        cout << "Enter " << columnSize << " number(s) for row "
             << "number " << row << ": ";
        for (int col = 0; col < columnSize; col++)
            cin >> p[row][col];
        cout << endl;
    }
}

void print(int **p, int rowSize, int columnSize)
{
    for (int row = 0; row < rowSize; row++)
    {
        for (int col = 0; col < columnSize; col++)
            cout << setw(5) << p[row][col];
        cout << endl;
    }
}
```

Sample Run: In this sample run, the user input is shaded.

```
Line 11: Enter the number of rows and columns: 3 4

Enter 4 number(s) for row number 0: 1 2 3 4

Enter 4 number(s) for row number 1: 5 6 7 8

Enter 4 number(s) for row number 2: 9 10 11 12

Line 18: Board:
    1     2     3     4
    5     6     7     8
    9    10    11    12
```

The preceding program contains the functions fill and print. The function fill prompts the user to enter the elements of a two-dimensional array of type int. The function print outputs the elements of a two-dimensional array of type int.

For the most part, the preceding output is self-explanatory. Let us look at the statements in the function `main`. The statement in Line 8 declares `board` to be a pointer to a pointer of type `int`. The statements in Lines 9 and 10 declare `int` variables `rows` and `columns`. The statement in Line 11 prompts the user to input the number of rows and number of columns. The statement in Line 12 stores the number of rows in the variable `rows` and the number of columns in the variable `columns`. The statement in Line 14 creates the rows of `board` and the `for` loop in Lines 15 and 16 creates the columns of `board`. The statement in Line 17 used the function `fill` to fill the array `board` and the statement in Line 19 uses the function `print` to output the elements of `board`.

Shallow Vs. Deep Copy and Pointers

In an earlier section, we discussed pointer arithmetic and explained that if we are not careful, one pointer might access the data of another (completely unrelated) pointer. This event might result in unsuspected or erroneous results. Here, we discuss another peculiarity of pointers. To facilitate the discussion, we will use diagrams to show pointers and their related memory.

Suppose that you have the following declarations:

```
int *first;
int *second;
```

Further suppose that `first` points to an **int** array, as shown in Figure 3-16.

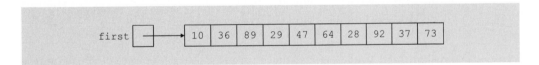

FIGURE 3-16 Pointer `first` and its array

Next, consider the following statement:

```
second = first;          //Line A
```

This statement copies the value of `first` into `second`. After this statement executes, both `first` and `second` point to the same array, as shown in Figure 3-17.

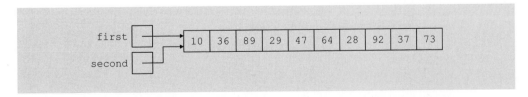

FIGURE 3-17 `first` and `second` after the statement `second = first;` executes

The statement first[4] = 10; not only changes the value of first[4], it also changes the value of second[4] because they point to the same array.

Let us execute the following statement:

delete [] second;

After this statement executes, the array to which second points is deleted. This action results in Figure 3-18.

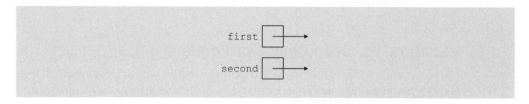

FIGURE 3-18 first and second after the statement delete [] second; executes

Because first and second pointed to the same array, after the statement

delete [] second;

executes, first becomes invalid, that is, first (as well as second) are now dangling pointers. Therefore, if the program later tries to access the memory to which first pointed, either the program will access the wrong memory or it will terminate in an error. This case is an example of a shallow copy. More formally, in a **shallow copy**, two or more pointers of the same type point to the same memory; that is, they point to the same data.

On the other hand, suppose that instead of the earlier statement, second = first; (in Line A), we have the following statements:

second = new int[10];

for (int j = 0; j < 10; j++)
    second[j] = first[j];

The first statement creates an array of 10 components of type **int**, and the base address of the array is stored in second. The second statement copies the array to which first points into the array to which second points. (See Figure 3-19.)

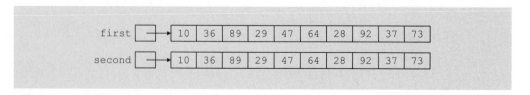

FIGURE 3-19 first and second both pointing to their own data

Both first and second now point to their own data. If second deletes its memory, there is no effect on first. This case is an example of a deep copy. More formally, in a **deep copy**, two or more pointers have their own data.

From the preceding discussion, it follows that you must know when to use a shallow copy and when to use a deep copy.

Classes and Pointers: Some Peculiarities

Because a class can have pointer member variables, this section discusses some peculiarities of such classes. To facilitate the discussion, we use the following class:

```
class pointerDataClass
{
public:
    .
    .
    .

private:
    int x;
    int lenP;
    int *p;
};
```

Also consider the following statements. (See Figure 3-20.)

```
pointerDataClass objectOne;
pointerDataClass objectTwo;
```

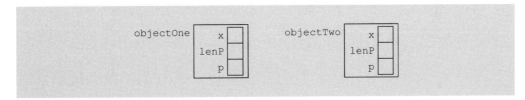

FIGURE 3-20   Objects objectOne and objectTwo

Destructor

The object objectOne has a pointer member variable p. Suppose that during program execution the pointer p creates a dynamic array. When objectOne goes out of scope, all the member variables of objectOne are destroyed. However, p created a dynamic array, and dynamic memory must be deallocated using the operator delete. Thus, if the pointer p does not use the delete operator to deallocate the dynamic array, the memory space of the dynamic array would stay marked as allocated, even though it cannot be accessed. How do we ensure that when p is destroyed, the dynamic memory created by p is also destroyed? Suppose that objectOne is as shown in Figure 3-21.

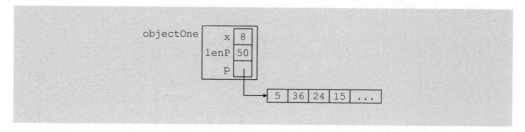

FIGURE 3-21 Object objectOne and its data

Recall that if a class has a destructor, the destructor automatically executes whenever a class object goes out of scope (see Chapter 1). Therefore, we can put the necessary code in the destructor to ensure that when objectOne goes out of scope, the memory created by the pointer p is deallocated. For example, the definition of the destructor for the class pointerDataClass is as follows:

```
pointerDataClass::~pointerDataClass()
{
    delete [] p;
}
```

Of course, you must include the destructor as a member of the class in its definition. Let us extend the definition of the class pointerDataClass by including the destructor. Moreover, the remainder of this section assumes that the definition of the destructor is as given previously—that is, the destructor deallocates the memory space pointed to by p.

```
class pointerDataClass
{
public:
    ~pointerDataClass();
        .
        .
        .

private:
    int x;
    int lenP;
    int *p;
};
```

NOTE   For the destructor to work properly, the pointer p must have a valid value. If p is not properly initialized (that is, if the value of p is garbage) and the destructor executes, either the program terminates with an error message or the destructor deallocates an unrelated memory space. For this reason, you should exercise extra caution while working with pointers.

Assignment Operator

This section describes the limitations of the built-in assignment operators for classes with pointer member variables. Suppose that `objectOne` and `objectTwo` are as shown in Figure 3-22.

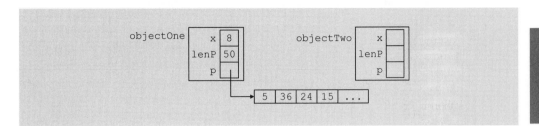

FIGURE 3-22 Objects `objectOne` and `objectTwo`

Recall that one of the built-in operations on classes is the assignment operator. For example, the statement:

```
objectTwo = objectOne;
```

copies the member variables of `objectOne` into `objectTwo`. That is, the value of `objectOne.x` is copied into `objectTwo.x`, and the value of `objectOne.p` is copied into `objectTwo.p`. Because `p` is a pointer, this memberwise copying of the data would lead to a shallow copying of the data. That is, both `objectTwo.p` and `objectOne.p` would point to the same memory space, as shown in Figure 3-23.

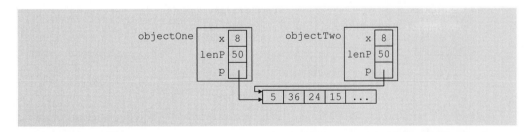

FIGURE 3-23 Objects `objectOne` and `objectTwo` after the statement `objectTwo = objectOne;` executes

Now, if `objectTwo.p` deallocates the memory space to which it points, `objectOne.p` would become invalid. This situation could very well happen, if the `class pointerDataClass` has a destructor that deallocates the memory space pointed to by `p` when an object of type `pointerDataClass` goes out of scope. It suggests that there must be a way to avoid this pitfall. To avoid this shallow copying of data for classes with a pointer member variable, C++ allows the programmer to extend the definition of the assignment operator. This process is called overloading the assignment operator. In the next section, we explain how to accomplish this task by using operator overloading. Once the assignment operator is properly overloaded, both `objectOne` and `objectTwo` have their own data, as shown in Figure 3-24.

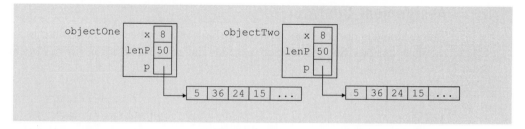

FIGURE 3-24 Objects objectOne and objectTwo

OVERLOADING THE ASSIGNMENT OPERATOR

Next we describe how to overload the assignment operator.

General Syntax to Overload the Assignment Operator = for a Class
Function Prototype (to be included in the definition of the class):

```
const className& operator=(const className&);
```

Function Definition:

```
const className& className::operator=(const className& rightObject)
{
        //local declaration, if any

        if (this != &rightObject)  //avoids self-assignment
        {
            //algorithm to copy rightObject into this object
        }

        //returns the object assigned
        return *this;
}
```

In the definition of the function operator=:

- There is only one formal parameter.
- The formal parameter is generally a const reference to a particular class.
- The return type of the function is a reference to a particular class.

Consider the statement

```
x = x;
```

Here, we are trying to copy the value of x into x; that is, this statement is a self-assignment. We must prevent such statements because they waste computer time.

The body of the function operator= does prevent such assignments. Let us see how.

Consider the if statement in the body of the operator function operator=:

```
if (this != &rightObject)  //avoids self-assignment
{
    //algorithm to copy rightObject into this object
}
```

Now the statement

```
x = x;
```

is compiled into the statement

```
x.operator=(x);
```

Because the function `operator=` is invoked by the object `x`, the pointer `this` in the body of the function `operator=` refers to the object `x`. Furthermore, because `x` is also a parameter to the function `operator=`, the formal parameter `rightObject` also refers to the object `x`. Therefore, in the expression

```
this != &rightObject
```

`this` means the address of `x`, and `&rightObject` also means the address of `x`. Thus, this expression will evaluate to `false` and, therefore, the body of the `if` statement will be skipped.

Notice that the return type of the function to overload the assignment operator is a reference. This is so that the statements such as `x = y = z;` can be executed, that is, the assignment operator can be used in a cascaded form.

In the section "Array-Based Lists," later in this chapter, we explicitly illustrate how to overload the assignment operator.

Copy Constructor

When declaring a class object, you can initialize it by using the value of an existing object of the same type. For example, consider the following statement:

```
pointerDataClass objectThree(objectOne);
```

The object `objectThree` is being declared and is also being initialized by using the value of `objectOne`. That is, the values of the member variables of `objectOne` are copied into the corresponding member variables of `objectThree`. This initialization is called the default memberwise initialization. The default memberwise initialization is due to the constructor, called the **copy constructor** (provided by the compiler). Just as in the case of the assignment operator, because the `class pointerDataClass` has pointer member variables, this default initialization would lead to a shallow copying of the data, as shown in Figure 3-25. (Assume that `objectOne` is given as before.)

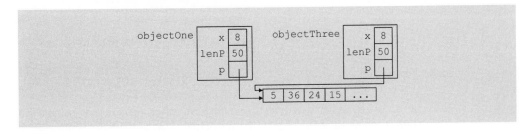

FIGURE 3-25 Objects `objectOne` and `objectThree`

Before describing how to overcome this deficiency, let us describe one more situation that could also lead to a shallow copying of the data. The solution to both these problems is the same.

Recall that, as parameters to a function, class objects can be passed either by reference or by value. Remember that the `class pointerDataClass` has the destructor, which deallocates the memory space pointed to by p. Suppose that `objectOne` is as shown in Figure 3-26.

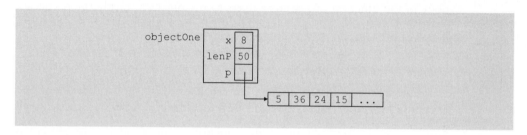

FIGURE 3-26 Object `objectOne`

Let us consider the following function prototype:

```
void destroyList(pointerDataClass paramObject);
```

The function `pointerDataClass` has a formal value parameter, `paramObject`. Now consider the following statement:

```
destroyList(objectOne);
```

In this statement, `objectOne` is passed as a parameter to the function `destroyList`. Because `paramObject` is a value parameter, the copy constructor copies the member variables of `objectOne` into the corresponding member variables of `paramObject`. Just as in the previous case, `paramObject.p` and `objectOne.p` would point to the same memory space, as shown in Figure 3-27.

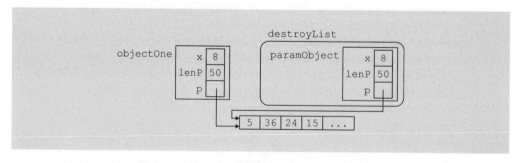

FIGURE 3-27 Pointer member variables of objects `objectOne` and `paramObject` pointing to the same array

Because `objectOne` is passed by value, the member variables of `paramObject` should have their own copy of the data. In particular, `paramObject.p` should have its own memory space. How do we ensure that this is, in fact, the case?

If a class has pointer member variables:

- During object declaration, the initialization of one object using the value of another object leads to a shallow copying of the data, if the default memberwise copying of data is allowed.

- If, as a parameter, an object is passed by value and the default memberwise copying of data is allowed, it leads to a shallow copying of the data.

In both cases, to force each object to have its own copy of the data, we must override the definition of the copy constructor provided by the compiler; that is, we must provide our own definition of the copy constructor. This is usually done by putting a statement that includes the copy constructor in the definition of the class, and then writing the definition of the copy constructor. Then, whenever the copy constructor needs to be executed, the system would execute the definition provided by us, not the one provided by the compiler. Therefore, for the **class pointerDataClass**, we can overcome this shallow copying problem by including the copy constructor in the **class pointerDataClass**.

The copy constructor automatically executes in three situations (the first two are described previously):

- When an object is declared and initialized by using the value of another object
- When, as a parameter, an object is passed by value
- When the return value of a function is an object

Therefore, once the copy constructor is properly defined for the **class pointerDataClass**, both **objectOne.p** and **objectThree.p** will have their own copies of the data. Similarly, **objectOne.p** and **paramObject.p** will have their own copies of the data, as shown in Figure 3-28.

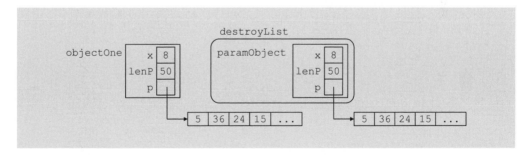

FIGURE 3-28 Pointer member variables of objects `objectOne` and `paramObject` with their own data

When the function **destroyList** exits, the formal parameter **paramObject** goes out of scope, and the destructor for the object **paramObject** deallocates the memory space pointed to by **paramObject.p**. However, this deallocation has no effect on **objectOne**.

The general syntax to include the copy constructor in the definition of a class is as follows:

```
className(const className& otherObject);
```

Notice that the formal parameter of the copy constructor is a constant reference parameter.

In the section, "Array-Based Lists," we explicitly illustrate how to include the copy constructor in a class and how it works.

For classes with pointer member variables, three things are normally done:

1. Include the destructor in the class.
2. Overload the assignment operator for the class.
3. Include the copy constructor.

Inheritance, Pointers, and Virtual Functions

Recall that, as a parameter, a class object can be passed either by value or by reference. Earlier chapters also said that the types of the actual and formal parameters must match. However, in the case of classes, C++ *allows the user to pass an object of a derived class to a formal parameter of the base class type.*

First, let us discuss the case when the formal parameter is either a reference parameter or a pointer. To be specific, let us consider the following classes:

```
class baseClass
{
public:
    void print();
    baseClass(int u = 0);

private:
    int x;
};

class derivedClass: public baseClass
{
public:
    void print();
    derivedClass(int u = 0, int v = 0);

private:
    int a;
};
```

The class baseClass has three members. The class derivedClass is derived from the class baseClass, and has three members of its own. Both classes have a member function print. Suppose that the definitions of the member functions of both classes are as follows:

```cpp
void baseClass::print()
{
    cout << "In baseClass x = " << x << endl;
}

baseClass::baseClass(int u)
{
    x = u;
}

void derivedClass::print()
{
    cout << "In derivedClass ***: ";
    baseClass::print();
    cout << "In derivedClass a = " << a << endl;
}

derivedClass::derivedClass(int u, int v)
                : baseClass(u)
{
    a = v;
}
```

Consider the following function in a user program (client code):

```cpp
void callPrint(baseClass& p)
{
    p.print();
}
```

The function `callPrint` has a formal reference parameter p of type `baseClass`. You can call the function `callPrint` by using an object of either type `baseClass` or type `derivedClass` as a parameter. Moreover, the body of the function `callPrint` calls the member function `print`. Consider the following function `main`:

```cpp
int main()                                //Line 1
{                                         //Line 2
    baseClass one(5);                     //Line 3
    derivedClass two(3, 15);              //Line 4

    one.print();                          //Line 5
    two.print();                          //Line 6

    cout << "*** Calling the function "
         << "callPrint  ***" << endl;     //Line 7

    callPrint(one);                       //Line 8
    callPrint(two);                       //Line 9

    return 0;                             //Line 10
}                                         //Line 11
```

Sample Run:

```
In baseClass x = 5
In derivedClass ***: In baseClass x = 3
In derivedClass a = 15
*** Calling the function callPrint   ***
In baseClass x = 5
In baseClass x = 3
```

The statements in Lines 3 through 7 are quite straightforward. Let us look at the statements in Lines 8 and 9. The statement in Line 8 calls the function `callPrint` and passes the object one as the parameter; it generates the fifth line of the output. The statement in Line 9 also calls the function `callPrint`, but passes the object two as the parameter; it generates the sixth line of the output. The output generated by the statements in Lines 8 and 9 shows only the value of **x**, even though in these statements a different class object is passed as a parameter. (Because in Line 9 object two is passed as a parameter to the function `callPrint`, one would expect that the output generated by the statement in Line 9 should be similar to the output in the second and third lines of the output.) What actually occurred is that for both statements (Lines 8 and 9), the member function `print` of the class `baseClass` is executed. This is due to the fact that the binding of the member function `print`, in the body of the function `callPrint`, occurred at compile time. Because the formal parameter p of the function `callPrint` is of type `baseClass`, for the statement `p.print();`, the compiler associates the function `print` of the class `baseClass`. More specifically, in **compile-time binding**, the necessary code to call a specific function is generated by the compiler. (Compile-time binding is also known as **static binding**.)

For the statement in Line 9, the actual parameter is of type `derivedClass`. Thus, when the body of the function `callPrint` executes, logically the `print` function of object two should execute, which is not the case. So, during program execution, how does C++ correct this problem of making the call to the appropriate function? C++ corrects this problem by providing the mechanism of **virtual functions**. The binding of virtual functions occurs at program execution time, not at compile time. This kind of binding is called **run-time binding**. More formally, in run–time binding, the compiler does not generate the code to call a specific function. Instead, it generates enough information to enable the run-time system to generate the specific code for the appropriate function call. Run-time binding is also known as **dynamic binding**.

In C++, virtual functions are declared using the reserved word `virtual`. Let us redefine the previous classes using this feature:

```
class baseClass
{
public:
    virtual void print();        //virtual function
    baseClass(int u = 0);

private:
    int x;
};
```

```
class derivedClass: public baseClass
{
public:
    void print();
    derivedClass(int u = 0, int v = 0);

private:
    int a;
};
```

3

Note that we need to declare a virtual function only in the base class.

The definition of the member function print is the same as before. If we execute the previous program with these modifications, the output is as follows.

Sample Run:

```
In baseClass x = 5
In derivedClass ***: In baseClass x = 3
In derivedClass a = 15
*** Calling the function callPrint  ***
In baseClass x = 5
In derivedClass ***: In baseClass x = 3
In derivedClass a = 15
```

This output shows that for the statement in Line 9, the print function of derivedClass is executed (see the last two lines of the output).

The previous discussion also applies when a formal parameter is a pointer to a class, and a pointer of the derived class is passed as an actual parameter. To illustrate this feature, suppose we have the preceding classes. (We assume that the definition of the class baseClass is in the header file baseClass.h, and the definition of the class derivedClass is in the header file derivedClass.h.) Consider the following program:

```
//****************************************************
// Author: D.S. Malik
//
// This program illustrates how virtual functions and
// pointer formal parameters work.
//****************************************************

#include <iostream>                              //Line 1

#include "derivedClass.h"                        //Line 2

using namespace std;                             //Line 3

void callPrint(baseClass *p);                    //Line 4

int main()                                       //Line 5
{                                                //Line 6
    baseClass *q;                                //Line 7
    derivedClass *r;                             //Line 8
```

```
    q = new baseClass(5);              //Line 9
    r = new derivedClass(3, 15);       //Line 10

    q->print();                        //Line 11
    r->print();                        //Line 12

    cout << "*** Calling the function "
         << "callPrint  ***" << endl;  //Line 13

    callPrint(q);                      //Line 14
    callPrint(r);                      //Line 15

    return 0;                          //Line 16
}                                      //Line 17

void callPrint(baseClass *p)
{
    p->print();
}
```

Sample Run:

```
In baseClass x = 5
In derivedClass ***: In baseClass x = 3
In derivedClass a = 15
*** Calling the function callPrint  ***
In baseClass x = 5
In derivedClass ***: In baseClass x = 3
In derivedClass a = 15
```

The preceding examples show that if a formal parameter, say p of a class type, is either a reference parameter or a pointer and p uses a virtual function of the base class, we can effectively pass a derived class object as an actual parameter to p.

However, if p is a *value parameter*, then this mechanism of passing a derived class object as an actual parameter to p does not work, even if p uses a virtual function. Recall that, if a formal parameter is a value parameter, the value of the actual parameter is copied into the formal parameter. Therefore, if a formal parameter is of a `class` type, the member variables of the actual object are copied into the corresponding member variables of the formal parameter.

Suppose that we have the classes defined above—that is, `baseClass` and `derivedClass`. Consider the following function definition:

```
void callPrint(baseClass p)   //p is a value parameter
{
    p.print();
}
```

Further suppose that we have the following declaration:

```
derivedClass two;
```

The object two has two member variables, x and a. The member variable x is inherited from the base class. Consider the following function call:

```
callPrint(two);
```

In this statement, because the formal parameter p is a value parameter, the member variables of two are copied into the member variables of p. However, because p is an object of type baseClass, it has only one member variable. Consequently, only the member variable x of two will be copied into the member variable x of p. Also, the statement:

```
p.print();
```

in the body of the function will result in executing the member function print of the class baseClass.

The output of the following program further illustrates this concept. (As before, we assume that the definition of the class baseClass is in the header file baseClass.h, and the definition of the class derivedClass is in the header file derivedClass.h.)

```
//**********************************************************
// Author: D.S. Malik
//
// This program illustrates how virtual functions and a
// pointer variable of base class as a formal parameter
// work.
//**********************************************************

#include <iostream>                        //Line 1

#include "derivedClass.h"                  //Line 2

using namespace std;                       //Line 3

void callPrint(baseClass p);               //Line 4

int main()                                 //Line 5
{                                          //Line 6
    baseClass one(5);                      //Line 7
    derivedClass two(3, 15);               //Line 8

    one.print();                           //Line 9
    two.print();                           //Line 10

    cout << "*** Calling the function "
         << "callPrint  ***" << endl;      //Line 11

    callPrint(one);                        //Line 12
    callPrint(two);                        //Line 13

    return 0;                              //Line 14
}                                          //Line 15
```

```
void callPrint(baseClass p)   //p is a value parameter
{
    p.print();
}
```

Sample Run:

```
In baseClass x = 5
In derivedClass ***: In baseClass x = 3
In derivedClass a = 15
*** Calling the function callPrint  ***
In baseClass x = 5
In baseClass x = 3
```

Look closely at the output of the statements in Lines 12 and 13 (the last two lines of output). In Line 13, because the formal parameter p is a value parameter, the member variables of two are copied into the corresponding member variables of p. However, because p is an object of type baseClass, it has only one member variable. Consequently, only the member variable x of two is copied into the member variable x of p. Moreover, the statement p.print(); in the function callPrint executes the function print of the class baseClass, not the class derivedClass. Therefore, the last line of the output shows only the value of x (the member variable of two).

> **NOTE** An object of the base class type cannot be passed to a formal parameter of the derived class type.

Classes and Virtual Destructors

One thing recommended for classes with pointer member variables is that these classes should have the destructor. The destructor is automatically executed when the class object goes out of scope. Thus, if the object creates dynamic objects, the destructor can be designed to deallocate the storage for them. If a derived class object is passed to a formal parameter of the base class type, the destructor of the base class executes regardless of whether the derived class object is passed by reference or by value. Logically, however, the destructor of the derived class should be executed when the derived class object goes out of scope.

To correct this problem, the destructor of the base class must be virtual. The **virtual destructor** of a base class automatically makes the destructor of a derived class virtual. When a derived class object is passed to a formal parameter of the base class type, then when the object goes out of scope, the destructor of the derived class executes. After executing the destructor of the derived class, the destructor of the base class executes. Therefore, when the derived class object is destroyed, the base class part (that is, the members inherited from the base class) of the derived class object is also destroyed.

If a base class contains virtual functions, make the destructor of the base class virtual.

Abstract Classes and Pure Virtual Functions

The preceding section discussed virtual functions. Other than enforcing run-time binding of functions, virtual functions also have another use, which is discussed in this section. Chapter 2 described the second principal of OOD—inheritance. Through inheritance we can derive new classes without designing them from scratch. The derived classes, in addition to inheriting the existing members of the base class, can add their own members and also redefine or override public and protected member functions of the base class. The base class can contain functions that you would want each derived class to implement. There are many scenarios when a class is desired to be served as a base class for a number of derived classes, however, the base class may contain certain functions that may not have meaningful definitions in the base class.

Let us consider the `class shape` given in Chapter 2. As noted in that chapter, from the `class shape` you can derive other `classes` such as `rectangle`, `circle`, `ellipse`, and so on. Some of the things common to every shape are its center, using the center to move a shape to a different location, and drawing the shape. Among others, we can include these in the `class shape`. For example, you could have the definition of the `class shape` similar to the following:

```
class shape
{
public:
    virtual void draw();
      //Function to draw the shape.

    virtual void move(double x, double y);
      //Function to move the shape at the position (x, y).
      .
      .
      .

};
```

Because the definitions of the functions `draw` and `move` are specific to a particular shape, each derived class can provide an appropriate definition of these functions. Note that we have made the functions `draw` and `move` **virtual** to enforce run-time binding of these functions.

The way the definition of the `class shape` is written when you write the definition of the functions of the `class shape`, you must also write the definitions of the functions `draw` and `move`. However, at this point there is no shape to draw or move. Therefore, these function bodies have no code. One way to handle this is to make the body of these functions empty. This solution would work, but it has another drawback. Once we write the definitions of the functions of the `class shape`, then we could create an object of this class. Because there is no shape to work with, we would like to prevent the user from creating objects of the `class shape`. It follows that we would like to do the following two things—to not include the definitions of the functions `draw` and `move`, and to prevent the user from creating objects of the `class shape`.

Because we do not want to include the definitions of the functions `draw` and `move` of the class shape, we must convert these functions to **pure virtual functions**. In this case, the prototypes of these functions are:

```
virtual void draw() = 0;
virtual void move(double x, double y) = 0;
```

Note the expression = 0 before the semicolon. Once you make these functions pure virtual functions in the `class shape`, you no longer need to provide the definitions of these functions for the `class shape`.

Once a class contains one or more pure virtual functions, then that class is called an **abstract class**. Thus, the abstract definition of the `class shape` is similar to the following:

```
class shape
{
public:
    virtual void draw() = 0;
        //Function to draw the shape. Note that this is a
        //pure virtual function.

    virtual void move(double x, double y) = 0;
        //Function to move the shape at the position (x, y).
        //Note that this is a pure virtual function.
        .
        .
        .
};
```

Because an abstract class is not a complete class, as it (or its implementation file) does not contain the definitions of certain functions, you cannot create objects of that class.

Now suppose that we derive the `class rectangle` from the `class shape`. To make `rectangle` a nonabstract class, so that we can create objects of this class, the class (or its implementation file) must provide the definitions of the pure `virtual` functions of its base class, which is the `class shape`.

Note that in addition to the pure virtual functions, an abstract class can contain instance variables, constructors, and functions that are not pure virtual. However, the abstract class must provide the definitions of constructor and functions that are not pure virtual.

Array-Based Lists

Everyone is familiar with the term *list*. You might have a list consisting of employee data, student data, sales data, or a list of rental properties. One thing common to all lists is that all the elements of a list are of the same type. More formally, we can define a list as follows:

List: A collection of elements of the same type.

The **length** of a list is the number of elements in the list.

Following are some of the operations performed on a list:

1. Create the list. The list is initialized to an empty state.
2. Determine whether the list is empty.
3. Determine whether the list is full.
4. Find the size of the list.
5. Destroy, or clear, the list.
6. Determine whether an item is the same as a given list element.
7. Insert an item in the list at the specified location.
8. Remove an item from the list at the specified location.
9. Replace an item at the specified location with another item.
10. Retrieve an item from the list from the specified location.
11. Search the list for a given item.

Before discussing how to implement these operations, we must first decide how to store the list in the computer's memory. Because all the elements of a list are of the same type, an effective and convenient way to process a list is to store it in an array. Initially, the size of the array holding the list elements is usually larger than the number of elements in the list so that, at a later stage, the list can grow. Thus, we must know how full the array is; that is, we must keep track of the number of list elements stored in the array. C++ allows the programmer to create dynamic arrays. Therefore, we leave it for the user to specify the size of the array. The size of the array can be specified when a list object is declared. It follows that, to maintain and process the list in an array, we need the following three variables:

- The array holding the list elements
- A variable to store the length of the list (that is, the number of list elements currently in the array)
- A variable to store the size of the array (that is, the maximum number of elements that can be stored in the array)

Suppose that the variable `length` indicates the number of elements in the list and that `maxSize` indicates the maximum number of elements that can be stored in the list. Then `length` and `maxSize` are nonnegative integers and, therefore, we can declare them to be of type `int`. What about the type of the array, that is, the data type of the array elements? If we have a list of numbers, the array elements could be of type `int` or `double`. If we have a list of names, the array elements are of type `string`. Similarly, if we have a list of students, the array elements are of type `studentType` (a data type you can define). As you can see, there are various types of lists.

A list of sales data or a list of students' data is empty if its length is zero. To insert an item at the end of a list of any type would require you to add the element after the current last element and then increment the length by one. Similarly, it can be seen that, for the most part, the algorithms to implement operations on a list of names, on a list of sales data, or on a list of students' data are the same. We do not want to spend time and efforts to develop separate code for each type of list we encounter. Instead, we want to develop a generic code that can be used to implement any type of list in a program. In other words, while designing the algorithms, we do not want to be concerned whether we are processing a list of numbers, a list of names, or a list of students' data. However, while illustrating a particular algorithm, we will consider a specific type of list. To develop generic algorithms to implement list operations, we make use of class templates.

Now that we know the operations to be performed on a list and how to store the list into the computer's memory, next we define the class implementing the list as an abstract data type (ADT). The following class, `arrayListType`, defines the list as an ADT:

```
//**********************************************************
// Author: D.S. Malik
//
// This class specifies the members to implement the basic
// properties of array-based lists.
//**********************************************************

template <class elemType>
class arrayListType
{
public:
    const arrayListType<elemType>& operator=
                        (const arrayListType<elemType>&);
    //Overloads the assignment operator
    bool isEmpty() const;
    //Function to determine whether the list is empty
    //Postcondition: Returns true if the list is empty;
    //    otherwise, returns false.
    bool isFull() const;
    //Function to determine whether the list is full.
    //Postcondition: Returns true if the list is full;
    //    otherwise, returns false.
    int listSize() const;
    //Function to determine the number of elements in the list
    //Postcondition: Returns the value of length.
    int maxListSize() const;
    //Function to determine the size of the list.
    //Postcondition: Returns the value of maxSize.
    void print() const;
    //Function to output the elements of the list
    //Postcondition: Elements of the list are output on the
    //    standard output device.
    bool isItemAtEqual(int location, const elemType& item) const;
    //Function to determine whether the item is the same
    //as the item in the list at the position specified by
    //Postcondition: Returns true if list[location]
    //    is the same as the item; otherwise,
    //    returns false.
    void insertAt(int location, const elemType& insertItem);
    //Function to insert an item in the list at the
    //position specified by location. The item to be inserted
    //is passed as a parameter to the function.
```

```
    //Postcondition: Starting at location, the elements of the
    //     list are shifted down, list[location] = insertItem;,
    //     and length++;. If the list is full or location is
    //     out of range, an appropriate message is displayed.
void insertEnd(const elemType& insertItem);
    //Function to insert an item at the end of the list.
    //The parameter insertItem specifies the item to be inserted.
    //Postcondition: list[length] = insertItem; and length++;
    //     If the list is full, an appropriate message is
    //     displayed.
void removeAt(int location);
    //Function to remove the item from the list at the
    //position specified by location
    //Postcondition: The list element at list[location] is removed
    //     and length is decremented by 1. If location is out of
    //     range, an appropriate message is displayed.
void retrieveAt(int location, elemType& retItem) const;
    //Function to retrieve the element from the list at the
    //position specified by location.
    //Postcondition: retItem = list[location]
    //     If location is out of range, an appropriate message is
    //     displayed.
void replaceAt(int location, const elemType& repItem);
    //Function to replace the elements in the list at the
    //position specified by location. The item to be replaced
    //is specified by the parameter repItem.
    //Postcondition: list[location] = repItem
    //     If location is out of range, an appropriate message is
    //     displayed.
void clearList();
    //Function to remove all the elements from the list.
    //After this operation, the size of the list is zero.
    //Postcondition: length = 0;
int seqSearch(const elemType& item) const;
    //Function to search the list for a given item.
    //Postcondition: If the item is found, returns the location
    //     in the array where the item is found; otherwise,
    //     returns -1.
void insert(const elemType& insertItem);
    //Function to insert the item specified by the parameter
    //insertItem at the end of the list. However, first the
    //list is searched to see whether the item to be inserted
    //is already in the list.
    //Postcondition: list[length] = insertItem and length++
    //     If the item is already in the list or the list
    //     is full, an appropriate message is displayed.
void remove(const elemType& removeItem);
    //Function to remove an item from the list. The parameter
    //removeItem specifies the item to be removed.
    //Postcondition: If removeItem is found in the list,
    //     it is removed from the list and length is
    //     decremented by one.
```

3

```
arrayListType(int size = 100);
  //constructor
  //Creates an array of the size specified by the
  //parameter size. The default array size is 100.
  //Postcondition: The list points to the array, length = 0,
  //     and maxSize = size

arrayListType(const arrayListType<elemType>& otherList);
  //copy constructor

~arrayListType();
  //destructor
  //Deallocates the memory occupied by the array.

protected:
  elemType *list;   //array to hold the list elements
  int length;       //to store the length of the list
  int maxSize;      //to store the maximum size of the list
};
```

Figure 3-29 shows the UML class diagram of the class arrayListType.

```
┌─────────────────────────────────────────────────────┐
│                    arrayListType                     │
├─────────────────────────────────────────────────────┤
│ #*list: elemType                                     │
│ #length: int                                         │
│ #maxSize: int                                        │
├─────────────────────────────────────────────────────┤
│ +isEmpty()const: bool                                │
│ +isFull()const: bool                                 │
│ +listSize()const: int                                │
│ +maxListSize()const: int                             │
│ +print() const: void                                 │
│ +isItemAtEqual(int, const elemType&)const: bool      │
│ +insertAt(int, const elemType&): void                │
│ +insertEnd(const elemType&): void                    │
│ +removeAt(int): void                                 │
│ +retrieveAt(int, elemType&)const: void               │
│ +replaceAt(int, const elemType&): void               │
│ +clearList(): void                                   │
│ +seqSearch(const elemType&)const: int                │
│ +insert(const elemType&): void                       │
│ +remove(const elemType&): void                       │
│ +arrayListType(int = 100)                            │
│ +arrayListType(const arrayListType<elemType>&)       │
│ +~arrayListType()                                    │
│ +operator=(const arrayListType<elemType>&):          │
│                    const arrayListType<elemType>&    │
└─────────────────────────────────────────────────────┘
```

FIGURE 3-29 UML class diagram of the class arrayListType

Notice that the data members of the class `arrayListType` are declared as `protected`. This is because we want to derive classes from this class to implement special lists such as an ordered list. Next, we write the definitions of these functions.

The list is empty if `length` is `zero`; it is full if `length` is equal to `maxSize`. Therefore, the definitions of the functions `isEmpty` and `isFull` are as follows:

```
template <class elemType>
bool arrayListType<elemType>::isEmpty() const
{
    return (length == 0);
}
```

```
template <class elemType>
bool arrayListType<elemType>::isFull() const
{
    return (length == maxSize);
}
```

The data member `length` of the class stores the number of elements currently in the list. Similarly, because the size of the array holding the list elements is stored in the data member `maxSize`, `maxSize` specifies the maximum size of the list. Therefore, the definitions of the functions `listSize` and `maxListSize` are as follows:

```
template <class elemType>
int arrayListType<elemType>::listSize() const
{
    return length;
}
```

```
template <class elemType>
int arrayListType<elemType>::maxListSize() const
{
    return maxSize;
}
```

Each of the functions `isEmpty`, `isFull`, `listSize`, and `maxListSize` contain only one statement, which is either a comparison statement or a statement returning a value. It follows that each of these functions is of $O(1)$.

The member function `print` outputs the elements of the list. We assume that the output is sent to the standard output device.

```
template <class elemType>
void arrayListType<elemType>::print() const
{
    for (int i = 0; i < length; i++)
        cout << list[i] << " ";

    cout << endl;
}
```

The function `print` uses a loop to output the elements of the list. The number of times the **for** loop executes depends on the number of elements of the list. If the list has 100 elements, the **for** loop executes 100 times. In general, suppose that the number of elements in the list is n. Then the function print is of $O(n)$.

The definition of the function isItemAtEqual is straightforward.

```
template <class elemType>
bool arrayListType<elemType>::isItemAtEqual
                         (int location, const elemType& item) const
{
    return(list[location] == item);
}
```

The body of function isItemAtEqual has only one statement, which is a comparison statement. It is easy to see that this function is of $O(1)$.

The function insertAt inserts an item at a specific location in the list. The item to be inserted and the insert location in the array are passed as parameters to this function. To insert the item somewhere in the middle of the list, we must first make room for the new item. That is, we need to move certain elements right one array slot. Suppose that the data member list of an arrayListType object is as shown in Figure 3-30. (Note that this figure does not show the data members length and maxSize.)

```
            [0]  [1]  [2]  [3]  [4]  [5]  [6]  [7]  [8]
    list    35   24   45   17   26   78                   ...
```

FIGURE 3-30 Array list

The number of elements currently in the list is 6, so length is 6. Thus, after inserting a new element, the length of the list is 7. If the item is to be inserted at, say location 6, we can easily accomplish this by copying the item into list[6]. On the other hand, if the item is to be inserted at, say location 3, we first need to move elements list[3], list[4], and list[5] one array slot right to make room for the new item. Thus, we must first copy list[5] into list[6], list[4] into list[5], and list[3] into list[4], in this order. Then we can copy the new item into list[3].

Of course, special cases such as trying to insert in a full list must be handled separately. Other member functions can handle some of these cases.

The definition of the function insertAt is as follows:

```
template <class elemType>
void arrayListType<elemType>::insertAt
                     (int location, const elemType& insertItem)
{
    if (location < 0 || location >= maxSize)
        cerr << "The position of the item to be inserted "
             << "is out of range" << endl;
```

```
    else
        if (length >= maxSize)   //list is full
            cerr << "Cannot insert in a full list" << endl;
        else
        {
            for (int i = length; i > location; i--)
                list[i] = list[i - 1];    //move the elements down

            list[location] = insertItem;   //insert the item at the
                                           //specified position

            length++;       //increment the length
        }
} //end insertAt
```

The function insertAt uses a **for** loop to shift the elements of the list. The number of times the **for** loop executes depends on where in the list the item is to be inserted. If the item is to be inserted at the first position, all the elements of the list are shifted. It can be easily shown that this function is of $O(n)$.

The function insertEnd can be implemented by using the function insertAt. However, the function insertEnd does not require the shifting of elements. Therefore, we give its definition directly.

```
template <class elemType>
void arrayListType<elemType>::insertEnd(const elemType& insertItem)
{
    if (length >= maxSize)   //the list is full
        cerr << "Cannot insert in a full list" << endl;
    else
    {
        list[length] = insertItem;    //insert the item at the end
        length++;    //increment the length
    }
} //end insertEnd
```

The number of statements and, hence, the number of operations executed in the body of the function insertEnd are fixed. Therefore, this function is of $O(1)$.

The function removeAt is the opposite of the function insertAt. The function removeAt removes an item from a specific location in the list. The location of the item to be removed is passed as a parameter to this function. After removing the item from the list, the length of the list is reduced by 1. If the item to be removed is somewhere in the middle of the list, after removing the item we must move certain elements left one array slot because we cannot leave holes in the portion of the array containing the list. Suppose that the data member list of an **arrayListType** object is as shown in Figure 3-31. (Note that this figure does not show the data members length and maxSize.)

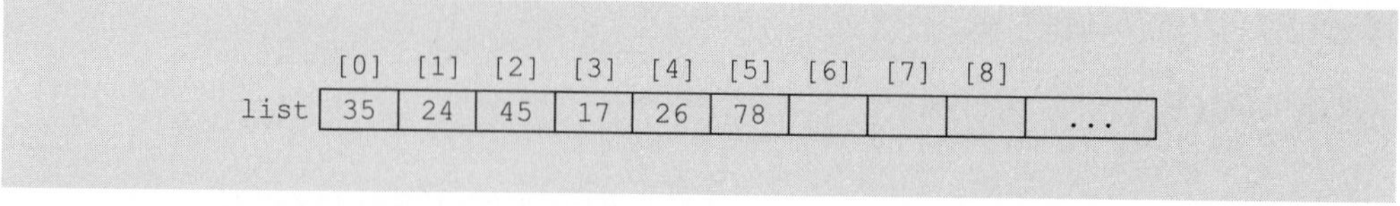

```
          [0]  [1]  [2]  [3]  [4]  [5]  [6]  [7]  [8]
list   |  35 | 24 | 45 | 17 | 26 | 78 |    |    |    |  ...  |
```

FIGURE 3-31 Array `list`

The number of elements currently in the list is 6, so `length` is 6. Thus, after removing an element, the `length` of the list is 5. Suppose that the item to be removed is at, say location 3. Clearly, we must move `list[4]` into `list[3]` and `list[5]` into `list[4]`, in this order.

The definition of the function `removeAt` is as follows:

```
template <class elemType>
void arrayListType<elemType>::removeAt(int location)
{
    if (location < 0 || location >= length)
        cerr << "The location of the item to be removed "
             << "is out of range" << endl;
    else
    {
        for (int i = location; i < length - 1; i++)
            list[i] = list[i+1];

        length--;
    }
} //end removeAt
```

Similar to the function `insertAt`, it is easily seen that the function `removeAt` is of $O(n)$.

The definition of the function `retrieveAt` is straightforward. The index of the item to be retrieved, and the location where to retrieve the item, are passed as parameters to this function. Similarly, the definition of the function `replaceAt` is straightforward. The definitions of these functions are as follows:

```
template <class elemType>
void arrayListType<elemType>::retrieveAt
                           (int location, elemType& retItem) const
{
    if (location < 0 || location >= length)
        cerr << "The location of the item to be retrieved is "
             << "out of range." << endl;
    else
        retItem = list[location];
} //end retrieveAt


template <class elemType>
void arrayListType<elemType>::replaceAt
                           (int location, const elemType& repItem)
```

```
{
    if (location < 0 || location >= length)
        cerr << "The location of the item to be replaced is "
            << "out of range." << endl;
    else
        list[location] = repItem;

} //end replaceAt
```

The function `clearList` removes the elements from the list, leaving it empty. Because the data member `length` indicates the number of elements in the list, the elements are removed by simply setting `length` to 0. Therefore, the definition of this function is as follows:

```
template <class elemType>
void arrayListType<elemType>::clearList()
{
    length = 0;
} //end clearList
```

We now discuss the definition of the constructor and the destructor. The constructor creates an array of the size specified by the user, and initializes the `length` of the list to 0 and the `maxSize` to the size of the array specified by the user. The size of the array is passed as a parameter to the constructor. The default array size is 100. The destructor deallocates the memory occupied by the array holding the list elements. The definition of the constructor and the destructor are as follows:

```
template <class elemType>
arrayListType<elemType>::arrayListType(int size)
{
    if (size < 0)
    {
        cerr << "The array size must be positive. Creating "
            << "an array of size 100. " << endl;

        maxSize = 100;
    }
    else
        maxSize = size;

    length = 0;

    list = new elemType[maxSize];
    assert(list != NULL);
}

template <class elemType>
arrayListType<elemType>::~arrayListType()
{
    delete [] list;
}
```

As before, it is easy to see that each of the functions retrieveAt, replaceAt, clearList, as well as the constructor and destructor is of $O(1)$.

Copy Constructor

Recall that the copy constructor is called when an object is passed as a (value) parameter to a function, and when an object is declared and initialized using the value of another object of the same type. It copies the data members of the actual object into the corresponding data members of the formal parameter and the object being created. Its definition is as follows:

```
template <class elemType>
arrayListType<elemType>::arrayListType
                (const arrayListType<elemType>& otherList)
{
    maxSize = otherList.maxSize;
    length = otherList.length;
    list = new elemType[maxSize];  //create the array
    assert(list != NULL);           //terminate if unable to allocate
                                    //memory space

    for (int j = 0; j < length; j++)  //copy otherList
        list [j] = otherList.list[j];
} //end copy constructor
```

Overloading the Assignment Operator

Next, because we are overloading the assignment operator for the class arrayListType, we give the definition of the function template to overload the assignment operator.

```
template <class elemType>
const arrayListType<elemType>& arrayListType<elemType>::operator=
                (const arrayListType<elemType>& otherList)
{
    if (this != &otherList)    //avoid self-assignment
    {
        delete [] list;
        maxSize = otherList.maxSize;
        length = otherList.length;

        list = new elemType[maxSize];  //create the array
        assert(list != NULL);     //if unable to allocate memory
                                  //space, terminate the program
        for (int i = 0; i < length; i++)
            list[i] = otherList.list[i];
    }

    return *this;
}
```

Similar to the function `print`, it is easy to see that both the copy constructor and the function to overload the assignment operator are of $O(n)$.

Search

The search algorithm described next is called a **sequential** or **linear** search.

Consider the list of seven elements shown in Figure 3-32.

	[0]	[1]	[2]	[3]	[4]	[5]	[6]	[7]
list	35	12	27	18	45	16	38		...

FIGURE 3-32 List of seven elements

Suppose that you want to determine whether 27 is in the list. The sequential search works as follows: First, you compare 27 with `list[0]`—that is, compare 27 with 35. Because `list[0]` ≠ 27, you then compare 27 with `list[1]` (that is, with 12, the second item in the list). Because `list[1]` ≠ 27, you compare 27 with the next element in the list—that is, compare 27 with `list[2]`. Because `list[2]` = 27, the search stops. This is a successful search.

Let us now search for 10. As before, the search starts with the first element in the list—that is, at `list[0]`. This time the search item, which is 10, is compared with every item in the list. Eventually, no more data is left in the list to compare with the search item. This is an unsuccessful search.

It now follows that, as soon as you find an element in the list that is equal to the search item, you must stop the search and report "success." (In this case, you usually also tell the location in the list where the search item was found.) Otherwise, after the search item is compared with every element in the list, you must stop the search and report "failure."

Suppose that the name of the array containing the list elements is `list`. The following function performs a sequential search on a list:

```cpp
template <class elemType>
int arrayListType<elemType>::seqSearch(const elemType& item) const
{
    int loc;
    bool found = false;

    for (loc = 0; loc < length; loc++)
        if (list[loc] == item)
        {
            found = true;
            break;
        }
```

```
        if (found)
            return loc;
        else
            return -1;
} //end seqSearch
```

Now that we know how to implement the (sequential) search algorithm, we can give the definitions of the functions `insert` and `remove`. Recall that the function `insert` inserts a new item at the end of the list if this item does not exist in the list and the list is not full. The function `remove` removes an item from the list if the list is not empty.

Chapter 9 explicitly shows that the function `seqSearch` is of $O(n)$.

Insert

The function `insert` inserts a new item in the list. Because duplicates are not allowed, this function first searches the list to determine whether the item to be inserted is already in the list. To determine whether the item to be inserted is already in the list, this function calls the member function `seqSearch`, described previously. If the item to be inserted is not in the list, the new item is inserted at the end of the list and the length of the list is increased by 1. Also, the item to be inserted is passed as a parameter to this function. The definition of this function is as follows:

```
template <class elemType>
void arrayListType<elemType>::insert(const elemType& insertItem)
{
    int loc;

    if (length == 0)    //list is empty
        list[length++] = insertItem;      //insert the item and
                                    //increment the length
    else if (length == maxSize)
        cerr << "Cannot insert in a full list." << endl;
    else
    {
        loc = seqSearch(insertItem);

        if (loc == -1)     //the item to be inserted
                            //does not exist in the list
            list[length++] = insertItem;
        else
            cerr << "the item to be inserted is already in "
                 << "the list. No duplicates are allowed." << endl;
    }
} //end insert
```

The function `insert` uses the function `seqSearch` to determine whether the `insertItem` is already in the list. Because the function `seqSearch` is of $O(n)$, it follows that the function `insert` is of $O(n)$.

Remove

The function `remove` deletes an item from the list. The item to be deleted is passed as a parameter to this function. To delete the item, the function calls the member function `seqSearch` to determine whether the item to be deleted is in the list. If the item to be deleted is found in the list, the item is removed from the list and the length of the list is decremented by 1. If the item to be removed is found in the list, the function `seqSearch` returns the `index` of the item in the list to be deleted. We can now use the `index` returned by the function `seqSearch`, and use the function `removeAt` to remove the item from the list. Therefore, the definition of the function `remove` is as follows:

```
template<class elemType>
void arrayListType<elemType>::remove(const elemType& removeItem)
{
    int loc;

    if (length == 0)
        cerr << "Cannot delete from an empty list." << endl;
    else
    {
        loc = seqSearch(removeItem);

        if (loc != -1)
            removeAt(loc);
        else
            cout << "The item to be deleted is not in the list."
                << endl;
    }
} //end remove
```

The function `remove` uses the functions `seqSearch` and `removeAt` to remove an item from the list. Because each of these functions is of $O(n)$ and because they are called in sequence, it follows that the function `remove` is of $O(n)$.

Time Complexity of List Operations

The following table summarizes the time complexity of list operations.

TABLE 3-1 Time complexity of list operations

Function	Time-complexity
isEmpty	$O(1)$
isFull	$O(1)$
listSize	$O(1)$
maxListSize	$O(1)$

TABLE 3-1 Time complexity of list operations (continued)

Function	Time-complexity
print	$O(n)$
isItemAtEqual	$O(1)$
insertAt	$O(n)$
insertEnd	$O(1)$
removeAt	$O(n)$
retrieveAt	$O(1)$
replaceAt	$O(n)$
clearList	$O(1)$
constructor	$O(1)$
destructor	$O(1)$
copy constructor	$O(n)$
overloading the assignment operator	$O(n)$
seqSearch	$O(n)$
insert	$O(n)$
remove	$O(n)$

The following program tests the various operations on array-based lists.

```
//********************************************************************
// Author: D.S. Malik
//
// This program illustrates how to use the class arrayListType.
//********************************************************************

#include <iostream>                                              //Line 1

#include <string>                                                //Line 2
#include "arrayListType.h"                                       //Line 3
```

```
using namespace std;                                        //Line 4

int main()                                                  //Line 5
{                                                           //Line 6
    arrayListType<int> intList(100);                        //Line 7
    arrayListType<string> stringList;                       //Line 8

    int number;                                             //Line 9

    cout << "List 10: Enter 5 integers: ";                  //Line 10

    for (int counter = 0; counter < 5; counter++)           //Line 11
    {                                                       //Line 12
        cin >> number;                                      //Line 13
        intList.insertAt(counter, number);                  //Line 14
    }                                                       //Line 15

    cout << endl;                                           //Line 16
    cout << "List 19: The list you entered is: ";           //Line 17
    intList.print();                                        //Line 18
    cout << endl;                                           //Line 19

    cout << "Line 20: Enter the item to be deleted: ";      //Line 20
    cin >> number;                                          //Line 21
    intList.remove(number);                                 //Line 22
    cout << "Line 23: After removing " << number
         << ", the list is:" << endl;                       //Line 23
    intList.print();                                        //Line 24
    cout << endl;                                           //Line 25

    string str;                                             //Line 26

    cout << "Line 27: Enter 5 strings: ";                   //Line 27

    for (int counter = 0; counter < 5; counter++)           //Line 28
    {                                                       //Line 29
        cin >> str;                                         //Line 30
        stringList.insertAt(counter, str);                  //Line 31
    }                                                       //Line 32

    cout << endl;                                           //Line 33
    cout << "Line 34: The list you entered is: " << endl;   //Line 34
    stringList.print();                                     //Line 35
    cout << endl;                                           //Line 36

    cout << "Line 37: Enter the string to be deleted: ";    //Line 37
    cin >> str;                                             //Line 38
    stringList.remove(str);                                 //Line 39
    cout << "Line 40: After removing " << str
         << ", the list is:" << endl;                       //Line 40
```

```
    stringList.print();                                      //Line 41
    cout << endl;                                            //Line 42

    return 0;                                                //Line 43
}                                                            //Line 44
```

Sample Run: In this sample run, the user input is shaded.

List 10: Enter 5 integers: 23 78 56 12 79

List 19: The list you entered is: 23 78 56 12 79

Line 20: Enter the item to be deleted: 56
Line 23: After removing 56, the list is:
23 78 12 79

Line 27: Enter 5 strings: hello sunny warm winter summer

Line 34: The list you entered is:
hello sunny warm winter summer

Line 37: Enter the string to be deleted: hello
Line 40: After removing hello, the list is:
sunny warm winter summer

The preceding program works as follows. The statement in Line 7 declares `intList` to be an object of type `arrayListType`. The data member `list` of `intList` is an array of 100 components and the component type is `int`. The statement in Line 8 declares `stringList` to be an object of type `arrayListType`. The data member `list` of `stringList` is an array of 100 components (the default size) and the component type is `string`. The statement in Line 10 prompts the user to enter five integers. The statement in Line 13 gets the next number from the input stream. The statement in Line 14 uses the member function `insertAt` of `intList` to store the number into `intList`. The statement in Line 18 uses the member function `print` of `intList` to output the elements of `intList`. The statement in Line 20 prompts the user to enter the number to be deleted from `intList`; the statement in Line 21 gets the number to be deleted from the input stream. The statement in Line 22 uses the member function `remove` of `intList` to remove the number from `intList`.

The statements in Lines 27 through 42 work the same way as the statements in Lines 10 through 25. These statements process a list of strings.

PROGRAMMING EXAMPLE: Polynomial Operations

You learned in a college algebra or calculus course that a polynomial, $p(x)$, in one variable, x, is an expression of the form:

$$p(x) = a_0 + a_1 x + \ldots + a_{n-1} x^{n-1} + a_n x^n,$$

where a_i are real (or complex) numbers and n is a nonnegative integer. If $p(x) = a_0$, $p(x)$ is called a **constant** polynomial. If $p(x)$ is a nonzero constant polynomial, the degree of $p(x)$ is defined to be 0. Even though, in mathematics, the degree of the zero polynomial is undefined, for the purpose of this program, we consider the degree of such polynomials to be zero. If $p(x)$ is not constant and $a_n \neq 0$, n is called the degree of $p(x)$; that is, the degree of a nonconstant polynomial is defined to be the exponent of the highest power of x. (Note that the symbol $\neq$ means not equal to.)

The basic operations performed on polynomials are add, subtract, multiply, divide, and evaluate a polynomial at any given point. For example, suppose that

$$p(x) = 1 + 2x + 3x^2,$$

and

$$q(x) = 4 + x.$$

The degree of $p(x)$ is 2 and the degree of $q(x)$ is 1. Moreover,

$$p(2) = 1 + 2 \cdot 2 + 3 \cdot 2^2 = 17$$
$$p(x) + q(x) = 5 + 3x + 3x^2$$
$$p(x) - q(x) = -3 + x + 3x^2$$
$$p(x)^* q(x) = 4 + 9x + 14x^2 + 3x^3$$

The purpose of this programming example is to design and implement the `class` `polynomialType` to perform the various polynomial operations in a program.

To be specific, in this program, we will implement the following operations on polynomials:

1. Evaluate a polynomial at a given value.
2. Add polynomials.
3. Subtract polynomials.
4. Multiply polynomials.

Furthermore, we assume that the coefficients of polynomials are real numbers. You will be asked in Programming Exercise 8 to generalize it so that the coefficients can also be complex numbers. To store a polynomial, we use a dynamic array as follows:

Suppose $p(x)$ is a polynomial of degree $n \geq 0$. Let `list` be an array of size $n + 1$. The coefficient a_i of x^i is stored in `list[i]`. See Figure 3-33.

	[0]	[1]		[i]		[n-1]	[n]
$p(x)$	a_0	a_1	...	a_i	...	a_{n-1}	a_n

FIGURE 3-33 Polynomial $p(x)$

Figure 3-33 shows that if $p(x)$ is a polynomial of degree n, we need an array of size $n+1$ to store the coefficients of $p(x)$. Suppose that $p(x) = 1 + 8x - 3x^2 + 5x^4 + 7x^8$. Then the array storing the coefficient of $p(x)$ is given in Figure 3-34.

	[0]	[1]	[2]	[3]	[4]	[5]	[6]	[7]	[8]
$p(x)$	1	8	-3	0	5	0	0	0	7

FIGURE 3-34 Polynomial $p(x)$ of degree 8 and its coefficients

Similarly, if $q(x) = -5x^2 + 16x^5$, the array storing the coefficient of $q(x)$ is given in Figure 3-35.

	[0]	[1]	[2]	[3]	[4]	[5]
$q(x)$	0	0	-5	0	0	16

FIGURE 3-35 Polynomial $q(x)$ of degree 5 and its coefficients

Next, we define the operations +, –, and *. Suppose that

$p(x) = a_0 + a_1x + \ldots + a_{n-1}x^{n-1} + a_nx^n$ and

$q(x) = b_0 + b_1x + \ldots + b_{m-1}x^{m-1} + a_mx^m$.

Let $t = max(n, m)$. Then

$p(x) + q(x) = c_0 + c_1x + \ldots + c_{t-1}x^{t-1} + c_tx^t$,

where for $i = 0, 1, 2, \ldots, t$

$$c_i = \begin{cases} a_i + b_i & if \ i \leq \min(n, m) \\ a_i & if \ i > m \\ b_i & if \ i > n \end{cases}$$

The difference, $p(x) - q(x)$, of $p(x)$ and $q(x)$ can be defined similarly. It follows that the degree of the polynomials is $\leq max(n, m)$.

The product, $p(x) \star q(x)$, of $p(x)$ and $q(x)$ is defined as follows:

$$p(x) * q(x) = d_0 + d_1 x + \ldots + d_{n+m} x^{n+m},$$

The coefficient d_k, for $k = 0, 1, 2, \ldots, t$, is given by the formula

$$d_k = a_0 * b_k + a_1 * b_{k-1} + \ldots + a_k * b_0,$$

where if either a_i or b_i does not exist, it is assumed to be zero. For example,

$$d_0 = a_0 b_0$$
$$d_1 = a_0 b_1 + a_1 b_0$$

$$\ldots$$

$$d_{n+m} = a_n b_m$$

In Chapter 2, you learned how to overload various operators. This program overloads the operators +, -, and * to perform polynomial addition, subtraction, and multiplication. Moreover, we also overload the function call operator, (), to evaluate a polynomial at a given value. To simplify the input and output of polynomials, the operators << and >> are also overloaded.

Because the coefficients of a polynomial are stored in a dynamic array, we use the class arrayListType to store and manipulate the coefficients of a polynomial. In fact, we derive the class polynomialType to implement polynomial operations from the class arrayListType, which requires us to implement only the operations needed to manipulate polynomials.

The following class defines polynomials as an ADT:

```
//*************************************************************
// Author: D.S. Malik
//
// This class specifies the members to implement the basic
// polynomial operations.
//*************************************************************

class polynomialType: public arrayListType<double>
{
    friend ostream& operator<<(ostream&, const polynomialType&);
        //Overloads the stream insertion operator
    friend istream& operator>>(istream&, polynomialType&);
        //Overloads the stream extraction operator
```

```
public:
    polynomialType operator+(const polynomialType&);
      //Overloads the operator +
    polynomialType operator-(const polynomialType&);
      //Overloads the operator -
    polynomialType operator*(const polynomialType&);
      //Overloads the operator *

    double operator() (double x);
      //Overloads the operator () to evaluate the polynomial at
      //a given point
      //Postcondition: The value of the polynomial at x is
      //       calculated and returned

    polynomialType(int size = 100);
      //constructor

    int min(int x, int y) const;
      //Function to return the smaller of x and y
    int max(int x, int y) const;
      //Function to return the larger of x and y
};
```

In Exercise 24 (at the end of this chapter), you are asked to draw the UML diagram of the class polynomialType.

If $p(x)$ is a polynomial of degree 3, we can create an object, say p, of type polynomialType and set the size of the array list to 4. The following statement declares such an object p:

```
polynomialType p(4);
```

The degree of the polynomial is stored in the data member length, which is inherited from the class arrayListType.

Next we discuss the definitions of the functions.

The constructor sets the value of length to the size of the array and initializes the array list to 0.

```
polynomialType::polynomialType(int size)
               : arrayListType<double>(size)
{
    length = size;

    for (int i = 0; i < size; i++)
        list[i] = 0;
}
```

The definition of the function to overload the operator () is quite straightforward and is given next.

```
double polynomialType::operator() (double x)
{
    double value = 0.0;

    for (int i = 0; i < length; i++)
    {
        if (list[i] != 0.0)
            value = value + list[i] * pow(x,i);
    }

    return value;
}
```

Suppose that $p(x)$ is a polynomial of degree n and $q(x)$ is a polynomial of degree m. If $n = m$, the operator + adds the corresponding coefficients of $p(x)$ and $q(x)$. If $n > m$, the first m coefficients of $p(x)$ are added with the corresponding coefficients of $q(x)$. The remaining coefficients of $p(x)$ are copied into the polynomial containing the sum of $p(x)$ and $q(x)$. Similarly, if $n < m$, the first n coefficients of $q(x)$ are added with the corresponding coefficients of $p(x)$. The remaining coefficients of $q(x)$ are copied into the polynomial containing the sum. The definition of the operator − is similar to the definition of the operator +. The definitions of these two operator functions are as follows:

```
polynomialType polynomialType::operator+
                            (const polynomialType& right)
{
    int size = max(length, right.length);

    polynomialType temp(size); //polynomial to store the sum

    for (int i = 0; i < min(length, right.length); i++)
        temp.list[i] = list[i] + right.list[i];

    if (size == length)
        for (int i = min(length, right.length); i < length; i++)
            temp.list[i] = list[i];
    else
        for (int i = min(length, right.length); i < right.length;
                                                 i++)
            temp.list[i] = right.list[i];

    return temp;
}

polynomialType polynomialType::operator-
                            (const polynomialType& right)
{
    int size = max(length, right.length);

    polynomialType temp(size); //polynomial to store the difference
```

```
        for (int i = 0; i < min(length, right.length); i++)
            temp.list[i] = list[i] - right.list[i];

        if (size == length)
            for (int i = min(length, right.length); i < length; i++)
                temp.list[i] = list[i];
        else
            for (int i = min(length, right.length); i < right.length;
                                                    i++)
                temp.list[i] = -right.list[i];

        return temp;
}
```

The definition of the function to overload the operator * to multiply two polynomials is left as an exercise for you. See Programming Exercise 6 at the end of this chapter. The definitions of the remaining functions of the class polynomialType are as follows:

```
int polynomialType::min(int x, int y) const
{
    if (x <= y)
        return x;
    else
        return y;
}

int polynomialType::max(int x, int y) const
{
    if (x >= y)
        return x;
    else
        return y;
}

ostream& operator<<(ostream& os, const polynomialType& p)
{
    int indexFirstNonzeroCoeff = 0;

    for (int i = 0; i < p.length; i++)  //determine the index of the
                                        //first nonzero coefficient
        if (p.list[i] != 0.0)
        {
            indexFirstNonzeroCoeff = i;
            break;
        }

    if (indexFirstNonzeroCoeff < p.length)
    {
        if (indexFirstNonzeroCoeff == 0)
            os << p.list[indexFirstNonzeroCoeff] << " ";
```

```
                else
                    os << p.list[indexFirstNonzeroCoeff] << "x^"
                        << indexFirstNonzeroCoeff << " ";

                for (int i = indexFirstNonzeroCoeff + 1; i < p.length; i++)
                {
                    if (p.list[i] != 0.0)
                        if (p.list[i] >= 0.0)
                            os << "+ " << p.list[i] << "x^" << i << " ";
                        else
                            os << "- " << -p.list[i] << "x^" << i << " ";
                }
            }
            else
                os << "0";

            return os;
        }

        istream& operator>>(istream& is, polynomialType& p)
        {
            cout << "The degree of this polynomial is: "
                << p.length - 1 << endl;

            for (int i = 0; i < p.length; i++)
            {
                cout << "Enter the coefficient of x^" << i << ": ";
                is >> p.list[i];
            }

            return is;
        }
```

MAIN PROGRAM

```
//************************************************************
// Author: D.S. Malik
//
// This program illustrates how to use the class polynomialType.
//************************************************************

#include <iostream>                              //Line 1

#include "polynomialType.h"                      //Line 2

using namespace std;                             //Line 3

int main()                                       //Line 4
{                                                //Line 5
    polynomialType p(8);                         //Line 6
    polynomialType q(4);                         //Line 7
    polynomialType t;                            //Line 8
```

```
cin >> p;                                              //Line 9
cout << endl << "Line 10: p(x): " << p << endl;        //Line 10

cout << "Line 11: p(5): " << p(5) << endl << endl;     //Line 11

cin >> q;                                              //Line 12
cout << endl << "Line 13: q(x): " << q << endl
     << endl;                                          //Line 13

t = p + q;                                             //Line 14

cout << "Line 15: p(x) + q(x): " << t << endl;         //Line 15

cout << "Line 16: p(x) - q(x): " << p - q << endl;     //Line 16

return 0;                                              //Line 17
}                                                      //Line 18
```

Sample Run: In this sample run, the user input is shaded.

```
The degree of this polynomial is: 7
Enter the coefficient of x^0: 0
Enter the coefficient of x^1: 1
Enter the coefficient of x^2: 4
Enter the coefficient of x^3: 0
Enter the coefficient of x^4: 0
Enter the coefficient of x^5: 0
Enter the coefficient of x^6: 0
Enter the coefficient of x^7: 6

Line 10: p(x): 1x^1 + 4x^2 + 6x^7
Line 11: p(5): 468855

The degree of this polynomial is: 3
Enter the coefficient of x^0: 1
Enter the coefficient of x^1: 2
Enter the coefficient of x^2: 0
Enter the coefficient of x^3: 3

Line 13: q(x): 1 + 2x^1 + 3x^3

Line 15: p(x) + q(x): 1 + 3x^1 + 4x^2 + 3x^3 + 6x^7
Line 16: p(x) - q(x): -1 - 1x^1 + 4x^2 - 3x^3 + 6x^7
```

QUICK REVIEW

1. Pointer variables contain the addresses of other variables as their values.

2. In C++, no name is associated with the pointer data type.

3. A pointer variable is declared using an asterisk, *, between the data type and the variable.

4. In C++, & is called the address of operator.

5. The address of operator returns the address of its operand. For example, if p is a pointer variable of type int and num is an int variable, the statement

```
p = &num;
```

sets the value of p to the address of num.

6. When used as a unary operator, * is called the dereferencing operator.

7. The memory location indicated by the value of a pointer variable is accessed by using the dereferencing operator, *. For example, if p is a pointer variable of type int, the statement

```
*p = 25;
```

sets the value of the memory location indicated by the value of p to 25.

8. You can use the member access operator arrow, ->, to access the component of an object pointed to by a pointer.

9. Pointer variables are initialized using either 0 (the integer zero), NULL, or the address of a variable of the same type.

10. The only integer value that can be directly assigned to a pointer variable is 0.

11. The only arithmetic operations allowed on pointer variables are increment (++), decrement (--), addition of an integer to a pointer variable, subtraction of an integer from a pointer variable, and subtraction of a pointer from another pointer.

12. Pointer arithmetic is different from ordinary arithmetic. When an integer is added to a pointer, the value added to the value of the pointer variable is the integer times the size of the object to which the pointer is pointing. Similarly, when an integer is subtracted from a pointer, the value subtracted from the value of the pointer variable is the integer times the size of the object to which the pointer is pointing.

13. Pointer variables can be compared using relational operators. (It makes sense to compare pointers of the same type.)

14. The value of one pointer variable can be assigned to another pointer variable of the same type.

15. A variable created during program execution is called a dynamic variable.

16. The operator new is used to create a dynamic variable.

17. The operator delete is used to deallocate the memory occupied by a dynamic variable.

18. In C++, both new and delete are reserved words.

19. The operator new has two forms: one to create a single dynamic variable, and another to create an array of dynamic variables.

20. If p is a pointer of type int, the statement

```
p = new int;
```

allocates storage of type int somewhere in memory and stores the address of the allocated storage in p.

3

21. The operator `delete` has two forms: one to deallocate the memory occupied by a single dynamic variable, and another to deallocate the memory occupied by an array of dynamic variables.

22. If `p` is a pointer of type `int`, the statement `delete p;` deallocates the memory to which p points.

23. The array name is a constant pointer. It always points to the same memory location, which is the location of the first array component.

24. To create a dynamic array, the form of the `new` operator that creates an array of dynamic variables is used. For example, if `p` is a pointer of type `int`, the statement

    `p = new int[10];`

    creates an array of 10 components of type `int`. The base address of the array is stored in **p**. We call **p** a dynamic array.

25. Array notation can be used to access the components of a dynamic array. For example, suppose **p** is a dynamic array of 10 components. Then `p[0]` refers to the first array component, `p[1]` refers to the second array component, and so on. In particular, `p[i]` refers to the $(i + 1)$th component of the array.

26. An array created during program execution is called a dynamic array.

27. If **p** is a dynamic array, then the statement

    `delete [] p;`

    deallocates the memory occupied by **p**—that is, the components of **p**.

28. In a shallow copy, two or more pointers of the same type point to the same memory space; that is, they point to the same data.

29. In a deep copy, two or more pointers of the same type have their own copies of the data.

30. If a class has a destructor, the destructor automatically executes whenever a class object goes out of scope.

31. If a class has pointer data members, the built-in assignment operators provide a shallow copy of the data.

32. A copy constructor executes when an object is declared and initialized by using the value of another object, and when an object is passed by value as a parameter.

33. C++ allows a user to pass an object of a derived class to a formal parameter of the base class type.

34. The binding of virtual functions occurs at execution time, not at compile time, and is called dynamic or run-time binding.

35. In C++, virtual functions are declared using the reserved word virtual.

36. A class is called an abstract class if it contains one or more pure virtual functions.

37. Because an abstract class is *not* a complete classas—it (or its implementation file) does not contain the definitions of certain functions as you cannot create objects of that class.

38. In addition to the pure virtual functions, an abstract class can contain instance variables, constructors, and functions that are not pure virtual. However, the abstract class must provide the definitions of constructors and functions that are not pure virtual.

39. A list is a collection of elements of the same type.

40. The commonly performed operations on a list are create the list, determine whether the list is empty, determine whether the list is full, find the size of the list, destroy or clear the list, determine whether an item is the same as a given list element, insert an item in the list at the specified location, remove an item from the list at the specified location, replace an item at the specified location with another item, retrieve an item from the list from the specified location, and search the list for a given item.

3

EXERCISES

1. Mark the following statements as true or false.

   a. In C++, `pointer` is a reserved word.

   b. In C++, pointer variables are declared using the reserved word `pointer`.

   c. The statement `delete p;` deallocates the variable pointer p.

   d. The statement `delete p;` deallocates the dynamic variable to which p points.

   e. Given the declaration

   ```
   int list[10];
   int *p;
   ```

   the statement

   ```
   p = list;
   ```

   is valid in C++.

   f. Given the declaration

   ```
   int *p;
   ```

   the statement

   ```
   p = new int[50];
   ```

   dynamically allocates an array of 50 components of type `int`, and p contains the base address of the array.

   g. The address of operator returns the address and value of its operand.

   h. If p is a pointer variable, the statement p = p * 2; is valid in C++.

2. Given the declaration

```
int x;
int *p;
int *q;
```

Mark the following statements as valid or invalid. If a statement is invalid, explain why.

a. `p = q;`

b. `*p = 56;`

c. `p = x;`

d. `*p = *q;`

e. `q = &x;`

f. `*p = q;`

3. What is the output of the following C++ code?

```
int x;
int y;
int *p = &x;
int *q = &y;
*p = 35;
*q = 98;
*p = *q;
cout << x << "   " << y << endl;
cout << *p << "   " << *q << endl;
```

4. What is the output of the following C++ code?

```
int x;
int y;
int *p = &x;
int *q = &y;
x = 35;   y = 46;
p = q;
*p = 78;
cout << x << "   " << y << endl;
cout << *p << "   " << *q << endl;
```

5. Given the declaration

```
int num = 6;
int *p = &num;
```

which of the following statement(s) increment the value of num?

a. `p++;`

b. `(*p)++;`

c. `num++`

d. `(*num)++;`

6. What is the output of the following code?

```
int *p;
int * q;
p = new int;
q = p;
*p = 46;
*q = 39;
cout << *p << " " << *q << endl;
```

7. What is the output of the following code?

```
int *p;
int *q;
p = new int;
*p = 43;
q = p;
*q = 52;
p = new int;
*p = 78;
q = new int;
*q = *p;
cout << *p << " " << *q << endl;
```

8. What is wrong with the following code?

```
int *p;                              //Line 1
int *q;                              //Line 2

p = new int;                         //Line 3
*p = 43;                             //Line 4

q = p;                               //Line 5
*q = 52;                             //Line 6

delete q;                            //Line 7

cout << *p << " " << *q << endl;     //Line 8
```

9. What is the output of the following code?

```
int x;
int *p;
int *q;
p = new int[10] ;
q = p;
*p = 4;

for(int j = 0; j < 10; j++)
{
    x = *p;
    p++;
    *p = x + j;
}
```

```
for (int k = 0; k < 10; k++)
{
    cout << *q << " ";
    q++;
}
cout << endl;
```

10. What is the output of the following code?

```
int *secret;

secret = new int[10];
secret[0] = 10;
for (int j = 1; j < 10; j++)
    secret[j] = secret[j -1] + 5;
for(int j = 0; j < 10; j++)
    cout << secret[j] << " ";
cout << endl;
```

11. Explain the difference between a shallow copy and a deep copy of data.

12. What is wrong with the following code?

```
int *p;                         //Line 1
int *q;                         //Line 2

p = new int [5];                //Line 3
*p = 2;                         //Line 4

for (int i = 1; i < 5; i++)     //Line 5
    p[i] = p[i-1] + i;          //Line 6

q = p;                          //Line 7

delete [] p;                    //Line 8

for (int j = 0; j < 5; j++)     //Line 9
    cout << q[j] << " ";        //Line 10

cout << endl;                   //Line 11
```

13. What is the output of the following code?

```
int *p;
int *q;

p = new int [5];
p[0] = 5;

for (int i = 1; i < 5; i++)
    p[i] = p[i - 1] + 2 * i;

cout << "Array p: ";
for (int i = 0; i < 5; i++)
    cout << p[i] << " ";
cout << endl;
```

```
q = new int[5];

for (int i = 0; i < 5; i++)
    q[i] = p[4 - i];

cout << "Array q: ";
for (int i = 0; i < 5; i++)
    cout << q[i] << " ";

cout << endl;
```

14. What is the output of the following code?

```
int **p;

p = new int* [5];

for (int i = 0; i < 5; i++)
    p[i] = new int[3];

for (int i = 1; i < 5; i++)
    for (int j = 0; j < 3; j++)
        p[i][j] = 2 * i + j;

for (int i = 1; i < 5; i++)
{
    for (int j = 0; j < 3; j++)
        cout << p[i][j] << " ";
    cout << endl;
}
```

15. What is the purpose of the copy constructor?

16. Name three situations when a copy constructor executes.

17. Name three things that you should do for classes with pointer data members.

18. Suppose that you have the following definition of a class.

```
class dummyClass
{
public:
    void print();

    ...
private:
    int listLength;
    int *list;
    double salary;
    string name;
}
```

a. Write the function prototype to overload the assignment operator for the class dummyClass.

b. Write the definition of the function to overload the assignment operator for the class dummyClass.

    c.   Write the function prototype to include the copy constructor for the class dummyClass.

    d.   Write the definition of the copy constructor for the class dummyClass.

19.   Suppose that you have the following classes, classA and classB:

```cpp
class classA
{
public:
    virtual void print() const;
    void doubleNum();
    classA(int a = 0);

private:
    int x;
};

void classA::print() const
{
    cout << "ClassA x: " << x << endl;
}

void classA::doubleNum()
{
    x = 2 * x;
}

classA::classA(int a)
{
    x = a;
}

class classB: public classA
{
public:
    void print() const;
    void doubleNum();
    classB(int a = 0, int b = 0);

private:
    int y;
};

void classB::print() const
{
    classA::print();
    cout << "ClassB y: " << y << endl;
}
```

3

```
void classB::doubleNum()
{
    classA::doubleNum();

    y = 2 * y;
}

classB::classB(int a, int b)
        : classA(a)
{
    y = b;
}
```

What is the output of the following function main?

```
int main()
{
    classA *ptrA;
    classA objectA(2);

    classB objectB(3, 5);

    ptrA = &objectA;
    ptrA->doubleNum();
    ptrA->print();
    cout << endl;

    ptrA = &objectB;

    ptrA->doubleNum();
    ptrA->print();
    cout << endl;

    return 0;
}
```

20. What is the output of the function main of Exercise 19, if the definition of classA is replaced by the following definition?

```
class classA
{
public:
    virtual void print() const;
    virtual void doubleNum();
    classA(int a = 0);

private:
    int x;
};
```

21. What is the difference between compile-time binding and run-time binding?

22. Consider the following definition of the `class student`.

```
public studentType: public personType
{
public:
    void print();
    void calculateGPA();
    void setID(long id);
    void setCourses(const string c[], int noOfC);
    void setGrades(const char cG[], int noOfC);

    void getID();
    void getCourses(string c[], int noOfC);
    void getGrades(char cG[], int noOfC);
    void studentType(string fName = "", string lastName = "",
                     long id, string c[] = NULL,
                     char cG[] = NULL, int noOfC = 0);

private:
    long studentId;
    string courses[6];
    char coursesGrade[6]
    int noOfCourses;
}
```

Rewrite the definition of the `class student` so that the functions `print` and `calculateGPA` are pure `virtual` functions.

23. What is the effect of the following statements?

a. `arrayListType<int> intList(100);`

b. `arrayListType<string> stringList(1000);`

c. `arrayListType<double> salesList(-10);`

24. Draw the UML diagram of the `class polynomialType`. Also show the inheritance hierarchy.

PROGRAMMING EXERCISES

1. The function `removeAt` of the `class arrayListType` removes an element from the list by shifting the elements of the list. However, if the element to be removed is at the beginning of the list and the list is fairly large, it could take a lot of computer time. Because the list elements are in no particular order, you could simply remove the element by swapping the last element of the list with the item to be removed and reducing the length of the list. Rewrite the definition of the function `removeAt` using this technique.

2. The function `remove` of the `class arrayListType` removes only the first occurrence of an element. Add the function `removeAll` to the `class arrayListType` that would remove all occurrences of a given element. Also, write the definition of the function `removeAll` and a program to test this function.

3. Add the function min to the **class arrayListType** to return the smallest element of the list. Also, write the definition of the function min and a program to test this function.

4. Add the function max to the **class arrayListType** to return the largest element of the list. Also, write the definition of the function max and a program to test this function.

5. The operators + and − are overloaded as member functions for the **class polynomialType**. Redo Programming Example Polynomial Operations so that these operators are overloaded as nonmember functions. Also write a test program to test these operators.

6. Write the definition of the function to overload the operator * (as a member function) for the **class polynomialType** to multiply two polynomials. Also write a test program to test the operator *.

7. Let $p(x) = a_0 + a_1x + \ldots + a_{n-1}x^{n-1} + a_nx^n$ be a polynomial of degree n, where a_i are real (or complex) numbers and n is a nonnegative integer. The derivative of $p(x)$, written $p'(x)$, is defined to be $p'(x) = a_1 + 2a_2x^2 + \ldots + na_nx^{n-1}$. If $p(x)$ is constant, then $p'(x) = 0$. Overload the operator $\sim$ as a member function for the **class polynomialType** so that $\sim$ returns the derivative of a polynomial.

8. The **class polynomialType** as given in the Programming Example Polynomial Operations processes polynomials with coefficients that are real numbers. Design and implement a similar class that can be used to process polynomials with coefficients as complex numbers. Your class must overload the operators +, −, * to perform addition, subtraction, and multiplication; and the operator () to evaluate a polynomial at a given complex number. Also write a program to test various operations.

9. Using classes, design an online address book to keep track of the names, addresses, phone numbers, and dates of birth of family members, close friends, and certain business associates. Your program should be able to handle a maximum of 500 entries.

   a. Define a **class, addressType,** that can store a street address, city, state, and zip code. Use the appropriate functions to print and store the address. Also, use constructors to automatically initialize the data members.

   b. Define a **class extPersonType** using the **class personType** (as defined in Example 1-12, Chapter 1), the **class dateType** (as designed in Programming Exercise 2 of Chapter 2), and the **class addressType**. Add a data member to this class to classify the person as a family member, friend, or business associate. Also, add a data member to store the phone number. Add (or override) the functions to print and store the appropriate information. Use constructors to automatically initialize the data members.

   c. Derive the **class addressBookType** from the **class arrayListType,** as defined in this chapter, so that an object of type addressBookType can store objects of type `extPersonType`. An object of type `addressBookType` should be able to process a maximum of 500 entries. Add necessary operations to the `class addressBookType` so that the program should perform the following operations:

   i.   Load the data into the address book from a disk.

   ii.   Search for a person by last name.

   iii.   Print the address, phone number, and date of birth (if it exists) of a given person.

   iv.   Print the names of the people whose birthdays are in a given month or between two given dates.

   v.   Print the names of all the people having the same status, such as family, friend, or business.

   vi.   Print the names of all the people between two last names.

10. **(Safe Arrays)** In C++, there is no check to determine whether the array index is out of bounds. During program execution, an out-of-bound array index can cause serious problems. Also, recall that in C++ the array index starts at 0.

    Design a `class safeArray` that solves the out-of-bound array index problem and allows the user to begin the array index starting at any integer, positive or negative. Every object of type `safeArray` should be an array of type `int`. During execution, when accessing an array component, if the index is out of bounds, the program must terminate with an appropriate error message. For example,

    ```
    safeArray list(2,13);
    safeArray yourList(-5,9);
    ```

    In this example, `list` is an array of 11 components, the component type is `int`, and the components are `list[2]`, `list[3]`, ..., `list[12]`. Also, `yourList` is an array of 15 components, the component type is `int`, and the components are `yourList[-5]`, `yourlist[-4]`, ..., `yourList[0]`, ..., `yourList[8]`.

11. Programming Exercise 10 processes only `int` arrays. Redesign the `class safeArray` using class templates so that the class can be used in any application that requires arrays to process data.

12. Design a class to perform various matrix operations. A matrix is a set of numbers arranged in rows and columns. Therefore, every element of a matrix has a row position and a column position. If A is a matrix of 5 rows and 6 columns, we say that matrix A is of the size 5×6 and sometimes denote it as $A_{5 \times 6}$. Clearly, a convenient place to store a matrix is in a two-dimensional array. Two matrices can be added and subtracted if they have the same size. Suppose that $A = [a_{ij}]$ and

$B = [b_{ij}]$ are two matrices of the size $m \times n$, where a_{ij} denotes the element of A in the ith row and the jth column, and so on. The sum and difference of A and B is given by

$$A + B = [a_{ij} + b_{ij}]; \qquad A - B = [a_{ij} - b_{ij}]$$

The multiplication of A and B ($A \star B$) is defined only if the number of columns of A are the same as the number of rows of B. If A is of the size $m \times n$ and B is of the size $n \times t$, then $A \star B = [c_{ik}]$ is of the size $m \times t$ and the element c_{ik} is given by the formula

$$c_{ik} = a_{i1}b_{1k} + a_{i2}b_{2k} + \ldots + a_{in}b_{nk}$$

Design and implement a **class matrixType** that can store a matrix of any size. Overload the operators +, -, and * to perform the addition, subtraction, and multiplication operations, respectively, and overload the operator << to output a matrix. Also, write a test program to test various operations on matrices.

13. The **class largeIntegers** in Programming Exercise 16, in Chapter 2, is designed to process large integers of at most 100 digits. Using dynamic arrays, redesign this class so that integers of any digits can be added and/or subtracted. Also overload the multiplication operator to multiply large integers.

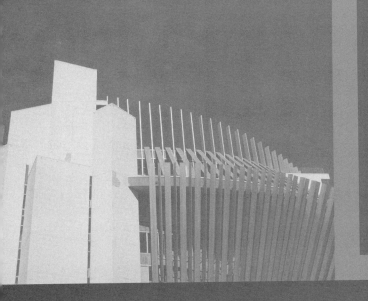

STANDARD TEMPLATE LIBRARY (STL) I

Chapter 2 introduced and examined templates. With the help of class templates, we developed (and used) a generic code to process lists. For example, in Chapter 3, we used the **class arrayListType** to process a list of integers and a list of strings. In Chapters 5, 7, and 8, we will study the three most important data structures: linked lists, stacks, and queues. In Chapter 5, using class templates, we will develop a generic code to process linked lists. In addition, using the second principle, inheritance, of object-oriented programming (OOP), we will develop a generic code to process ordered lists. Then, in Chapters 7 and 8, we will use class templates to develop a generic code to implement stacks and queues. Along the way, you will see that a template is a powerful tool that promotes code reuse.

C++ is equipped with a Standard Template Library (STL). Among other things, the STL provides class templates to process lists (contiguous or linked), stacks, and queues. This chapter discusses some of the STL's important features, and shows how to use certain tools provided by the STL in a program. Chapter 13 describes the features of the STL not described in this chapter.

In the ensuing chapters, you will learn how to develop your own code to implement and manipulate data, as well as how to use professionally written code.

Components of the STL

The main objective of a program is to manipulate data and generate results. Achieving this goal requires the ability to store data into computer memory, access a particular piece of data, and write algorithms to manipulate the data.

For example, if all the data items are of the same type and we have some idea of the number of data items, we could use an array to store the data. We can then use an index to access a particular component of the array. Using a loop and the array index, we can step through the elements of the array. Algorithms, such as those for initializing the array, sorting, and searching, are used to manipulate the data stored in an array. On the other hand, if we do not want to worry about the size of the data, we can use a linked list, as is described in Chapter 5, to process it. If the data needs to be processed in a Last In First Out (LIFO) manner, we can use a stack (Chapter 7). Similarly, if the data needs to be processed in a First In First Out (FIFO) manner, we can use a queue (Chapter 8).

The STL is equipped with these features to effectively manipulate data. More formally, the STL has three main components:

- Containers
- Iterators
- Algorithms

Containers and iterators are class templates. Iterators are used to step through the elements of a container. Algorithms are used to manipulate data. This chapter discusses some of the containers and iterators. Algorithms are discussed in Chapter 13.

Container Types

Containers are used to manage objects of a given type. The STL containers are classified into three categories:

- Sequence containers (also called sequential containers)
- Associative containers
- Container adapters

Associative containers are described in Chapter 13, and container adapters are described in Chapters 7 and 8.

Sequence Containers

Every object in a sequence container has a specific position. The three predefined sequence containers are as follows:

- `vector`
- `deque`
- `list`

Before discussing container types in general, let us first briefly describe the sequence container `vector`. We do so because vector containers are logically the same as arrays and, therefore, they can be processed like arrays. Also, with the help of vector containers, we can describe several properties that are common to all containers. In fact, all containers use the same names for the common operations. Of course, there are operations that are specific to a container. These operations are discussed when describing a specific container. This chapter discusses `vector` and `deque` containers. Chapter 5 discusses `list` containers.

Sequence Container: `vector`

A vector container stores and manages its objects in a dynamic array. Because an array is a random access data structure, the elements of a vector can be accessed randomly. Item insertion in the middle or beginning of an array is time consuming, especially if the array is large. However, inserting an item at the end is fast.

The name of the class that implements the vector container is `vector`. (Recall that containers are class templates.) The name of the header file containing the `class vector` is `vector`. Thus, to use a vector container in a program, the program must include the following statement:

```
#include <vector>
```

Furthermore, to define an object of type `vector`, we must specify the type of the object because the **class** `vector` is a class template. For example, the statement

```
vector<int> intList;
```

declares `intList` to be a vector and the component type to be **int**. Similarly, the statement

```
vector<string> stringList;
```

declares `stringList` to be a `vector` container and the component type to be `string`.

DECLARING VECTOR OBJECTS

The **class** `vector` contains several constructors, including the default constructor. Therefore, a vector container can be declared and initialized in several ways. Table 4-1 describes how a vector container of a specific type can be declared and initialized.

TABLE 4-1   Various ways to declare and initialize a vector container

Statement	Effect
`vector<elementType> vecList;`	Creates an empty vector, `vecList`, without any elements. (The default constructor is invoked.)
`vector<elementType>` `vecList(otherVecList);`	Creates a vector, `vecList`, and initializes `vecList` to the elements of the vector `otherVecList`. `vecList` and `otherVecList` are of the same type.
`vector<elementType>` `vecList(size);`	Creates a vector, `vecList`, of size `size`. `vecList` is initialized using the default constructor.
`vector<elementType>` `vecList(n, elem);`	Creates a vector, `vecList`, of size n. `vecList` is initialized using n copies of the element `elem`.
`vector<elementType>` `vecList(begin, end);`	Creates a vector, `vecList`. `vecList` is initialized to the elements in the range `[begin, end)`, that is, all elements in the range `begin...end-1`.

EXAMPLE 4-1

a. The following statement declares `intList` to be an empty vector container and the element type is **int**.

```
vector<int> intList;
```

b. The following statement declares `intList` to be a vector container of size 10 and the element type is **int**. The elements of `intList` are initialized to 0.

```
vector<int> intList(10);
```

c. The following statement declares `intList` to be a vector container of size 5 and the element type is **int**. The container `intList` is initialized using the elements of the array.

```
int intArray[5] = {2,4,6,8,10};
vector<int> intList(intArray, intArray + 5);
```

The container `intList` is initialized using the elements of the array `intArray`. That is, `intList = {2,4,6,8,10}`.

Now that we know how to declare a vector sequence container, let us now discuss how to manipulate data stored in a vector container. To do so, we must know the following basic operations:

- Item insertion
- Item deletion
- Stepping through the elements of a vector container

The elements in a vector container can be accessed directly by using the operations given in Table 4-2.

TABLE 4-2 Operations to access the elements of a vector container

Expression	Effect
vecList.**at**(index)	Returns the element at the position specified by index.
vecList[index]	Returns the element at the position specified by index.
vecList.**front**()	Returns the first element. (Does not check whether the container is empty.)
vecList.**back**()	Returns the last element. (Does not check whether the container is empty.)

From Table 4-2, it follows that that the elements in a vector can be processed just as they can in an array. (Recall that in C++, arrays start at location 0. Similarly, the first element in a vector container is at location 0.)

EXAMPLE 4-2

Consider the following statement, which declares `intList` to be a vector container of size 5 and the element type is `int`.

```
vector<int> intList(5);
```

You can use a loop, such as the following, to store elements into `intList`:

```
for (int j = 0; j < 5; j++)
    intList[j] = j;
```

Similarly, you can use a `for` loop to output the elements of `intList`.

The `class vector` provides various operations to process the elements of a vector container. Suppose that `vecList` is a container of type `vector`. Item insertion and deletion in `vecList` can be accomplished using the operations given in Table 4-3. These operations are implemented as member functions of the `class vector` and are shown in bold. Table 4-3 also shows how these operations are used.

TABLE 4-3 Various operations on a vector container

Expression	Effect
vecList.**clear**()	Deletes all elements from the container.
vecList.**erase**(position)	Deletes the element at the position specified by position.
vecList.**erase**(beg, end)	Deletes all elements starting at beg until end−1.
vecList.**insert**(position, elem)	A copy of elem is inserted at the position specified by position. The position of the new element is returned.
vecList.**insert**(position, n, elem)	n copies of elem are inserted at the position specified by position.
vecList.**insert**(position, beg, end)	A copy of the elements, starting at beg until end−1, is inserted into vecList at the position specified by position.

TABLE 4-3 Various operations on a vector container (continued)

Expression	Effect
vecList.**push_back**(elem)	A copy of elem is inserted into vecList at the end.
vecList.**pop_back**()	Deletes the last element.
vecList.**resize**(num)	Changes the number of elements to **num**. If size(), that is, the number of elements in the container increases, the default constructor creates the new elements.
vecList.**resize**(num, elem)	Changes the number of elements to num. If size() increases, the default constructor creates the new elements.

NOTE In Table 4-3, the argument position in STL terminology is called an **iterator**. An iterator works just like a pointer. In general, iterators are used to step through the elements of a container. In other words, with the help of an iterator, we can walk through the elements of a container and process them one at a time. In the next section, we describe how to declare an iterator in a vector container and how to manipulate the data stored in a container. Because iterators are an integral part of the STL, they are discussed in detail in the section "Iterators," located later in this chapter.

The function push_back is quite useful. This function is used to add an element at the end of a container. The container intList of size 5 was declared in Example 4-2. You might think that you can only add five elements to the container intList. However, this is not the case. If you need to add more than five elements, you can use the function push_back. You cannot use the array subscripting operator, as in Example 4-2, to add elements past the position 4 unless you increase the size of the container.

If you do not know the number of elements you need to store in a vector container, then when you declare the vector container you do not need to specify its size (see Example 4-3). In this case, you can use the function push_back, as shown in Examples 4-3 and 4-5, to add elements into a vector container.

EXAMPLE 4-3

The following statement declares `intList` to be a vector container of size 0.

```
vector<int> intList;
```

To add elements into `intList`, we can use the function `push_back` as follows:

```
intList.push_back(34);
intList.push_back(55);
```

After these statements execute, the size of `intList` is 2 and `intList` = {34, 55}. Of course, you could have used the `resize` function to increase the size of `intList` and then use the array subscripting operator. However, at times, the `push_back` function is more convenient because it does not need to know the size of the container; it simply adds elements at the end.

Declaring an Iterator to a Vector Container

Even though we can process a vector container just like an array using the array subscripting operator, there are situations where we would like to process the elements of a vector container using an iterator. (Recall that an iterator is just like a pointer.) For example, suppose that we want to insert an element at a specific position in a vector container. Because the element is to be inserted at a specific position, this would require shifting the elements of the container (unless the element is added at the end). Of course, we must also think about the size of the container. To make element(s) insertion convenient, the **class vector** provides the function `insert` to insert the elements at a specific position in a vector container. However, to use the function `insert`, the position where to insert the element(s) must be specified by an iterator. Similarly, the function `erase`, to remove an element, also requires the use of an iterator. This section describes how to declare and use an iterator on a vector container.

The **class** vector contains a **typedef** iterator, which is declared as a **public** member. An iterator to a vector container is declared using the **typedef** iterator. For example, the statement

```
vector<int>::iterator intVecIter;
```

declares `intVecIter` to be an iterator into a vector container of type `int`.

Because `iterator` is a `typedef` defined inside the `class vector`, we must use the container name (`vector`), container element type, and scope resolution operator to use the `typedef iterator`.

Suppose that the iterator `intVecIter` points to an element of a vector container whose elements are of type `int`. The expression

```
++intVecIter
```

advances the iterator `intVecIter` to the next element into the container. The expression

```
*intVecIter
```

returns the element at the current iterator position.

Note that these operations are the same as the operations on pointers, discussed in Chapter 3. Recall that when used as a unary operator, `*` is called the dereferencing operator.

We now discuss how to use an iterator into a vector container to manipulate the data stored into it. Suppose that we have the following statements:

```
vector<int> intList;                    //Line 1
vector<int>::iterator intVecIter;       //Line 2
```

The statement in Line 1 declares `intList` to be a `vector` container and the element type to be `int`. The statement in Line 2 declares `intVecIter` to be an iterator into a `vector` container whose element type is `int`.

Containers and the Functions begin and end

Every container contains the member functions **begin** and **end**. The function `begin` returns the position of the first element into the container; the function `end` returns the position of the last element into the container. These functions have no parameters.

After the following statement executes:

```
intVecIter = intList.begin();
```

the iterator `intVecIter` points to the first element into the container `intList`.

The following `for` loop uses an iterator to output the elements of `intList` onto the standard output device:

```
for (intVecIter = intList.begin(); intVecIter != intList.end();
                                   intVecList)
    cout << *intVecIter << " ";
```

EXAMPLE 4-4

Consider the following statements:

```
int intArray[7] = {1, 3, 5, 7, 9, 11, 13};      //Line 1
vector<int> vecList(intArray, intArray + 7};    //Line 2
vector<int>::iterator  intVecIter;              //Line 3
```

The statement in Line 2 declares and initializes the vector container `vecList`. Now consider the following statements:

```
intVecIter = vecList.begin();       //Line 4
++intVecIter;                       //Line 5
vecList.insert(intVecIter, 22};     //Line 6
```

The statement in Line 4 initializes the iterator `intVecIter` to the first element of `vecList`. The statement in Line 5 advances `intVecIter` to the second element of `vecList`. The statement in Line 6 inserts 22 at the position specified by `intVecIter`. After the statement in Line 6 executes, `vecList = {1, 22, 3, 5, 7, 9, 11, 13}`. Notice that the size of the container also increases.

The `class vector` also contains member functions that can be used to find the number of elements currently in the container, the maximum number of elements that can be inserted in a container, and so on. Table 4-4 describes some of these operations. (Suppose that `vecCont` is a vector container.)

TABLE 4-4 Functions to determine the size of a vector container

Expression	Effect
vecCont.**capacity**()	Returns the maximum number of elements that can be inserted into the container **vecCont** without reallocation.
vecCont.**empty**()	Returns **true** if the container **vecCont** is empty and **false** otherwise.
vecCont.**size**()	Returns the number of elements currently in the container **vecCont**.
vecCont.**max_size**()	Returns the maximum number of elements that can be inserted into the container **vecCont**.

Example 4-5 illustrates how to use a vector container in a program and how to process the elements into a vector container.

EXAMPLE 4-5

```
//************************************************************
// Author: D.S. Malik
//
// This program illustrates how to use a vector container in a
// program.
//************************************************************

#include <iostream>                              //Line 1
#include <vector>                                //Line 2

using namespace std;                             //Line 3
```

```
int main()                                              //Line 4
{                                                       //Line 5
    vector<int>  intList;                               //Line 6

    intList.push_back(13);                              //Line 7
    intList.push_back(75);                              //Line 8
    intList.push_back(28);                              //Line 9
    intList.push_back(35);                              //Line 10

    cout << "Line 11: List Elements: ";                 //Line 11
    for (int i = 0; i < 4; i++)                         //Line 12
        cout << intList[i] << " ";                      //Line 13
    cout << endl;                                       //Line 14

    for (int i = 0; i < 4; i++)                         //Line 15
        intList[i] *= 2;                                //Line 16

    cout << "Line 17: List Elements: ";                 //Line 17
    for (int i = 0; i < 4; i++)                         //Line 18
        cout << intList[i] << " ";                      //Line 19
    cout << endl;                                       //Line 20

    vector<int>::iterator  listIt;                      //Line 21

    cout << "Line 22: List Elements: ";                 //Line 22
    for (listIt = intList.begin();
              listIt != intList.end(); ++listIt)        //Line 23
        cout << *listIt << " ";                         //Line 24
    cout << endl;                                       //Line 25

    listIt = intList.begin();                           //Line 26
    ++listIt;                                           //Line 27
    ++listIt;                                           //Line 28
    intList.insert(listIt, 88);                         //Line 29

    cout << "Line 30: List Elements: ";                 //Line 30
    for (listIt = intList.begin();
              listIt != intList.end(); ++listIt)        //Line 31
        cout << *listIt << " ";                         //Line 32
    cout << endl;                                       //Line 33

    return 0;                                           //Line 34
}                                                       //Line 35
```

Sample Run:

```
Line 11: List Elements: 13 75 28 35
Line 17: List Elements: 26 150 56 70
Line 22: List Elements: 26 150 56 70
Line 30: List Elements: 26 150 88 56 70
```

The statement in Line 6 declares a vector container (or vector for short), `intList`, of type `int`. The statements in Lines 7 through 10 use the operation `push_back` to insert four numbers—13, 75, 28, and 35—into `intList`. The statements in Lines 12 and 13 use the `for` loop and the array subscripting operator `[]` to output the elements of `intList`. In the output, see the line marked Line 11, which contains the output of Lines 11 through 14 of the program. The statements in Lines 15 and 16 use a **for** loop to double the value of each element of `intList`; the statements in Lines 18 and 19 output the elements of `intList`. In the output, see the line marked Line 17, which contains the output of Lines 17 through 20 of the program.

The statement in Line 21 declares `listIt` to be a vector iterator that processes any vector container whose elements are of type `int`. Using the iterator `listIt`, the statements in Lines 23 and 24 output the elements of `intList`. After the statement in Line 26 executes, `listIt` points to the first element of `intList`. The statements in Lines 27 and 28 advance `listIt` twice; after these statements execute, `listIt` points to the third element of `intList`. The statement in Line 29 inserts 88 into `intList` at the position specified by the iterator `listIt`. Because `listIt` points to the component at position 2 (the third element of `intList`), 88 is inserted at position 2 in `intList`; that is, 88 becomes the third element of `intList`. The statements in Lines 31 and 32 output the modified `intList`.

Member Functions Common to All Containers

The previous section discussed vector containers. We now look at operations that are common to all containers. For example, every container class has a default constructor, several constructors with parameters, a destructor, a function to insert an element into a container, and so on.

Recall that a class encapsulates data, and operations on that data, into a single unit. Because every container is a class, several operations are directly defined for a container and are provided as part of the class definition. Also, recall that the operations to manipulate the data are implemented with the help of functions and are called member functions of the class. Table 4-5 describes the member functions that are common to all containers; that is, these functions are included as members of the class template implementing the container.

Suppose that `ct`, `ct1`, and `ct2` are containers of the same type. Table 4-5 shows the name of the function in bold, and shows how a function is called.

TABLE 4-5 Member functions common to all containers

Member function	Effect
Default constructor	Initializes the object to an empty state.
Constructor with parameters	In addition to the default constructor, every container has constructors with parameters. We describe these constructors when we discuss a specific container.
Copy constructor	Executes when an object is passed as a parameter by value, and when an object is declared and initialized using another object of the same type.
Destructor	Executes when the object goes out of scope.
ct.**empty**()	Returns true if container ct is empty and false otherwise.
ct.**size**()	Returns the number of elements currently in container ct.
ct.**max_size**()	Returns the maximum number of elements that can be inserted into container ct.
ct1.**swap**(ct2)	Swaps the elements of containers ct1 and ct2.
ct.**begin**()	Returns an iterator to the first element into container ct.
ct.**end**()	Returns an iterator to the last element into container ct.
ct.**rbegin**()	Reverse begin. Returns a pointer to the last element into container ct. This function is used to process the elements of ct in reverse.
ct.**rend**()	Reverse end. Returns a pointer to the first element into container ct.
ct.**insert**(position, elem)	Inserts elem into container ct at the position specified by the argument position. Note that here position is an iterator.
ct.**erase**(begin, end)	Deletes all elements between begin...end-1 from container ct.

4

TABLE 4-5 Member functions common to all containers (continued)

Member function	Effect
ct.**clear**()	Deletes all elements from the container. After a call to this function, container ct is empty.
Operator functions	
ct1 = ct2	Copies the elements of ct2 into ct1. After this operation, the elements in both containers are the same.
ct1 == ct2	Returns true if containers ct1 and ct2 are equal and false otherwise.
ct1 != ct2	Returns true if containers ct1 and ct2 are not equal and false otherwise.
ct1 < ct2	Returns true if container ct1 is less than container ct2 and false otherwise.
ct1 <= ct2	Returns true if container ct1 is less than or equal to container ct2 and false otherwise.
ct1 > ct2	Returns true if container ct1 is greater than container ct2 and false otherwise.
ct1 >= ct2	Returns true if container ct1 is greater than or equal to container ct2 and false otherwise.

NOTE | Because these operations are common to all containers, when discussing a specific container, to save space, these operations are not listed again.

Member Functions Common to Sequence Containers

The previous section described the member functions that are common to all containers. In addition to these member functions, Table 4-6 describes the member functions that are common to all sequence containers—that is, containers of type vector, deque, and list. (Suppose that seqCont is a sequence container.)

TABLE 4-6 Member functions common to all sequence containers

Expression	Effect
seqCont.**insert**(position, elem)	A copy of elem is inserted at the position specified by position. The position of the new element is returned.
seqCont.**insert**(position, n, elem)	n copies of elem are inserted at the position specified by position.
seqCont.**insert**(position, beg, end)	A copy of the elements, starting at beg until end−1, are inserted into seqCont at the position specified by position.
seqCont.**push_back**(elem)	A copy of elem is inserted into seqCont at the end.
seqCont.**pop_back**()	Deletes the last element.
seqCont.**erase**(position)	Deletes the element at the position specified by position.
seqCont.**erase**(beg, end)	Deletes all elements starting at beg until end−1.
seqCont.**clear**()	Deletes all elements from the container.
seqCont.**resize**(num)	Changes the number of elements to num. If size() grows, the new elements are created by their default constructor.
seqCont.**resize**(num, elem)	Changes the number of elements to num. If size() grows, the new elements are copies of elem.

The copy Algorithm

Example 4-5 used a for loop to output the elements of a vector container. The STL provides a convenient way to output the elements of a container with the help of the function copy. The function copy is provided as a part of the generic algorithms of the STL and can be used with any container type as well as arrays. Because we frequently need to output the elements of a container, before continuing with our discussion of containers, let us describe this function.

NOTE Like the function copy, the STL contains many functions as part of generic algorithms, which are described in Chapter 13.

The function copy does more than output the elements of a container. In general, it allows us to copy the elements from one place to another. For example, to output the elements of a vector or to copy the elements of a vector into another vector, we can use the function copy. The prototype of the function template copy is as follows:

```
template <class inputIterator, class outputIterator>
outputItr copy(inputIterator first1, inputIterator last,
               outputIterator first2);
```

The parameter first1 specifies the position from which to begin copying the elements; the parameter last specifies the end position. The parameter first2 specifies where to copy the elements. Therefore, the parameters first1 and last specify the source, and the parameter first2 specifies the destination. Note that the elements within the range first1...last−1 are copied.

The definition of the function template copy is contained in the header file algorithm. Thus, to use the function copy, the program must include the statement

```
#include <algorithm>
```

The function copy works as follows. Consider the following statement:

```
int intArray[] = {5, 6, 8, 3, 40, 36, 98, 29, 75};    //Line 1
vector<int> vecList(9);                                //Line 2
```

This statement in Line 1 creates the array intArray of nine components—that is,

```
intArray = {5, 6, 8, 3, 40, 36, 98, 29, 75}
```

Here intArray[0] = 5, intArray[1] = 6, and so on.

The statement in Line 2 creates an empty container of nine components of type vector and the element type int.

Recall that the array name, intArray, is actually a pointer and contains the base address of the array. Therefore, intArray points to the first component of the array, intArray + 1 points to the second component of the array, and so on.

Now consider the statement

```
copy(intArray, intArray+9, vecList.begin());    //Line 3
```

This statement copies the elements starting at the location intArray, which is the first component of the array intArray, until intArray + 9 − 1 (that is, intArray + 8), which is the last element of the array intArray, into the container vecList. (Note that here first1 is intArray, last is intArray + 9, and first2 is vecList.begin().) After the statement in Line 3 executes,

```
vecList = {5, 6, 8, 3, 40, 36, 98, 29, 75}   //Line 4
```

Next, consider the statement

```
copy(intArray + 1, intArray + 9, intArray);   //Line 5
```

Here `first1` is `intArray + 1`; that is, `first1` points to the location of the second element of the array `intArray`, and `last` is `intArray + 9`. Also, `first2` is `intArray`; that is, `first2` points to the location of the first element of the array `intArray`. Therefore, the second array element is copied into the first array component, the third array element into the second array component, and so on. After the statement in Line 5 executes,

```
intArray[] = {6, 8, 3, 40, 36, 98, 29, 75, 75}     //Line 6
```

Notice that the elements of the array `intArray` are shifted to the left by one position.

Suppose that `vecList` is as in Line 4. Consider the statement

```
copy(vecList.rbegin() + 2, vecList.rend(),
                         vecList.rbegin());  //Line 7
```

Recall that the function `rbegin` (reverse begin) returns a pointer to the last element into a container; it is used to process the elements of a container in reverse. Therefore, `vecList.rbegin() + 2` returns a pointer to the third-to-last element into the container `vecList`. Similarly, the function `rend` (reverse end) returns a pointer to the first element of a container. The previous statement shifts the elements of the container `vecList` to the right by two positions. After the statement in Line 7 executes, the container `vecList` is as follows:

```
vecList = {5, 6, 5, 6, 8, 3, 40, 36, 98}
```

Example 4-6 shows the effect of the preceding statements using a C++ program. Before discussing Example 4-6, let us describe a special type of iterator, called **ostream iterators**, which work well with the function `copy` to copy the elements of a container to an output device.

ostream Iterator and Function copy

One way to output the contents of a container is to use a **for** loop and the function `begin` to initialize the **for** loop control variable, and to use the function `end` to set the limit. Alternatively, the function `copy` can be used to output the elements of a container. In this case, an iterator of type `ostream` specifies the destination (`ostream` iterators are discussed in detail later in this chapter). When we create an iterator of type `ostream`, we also specify the type of element the iterator will output.

The following statement illustrates how to create an `ostream` iterator of type **int**:

```
ostream_iterator<int> screen(cout, " "); //Line A
```

This statement creates `screen` to be an `ostream` iterator with the element type `int`. The iterator `screen` has two arguments: the object `cout` and a space. Thus, the iterator `screen` is initialized using the object `cout`, and when this iterator outputs the elements they are separated by a space.

The statement

```
copy(intArray, intArray+9, screen);
```

outputs the elements of `intArray` on the screen.

Similarly, the statement

```
copy(vecList.begin(), vecList.end(), screen);
```

outputs the elements of the container `vecList` on the screen.

We will frequently use the function `copy` to output the elements of a container by using an `ostream` iterator. Also, until we discuss `ostream` iterators in detail, we will use statements similar to the statement in Line A to create an `ostream` iterator.

Of course, we can directly specify an `ostream` iterator in the function `copy`. For example, the statement (shown previously)

```
copy(vecList.begin(), vecList.end(), screen);
```

is equivalent to the statement

```
copy(vecList.begin(), vecList.end(), ostream_iterator<int>(cout, " "));
```

Finally, the statement

```
copy(vecList.begin(), vecList.end(),
                     ostream_iterator<int>(cout, ", "));
```

outputs the elements of `vecList` with a comma and space between them.

Example 4-6 illustrates how to use the function `copy` and an `ostream` iterator in a program.

EXAMPLE 4-6

```
//**********************************************************
// Author: D.S. Malik
//
// This program illustrates how to use the function copy and
// an ostream iterator in a program.
//**********************************************************

#include <algorithm>                                     //Line 1
#include <vector>                                         //Line 2
#include <iterator>                                       //Line 3
#include <iostream>                                       //Line 4
```

```
using namespace std;                                        //Line 5

int main()                                                  //Line 6
{                                                           //Line 7
    int intArray[] = {5, 6, 8, 3, 40, 36, 98, 29, 75};      //Line 8

    vector<int> vecList(9);                                 //Line 9

    ostream_iterator<int> screen(cout, " ");                //Line 10

    cout << "Line 11: intArray: ";                          //Line 11
    copy(intArray, intArray + 9, screen);                   //Line 12
    cout << endl;                                           //Line 13

    copy(intArray, intArray + 9, vecList.begin());          //Line 14

    cout << "Line 15: vecList: ";                           //Line 15
    copy(vecList.begin(), vecList.end(), screen);           //Line 16
    cout << endl;                                           //Line 17

    copy(intArray + 1, intArray + 9, intArray);             //Line 18
    cout << "Line 19: After shifting the elements one "
         << "position to the left, intArray: " << endl;     //Line 19
    copy(intArray, intArray + 9, screen);                   //Line 20
    cout << endl;                                           //Line 21

    copy(vecList.rbegin() + 2, vecList.rend(),
                        vecList.rbegin());                  //Line 22
    cout << "Line 23: After shifting the elements down "
         << "by two positions, vecList:" << endl;           //Line 23
    copy(vecList.begin(), vecList.end(), screen);           //Line 24
    cout << endl;                                           //Line 25

    return 0;                                               //Line 26
}                                                           //Line 27
```

Sample Run:

```
Line 11: intArray: 5 6 8 3 40 36 98 29 75
Line 15: vecList: 5 6 8 3 40 36 98 29 75
Line 19: After shifting the elements one position to the left, intArray:
6 8 3 40 36 98 29 75 75
Line 23: After shifting the elements down by two positions, vecList:
5 6 5 6 8 3 40 36 98
```

Sequence Container: deque

This section describes the deque sequence containers. The term **deque** stands for double-ended queue. Deque containers are implemented as dynamic arrays in such a way that the elements can be inserted at both ends. Thus, a deque can expand in either direction. Elements can also be inserted in the middle. Inserting elements at the beginning or at the end is fast; inserting elements in the middle, however, is time consuming because the elements in the queue need to be shifted.

The name of the class defining the deque containers is deque. The definition of the class deque, and the functions to implement the various operations on a deque object, are also contained in the header file deque. Therefore, to use a deque container in a program, the program must include the following statement:

```
#include <deque>
```

The class deque contains several constructors. Thus, a deque object can be initialized in various ways when it is declared, as described in Table 4–7.

TABLE 4-7 Various ways to declare a deque object

Statement	Effect
deque<elementType> deq;	Creates an empty deque container without any elements. (The default constructor is invoked.)
deque<elementType> deq(otherDeq);	Creates a deque container, deq, and initializes deq to the elements of otherDeq; deq and otherDeq are of the same type.
deque<elementType> deq(size);	Creates a deque container, deq, of size size. deq is initialized using the default constructor.
deque<elementType> deq(n, elem);	Creates a deque container, deq, of size n. deq is initialized using n copies of the element elem.
deque<elementType> deq(begin, end);	Creates a deque container, deq. deq is initialized to the elements in the range [begin, end)—that is, all elements in the range begin...end-1.

In addition to the operations that are common to all containers (see Table 4-6), Table 4-8 describes the operations that can be used to manipulate the elements of a deque container. The name of the function implementing the operations is shown in bold. The statement also shows how to use a particular function. Suppose that deq is a deque container.

TABLE 4-8 Various operations that can be performed on a deque object

Expression	Effect
deq.**assign**(n,elem)	Assigns n copies of elem.
deq.**assign**(beg,end)	Assigns all the elements in the range beg...end-1.
deq.**push_front**(elem)	Inserts elem at the beginning of deq.
deq.**pop_front**()	Removes the first element from deq.
deq.**at**(index)	Returns the element at the position specified by index.
deq[index]	Returns the element at the position specified by index.
deq.**front**()	Returns the first element. (Does not check whether the container is empty.)
deq.**back**()	Returns the last element. (Does not check whether the container is empty.)

Example 4-7 illustrates how to use a deque container in a program.

EXAMPLE 4-7

```
//*************************************************************
// Author: D.S. Malik
//
// This program illustrates how to use a deque container in a
// program.
//*************************************************************

#include <iostream>                                   //Line 1
#include <deque>                                      //Line 2
#include <algorithm>                                  //Line 3
#include <iterator>                                   //Line 4

using namespace std;                                  //Line 5

int main()                                            //Line 6
{                                                     //Line 7
    deque<int>  intDeq;                               //Line 8
    ostream_iterator<int> screen(cout, " ");          //Line 9

    intDeq.push_back(13);                             //Line 10
    intDeq.push_back(75);                             //Line 11
```

```
    intDeq.push_back(28);                                 //Line 12
    intDeq.push_back(35);                                 //Line 13

    cout << "Line 14: intDeq: ";                          //Line 14
    copy(intDeq.begin(), intDeq.end(), screen);           //Line 15
    cout << endl;                                         //Line 16

    intDeq.push_front(0);                                 //Line 17
    intDeq.push_back(100);                                //Line 18

    cout << "Line 19: After adding two more "
         << "elements, one at the front " << endl
         << "          and one at the back, intDeq: ";    //Line 19
    copy(intDeq.begin(), intDeq.end(), screen);           //Line 20
    cout << endl;                                         //Line 21

    intDeq.pop_front();                                   //Line 22
    intDeq.pop_front();                                   //Line 23

    cout << "Line 24: After removing the first "
         << "two elements, intDeq: ";                     //Line 24
    copy(intDeq.begin(), intDeq.end(), screen);           //Line 25
    cout << endl;                                         //Line 26

    intDeq.pop_back();                                    //Line 27
    intDeq.pop_back();                                    //Line 28

    cout << "Line 29: After removing the last "
         << "two elements, intDeq = ";                    //Line 29
    copy(intDeq.begin(), intDeq.end(), screen);           //Line 30
    cout << endl;                                         //Line 31

    deque<int>::iterator  deqIt;                          //Line 32

    deqIt = intDeq.begin();                               //Line 33
    ++deqIt;    //deqIt points to the second element      //Line 34
    intDeq.insert(deqIt, 444);                            //Line 35
    cout << "Line 36: After inserting 444, intDeq:  ";    //Line 36
    copy(intDeq.begin(), intDeq.end(), screen);           //Line 37
    cout << endl;                                         //Line 38

    return 0;                                             //Line 39
}                                                         //Line 40
```

Sample Run:

```
Line 14:  intDeq: 13 75 28 35
Line 19: After adding two more elements, one at the front
         and one at the back, intDeq: 0 13 75 28 35 100
Line 24: After removing the first two elements, intDeq: 75 28 35 100
Line 29: After removing the last two elements, intDeq = 75 28
Line 36: After inserting 444, intDeq:  75 444 28
```

The statement in Line 8 declares a `deque` container `intDeq` of type `int`; that is, all the elements of `intDeq` are of type `int`. The statement in Line 9 declares `screen` to be an `ostream` iterator initialized to the standard output device. The statements in Lines 10 through 13 use the `push_back` operation to insert four numbers—13, 75, 28, and 35—into `intDeq`. The statement in Line 15 outputs the elements of `intDeq`. In the output, see the line marked Line 14, which contains the output of the statements in Lines 14 through 16 of the program.

The statement in Line 17 inserts 0 at the beginning of `intDeq`. The statement in Line 18 inserts 100 at the end of `intDeq`. The statement in Line 20 outputs the modified `intDeq`.

The statements in Lines 22 and 23 use the operation `pop_front` to remove the first two elements of `intDeq`; the statement in Line 25 outputs the modified `intDeq`. The statements in Lines 27 and 28 use the operation `pop_back` to remove the last two elements of `intDeq`; the statement in Line 30 outputs the modified `intDeq`.

The statement in Line 32 declares `deqIt` to be a `deque` iterator that processes all `deque` containers whose elements are of type `int`. After the statement in Line 33 executes, `deqIt` points to the first element of `intDeq`. The statement in Line 34 advances `deqIt` to the next element of `intDeq`. The statement in Line 35 inserts 444 into `intDeq` at the position specified by `deqIt`. The statement in Line 37 outputs `intDeq`.

Iterators

Examples 4-5 through 4-7 further clarify that iterators are quite important to efficiently process the elements of a container. Let us discuss iterators in some detail.

Iterators work just like pointers. In general, an iterator points to the elements of a container (sequence or associative). Thus, with the help of iterators, we can successively access each element of a container.

The two most common operations on iterators are ++ (the increment operator) and * (the dereferencing operator). Suppose that `cntItr` is an iterator into a container. The statement

```
++cntItr;
```

advances `cntItr` so that it points to the next element in the container. The statement

```
*cntItr;
```

returns the value of the element of the container pointed to by `cntItr`.

Types of Iterators

There are five types of iterators: input iterators, output iterators, forward iterators, bidirectional iterators, and random access iterators. In the next few sections, we describe these iterators.

Input Iterators

Input iterators, with read access, step forward element-by-element and so return the values element-by-element. These iterators are provided for reading data from an input stream.

Suppose `inputIterator` is an input iterator. Table 4-9 describes the operations on `inputIterator`.

TABLE 4-9   Operations on an input iterator

Expression	Effect
`*inputIterator`	Gives access to the element to which `inputIterator` points.
`inputIterator->member`	Gives access to the member of the element.
`++inputIterator`	Moves forward, returns the new position (preincrement).
`inputIterator++`	Moves forward, returns the old position (postincrement).
`inputIt1 == inputIt2`	Returns `true` if the two iterators are the same and `false` otherwise.
`inputIt1 != inputIt2`	Returns `true` if the two iterators are not the same and `false` otherwise.
`Type(inputIterator)`	Copies the iterators.

Output Iterators

Output iterators, with write access, step forward element-by-element. These iterators are typically used for writing data to an output stream.

Suppose `outputIterator` is an output iterator. Table 4-10 describes the operations on `outputIterator`.

TABLE 4-10 Operations on an output iterator

Expression	Effect
`*outputIterator = value;`	Writes the `value` at the position specified by the `outputIterator`.
`++outputIterator`	Moves forward, returns the new position (preincrement).
`outputIterator++`	Moves forward, returns the old position (postincrement).
`Type(outputIterator)`	Copies the iterators.

 NOTE Output iterators cannot be used to iterate over a range twice. Thus, if we write data at the same position twice, there is no guarantee that the new value will replace the old value.

Forward Iterators

Forward iterators combine all of the functionality of input iterators and almost all of the functionality of output iterators. Suppose `forwardIterator` is a forward iterator. Table 4-11 describes the operations on `forwardIterator`.

TABLE 4-11 Operations on a forward iterator

Expression	Effect
`*forwardIterator`	Gives access to the element to which `forwardIterator` points.
`forwardIterator->member`	Gives access to the member of the element.
`++forwardIterator`	Moves forward, returns the new position (preincrement).
`forwardIterator++`	Moves forward, returns the old position (postincrement).
`forwardIt1 == forwardIt2`	Returns `true` if the two iterators are the same and `false` otherwise.
`forwardIt1 != forwardIt2`	Returns `true` if the two iterators are not the same and `false` otherwise.
`forwardIt1 = forwardIt2`	Assignment.

NOTE A forward iterator can refer to the same element in the same collection and process the same element more than once.

Bidirectional Iterators

Bidirectional iterators are forward iterators that can also iterate backward over the elements. Suppose `biDirectionalIterator` is a bidirectional iterator. The operations defined for forward iterators (Table 4-11) are also applicable to bidirectional iterators. To step backward, the decrement operations are also defined for `biDirectionalIterator`. Table 4-12 shows additional operations on a bidirectional iterator.

TABLE 4-12 Additional operations on a bidirectional iterator

Expression	Effect
`--biDirectionalIterator`	Moves backward, returns the new position (predecrement).
`biDirectionalIterator--`	Moves backward, returns the old position (postdecrement).

 NOTE Bidirectional iterators can be used only with containers of type `vector`, `deque`, `list`, `set`, `multiset`, `map`, and `multimap`.

Random Access Iterators

Random access iterators are bidirectional iterators that can randomly process the elements of a container. These iterators can be used with containers of type `vector`, `deque`, `string`, and arrays. The operations defined for bidirectional iterators (for example, Tables 4-11 and 4-12) are also applicable to random access iterators. Table 4-13 describes the additional operations that are defined for random access iterators. (Suppose `rAccessIterator` is a random access iterator.)

TABLE 4-13 Additional operations on a random access iterator

Expression	Effect
rAccessIterator[n]	Accesses the nth element.
rAccessIterator += n	Moves rAccessIterator forward n elements if n >= 0 and backward if n < 0.
rAccessIterator -= n	Moves rAccessIterator backward n elements if n >= 0 and forward if n < 0.
rAccessIterator + n	Returns the iterator of the next nth element.
n + rAccessIterator	Returns the iterator of the next nth element.
rAccessIterator - n	Returns the iterator of the previous nth element.
rAccessIt1 - rAccessIt2	Returns the distance between the iterators rAccessIt1 and rAccessIt2.
rAccessIt1 < rAccessIt2	Returns true if rAccessIt1 is before rAccessIt2 and false otherwise.
rAccessIt1 <= rAccessIt2	Returns true if rAccessIt1 is before or equal to rAccessIt2 and false otherwise.
rAccessIt1 > rAccessIt2	Returns true if rAccessIt1 is after rAccessIt2 and false otherwise.
rAccessIt1 >= rAccessIt2	Returns true if rAccessIt1 is after or equal to rAccessIt2 and false otherwise.

4

Figure 4-1 shows the iterator hierarchy.

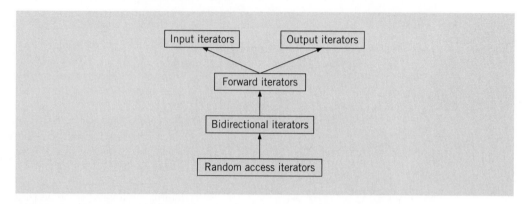

Now that you know the different types of iterators, next we describe how to declare an iterator to a container.

typedef iterator   Every container (sequence or associative) contains a `typedef` `iterator`. Thus, an iterator into a container is declared using the `typedef iterator`. For example, the statement

`vector<int>::iterator intVecIter;`

declares `intVecIter` to be an iterator into a `vector` container of type `int`. Moreover, the iterator `intVecIter` can be used on any `vector<int>`, but not on any other container, such as `vector<double>`, `vector<string>`, and `deque`.

Because `iterator` is a `typedef` defined inside a container (that is, a class) such as `vector`, we must use the appropriate container name, container element type, and the scope resolution operator to use the `typedef iterator`.

typedef const_iterator   Because an iterator works like a pointer, with the help of an iterator into a container and the dereferencing operator, `*`, we can modify the elements of the container. However, if a container is declared as **const**, then we must prevent the iterator from modifying the elements of the container, especially accidentally. To handle this situation, every container contains another **typedef** `const_iterator`. For example, the statement

`vector<int>::const_iterator  intConstVecIt;`

declares `intConstVecIt` to be an iterator into a `vector` container whose elements are of type **int**. The iterator `intConstVecIt` is used to process the elements of those vector containers that are declared as constant vector containers of type `vector<int>`.

An iterator of type `const_iterator` is a read-only iterator.

typedef reverse_iterator Every container also contains the typedef reverse_iterator. An iterator of this type is used to iterate through the elements of a container in reverse.

typedef const_reverse_iterator An iterator of this type is a read-only iterator and is used to iterate through the elements of a container in reverse. It is required if the container is declared as const and we need to iterate through the elements of the container in reverse.

In addition to the previous four typedefs, several other typedefs are common to all containers. Table 4-14 describes them.

TABLE 4-14 Various typedefs common to all containers

typedef	Effect
difference_type	The type of result from subtracting two iterators referring to the same container.
pointer	A pointer to the type of elements stored in the container.
reference	A reference to the type of elements stored in the container.
const_reference	A constant reference to the type of elements stored in the container. A constant reference is read-only.
size_type	The type used to count the elements in a container. This type is also used to index through sequence containers, except list containers.
value_type	The type of container elements.

Stream Iterators

Another useful set of iterators is stream iterators—istream iterators and ostream iterators. This section describes both types of iterators.

istream_iterator The istream iterator is used to input data into a program from an input stream. The class istream_iterator contains the definition of an input stream iterator. The general syntax to use an istream iterator is as follows:

```
istream_iterator<Type> isIdentifier(istream&);
```

where `Type` is either a built-in type or a user-defined class type, for which an input iterator is defined. The identifier `isIdentifier` is initialized using the constructor whose argument is either an `istream` class object such as `cin`, or any publicly defined `istream` subtype, such as `ifstream`.

ostream_iterator The `ostream` iterators are used to output data from a program into an output stream. These iterators were defined earlier in this chapter. We review them here for the sake of completeness.

The `class ostream_iterator` contains the definition of an output stream iterator. The general syntax to use an `ostream` iterator is as follows:

```
ostream_iterator<Type> osIdentifier(ostream&);
```

or

```
ostream_iterator<Type> osIdentifier(ostream&, char* deLimit);
```

where `Type` is either a built-in type or a user-defined class type, for which an output iterator is defined. The identifier `osIdentifier` is initialized using the constructor whose argument is either an `ostream` class object such as `cout`, or any publicly defined `ostream` subtype, such as `ofstream`. In the second form used for declaring an `ostream` iterator, by using the second argument (`deLimit`) of the initializing constructor, we can specify a character separating the output.

PROGRAMMING EXAMPLE: Grade Report

The midsemester point at your local university is approaching. The registrar's office wants to prepare the grade reports as soon as the students' grades are recorded. Some of the students enrolled have not yet paid their tuition, however.

If a student has paid the tuition, the grades are shown on the grade report together with the grade point average (GPA). If a student has not paid the tuition, the grades are not printed. For these students, the grade report contains a message indicating that the grades have been held for nonpayment of the tuition. The grade report also shows the billing amount.

The registrar's office and the business office want your help in writing a program that can analyze the students' data and print the appropriate grade reports. The data is stored in a file in the following form:

```
345
studentName studentID isTuitionPaid numberOfCourses
courseName courseNumber creditHours grade
```

```
courseName courseNumber creditHours grade
...
studentName studentID isTuitionPaid numberOfCourses
courseName courseNumber creditHours grade
courseName courseNumber creditHours grade
...
```

The first line indicates the tuition rate per credit hour. The students' data is given thereafter.

A sample input file follows:

```
345
Lisa Miller 890238 Y 4
Mathematics MTH345 4 A
Physics PHY357 3 B
ComputerSci CSC478 3 B
History HIS356 3 A
...
```

The first line indicates that the tuition rate is $345 per credit hour. Next, the course data for student Lisa Miller is given: Lisa Miller's ID is 890238, she has paid the tuition, and is taking 4 courses. The course number for the mathematics class she is taking is MTH345, the course has 4 credit hours, her midsemester grade is A, and so on.

The desired output for each student is in the following form:

```
Student Name: Lisa Miller
Student ID: 890238
Number of courses enrolled: 4

Course No  Course Name  Credits Grade
CSC478     ComputerSci     3       B
HIS356     History         3       A
MTH345     Mathematics     4       A
PHY357     Physics         3       B

Total number of credits: 13
Midsemester GPA: 3.54
```

This output shows that the courses must be ordered according to the course number. To calculate the GPA, we assume that the grade A is equivalent to 4 points, B is equivalent to 3 points, C is equivalent to 2 points, D is equivalent to 1 point, and F is equivalent to 0 points.

Input A file containing the data in the form given previously. For easy reference in the rest of the discussion, let us assume that the name of the input file is stData.txt.

Output A file containing the output of the form given previously. Let us assume that the name of the output file is stDataOut.txt.

PROBLEM
ANALYSIS
AND
ALGORITHM
DESIGN

We must first identify the main components of the program. The university has students, and every student takes courses. Thus, the two main components are the student and the course.

Let us first describe the component course.

Course

The main characteristics of a course are the course name, course number, and number of credit hours. Although the grade a student receives is not really a characteristic of a course, to simplify the program this component also includes the student's grade.

Some of the basic operations that need to be performed on an object of the course type are as follows:

1. Set the course information.
2. Print the course information.
3. Show the credit hours.
4. Show the course number.
5. Show the grade.

The following class defines the course as an ADT:

```
class courseType
{
public:
    void setCourseInfo(string cName, string cNo,
                       char grade, int credits);
      //Function to set the course information
      //The course information is set according to the
      //incoming parameters.
      //Postcondition: courseName = cName; courseNo = cNo;
      //       courseGrade = grade; courseCredits = credits;

    void print(ostream& outp, bool isGrade);
      //Function to print the course information
      //If the bool parameter isGrade is true, the grade is
      //shown, otherwise three stars are printed.

    int getCredits();
      //Function to return the credit hours
      //The value of the private data member courseCredits
      //is returned.

    void getCourseNumber(string& cNo);
      //Function to return the course number
      //Postcondition:  cNo = courseNo;

    char getGrade();
      //Function to return the grade for the course
      //The value of the private data member courseGrade
      //is returned.
```

```
    bool operator==(const courseType&) const;
    bool operator!=(const courseType&) const;
    bool operator<=(const courseType&) const;
    bool operator<(const courseType&) const;
    bool operator>=(const courseType&) const;
    bool operator>(const courseType&) const;

    courseType(string cName = "", string cNo = "",
                  char grade = '*', int credits = 0);
      //Constructor
      //The object is initialized according to the parameters.
      //Postcondition: courseName = cName; courseNo = cNo;
      //      courseGrade = grade; courseCredits = credits;

private:
    string courseName;   //variable to store the course name
    string courseNo;     //variable to store the course number
    char courseGrade;    //variable to store the grade
    int courseCredits;   //variable to store the course credits
};
```

Figure 4-2 shows the UML class diagram of the class courseType.

```
                        courseType

-courseName: string
-courseNo: string
-courseGrade: char
-courseCredits: int

+setCourseInfo(string, string, char, int): void
+print(ostream&, bool): void
+getCredits(): int
+getCourseNumber(string&): void
+getGrade(): char
+operator==(const courseType&) const: bool
+operator!=(const courseType&) const: bool
+operator<=(const courseType&) const: bool
+operator<(const courseType&) const: bool
+operator>=(const courseType&) const: bool
+operator>(const courseType&) const: bool
+courseType(string = "", string = "", char = '*', int = 0)
```

FIGURE 4-2 UML class diagram of the class courseType

Next, we discuss the definition of the functions to implement the operations of the class courseType. These definitions are quite straightforward and easy to follow.

The function setCourseInfo sets the values of the private data members according to the values of the parameters. Its definition is as follows:

```
void courseType::setCourseInfo(string cName, string cNo,
                                char grade, int credits)
{
    courseName = cName;
    courseNo = cNo;
    courseGrade = grade;
    courseCredits = credits;
}
```

The function `print` prints the course information. If the `bool` parameter `isGrade` is `true`, the grade is printed on the screen; otherwise, three stars are shown in place of the grade. Also, we print the course name and course number left-justified rather than right-justified (the default). Thus, we need to set the `left` manipulator. This manipulator will be unset before we print the grade and the credit hours. The following steps describe this function:

1. Set the `left` manipulator.

2. Print the course number.

3. Print the course name.

4. Unset the `left` manipulator.

5. Print the credit hours.

6. If `isGrade` is true

    Output the grade
   else
    Output three stars.

The definition of the function `print` is as follows:

```
void courseType::print(ostream& outp, bool isGrade)
{
    outp << left;                               //Step 1
    outp << setw(8) << courseNo << "   ";       //Step 2
    outp << setw(15) << courseName;             //Step 3
    outp.unsetf(ios::left);                     //Step 4
    outp << setw(3) << courseCredits << "   ";  //Step 5

    if (isGrade)                                //Step 6
        outp << setw(4) << courseGrade << endl;
    else
        outp << setw(4) << "***" << endl;
}
```

The constructor is declared with default values. If no values are specified when a `courseType` object is declared, the constructor uses the default to initialize the object. Using the default values, the object's data members are initialized as follows: `courseNo` to blank, `courseName` to blank, `courseGrade` to *, and `creditHours` to 0. Otherwise, the values specified in the object declaration are used to initialize the object. Its definition is as follows:

```
courseType::courseType(string cName, string cNo,
                       char grade, int credits)
{
    setCourseInfo(cName, cNo, grade, credits);
}
```

The definitions of the remaining functions are straightforward.

```
int courseType::getCredits()
{
    return courseCredits;
}
```

```
char courseType::getGrade()
{
    return courseGrade;
}
```

```
void courseType::getCourseNumber(string& cNo)
{
    cNo = courseNo;
}
```

```
bool courseType::operator==(const courseType& right) const
{
    return (courseNo == right.courseNo);
}
```

```
bool courseType::operator!=(const courseType& right) const
{
    return (courseNo != right.courseNo);
}
```

```
bool courseType::operator<=(const courseType& right) const
{
    return (courseNo <= right.courseNo);
}
```

```
bool courseType::operator<(const courseType& right) const
{
    return (courseNo < right.courseNo);
}
```

```
bool courseType::operator>=(const courseType& right) const
{
    return (courseNo >= right.courseNo);
}
```

```
bool courseType::operator>(const courseType& right) const
{
    return (courseNo > right.courseNo);
}
```

Next we discuss the component student.

Student   The main characteristics of a student are the student name, student ID, number of courses in which enrolled, courses in which enrolled, and the grade for each course. Because every student has to pay tuition, we also include a member to indicate whether the student has paid the tuition.

Every student is a person, and every student takes courses. We have already designed a `class personType` to process a person's first name and last name. We have also designed a class to process the information of a course. Thus, we see that we can derive the `class studentType` to keep track of a student's information from the `class personType`, and one member of this class is of type `courseType`. We can add more members as needed.

The basic operations to be performed on an object of type `studentType` are as follows:

1. Set the student information.
2. Print the student information.
3. Calculate the number of credit hours taken.
4. Calculate the GPA.
5. Calculate the billing amount.
6. Because the grade report will print the courses in ascending order, sort the courses according to the course number.

The following class defines `studentType` as an ADT. We assume that a student takes no more than six courses per semester:

```
class studentType: public personType
{
public:
    void setInfo(string fname, string lName, int ID,
                 bool isTPaid,
                 vector<courseType> courses);
      //Function to set the student's information
      //The private data members are set according
      //to the parameters.

    void print(ostream& out, double tuitionRate);
      //Function to print the student's grade report
      //The output is stored in a file specified by the
      //parameter out.

    studentType();
      //Default constructor
      //Postcondition: Data members are initialized to
       //the default values.
```

```
    int getHoursEnrolled();
      //Function to return the credit hours a student
      //is enrolled in.
      //Postcondition: The number of credit hours in which a
      //   student is enrolled is calculated and returned.

    double getGpa();
      //Function to return the grade point average.
      //Postcondition: The GPA is calculated and returned.

    double billingAmount(double tuitionRate);
      //Function to return the tuition fees
      //Postcondition: The tuition fees due is calculated
      //                 and returned.

private:
    int sId;                //variable to store the student ID
    int numberOfCourses;    //variable to store the number
                            //of courses
    bool isTuitionPaid;     //variable to indicate if the tuition
                            //is paid
    vector<courseType> coursesEnrolled; //vector to store the courses
};
```

Figure 4-3 shows the UML class diagram of the class studentType and the inheritance hierarchy.

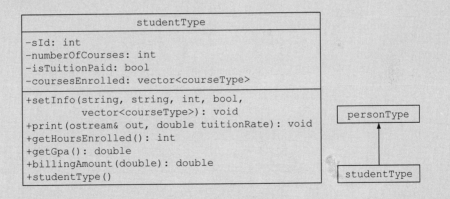

FIGURE 4-3 UML class diagram of the class studentType and the inheritance hierarchy

Next, we discuss the definitions of the functions to implement the operations of the class studentType.

The function setInfo first initializes the private data members according to the incoming parameters. The class studentType is derived from the class personType, and the variables to store the first name and last name are private data members of that class. Therefore, we call the member function `setName` of the class `personType`, and we pass the appropriate variables to set the first and last names. To sort the array `coursesEnrolled` we use the algorithm `sort` provided by the STL.

To use the algorithm `sort`, to sort the vector `coursesEnrolled`, we need to know the position of the first element and last element in the vector `coursesEnrolled`. When we declare the vector `coursesEnrolled`, we did not specify its size. The function `begin` of the `class vector` returns the position of the first element in a vector container; the function `end` specifies the position of the last element. Therefore, `coursesEnrolled.begin()` specifies the position of the first element of the vector `coursesEnrolled`, and `coursesEnrolled.end()` specifies the position of the last element. Now the operator `<=` is overloaded for the `class courseType` and it compares the courses by the course number; the `sort` algorithm will use this criteria to sort the vector `coursesEnrolled`. The following statement sorts the vector `coursesEnrolled`.

```
sort(coursesEnrolled.begin(), coursesEnrolled.end());
```

The definition of the function `setInfo` is as follows:

```
void studentType::setInfo(string fName, string lName, int ID,
                          bool isTPaid,
                          vector<courseType> courses)
{
    setName(fName, lName);

    sId = ID;
    isTuitionPaid = isTPaid;
    numberOfCourses = courses.size();

    coursesEnrolled = courses;

    sort(coursesEnrolled.begin(), coursesEnrolled.end());
}
```

The default constructor initializes the `private` data members to the default values. Note that because the `private` data member `coursesEnrolled` is of type `vector`, the default constructor of the `class vector` executes automatically and initializes `coursesEnrolled`.

```
studentType::studentType()
{
    numberOfCourses = 0;
    sId = 0;
    isTuitionPaid = false;
}
```

The function `print` prints the grade report. If the student has paid his or her tuition, the grades and the GPA are shown. Otherwise, three stars are printed in place of each grade, the GPA is not shown, a message indicates that the grades are being held for nonpayment of the tuition, and the amount due is shown. This function has the following steps:

1. Output the student's name.
2. Output the student's ID.
3. Output the number of courses in which enrolled.
4. Output heading: `CourseNo CourseName Credits Grade`
5. Print each course's information.
6. Print the total credit hours.
7. To output the GPA and billing amount in a fixed decimal format with the decimal point and trailing zeros, set the necessary flag. Also, set the precision to two decimal places.
8. `if isTuitionPaid is true`
   Output the GPA
   `else`
   Output the billing amount and a message about withholding the grades.

This definition of the function `print` is as follows:

```
void studentType::print(ostream& outp, double tuitionRate)
{
    outp << "Student Name: " << personType::getFirstName()
         << " " << personType::getLastName() << endl;    //Step 1

    outp << "Student ID: " << sId << endl;                //Step 2

    outp << "Number of courses enrolled: "
         << numberOfCourses << endl << endl;              //Step 3

    outp << left;
    outp << "Course No" << setw(15) << "  Course Name"
         << setw(8) << "Credits"
         << setw(6) << "Grade" << endl;                   //Step 4

    outp.unsetf(ios::left);

    for (int i = 0; i < numberOfCourses; i++)
        coursesEnrolled[i].print(outp, isTuitionPaid);    //Step 5
    outp << endl;

    outp << "Total number of credit hours: "
         << getHoursEnrolled() << endl;                   //Step 6

    outp << fixed << showpoint << setprecision(2);        //Step 7
```

```
        if (isTuitionPaid)                                      //Step 8
            outp << "Midsemester GPA: " << getGpa() << endl;
        else
        {
            outp << "*** Grades are being held for not paying "
                 << "the tuition. ***" << endl;
            outp << "Amount Due: $" << billingAmount(tuitionRate)
                 << endl;
        }

        outp << "-*-*-*-*-*-*-*-*-*-*-*-*-*-*-*-*-*-*-*-* "
             << "-*-*-*-*-" << endl << endl;
}
```

The function `getHoursEnrolled` calculates and returns the total credit hours that a student is taking. These credit hours are needed to calculate both the GPA and the billing amount. The total credit hours are calculated by adding the credit hours of each course in which the student is enrolled. The credit hours for a course are in the `private` data member of an object of type `courseType`. Therefore, we use the member function `getCredits` of the `class courseType` to retrieve the credit hours. The definition of this function is as follows:

```
int studentType::getHoursEnrolled()
{
    int totalCredits = 0;

    for (int i = 0; i < numberOfCourses; i++)
        totalCredits += coursesEnrolled[i].getCredits();
    return totalCredits;
}
```

If a student has not paid the tuition, the function `billingAmount` calculates and returns the amount due, based on the number of credit hours enrolled. The definition of this function is as follows:

```
double studentType::billingAmount(double tuitionRate)
{
    return tuitionRate * getHoursEnrolled();
}
```

We now discuss the function `getGpa`. This function calculates a student's GPA. To find the GPA, we find the equivalent points for each grade, add the points, and then divide the sum by the total credit hours the student is taking. The definition of this function is as follows:

```
double studentType::getGpa()
{
    double sum = 0.0;
```

```
for (int i = 0; i < numberOfCourses; i++)
{
    switch (coursesEnrolled[i].getGrade())
    {
    case 'A':
        sum += coursesEnrolled[i].getCredits() * 4;
        break;

    case 'B':
        sum += coursesEnrolled[i].getCredits() * 3;
        break;

    case 'C':
        sum += coursesEnrolled[i].getCredits() * 2;
        break;

    case 'D':
        sum += coursesEnrolled[i].getCredits() * 1;
        break;

    case 'F':
        break;

    default:
        cout << "Invalid Course Grade" << endl;
    }
}

if (getHoursEnrolled() != 0)
    return sum / getHoursEnrolled();
else
    return 0;
}
```

MAIN PROGRAM   Now that we have designed the classes courseType and studentType, we will use these classes to complete the program.

Because the function print of the class does the necessary computations to print the final grade report, the main program has very little work to do. In fact, all that is left for the main program is to declare the objects to hold the students' data, load the data into these objects, and then print the grade reports. Because the input is in a file and the output will be sent to a file, we declare stream variables to access the input and output files. Essentially, the main algorithm for the program is as follows:

1. Declare the variables.
2. Open the input file.
3. If the input file does not exist, exit the program.
4. Open the output file.

5. Get the tuition rate.
6. Load the students' data.
7. Print the grade reports.

Variables

To store students' data, we use the vector container, `studentList`, whose elements are of type `studentType`. We also need to store the tuition rate. Because the data will be read from a file, and because the output is sent to a file, we need two stream variables to access the input and output files. Thus, we need the following variables:

```
vector<studentType> studentList; //vector to store the
                                 // students' data

double tuitionRate;     //variable to store the tuition rate

ifstream infile;        //input stream variable
ofstream outfile;       //output stream variable
```

To simplify the complexity of the function `main`, we write a function, `getStudentData`, to load the students' data and another function, `printGradeReports`, to print the grade reports. The next two sections describe these functions.

Function getStudentData

This function has two parameters: a parameter to access the input file and a parameter to access the vector container `studentList`. In pseudocode, the definition of this function is as follows:

For each student in the university,

1. Get the first name, last name, student ID, and `isPaid`.
2. `if isPaid is 'Y'`

        set `isTuitionPaid` to true

    `else`

        set `isTuitionPaid` to false
3. Get the number of courses the student is taking.
4. For each course

    a. Get the course name, course number, credit hours, and grade.

    b. Load the course information into a `courseType` object.

    c. Push the object containing course information into the vector container that stores course data.
5. Load the data into a `studentType` object.
6. Push the object containing student's data into `studentList`.

We need to declare several local variables to read and store the data. The definition of the function `getStudentData` is as follows:

```cpp
void getStudentData(ifstream& infile,
                    vector<studentType> &studentList)
{
        //Local variable
    string fName;       //variable to store the first name
    string lName;       //variable to store the last name
    int ID;             //variable to store the student ID
    int noOfCourses;    //variable to store the number of courses
    char isPaid;        //variable to store Y/N, that is,
                        //is tuition paid
    bool isTuitionPaid; //variable to store true/false

    string cName;   //variable to store the course name
    string cNo;     //variable to store the course number
    int credits;    //variable to store the course credit hours
    char grade;     //variable to store the course grade

    vector<courseType> courses; //vector of objects to store course
                                //information
    courseType cTemp;
    studentType sTemp;

    infile >> fName;                                    //Step 1

    while (infile)
    {
        infile >> lName >> ID >> isPaid;                //Step 1

        if (isPaid == 'Y')                              //Step 2
            isTuitionPaid = true;
        else
            isTuitionPaid = false;

        infile >> noOfCourses;                          //Step 3

        courses.clear();

        for (int i = 0; i < noOfCourses; i++)           //Step 4
        {
            infile >> cName >> cNo >> credits >> grade; //Step 4.a
            cTemp.setCourseInfo(cName, cNo,
                                grade, credits);        //Step 4.b
            courses.push_back(cTemp);                   //Step 4.c
        }

        sTemp.setInfo(fName, lName, ID, isTuitionPaid,
                      courses);                         //Step 5
        studentList.push_back(sTemp);                   //Step 6

        infile >> fName;                                //Step 1
    }//end while
}
```

4

Function printGrade Reports

This function prints the grade reports. For each student, it calls the function `print` of the `class studentType` to print the grade report. The definition of the function `printGradeReports` is as follows:

```cpp
void printGradeReports(ofstream& outfile,
                       vector<studentType> studentList,
                       double tuitionRate)
{
    for (int count = 0; count < studentList.size(); count++)
        studentList[count].print(outfile, tuitionRate);
}
```

MAIN PROGRAM

```cpp
//****************************************************************
// Author: D.S. Malik
//
// This program illustrates how to use the classes courseType,
// studentType, and vector.
//****************************************************************

#include <iostream>
#include <fstream>
#include <string>
#include <algorithm>
#include <vector>
#include <iterator>

#include "studentType.h"

using namespace std;

void getStudentData(ifstream& infile,
                    vector<studentType> &studentList);

void printGradeReports(ofstream& outfile,
                       vector<studentType> studentList,
                       double tuitionRate);

int main()
{
    vector<studentType> studentList;

    double tuitionRate;

    ifstream infile;
    ofstream outfile;

    infile.open("stData.txt");
```

```
        if (!infile)
        {
            cout << "Input file does not exist. "
                 << "Program terminates." << endl;
            return 1;
        }

        outfile.open("stDataOut.txt");

        infile >> tuitionRate;      //get the tuition rate

        getStudentData(infile, studentList);
        printGradeReports(outfile, studentList, tuitionRate);

        return 0;
    }

    //Place the definition of the function getStudentData here
    //Place the definition of the function printGradeReports here
```

Sample Run:

```
Student Name: Lisa Miller
Student ID: 890238
Number of courses enrolled: 4

Course No  Course Name  Credits Grade
CSC478     ComputerSci     3       B
HIS356     History         3       A
MTH345     Mathematics     4       A
PHY357     Physics         3       B

Total number of credit hours: 13
Midsemester GPA: 3.54
-*-*-*-*-*-*-*-*-*-*-*-*-*-*-*-*-*-*-*-*-*-*-*-*-


Student Name: Bill Wilton
Student ID: 798324
Number of courses enrolled: 5

Course No  Course Name  Credits Grade
BIO234     Biology         4      ***
CHM256     Chemistry       4      ***
ENG378     English         3      ***
MTH346     Mathematics     3      ***
PHL534     Philosophy      3      ***

Total number of credit hours: 17
*** Grades are being held for not paying the tuition. ***
Amount Due: $5865.00
-*-*-*-*-*-*-*-*-*-*-*-*-*-*-*-*-*-*-*-*-*-*-*-*-
```

```
Student Name: Dandy Goat
Student ID: 746333
Number of courses enrolled: 6

Course No  Course Name  Credits Grade
BUS128     Business        3      C
CHM348     Chemistry       4      B
CSC201     ComputerSci     3      B
ENG328     English         3      B
HIS101     History         3      A
MTH137     Mathematics     3      A

Total number of credit hours: 19
Midsemester GPA: 3.16
```
_*_

Input File

```
345
Lisa Miller 890238 Y 4
Mathematics MTH345 4 A
Physics PHY357 3 B
ComputerSci CSC478 3 B
History HIS356 3 A

Bill Wilton 798324 N 5
English ENG378 3 B
Philosophy PHL534 3 A
Chemistry CHM256 4 C
Biology BIO234 4 A
Mathematics MTH346 3 C

Dandy Goat 746333 Y 6
History HIS101 3 A
English ENG328 3 B
Mathematics MTH137 3 A
Chemistry CHM348 4 B
ComputerSci CSC201 3 B
Business BUS128 3 C
```

QUICK REVIEW

1. The STL provides class templates that process lists, stacks, and queues.
2. The three main components of the STL are containers, iterators, and algorithms.
3. STL containers are class templates.
4. Iterators are used to step through the elements of a container.

5. Algorithms are used to manipulate the elements in a container.

6. The main categories of containers are sequence containers, associative containers, and container adapters.

7. The three predefined sequence containers are `vector`, `deque`, and `list`.

8. A vector container stores and manages its objects in a dynamic array.

9. Because an array is a random access data structure, elements of a vector can be accessed randomly.

10. The name of the class that implements the vector container is `vector`.

11. Item insertion in a vector container is accomplished by using the operations `insert` and `push_back`.

12. Item deletion in a vector container is accomplished by using the operations `pop_back`, `erase`, and `clear`.

13. An iterator to a vector container is declared using the `typedef iterator`, which is declared as a `public` member of the `class vector`.

14. Member functions common to all containers are the default constructor, constructors with parameters, the copy constructor, the destructor, `empty`, `size`, `max_size`, `swap`, `begin`, `end`, `rbegin`, `rend`, `insert`, `erase`, `clear`, and the relational operator functions.

15. The member function `begin` returns an iterator to the first element into the container.

16. The member function `end` returns an iterator to the last element into the container.

17. In addition to the member functions listed in 14, the other member functions common to all sequence containers are `insert`, `push_back`, `pop_back`, `erase`, `clear`, and `resize`.

18. The `copy` algorithm is used to copy the elements in a given range to another place.

19. The function `copy`, using an `ostream` iterator, can also be used to output the elements of a container.

20. When we create an iterator of the type `ostream`, we also specify the type of element that the iterator will output.

21. Deque containers are implemented as dynamic arrays in such a way that the elements can be inserted at both ends of the array.

22. A `deque` can expand in either direction.

23. The name of the header file containing the definition of the `class deque` is `deque`.

24. In addition to the operations that are common to all containers, the other operations that can be used to manipulate the elements of a `deque` are `assign`, `push_front`, `pop_front`, `at`, array subscripting operator `[]`, `front`, and `back`.

25. The five categories of iterators are: input, output, forward, bidirectional, and random access iterator.

26. Input iterators are used to input data from an input stream.

27. Output iterators are used to output data to an output stream.

28. A forward iterator can refer to the same element in the same collection and process the same element more than once.

29. Bidirectional iterators are forward iterators that can also iterate backwards over the elements.

30. Bidirectional iterators can be used with containers of type `list`, `set`, `multiset`, `map`, and `multimap`.

31. Random access iterators are bidirectional iterators that can randomly process the elements of a container.

32. Random access iterators can be used with containers of type `vector`, `deque`, `string`, and arrays.

EXERCISES

1. What are the three main components of the STL?

2. What is the difference between an STL container and an STL iterator?

3. Write a statement that declares a vector object that can store 50 decimal numbers.

4. Write a statement that declares and stores the elements of the following array into a `vector` object:

   ```
   char vowels[5] = {'a', 'e', 'i', 'o', 'u'};
   ```

5. Write a statement to declare `screen` to be an `ostream_iterator` initialized to the standard output device that outputs the elements of an `int` vector object.

6. Consider the following statements:

   ```
   vector<int> intVector;
   ```

   Suppose that `intVector = {5, 7, 9, 11, 13}`. Moreover, suppose that `screen` is an `ostream_iterator` initialized to the standard output device to output the elements of an `int` vector object. What is the effect of the following statement?

   ```
   copy(vecList.begin(), vecList.end(), screen);
   ```

7. What is the output of the following program segment?

   ```
   vector<int> vecList(5);

   for (int j = 0; j < 5; j++)
       vecList[j] = 2 * j;
   for (int j = 0; j < 5; j++)
       cout << vecList[j] << " ";
   cout << endl;
   ```

8. What is the output of the following program segment? (Assume that screen is an `ostream_iterator` initialized to the standard output device to output elements of type int.)

```
int list[5] = {2,4,6,8,10};
vector<int> vecList(5);

copy(list, list + 5, vecList.begin());

copy(vecList.begin(), vecList.end(), screen);
cout << endl;
```

9. What is the output of the following program segment? (Assume that screen is an `ostream_iterator` initialized to the standard output device to output elements of type int.)

```
vector<int> vecList;
vector<int>::iterator vecIt;

vecList.push_back(3);
vecList.push_back(5);
vecList.push_back(7);
vecIt = vecList.begin();
++vecIt;
vecList.erase(vecIt);
vecList.push_back(9);

copy(vecList.begin(), vecList.end(), screen);
cout << endl;
```

10. What is the output of the following program segment? (Assume that screen is an `ostream_iterator` initialized to the standard output device to output elements of type int.)

```
int list[5] = {2,4,6,8,10};
vector<int> vecList(7);

copy(list, list + 5, vecList.begin());

vecList.push_back(12);

copy(vecList.begin(), vecList.end(), screen);
cout << endl;
```

11. What is the output of the following program segment? (Assume that screen is an `ostream_iterator` initialized to the standard output device to output elements of type double.)

```
vector<double> sales(3);

sales[0] = 50.00;
sales[1] = 75.00;
sales[2] = 100.00;
```

4

```
sales.resize(5);

sales[3] = 200.00;
sales[4] = 95.00;

copy(sales.begin(), sales.end(), screen);
cout << endl;
```

12. What is the output of the following program segment? (Assume that screen is an ostream_iterator initialized to the standard output device that outputs elements of type int.)

```
vector<int> intVector;
vector<int>::iterator vecIt;

intVector.push_back(15);
intVector.push_back(2);
intVector.push_back(10);
intVector.push_back(7);
vecIt = intVector.begin();
vecIt++;
intVector.erase(vecIt);
intVector.pop_back();

copy(intVector.begin(),intVector.end(), screen);
```

13. Suppose that vecList is a vector container and

    vecList = {12, 16, 8, 23, 40, 6, 18, 9, 75}

    Show vecList after the following statement executes:

    ```
    copy(vecList.begin() + 2, vecList.end(), vecList.begin());
    ```

14. Suppose that vecList is a vector container and

    vecList = {12, 16, 8, 23, 40, 6, 18, 9, 75}

    Show vecList after the following statement executes:

    ```
    copy(vecList.rbegin() + 3, vecList.rend(), vecList.rbegin());
    ```

15. What is the output of the following program segment?

```
deque<int>   intDeq;
ostream_iterator<int> screen(cout, " ");
deque<int>::iterator deqIt;

intDeq.push_back(5);
intDeq.push_front(23);
intDeq.push_front(45);
intDeq.push_back(35);
intDeq.push_front(0);
intDeq.push_back(50);
intDeq.push_front(34);

deqIt = intDeq.begin();
intDeq.insert(deqIt,76);
intDeq.pop_back();
```

```
deqIt = intDeq.begin();
++deqIt;
++deqIt;

intDeq.erase(deqIt);
intDeq.push_front(2 * intDeq.back());
intDeq.push_back(3 * intDeq.front());

copy(intDeq.begin(), intDeq.end(), screen);
cout << endl;
```

4

PROGRAMMING EXERCISES

1. Write a program that allows the user to enter the last names of five candidates in a local election and the votes received by each candidate. The program should then output each candidate's name, votes received by that candidate, and the percentage of the total votes received by the candidate. Your program should also output the winner of the election. A sample output is as follows:

```
Candidate       Votes Received      % of Total Votes
Johnson            5000                 25.91
Miller             4000                 20.72
Duffy              6000                 31.09
Robinson           2500                 12.95
Sam                1800                  9.33
Total             19300
The Winner of the Election is Duffy.
```

2. Write a program that allows the user to input the students' names followed by their test scores and outputs the following:

   a. Class average

   b. Names of all students whose test scores are below the class average with an appropriate message

   c. Highest test score and the names of all students having the highest score

3. Write a program that uses a vector object to store a set of real numbers. The program outputs the smallest, largest, and average of the numbers. When declaring the vector object, do not specify its size. Use the function push_back to insert elements in the vector object.

4. Write the definition of the function template reverseVector to reverse the elements of a vector object.

```
template<class elemType>
void reverseVector(vector<elemType> &list);
   //Reverses the elements of the vector list.
   //Example: Suppose list = {4, 8, 2, 5}.
   //         After a call to this function, list = {5, 2, 8, 4}.
```

Also, write a program to test the function `reverseVector`. When declaring the vector object, do not specify its size. Use the function `push_back` to insert elements in the vector object.

5. Write the definition of the function template `seqSearch` to implement the sequential search on a vector object.

```
template<class elemType>
int seqSearch(const vector<elemType> &list, const elemType& item);
   //If item is found in the list, returns the
   //position of the item in the list; otherwise, returns -1.
```

Also, write a program to test the function `seqSearch`. Use the function `push_back` to insert elements in the vector object.

6. Write a program to find the mean and standard deviation of numbers. The mean (average) of n numbers $x_1, x_2, \ldots, x_n$ is $x = (x_1 + x_2 + \ldots + x_n) / n$. The standard deviation of these numbers is as follows:

$$s = \sqrt{\frac{(x_1 - x)^2 + (x_2 - x)^2 + \cdots + (x_i - x)^2 + \cdots + (x_n - x)^2}{n}}$$

Use a vector object to store the numbers.

7. a. Some of the characteristics of a book are the title, author(s), publisher, ISBN, price, and year of publication. Design the `class bookType` that defines the book as an ADT.

   Each object of the `class bookType` can hold the following information about a book: title, up to four authors, publisher, ISBN, price, and number of copies in stock. To keep track of the number of authors, add another data member.

   Include the member functions to perform the various operations on the objects of `bookType`. For example, the typical operations that can be performed on the title are to show the title, set the title, and check whether a title is the same as the actual title of the book. Similarly, the typical operations that can be performed on the number of copies in stock are to show the number of copies in stock, set the number of copies in stock, update the number of copies in stock, and return the number of copies in stock. Add similar operations for the publisher, ISBN, book price, and authors. Add the appropriate constructors and a destructor (if one is needed).

   b. Write the definitions of the member functions of the `class bookType`.

   c. Write a program that uses the `class bookType` and tests the various operations on the objects of `class bookType`. Declare a vector container of type `bookType`. Some of the operations that you should perform are to search for a book by its title, search by ISBN, and update the number of copies in stock.

8. a. In the first part of this exercise, you will design a class memberType.

      i. Each object of memberType can hold the name of a person, member ID, number of books bought, and amount spent.

      ii. Include the member functions to perform the various operations on the objects of memberType—for example, modify, set, and show a person's name. Similarly, update, modify, and show the number of books bought and the amount spent.

      iii. Add the appropriate constructors and a destructor (if one is needed).

      iv. Write the definitions of the member functions of memberType.

  b. Using the classes designed in Programming Exercise 7 and part (8a), write a program to simulate a bookstore. The bookstore has two types of customers: those who are members of the bookstore and those who buy books from the bookstore only occasionally. Each member has to pay a $10 yearly membership fee and receives a 5% discount on each book bought.

    For each member, the bookstore keeps track of the number of books bought and the total amount spent. For every eleventh book that a member buys, the bookstore takes the average of the total amount of the last 10 books bought, applies this amount as a discount, and then resets the total amount spent to 0.

    Your program should contain a menu that gives the user different choices to effectively run the program; in other words, your program should be self-driven.

9. Redo Programming Exercise 9 of Chapter 3 so that the address book is stored in a vector object.

10. (**Stock Market**) Write a program to help a local stock trading company automate its systems. The company invests only in the stock market. At the end of each trading day, the company would like to generate and post the listing of its stocks so that investors can see how their holdings performed that day. We assume that the company invests in, say, 10 different stocks. The desired output is to produce two listings, one sorted by stock symbol and another sorted by percent gain from highest to lowest.
The input data is stored in a file in the following format:

```
symbol openingPrice closingPrice todayHigh todayLow prevClose
volume
```

For example, the sample data is as follows:

```
MSMT 112.50 115.75 116.50 111.75 113.50 6723823
CBA 67.50 75.50 78.75 67.50 65.75 378233
  .
  .
  .
```

The first line indicates that the stock symbol is MSMT, today's opening price was 112.50, the closing price was 115.75, today's high price was 116.50, today's low price was 111.75, yesterday's closing price was 113.50, and the number of shares currently being held is 6723823.

The listing sorted by stock symbols must be in the following form:

```
*********  First Investor's Heaven  **********
*********     Financial Report          **********
Stock          Today                Previous  Percent
Symbol Open   Close  High    Low   Close  Gain Volume
------ ----   -----  ----    ---   -----  ---- ------
ABC    123.45 130.95 132.00 125.00 120.50  8.67% 10000
AOLK    80.00  75.00  82.00  74.00  83.00 -9.64%  5000
CSCO   100.00 102.00 105.00  98.00 101.00  0.99% 25000
IBD     68.00  71.00  72.00  67.00  75.00 -5.33% 15000
MSET   120.00 140.00 145.00 140.00 115.00 21.74% 30920
Closing Assets: $9628300.00
-*-*-*-*-*-*-*-*-*-*-*-*-*-*-*-*-*-*-*-*-*-*-*-*
```

Develop this programming exercise in two steps. In the first step (part a), design and implement a stock object. In the second step (part b), design and implement an object to maintain a list of stocks.

a.   **(Stock Object)** Design and implement the stock object. Call the class that captures the various characteristics of a stock object stockType.

The main components of a stock are the stock symbol, stock price, and number of shares. Moreover, we need to output the opening price, high price, low price, previous price, and the percent gain/loss for the day. These are also all the characteristics of a stock. Therefore, the stock object should store all this information.

Perform the following operations on each stock object:

   i.   Set the stock information.
   ii. Print the stock information.
   iii. Show the different prices.
   iv. Calculate and print the percent gain/loss.
   v.   Show the number of shares.

   a.1.   The natural ordering of the stock list is by stock symbol. Overload the relational operators to compare two stock objects by their symbols.

   a.2.   Overload the insertion operator, <<, for easy output.

   a.3.   Because data is stored in a file, overload the stream extraction operator, >>, for easy input.
   For example, suppose infile is an ifstream object and the input file was opened using the object infile. Further suppose that myStock is a stock object. Then, the statement

   infile >> myStock;

reads data from the input file and stores it in the object myStock. (Note that this statement reads and stores data in relevant components of myStock.)

b. Now that you have designed and implemented the **class stockType** to implement a stock object in a program, it is time to create a list of stock objects. Let us call the class to implement a list of stock objects **stockListType**. To store the list of stocks, you need to declare a vector. The component type of this vector is stockType.

Because the company also requires you to produce the list ordered by the percent gain/loss, you need to sort the stock list by this component. However, you are not to physically sort the list by the component percent gain/loss; instead, you will provide a logical ordering with respect to this component.

To do so, add a data member, a vector, to hold the indices of the stock list ordered by the component percent gain/loss. Call this array indexByGain. When printing the list ordered by the component percent gain/loss, use the array indexByGain to print the list. The elements of the array indexByGain will tell which component of the stock list to print next. In skeleton form, the definition of the **class stockListType** is as follows:

```
class stockListType
{
public:
    void insert(const stockType& item));
        //Function to insert a stock in the list.
...

private:
    vector<int> indexByGain;
    vector<stockType> list; //vector to store the list //of stocks
};
```

c. Write a program that uses these two classes to automate the company's analysis of stock data.

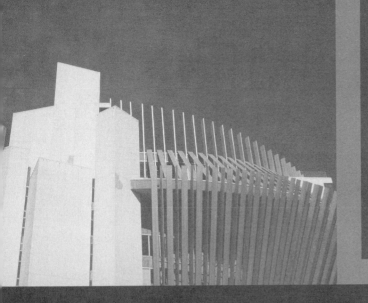

LINKED LISTS

IN THIS CHAPTER, YOU WILL:

- ·   Learn about linked lists
- ·   Become aware of the basic properties of linked lists
- ·   Explore the insertion and deletion operations on linked lists
- ·   Discover how to build and manipulate a linked list
- ·   Learn how to construct a doubly linked list
- ·   Discover how to use the STL container `list`
- ·   Learn about linked lists with header and trailer nodes
- ·   Become aware of circular linked lists

You have already seen how data is organized and processed sequentially using an array, called a *sequential list*. You have performed several operations on sequential lists, such as sorting, inserting, deleting, and searching. You also found that if data is not sorted, searching for an item in the list can be very time consuming, especially with large lists. Once the data is sorted, you can use a binary search and improve the search algorithm. However, in this case, insertion and deletion become time consuming, especially with large lists because these operations require data movement. Also, because the array size must be fixed during execution, new items can be added only if there is room. Thus, there are limitations when you organize data in an array.

This chapter helps you to overcome some of these problems. Chapter 3 showed how memory (variables) can be dynamically allocated and deallocated using pointers. This chapter uses pointers to organize and process data in lists, called **linked lists**. Recall that when data is stored in an array, memory for the components of the array is contiguous—that is, the blocks are allocated one after the other. However, as we will see, the components (called nodes) of a linked list need not be contiguous.

Linked Lists

A linked list is a collection of components, called **nodes**. Every node (except the last node) contains the address of the next node. Thus, every node in a linked list has two components: one to store the relevant information (that is, data) and one to store the address, called the **link**, of the next node in the list. The address of the first node in the list is stored in a separate location, called the **head** or **first**. Figure 5-1 is a pictorial representation of a node.

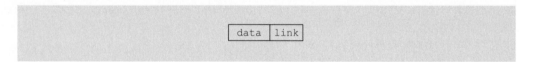

FIGURE 5-1   Structure of a node

Linked list: A list of items, called **nodes**, in which the order of the nodes is determined by the address, called the **link**, stored in each node.

The list in Figure 5-2 is an example of a linked list.

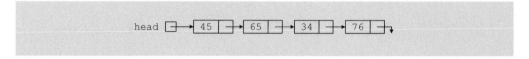

FIGURE 5-2   Linked list

The arrow in each node indicates that the address of the node to which it is pointing is stored in that node. The down arrow in the last node indicates that this link field is NULL.

For a better understanding of this notation, suppose that the first node is at memory location 1200, and the second node is at memory location 1575, see Figure 5-3.

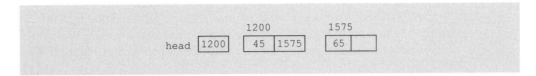

FIGURE 5-3 Linked list and values of the links

The value of the head is 1200, the data part of the first node is 45, and the link component of the first node contains 1575, the address of the second node. If no confusion arises, we will use the arrow notation whenever we draw the figure of a linked list.

For simplicity and for the ease of understanding and clarity, Figures 5-3 through 5-5 use decimal integers as the values of memory addresses. However, in computer memory the memory addresses are in binary.

Because each node of a linked list has two components, we need to declare each node as a class or struct. The data type of each node depends on the specific application—that is, what kind of data is being processed. However, the link component of each node is a pointer. The data type of this pointer variable is the node type itself. For the previous linked list, the definition of the node is as follows. (Suppose that the data type is int.)

```
struct nodeType
{
    int info;
    nodeType *link;
};
```

The variable declaration is as follows:

```
nodeType *head;
```

Linked Lists: Some Properties

To better understand the concept of a linked list and a node, some important properties of linked lists are described next.

Consider the linked list in Figure 5-4.

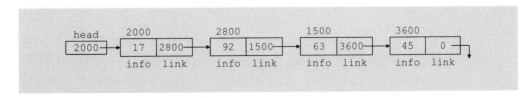

FIGURE 5-4 Linked list with four nodes

This linked list has four nodes. The address of the first node is stored in the pointer `head`. Each node has two components: `info`, to store the info, and `link`, to store the address of the next node. For simplicity, we assume that `info` is of type `int`.

Suppose that the first node is at location 2000, the second node is at location 2800, the third node is at location 1500, and the fourth node is at location 3600. Table 5-1 shows the values of `head` and some other nodes in the list shown in Figure 5-4.

TABLE 5-1 Values of `head` and some of the nodes of the linked list in Figure 5-4

	Value	Explanation
head	2000	
head->info	17	Because `head` is 2000 and the `info` of the node at location 2000 is 17
head->link	2800	
head->link->info	92	Because `head->link` is 2800 and the `info` of the node at location 2800 is 92

Suppose that `current` is a pointer of the same type as the pointer `head`. Then the statement

`current = head;`

copies the value of `head` into `current`. Now consider the following statement:

`current = current->link;`

This statement copies the value of `current->link`, which is 2800, into `current`. Therefore, after this statement executes, `current` points to the second node in the list. (When working with linked lists, we typically use these types of statements to advance a pointer to the next node in the list.) See Figure 5-5.

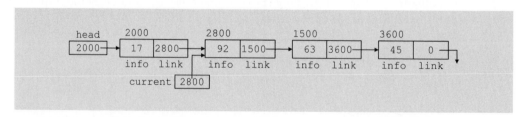

FIGURE 5-5 List after the statement `current = current->link;` executes

Table 5-2 shows the values of current, head, and some other nodes in Figure 5-5.

TABLE 5-2 Values of current, head, and some of the nodes of the linked list in Figure 5-5

	Value
current	2800
current->info	92
current->link	1500
current->link->info	63
head->link->link	1500
head->link->link->info	63
head->link->link->link	3600
current->link->link->link	0 (that is, NULL)
current->link->link->link->info	Does not exist (run-time error)

From now on, when working with linked lists, we will use only the arrow notation.

TRAVERSING A LINKED LIST

The basic operations of a linked list are as follows: Search the list to determine whether a particular item is in the list, insert an item in the list, and delete an item from the list. These operations require the list to be traversed. That is, given a pointer to the first node of the list, we must step through the nodes of the list.

Suppose that the pointer head points to the first node in the list, and the link of the last node is NULL. We cannot use the pointer head to traverse the list because if we use the head to traverse the list, we would lose the nodes of the list. This problem occurs because the links are in only one direction. The pointer head contains the address of the first node, the first node contains the address of the second node, the second node contains the address of the third node, and so on. If we move head to the second node, the first node is lost (unless we save a pointer to this node). If we keep advancing head to the next node, we will lose all the nodes of the list (unless we save a pointer to each node before advancing head, which is impractical because it would require additional computer time and memory space to maintain the list).

Therefore, we always want head to point to the first node. It now follows that we must traverse the list using another pointer of the same type. Suppose that current is a pointer of the same type as head. The following code traverses the list:

```
current = head;

while (current != NULL)
{
    //Process current
    current = current->link;
}
```

For example, suppose that head points to a linked list of numbers. The following code outputs the data stored in each node:

```
current = head;

while (current != NULL)
{
    cout << current->info << " ";
    current = current->link;
}
```

Item Insertion and Deletion

This section discusses how to insert an item into, and delete an item from, a linked list. Consider the following definition of a node. (For simplicity, we assume that the info type is int. The next section, which discusses linked lists as an abstract data type (ADT) using templates, uses the generic definition of a node.)

```
struct nodeType
{
    int info;
    nodeType *link;
};
```

We will use the following variable declaration:

```
nodeType *head, *p, *q, *newNode;
```

INSERTION

Consider the linked list shown in Figure 5-6.

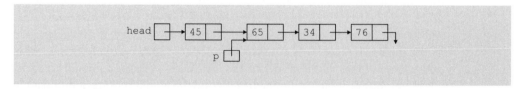

FIGURE 5-6 Linked list before item insertion

Suppose that p points to the node with info 65, and a new node with info 50 is to be created and inserted after p. Consider the following statements:

```
newNode = new nodeType;  //create newNode
newNode->info = 50;      //store 50 in the new node
newNode->link = p->link;
p->link = newNode;
```

Table 5-3 shows the effect of these statements.

TABLE 5-3 Inserting a node in a linked list

Statement	Effect
`newNode = new nodeType;`	
`newNode->info = 50;`	
`newNode->link = p->link;`	
`p->link = newNode;`	

Note that the sequence of statements to insert the node, that is,

```
newNode->link = p->link;
p->link = newNode;
```

is very important because to insert **newNode** in the list we use only one pointer, **p**, to adjust the links of the nodes of the linked list. Suppose that we reverse the sequence of the statements and execute the statements in the following order:

```
p->link = newNode;
newNode->link = p->link;
```

Figure 5-7 shows the resulting list after these statements execute.

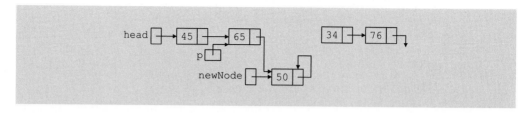

FIGURE 5-7 List after the execution of the statement p->link = newNode; followed by the execution of the statement newNode->link = p->link;

From Figure 5-7, it is clear that **newNode** points back to itself and the remainder of the list is lost.

Using two pointers, we can simplify the insertion code somewhat. Suppose **q** points to the node with **info** 34. (See Figure 5-8.)

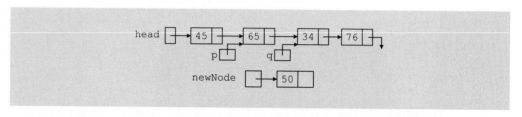

FIGURE 5-8 List with pointers p and q

The following statements insert **newNode** between **p** and **q**:

```
newNode->link = q;
p->link = newNode;
```

The order in which these statements execute does not matter. To illustrate this, suppose that we execute the statements in the following order:

```
p->link = newNode;
newNode->link = q;
```

Table 5-4 shows the effect of these statements.

TABLE 5-4 Inserting a node in a linked list using two pointers

Statement	Effect
p->link = newNode;	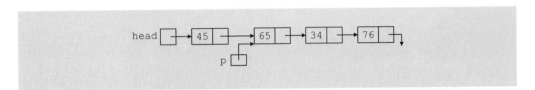
newNode->link = q;	

DELETION

Consider the linked list shown in Figure 5-9.

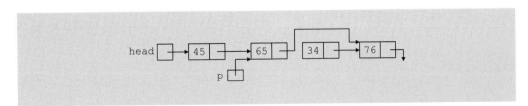

FIGURE 5-9 Node to be deleted is with `info 34`

Suppose that the node with `info 34` is to be deleted from the list. The following statement removes the node from the list:

`p->link = p->link->link;`

Figure 5-10 shows the resulting list after the preceding statement executes.

FIGURE 5-10 List after the statement `p->link = p->link->link;` executes

From Figure 5-10, it is clear that the node with `info 34` is removed from the list. However, the memory is still occupied by this node and this memory is inaccessible; that is, this node is dangling. To deallocate the memory, we need a pointer to this node. The following statements delete the node from the list and deallocate the memory occupied by this node:

```
q = p->link;
p->link = q->link;
delete q;
```

Table 5-5 shows the effect of these statements.

TABLE 5-5 Deleting a node from a linked list

Statement	Effect
`q = p->link;`	head → 45 → 65 → 34 → 76 p q
`p->link = q->link;`	head → 45 → 65 → 34 → 76 p q
`delete q;`	head → 45 → 65 → 76 p

Building a Linked List

Now that we know how to insert a node in a linked list, let us see how to build a linked list. First, we consider a linked list in general. If the data we read is unsorted, the linked list will be unsorted. Such a list can be built in two ways: forward and backward. In the forward manner, a new node is always inserted at the end of the linked list. In the backward manner, a new node is always inserted at the beginning of the list. We will consider both cases.

BUILDING A LINKED LIST FORWARD

Suppose that the nodes are in the usual `info-link` form and `info` is of type `int`. Let us assume that we process the following data:

```
2 15 8 24 34
```

We need three pointers to build the list: one to point to the first node in the list, which cannot be moved, one to point to the last node in the list, and one to create the new node. Consider the following variable declaration:

```
nodeType *first, *last, *newNode;
int num;
```

Suppose that `first` points to the first node in the list. Initially, the list is empty, so both `first` and `last` are `NULL`. Thus, we must have the statements

```
first = NULL;
last = NULL;
```

to initialize `first` and `last` to `NULL`.

Next, consider the following statements:

```
1   cin >> num;               //read and store a number in num
2   newNode = new nodeType;   //allocate memory of type nodeType
                              //and store the address of the
                              //allocated memory in newNode
3   newNode->info = num;      //copy the value of num into the
                              //info field of newNode
4   newNode->link = NULL;     //initialize the link field of
                              //newNode to NULL
5   if (first == NULL)        //if first is NULL, the list is empty;
                              //make first and last point to newNode

    {
5a      first = newNode;
5b      last = newNode;
    }
6   else                      //list is not empty
    {
6a      last->link = newNode; //insert newNode at the end of the list
6b      last = newNode;       //set last so that it points to the
                              //actual last node in the list

    }
```

Let us now execute these statements. Initially, both `first` and `last` are `NULL`. Therefore, we have the list as shown in Figure 5-11.

```
                            first ⊟↴
                             last ⊟↴
```

FIGURE 5-11 Empty list

After statement 1 executes, num is 2. Statement 2 creates a node and stores the address of that node in `newNode`. Statement 3 stores 2 in the `info` field of `newNode`, and statement 4 stores `NULL` in the link field of `newNode`. (See Figure 5-12.)

FIGURE 5-12 newNode with info 2

Because `first` is NULL, we execute statements 5a and 5b. Figure 5-13 shows the resulting list.

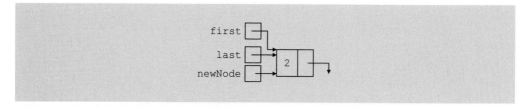

FIGURE 5-13 List after inserting `newNode` in it

We now repeat statements 1 through 6b. After statement 1 executes, `num` is 15. Statement 2 creates a node and stores the address of this node in `newNode`. Statement 3 stores 15 in the `info` field of `newNode`, and statement 4 stores NULL in the link field of `newNode`. (See Figure 5-14.)

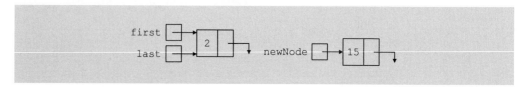

FIGURE 5-14 List and `newNode` with `info` 15

Because `first` is not NULL, we execute statements 6a and 6b. Figure 5-15 shows the resulting list.

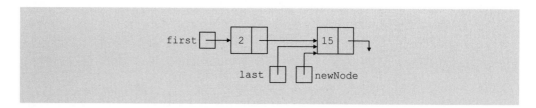

FIGURE 5-15 List after inserting `newNode` at the end

We now repeat statements 1 through 6b three more times. Figure 5-16 shows the resulting list.

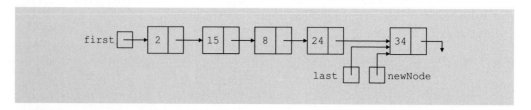

FIGURE 5-16 List after inserting 8, 24, and 34

We can put the previous statements in a loop, and execute the loop until certain conditions are met, to build the linked list. We can, in fact, write a C++ function to build a linked list.

Suppose that we read a list of integers ending with −999. The following function, `buildListForward`, builds a linked list (in a forward manner) and returns the pointer of the built list:

```cpp
nodeType* buildListForward()
{
    nodeType *first, *newNode, *last;
    int num;

    cout << "Enter a list of integers ending with -999."
         << endl;
    cin >> num;
    first = NULL;

    while (num != -999)
    {
        newNode = new nodeType;
        newNode->info = num;
        newNode->link = NULL;

        if (first == NULL)
        {
            first = newNode;
            last = newNode;
        }
        else
        {
            last->link = newNode;
            last = newNode;
        }
        cin >> num;
    } //end while

    return first;
} //end buildListForward
```

BUILDING A LINKED LIST BACKWARD

Now we consider the case of building a linked list backward. For the previously given data—2, 15, 8, 24, and 34—the linked list is as shown in Figure 5-17.

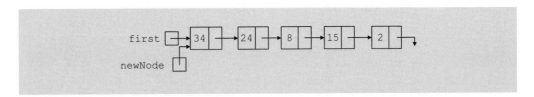

FIGURE 5-17 List after building it backward

Because the new node is always inserted at the beginning of the list, we do not need to know the end of the list, so the pointer last is not needed. Also, after inserting the new node at the beginning, the new node becomes the first node in the list. Thus, we need to update the value of the pointer first to correctly point to the first node in the list. We see, then, that we need only two pointers to build the linked list: one to point to the list and one to create the new node. Because initially the list is empty, the pointer first must be initialized to NULL. The following C++ function builds the linked list backward and returns the pointer of the built list:

```cpp
nodeType* buildListBackward()
{
    nodeType *first, *newNode;
    int num;

    cout << "Enter a list of integers ending with -999."
         << endl;
    cin >> num;
    first = NULL;

    while (num != -999)
    {
        newNode = new nodeType;    //create a node
        newNode->info = num;       //store the data in newNode
        newNode->link = first;     //put newNode at the beginning
                                   //of the list
        first = newNode;           //update the head pointer of
                                   //the list, that is, first
        cin >> num;                //read the next number
    }

    return first;
} //end buildListBackward
```

Linked List as an ADT

The previous sections taught you the basic properties of linked lists and how to construct and manipulate linked lists. Because a linked list is a very important data structure, rather than discuss specific lists such as a list of integers or a list of strings, this section discusses linked lists as an abstract data type (ADT). Using templates, this section gives a generic definition of linked lists, which is then used in the next section and later in this book. The programming example at the end of this chapter also uses this generic definition of linked lists.

The basic operations on linked lists are as follows:

1. Initialize the list.
2. Determine whether the list is empty.
3. Print the list.
4. Find the length of the list.
5. Destroy the list.

6. Retrieve the `info` contained in the first node.

7. Retrieve the `info` contained in the last node.

8. Search the list for a given item.

9. Insert an item in the list.

10. Delete an item from the list.

11. Make a copy of the linked list.

In general, there are two types of linked lists—sorted lists, whose elements are arranged according to some criteria, and unsorted lists, whose elements are in no particular order. The algorithms to implement the operations search, insert, and remove slightly differ for sorted and unsorted lists. Therefore, we will define the `class linkedListType` to implement the basic operations on a linked list as an `abstract class`. Using the principal of inheritance, we derive two `classes`— `unorderedLinkedList` and `orderedLinkedList`—from the `class linkedListType`.

Objects of the `class unorderedLinkedList` would arrange list elements in no particular order, that is, these lists may not be sorted. On the other hand, objects of the `class orderedLinkedList` would arrange elements according to some comparison criteria, usually less than or equal to. That is, these lists will be in ascending order. Moreover, after inserting an element into or removing an element from an ordered list, the resulting list will be ordered.

If a linked list is unordered, we can insert a new item at either the end or the beginning. Furthermore, you can build such a list in either a forward manner or a backward manner. The function `buildListForward` inserts the new item at the end, whereas the function `buildListBackward` inserts the new item at the beginning. To accommodate both operations, we will write two functions: `insertFirst` to insert the new item at the beginning of the list and `insertLast` to insert the new item at the end of the list. Also, to make the algorithms more efficient, we will use two pointers in the list: `first`, which points to the first node in the list, and `last`, which points to the last node in the list.

Structure of Linked List Nodes

Recall that each node of a linked list must store the data as well as the address for the next node in the list (except the last node of the list). Therefore, the node has two instance variables. To simplify operations such as insert and delete, we define the class to implement the node of a linked list as a `struct`. The definition of the `struct nodeType` is as follows:

```
//Definition of the node

template <class Type>
struct nodeType
{
    Type info;
    nodeType<Type> *link;
};
```

NOTE The class to implement the node of a linked list is declared as a `struct`. Programming Exercise 8, at the end of this chapter, asks you to redefine the class to implement the nodes of a linked list so that the instance variables of the `class nodeType` are `private`.

Member Variables of the `class linkedListType`

To maintain a linked list, we use two pointers—`first` and `last`. The pointer `first` points to the first node in the list, and `last` points to the last node in the list. We also keep a count of the number of nodes in the list. Therefore, the `class linkedListType` has three instance variables, as follows:

```
protected:
    int count; //variable to store the number of elements in the list
    nodeType<Type> *first; //pointer to the first node of the list
    nodeType<Type> *last;  //pointer to the last node of the list
```

Linked List Iterators

One of the basic operations performed on a list is to process each node of the list. This requires the list to be traversed starting at the first node. Moreover, a specific application requires each node to be processed in a very specific way. A common technique to accomplish this is to provide an iterator. So what is an iterator? An **iterator** is an object that produces each element of a container, such as a linked list, one element at a time. The two most common operations on iterators are ++ (the increment operator) and * (the dereferencing operator). The increment operator advances the iterator to the next node in the list while the dereferencing operator returns the `info` of the current node.

Note that an iterator is an object. So we need to define a class, which we will call `linkedListIterator`, to create iterators to objects of the `class linkedListType`. The iterator class would have one member variable pointing to (the current) node.

```
//************************************************************
// Author: D.S. Malik
//
// This class specifies the members to implement an iterator
// to a linked list.
//************************************************************

template <class Type>
class linkedListIterator
{
public:
    linkedListIterator();
      //Default constructor
      //Postcondition: current = NULL;

    linkedListIterator(nodeType<Type> *ptr);
      //Constructor with a parameter.
      //Postcondition: current = ptr;

    Type operator*();
      //Function to overload the dereferencing operator *.
      //Postcondition: Returns the info contained in the node.

    linkedListIterator<Type> operator++();
      //Overload the preincrement operator.
      //Postcondition: The iterator is advanced to the next node.
```

```
    bool operator==(const linkedListIterator<Type>& right) const;
      //Overload the equality operator.
      //Postcondition: Returns true if this iterator is equal to
      //    the iterator specified by right, otherwise it returns
      //    false.

    bool operator!=(const linkedListIterator<Type>& right) const;
      //Overload the not equal to operator.
      //Postcondition: Returns true if this iterator is not equal to
      //    the iterator specified by right, otherwise it returns
      //    false.

private:
    nodeType<Type> *current; //pointer to point to the current
                             //node in the linked list
};
```

Figure 5-18 shows the UML class diagram of the class linkedListIterator.

```
+-------------------------------------------------------------+
|             linkedListIterator<Type>                        |
+-------------------------------------------------------------+
| - *current: nodeType<Type>                                  |
+-------------------------------------------------------------+
|+linkedListIterator()                                        |
|+linkedListIterator(nodeType<Type>)                          |
|+operator*(): Type                                           |
|+operator++(): linkedListIterator<Type>                      |
|+operator==(const linkedListIterator<Type>&) const: bool     |
|+operator!=(const linkedListIterator<Type>&) const: bool     |
+-------------------------------------------------------------+
```

FIGURE 5-18 UML class diagram of the class linkedListIterator

The definitions of the functions of the class linkedListIterator are as follows:

```
template <class Type>
linkedListIterator<Type>::linkedListIterator()
{
    current = NULL;
}

template <class Type>
linkedListIterator<Type>::
                linkedListIterator(nodeType<Type> *ptr)
{
    current = ptr;
}

template <class Type>
Type linkedListIterator<Type>::operator*()
{
    return current->info;
}
```

```
template <class Type>
linkedListIterator<Type> linkedListIterator<Type>::operator++()
{
    current = current->link;

    return *this;
}

template <class Type>
bool linkedListIterator<Type>::operator==
              (const linkedListIterator<Type>& right) const
{
    return (current == right.current);
}

template <class Type>
bool linkedListIterator<Type>::operator!=
              (const linkedListIterator<Type>& right) const
{
    return (current != right.current);
}
```

From the definitions of the functions and constructors of the class linkedListIterator, it follows that each function and the constructors are of $O(1)$.

Now that we have defined the classes to implement the node of a linked list and an iterator to a linked list, next, we describe the class linkedListType to implement the basic porperties of a linked list.

The following abstract class defines the basic properties of a linked list as an ADT:

```
//***************************************************************
// Author: D.S. Malik
//
// This class specifies the members to implement the basic
// properties of a linked list. This is an abstract class.
// We cannot instantiate an object of this class.
//***************************************************************

template <class Type>
class linkedListType
{
public:
    const linkedListType<Type>& operator=
                        (const linkedListType<Type>&);
        //Overload the assignment operator.

    void initializeList();
        //Initialize the list to an empty state.
        //Postcondition: first = NULL, last = NULL, count = 0;
```

```
bool isEmptyList() const;
   //Function to determine whether the list is empty.
   //Postcondition: Returns true if the list is empty, otherwise
   //    it returns false.

void print() const;
   //Function to output the data contained in each node.
   //Postcondition: none

int length() const;
   //Function to return the number of nodes in the list.
   //Postcondition: The value of count is returned.

void destroyList();
   //Function to delete all the nodes from the list.
   //Postcondition: first = NULL, last = NULL, count = 0;

Type front() const;
   //Function to return the first element of the list.
   //Precondition: The list must exist and must not be empty.
   //Postcondition: If the list is empty, the program terminates;
   //    otherwise, the first element of the list is returned.

Type back() const;
   //Function to return the last element of the list.
   //Precondition: The list must exist and must not be empty.
   //Postcondition: If the list is empty, the program
   //                terminates; otherwise, the last
   //                element of the list is returned.

virtual bool search(const Type& searchItem) const = 0;
   //Function to determine whether searchItem is in the list.
   //Postcondition: Returns true if searchItem is in the list,
   //    otherwise the value false is returned.

virtual void insertFirst(const Type& newItem) = 0;
   //Function to insert newItem at the beginning of the list.
   //Postcondition: first points to the new list, newItem is
   //    inserted at the beginning of the list, last points to
   //    the last node in the list, and count is incremented by
   //    1.

virtual void insertLast(const Type& newItem) = 0;
   //Function to insert newItem at the end of the list.
   //Postcondition: first points to the new list, newItem is
   //    inserted at the end of the list, last points to the
   //    last node in the list, and count is incremented by 1.

virtual void deleteNode(const Type& deleteItem) = 0;
   //Function to delete deleteItem from the list.
   //Postcondition: If found, the node containing deleteItem is
   //    deleted from the list. first points to the first node,
   //    last points to the last node of the updated list, and
   //    count is decremented by 1.
```

5

```
linkedListIterator<Type> begin();
   //Function to return an iterator at the beginning of the
   //linked list.
   //Postcondition: Returns an iterator such that current is set
   //    to first.

linkedListIterator<Type> end();
   //Function to return an iterator one element past the
   //last element of the linked list.
   //Postcondition: Returns an iterator such that current is set
   //    to NULL.

linkedListType();
   //default constructor
   //Initializes the list to an empty state.
   //Postcondition: first = NULL, last = NULL, count = 0;

linkedListType(const linkedListType<Type>& otherList);
   //copy constructor

~linkedListType();
   //destructor
   //Deletes all the nodes from the list.
   //Postcondition: The list object is destroyed.

protected:
    int count; //variable to store the number of list elements
               //
    nodeType<Type> *first; //pointer to the first node of the list
    nodeType<Type> *last;  //pointer to the last node of the list

private:
    void copyList(const linkedListType<Type>& otherList);
       //Function to make a copy of otherList.
       //Postcondition: A copy of otherList is created and assigned
       //    to this list.
};
```

Figure 5-19 shows the UML class diagram of the `class linkedListType`.

```
                  linkedListType<Type>
-count: int
-*first: nodeType<Type>
-*last: nodeType<Type>

+operator=(const linkedListType<Type>&):
                       const linkedListType<Type>&
+initializeList(): void
+isEmptyList() const: bool
+print() const: void
+length() const: int
+destroyList(): void
+front() const: Type
+back() const: Type
+search(const Type&) const = 0: bool
+insertFirst(const Type&) = 0: void
+insertLast(const Type&) = 0: void
+deleteNode(const Type&) = 0: void
+begin(): linkedListIterator<Type>
+end(): linkedListIterator<Type>
+linkedListType()
+linkedListType(const linkedListType<Type>&)
+~linkedListType()
-copyList(const linkedListType<Type>&): void
```

FIGURE 5-19 UML class diagram of the `class linkedListType`

Note that, typically, in the UML class diagram the names of an abstract class and abstract function are shown in italic.

The instance variables `first` and `last`, as defined earlier, of the `class linkedListType` are `protected`, not `private`, because as noted previously, we will derive the `classes unorderedLinkedList` and `orderedLinkedList` from the `class linkedListType`. Because each of the `classes unorderedLinkedList` and `orderedLinkedList` will provide separate definitions of the functions `search`, `insertFirst`, `insertLast`, and `deleteNode`, and because these functions would access the instance variable, to provide direct access to the instance variables, the instance variables are declared as `protected`.

The definition of the `class linkedListType` includes a member function to overload the assignment operator. For classes that include pointer data members, the assignment operator must be explicitly overloaded (see Chapters 2 and 3). For the same reason, the definition of the class also includes a copy constructor.

Notice that the definition of the `class linkedListType` contains the member function `copyList`, which is declared as a `private` member. This is because this function is used only to implement the copy constructor and overload the assignment operator.

Next, we write the definitions of the nonabstract functions of the class `LinkedListClass`.

The list is empty if `first` is `NULL`. Therefore, the definition of the function `isEmptyList` to implement this operation is as follows:

```
template <class Type>
bool linkedListType<Type>::isEmptyList() const
{
    return (first == NULL);
}
```

Default Constructor

The default constructor, `linkedListType`, is quite straightforward. It simply initializes the list to an empty state. Recall that when an object of the `linkedListType` type is declared and no value is passed, the default constructor is executed automatically.

```
template <class Type>
linkedListType<Type>::linkedListType() //default constructor
{
    first = NULL;
    last = NULL;
    count = 0;
}
```

From the definitions of the functions `isEmptyList` and the default constructor, it follows that each of these functions is of $O(1)$.

Destroy the List

The function `destroyList` deallocates the memory occupied by each node. We traverse the list starting from the first node and deallocate the memory by calling the operator `delete`. We need a temporary pointer to deallocate the memory. Once the entire list is destroyed, we must set the pointers `first` and `last` to `NULL` and count to 0.

```
template <class Type>
void linkedListType<Type>::destroyList()
{
    nodeType<Type> *temp;    //pointer to deallocate the memory
                             //occupied by the node
    while (first != NULL)    //while there are nodes in the list
    {
        temp = first;           //set temp to the current node
        first = first->link; //advance first to the next node
        delete temp;    //deallocate the memory occupied by temp
    }

    last = NULL; //initialize last to NULL; first has already
                 //been set to NULL by the while loop
    count = 0;
}
```

If the list has *n* items, the **while** loop executes *n* times. From this, it follows that the function destroyList is of $O(n)$.

Initialize the List

The function initializeList initializes the list to an empty state. Note that the default constructor or the copy constructor has already initialized the list when the list object was declared. This operation, in fact, reinitializes the list to an empty state, and so it must delete the nodes (if any) from the list. This task can be accomplished by using the destroyList operation, which also resets the pointers first and last to NULL and sets count to 0.

```
template <class Type>
void linkedListType<Type>::initializeList()
{
    destroyList(); //if the list has any nodes, delete them
}
```

The function initializeList uses the function destroyList, which is of $O(n)$. Therefore, the function initializeList is of $O(n)$.

Print the List

The member function print prints the data contained in each node. To print the data contained in each node, we must traverse the list starting at the first node. Because the pointer first always points to the first node in the list, we need another pointer to traverse the list. (If we use first to traverse the list, the entire list will be lost.)

```
template <class Type>
void linkedListType<Type>::print() const
{
    nodeType<Type> *current; //pointer to traverse the list

    current = first; //set current point to the first node
    while (current != NULL) //while more data to print
    {
        cout << current->info << " ";
        current = current->link;
    }
}//end print
```

As in the case of the function destroyList, the function print is of $O(n)$.

Length of a List

The length of a linked list (that is, how many nodes are in the list) is stored in the variable count. Therefore, this function returns the value of this variable.

```
template <class Type>
int linkedListType<Type>::length() const
{
    return count;
}
```

Retrieve the Data of the First Node

The function `front` returns the `info` contained in the first node, and its definition is straightforward.

```
template <class Type>
Type linkedListType<Type>::front() const
{
    assert(first != NULL);

    return first->info; //return the info of the first node
}//end front
```

Notice that if the list is empty, the `assert` statement terminates the program. Therefore, before calling this function check, you have to check to see whether the list is nonempty.

Retrieve the Data of the Last Node

The function `back` returns the `info` contained in the last node. Its definition is as follows:

```
template <class Type>
Type linkedListType<Type>::back() const
{
    assert(last != NULL);

    return last->info; //return the info of the last node
}//end back
```

Notice that if the list is empty, the `assert` statement terminates the program. Therefore, before calling this function, you have to check to see whether the list is nonempty.

From the definitions of the functions `length`, `front`, and `back`, it follows easily that each of these functions are of O(1).

Begin and End

The function `begin` returns an iterator to the first node in the linked list and the function `end` returns an iterator to the last node in the linked list. Their definitions are as follows:

```
template <class Type>
linkedListIterator<Type> linkedListType<Type>::begin()
{
    linkedListIterator<Type> temp(first);

    return temp;
}

template <class Type>
linkedListIterator<Type> linkedListType<Type>::end()
{
    linkedListIterator<Type> temp(NULL);

    return temp;
}
```

From the definitions of the functions `length`, `front`, `back`, `begin`, and `end`, it follows easily that each of these functions are of $O(1)$.

Copy the List

The function `copyList` makes an identical copy of a linked list. Therefore, we traverse the list to be copied starting at the first node. Corresponding to each node in the original list, we do the following:

1. Create a node and call it `newNode`.
2. Copy the `info` of the node (in the original list) into `newNode`.
3. Insert `newNode` at the end of the list being created.

The definition of the function `copyList` is as follows:

```cpp
template <class Type>
void linkedListType<Type>::copyList
                    (const linkedListType<Type>& otherList)
{
    nodeType<Type> *newNode; //pointer to create a node
    nodeType<Type> *current; //pointer to traverse the list

    if (first != NULL) //if the list is nonempty, make it empty
        destroyList();

    if (otherList.first == NULL) //otherList is empty
    {
        first = NULL;
        last = NULL;
        count = 0;
    }
    else
    {
        current = otherList.first; //current points to the
                                   //list to be copied
        count = otherList.count;

            //copy the first node
        first = new nodeType<Type>;   //create the node
        first->info = current->info; //copy the info
        first->link = NULL; //set the link field of the node to NULL
        last = first;    //make last point to the first node
        current = current->link; //make current point to the next
                                 // node

            //copy the remaining list
        while (current != NULL)
        {
            newNode = new nodeType<Type>;   //create a node
            newNode->info = current->info; //copy the info
            newNode->link = NULL; //set the link of newNode to NULL
```

5

```
                last->link = newNode; //attach newNode after last
                last = newNode; //make last point to the actual last
                                     //node
                current = current->link; //make current point to the
                                             //next node
        }//end while
    }//end else
}//end copyList
```

The function `copyList` contains a `while` loop. The number of times the `while` loop executes depends on the number of items in the list. If the list contains *n* items, the `while` loop executes *n* times. Therefore, the function `copyList` is of $O(n)$.

Destructor

The destructor deallocates the memory occupied by the nodes of a list when the class object goes out of scope. Because memory is allocated dynamically, resetting the pointers `first` and `last` does not deallocate the memory occupied by the nodes in the list. We must traverse the list, starting at the first node, and delete each node in the list. The list can be destroyed by calling the function `destroyList`. Therefore, the definition of the destructor is as follows:

```
template <class Type>
linkedListType<Type>::~linkedListType() //destructor
{
    destroyList();
}
```

Copy Constructor

Because the `class linkedListType` contains pointer data members, the definition of this class contains the copy constructor. Recall that, if a formal parameter is a value parameter, the copy constructor provides the formal parameter with its own copy of the data. The copy constructor also executes when an object is declared and initialized using another object.

The copy constructor makes an identical copy of the linked list. This can be done by calling the function `copyList`. Because the function `copyList` checks whether the original is empty by checking the value of `first`, we must first initialize the pointer `first` to NULL before calling the function `copyList`.

The definition of the copy constructor is as follows:

```
template <class Type>
linkedListType<Type>::linkedListType
                    (const linkedListType<Type>& otherList)
{
    first = NULL;
    copyList(otherList);
}//end copy constructor
```

Overloading the Assignment Operator

The definition of the function to overload the assignment operator for the **class** linkedListType is similar to the definition of the copy constructor. We give its definition for the sake of completeness.

```
    //overload the assignment operator
template <class Type>
const linkedListType<Type>& linkedListType<Type>::operator=
                    (const linkedListType<Type>& otherList)
{
    if (this != &otherList) //avoid self-copy
    {
        copyList(otherList);
    }//end else

    return *this;
}
```

The destructor uses the function destroyList, which is of $O(n)$. The copy constructor and the function to overload the assignment operator use the function copyList, which is of $O(n)$. Therefore, each of these functions are of $O(n)$.

TABLE 5-6 Time-complexity of the operations of the class linkedListType

Function	Time-complexity
isEmptyList	$O(1)$
default constructor	$O(1)$
destroyList	$O(n)$
front	$O(1)$
end	$O(1)$
initializeList	$O(n)$
print	$O(n)$
length	$O(1)$
front	$O(1)$
back	$O(1)$
copyList	$O(n)$

TABLE 5-6 Time-complexity of the operations of the `class linkedListType` (continued)

Function	Time-complexity
destructor	$O(n)$
copy constructor	$O(n)$
Overloading the assignment operator	$O(n)$

Unordered Linked Lists

As described in the previous section, we derive the `class unorderedLinkedList` from the abstract `class linkedListType` and implement the operations `search`, `insertFirst`, `insertLast`, and `deleteNode`.

The following class defines an unordered linked list as an ADT:

```
//************************************************************
// Author: D.S. Malik
//
// This class specifies the members to implement the basic
// properties of an unordered linked list. This class is
// derived from the class linkedListType.
//************************************************************

template <class Type>
class unorderedLinkedList: public linkedListType<Type>
{
public:
    bool search(const Type& searchItem) const;
        //Function to determine whether searchItem is in the list.
        //Postcondition: Returns true if searchItem is in the list,
        //    otherwise the value false is returned.

    void insertFirst(const Type& newItem);
        //Function to insert newItem at the beginning of the list.
        //Postcondition: first points to the new list, newItem is
        //    inserted at the beginning of the list, last points to
        //    the last node, and count is incremented by 1.
        //

    void insertLast(const Type& newItem);
        //Function to insert newItem at the end of the list.
        //Postcondition: first points to the new list, newItem is
        //    inserted at the end of the list, last points to the
        //    last node, and count is incremented by 1.

    void deleteNode(const Type& deleteItem);
        //Function to delete deleteItem from the list.
        //Postcondition: If found, the node containing deleteItem
```

```
        //      is deleted from the list. first points to the first
        //      node, last points to the last node of the updated
        //      list, and count is decremented by 1.
};
```

Figure 5-20 shows a UML class diagram of the class unorderedLinkedList and the inheritance hierarchy.

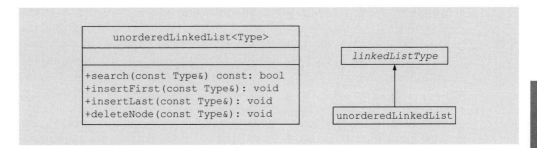

FIGURE 5-20 UML class diagram of the class unorderedLinkedList and the inheritance hierarchy

Next we give the definitions of the member functions of the class unorderedLinkedList.

Search the List

The member function search searches the list for a given item. If the item is found, it returns true; otherwise, it returns false. Because a linked list is not a random access data structure, we must sequentially search the list starting from the first node.

This function has the following steps:

1. Compare the search item with the current node in the list. If the info of the current node is the same as the search item, stop the search; otherwise, make the next node the current node.

2. Repeat Step 1 until either the item is found or no more data is left in the list to compare with the search item.

```
template <class Type>
bool unorderedLinkedList<Type>::
                  search(const Type& searchItem) const
{
    nodeType<Type> *current; //pointer to traverse the list
    bool found = false;

    current = first; //set current to point to the first
                     //node in the list

    while (current != NULL && !found)      //search the list
        if (current->info == searchItem) //searchItem is found
            found = true;
```

```
        else
            current = current->link; //make current point to
                                     //the next node
    return found;
}//end search
```

The number of times the `while` loop executes, in the function search, depends on where in the list the search item is located. Suppose the list has n items. If the search item is not in the list, the while loop executes n times. On the other hand, if the search item is the first item, the `while` loop executes 1 time. Similarly, if the search item is the ith item in the list, the while loop executes i times. From these observations, we can show that the function `search` is of $O(n)$. We will explicitly analyze the sequential search algorithm in Chapter 9.

Insert the First Node

The function `insertFirst` inserts the new item at the beginning of the list—that is, before the node pointed to by `first`. The steps needed to implement this function are as follows:

1. Create a new node.
2. If unable to create the node, terminate the program.
3. Store the new item in the new node.
4. Insert the node before `first`.
5. Increment count by 1.

```
template <class Type>
void unorderedLinkedList<Type>::insertFirst(const Type& newItem)
{
    nodeType<Type> *newNode; //pointer to create the new node

    newNode = new nodeType<Type>; //create the new node
    newNode->info = newItem;    //store the new item in the node
    newNode->link = first;      //insert newNode before first
    first = newNode;    //make first point to the actual first node
    count++;    //increment count

    if (last == NULL)   //if the list was empty, newNode is also
                        //the last node in the list
        last = newNode;
}//end insertFirst
```

Insert the Last Node

The definition of the member function `insertLast` is similar to the definition of the member function `insertFirst`. Here, we insert the new node after `last`. Essentially, the function `insertLast` is as follows:

```
template <class Type>
void unorderedLinkedList<Type>::insertLast(const Type& newItem)
{
    nodeType<Type> *newNode; //pointer to create the new node
```

```
    newNode = new nodeType<Type>; //create the new node
    newNode->info = newItem;    //store the new item in the node
    newNode->link = NULL; //set the link field of newNode to NULL

    if (first == NULL)  //if the list is empty, newNode is
                        //both the first and last node
    {
        first = newNode;
        last = newNode;
        count++;            //increment count
    }
    else    //the list is not empty, insert newNode after last
    {
        last->link = newNode; //insert newNode after last
        last = newNode; //make last point to the actual
                        //last node in the list
        count++;            //increment count
    }
}//end insertLast
```

From the definitions of the functions insertFirst and insertLast, it follows that each of these functions is of $O(1)$.

DELETE A NODE

Next, we discuss the implementation of the member function deleteNode, which deletes a node from the list with a given info. We need to consider the following cases:

- The list is empty.
- The node is nonempty and the node to be deleted is the first node.
- The node is nonempty and the node to be deleted is not the first node, it is somewhere in the list.
- The node to be deleted is not in the list.

If list is empty, we can simply print a message indicating that the list is empty. If list is not empty, we search the list for the node with the given info and, if such a node is found, we delete this node. After deleting the node, count is decremented by 1. In pseudocode, the algorithm is as follows:

```
if list is empty
   Output(cannot delete from an empty list);
else
{
   if the first node is the node with the given info
       adjust the head pointer, that is, first, and deallocate
       the memory;
   else
   {
       search the list for the node with the given info
       if such a node is found, delete it and adjust the
       values of last (if necessary) and count.
   }
}
```

Case 1: The list is empty. If the list is empty, output an error message as shown in the pseudocode.

Case 2: The list is not empty and the node to be deleted is the first node. This case has two scenarios: `list` has only one node, and `list` has more than one node. If `list` has only one node, then after deletion, the list becomes empty. Therefore, after deletion, both `first` and `last` are set to `NULL` and `count` is set to `0`.

Suppose that the node to be deleted is the first node and `list` has more than one node. Then after deleting this node, the second node becomes the first node. Therefore, after deleting the node the value of the pointer `first` changes and it contains the address of the second node.

Case 3: The node to be deleted is not the first node, but is somewhere in the list.

This case has two subcases: (a) the node to be deleted is not the last node, and (b) the node to be deleted is the last node. Let us illustrate the first cases.

Case 3a: The node to be deleted is not the last node.

Consider the list shown in Figure 5-21.

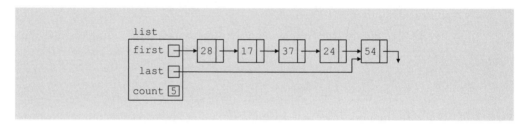

FIGURE 5-21 `list` before deleting 37

Suppose that the node to be deleted is 37. After deleting this node, the resulting list is as shown in Figure 5-22. (Notice that the deletion of 37 does not require us to change the values of `first` and `last`. The link field of the previous node—that is, 17—changes. After deletion, the node with `info` 17 contains the address of the node with 24.)

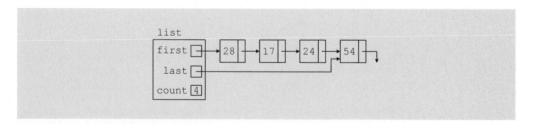

FIGURE 5-22 `list` after deleting 37

Case 3b: The node to be deleted is the last node. In this case, after deleting the node, the value of the pointer `last` changes. It contains the address of the node just before the node to be deleted. For example, consider the list given in Figure 5-21 and the node to be deleted is 54. After deleting 54, `last` contains the address of the node with `info` 24. Also, `count` is decremented by 1.

Case 4: The node to be deleted is not in the list. In this case, the list requires no adjustment. We simply output an error message, indicating that the item to be deleted is not in the list.

From cases 2, 3, and 4, it follows that the deletion of a node requires us to traverse the list. Because a linked list is not a random access data structure, we must sequentially search the list. We handle case 1 separately because it does not require us to traverse the list. We sequentially search the list starting at the second node. If the node to be deleted is in the middle of the list, we need to adjust the link field of the node just before the node to be deleted. Thus, we need a pointer to the previous node. When we search the list for the given `info`, we use two pointers: one to check the `info` of the current node, and one to keep track of the node just before the current node. If the node to be deleted is the last node, we must adjust the pointer `last`.

The definition of the function `deleteNode` is as follows:

```
template <class Type>
void unorderedLinkedList<Type>::deleteNode(const Type& deleteItem)
{
    nodeType<Type> *current; //pointer to traverse the list
    nodeType<Type> *trailCurrent; //pointer just before current
    bool found;

    if (first == NULL)     //Case 1; the list is empty.
        cout << "Cannot delete from an empty list."
             << endl;
    else
    {
        if (first->info == deleteItem) //Case 2
        {
            current = first;
            first = first->link;
            count--;

            if (first == NULL)     //the list has only one node
                last = NULL;

            delete current;
        }
        else //search the list for the node with the given info
        {
            found = false;
            trailCurrent = first;   //set trailCurrent to point
                                    //to the first node
            current = first->link; //set current to point to
                                   //the second node
```

```
            while (current != NULL && !found)
            {
                if (current->info != deleteItem)
                {
                    trailCurrent = current;
                    current = current-> link;
                }
                else
                    found = true;
            }//end while

            if (found) //Case 3; if found, delete the node
            {
                trailCurrent->link = current->link;
                count--;

                if (last == current) //node to be deleted was the
                                     //last node
                    last = trailCurrent; //update the value of last
                delete current;  //delete the node from the list
            }
            else
                cout << "The item to be deleted is not in "
                     << "the list." << endl;
        }//end else
    }//end else
}//end deleteNode
```

From the definition of the function `deleteNode`, it can be shown that this function is of $O(n)$.

Table 5-7 gives the time-complexity of the operations of the `class unorderedLinkedList`.

TABLE 5-7 Time-complexity of the operations of the `class unorderedLinkedList`

Function	Time-complexity
search	$O(n)$
insertFirst	$O(1)$
insertLast	$O(1)$
deleteNode	$O(n)$

Header File of the Unordered Linked List

For the sake of completeness, we show how to create the header file that defines the `class unorderedListType` and the operations on such lists. (We assume that the definition of the `class linkedListType` and the definitions of the functions to implement the operations are in the header file `linkedList.h`.)

```
#ifndef H_UnorderedLinkedList
#define H_UnorderedLinkedList

//*************************************************************
// Author: D.S. Malik
//
// This class specifies the members to implement the basic
// properties of an unordered linked list. This class is
// derived from the class linkedListType.
//*************************************************************

#include "linkedList.h"

using namespace std;

template <class Type>
class unorderedLinkedList: public linkedListType<Type>
{
public:
    bool search(const Type& searchItem) const;
      //Function to determine whether searchItem is in the list.
      //Postcondition: Returns true if searchItem is in the list,
      //     otherwise the value false is returned.

    void insertFirst(const Type& newItem);
      //Function to insert newItem at the beginning of the list.
      //Postcondition: first points to the new list, newItem is
      //     inserted at the beginning of the list, last points to
      //     the last node, and count is incremented by 1.

    void insertLast(const Type& newItem);
      //Function to insert newItem at the end of the list.
      //Postcondition: first points to the new list, newItem is
      //     inserted at the end of the list, last points to the
      //     last node, and count is incremented by 1.

    void deleteNode(const Type& deleteItem);
      //Function to delete deleteItem from the list.
      //Postcondition: If found, the node containing deleteItem
      //     is deleted from the list. first points to the first
      //     node, last points to the last node of the updated list,
      //     and count is decremented by 1.
};

//Place the definitions of the functions search, insertNode,
//insertFirst, insertLast, and deleteNode here.
  .
  .
  .
#endif
```

NOTE   The Web site accompanying this book contains several programs illustrating how to use the class unorderedLinkedList.

Ordered Linked Lists

The preceding section described the operations on an unordered linked list. This section deals with ordered linked lists. As noted earlier, we derive the class `orderedLinkedList` from the class `linkedListType` and provide the definitions of the abstract functions `insertFirst`, `insertLast`, `search`, and `deleteNode` to take advantage of the fact that the elements of an ordered linked list are arranged using some ordering criteria. For simplicity, we assume that elements of an ordered linked list are arranged in ascending order.

Because the elements of an ordered linked list are in order, we include the function `insert` to insert an element in an ordered list at the proper place.

The following class defines an ordered linked list as an ADT:

```
//***********************************************************
// Author: D.S. Malik
//
// This class specifies the members to implement the basic
// properties of an ordered linked list. This class is
// derived from the class linkedListType.
//***********************************************************

template <class Type>
class orderedLinkedList: public linkedListType<Type>
{
public:
    bool search(const Type& searchItem) const;
      //Function to determine whether searchItem is in the list.
      //Postcondition: Returns true if searchItem is in the list,
      //    otherwise the value false is returned.

    void insert(const Type& newItem);
      //Function to insert newItem in the list.
      //Postcondition: first points to the new list, newItem
      //    is inserted at the proper place in the list, and
      //    count is incremented by 1.

    void insertFirst(const Type& newItem);
      //Function to insert newItem at the beginning of the list.
      //Postcondition: first points to the new list, newItem is
      //    inserted at the beginning of the list, last points to the
      //    last node in the list, and count is incremented by 1.

    void insertLast(const Type& newItem);
      //Function to insert newItem at the end of the list.
      //Postcondition: first points to the new list, newItem is
      //    inserted at the end of the list, last points to the
      //    last node in the list, and count is incremented by 1.

    void deleteNode(const Type& deleteItem);
      //Function to delete deleteItem from the list.
      //Postcondition: If found, the node containing deleteItem is
```

```
//      deleted from the list; first points to the first node
//      of the new list, and count is decremented by 1. If
//      deleteItem is not in the list, an appropriate message
//      is printed.
};
```

Figure 5-23 shows a UML class diagram of the class orderedLinkedList and the inheritance hierarchy.

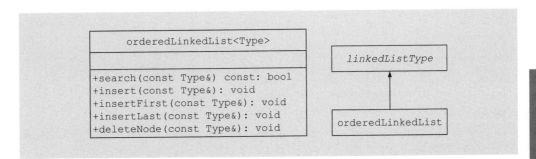

FIGURE 5-23   UML class diagram of the class orderedLinkedList and the inheritance hierarchy

Next we give the definitions of the member functions of the class orderedLinkedList.

Search the List

First, we discuss the search operation. The algorithm to implement the search operation is similar to the search algorithm for general lists discussed earlier. Here, because the list is sorted, we can improve the search algorithm somewhat. As before, we start the search at the first node in the list. We stop the search as soon as we find a node in the list with info greater than or equal to the search item, or we have searched the entire list.

The following steps describe this algorithm:

1. Compare the search item with the current node in the list. If the info of the current node is greater than or equal to the search item, stop the search; otherwise, make the next node the current node.

2. Repeat Step 1 until either an item in the list that is greater than or equal to the search item is found, or no more data is left in the list to compare with the search item.

Note that the loop does not explicitly check whether the search item is equal to an item in the list. Thus, after the loop executes, we must check whether the search item is equal to the item in the list.

```
template <class Type>
bool orderedLinkedList<Type>::
                        search(const Type& searchItem) const
```

```
{
    bool found = false;
    nodeType<Type> *current; //pointer to traverse the list

    current = first;   //start the search at the first node

    while (current != NULL && !found)
        if (current->info >= searchItem)
            found = true;
        else
            current = current->link;

    if (found)
        found = (current->info == searchItem); //test for equality

    return found;
}//end search
```

As in the case of the search function of the `class unorderedLinkedList`, the search function of the `class orderedLinkedList` is also of $O(n)$.

Insert a Node

To insert an item in an ordered linked list, we first find the place where the new item is supposed to go, then we insert the item in the list. To find the place for the new item in the list, as before, we search the list. Here we use two pointers, `current` and `trailCurrent`, to search the list. The pointer `current` points to the node whose `info` is being compared with the item to be inserted, and `trailCurrent` points to the node just before `current`. Because the list is in order, the search algorithm is the same as before. The following cases arise:

Case 1: The list is initially empty. The node containing the new item is the only node and, thus, the first node in the list.

Case 2: The new item is smaller than the smallest item in the list. The new item goes at the beginning of the list. In this case, we need to adjust the list's head pointer—that is, `first`. Also, `count` is incremented by 1.

Case 3: The item is to be inserted somewhere in the list.

Case 3a: The new item is larger than all the items in the list. In this case, the new item is inserted at the end of the list. Thus, the value of `current` is `NULL` and the new item is inserted after `trailCurrent`. Also, `count` is incremented by 1.

Case 3b: The new item is to be inserted somewhere in the middle of the list. In this case, the new item is inserted between `trailCurrent` and `current`. Also, `count` is incremented by 1.

The following statements can accomplish both cases 3a and 3b. Assume `newNode` points to the new node.

```
trailCurrent->link = newNode;
newNode->link = current;
```

Let us next illustrate Case 3.

Case 3: The list is not empty, and the item to be inserted is larger than the first item in the list. As indicated previously, this case has two scenarios.

Case 3a: The item to be inserted is larger than the largest item in the list; that is, it goes at the end of the list. Consider the list shown in Figure 5-24.

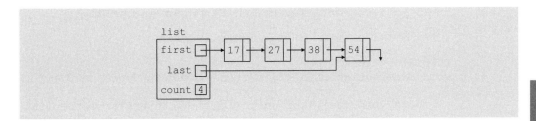

FIGURE 5-24 `list` before inserting 65

Suppose that we want to insert 65 in the list. After inserting 65, the resulting list is as shown in Figure 5-25.

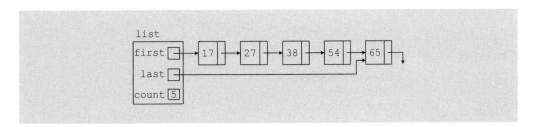

FIGURE 5-25 `list` after inserting 65

Case 3b: The item to be inserted goes somewhere in the middle of the list. Again consider the list shown in Figure 5-24. Suppose that we want to insert 25 in this list. Clearly, 25 goes between 17 and 27, which would require the link of the node with `info` 17 to be changed. After inserting 25, the resulting list is as shown in Figure 5-26.

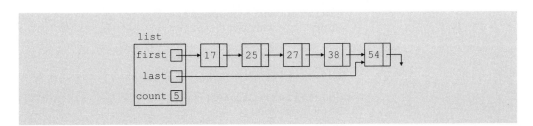

FIGURE 5-26 `list` after inserting 25 in the list in Figure 5-24

From case 3, it follows that we must first traverse the list to find the place where the new item is to be inserted. It also follows that we should traverse the list with two pointers— say, current and trailCurrent. The pointer current is used to traverse the list and compare the info of the node in the list with the item to be inserted. The pointer trailCurrent points to the node just before current. For example, in case 3b, when the search stops, trailCurrent points to node 17 and current points to node 27. The item is inserted after trailCurrent. In case 3a, after searching the list to find the place for 65, trailCurrent points to node 54 and current is NULL.

The definition of the function insert is as follows:

```
template <class Type>
void orderedLinkedList<Type>::insert(const Type& newItem)
{
    nodeType<Type> *current; //pointer to traverse the list
    nodeType<Type> *trailCurrent; //pointer just before current
    nodeType<Type> *newNode;  //pointer to create a node

    bool found;

    newNode = new nodeType<Type>; //create the node
    newNode->info = newItem;    //store newItem in the node
    newNode->link = NULL;       //set the link field of the node
                                //to NULL

    if (first == NULL)  //Case 1
    {
        first = newNode;
        last = newNode;
        count++;
    }
    else
    {
        current = first;
        found = false;

        while (current != NULL && !found) //search the list
            if (current->info >= newItem)
                found = true;
            else
            {
                trailCurrent = current;
                current = current->link;
            }

        if (current == first)        //Case 2
        {
            newNode->link = first;
            first = newNode;
            count++;
        }
```

```
        else                        //Case 3
        {
            trailCurrent->link = newNode;
            newNode->link = current;

            if (current == NULL)
                last = newNode;

            count++;
        }
    }//end else
}//end insert
```

The function `insert` uses a `while` loop to find the place where the new item is to be inserted and this loop is similar to the `while` loop used in the `search` function. It can be shown that the function `insert` is of $O(n)$.

 NOTE   The function `insert` does not check if the item to be inserted is already in the list, that is, it does not check for duplicates. In Programming Exercise 7 at the end of this chapter you are asked to revise the definition of the function `insert` so that before inserting the item it checks whether the item to be inserted is already in the list. If the item to be inserted is already in the list, the function outputs an appropriate error message. In other words, duplicates are not allowed.

Insert First and Insert Last

The function `insertFirst` inserts the new item at the beginning of the list. However, because the resulting list must be sorted, the new item must be inserted at the proper place. Similarly, the function `insertLast` must insert the new item at the proper place. We, therefore, use the function `insert` to insert the new item at its proper place. The definitions of these functions are as follows:

```
template <class Type>
void orderedLinkedList<Type>::insertFirst(const Type& newItem)
{
    insert(newItem);
}//end insertFirst
```

```
template <class Type>
void orderedLinkedList<Type>::insertLast(const Type& newItem)
{
    insert(newItem);
}//end insertLast
```

Note that in reality, the functions `insertFirst` and `insertLast` do not apply to an ordered linked list because the new item must be inserted at the proper place in the list. However, you must provide its definition as these functions are declared as abstract in the parent class.

The functions `insertFirst` and `insertLast` use the function `insert`, which is of $O(n)$. It follows that these functions are of $O(n)$.

Delete a Node

To delete a given item from an ordered linked list, first we search the list to see whether the item to be deleted is in the list. The function to implement this operation is the same as the delete operation on general linked lists. Here, because the list is sorted, we can somewhat improve the algorithm for ordered linked lists.

As in the case of `insertNode`, we search the list with two pointers, `current` and `trailCurrent`. Similar to the operation `insertNode`, several cases arise:

Case 1: The list is initially empty. We have an error. We cannot delete from an empty list.

Case 2: The item to be deleted is contained in the first node of the list. We must adjust the head pointer of the list—that is, `first`.

Case 3: The item to be deleted is somewhere in the list. In this case, `current` points to the node containing the item to be deleted, and `trailCurrent` points to the node just before the node pointed to by `current`.

Case 4: The list is not empty, but the item to be deleted is not in the list.

After deleting a node, `count` is decremented by 1. The definition of the function `deleteNode` is as follows:

```
template <class Type>
void orderedLinkedList<Type>::deleteNode(const Type& deleteItem)
{
    nodeType<Type> *current; //pointer to traverse the list
    nodeType<Type> *trailCurrent; //pointer just before current
    bool found;

    if (first == NULL) //Case 1
        cout << "Cannot delete from an empty list." << endl;
    else
    {
        current = first;
        found = false;

        while (current != NULL && !found)  //search the list
            if (current->info >= deleteItem)
                found = true;
            else
            {
                trailCurrent = current;
                current = current->link;
            }

        if (current == NULL)    //Case 4
            cout << "The item to be deleted is not in the list."
                 << endl;
        else
            if (current->info == deleteItem) //the item to be
                                             //deleted is in the list
```

```
    {
        if (first == current)        //Case 2
        {
            first = first->link;

            if (first == NULL)
                last = NULL;

            delete current;
        }
        else                            //Case 3
        {
            trailCurrent->link = current->link;

            if (current == last)
                last = trailCurrent;

            delete current;
        }
        count--;
    }
    else                                //Case 4
        cout << "The item to be deleted is not in the "
             << "list." << endl;
    }
}//end deleteNode
```

From the definition of the function `deleteNode`, it can be shown that this function is of $O(n)$.

Table 5-8 gives the time-complexity of the operations of the `class orderedLinkedList`.

TABLE 5-8 Time-complexity of the operations of the `class orderedLinkedList`

Function	Time-complexity
search	$O(n)$
insert	$O(n)$
insertFirst	$O(n)$
insertLast	$O(n)$
deleteNode	$O(n)$

Header File of the Ordered Linked List

For the sake of completeness, we show how to create the header file that defines the `class orderedListType` and the operations on such lists. (We assume that the definition of the class linkedListType and the definitions of the functions to implement the operations are in the header file linkedList.h.)

```cpp
#ifndef H_orderedListType
#define H_orderedListType

//**********************************************************
// Author: D.S. Malik
//
// This class specifies the members to implement the basic
// properties of an ordered linked list. This class is
// derived from the class linkedListType.
//**********************************************************

#include "linkedList.h"

using namespace std;

template <class Type>
class orderedLinkedList: public linkedListType<Type>
{
public:
    bool search(const Type& searchItem) const;
      //Function to determine whether searchItem is in the list.
      //Postcondition: Returns true if searchItem is in the list,
      //     otherwise the value false is returned.

    void insert(const Type& newItem);
      //Function to insert newItem in the list.
      //Postcondition: first points to the new list, newItem is
      //     inserted at the proper place in the list, and count
      //     is incremented by 1.

    void insertFirst(const Type& newItem);
      //Function to insert newItem at the beginning of the list.
      //Postcondition: first points to the new list, newItem is
      //     inserted at the beginning of the list, last points to the
      //     last node in the list, and count is incremented by 1.
      //

    void insertLast(const Type& newItem);
      //Function to insert newItem at the end of the list.
      //Postcondition: first points to the new list, newItem is
      //     inserted at the end of the list, last points to the
      //     last node in the list, and count is incremented by 1.

    void deleteNode(const Type& deleteItem);
      //Function to delete deleteItem from the list.
      //Postcondition: If found, the node containing deleteItem is
      //     deleted from the list; first points to the first node of
      //     the new list, and count is decremented by 1. If
      //     deleteItem is not in the list, an appropriate message
      //     is printed.
};
```

```
//Place the definitions of the functions search, insert,
//insertfirst, insertLast, and deleteNode here.
   .
   .
   .
#endif
```

The following program tests various operations on an ordered linked list:

```
//************************************************************
// Author: D.S. Malik
//
// This program tests the various operations on an ordered
// linked list.
//************************************************************

#include <iostream>                          //Line 1
#include "orderedLinkedList.h"               //Line 2

using namespace std;                         //Line 3

int main()                                   //Line 4
{
    orderedLinkedList<int> list1, list2;     //Line 5
    int num;                                 //Line 6

    cout << "Line 7: Enter numbers ending "
         << "with -999." << endl;            //Line 7
    cin >> num;                              //Line 8

    while (num != -999)                      //Line 9
    {                                        //Line 10
        list1.insert(num);                   //Line 11
        cin >> num;                          //Line 12
    }                                        //Line 13

    cout << endl;                            //Line 14

    cout << "Line 15: list1: ";              //Line 15
    list1.print();                           //Line 16
    cout << endl;                            //Line 17

    list2 = list1; //test the assignment operator Line 18

    cout << "Line 19: list2: ";              //Line 19
    list2.print();                           //Line 20
    cout << endl;                            //Line 21

    cout << "Line 22: Enter the number to be "
         << "deleted: ";                     //Line 22
    cin >> num;                              //Line 23
    cout << endl;                            //Line 24
```

```
        list2.deleteNode(num);                          //Line 25

        cout << "Line 26: After deleting "
             << num << ", list2: " << endl;             //Line 26
        list2.print();                                  //Line 27
        cout << endl;                                   //Line 28

        return 0;                                       //Line 29
}                                                       //Line 30
```

Sample Run: In this sample run, the user input is shaded:

```
Line 7: Enter numbers ending with -999.
23 65 34 72 12 82 36 55 29 -999

Line 15: list1: 12 23 29 34 36 55 65 72 82
Line 19: list2: 12 23 29 34 36 55 65 72 82
Line 22: Enter the number to be deleted: 34

Line 26: After deleting 34, list2:
12 23 29 36 55 65 72 82
```

The preceding output is self-explanatory. The details are left as an exercise for you.

> **NOTE** Notice that the function `insert` does not check whether the item to be inserted is already in the list, that is, it does not check for duplicates. Programming Exercise 7 at the end of this chapter asks you to revise the definition of the function `insert` so that before inserting the item it checks whether it is already in the list. If the item to be inserted is already in the list, the function outputs an appropriate error message. In other words, duplicates are not allowed.

Doubly Linked Lists

A doubly linked list is a linked list in which every node has a next pointer and a back pointer. In other words, every node contains the address of the next node (except the last node), and every node contains the address of the previous node (except the first node). (See Figure 5-27.)

FIGURE 5-27 Doubly linked list

A doubly linked list can be traversed in either direction. That is, we can traverse the list starting at the first node or, if a pointer to the last node is given, we can traverse the list starting at the last node.

As before, the typical operations on a doubly linked list are as follows: Initialize the list, destroy the list, determine whether the list is empty, search the list for a given item, insert an item, delete an item, and so on. The following class defines a doubly linked list as an ADT and specifies the basic operations on a doubly linked list:

```cpp
//************************************************************
// Author: D.S. Malik
//
// This class specifies the members to implement the basic
// properties of an ordered doubly linked list.
//************************************************************

    //Definition of the node
template <class Type>
struct nodeType
{
    Type info;
    nodeType<Type> *next;
    nodeType<Type> *back;
};

template <class Type>
class doublyLinkedList
{
public:
    const doublyLinkedList<Type>& operator=
                         (const doublyLinkedList<Type> &);
      //Overload the assignment operator.

    void initializeList();
      //Function to initialize the list to an empty state.
      //Postcondition: first = NULL; last = NULL; count = 0;

    bool isEmptyList() const;
      //Function to determine whether the list is empty.
      //Postcondition: Returns true if the list is empty,
      //                otherwise returns false.

    void destroy();
      //Function to delete all the nodes from the list.
      //Postcondition: first = NULL; last = NULL; count = 0;

    void print() const;
      //Function to output the info contained in each node.

    void reversePrint() const;
      //Function to output the info contained in each node
      //in reverse order.
```

```
int length() const;
    //Function to return the number of nodes in the list.
    //Postcondition: The value of count is returned.

Type front() const;
    //Function to return the first element of the list.
    //Precondition: The list must exist and must not be empty.
    //Postcondition: If the list is empty, the program terminates;
    //    otherwise, the first element of the list is returned.

Type back() const;
    //Function to return the last element of the list.
    //Precondition: The list must exist and must not be empty.
    //Postcondition: If the list is empty, the program terminates;
    //    otherwise, the last element of the list is returned.

bool search(const Type& searchItem) const;
    //Function to determine whether searchItem is in the list.
    //Postcondition: Returns true if searchItem is found in the
    //    list, otherwise returns false.

void insert(const Type& insertItem);
    //Function to insert insertItem in the list.
    //Precondition: If the list is nonempty, it must be in order.
    //Postcondition: insertItem is inserted at the proper place
    //    in the list, first points to the first node, last points
    //    to the last node of the new list, and count is
    //    incremented by 1.

void deleteNode(const Type& deleteItem);
    //Function to delete deleteItem from the list.
    //Postcondition: If found, the node containing deleteItem is
    //    deleted from the list; first points to the first node of
    //    the new list, last points to the last node of the new
    //    list, and count is decremented by 1; otherwise an
    //    appropriate message is printed.

doublyLinkedList();
    //default constructor
    //Initializes the list to an empty state.
    //Postcondition: first = NULL; last = NULL; count = 0;

doublyLinkedList(const doublyLinkedList<Type>& otherList);
    //copy constructor
~doublyLinkedList();
    //destructor
    //Postcondition: The list object is destroyed.

protected:
    int count;
    nodeType<Type> *first; //pointer to the first node
    nodeType<Type> *last;  //pointer to the last node
```

```
private:
    void copyList(const doublyLinkedList<Type>& otherList);
        //Function to make a copy of otherList.
        //Postcondition: A copy of otherList is created and assigned
        //     to this list.
};
```

We leave the UML class diagram of the `class doublyLinkedList` as an exercise for you, see Exercise 11 at the end of this chapter.

The functions to implement the operations of a doubly linked list are similar to the ones discussed earlier. Here, because every node has two pointers, `back` and `next`, some of the operations require the adjustment of two pointers in each node. For the insert and delete operations, because we can traverse the list in either direction, we use only one pointer to traverse the list. Let us call this pointer `current`. We can set the value of `trailCurrent` by using both the `current` pointer and the `back` pointer of the node pointed to by `current`. We give the definition of each function here, with four exceptions. Definitions of the functions `copyList`, the copy constructor, overloading the assignment operator, and the destructor are left as exercises for you. (See Programming Exercise 10 at the end of this chapter.) Furthermore, the function `copyList` is used only to implement the copy constructor and overload the assignment operator.

Default Constructor

The default constructor initializes the doubly linked list to an empty state. It sets `first` and `last` to `NULL` and `count` to 0.

```
template <class Type>
doublyLinkedList<Type>::doublyLinkedList()
{
    first= NULL;
    last = NULL;
    count = 0;
}
```

isEmptyList

This operation returns `true` if the list is empty; otherwise, it returns `false`. The list is empty if the pointer `first` is `NULL`.

```
template <class Type>
bool doublyLinkedList<Type>::isEmptyList() const
{
    return (first == NULL);
}
```

Destroy the List

This operation deletes all the nodes in the list, leaving the list in an empty state. We traverse the list starting at the first node and then delete each node. Furthermore, `count` is set to 0.

```
template <class Type>
void doublyLinkedList<Type>::destroy()
{
    nodeType<Type> *temp; //pointer to delete the node

    while (first != NULL)
    {
        temp = first;
        first = first->next;
        delete temp;
    }

    last = NULL;
    count = 0;
}
```

Initialize the List

This operation reinitializes the doubly linked list to an empty state. This task can be done by using the operation destroy. The definition of the function initializeList is as follows:

```
template <class Type>
void doublyLinkedList<Type>::initializeList()
{
    destroy();
}
```

Length of the List

The length of a linked list (that is, how many nodes are in the list) is stored in the variable count. Therefore, this function returns the value of this variable.

```
template <class Type>
int doublyLinkedList<Type>::length() const
{
    return count;
}
```

Print the List

The function print outputs the info contained in each node. We traverse the list starting from the first node.

```
template <class Type>
void doublyLinkedList<Type>::print() const
{
    nodeType<Type> *current; //pointer to traverse the list

    current = first;  //set current to point to the first node

    while (current != NULL)
```

```
    {
        cout << current->info << "   ";   //output info
        current = current->next;
    }//end while
}//end print
```

Reverse Print the List

This function outputs the `info` contained in each node in reverse order. We traverse the list in reverse order starting from the last node. Its definition is as follows:

```
template <class Type>
void doublyLinkedList<Type>::reversePrint() const
{
    nodeType<Type> *current; //pointer to traverse the list

    current = last;  //set current to point to the last node

    while (current != NULL)
    {
        cout << current->info << "   ";
        current = current->back;
    }//end while
}//end reversePrint
```

Search the List

The function `search` returns `true` if `searchItem` is found in the list; otherwise, it returns `false`. The search algorithm is exactly the same as the search algorithm for an ordered linked list.

```
template <class Type>
bool doublyLinkedList<Type>::search(const Type& searchItem) const
{
    bool found = false;
    nodeType<Type> *current; //pointer to traverse the list

    current = first;

    while (current != NULL && !found)
        if (current->info >= searchItem)
            found = true;
        else
            current = current->next;

    if (found)
        found = (current->info == searchItem); //test for equality

    return found;
}//end search
```

First and Last Elements

The function `front` returns the first element of the list and the function `back` returns the last element of the list. If the list is empty, both functions terminate the program. Their definitions are as follows:

```
template <class Type>
Type doublyLinkedList<Type>::front() const
{
    assert(first != NULL);

    return first->info;
}

template <class Type>
Type doublyLinkedList<Type>::back() const
{
    assert(last != NULL);

    return last->info;
}
```

INSERT A NODE

Because we are inserting an item in a doubly linked list, the insertion of a node in the list requires the adjustment of two pointers in certain nodes. As before, we find the place where the new item is supposed to be inserted, create the node, store the new item, and adjust the link fields of the new node and other particular nodes in the list. There are four cases:

Case 1: Insertion in an empty list

Case 2: Insertion at the beginning of a nonempty list

Case 3: Insertion at the end of a nonempty list

Case 4: Insertion somewhere in a nonempty list

Both cases 1 and 2 require us to change the value of the pointer `first`. Cases 3 and 4 are similar. After inserting an item, `count` is incremented by 1. Next, we show case 4.

Consider the doubly linked list shown in Figure 5-28.

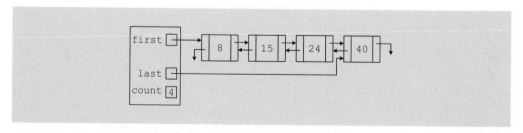

FIGURE 5-28 Doubly linked list before inserting 20

Suppose that 20 is to be inserted in the list. After inserting 20, the resulting list is as shown in Figure 5-29.

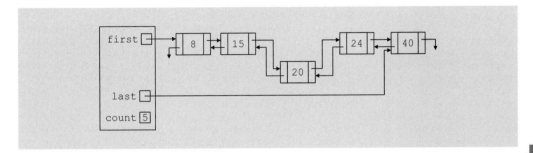

FIGURE 5-29 Doubly linked list after inserting 20

From Figure 5-29, it follows that the next pointer of node 15, the back pointer of node 24, and both the next and back pointers of node 20 need to be adjusted.

The definition of the function insert is as follows:

```
template <class Type>
void doublyLinkedList<Type>::insert(const Type& insertItem)
{
    nodeType<Type> *current;      //pointer to traverse the list
    nodeType<Type> *trailCurrent; //pointer just before current
    nodeType<Type> *newNode;      //pointer to create a node
    bool found;

    newNode = new nodeType<Type>; //create the node
    newNode->info = insertItem;   //store the new item in the node
    newNode->next = NULL;
    newNode->back = NULL;

    if (first == NULL) //if list is empty, newNode is the only node
    {
        first = newNode;
        last = newNode;
        count++;
    }
    else
    {
        found = false;
        current = first;

        while (current != NULL && !found) //search the list
            if (current->info >= insertItem)
                found = true;
            else
            {
                trailCurrent = current;
                current = current->next;
            }
```

```
        if (current == first) //insert newNode before first
        {
            first->back = newNode;
            newNode->next = first;
            first = newNode;
            count++;
        }
        else
        {
            //insert newNode between trailCurrent and current
            if (current != NULL)
            {
                trailCurrent->next = newNode;
                newNode->back = trailCurrent;
                newNode->next = current;
                current->back = newNode;
            }
            else
            {
                trailCurrent->next = newNode;
                newNode->back = trailCurrent;
                last = newNode;
            }

            count++;
        }//end else
    }//end else
}//end insert
```

DELETE A NODE

This operation deletes a given item (if found) from the doubly linked list. As before, we first search the list to see whether the item to be deleted is in the list. The search algorithm is the same as before. Similar to the insert operation, this operation (if the item to be deleted is in the list) requires the adjustment of two pointers in certain nodes. The delete operation has several cases:

Case 1: The list is empty.

Case 2: The item to be deleted is in the first node of the list, which would require us to change the value of the pointer first.

Case 3: The item to be deleted is somewhere in the list.

Case 4: The item to be deleted is not in the list.

After deleting a node, `count` is decremented by 1. Let us demonstrate case 3. Consider the list shown in Figure 5–30.

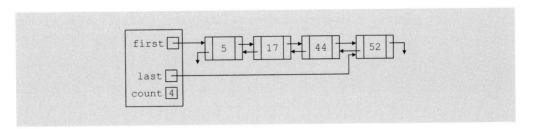

FIGURE 5-30 Doubly linked list before deleting `17`

Suppose that the item to be deleted is 17. First, we search the list with two pointers and find the node with `info` 17, and then adjust the link field of the affected nodes. (See Figure 5–31.)

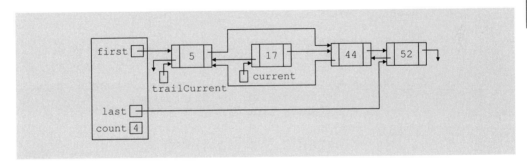

FIGURE 5-31 List after adjusting the links of the nodes before and after the node with `info` 17

Next, we delete the node pointed to by `current`. (See Figure 5–32.)

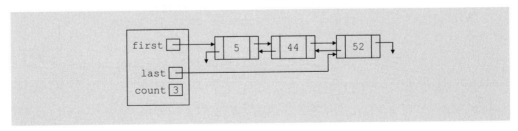

FIGURE 5-32 List after deleting the node with `info` 17

The definition of the function `deleteNode` is as follows:

```
template <class Type>
void doublyLinkedList<Type>::deleteNode(const Type& deleteItem)
{
    nodeType<Type> *current; //pointer to traverse the list
    nodeType<Type> *trailCurrent; //pointer just before current
```

```
    bool found;

    if (first == NULL)
        cout << "Cannot delete from an empty list." << endl;
    else if (first->info == deleteItem) //node to be deleted is
                                        //the first node
    {
        current = first;
        first = first->next;

        if (first != NULL)
            first->back = NULL;
        else
            last = NULL;

        count--;

        delete current;
    }
    else
    {
        found = false;
        current = first;

        while (current != NULL && !found)  //search the list
            if (current->info >= deleteItem)
                found = true;
            else
                current = current->next;

        if (current == NULL)
            cout << "The item to be deleted is not in "
                 << "the list." << endl;
        else if (current->info == deleteItem) //check for equality
        {
            trailCurrent = current->back;
            trailCurrent->next = current->next;

            if (current->next != NULL)
                current->next->back = trailCurrent;

            if (current == last)
                last = trailCurrent;

            count--;
            delete current;
        }
        else
            cout << "The item to be deleted is not in list." endl;
    }//end else
}//end deleteNode
```

STL Sequence Container: `list`

Chapter 4 listed three types of sequence containers—vector, deque, and list. The sequence containers vector and deque are described in Chapter 4. This section describes the STL sequence container list. List containers are implemented as doubly linked lists. Thus, every element in a list points to its immediate predecessor and to its immediate successor (except the first and last elements). Recall that a linked list is not a random access data structure such as an array. Therefore, to access, for example, the fifth element in the list, we must first traverse the first four elements.

The name of the class containing the definition of the class list is list. The definition of the class list, and the definitions of the functions to implement the various operations on a list, are contained in the header file list. Therefore, to use list in a program, the program must include the following statement:

```
#include <list>
```

Like other container classes, the class list contains several constructors. Thus, a list object can be initialized in several ways when it is declared, as described in Table 5-9.

TABLE 5-9 Various ways to declare a `list` object

Statement	Description
`list<elemType> listCont;`	Creates the empty list container listCont. (The default constructor is invoked.)
`list<elemType> listCont(otherList);`	Creates the list container listCont and initializes it to the elements of otherList. listCont and otherList are of the same type.
`list<elemType> listCont(size);`	Creates the list container listCont of size size. listCont is initialized using the default constructor.
`list<elemType> listCont(n, elem);`	Creates the list container listCont of size n. listCont is initialized using n copies of the element elem.
`list<elemType> listCont(beg, end);`	Creates the list container listCont. listCont is initialized to the elements in the range [beg, end), that is, all the elements in the range beg...end-1. Both beg and end are iterators.

Table 4-5 describes the operations that are common to all containers, and Table 4-6 describes the operations that are common to all sequence containers. In addition to these common operations, Table 5-10 describes the operations that are specific to a `list` container. The name of the function implementing the operation is shown in bold. (Suppose that `listCont` is a container of type `list`.)

TABLE 5-10 Operations specific to a `list` container

Expression	Description
listCont.**assign**(n, elem)	Assigns n copies of elem.
listCont.**assign**(beg, end)	Assigns all the elements in the range beg...end−1. Both beg and end are iterators.
listCont.**push_front**(elem)	Inserts elem at the beginning of listCont.
listCont.**pop_front**()	Removes the first element from listCont.
listCont.**front**()	Returns the first element. (Does not check whether the container is empty.)
listCont.**back**()	Returns the last element. (Does not check whether the container is empty.)
listCont.**remove**(elem)	Removes all the elements that are equal to elem.
listCont.**remove_if**(oper)	Removes all the elements for which oper is true.
listCont.**unique**()	If the consecutive elements in listCont have the same value, removes the duplicates.
listCont.**unique**(oper)	If the consecutive elements in listCont have the same value, removes the duplicates, for which oper is true.
listCont1.**splice**(pos, listCont2)	All the elements of listCont2 are moved to listCont1 before the position specified by the iterator pos. After this operation, listCont2 is empty.

TABLE 5-10 Operations specific to a list container (continued)

Expression	Description
listCont1.**splice**(pos, listCont2, pos2)	All the elements starting at pos2 of listCont2 are moved to listCont1 before the position specified by the iterator pos.
listCont1.**splice**(pos, listCont2, beg, end)	All the elements in the range beg...end-1 of listCont2 are moved to listCont1 before the position specified by the iterator pos. Both beg and end are iterators.
listCont.**sort**()	The elements of listCont are sorted. The sort criterion is <.
listCont.**sort**(oper)	The elements of listCont are sorted. The sort criterion is specified by oper.
listCont1.**merge**(listCont2)	Suppose that the elements of listCont1 and listCont2 are sorted. This operation moves all the elements of listCont2 into listCont1. After this operation, the elements in listCont1 are sorted. Moreover, after this operation, listCont2 is empty.
listCont1.**merge**(listCont2, oper)	Suppose that the elements of listCont1 and listCont2 are sorted according to the sort criteria oper. This operation moves all the elements of listCont2 into listCont1. After this operation, the elements in listCont1 are sorted according to the sort criteria oper.
listCont.**reverse**()	The elements of listCont are reversed.

Example 5-1 shows how to use various operations on a list container.

EXAMPLE 5-1

```
//************************************************************
// Author: D.S. Malik
//
// This program illustrates how to use a list container in a
// program.
//************************************************************
```

```
#include <iostream>                                         //Line 1
#include <list>                                             //Line 2
#include <iterator>                                         //Line 3
#include <algorithm>                                        //Line 4

using namespace std;                                        //Line 5

int main()                                                  //Line 6
{                                                           //Line 7
    list<int> intList1, intList2;                           //Line 8

    ostream_iterator<int> screen(cout, " ");                //Line 9

    intList1.push_back(23);                                 //Line 10
    intList1.push_back(58);                                 //Line 11
    intList1.push_back(58);                                 //Line 12
    intList1.push_back(36);                                 //Line 13
    intList1.push_back(15);                                 //Line 14
    intList1.push_back(98);                                 //Line 15
    intList1.push_back(58);                                 //Line 16

    cout << "Line 17: intList1: ";                          //Line 17
    copy(intList1.begin(), intList1.end(), screen);         //Line 18
    cout << endl;                                           //Line 19

    intList2 = intList1;                                    //Line 20

    cout << "Line 21: intList2: ";                          //Line 21
    copy(intList2.begin(), intList2.end(), screen);         //Line 22
    cout << endl;                                           //Line 23

    intList1.unique();                                      //Line 24

    cout << "Line 25: After removing the consecutive "
         << "duplicates," << endl
         << "          intList1: ";                         //Line 25
    copy(intList1.begin(), intList1.end(), screen);         //Line 26
    cout << endl;                                           //Line 27

    intList2.sort();                                        //Line 28

    cout << "Line 29: After sorting, intList2: ";           //Line 29
    copy(intList2.begin(), intList2.end(), screen);         //Line 30
    cout << endl;                                           //Line 31

    return 0;                                               //Line 32
}                                                           //Line 33
```

Sample Run:

```
Line 17: intList1: 23 58 58 36 15 98 58
Line 21: intList2: 23 58 58 36 15 98 58
Line 25: After removing the consecutive duplicates,
         intList1: 23 58 36 15 98 58
Line 29: After sorting, intList2: 15 23 36 58 58 58 98
```

For the most part, the output of the preceding program is straightforward. The statements in Lines 10 through 16 insert the element numbers 23, 58, 58, 36, 15, 98, and 58 (in that order) into `intList1`. The statement in Line 20 copies the elements of `intList1` into `intList2`. After this statement executes, `intList1` and `intList2` are identical. The statement in Line 24 removes any consecutive occurrences of the same elements. For example, the number 58 appears consecutively two times. The operation unique removes two occurrences of 58. Note that this operation has no effect on the 58 that appears at the end of `intList1`. The statement in Line 28 sorts `intList2`.

Linked Lists with Header and Trailer Nodes

When inserting and deleting items from a linked list (especially an ordered list), we saw that there are special cases, such as inserting (or deleting) at the beginning (the first node) of the list or in an empty list. These cases needed to be handled separately. As a result, the insertion and deletion algorithms were not as simple and straightforward as we would like. One way to simplify these algorithms is to never insert an item before the first or last item and to never delete the first node. Next we discuss how to accomplish this.

Suppose the nodes of a list are in order; that is, they are arranged with respect to a given key. Suppose it is possible for us to determine what the smallest and largest keys are in the given data set. In this case, we can set up a node, called the **header**, at the beginning of the list containing a value smaller than the smallest value in the data set. Similarly, we can set up a node, called the **trailer**, at the end of the list containing a value larger than the largest value in the data set. These two nodes, header and trailer, serve merely to simplify the insertion and deletion algorithms and are not part of the actual list. The actual list is between these two nodes.

For example, suppose the data are ordered according to the last name. Further, assume that the last name is a string of at most 8 characters. The smallest last name is larger than the string `"A"` and the largest last name is smaller than the string `"zzzzzzzz"`. We can set up the header node with the value `"A"` and the trailer node with the value `"zzzzzzzz"`. Figure 5-33 shows an empty and a nonempty linked list with header and trailer nodes.

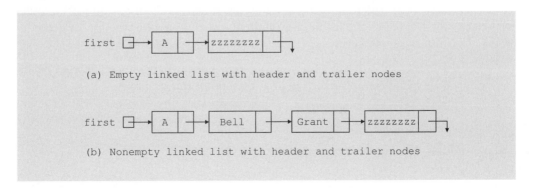

(a) Empty linked list with header and trailer nodes

(b) Nonempty linked list with header and trailer nodes

FIGURE 5-33 Linked list with header and trailer nodes

As before, the usual operations on lists with header and trailer nodes are as follows: Initialize the list (to an empty state), destroy the list, print the list, find the length of the list, search the list for a given item, insert an item in the list, delete an item from the list, and copy the list.

We leave it as an exercise for you to design a class to implement a linked list with header and trailer nodes. (See Programming Exercise 12 at the end of this chapter.)

Circular Linked Lists

A linked list in which the last node points to the first node is called a **circular linked list**. Figure 5-34 shows various circular linked lists.

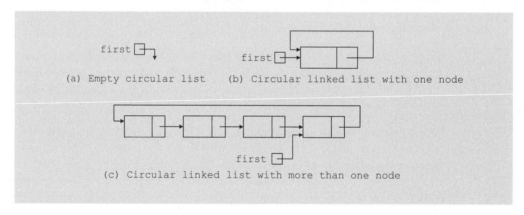

(a) Empty circular list   (b) Circular linked list with one node

(c) Circular linked list with more than one node

FIGURE 5-34 Circular linked lists

In a circular linked list with more than one node, as in Figure 5-34(c), it is convenient to make the pointer `first` point to the last node of the list. Then by using `first` you can access both the first and the last node of the list. For example, first points to the last node and `first->link` points to the first node.

As before, the usual operations on a circular list are as follows: Initialize the list (to an empty state), determine if the list is empty, destroy the list, print the list, find the length of the list, search the list for a given item, insert an item in the list, delete an item from the list, and copy the list.

We leave it as exercise for you to design a class to implement a sorted circular linked list. (See Programming Exercise 13 at the end of this chapter.)

PROGRAMMING EXAMPLE: Video Store

During holidays or on weekends, a family or an individual typically rents a movie either from a local store or online. Therefore, we write a program that does the following:

1. Rent a video; that is, check out a video.
2. Return, or check in, a video.
3. Create a list of videos owned by the store.
4. Show the details of a particular video.
5. Print a list of all the videos in the store.
6. Check whether a particular video is in the store.
7. Maintain a customer database.
8. Print a list of all the videos rented by each customer.

Let us write a program for the video store. This example further illustrates the object-oriented design methodology and, in particular, inheritance and overloading.

The programming requirement tells us that the video store has two major components: videos and customers. We will describe these two components in detail. We also need to maintain various lists:

- A list of all the videos in the store
- A list of all the store's customers
- Lists of the videos currently rented by each customer

We will develop the program in two parts. In part 1, we design, implement, and test the video component. In part 2, we design and implement the customer component, which is then added to the video component developed in part 1. That is, after completing parts 1 and 2, we can perform all the operations listed previously.

PART 1: VIDEO COMPONENT

Video Object

This is the first stage, wherein we discuss the video component. The common things associated with a video are as follows:

- Name of the movie
- Names of the stars
- Name of the producer
- Name of the director
- Name of the production company
- Number of copies in the store

From this list, we see that some of the operations to be performed on the video object are as follows:

1. Set the video information—that is, the title, stars, production company, and so on.

2. Show the details of a particular video.

3. Check the number of copies in the store.

4. Check out (that is, rent) the video. In other words, if the number of copies is greater than zero, decrement the number of copies by one.

5. Check in (that is, return) the video. To check in a video, first we must check whether the store owns such a video and, if it does, increment the number of copies by one.

6. Check whether a particular video is available—that is, check whether the number of copies currently in the store is greater than zero.

The deletion of a video from the video list requires that the video list be searched for the video to be deleted. Thus, we need to check the title of a video to find out which video is to be deleted from the list. For simplicity, we assume that two videos are the same if they have the same title.

The following class defines the video object as an ADT:

```cpp
//***********************************************************
// Author: D.S. Malik
//
// class videoType
// This class specifies the members to implement a video.
//***********************************************************

#include <iostream>
#include <string>

using namespace std;

class videoType
{
    friend ostream& operator<< (ostream&, const videoType&);

public:
    void setVideoInfo(string title, string star1,
                      string star2, string producer,
                      string director, string productionCo,
                      int setInStock);
    //Function to set the details of a video.
    //The private member variables are set according to the
    //parameters.
```

```
    //Postcondition: videoTitle = title; movieStar1 = star1;
    //      movieStar2 = star2; movieProducer = producer;
    //      movieDirector = director;
    //      movieProductionCo = productionCo;
    //      copiesInStock = setInStock;

int getNoOfCopiesInStock() const;
    //Function to check the number of copies in stock.
    //Postcondition: The value of copiesInStock is returned.

void checkOut();
    //Function to rent a video.
    //Postcondition: The number of copies in stock is
    //      decremented by one.

void checkIn();
    //Function to check in a video.
    //Postcondition: The number of copies in stock is
    //      incremented by one.

void printTitle() const;
    //Function to print the title of a movie.

void printInfo() const;
    //Function to print the details of a video.
    //Postcondition: The title of the movie, stars, director,
    //      and so on are displayed on the screen.

bool checkTitle(string title);
    //Function to check whether the title is the same as the
    //title of the video.
    //Postcondition: Returns the value true if the title is the
    //      same as the title of the video; false otherwise.

void updateInStock(int num);
    //Function to increment the number of copies in stock by
    //adding the value of the parameter num.
    //Postcondition: copiesInStock = copiesInStock + num;

void setCopiesInStock(int num);
    //Function to set the number of copies in stock.
    //Postcondition: copiesInStock = num;

string getTitle() const;
    //Function to return the title of the video.
    //Postcondition: The title of the video is returned.

videoType(string title = "", string star1 = "",
          string star2 = "", string producer = "",
          string director = "", string productionCo = "",
          int setInStock = 0);
```

```
        //constructor
        //The member variables are set according to the
        //incoming parameters. If no values are specified, the
        //default values are assigned.
        //Postcondition: videoTitle = title; movieStar1 = star1;
        //     movieStar2 = star2; movieProducer = producer;
        //     movieDirector = director;
        //     movieProductionCo = productionCo;
        //     copiesInStock = setInStock;

        //Overload the relational operators.
    bool operator==(const videoType&) const;
    bool operator!=(const videoType&) const;

private:
    string videoTitle;   //variable to store the name of the movie
    string movieStar1;   //variable to store the name of the star
    string movieStar2;   //variable to store the name of the star
    string movieProducer; //variable to store the name of the
                          //producer
    string movieDirector; //variable to store the name of the
                          //director
    string movieProductionCo; //variable to store the name
                              //of the production company
    int copiesInStock;   //variable to store the number of
                         //copies in stock
};
```

We leave the UML diagram of the class videoType as an exercise for you, see Exercise 15 at the end of this chapter.

For easy output, we will overload the output stream insertion operator, <<, for the class videoType.

Next, we write the definitions of each function in the **class** videoType. The definitions of these functions, as shown here, are quite straightforward and easy to follow:

```
void videoType::setVideoInfo(string title, string star1,
                             string star2, string producer,
                             string director,
                             string productionCo,
                             int setInStock)
{
    videoTitle = title;
    movieStar1 = star1;
    movieStar2 = star2;
    movieProducer = producer;
    movieDirector = director;
    movieProductionCo = productionCo;
    copiesInStock = setInStock;
}
```

```cpp
void videoType::checkOut()
{
    if (getNoOfCopiesInStock() > 0)
        copiesInStock--;
    else
        cout << "Currently out of stock" << endl;
}

void videoType::checkIn()
{
    copiesInStock++;
}

int videoType::getNoOfCopiesInStock() const
{
    return copiesInStock;
}

void videoType::printTitle() const
{
    cout << "Video Title: " << videoTitle << endl;
}

void videoType::printInfo() const
{
    cout << "Video Title: " << videoTitle << endl;
    cout << "Stars: " << movieStar1 << " and "
         << movieStar2 << endl;
    cout << "Producer: " << movieProducer << endl;
    cout << "Director: " << movieDirector << endl;
    cout << "Production Company: " << movieProductionCo << endl;
    cout << "Copies in stock: " << copiesInStock << endl;
}

bool videoType::checkTitle(string title)
{
    return (videoTitle == title);
}

void videoType::updateInStock(int num)
{
    copiesInStock += num;
}

void videoType::setCopiesInStock(int num)
{
    copiesInStock = num;
}
```

5

```cpp
string videoType::getTitle() const
{
    return videoTitle;
}

videoType::videoType(string title, string star1,
                     string star2, string producer,
                     string director,
                     string productionCo, int setInStock)
{
    setVideoInfo(title, star1, star2, producer, director,
                 productionCo, setInStock);
}

bool videoType::operator==(const videoType& other) const
{
    return (videoTitle == other.videoTitle);
}

bool videoType::operator!=(const videoType& other) const
{
    return (videoTitle != other.videoTitle);
}

ostream& operator<< (ostream& osObject, const videoType& video)
{
    osObject << endl;
    osObject << "Video Title: " << video.videoTitle << endl;
    osObject << "Stars: " << video.movieStar1 << " and "
             << video.movieStar2 << endl;
    osObject << "Producer: " << video.movieProducer << endl;
    osObject << "Director: " << video.movieDirector << endl;
    osObject << "Production Company: "
             << video.movieProductionCo << endl;
    osObject << "Copies in stock: " << video.copiesInStock
             << endl;
    osObject << "_____" << endl;

    return osObject;
}
```

Video List

This program requires us to maintain a list of all the videos in the store, and we should be able to add a new video to our list. In general, we would not know how many videos are in the store, and adding or deleting a video from the store would change the number of videos in the store. Therefore, we will use a linked list to create a list of videos.

Earlier in this chapter, we defined the class unorderedLinkedList to create a linked list of objects. We also defined the basic operations such as insertion and deletion of a video in the list. However, some operations are very specific to the video list, such as check out a video, check in a video, set the number of copies of a video, and so on. These operations are not available in the class `unorderedLinkedList`. We, therefore, derive a class `videoListType` from the class `unorderedLinkedList` and add these operations.

The definition of the class `videoListType` is as follows:

```
//*****************************************************************
// Author: D.S. Malik
//
// class videoListType
// This class specifies the members to implement a list of videos.
//*****************************************************************

#include <string>
#include "unorderedLinkedList.h"
#include "videoType.h"

using namespace std;

class videoListType:public unorderedLinkedList<videoType>
{
public:
    bool videoSearch(string title) const;
      //Function to search the list to see whether a
      //particular title, specified by the parameter title,
      //is in the store.
      //Postcondition: Returns true if the title is found, and
      //    false otherwise.

    bool isVideoAvailable(string title) const;
      //Function to determine whether a copy of a particular
      //video is in the store.
      //Postcondition: Returns true if at least one copy of the
      //    video specified by title is in the store, and false
      //    otherwise.

    void videoCheckOut(string title);
      //Function to check out a video, that is, rent a video.
      //Postcondition: copiesInStock is decremented by one.

    void videoCheckIn(string title);
      //Function to check in a video returned by a customer.
      //Postcondition: copiesInStock is incremented by one.

    bool videoCheckTitle(string title) const;
      //Function to determine whether a particular video is in
      //the store.
      //Postcondition: Returns true if the video's title is the
      //    same as title, and false otherwise.
```

5

```
    void videoUpdateInStock(string title, int num);
      //Function to update the number of copies of a video
      //by adding the value of the parameter num. The
      //parameter title specifies the name of the video for
      //which the number of copies is to be updated.
      //Postcondition: copiesInStock = copiesInStock + num;

    void videoSetCopiesInStock(string title, int num);
      //Function to reset the number of copies of a video.
      //The parameter title specifies the name of the video
      //for which the number of copies is to be reset, and the
      //parameter num specifies the number of copies.
      //Postcondition: copiesInStock = num;

    void videoPrintTitle() const;
      //Function to print the titles of all the videos in the store.

  private:
    void searchVideoList(string title, bool& found,
                         nodeType<videoType>* &current) const;
      //This function searches the video list for a particular
      //video, specified by the parameter title.
      //Postcondition: If the video is found, the parameter found is
      //    set to true, otherwise it is set to false. The parameter
      //    current points to the node containing the video.
};
```

Note that the class videoListType is derived from the class unorderedLinkedList via a public inheritance. Furthermore, unorderedLinkedList is a class template and we have passed the class videoType as a parameter to this class. That is, the class videoListType is not a template. Because we are now dealing with a very specific data type, the class videoListType is no longer needed to be a template. Thus, the info type of each node in the linked list is now videoType. Through the member functions of the class videoType, certain members—such as videoTitle and copiesInStock of an object of type videoType—can now be accessed.

The definitions of the functions to implement the operations of the class videoListType are given next.

The primary operations on the video list are to check in a video and to check out a video. Both operations require the list to be searched and the location of the video being checked in or checked out to be found in the video list. Other operations such as seeing whether a particular video is in the store, updating the number of copies of a video, and so on also require the video list to be searched. To simplify the search process, we will write a function that searches the video list for a particular video. If the video is found, it sets a parameter found to true and returns a pointer to the video so that check-in, check-out, and other operations on the video object can be performed. Note that the function searchVideoList is a private data member of the class videoListType because it is used only for internal manipulation. First, we describe the search procedure.

The following function definition performs the desired search:

```
void videoListType::searchVideoList(string title, bool& found,
                            nodeType<videoType>* &current) const
{
    found = false;    //set found to false

    current = first; //set current to point to the first node

    while (current != NULL && !found)       //search the list
        if (current->info.checkTitle(title)) //the item is found
            found = true;
        else
            current = current->link; //advance current to
                                     //the next node
}//end searchVideoList
```

If the search is successful, the parameter found is set to true and the parameter current points to the node containing the video info. If it is unsuccessful, found is set to false and current will be NULL.

The definitions of the other functions of the class videoListType follow:

```
bool videoListType::isVideoAvailable(string title) const
{
    bool found;
    nodeType<videoType> *location;

    searchVideoList(title, found, location);

    if (found)
        found = (location->info.getNoOfCopiesInStock() > 0);
    else
        found = false;

    return found;
}

void videoListType::videoCheckIn(string title)
{
    bool found = false;
    nodeType<videoType> *location;

    searchVideoList(title, found, location); //search the list

    if (found)
        location->info.checkIn();
```

```cpp
    else
        cout << "The store does not carry " << title
             << endl;
}

void videoListType::videoCheckOut(string title)
{
    bool found = false;
    nodeType<videoType> *location;

    searchVideoList(title, found, location); //search the list

    if (found)
        location->info.checkOut();
    else
        cout << "The store does not carry " << title
             << endl;
}

bool videoListType::videoCheckTitle(string title) const
{
    bool found = false;
    nodeType<videoType> *location;

    searchVideoList(title, found, location); //search the list

    return found;
}

void videoListType::videoUpdateInStock(string title, int num)
{
    bool found = false;
    nodeType<videoType> *location;

    searchVideoList(title, found, location); //search the list

    if (found)
        location->info.updateInStock(num);
    else
        cout << "The store does not carry " << title
             << endl;
}

void videoListType::videoSetCopiesInStock(string title, int num)
{
    bool found = false;
    nodeType<videoType> *location;

    searchVideoList(title, found, location);

    if (found)
        location->info.setCopiesInStock(num);
```

```
        else
            cout << "The store does not carry " << title
                << endl;
}

bool videoListType::videoSearch(string title) const
{
    bool found = false;
    nodeType<videoType> *location;

    searchVideoList(title, found, location);

    return found;
}

void videoListType::videoPrintTitle() const
{
    nodeType<videoType>* current;

    current = first;
    while (current != NULL)
    {
        current->info.printTitle();
        current = current->link;
    }
}
```

PART 2:
CUSTOMER
COMPONENT

Customer
Object

The customer object stores information about a customer, such as the first name, last name, account number, and a list of videos rented by the customer.

Every customer is a person. We have already designed the class personType in Example 1-12 (Chapter 1) and described the necessary operations on the name of a person. Therefore, we can derive the class customerType from the class personType and add the additional members that we need. First, however, we must redefine the class personType to take advantage of the new features of object-oriented design that you have learned, such as operator overloading, and then derive the class customerType.

The basic operations on an object of type customerType are as follows:

1. Print the name, the account number, and the list of rented videos.
2. Set the name and the account number.
3. Rent a video; that is, add the rented video to the list.
4. Return a video; that is, delete the rented video from the list.
5. Show the account number.

The details of implementing the customer component are left as an exercise for you. (See Programming Exercise 14 at the end of this chapter.)

MAIN PROGRAM

We will now write the main program to test the video object. We assume that the necessary data for the videos are stored in a file. We will open the file and create the list of videos owned by the video store. The data in the input file is in the following form:

```
video title (that is, the name of the movie)
movie star1
movie star2
movie producer
movie director
movie production co.
number of copies
  .
  .
  .
```

We will write a function, `createVideoList`, to read the data from the input file and create the list of videos. We will also write a function, `displayMenu`, to show the different choices—such as check in a movie or check out a movie—that the user can make. The algorithm of the function `main` is as follows:

1. Open the input file.

   If the input file does not exist, exit the program.
2. Create the list of videos (`createVideoList`).
3. Show the menu (`displayMenu`).
4. While not done

Perform various operations.

Opening the input file is straightforward. Let us describe Steps 2 and 3, which are accomplished by writing two separate functions: `createVideoList` and `displayMenu`.

createVideoList

This function reads the data from the input file and creates a linked list of videos. Because the data will be read from a file and the input file was opened in the function `main`, we pass the input file pointer to this function. We also pass the video list pointer, declared in the function `main`, to this function. Both parameters are reference parameters. Next, we read the data for each video and then insert the video in the list. The general algorithm is as follows:

1. Read the data and store it in a video object.
2. Insert the video in the list.
3. Repeat Steps a and b for each video's data in the file.

displayMenu This function informs the user what to do. It contains the following output statements:

Select one of the following:

1: To check whether the store carries a particular video

2: To check out a video

3: To check in a video

4: To check whether a particular video is in stock

5: To print only the titles of all the videos

6: To print a list of all the videos

9: To exit

PROGRAM LISTING

```cpp
//****************************************************************
// Author: D.S. Malik
//
// This program illustrates how to use the classes videoType and
// videListType to create and process a list of videos.
//****************************************************************

#include <iostream>
#include <fstream>
#include <string>
#include "videoType.h"
#include "videoListType.h"

using namespace std;

void createVideoList(ifstream& infile,
                     videoListType& videoList);
void displayMenu();

int main()
{
    videoListType videoList;
    int choice;
    char ch;
    string title;

    ifstream infile;

            //open the input file
    infile.open("videoDat.txt");
    if (!infile)
```

```cpp
{
    cout << "The input file does not exist. "
         << "The program terminates!!!" << endl;
    return 1;
}

    //create the video list
createVideoList(infile, videoList);
infile.close();

    //show the menu
displayMenu();
cout << "Enter your choice: ";
cin >> choice;      //get the request
cin.get(ch);
cout << endl;

    //process the requests
while (choice != 9)
{
    switch (choice)
    {
    case 1:
        cout << "Enter the title: ";
        getline(cin, title);
        cout << endl;

        if (videoList.videoSearch(title))
            cout << "The store carries " << title
                 << endl;
        else
            cout << "The store does not carry "
                 << title << endl;
        break;

    case 2:
        cout << "Enter the title: ";
        getline(cin, title);
        cout << endl;

        if (videoList.videoSearch(title))
        {
            if (videoList.isVideoAvailable(title))
            {
                videoList.videoCheckOut(title);
                cout << "Enjoy your movie: "
                     << title << endl;
            }
            else
                cout << "Currently " << title
                     << " is out of stock." << endl;
        }
```

```
            else
                cout << "The store does not carry "
                    << title << endl;
            break;

    case 3:
        cout << "Enter the title: ";
        getline(cin, title);
        cout << endl;

        if (videoList.videoSearch(title))
        {
            videoList.videoCheckIn(title);
            cout << "Thanks for returning "
                << title << endl;
        }
        else
            cout << "The store does not carry "
                << title << endl;
        break;

    case 4:
        cout << "Enter the title: ";
        getline(cin, title);
        cout << endl;

        if (videoList.videoSearch(title))
        {
            if (videoList.isVideoAvailable(title))
                cout << title << " is currently in "
                    << "stock." << endl;
            else
                cout << title << " is currently out "
                    << "of stock." << endl;
        }
        else
            cout << "The store does not carry "
                << title << endl;
        break;

    case 5:
        videoList.videoPrintTitle();
        break;

    case 6:
        videoList.print();
        break;

    default:
        cout << "Invalid selection." << endl;
    }//end switch
```

```
            displayMenu();        //display menu

            cout << "Enter your choice: ";
            cin >> choice;         //get the next request
            cin.get(ch);
            cout << endl;
    }//end while

    return 0;
}

void createVideoList(ifstream& infile,
                     videoListType& videoList)
{
    string title;
    string star1;
    string star2;
    string producer;
    string director;
    string productionCo;
    char ch;
    int inStock;

    videoType newVideo;

    getline(infile, title);

    while (infile)
    {
        getline(infile, star1);
        getline(infile, star2);
        getline(infile, producer);
        getline(infile, director);
        getline(infile, productionCo);
        infile >> inStock;
        infile.get(ch);
        newVideo.setVideoInfo(title, star1, star2, producer,
                              director, productionCo, inStock);
        videoList.insertFirst(newVideo);

        getline(infile, title);
    }//end while
}//end createVideoList

void displayMenu()
{
    cout << "Select one of the following:" << endl;
    cout << "1: To check whether the store carries a "
         << "particular video." << endl;
    cout << "2: To check out a video." << endl;
    cout << "3: To check in a video." << endl;
```

```
        cout << "4: To check whether a particular video is "
             << "in stock." << endl;
        cout << "5: To print only the titles of all the videos."
             << endl;
        cout << "6: To print a list of all the videos." << endl;
        cout << "9: To exit" << endl;
} //end createVideoList
```

QUICK REVIEW

1. A linked list is a list of items, called nodes, in which the order of the nodes is determined by the address, called a link, stored in each node.

2. The pointer to a linked list—that is, the pointer to the first node in the list—is stored in a separate location, called the head or first.

3. A linked list is a dynamic data structure.

4. The length of a linked list is the number of nodes in the list.

5. Item insertion and deletion from a linked list does not require data movement; only the pointers are adjusted.

6. A (single) linked list is traversed in only one direction.

7. The search on a linked list is sequential.

8. The first (or head) pointer of a linked list is always fixed, pointing to the first node in the list.

9. To traverse a linked list, the program must use a pointer different than the head pointer of the list, initialized to the first node in the list.

10. In a doubly linked list, every node has two links: one points to the next node, and one points to the previous node.

11. A doubly linked list can be traversed in either direction.

12. In a doubly linked list, item insertion and deletion requires the adjustment of two pointers in a node.

13. The name of the class containing the definition of the `class list` is `list`.

14. In addition to the operations that are common to sequence containers (see Chapter 4), the other operations that can be used to manipulate the elements in a list container are `assign`, `push_front`, `pop_front`, `front`, `back`, `remove`, `remove_if`, `unique`, `splice`, `sort`, `merge`, and `reverse`.

15. A linked list with header and trailer nodes simplifies the insertion and deletion operations.

16. The header and trailer nodes are not part of the actual list. The actual list elements are between the header and trailer nodes.

17. A linked list with header and trailer nodes is empty if the only nodes in the list are the header and the trailer.

18. A circular linked list is a list in which, if the list is nonempty, the last node points to the first node.

EXERCISES

1. Mark the following statements as true or false.

   a. In a linked list, the order of the elements is determined by the order in which the nodes were created to store the elements.

   b. In a linked list, memory allocated for the nodes is sequential.

   c. A single linked list can be traversed in either direction.

   d. In a linked list, nodes are always inserted either at the beginning or the end because a linked link is not a random access data structure.

   e. The head pointer of a linked list cannot be used to traverse the list.

   Consider the linked list shown in Figure 5-35. Assume that the nodes are in the usual `info-link` form. Use this list to answer Exercises 2 through 7. If necessary, declare additional variables. (Assume that `list`, `p`, `s`, `A`, and `B` are pointers of type `nodeType`.)

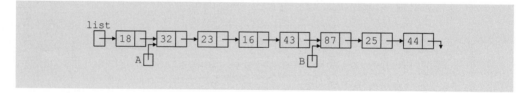

FIGURE 5-35 Linked list for Exercises 2–7

2. What is the output of each of the following C++ statements?

   a. `cout << list->info;`

   b. `cout << A->info;`

   c. `cout << B->link->info;`

   d. `cout << list->link->link->info`

3. What is the value of each of the following relational expressions?

   a. `list->info >= 18`

   b. `list->link == A`

   c. `A->link->info == 16`

   d. `B->link == NULL`

   e. `list->info == 18`

4. Mark each of the following statements as valid or invalid. If a statement is invalid, explain why.

   a. `A = B;`

   b. `list->link = A->link;`

   c. `list->link->info = 45;`

   d. `*list = B;`

   e. `*A = *B;`

   f. `B = A->link->info;`

   g. `A->info = B->info;`

   h. `list = B->link->link;`

   i. `B = B->link->link->link;`

5. Write C++ statements to do the following:

   a. Make `A` point to the node containing info 23.

   b. Make `list` point to the node containing 16.

   c. Make `B` point to the last node in the list.

   d. Make `list` point to an empty list.

   e. Set the value of the node containing 25 to 35.

   f. Create and insert the node with info 10 after the node pointed to by `A`.

   g. Delete the node with info 23. Also, deallocate the memory occupied by this node.

6. What is the output of the following C++ code?

```
p = list;

while (p != NULL)
    cout << p->info << " ";
    p = p->link;
cout << endl;
```

7. If the following C++ code is valid, show the output. If it is invalid, explain why.

   a.
```
s = A;
p = B;
s->info = B;
p = p->link;
cout << s->info << " " << p->info << endl;
```

   b.
```
p = A;
p = p->link;
s = p;
p->link = NULL;
s = s->link;
cout << p->info << " " << s->info << endl;
```

8. Show what is produced by the following C++ code. Assume the node is in the usual `info-link` form with the `info` of type `int`. (`list` and `ptr` are pointers of type `nodeType`.)

   a.
   ```cpp
   list = new nodeType;
   list->info = 10;
   ptr = new nodeType;
   ptr->info = 13;
   ptr->link = NULL;
   list->link = ptr;
   ptr = new nodeType;
   ptr->info = 18;
   ptr->link = list->link;
   list->link = ptr;
   cout << list->info << " " << ptr->info << " ";
   ptr = ptr->link;
   cout << ptr->info << endl;
   ```

   b.
   ```cpp
   list = new nodeType;
   list->info = 20;
   ptr = new nodeType;
   ptr->info = 28;
   ptr->link = NULL;
   list->link = ptr;
   ptr = new nodeType;
   ptr->info = 30;
   ptr->link = list;
   list = ptr;
   ptr = new nodeType;
   ptr->info = 42;
   ptr->link = list->link;
   list->link = ptr;
   ptr = List;
   while (ptr != NULL)
   {
       cout << ptr->info << endl;
       ptr = ptr->link;
   }
   ```

9. Consider the following C++ statements. (The class `unorderedLinkedList` is as defined in this chapter.)

   ```cpp
   unorderedLinkedList<int> list;
   ```

   ```cpp
   list.insertFirst(15);
   list.insertLast(28);
   list.insertFirst(30);
   list.insertFirst(2);
   list.insertLast(45);
   list.insertFirst(38);
   list.insertLast(25);
   list.deleteNode(30);
   list.insertFirst(18);
   list.deleteNode(28);
   ```

```
list.deleteNode(12);
list.print();
```

What is the output of this program segment?

10. Suppose the input is:

```
18 30 4 32 45 36 78 19 48 75 -999
```

What is the output of the following C++ code? (The class unorderedLinkedList is as defined in this chapter.)

```
unorderedLinkedList<int> list;
unorderedLinkedList<int> copyList;
int num;

cin >> num;
while (num != -999)
{
    if (num % 5 == 0 || num % 5 == 3)
        list.insertFirst(num);
    else
        list.insertLast(num);
    cin >> num;
}

list.print();
cout << endl;

copyList = list;

copyList.deleteNode(78);
copyList.deleteNode(35);

cout << "Copy List = ";
copyList.print();
cout << endl;
```

11. Draw the UML diagram of the class doublyLinkedList as discussed in this chapter.

12. Suppose that intList is a list container and

```
intList = {3, 23, 23, 43, 56, 11, 11, 23, 25}
```

Show intList after the following statement executes: intList.unique();

13. Suppose that intList1 and intList2 are list containers and

```
intList1 = {3, 58, 78, 85, 6, 15, 93, 98, 25}
intList2 = {5, 24, 16, 11, 60, 9}
```

Show intList1 after the following statement executes:

```
intList1.splice(intList1.begin(), intList2);
```

14. What is the output of the following program segment?

```
list<int>  intList;
ostream_iterator<int> screen(cout, " ");
list<int>::iterator listIt;

intList.push_back(5);
intList.push_front(23);
intList.push_front(45);
intList.pop_back();
intList.push_back(35);

intList.push_front(0);
intList.push_back(50);
intList.push_front(34);

copy(intList.begin(), intList.end(), screen);
cout << endl;

listIt = intList.begin();
intList.insert(listIt,76);

++listIt;
++listIt;
intList.insert(listIt,38);

intList.pop_back();

++listIt;
++listIt;

intList.erase(listIt);
intList.push_front(2 * intList.back());
intList.push_back(3 * intList.front());

copy(intList.begin(), intList.end(), screen);
cout << endl;
```

15. Draw the UML diagram of the class `videoType` of the Programming Example Video Store.

16. Draw the UML diagram of the class `videoListType` of the Programming Example Video Store.

PROGRAMMING EXERCISES

1. (**Online Address Book Revisited**) Programming Exercise 9 in Chapter 3 could handle a maximum of only 500 entries. Using linked lists, redo the program to handle as many entries as required. Add the following operations to your program:

   a. Add or delete a new entry to the address book.

   b. When the program terminates, write the data in the address book to a disk.

2. Extend the class `linkedListType` by adding the following operations:

    a. Find and delete the node with the smallest `info` in the list. (Delete only the first occurrence and traverse the list only once.)

    b. Find and delete all occurrences of a given `info` from the list. (Traverse the list only once.) Add these as abstract functions in the class `linkedListType` and provide the definitions of these functions in the class `unorderedLinkedList`. Also write a program to test these functions.

3. Extend the class `linkedListType` by adding the following operations:

    a. Write a function that returns the info of the kth element of the linked list. If no such element exists, terminate the program.

    b. Write a function that deletes the kth element of the linked list. If no such element exists, output an appropriate message. Provide the definitions of these functions in the class `linkedListType`. Also write a program to test these functions. (Use either the class `unorderedLinkedList` or the class `orderedLinkedList` to test your function.)

4. **(Dividing a linked list into two sublists of almost equal sizes)**

    a. Add the operation `divideMid` to the class `linkedListType` as follows:

    ```
    void divideMid(linkedListType<Type> &sublist);
        //This operation divides the given list into two sublists
        //of (almost) equal sizes.
        //Postcondition: first points to the first node and last
        //    points to the last node of the first sublist.
        //    sublist.first points to the first node and sublist.last
        //    points to the last node of the second sublist.
    ```

    Consider the following statements:

    ```
    unorderedLinkedList<int> myList;
    unorderedLinkedList<int> subList;
    ```

    Suppose `myList` points to the list with elements 34 65 27 89 12 (in this order). The statement:

    ```
    myList.divideMid(subList);
    ```

    divides `myList` into two sublists: `myList` points to the list with the elements 34 65 27, and `subList` points to the sublist with the elements 89 12.

    b. Write the definition of the function template to implement the operation `divideMid`. Also write a program to test your function.

5

5. **(Splitting a linked list, at a given node, into two sublists)**

   a. Add the following operation to the `class linkedListType`:

   ```
   void divideAt(linkedListType<Type> &secondList,
                 const Type& item);
       //Divide the list at the node with the info item into two
       //sublists.
       //Postcondition: first and last point to the first and last
       //    nodes of the first sublist.
       //    secondList.first and secondList.last point to the
       //    first and last nodes of the second sublist.
   ```

   Consider the following statements:

   ```
   unorderedLinkedList<int> myList;
   unorderedLinkedList<int> otherList;
   ```

   Suppose `myList` points to the list with the elements:

   ```
   34 65 18 39 27 89 12
   ```

   (in this order). The statement:

   ```
   myList.divideAt(otherList, 18);
   ```

   divides `myList` into two sublists: `myList` points to the list with the elements 34 65, and `otherList` points to the sublist with the elements 18 39 27 89 12.

   b. Write the definition of the function template to implement the operation `divideAt`. Also write a program to test your function.

6. a. Add the following operation to the `class orderedLinkedList`:

   ```
   void mergeLists(orderedLinkedList<Type> &list1,
                   orderedLinkedList<Type> &list2);
       //This function creates a new list by merging the
       //elements of list1 and list2.
       //Postcondition: first points to the merged list; list1
       //    and list2 are empty
   ```

   Example: Consider the following statements:

   ```
   orderedLinkedList<int> newList;
   orderedLinkedList<int> list1;
   orderedLinkedList<int> list2;
   ```

   Suppose `list1` points to the list with the elements 2 6 7 and `list2` points to the list with the elements 3 5 8. The statement:

   ```
   newList.mergeLists(list1, list2);
   ```

creates a new linked list with the elements in the order 2 3 5 6 7 8 and the object newList points to this list. Also, after the preceding statement executes, list1 and list2 are empty.

b. Write the definition of the function template mergeLists to implement the operation mergeLists. Also write a program to test your function.

7. The function insert of the class orderedLinkedList does not check if the item to be inserted is already in the list; that is, it does not check for duplicates. Rewrite the definition of the function insert so that before inserting the item it checks whether the item to be inserted is already in the list. If the item to be inserted is already in the list, the function outputs an appropriate error message. Also write a program to test your function.

8. In this chapter, the class to implement the nodes of a linked list is defined as a struct. The following rewrites the definition of the struct nodeType so that it is declared as a class and the member variables are private.

```
template <class Type>
class nodeType
{
public:
    const nodeType<Type>& operator=(const nodeType<Type>&);
        //Overload the assignment operator.

    void setInfo(const Type& elem);
        //Function to set the info of the node.
        //Postcondition: info = elem;

    Type getInfo() const;
        //Function to return the info of the node.
        //Postcondition: The value of info is returned.

    void setLink(nodeType<Type> *ptr);
        //Function to set the link of the node.
        //Postcondition: link = ptr;

    nodeType<Type>* getLink() const;
        //Function to return the link of the node.
        //Postcondition: The value of link is returned.

    nodeType();
        //Default constructor
        //Postcondition: link = NULL;

    nodeType(const Type& elem, nodeType<Type> *ptr);
        //Constructor with parameters
        //Sets info point to the object elem points to and
        //link is set to point to the object ptr points to.
        //Postcondition: info = elem; link = ptr
```

```
nodeType(const nodeType<Type> &otherNode);
   //Copy constructor

~nodeType();
   //Destructor

private:
    Type info;
    nodeType<Type> *link;
};
```

Write the definitions of the member functions of the class nodeType. Also write a program to test your class.

9. Programming Exercise 8 asks you to redefine the class to implement the nodes of a linked list so that the instance variables are private. Therefore, the class linkedListType and its derived classes unorderedLinkedList and orderedLinkedList can no longer directly access the instance variables of the class nodeType. Rewrite the definitions of these classes so that these classes use the member functions of the class nodeType to access the info and link fields of a node. Also write programs to test various operations of the classes unorderedLinkedList and orderedLinkedList.

10. Write the definitions of the function copyList, the copy constructor, and the function to overload the assignment operator for the class doublyLinkedList.

11. Write a program to test various operations of the class doublyLinkedList.

12. (**Linked List with Header and Trailer Nodes**) This chapter defined and identified various operations on a linked list with header and trailer nodes.

   a. Write the definition of the class that defines a linked list with header and trailer nodes as an ADT.

   b. Write the definitions of the member functions of the class defined in (a). (You may assume that the elements of the linked list with header and trailer nodes are in ascending order.)

   c. Write a program to test various operations of the class defined in (a).

13. (**Circular Linked Lists**) This chapter defined and identified various operations on a circular linked list.

   a. Write the definitions of the class circularLinkedList and its member functions. (You may assume that the elements of the circular linked list are in ascending order.)

   b. Write a program to test various operations of the class defined in (a).

14. (**Programming Example Video Store**)

   a. Complete the design and implementation of the class customerType defined in the Programming Example Video Store.

   b. Design and implement the class customerListType to create and maintain a list of customers for the video store.

15. (**Programming Example Video Store**) Complete the design and implementation of the video store program. In other words, write a program that uses the classes designed in the Programming Example Video Store and in Programming Exercise 14 to make a video store operational.

16. Redo the video store program so that the list of videos, the list of customers, and the list of videos rented by a customer are kept in a `list` container.

17. Extend the `class linkedListType` by adding the following function:

```
void rotate();
   //Function to remove the first node of a linked list and put it
   //at the end of the linked list.
```

18. Write a program that prompts the user to input a string and then outputs the string in the pig Latin form. The rules for converting a string into pig Latin form are as follows:

   a. If the string begins with a vowel, add the string `"-way"` at the end of the string. For example, the pig Latin form of the string `"eye"` is `"eye-way"`.

   b. If the string does not begin with a vowel, first add `"-"` at the end of the string. Then rotate the string one character at a time; that is, move the first character of the string to the end of the string until the first character of the string becomes a vowel. Then add the string `"ay"` at the end. For example, the pig Latin form of the string `"There"` is `"ere-Thay"`.

   c. Strings such as `"by"` contain no vowels. In cases like this, the letter y can be considered a vowel. So, for this program the vowels are a, e, i, o, u, y, A, E, I, O, U, and Y. Therefore, the pig Latin form of `"by"` is `"y-bay"`.

   d. Strings such as `"1234"` contain no vowels. The pig Latin form of the string `"1234"` is `"1234-way"`. That is, the pig Latin form of a string that has no vowels in it is the string followed by the string `"-way"`.

   Your program must store the characters of a string into a linked list and use the function `rotate`, as described in Programming Exercise 17, to rotate the string.

5

CHAPTER 6

RECURSION

In previous chapters, to devise solutions to problems we used the most common technique, called iteration. For certain problems, however, using the iterative technique to obtain the solution is quite complicated. This chapter introduces another problem-solving technique, called recursion, and provides several examples demonstrating how recursion works.

Recursive Definitions

The process of solving a problem by reducing it to smaller versions of itself is called **recursion**. Recursion is a very powerful way to solve certain problems for which the solution would otherwise be very complicated. Let us consider a problem that is familiar to most everyone.

In an algebra course, you probably learned how to find the factorial of a nonnegative integer. For example, the factorial of 5, written 5!, is $5 \times 4 \times 3 \times 2 \times 1 = 120$. Similarly, $4! = 4 \times 3 \times 2 \times 1 = 24$. Also, factorial of 0 is defined to be $0! = 1$. Note that $5! = 5 \times 4 \times 3 \times 2 \times 1 = 5 \times (4 \times 3 \times 2 \times 1) = 5 \times 4!$. In general, if n is a nonnegative, the factorial of n, written as $n!$ can be defined as follows:

$$0! = 1 \qquad\qquad\qquad \text{(Equation 6-1)}$$

$$n! = n \times (n-1)! \quad \text{if} \quad n > 0 \qquad \text{(Equation 6-2)}$$

In this definition, 0! is defined to be 1, and if n is an integer greater than 0, first we find $(n-1)!$ and then multiply it by n. To find $(n-1)!$, we apply the definition again. If $(n-1) > 0$, then we use Equation 6-2; otherwise, we use Equation 6-1. Thus, for an integer n greater than 0, $n!$ is obtained by first finding $(n-1)!$ and then multiplying $(n-1)!$ by n.

Let us apply this definition to find 3!. Here $n = 3$. Because $n > 0$, we use Equation 6-2 to obtain:

$$3! = 3 \times 2!$$

Next, we find 2! Here $n = 2$. Because $n > 0$, we use Equation 6-2 to obtain:

$$2! = 2 \times 1!$$

Now to find 1!, we again use Equation 6-2 because $n = 1 > 0$. Thus:

$$1! = 1 \times 0!$$

Finally, we use Equation 6-1 to find 0!, which is 1. Substituting 0! into 1! gives $1! = 1$. This gives $2! = 2 \times 1! = 2 \times 1 = 2$, which in turn gives $3! = 3 \times 2! = 3 \times 2 = 6$.

The solution in Equation 6-1 is direct—that is, the right side of the equation contains no factorial notation. The solution in Equation 6-2 is given in terms of a *smaller version of itself*. The definition of the factorial given in Equations 6-1 and 6-2 is called a **recursive definition**. Equation 6-1 is called the **base case** (that is, the case for which the solution is obtained directly); Equation 6-2 is called the **general case**.

Recursive definition: A definition in which something is defined in terms of a smaller version of itself.

From the previous example (factorial), it is clear that:

1. Every recursive definition must have one (or more) base cases.
2. The general case must eventually be reduced to a base case.
3. The base case stops the recursion.

The concept of recursion in computer science works similarly. Here, we talk about recursive algorithms and recursive functions. An algorithm that finds the solution to a given problem by reducing the problem to smaller versions of itself is called a **recursive algorithm**. The recursive algorithm must have one or more base cases, and the general solution must eventually be reduced to a base case.

A function that calls itself is called a **recursive function**. That is, the body of the recursive function contains a statement that causes the same function to execute again before completing the current call. Recursive algorithms are implemented using recursive functions.

Next, let us write the recursive function that implements the factorial function.

```
int fact(int num)
{
    if (num == 0)
        return 1;
    else
        return num * fact(num - 1);
}
```

Figure 6-1 traces the execution of the following statement:

```
cout << fact(3) << endl;
```

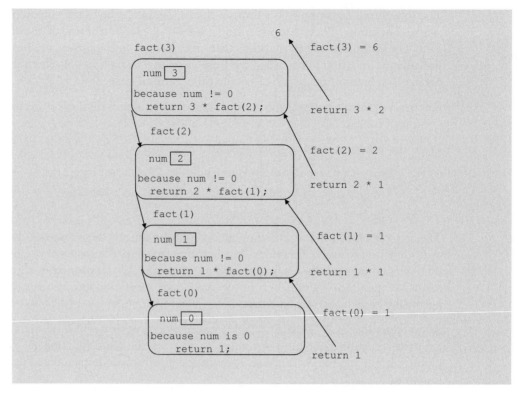

FIGURE 6-1 Execution of `fact(4)`

The output of the previous `cout` statement is: 6

In Figure 6-1, the down arrow represents the successive calls to the function `fact`, and the upward arrows represent the values returned to the caller, that is, the calling function.

Let us note the following from the previous example, involving the factorial function:

- Logically, you can think of a recursive function as having an unlimited number of copies of itself.
- Every call to a recursive function—that is, every recursive call—has its own code and its own set of parameters and local variables.
- After completing a particular recursive call, control goes back to the calling environment, which is the previous call. The current (recursive) call must execute completely before control goes back to the previous call. The execution in the previous call begins from the point immediately following the recursive call.

Direct and Indirect Recursion

A function is called **directly recursive** if it calls itself. A function that calls another function and eventually results in the original function call is said to be **indirectly**

recursive. For example, if a function A calls a function B and function B calls function A, then function A is indirectly recursive. Indirect recursion can be several layers deep. For example, suppose that function A calls function B, function B calls function C, function C calls function D, and function D calls function A. Function A is then indirectly recursive.

Indirect recursion requires the same careful analysis as direct recursion. The base cases must be identified and appropriate solutions to them must be provided. However, tracing through indirect recursion can be tedious. You must, therefore, exercise extra care when designing indirect recursive functions. For simplicity, the problems in this book involve only direct recursion.

A recursive function in which the last statement executed is the recursive call is called a **tail recursive function**. The function `fact` is an example of a tail recursive function.

Infinite Recursion

Figure 6–1 shows that the sequence of recursive calls eventually reached a call that made no further recursive calls. That is, the sequence of recursive calls eventually reached a base case. On the other hand, if every recursive call results in another recursive call, the recursive function (algorithm) is said to have infinite recursion. In theory, infinite recursion executes forever. Every call to a recursive function requires the system to allocate memory for the local variables and formal parameters. The system also saves this information so that after completing a call, control can be transferred back to the right caller. Therefore, because computer memory is finite, if you execute an infinite recursive function on a computer, the function executes until the system runs out of memory and results in an abnormal termination of the program.

Recursive functions (algorithms) must be carefully designed and analyzed. You must make sure that every recursive call eventually reduces to a base case. This chapter provides several examples that illustrate how to design and implement recursive algorithms.

To design a recursive function, you must do the following:

1. Understand the problem requirements.
2. Determine the limiting conditions. For example, for a list, the limiting condition is the number of elements in the list.
3. Identify the base cases and provide a direct solution to each base case.
4. Identify the general cases and provide a solution to each general case in terms of smaller versions of itself.

Problem Solving Using Recursion

The next few sections illustrate how recursive algorithms are developed and implemented in C++ using recursive functions.

Largest Element in an Array

In this example, we use a recursive algorithm to find the largest element in an array. Consider the list given in Figure 6-2.

```
          [0]  [1]  [2]  [3]  [4]  [5]  [6]
list     | 5 |  8 |  2 | 10 |  9 |  4 |   |
```

FIGURE 6-2 `list` with six elements

The largest element in the list in Figure 6-2 is 10.

Suppose `list` is the name of the array containing the list elements. Also, suppose that `list[a]...list[b]` stands for the array elements `list[a]`, `list[a + 1]`, ..., `list[b]`. For example, `list[0]...list[5]` represents the array elements `list[0]`, `list[1]`, `list[2]`, `list[3]`, `list[4]`, and `list[5]`. Similarly, `list[1]...list[5]` represents the array elements `list[1]`, `list[2]`, `list[3]`, `list[4]`, and `list[5]`. To write a recursive algorithm to find the largest element in `list`, let us think in terms of recursion.

If `list` is of length 1, then `list` has only one element, which is the largest element. Suppose the length of `list` is greater than 1. To find the largest element in `list[a]...list[b]`, we first find the largest element in `list[a + 1]...list[b]` and then compare this largest element with `list[a]`. That is, the largest element in `list[a]...list[b]` is given by:

```
maximum(list[a], largest(list[a + 1]...list[b]))
```

Let us apply this formula to find the largest element in the list shown in Figure 6-2. This list has six elements, given by `list[0]...list[5]`. Now the largest element in `list` is given by:

```
maximum(list[0], largest(list[1]...list[5]))
```

That is, the largest element in `list` is the maximum of `list[0]` and the largest element in `list[1]...list[5]`. To find the largest element in `list[1]...list[5]`, we use the same formula again because the length of this list is greater than 1. The largest element in `list[1]...list[5]` is then:

```
maximum(list[1], largest(list[2]...list[5]))
```

and so on. We see that every time we use the previous formula to find the largest element in a sublist, the length of the sublist in the next call is reduced by one. Eventually, the sublist is of length 1, in which case the sublist contains only one element, which is the largest element in the sublist. From this point onward, we backtrack through the recursive calls. This discussion translates into the following recursive algorithm, which is presented in pseudocode:

Base Case: The size of the list is 1
         The only element in the list is the largest element

General Case: The size of the list is greater than 1
       To find the largest element in list[a]...list[b]

    1. Find the largest element in list[a + 1]...list[b]
       and call it max
    2. Compare the elements list[a] and max
       if (list[a] >= max)
          the largest element in list[a]...list[b] is list[a]
       otherwise
          the largest element in list[a]...list[b] is max

This algorithm translates into the following C++ function to find the largest element in an array:

```
int largest(const int list[], int lowerIndex, int upperIndex)
{
    int max;

    if (lowerIndex == upperIndex)  //size of the sublist is one
        return list[lowerIndex];
    else
    {
        max = largest(list, lowerIndex + 1, upperIndex);

        if (list[lowerIndex] >= max)
            return list[lowerIndex];
        else
            return max;
    }
}
```

Consider the list given in Figure 6-3.

                             [0] [1] [2] [3]
                    list   5   10   12   8

FIGURE 6-3 list with four elements

Let us trace the execution of the following statement:

```
cout << largest(list, 0, 3) << endl;
```

Here `upperIndex` = 3 and the list has four elements. Figure 6-4 traces the execution of `largest(list, 0, 3)`.

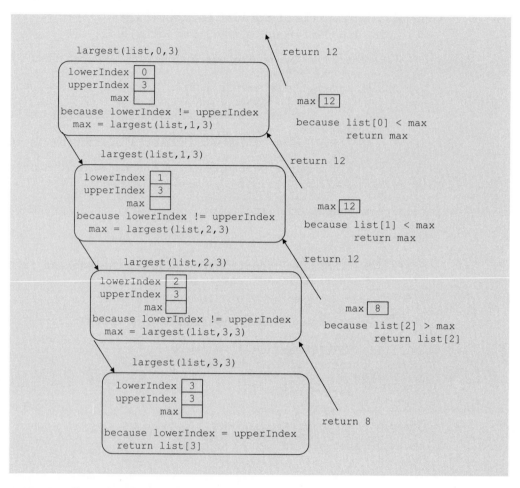

FIGURE 6-4 Execution of `largest(list, 0, 3)`

The value returned by the expression `largest(list, 0, 3)` is 12, which is the largest element in `list`.

The following C++ program uses the function `largest` to determine the largest element in a list:

```
//****************************************************************
// Author: D.S. Malik
//
// This program uses a recursive function to find the largest
// element in a list.
//****************************************************************

#include <iostream>

using namespace std;
```

```
int largest(const int list[], int lowerIndex, int upperIndex);

int main()
{
    int intArray[10] = {23, 43, 35, 38, 67, 12, 76, 10, 34, 8};

    cout << "The largest element in intArray: "
         << largest(intArray, 0, 9);
    cout << endl;

    return 0;
}

int largest(const int list[], int lowerIndex, int upperIndex)
{
    int max;

    if (lowerIndex == upperIndex) //size of the sublist is one
        return list[lowerIndex];
    else
    {
        max = largest(list, lowerIndex + 1, upperIndex);

        if (list[lowerIndex] >= max)
            return list[lowerIndex];
        else
            return max;
    }
}
```

Sample Run:

```
The largest element in intArray: 76
```

Print a Linked List in Reverse Order

The nodes of an ordered linked list (as constructed in Chapter 5) are in ascending order. Certain applications, however, might require the data to be printed in descending order, which means that we must print the list backward. We now discuss the function `reversePrint`. Given a pointer to a list, this function prints the elements of the list in reverse order.

Consider the linked list shown in Figure 6-5.

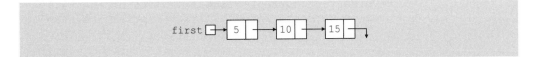

FIGURE 6-5 Linked list

For the list in Figure 6-5, the output should be in the following form:

```
15 10 5
```

Because the links are in only one direction, we cannot traverse the list backward starting from the last node. Let us see how we can effectively use recursion to print the list in reverse order.

Let us think in terms of recursion. We cannot print the info of the first node until we have printed the remainder of the list (that is, the tail of the first node). Similarly, we cannot print the info of the second node until we have printed the tail of the second node, and so on. Every time we consider the tail of a node, we reduce the size of the list by 1. Eventually, the size of the list is reduced to zero, in which case the recursion stops.

Base Case: List is empty: no action

General Case: List is nonempty

     1.   Print the tail

     2.   Print the element

Let us write this algorithm. (Suppose that current is a pointer to a linked list.)

```
if (current != NULL)
{
   reversePrint(current->link);      //print the tail
   cout << current->info << endl;    //print the node
}
```

Here, we do not see the base case; it is hidden. The list is printed only if the pointer, current, to the list is not NULL. Also, inside the if statement the recursive call is on the tail of the list. Because eventually the tail of a list will be empty, the if statement in the next call fails and the recursion stops. Also, note that statements (for example, printing the info of the node) appear after the recursive call; thus, when the transfer comes back to the calling function, we must execute the remaining statements. Recall that the function exits only after the last statement executes. (By the "last statement," we do not mean the physical last statement, but rather the logical last statement.)

Let us write a function template to implement the previous algorithm and then apply it to a list.

```
template <class Type>
void linkedListType<Type>::reversePrint
                         (nodeType<Type> *current) const
{
    if (current != NULL)
    {
        reversePrint(current->link);     //print the tail
        cout << current->info << " ";    //print the node
    }
}
```

Consider the statement

```
reversePrint(first);
```

where first is a pointer of type nodeType<Type>.

Let us trace the execution of this statement; which is a function call, for the list shown in Figure 6-5. Because the formal parameter is a value parameter, the value of the actual parameter is passed to the formal parameter. See Figure 6-6.

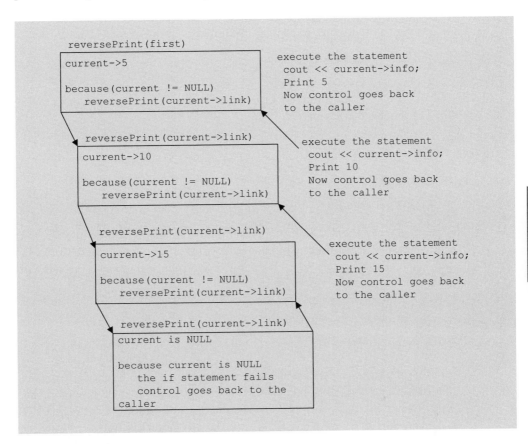

FIGURE 6-6 Execution of the statement `reversePrint(first);`

THE FUNCTION `printListReverse`

Now that we have written the function `reversePrint`, we can write the definition of the function `printListReverse`, which can be used to print an ordered linked list contained in an object of the type `linkedListType`. Its definition is as follows:

```cpp
template <class Type>
void linkedListType<Type>::printListReverse() const
{
    reversePrint(first);
    cout << endl;
}
```

We can include the function `printListReverse` as a `public` member in the definition of the class and the function `reversePrint` as a `private` member. We include the function `reversePrint` as a `private` member because it is used only to implement the function `printListReverse`.

Fibonacci Number

Consider the following sequence of numbers:

$$1, 1, 2, 3, 5, 8, 13, 21, 34, \ldots.$$

Given the first two numbers of the sequence (say a_1 and a_2), the nth number a_n, $n >= 3$, of this sequence is given by:

$$a_n = a_{n-1} + a_{n-2}$$

Thus:

$a_3 = a_2 + a_1 = 1 + 1 = 2$, $a_4 = a_3 + a_2 = 2 + 1 = 3$, and so on.

Such a sequence is called a **Fibonacci sequence**. In the previous sequence, $a_2 = 1$ and $a_1 = 1$. However, given any first two numbers, using this process, you can determine the nth number, a_n, $n >= 3$, of such a sequence. The number determined this way is called the **nth Fibonacci number**. Suppose $a_2 = 6$ and $a_1 = 3$.

Then:

$a_3 = a_2 + a_1 = 6 + 3 = 9;$ $\qquad\qquad a_4 = a_3 + a_2 = 9 + 6 = 15.$

In this example, we write a recursive function, `rFibNum`, to determine the desired Fibonacci number. The function `rFibNum` takes as parameters three numbers representing the first two numbers of the Fibonacci sequence and a number n, the desired nth Fibonacci number. The function `rFibNum` returns the nth Fibonacci number in the sequence.

Recall that the third Fibonacci number is the sum of the first two Fibonacci numbers. The fourth Fibonacci number in a sequence is the sum of the second and third Fibonacci numbers. Therefore, to calculate the fourth Fibonacci number, we add the second Fibonacci number and the third Fibonacci number (which is itself the sum of the first two Fibonacci numbers). The following recursive algorithm calculates the nth Fibonacci number, where a denotes the first Fibonacci number, b the second Fibonacci number, and n the nth Fibonacci number:

$$rFibNum(a, b, n) = \begin{cases} a & \text{if } n = 1 \\ b & \text{if } n = 2 \quad \text{(Equation 6-3)} \\ rFibNum(a, b, n - 1) + \\ rFibNum(a, b, n - 2) & \text{if } n > 2. \end{cases}$$

The following recursive function implements this algorithm:

```
int rFibNum(int a, int b, int n)
{
    if (n == 1)
        return a;
    else if (n == 2)
        return b;
    else
        return rFibNum(a, b, n - 1) + rFibNum(a, b, n - 2);
}
```

Let us trace the execution of the following statement:

```
cout << rFibNum(2, 3, 4) << endl;
```

In this statement, the first number is 2, the second number is 3, and we want to determine the 4th Fibonacci number of the sequence. Figure 6-7 traces the execution of the expression rFibNum(2,3,4). The value returned is 8, which is the 4th Fibonacci number of the sequence whose first number is 2 and whose second number is 3.

6

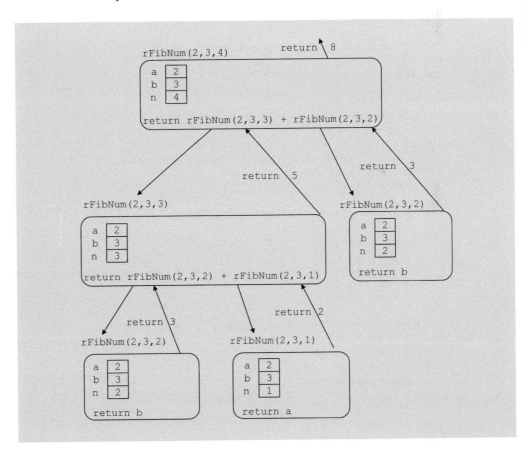

FIGURE 6-7 Execution of rFibNum(2, 3, 4)

Figure 6-7 reveals that the execution of the recursive version of the program to calculate a Fibonacci number is not as efficient as the execution of the nonrecursive version, even though the algorithm and the method implementing the algorithm might be simpler. In the recursive version, some values are calculated more than once. For example, to calculate rFibNum(2, 3, 4), the value rFibNum(2, 3, 2) is calculated twice. So a recursive method might be easier to write, but might not execute as efficiently. The section "Recursion or Iteration?", presented later in this chapter, discusses these two alternatives.

The following C++ program uses the function rFibNum:

```cpp
//*************************************************************
// Author: D.S. Malik
//
// Given the first two numbers of a Fibonacci sequence, this
// program uses a recursive function to determine a specific
// number(s) of a Fibonacci sequence.
//*************************************************************

#include <iostream>

using namespace std;

int rFibNum(int a, int b, int n);

int main()
{
    int firstFibNum;
    int secondFibNum;
    int nth;

    cout << "Enter the first Fibonacci number: ";
    cin >> firstFibNum;
    cout << endl;

    cout << "Enter the second Fibonacci number: ";
    cin >> secondFibNum;
    cout << endl;

    cout << "Enter the position of the desired Fibonacci number: ";
    cin >> nth;
    cout << endl;

    cout << "The Fibonacci number at position " << nth
         << " is: " << rFibNum(firstFibNum, secondFibNum, nth)
         << endl;

    return 0;
}
```

```
int rFibNum(int a, int b, int n)
{
    if (n == 1)
        return a;
    else if (n == 2)
        return b;
    else
        return rFibNum(a, b, n - 1) + rFibNum(a, b, n - 2);
}
```

Sample Run: In this sample run, the user input is shaded.

Enter the first Fibonacci number: 2

Enter the second Fibonacci number: 5

Enter the position of the desired Fibonacci number: 6

The Fibonacci number at position 6 is: 31

Tower of Hanoi

In the nineteenth century, a game called the Tower of Hanoi became popular in Europe. This game represents work that is under way in the temple of Brahma. At the creation of the universe, priests in the temple of Brahma were supposedly given three diamond needles, with one needle containing 64 golden disks. Each golden disk is slightly smaller than the disk below it. The priests' task is to move all 64 disks from the first needle to the third needle. The rules for moving the disks are as follows:

1. Only one disk can be moved at a time.
2. The removed disk must be placed on one of the needles.
3. A larger disk cannot be placed on top of a smaller disk.

The priests were told that once they had moved all the disks from the first needle to the third needle, the universe would come to an end.

Our objective is to write a program that prints the sequence of moves needed to transfer the disks from the first needle to the third needle. Figure 6-8 shows the Tower of Hanoi problem with three disks.

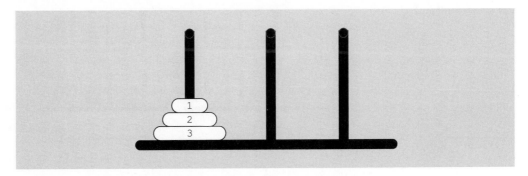

FIGURE 6-8 Tower of Hanoi problem with three disks

As before, we think in terms of recursion. Let us first consider the case when the first needle contains only one disk. In this case, the disk can be moved directly from needle 1 to needle 3. So let us consider the case when the first needle contains only two disks. In this case, first we move the first disk from needle 1 to needle 2, and then we move the second disk from needle 1 to needle 3. Finally, we move the first disk from needle 2 to needle 3. Next, we consider the case when the first needle contains three disks, and then generalize this to the case of 64 disks (in fact, to an arbitrary number of disks).

Suppose that needle 1 contains three disks. To move disk number 3 to needle 3, the top two disks must first be moved to needle 2. Disk number 3 can then be moved from needle 1 to needle 3. To move the top two disks from needle 2 to needle 3, we use the same strategy as before. This time we use needle 1 as the intermediate needle. Figure 6-9 shows a solution to the Tower of Hanoi problem with three disks.

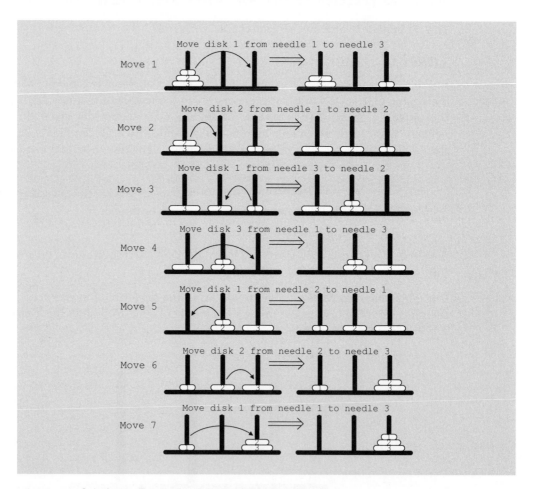

FIGURE 6-9 Solution to Tower of Hanoi problem with three disks

Let us now generalize this problem to the case of 64 disks. To begin, the first needle contains all 64 disks. Disk number 64 cannot be moved from needle 1 to needle 3 unless the top 63 disks are on the second needle. So first we move the top 63 disks from needle 1 to needle 2, and then we move disk number 64 from needle 1 to needle 3. Now the top 63 disks are all on needle 2. To move disk number 63 from needle 2 to needle 3, we first move the top 62 disks from needle 2 to needle 1, and then we move disk number 63 from needle 2 to needle 3. To move the remaining 62 disks, we use a similar procedure. This discussion translates into the following recursive algorithm given in pseudocode. Suppose that needle 1 contains n disks, where $n \geq 1$.

1. Move the top $n - 1$ disks from needle 1 to needle 2, using needle 3 as the intermediate needle.

2. Move disk number n from needle 1 to needle 3.

3. Move the top $n - 1$ disks from needle 2 to needle 3, using needle 1 as the intermediate needle.

This recursive algorithm translates into the following C++ function:

```cpp
void moveDisks(int count, int needle1, int needle3, int needle2)
{
    if (count > 0)
    {
        moveDisks(count - 1, needle1, needle2, needle3);

        cout << "Move disk " << count << " from " << needle1
             << " to " << needle3 << "." << endl;

        moveDisks(count - 1, needle2, needle3, needle1);
    }
}
```

TOWER OF HANOI: ANALYSIS

Let us determine how long it would take to move all 64 disks from needle 1 to needle 3. If needle 1 contains 3 disks, then the number of moves required to move all 3 disks from needle 1 to needle 3 is $2^3 - 1 = 7$. Similarly, if needle 1 contains 64 disks, then the number of moves required to move all 64 disks from needle 1 to needle 3 is $2^{64} - 1$. Because $2^{10} = 1024 \approx 1000 = 10^3$, we have

$$2^{64} = 2^4 \times 2^{60} \approx 2^4 \times 10^{18} = 1.6 \times 10^{19}$$

The number of seconds in one year is approximately 3.2×10^7. Suppose the priests move one disk per second and they do not rest. Now:

$$1.6 \times 10^{19} = 5 \times 3.2 \times 10^{18} = 5 \times (3.2 \times 10^7) \times 10^{11} = (3.2 \times 10^7) \times (5 \times 10^{11})$$

The time required to move all 64 disks from needle 1 to needle 3 is roughly 5×10^{11} years. It is estimated that our universe is about 15 billion years old (1.5×10^{10}). Also,

$5 \times 10^{11} = 50 \times 10^{10} \approx 33 \times (1.5 \times 10^{10})$. This calculation shows that our universe would last about 33 times as long as it already has.

Assume that a computer can generate 1 billion (10^9) moves per second. Then the number of moves that the computer can generate in one year is:

$$(3.2 \times 10^7) \times 10^9 = 3.2 \times 10^{16}$$

So the computer time required to generate 2^{64} moves is:

$$2^{64} \approx 1.6 \times 10^{19} = 1.6 \times 10^{16} \times 10^3 = (3.2 \times 10^{16}) \times 500$$

Thus, it would take about 500 years for the computer to generate 2^{64} moves at the rate of 1 billion moves per second.

Converting a Number from Decimal to Binary

In this example, we design a program that uses recursion to convert a nonnegative integer in decimal format—that is, base 10—into the equivalent binary number—that is, base 2. First we define some terms.

Let x be an integer. We call the remainder of x after division by 2 the **rightmost bit** of x. Thus, the rightmost bit of 33 is 1 because 33 % 2 is 1, and the rightmost bit of 28 is 0 because 28 % 2 is 0. (Recall that in C++, % is the mod operator; it produces the remainder of the integer division.)

We first illustrate the algorithm to convert an integer in base 10 to the equivalent number in binary format with the help of an example.

Suppose we want to find the binary representation of 35. First, we divide 35 by 2. The quotient is 17 and the remainder—that is, the rightmost bit of 35—is 1. Next, we divide 17 by 2. The quotient is 8 and the remainder—that is, the rightmost bit of 17—is 1. Next, we divide 8 by 2. The quotient is 4 and the remainder—that is, the rightmost bit of 8—is 0. We continue this process until the quotient becomes 0.

The rightmost bit of 35 cannot be printed until we have printed the rightmost bit of 17. The rightmost bit of 17 cannot be printed until we have printed the rightmost bit of 8, and so on. Thus, the binary representation of 35 is the binary representation of 17 (that is, the quotient of 35 after division by 2), followed by the rightmost bit of 35.

Thus, to convert an integer *num* in base 10 into the equivalent binary number, we first convert the quotient *num* / 2 into an equivalent binary number, and then append the rightmost bit of *num* to the binary representation of *num* / 2.

This discussion translates into the following recursive algorithm, where `binary(num)` denotes the binary representation of num:

1. `binary(num)` = num if num = 0.

2. `binary(num)` = `binary(num / 2)` followed by num % 2 if num > 0.

The following recursive function implements this algorithm:

```
void decToBin(int num, int base)
{
    if (num > 0)
    {
        decToBin(num / base, base);
        cout << num % base;
    }
}
```

Figure 6-10 traces the execution of the following statement:

```
decToBin(13, 2);
```

where num is 13 and base is 2.

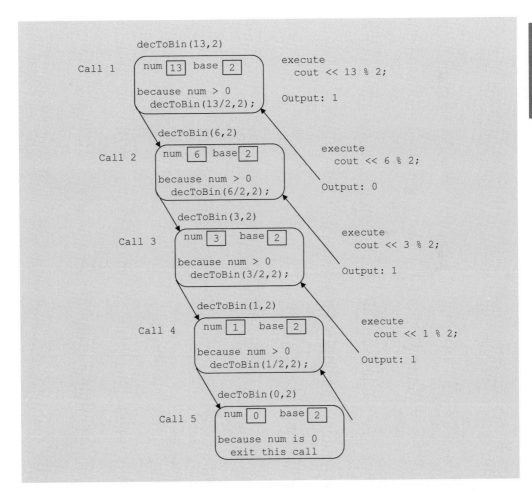

FIGURE 6-10 Execution of decToBin(13, 2)

Because the **if** statement in call 5 fails, this call does not print anything. The first output is produced by call 4, which prints 1; the second output is produced by call 3, which prints 1; the third output is produced by call 2, which prints 0; and the fourth output is produced by call 1, which prints 1. Thus, the output of the statement:

```
decToBin(13, 2);
```

is:

```
1101
```

The following C++ program tests the function decToBin:

```
//*********************************************************
// Author: D. S. Malik
//
// Program: Decimal to binary
// This program uses recursion to find the binary
// representation of a nonnegative integer.
//*********************************************************

#include <iostream>

using namespace std;

void decToBin(int num, int base);

int main()
{
    int decimalNum;
    int base;

    base = 2;

    cout << "Enter number in decimal: ";
    cin >> decimalNum;
    cout << endl;

    cout << "Decimal " << decimalNum << " = ";
    decToBin(decimalNum, base);
    cout << " binary" << endl;

    return 0;
}

void decToBin(int num, int base)
{
    if (num > 0)
    {
        decToBin(num / base, base);
        cout << num % base;
    }
}
```

Sample Run: In this sample run, the user input is shaded.

```
Enter a number in decimal: 57
```

```
Decimal 57 = 111001 binary
```

Recursion or Iteration?

Often there are two ways to solve a particular problem—recursion or iteration. The programs in the previous chapters used a loop to repeat a set of statements to perform certain calculations. In other words, the programs in the previous chapters used an iterative control structure to repeat a set of statements. Formally, **iterative control structures** use a looping structure, such as **while**, **for**, or **do...while**, to repeat a set of statements.

This chapter began by designing a recursive method to find the factorial of a nonnegative integer. Using an iterative control structure, we can easily write an algorithm to find the factorial of a nonnegative integer. Given our familiarity with iterative techniques, the iterative solution will seem simpler than the recursive solution. The only reason we gave a recursive solution to the factorial problem was to illustrate how recursion works using a simple example.

In this chapter, we also used recursion to determine the largest element in a list, determining a Fibonacci number. Using an iterative control structure, we can also write an algorithm to find the largest number in an array. Similarly, an algorithm that uses an iterative control structure can be designed to find the Fibonacci number.

The obvious question becomes, which approach is better? There is no general answer, but there are some guidelines. In addition to the nature of the solution, efficiency is the other key factor in determining the better approach.

When a function is called, memory space is allocated for its formal parameters and local variables. When the function terminates, that memory space is deallocated. In this chapter, while tracing the execution of recursive methods, we saw that every recursive call had its own set of parameters and local variables. That is, every recursive call required the system to allocate memory space for its formal parameters and local variables, and then deallocate the memory space when the function exited. Even though we don't need to write program statements to allocate and deallocate memory, overhead is associated with executing a recursive function, both in terms of memory space and execution time. Therefore, a recursive function executes more slowly than its iterative counterpart. On slower computers, especially those with limited memory space, the (relatively slow) execution of a recursive function is noticeable. Clearly, a recursive function is less efficient than a corresponding iterative function in terms of execution time and memory usage.

Efficiency is not determined solely by execution time and memory usage. Chances are that you *have never* been concerned with either execution time or memory usage as you have been writing C++ programs. Efficient use of a programmer's time also is an important consideration. Chances are that you *have* considered carefully what you can do to minimize the time required to produce C++ programs. Often this is entirely appropriate. As a professional programmer, your time typically is far more expensive than the cost of the

6

computer you use to produce programs. Of course, if you are developing software that will be used many times a day by large numbers of users, then execution time and memory usage become important considerations.

Today's computers are fast and have abundant memory. Therefore, the additional execution time and the memory consumed by a recursive function might not be noticeable. Given the ever-increasing speed and memory capacity of today's computers, the choice between iteration and recursion depends more and more on how the programmer envisions the solution to the problem, and less on execution time and memory usage. In rare instances where execution time must be minimized or the demand for memory is inordinately high, iteration might be better than recursion even when the recursive solution is more obvious. Fortunately, any program that can be written recursively also can be written iteratively.

As a general rule, if you think an iterative solution is at least as obvious and easy to construct as a recursive solution, choose the iterative solution. On the other hand, if the recursive solution is more obvious and easier to construct, such as the solution to the Towers of Hanoi problem, choose the recursive solution.

If you question the existence of problems for which a recursive solution is more obvious and easier to construct than an iterative solution, attempt to solve the Towers of Hanoi problem without using recursion. You'll quickly gain an increased appreciation for recursion. The ability to write recursive solutions is an important programming skill.

Recursion and Backtracking: 8-Queens Puzzle

This section describes a problem-solving and algorithm design technique called backtracking. Let us consider the following 8-queens puzzle: Place 8 queens on a chess-board (8 by 8 square board) so that no two queens can attack each other. For any two queens to be nonattacking, they cannot be in the same row, same column, or same diagonals. Figure 6-11 gives one possible solution to the 8-queens puzzle.

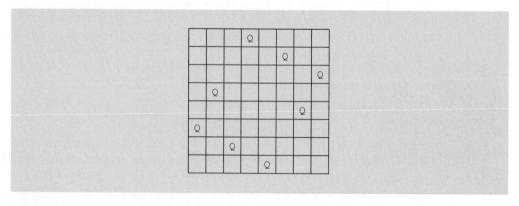

FIGURE 6-11 A solution to the 8-queens puzzle

In 1850, the 8-queens puzzle was considered by the great C. F. Gauss, who was unable to obtain a complete solution. The term backtrack was first coined by D. H. Lehmer in 1950. In 1960, R. J. Walker gave an algorithmic account of backtracking. A general description of backtracking with a variety of applications was presented by S. Golomb and L. Baumert.

Backtracking

The backtracking algorithm attempts to find solutions to a problem by constructing partial solutions and making sure that any partial solution does not violate the problem requirements. The algorithm tries to extend a partial solution toward completion. However, if it is determined that the partial solution would not lead to a solution, that is, the partial solution would end in a dead end, then the algorithm backs up by removing the most recently added part and trying other possibilities.

n-Queens Puzzle

In backtracking, the solution of the n-queens puzzle, because each queen must be placed in a different row, can be represented as an n-tuple $(x_1, x_2, \ldots, x_n)$, where x_i is an integer such that $1 \leq x_i \leq n$. In this tuple, x_i specifies the column number, where to place the ith queen in the ith row. Therefore, for the 8-queens puzzle the solution is an 8-tuple $(x_1, x_2, x_3, x_4, x_5, x_6, x_7, x_8)$, where x_i is the column where to place the ith queen in the ith row. For example, the solution in Figure 6-11 can be represented as the 8-tuple (4,6,8,2,7,1,3,5). That is, the first queen is placed in the first row and fourth column, the second queen is placed in the second row and sixth column, and so on. Clearly, each x_i is an integer such that $1 \leq x_i \leq 8$.

Let us again consider the 8-tuple $(x_1, x_2, x_3, x_4, x_5, x_6, x_7, x_8)$, where x_i is an integer such that $1 \leq x_i \leq 8$. Because each x_i has 8 choices, there are 8^8 such tuples, and so possibly 8^8 solutions. However, because no two queens can be placed in the same row, no two elements of the 8-tuple $(x_1, x_2, x_3, x_4, x_5, x_6, x_7, x_8)$ are the same. From this, it follows that the number of 8-tuples possibly representing solutions are 8!.

The solution that we develop can, in fact, be applied to any number of queens. Therefore, to illustrate the backtracking technique, we consider the 4-queens puzzle. That is, you are given a 4 by 4 square board (see Figure 6-12) and you are to place 4 queens on the board so that no two queens attack each other.

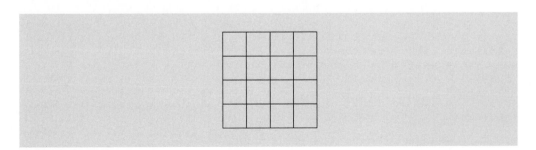

FIGURE 6-12 Square board for the 4-queens puzzle

We start by placing the first queen in the first row and first column as shown in Figure 6-13(a). (A cross in a box means no other queen can be placed in that box.)

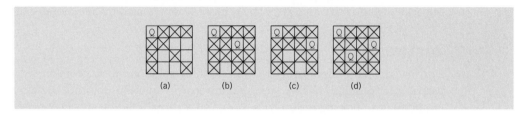

(a)   (b)   (c)   (d)

FIGURE 6-13 Finding a solution to the 4-queens puzzle

After placing the first queen, we try to place the second queen in the second row. Clearly, the first square in the second row where the second queen can be placed is the third column. So we place the second queen in that column; see Figure 6-13(b).

Next, we try to place the third queen in the third row. We find that the third queen cannot be placed in the third row and so we arrive at a dead end. At this point we backtrack to the previous board configuration and place the second queen in the fourth column; see Figure 6-13(c). Next, we try to place the third queen in the third row. This time, we successfully place the third queen in the second column of the third row; see Figure 6-13(d). After placing the third queen in the third row, when we try to place the fourth queen, we discover that the fourth queen cannot be placed in the fourth row.

We backtrack to the third row and try placing the queen in any other column. Because no other column is available for queen three, we backtrack to row two and try placing the second queen in any other column, which cannot be done. We, therefore, backtrack to the first row and place the first queen in the next column. After placing the first queen in the second column, we place the remaining queens in the successive rows. This time we obtain the solution, as shown by Figure 6-14.

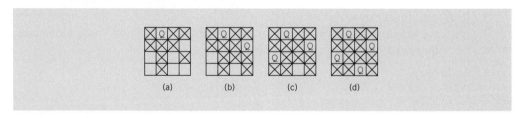

(a)   (b)   (c)   (d)

FIGURE 6-14 A solution to the 4-queens puzzle

Backtracking and the 4-Queens Puzzle

Suppose that the rows of the square board of the 4-queens puzzle are numbered 0 through 3 and the columns are numbered 0 through 3. (Recall that in C++, an array index starts at 0.)

For the 4-queens puzzle, we start by placing the first queen in the first row and first column, thus generating the tuple (0). We then place the second queen in the third column of the second row and so generate the tuple (0,2). When we try to place the third queen in the third row, we determined that the third queen cannot be placed in the third row and so we back up to the partial solution (0,2), remove 2 from the tuple and then generate the tuple (0,3), that is, the third queen is placed in the fourth column of the second row. With the partial solution (0,3), we then try to place the third queen in the third row and generate the tuple (0,3,1). Next, with the partial solution (0,3,1), when we try to place the fourth queen in the fourth row, it is determined that it cannot be done and so the partial solution (0,3,1) ends up in a dead end.

From the partial solution (0,3,1), the backtracking algorithm, in fact, backs up to placing the first queen and so removes all the elements of the tuple. The algorithm then places the first queen in the second column of the first row and thus generates the partial solution (1). In this case, the sequence of partial solution generated is, (1), (1,3), (1,3,0), and (1,3,0,2), which represents a solution to the 4-queens puzzle. The solutions generated by the backtracking algorithm can be represented by a tree, as shown in Figure 6-15.

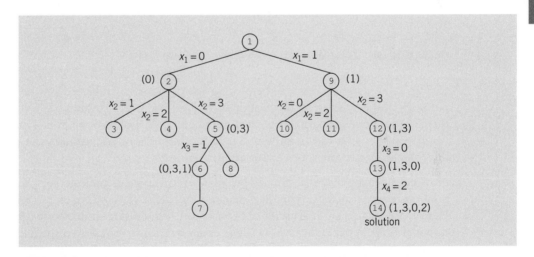

FIGURE 6-15   4-queens tree

8-Queens Puzzle

Let us now consider the 8-queens puzzle. Like the 4-queens puzzle, no two queens can be in the same row, same columns, and same diagonals. Determining whether two queens are in the same row or column is easy because we can check their row and column position. Let us describe how to determine whether two queens are in the same diagonal or not.

Consider the 8 by 8 square board shown in Figure 6-16. The rows are numbered 0 through 7; the columns are numbered 0 through 7. (Recall that, in C++, the array index starts at 0.)

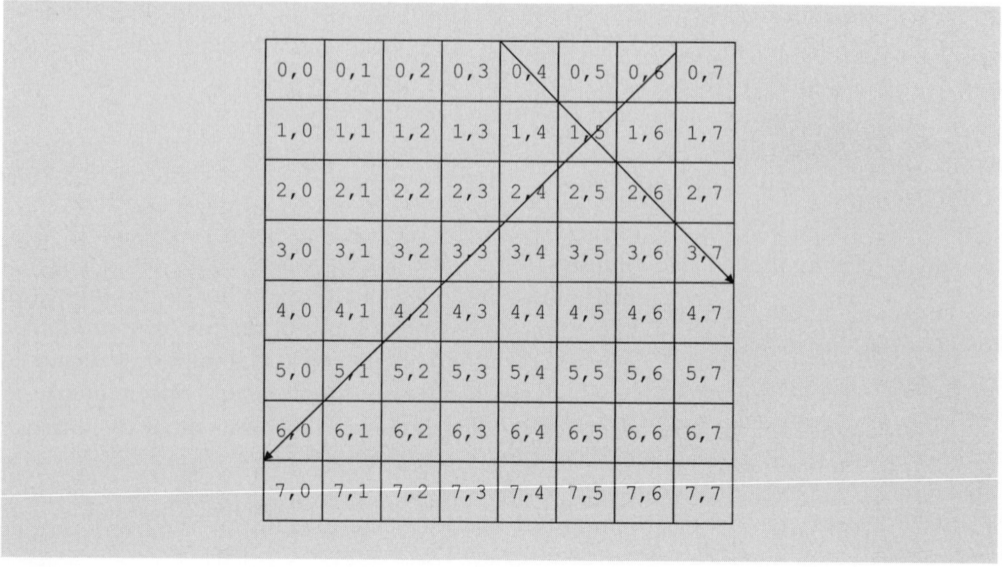

FIGURE 6-16 8 × 8 square board

Consider the diagonal from upper left to lower right, as indicated by the arrow. The positions of the squares on this diagonal are (0,4), (1,5), (2,6), and (3,7). Notice that for these entries `rowPosition − columnPosition` is − 4. For example, $0 - 4 = 1 - 5 = 2 - 6 = 3 - 7 = - 4$. It can be shown that for each square on a diagonal from upper left to lower right, `rowPosition − columnPosition` is the same.

Now consider the diagonal from upper right to lower left as indicated by the arrow. The positions of the squares on this diagonal are (0,6), (1,5), (2,4), (3,3), (4,2), (5,1), and (6,0). Here `rowPosition + columnPosition = 6`. It can be shown that for each square on a diagonal from upper right to lower left, `rowPosition + columnPosition` is the same.

We can use these results to determine whether two queens are on the same diagonal or not. Suppose a queen is at position (i, j), (row i and column j), and another queen is at position (k, l) , (row k and column l). These queens are on the same diagonal if either $i + j = k + l$ or $i - j = k - l$. The first equation implies that $j - l = i - k$ and the second equation implies that $j - l = k - i$. From this it follows that the two queens are on the same diagonal if $|j - l| = |i - k|$, where $|j - l|$ is the absolute value of $j - l$ and so on.

Because a solution to the 8-queens puzzle is represented as an 8-tuple, we use the array `queensInRow` of size 8, where `queensInRow[k]` specifies the column position of the kth queen in row k. For example, `queensInRow[0]` = 3 means the first queen is placed in column 3 (which is the fourth column) of row 0 (which is the first row).

Suppose that we place the first k-1 queens in the first $k − 1$ rows. Next we try to place the kth queen in a column of the kth row. We write the function `canPlaceQueen(k, i)`, which returns `true` if the kth queen can be placed in the ith column of row k; otherwise, it returns `false`.

The first k-1 queens are in the first k-1 rows and we are trying to place the kth queen in the kth row. The kth row, therefore, must first be empty. It thus follows that the kth queen can be placed in column i of row k, provided no other queen is in column i and no queens are on the diagonals on which square (k, i) lies. The general algorithm for the function `canPlaceQueen(k, i)` is as follows:

```
for (int j = 0; j < k; j++)
    if((queensInRow[j] == i)   //there is already a queen in column i
       || (abs(queensInRow[j] - i) == abs(j-k))) //there is already
                                    //a queen in one of the diagonals
                                    //on which square (k,i) lies

        return false;

return true;
```

The `for` loop checks whether there is already a queen either in column i or in one of the diagonals on which square (k, i) lies. If it finds a queen at any of such positions, the `for` loop returns the value `false`. Otherwise, the value `true` is returned.

The following class defines the *n*-queens puzzle as an ADT:

```
//****************************************************************
// D.S. Malik
//
// This class specifies the functions to solve the n-queens puzzle.
//****************************************************************

class nQueensPuzzle
{
public:
    nQueensPuzzle(int queens = 8);
      //constructor
      //Postcondition: noOfSolutions = 0; noOfQueens = queens;
      //    queensInRow is a pointer to the array to store the
      //    n-tuple

    bool canPlaceQueen(int k, int i);
      //Function to determine whether a queen can be placed
      //in row k and column i.
      //Postcondition: returns true if a queen can be placed in
      //    row k and column i; otherwise it returns false

    void queensConfiguration(int k);
      //Function to determine all solutions to the n-queens
      //puzzle using backtracking.
      //The function is called with the value 0.
      //Postcondition: All n-tuples representing solutions of
      //    n-queens puzzle are generated and printed.
```

6

```
void printConfiguration();
   //Function to output an n-tuple containing a solution
   //to the n-queens puzzle.

int solutionsCount();
   //Function to return the total number of solutions.
   //Postcondition: The value of noOfSolution is returned.

private:
   int noOfSolutions;
   int noOfQueens;
   int *queensInRow;
};
```

The definitions of the member functions of the class nQueensPuzzle are given next:

```
nQueensPuzzle::nQueensPuzzle(int queens)
{
   noOfQueens = queens;
   queensInRow = new int[noOfQueens];
   noOfSolutions = 0;
}

bool nQueensPuzzle::canPlaceQueen(int k, int i)
{
   for (int j = 0; j < k; j++)
      if ((queensInRow[j] == i)
          || (abs(queensInRow[j] - i) == abs(j-k)))
         return false;
   return true;
}
```

Using recursion, the function queensConfiguration implements the backtracking technique to determine all solutions to the *n*-queens puzzle. The parameter *k* specifies the queen to be placed in the *k*th row. Its definition is straightforward and is given next.

```
void nQueensPuzzle::queensConfiguration(int k)
{
   for (int i = 0; i < noOfQueens; i++)
   {
      if (canPlaceQueen(k, i))
      {
         queensInRow[k] = i;   //place the kth queen in column i
         if (k == noOfQueens - 1)   //all the queens are placed
            printConfiguration(); //print the n-tuple
         else
            queensConfiguration(k + 1); //determine the place
                                        //for the (k+1)th queen
      }
   }
}
```

```
void nQueensPuzzle::printConfiguration()
{
    noOfSolutions++;
    cout << "(";
    for (int i = 0; i < noOfQueens - 1; i++)
        cout << queensInRow[i] << ", ";

    cout << queensInRow[noOfQueens - 1] << ")" << endl;
}

int nQueensPuzzle::solutionsCount()
{
    return noOfSolutions;
}
```

We leave it as an exercise for you to write a program to test the *n*-queens puzzle class for various board sizes; see Programming Exercise 17 at the end of this chapter.

Recursion, Backtracking, and Sudoku

In the previous section, we used recursion and backtracking to solve the 8-queens problem. In this section, we introduce the well-known sudoku problem, which can be solved using recursion and backtracking. This problem involves filling numbers 1 to 9 in a partially filled, 9 × 9 grid with constraints described in this section. Figure 6-17(a) shows a partially filled grid.

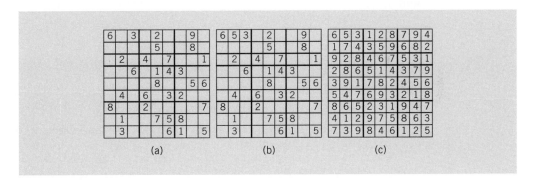

(a)   (b)   (c)

FIGURE 6-17 Sudoku problem and its solution

The sudoku grid is a 9 × 9 grid consisting of nine rows, nine columns, and nine 3 × 3 smaller grids. In Figure 6-17, the nine 3 × 3 smaller grids are separated by darker horizontal and vertical lines. The first 3 × 3 smaller grid is in rows 1 to 3 and columns 1 to 3, the second 3 × 3 smaller grid is in rows 1 to 3 and columns 4 to 6, and so on.

The objective is to fill the entire grid with numbers 1 to 9 such that each number appears exactly once in each row, each column, and each 3 × 3 smaller grid. For example, the solution to the sudoku problem in Figure 6-17(a) is shown in Figure 6-17(c).

Next, we describe, a simple recursive backtracking algorithm to find the solution to the sudoku problem in Figure 6-17(a).

Starting at the first row, we find the first empty grid slot. For example, in Figure 6-17(a), the first empty grid slot is in the second row and second column. Next we find the first number, between 1 and 9, that can be placed in this slot. (Note that before placing a number in an empty slot, we must check that the number does not appear in the row, column, and the 3 × 3 grid containing the slot.) For example, in Figure 6-17(a), the first number that can be placed in the second row and second column is 5; see Figure 6-17(b). After placing a number in the first empty slot, we find the next empty slot and try to place a number in that slot. If a number cannot be placed in a slot, then we must backtrack to the previous slot, where the number was placed, place a different number, and continue. If we arrive at a slot where no number can be placed, then the sudoku problem has no solutions.

The following class implements the sudoku problem as an ADT:

```
//*****************************************************************
// D.S. Malik
//
// This class specifies the functions to solve a sudoku problem.
//*****************************************************************

class sudoku
{
public:
    sudoku();
      //default constructor
      //Postcondition: grid is initialized to 0

    sudoku(int g[][9]);
      //constructor
      //Postcondition: grid = g

    void initializeSudokuGrid();
      //Function to prompt the user to specify the numbers of the
      //partially filled grid.
      //Postcondition: grid is initialized to the numbers
      //    specified by the user.

    void initializeSudokuGrid(int g[][9]);
      //Function to initialize grid to g
      //Postcondition: grid = g;

    void printSudokuGrid();
      //Function to print the sudoku grid.

    bool solveSudoku();
      //Funtion to solve the sudoku problem.
      //Postcondition: If a solution exits, it returns true,
      //    otherwise it returns false.
```

```
bool findEmptyGridSlot(int &row, int &col);
  //Function to determine if the grid slot specified by
  //row and col is empty.
  //Postcondition: Returns true if grid[row][col] = 0;

bool canPlaceNum(int row, int col, int num);
  //Function to determine if num can be placed in
  //grid[row][col]
  //Postcondition: Returns true if num can be placed in
  //    grid[row][col], otherwise it returns false.

bool numAlreadyInRow(int row, int num);
  //Function to determine if num is in grid[row][]
  //Postcondition: Returns true if num is in grid[row][],
  //    otherwise it returns false.

bool numAlreadyInCol(int col, int num);
  //Function to determine if num is in grid[row][]
  //Postcondition: Returns true if num is in grid[row][],
  //    otherwise it returns false.

bool numAlreadyInBox(int smallGridRow, int smallGridCol,
                     int num);
  //Function to determine if num is in the small grid
  //Postcondition: Returns true if num is in small grid,
  //    otherwise it returns false.

private:
    int grid[9][9];
};
```

Note that we use the digit 0 to specify an empty grid. For example, the partially filled sudoku grid in Figure 6-17(a) is entered and stored as:

```
6 0 3 0 2 0 0 9 0
0 0 0 0 5 0 0 8 0
0 2 0 4 0 7 0 0 1
0 0 6 0 1 4 3 0 0
0 0 0 0 8 0 0 5 6
0 4 0 6 0 3 2 0 0
8 0 0 2 0 0 0 0 7
0 1 0 0 7 5 8 0 0
0 3 0 0 0 6 1 0 5
```

Next we write the definition of the function solveSudoku.

The function solveSudoku uses recursion and backtracking to find a solution, if one exists, of the partially filled sudoku grid. The general algorithm is as follows:

1. Find the position of the first empty slot in the partially filled grid. If the grid has no empty slots, return true and print the solution.

2. Suppose the variables row and col specify the position of the empty grid position.

6

```
            for (int digit = 1; digit <= 9; digit++)
            {
                if (grid[row][col] <> digit)
                {
                    grid[row][col] = digit;
                    recursively fill the updated grid;
                    if the grid is filled successfully, return true,
                    otherwise remove the assigned digit from grid[row][col]
                    and try another digit.
                }
            If all the digits have been tried and nothing worked, return false.
```

The definition of the function is as follows:

```
bool sudoku::solveSudoku()
{
    int row, col;

    if (findEmptyGridSlot(row, col))
    {
        for (int num = 1; num <= 9; num++)
        {
            if (canPlaceNum(row, col, num))
            {
                grid[row][col] = num;
                if (solveSudoku()) //recursive call
                    return true;
                grid[row][col] = 0;
            }
        }

        return false; //backtrack
    }
    else
        return true; //there are no empty slots
}
```

We leave it is as an exercise for you to write the definitions of the remaining functions of the **class sudoku** and program that solves sudoku problems; see Programming Exercise 18 at end of this chapter.

QUICK REVIEW

1. The process of solving a problem by reducing it to smaller versions of itself is called recursion.

2. A recursive definition defines a problem in terms of smaller versions of itself.

3. Every recursive definition has one or more base cases.

4. A recursive algorithm solves a problem by reducing it to smaller versions of itself.

5. Every recursive algorithm has one or more base cases.

6. The solution to the problem in a base case is obtained directly.

7. A function is called recursive if it calls itself.

8. Recursive algorithms are implemented using recursive functions.

9. Every recursive function must have one or more base cases.

10. The general solution breaks the problem into smaller versions of itself.

11. The general case must eventually be reduced to a base case.

12. The base case stops the recursion.

13. While tracing a recursive function:

   - Logically, you can think of a recursive function as having an unlimited number of copies of itself.

   - Every call to a recursive function—that is, every recursive call—has its own code and its own set of parameters and local variables.

   - After completing a particular recursive call, control goes back to the calling environment, which is the previous call. The current (recursive) call must execute completely before control goes back to the previous call. The execution in the previous call begins from the point immediately following the recursive call.

14. A function is called directly recursive if it calls itself.

15. A function that calls another function and eventually results in the original function call is said to be indirectly recursive.

16. A recursive function in which the last statement executed is the recursive call is called a tail recursive function.

17. To design a recursive function, you must do the following:

   a. Understand the problem requirements.

   b. Determine the limiting conditions. For example, for a list the limiting condition is the number of elements in the list.

   c. Identify the base cases and provide a direct solution to each base case.

   d. Identify the general cases and provide a solution to each general case in terms of smaller versions of itself.

EXERCISES

1. Mark the following statements as true or false.

   a. Every recursive definition must have one or more base cases.

   b. Every recursive function must have one or more base cases.

   c. The general case stops the recursion.

   d. In the general case, the solution to the problem is obtained directly.

   e. A recursive function always returns a value.

2. What is a base case?

3. What is a recursive case?

4. What is direct recursion?

5. What is indirect recursion?

6. What is tail recursion?

7. Consider the following recursive function:

```
int mystery(int number)                          //Line 1
{                                                //Line 2
    if (number == 0)                             //Line 3
        return number;                           //Line 4
    else                                         //Line 5
        return(number + mystery(number - 1));    //Line 6
}                                                //Line 7
```

  a. Identify the base case.

  b. Identify the general case.

  c. What valid values can be passed as parameters to the function mystery?

  d. If mystery(0) is a valid call, what is its value? If not, explain why.

  e. If mystery(5) is a valid call, what is its value? If not, explain why.

  f. If mystery(-3) is a valid call, what is its value? If not, explain why.

8. Consider the following recursive function:

```
void funcRec(int u, char v)             //Line 1
{                                       //Line 2
    if (u == 0)                         //Line 3
        cout << v;                      //Line 4
    else if (u == 1)                    //Line 5
        cout << static_cast<char>
                  (static_cast<int>(v) + 1);   //Line 6
    else                                //Line 7
        funcRec(u - 1, v);              //Line 8
}                                       //Line 9
```

  Answer the following questions:

  a. Identify the base case.

  b. Identify the general case.

  c. What is the output of the following statement?

  ```
  funcRec(5, 'A');
  ```

9. Consider the following recursive function:

```
void exercise(int x)
{
    if (x > 0 && x < 10)
    {
        cout << x << " ";
        exercise(x + 1);
    }
}
```

What is the output of the following statements?

a. `exercise(0);`

b. `exercise(5);`

c. `exercise(10);`

d. `exercise(-5);`

10. Consider the following function:

```
int test(int x, int y)
{
    if (x == y)
        return x;
    else if (x > y)
        return (x + y);
    else
        return test(x + 1, y - 1);
}
```

What is the output of the following statements?

a. `cout << test(5, 10) << endl;`

b. `cout << test(3, 9) << endl;`

11. Consider the following function:

```
int func(int x)
{
    if (x == 0)
        return 2;
    else if (x == 1)
        return 3;
    else
        return (func(x - 1) + func(x - 2));
}
```

What is the output of the following statements?

a. `cout << func(0) << endl;`

b. `cout << func(1) << endl;`

c. `cout << func(2) << endl;`

d. `cout << func(5) << endl;`

12. Suppose that `intArray` is an array of integers, and `length` specifies the number of elements in `intArray`. Also, suppose that `low` and `high` are two integers such that 0 <= low < length, 0 <= high < length, and low < high. That is, `low` and `high` are two indices in `intArray`. Write a recursive definition that reverses the elements in `intArray` between `low` and `high`.

13. Write a recursive algorithm to multiply two positive integers *m* and *n* using repeated addition. Specify the base case and the recursive case.

14. Consider the following problem: How many ways can a committee of four people be selected from a group of 10 people? There are many other similar problems, where you are asked to find the number of ways to select a set of items from a given set of items. The general problem can be stated as follows: Find the number of ways r different things can be chosen from a set of n items, where r and n are nonnegative integers and $r \leq n$. Suppose $C(n, r)$ denotes the number of ways r different things can be chosen from a set of n items. Then $C(n, r)$ is given by the following formula:

$$C(n, r) = \frac{n!}{r!(n - r)!}$$

where the exclamation point denotes the factorial function. Moreover, $C(n, 0) = C(n, n) = 1$. It is also known that $C(n, r) = C(n - 1, r - 1) + C(n - 1, r)$.

a. Write a recursive algorithm to determine $C(n, r)$. Identify the base case(s) and the general case(s).

b. Using your recursive algorithm, determine $C(5, 3)$ and $C(9, 4)$.

PROGRAMMING EXERCISES

1. Write a recursive function that takes as a parameter a nonnegative integer and generates the following pattern of stars. If the nonnegative integer is 4, the pattern generated is as follows:

```
★★★★
★★★
★★
★
★
★★
★★★
★★★★
```

Also, write a program that prompts the user to enter the number of lines in the pattern and uses the recursive function to generate the pattern. For example, specifying 4 as the number of lines generates the preceding pattern.

2. Write a recursive function to generate a pattern of stars such as the following:

```
★
★★
★★★
★★★★
★★★★
★★★
★★
★
```

Also, write a program that prompts the user to enter the number of lines in the pattern and uses the recursive function to generate the pattern. For example, specifying 4 as the number of lines generates the preceding pattern.

3. Write a recursive a function to generate the following pattern of stars:

```
      *
    *   *
  *   *   *
*   *   *   *
  *   *   *
    *   *
      *
```

Also, write a program that prompts the user to enter the number of lines in the pattern and uses the recursive function to generate the pattern. For example, specifying 4 as the number of lines generates the preceding pattern.

4. Write a recursive function, `vowels`, that returns the number of vowels in a string. Also, write a program to test your function.

5. Write a recursive function that finds and returns the sum of the elements of an `int` array. Also, write a program to test your function.

6. A palindrome is a string that reads the same both forward and backward. For example, the string `"madam"` is a palindrome. Write a program that uses a recursive function to check whether a string is a palindrome. Your program must contain a value-returning recursive function that returns `true` if the string is a palindrome and `false` otherwise. Do not use any global variables; use the appropriate parameters.

7. Write a program that uses a recursive function to print a string backward. Do not use any global variables; use the appropriate parameters.

8. Write a recursive function, `reverseDigits`, that takes an integer as a parameter and returns the number with the digits reversed. Also, write a program to test your function.

9. Write a recursive function, `power`, that takes as parameters two integers x and y such that x is nonzero and returns x^y. You can use the following recursive definition to calculate x^y. If $y \geq 0$,

$$power(x, y) = \begin{cases} 1 & \text{if } y = 0 \\ x & \text{if } y = 1 \\ x \times power(x, y - 1) & \text{if } y > 1. \end{cases}$$

If $y < 0$,

$$power(x, y) = \frac{1}{power(x, -y)}.$$

Also, write a program to test your function.

10. **(Greatest Common Divisor)** Given two integers x and y, the following recursive definition determines the greatest common divisor of x and y, written $\gcd(x,y)$:

$$\gcd(x, y) = \begin{cases} x & \text{if} \quad y = 0 \\ \gcd(y, x\%y) & \text{if} \quad y \neq 0 \end{cases}$$

Note: In this definition, % is the mod operator.

Write a recursive function, gcd, that takes as parameters two integers and returns the greatest common divisor of the numbers. Also, write a program to test your function.

11. Write a recursive function to implement the recursive algorithm of Exercise 12 (reversing the elements of an array between two indices). Also, write a program to test your function.

12. Write a recursive function to implement the recursive algorithm of Exercise 13 (multiplying two positive integers using repeated addition). Also, write a program to test your function.

13. Write a recursive function to implement the recursive algorithm of Exercise 14 (determining the number of ways to select a set of things from a given set of things). Also, write a program to test your function.

14. In the section "Converting a Number from Decimal to Binary," in this chapter, you learned how to convert a decimal number into the equivalent binary number. Two more number systems, octal (base 8) and hexadecimal (base 16), are of interest to computer scientists. In fact, in C++, you can instruct the computer to store a number in octal or hexadecimal.

The digits in the octal number system are 0, 1, 2, 3, 4, 5, 6, and 7. The digits in the hexadecimal number system are 0, 1, 2, 3, 4, 5, 6, 7, 8, 9, A, B, C, D, E, and F. So A in hexadecimal is 10 in decimal, B in hexadecimal is 11 in decimal, and so on.

The algorithm to convert a positive decimal number into an equivalent number in octal (or hexadecimal) is the same as discussed for binary numbers. Here, we divide the decimal number by 8 (for octal) and by 16 (for hexadecimal). Suppose a_b represents the number a to the base b. For example, 75_{10} means 75 to the base 10 (that is decimal), and 83_{16} means 83 to the base 16 (that is, hexadecimal). Then:

$$753_{10} = 1361_8$$
$$753_{10} = 2F1_{16}$$

The method of converting a decimal number to base 2, or 8, or 16 can be extended to any arbitrary base. Suppose you want to convert a decimal number n into an equivalent number in base b, where b is between 2 and 36. You then divide the decimal number n by b as in the algorithm for converting decimal to binary.

Note that the digits in, say base 20, are 0, 1, 2, 3, 4, 5, 6, 7, 8, 9, A, B, C, D, E, F, G, H, I, and J.

Write a program that uses a recursive function to convert a number in decimal to a given base b, where b is between 2 and 36. Your program should prompt the user to enter the number in decimal and in the desired base.

Test your program on the following data:

9098 and base 20

692 and base 2

753 and base 16

15. **(Recursive Sequential Search)** The sequential search algorithm given in Chapter 3 is nonrecursive. Write and implement a recursive version of the sequential search algorithm.

16. The function `sqrt` from the header file `cmath` can be used to find the square root of a nonnegative real number. Using Newton's method, you can also write an algorithm to find the square root of a nonnegative real number within a given tolerance as follows: Suppose x is a nonnegative real number, a is the approximate square root of x, and *epsilon* is the tolerance. Start with $a = x$;

   a. If $|a^2 - x| \leq$ *epsilon*, then a is the square root of x within the tolerance; otherwise:

   b. Replace a with $(a^2 + x) / (2a)$ and repeat Step a

   where $|a^2 - x|$ denotes the absolute value of $a^2 - x$.

   Write a recursive function to implement this algorithm to find the square root of a nonnegative real number. Also, write a program to test your function.

17. Write a program to find solutions to the n-queens puzzle for various values of n. To be specific, test your program for $n = 4$ and $n = 8$.

18. Write the definitions of the remaining functions of the `class sudoku`. Also write a program to solve some sudoku problems.

19. **(Knight's Tour)** This chapter described the backtracking algorithm and how to use recursion to implement it. Another well-known chessboard problem that can be solved using the backtracking algorithm is a knight's tour. Given an initial board position, determine a sequence of moves by a knight that visits every square of the chessboard exactly once. For example, for a 5 × 5 and 6 × 6 square board, the sequence of moves are shown in Figure 6-18:

6

1	6	15	10	21
14	9	20	5	16
19	2	7	22	11
8	13	24	17	4
25	18	3	12	23

1	16	7	26	11	14
34	25	12	15	6	27
17	2	33	8	13	10
32	35	24	21	8	5
23	18	3	30	9	20
36	31	22	19	4	29

FIGURE 6-18 Knight's tour

A knight moves by jumping two positions either vertically or horizontally and one position in the perpendicular direction. Write a recursive backtracking program that takes as input an initial board position and determines a sequence of moves by a knight that visits each square of the board exactly once.

CHAPTER 7

STACKS

IN THIS CHAPTER, YOU WILL:

- Learn about stacks
- Examine various stack operations
- Learn how to implement a stack as an array
- Learn how to implement a stack as a linked list
- Discover stack applications
- Learn how to use a stack to remove recursion

This chapter discusses a very useful data structure called a stack. It has numerous applications in computer science.

Stacks

Suppose that you have a program with several functions. To be specific, suppose that you have the functions A, B, C, and D in your program. Now suppose that function A calls function B, function B calls function C, and function C calls function D. When function D terminates, control goes back to function C; when function C terminates, control goes back to function B; and when function B terminates, control goes back to function A. During program execution, how do you think the computer keeps track of the function calls? What about recursive functions? How does the computer keep track of the recursive calls? In Chapter 6, we designed a recursive function to print a linked list backward. What if you want to write a nonrecursive algorithm to print a linked list backward?

This section discusses the data structure called the **stack**, which the computer uses to implement function calls. You can also use stacks to convert recursive algorithms into nonrecursive algorithms, especially recursive algorithms that are not tail recursive. Stacks have numerous other applications in computer science. After developing the tools necessary to implement a stack, we will examine some applications of stacks.

A stack is a list of homogenous elements in which the addition and deletion of elements occurs only at one end, called the **top** of the stack. For example, in a cafeteria, the second tray in a stack of trays can be removed only if the first tray has been removed. For another example, to get to your favorite computer science book, which is underneath your math and history books, you must first remove the math and history books. After removing these books, the computer science book becomes the top book—that is, the top element of the stack. Figure 7-1 shows some examples of stacks.

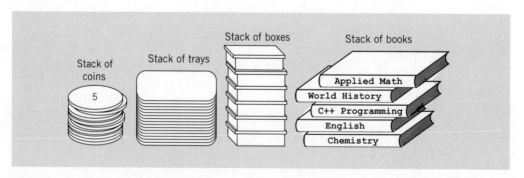

FIGURE 7-1 Various examples of stacks

The elements at the bottom of the stack have been in the stack the longest. The top element of the stack is the last element added to the stack. Because the elements are added and removed from one end (that is, the top), it follows that the item that is added last will be removed first. For this reason, a stack is also called a **Last In First Out (LIFO)** data structure.

Stack: A data structure in which the elements are added and removed from one end only; a Last In First Out (LIFO) data structure.

Now that you know what a stack is, let us see what kinds of operations can be performed on a stack. Because new items can be added to the stack, we can perform the add operation, called **push**, to add an element onto the stack. Similarly, because the top item can be retrieved and/or removed from the stack, we can perform the operation **top** to retrieve the top element of the stack, and the operation **pop** to remove the top element from the stack.

The push, top, and pop operations work as follows: Suppose there are boxes lying on the floor that need to be stacked on a table. Initially, all of the boxes are on the floor and the stack is empty. (See Figure 7-2.)

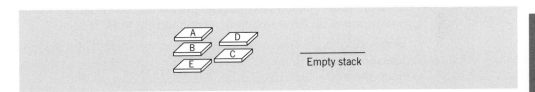

FIGURE 7-2 Empty stack

First we push box **A** onto the stack. After the push operation, the stack is as shown in Figure 7-3(a).

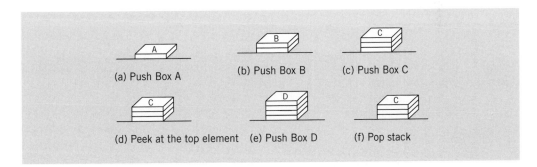

FIGURE 7-3 Stack operations

We then push box **B** onto the stack. After this push operation, the stack is as shown in Figure 7-3(b). Next, we push box **C** onto the stack. After this push operation, the stack is as shown in Figure 7-3(c). Next, we look at the top element of the stack. After this operation, the stack is unchanged and shown in Figure 7-3(d). We then push box **D** onto the stack. After this push operation, the stack is as shown in Figure 7-3(e). Next, we pop the stack. After the pop operation, the stack is as shown in Figure 7-3(f).

An element can be removed from the stack only if there is something in the stack, and an element can be added to the stack only if there is room. The two operations that immediately follow from push, top, and pop are **isFullStack** (checks whether the stack is full) and **isEmptyStack** (checks whether the stack is empty). Because a stack keeps changing as we add and remove elements, the stack must be empty before we first start using it. Thus, we need another operation, called **initializeStack**, which initializes the stack to an empty state. Therefore, to successfully implement a stack, we need at least these six operations, which are described next. (We might also need other operations on a stack, depending on the specific implementation.)

- **initializeStack**—Initializes the stack to an empty state.
- **isEmptyStack**—Determines whether the stack is empty. If the stack is empty, it returns the value true; otherwise, it returns the value false.
- **isFullStack**—Determines whether the stack is full. If the stack is full, it returns the value true; otherwise, it returns the value false.
- **push**—Adds a new element to the top of the stack. The input to this operation consists of the stack and the new element. Prior to this operation, the stack must exist and must not be full.
- **top**—Returns the top element of the stack. Prior to this operation, the stack must exist and must not be empty.
- **pop**—Removes the top element of the stack. Prior to this operation, the stack must exist and must not be empty.

The following abstract class stackADT defines these operations as an ADT:

```
//****************************************************************
// Author: D.S. Malik
//
// This class specifies the basic operations on a stack.
//****************************************************************

template <class Type>
class stackADT
{
public:
    virtual void initializeStack() = 0;
        //Method to initialize the stack to an empty state.
        //Postcondition: Stack is empty.

    virtual bool isEmptyStack() const = 0;
        //Function to determine whether the stack is empty.
        //Postcondition: Returns true if the stack is empty,
        //    otherwise returns false.
```

```
    virtual bool isFullStack() const = 0;
        //Function to determine whether the stack is full.
        //Postcondition: Returns true if the stack is full,
        //     otherwise returns false.

    virtual void push(const Type& newItem) = 0;
        //Function to add newItem to the stack.
        //Precondition: The stack exists and is not full.
        //Postcondition: The stack is changed and newItem is added
        //     to the top of the stack.

    virtual Type top() const = 0;
        //Function to return the top element of the stack.
        //Precondition: The stack exists and is not empty.
        //Postcondition: If the stack is empty, the program
        //     terminates; otherwise, the top element of the stack
        //     is returned.

    virtual void pop() = 0;
        //Function to remove the top element of the stack.
        //Precondition: The stack exists and is not empty.
        //Postcondition: The stack is changed and the top element
        //     is removed from the stack.
};
```

Figure 7-4 shows the UML class diagram of the class stackADT.

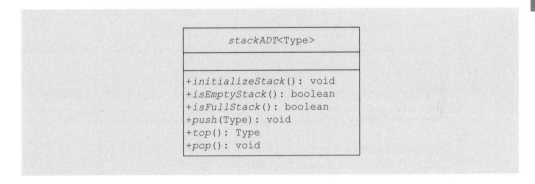

FIGURE 7-4 UML class diagram of the class stackADT

We now consider the implementation of our abstract stack data structure. Functions such as push and pop that are required to implement a stack are not available to C++ programmers. We must write the functions to implement the stack operations.

Because all the elements of a stack are of the same type, a stack can be implemented as either an array or a linked structure. Both implementations are useful and are discussed in this chapter.

Implementation of Stacks as Arrays

Because all the elements of a stack are of the same type, you can use an array to implement a stack. The first element of the stack can be put in the first array slot, the second element of the stack in the second array slot, and so on. The top of the stack is the index of the last element added to the stack.

In this implementation of a stack, stack elements are stored in an array, and an array is a random access data structure; that is, you can directly access any element of the array. However, by definition, a stack is a data structure in which the elements are accessed (popped or pushed) at only one end—that is, a Last In First Out data structure. Thus, a stack element is accessed only through the top, not through the bottom or middle. This feature of a stack is extremely important and must be recognized in the beginning.

To keep track of the top position of the array, we can simply declare another variable, called **stackTop**.

The following class, stackType, implements the functions of the abstract class stackADT. By using a pointer, we can dynamically allocate arrays, so we will leave it for the user to specify the size of the array (that is, the stack size). We assume that the default stack size is 100. Because the class stackType has a pointer member variable (the pointer to the array to store the stack elements), we must overload the assignment operator and include the copy constructor and destructor. Moreover, we give a generic definition of the stack. Depending on the specific application, we can pass the stack element type when we declare a stack object.

```
//*****************************************************************
// Author: D.S. Malik
//
// This class specifies the basic operation on a stack as an
// array.
//*****************************************************************

template <class Type>
class stackType: public stackADT<Type>
{
public:
    const stackType<Type>& operator=(const stackType<Type>&);
      //Overload the assignment operator.

    void initializeStack();
      //Function to initialize the stack to an empty state.
      //Postcondition: stackTop = 0;

    bool isEmptyStack() const;
      //Function to determine whether the stack is empty.
      //Postcondition: Returns true if the stack is empty,
      //    otherwise returns false.
```

```
    bool isFullStack() const;
        //Function to determine whether the stack is full.
        //Postcondition: Returns true if the stack is full,
        //    otherwise returns false.

    void push(const Type& newItem);
        //Function to add newItem to the stack.
        //Precondition: The stack exists and is not full.
        //Postcondition: The stack is changed and newItem is
        //    added to the top of the stack.

    Type top() const;
        //Function to return the top element of the stack.
        //Precondition: The stack exists and is not empty.
        //Postcondition: If the stack is empty, the program
        //    terminates; otherwise, the top element of the stack
        //    is returned.

    void pop();
        //Function to remove the top element of the stack.
        //Precondition: The stack exists and is not empty.
        //Postcondition: The stack is changed and the top element is
        //    removed from the stack.

    stackType(int stackSize = 100);
        //Constructor
        //Create an array of the size stackSize to hold
        //the stack elements. The default stack size is 100.
        //Postcondition: The variable list contains the base address
        //    of the array, stackTop = 0, and maxStackSize = stackSize

    stackType(const stackType<Type>& otherStack);
        //Copy constructor

    ~stackType();
        //Destructor
        //Remove all the elements from the stack.
        //Postcondition: The array (list) holding the stack
        //    elements is deleted.

private:
    int maxStackSize; //variable to store the maximum stack size
    int stackTop;     //variable to point to the top of the stack
    Type *list; //pointer to the array that holds the stack elements

    void copyStack(const stackType<Type>& otherStack);
        //Function to make a copy of otherStack.
        //Postcondition: A copy of otherStack is created and assigned
        //    to this stack.
};
```

7

Figure 7-5 shows the UML class diagram of the `class stackType`.

```
                        stackType<Type>
-maxStackSize: int
-stackTop: int
-*list: Type
+operator=(const stackType<Type>&): const stackType<Type>&
+initializeStack(): void
+isEmptyStack() const: bool
+isFullStack() const: bool
+push(const Type&): void
+top() const: Type
+pop(): void
-copyStack(const stackType<Type>&): void
+stackType(int = 100)
+stackType(const stackType<Type>&)
+~stackType()
```

FIGURE 7-5 UML class diagram of the `class stackType`

NOTE If `stackTop` is 0, the stack is empty. If `stackTop` is nonzero, the stack is nonempty and the top element of the stack is given by `stackTop – 1` because the first stack element is at position 0.

NOTE The function `copyStack` is included as a `private` member. It contains the code that is common to the functions to overload the assignment operator and the copy constructor. We use this function only to implement the copy constructor and overload the assignment operator. To copy a stack into another stack, the program can use the assignment operator.

Figure 7-6 shows this data structure, wherein `stack` is an object of type `stackType`. Note that `stackTop` can range from 0 to `maxStackSize`. If `stackTop` is nonzero, then `stackTop – 1` is the index of the top element of the stack. Suppose that `maxStackSize = 100`.

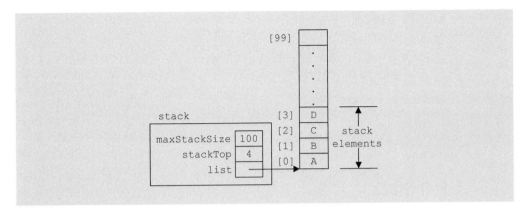

FIGURE 7-6 Example of a stack

Note that the pointer `list` contains the base address of the array (holding the stack elements)—that is, the address of the first array component. Next we discuss how to implement the member functions of the `class stackType`.

Initialize Stack

Let us consider the `initializeStack` operation. Because the value of `stackTop` indicates whether the stack is empty, we can simply set `stackTop` to 0 to initialize the stack. (See Figure 7-7.)

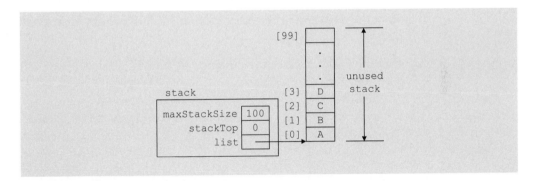

FIGURE 7-7 Empty stack

The definition of the function `initializeStack` is as follows:

```
template <class Type>
void stackType<Type>::initializeStack()
{
    stackTop = 0;
}//end initializeStack
```

Empty Stack

We have seen that the value of `stackTop` indicates whether the stack is empty. If `stackTop` is 0, the stack is empty; otherwise, the stack is not empty. The definition of the function `isEmptyStack` is as follows:

```
template <class Type>
bool stackType<Type>::isEmptyStack() const
{
    return(stackTop == 0);
}//end isEmptyStack
```

Full Stack

Next, we consider the operation `isFullStack`. It follows that the stack is full if `stackTop` is equal to `maxStackSize`. The definition of the function `isFullStack` is as follows:

```
template <class Type>
bool stackType<Type>::isFullStack() const
{
    return(stackTop == maxStackSize);
} //end isFullStack
```

Push

Adding, or pushing, an element onto the stack is a two-step process. Recall that the value of `stackTop` indicates the number of elements in the stack, and `stackTop - 1` gives the position of the top element of the stack. Therefore, the `push` operation is as follows:

1. Store the `newItem` in the array component indicated by `stackTop`.
2. Increment `stackTop`.

Figure 7-8(a) shows the stack before pushing `'y'` into the stack. Figure 7-8(b) shows the stack after pushing `'y'` into the stack.

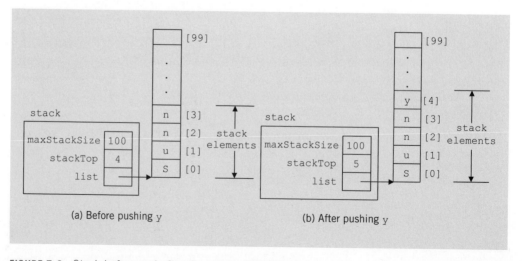

(a) Before pushing y   (b) After pushing y

FIGURE 7-8 Stack before and after the push operation

The definition of the function push is as follows:

```
template <class Type>
void stackType<Type>::push(const Type& newItem)
{
    if (!isFullStack())
    {
        list[stackTop] = newItem;   //add newItem at the top
        stackTop++; //increment stackTop
    }
    else
        cout << "Cannot add to a full stack." << endl;
}//end push
```

If we try to add a new item to a full stack, the resulting condition is called an **overflow**. Error checking for an overflow can be handled in different ways. One way is as shown previously. Or, we can check for an overflow before calling the function push, as shown next (assuming stack is an object of type stackType).

```
if (!stack.isFullStack())
    stack.push(newItem);
```

Return the Top Element

The operation top returns the top element of the stack. Its definition is as follows:

```
template <class Type>
Type stackType<Type>::top() const
{
    assert(stackTop != 0);   //if stack is empty, terminate the
                             //program
    return list[stackTop - 1]; //return the element of the stack
                               //indicated by stackTop - 1
}//end top
```

Pop

To remove, or pop, an element from the stack, we simply decrement stackTop by 1.

Figure 7-9(a) shows the stack before popping 'D' from the stack. Figure 7-9(b) shows the stack after popping 'D' from the stack.

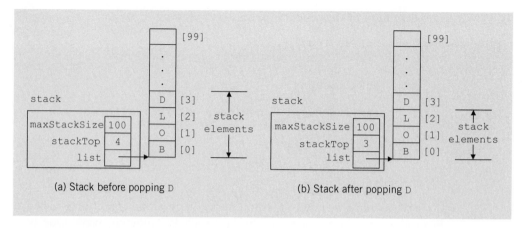

FIGURE 7-9 Stack before and after the pop operation

The definition of the function pop is as follows:

```
template <class Type>
void stackType<Type>::pop()
{
    if (!isEmptyStack())
        stackTop--;      //decrement stackTop
    else
        cout << "Cannot remove from an empty stack." << endl;
}//end pop
```

If we try to remove an item from an empty stack, the resulting condition is called an **underflow**. Error checking for an underflow can be handled in different ways. One way is as shown previously. Or, we can check for an underflow before calling the function pop, as shown next (assuming stack is an object of type stackType).

```
if (!stack.isEmptyStack())
    stack.pop();
```

Copy Stack

The function copyStack makes a copy of a stack. The stack to be copied is passed as a parameter to the function copyStack. We will, in fact, use this function to implement the copy constructor and overload the assignment operator. The definition of this function is as follows:

```
template <class Type>
void stackType<Type>::copyStack(const stackType<Type>& otherStack)
{
    delete [] list;
    maxStackSize = otherStack.maxStackSize;
    stackTop = otherStack.stackTop;
```

```
    list = new Type[maxStackSize];

        //copy otherStack into this stack
    for (int j = 0; j < stackTop; j++)
        list[j] = otherStack.list[j];
} //end copyStack
```

Constructor and Destructor

The functions to implement the constructor and the destructor are straightforward. The constructor with parameters sets the stack size to the size specified by the user, sets stackTop to 0, and creates an appropriate array in which to store the stack elements. If the user does not specify the size of the array in which to store the stack elements, the constructor uses the default value, which is 100, to create an array of size 100. The destructor simply deallocates the memory occupied by the array (that is, the stack) and sets stackTop to 0. The definitions of the constructor and destructor are as follows:

```
template <class Type>
stackType<Type>::stackType(int stackSize)
{
    if (stackSize <= 0)
    {
        cout << "Size of the array to hold the stack must "
             << "be positive." << endl;
        cout << "Creating an array of size 100." << endl;

        maxStackSize = 100;
    }
    else
        maxStackSize = stackSize;    //set the stack size to
                                     //the value specified by
                                     //the parameter stackSize

    stackTop = 0;                    //set stackTop to 0
    list = new Type[maxStackSize];   //create the array to
                                     //hold the stack elements
}//end constructor

template <class Type>
stackType<Type>::~stackType() //destructor
{
    delete [] list; //deallocate the memory occupied
                    //by the array
}//end destructor
```

Copy Constructor

The copy constructor is called when a stack object is passed as a (value) parameter to a function. It copies the values of the member variables of the actual parameter into the corresponding member variables of the formal parameter. Its definition is as follows:

```
template <class Type>
stackType<Type>::stackType(const stackType<Type>& otherStack)
{
    list = NULL;

    copyStack(otherStack);
}//end copy constructor
```

Overloading the Assignment Operator (=)

Recall that for classes with pointer member variables, the assignment operator must be explicitly overloaded. The definition of the function to overload the assignment operator for the class stackType is as follows:

```
template <class Type>
const stackType<Type>& stackType<Type>::operator=
                            (const stackType<Type>& otherStack)
{
    if (this != &otherStack) //avoid self-copy
        copyStack(otherStack);

    return *this;
} //end operator=
```

Stack Header File

Now that you know how to implement the stack operations, you can put the definitions of the class and the functions to implement the stack operations together to create the stack header file. For the sake of completeness, we next describe the header file. Suppose that the name of the header file containing the definition of the class stackType is myStack.h. We will refer to this header file in any program that uses a stack.

```
//Header file: myStack.h

#ifndef H_StackType
#define H_StackType

#include <iostream>
#include <cassert>

#include "stackADT.h"

using namespace std;

//Place the definition of the class template stackType, as given
//previously in this chapter, here.

//Place the definitions of the member functions as discussed here.
#endif
```

The analysis of the stack operations is similar to the operations of the **class arrayListType** (Chapter 3). We, therefore, provide only a summary in Table 7-1.

TABLE 7-1 Time complexity of the operations of the class stackType on a stack with *n* elements

Function	Time complexity
isEmptyStack	$O(1)$
isFullStack	$O(1)$
initializeStack	$O(1)$
constructor	$O(1)$
top	$O(1)$
push	$O(1)$
pop	$O(1)$
copyStack	$O(n)$
destructor	$O(1)$
copy constructor	$O(n)$
Overloading the assignment operator	$O(n)$

EXAMPLE 7-1

Before we give a programming example, let us first write a simple program that uses the **class** stackType and tests some of the stack operations. Among others, we will test the assignment operator and the copy constructor. The program and its output are as follows:

```
//**************************************************************
// Author: D.S. Malik
//
// This program tests various operations of a stack.
//**************************************************************

#include <iostream>
#include "myStack.h"

using namespace std;
```

```
void testCopyConstructor(stackType<int> otherStack);

int main()
{
    stackType<int> stack(50);
    stackType<int> copyStack(50);
    stackType<int> dummyStack(100);

    stack.initializeStack();
    stack.push(23);
    stack.push(45);
    stack.push(38);
    copyStack = stack;   //copy stack into copyStack

    cout << "The elements of copyStack: ";

    while (!copyStack.isEmptyStack())  //print copyStack
    {
        cout << copyStack.top() << " ";
        copyStack.pop();
    }
    cout << endl;

    copyStack = stack;
    testCopyConstructor(stack);   //test the copy constructor

    if (!stack.isEmptyStack())
        cout << "The original stack is not empty." << endl
             << "The top element of the original stack: "
             << copyStack.top() << endl;

    dummyStack = stack;   //copy stack into dummyStack

    cout << "The elements of dummyStack: ";

    while (!dummyStack.isEmptyStack())  //print dummyStack
    {
        cout << dummyStack.top() << " ";
        dummyStack.pop();
    }

    cout << endl;

    return 0;
}

void testCopyConstructor(stackType<int> otherStack)
{
    if (!otherStack.isEmptyStack())
        cout << "otherStack is not empty." << endl
             << "The top element of otherStack: "
             << otherStack.top() << endl;
}
```

Sample Run:

```
The elements of copyStack: 38 45 23
otherStack is not empty.
The top element of otherStack: 38
The original stack is not empty.
The top element of the original stack: 38
The elements of dummyStack: 38 45 23
```

It is recommended that you do a walk-through of this program.

PROGRAMMING EXAMPLE: Highest GPA

In this example, we write a C++ program that reads a data file consisting of each student's GPA followed by the student's name. The program then prints the highest GPA and the names of all the students who received that GPA. The program scans the input file only once. Moreover, we assume that there are a maximum of 100 students in the class.

Input The program reads an input file consisting of each student's GPA, followed by the student's name. Sample data is as follows:

```
3.5 Bill
3.6 John
2.7 Lisa
3.9 Kathy
3.4 Jason
3.9 David
3.4 Jack
```

Output The program outputs the highest GPA and all the names associated with the highest GPA. For example, for the preceding data, the highest GPA is 3.9 and the students with that GPA are Kathy and David.

PROGRAM
ANALYSIS AND
ALGORITHM
DESIGN

We read the first GPA and the name of the student. Because this data is the first item read, it is the highest GPA so far. Next, we read the second GPA and the name of the student. We then compare this (second) GPA with the highest GPA so far. Three cases arise:

1. The new GPA is greater than the highest GPA so far. In this case, we do the following:

   a. Update the value of the highest GPA so far.

   b. Initialize the stack—that is, remove the names of the students from the stack.

   c. Save the name of the student having the highest GPA so far in the stack.

2. The new GPA is equal to the highest GPA so far. In this case, we add the name of the new student to the stack.

3. The new GPA is smaller than the highest GPA so far. In this case, we discard the name of the student having this grade.

We then read the next GPA and the name of the student, and repeat Steps 1 through 3. We continue this process until we reach the end of file.

From this discussion, it is clear that we need the following variables:

```
double GPA;          //variable to hold the current GPA
double highestGPA;   //variable to hold the highest GPA
string name;         //variable to hold the name of the student
stackType<string> stack(100); //object to implement the stack
```

The previous discussion translates into the following algorithm:

1. Declare the variables and initialize stack.

2. Open the input file.

3. If the input file does not exist, exit the program.

4. Set the output of the floating-point numbers to a fixed decimal format with a decimal point and trailing zeroes. Also, set the precision to two decimal places.

5. Read the GPA and the student name.

6. `highestGPA = GPA;`

7. `while` (not end of file)
   `{`

   7.1. `if (GPA > highestGPA)`

      `{`

      7.1.1. `initializeStack(stack);`

      7.1.2. `push(stack, student name);`

      7.1.3. `highestGPA = GPA;`

      `}`

   7.2. `else`
      `if (GPA is equal to highestGPA)`
      `push(stack, student name);`

   7.3. Read `GPA` and `student name;`
   `}`

8. Output the highest GPA.

9. Output the names of the students having the highest GPA.

PROGRAM LISTING

```cpp
//**************************************************************
// Author: D.S. Malik
//
// This program reads a data file consisting of students' GPAs
// followed by their names. The program then prints the highest
// GPA and the names of the students with the highest GPA.
//**************************************************************

#include <iostream>
#include <iomanip>
#include <fstream>
#include <string>

#include "myStack.h"

using namespace std;

int main()
{
        //Step 1
    double GPA;
    double highestGPA;
    string name;

    stackType<string> stack(100);

    ifstream infile;

    infile.open("HighestGPAData.txt");              //Step 2

    if (!infile)                                     //Step 3
    {
        cout << "The input file does not "
            << "exist. Program terminates!" << endl;
        return 1;
    }

    cout << fixed << showpoint;                      //Step 4
    cout << setprecision(2);                         //Step 4

    infile >> GPA >> name;                           //Step 5

    highestGPA = GPA;                                //Step 6

    while (infile)                                   //Step 7
    {
        if (GPA > highestGPA)                        //Step 7.1
        {
            stack.initializeStack();                 //Step 7.1.1
```

7

```
                    if (!stack.isFullStack())          //Step 7.1.2
                        stack.push(name);

                    highestGPA = GPA;                   //Step 7.1.3
            }
        else if (GPA == highestGPA)                     //Step 7.2
            if (!stack.isFullStack())
                stack.push(name);
            else
            {
                cout << "Stack overflows. "
                    << "Program terminates!" << endl;
                return 1;   //exit program
            }

        infile >> GPA >> name;                          //Step 7.3
    }

    cout << "Highest GPA = " << highestGPA << endl;//Step 8
    cout << "The students holding the "
        << "highest GPA are:" << endl;

    while (!stack.isEmptyStack())                       //Step 9
    {
        cout << stack.top() << endl;
        stack.pop();
    }

    cout << endl;

    return 0;
}
```

Sample Run:

Input File (HighestGPAData.txt)

```
3.4 Randy
3.2 Kathy
2.5 Colt
3.4 Tom
3.8 Ron
3.8 Mickey
3.6 Peter
3.5 Donald
3.8 Cindy
3.7 Dome
3.9 Andy
3.8 Fox
3.9 Minnie
2.7 Gilda
3.9 Vinay
3.4 Danny
```

Output

```
Highest GPA = 3.90
The students holding the highest GPA are:
Vinay
Minnie
Andy
```

Note that the names of the students with the highest GPA are output in the reverse order, relative to the order they appear in the input because the top element of the stack is the last element added to the stack.

Linked Implementation of Stacks

Because an array size is fixed, in the array (linear) representation of a stack, only a fixed number of elements can be pushed onto the stack. If in a program the number of elements to be pushed exceeds the size of the array, the program might terminate in an error. We must overcome this problem.

We have seen that by using pointer variables we can dynamically allocate and deallocate memory, and by using linked lists we can dynamically organize data (such as an ordered list). Next, we will use these concepts to implement a stack dynamically.

Recall that in the linear representation of a stack, the value of `stackTop` indicates the number of elements in the stack, and the value of `stackTop - 1` points to the top item in the stack. With the help of `stackTop`, we can do several things: Find the top element, check whether the stack is empty, and so on.

Similar to the linear representation, in a linked representation `stackTop` is used to locate the top element in the stack. However, there is a slight difference. In the former case, `stackTop` gives the index of the array. In the latter case, `stackTop` gives the address (memory location) of the top element of the stack.

The following class implements the functions of the abstract `class stackADT`:

```
//************************************************************
// Author: D.S. Malik
//
// This class specifies the basic operation on a stack as a
// linked list.
//************************************************************

    //Definition of the node
template <class Type>
struct nodeType
{
    Type info;
    nodeType<Type> *link;
};
```

```
template <class Type>
class linkedStackType: public stackADT<Type>
{
public:
    const linkedStackType<Type>& operator=
                              (const linkedStackType<Type>&);
      //Overload the assignment operator.

    bool isEmptyStack() const;
      //Function to determine whether the stack is empty.
      //Postcondition: Returns true if the stack is empty;
      //    otherwise returns false.

    bool isFullStack() const;
      //Function to determine whether the stack is full.
      //Postcondition: Returns false.

    void initializeStack();
      //Function to initialize the stack to an empty state.
      //Postcondition: The stack elements are removed;
      //    stackTop = NULL;

    void push(const Type& newItem);
      //Function to add newItem to the stack.
      //Precondition: The stack exists and is not full.
      //Postcondition: The stack is changed and newItem is
      //    added to the top of the stack.

    Type top() const;
      //Function to return the top element of the stack.
      //Precondition: The stack exists and is not empty.
      //Postcondition: If the stack is empty, the program
      //    terminates; otherwise, the top element of
      //    the stack is returned.

    void pop();
      //Function to remove the top element of the stack.
      //Precondition: The stack exists and is not empty.
      //Postcondition: The stack is changed and the top
      //    element is removed from the stack.

    linkedStackType();
      //Default constructor
      //Postcondition: stackTop = NULL;

    linkedStackType(const linkedStackType<Type>& otherStack);
      //Copy constructor

    ~linkedStackType();
      //Destructor
      //Postcondition: All the elements of the stack are removed.
```

```
private:
    nodeType<Type> *stackTop; //pointer to the stack

    void copyStack(const linkedStackType<Type>& otherStack);
      //Function to make a copy of otherStack.
      //Postcondition: A copy of otherStack is created and
      //     assigned to this stack.
};
```

 NOTE In this linked implementation of stacks, the memory to store the stack elements is allocated dynamically. Logically, the stack is never full. The stack is full only if we run out of memory space. Therefore, in reality, the function isFullStack does not apply to linked implementations of stacks. However, the class linkedStackType must provide the definition of the function isFullStack because it is defined in the parent abstract class stackADT.

We leave the UML class diagram of the class linkedStackType as an exercise for you. (See Exercise 12 at the end of this chapter.)

7

EXAMPLE 7-2

Suppose that stack is an object of type linkedStackType. Figure 7-10(a) shows an empty stack and Figure 7-10(b) shows a nonempty stack.

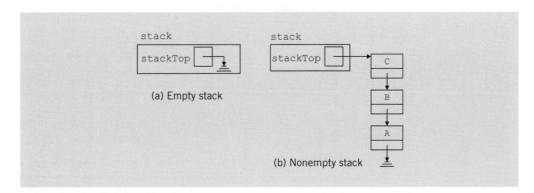

FIGURE 7-10 Empty and nonempty linked stacks

In Figure 7-10(b), the top element of the stack is C; that is, the last element pushed onto the stack is C.

Next, we discuss the definitions of the functions to implement the operations of a linked stack.

Default Constructor

The first operation that we consider is the default constructor. The default constructor initializes the stack to an empty state when a stack object is declared. Thus, this function sets `stackTop` to `NULL`. The definition of this function is as follows:

```
template  <class Type>
linkedStackType<Type>::linkedStackType()
{
    stackTop = NULL;
}
```

Empty Stack and Full Stack

The operations `isEmptyStack` and `isFullStack` are quite straightforward. The stack is empty if `stackTop` is `NULL`. Also, because the memory for a stack element is allocated and deallocated dynamically, the stack is never full. (The stack is full only if we run out of memory.) Thus, the function `isFullStack` always returns the value `false`. The definitions of the functions to implement these operations are as follows:

```
template <class Type>
bool linkedStackType<Type>::isEmptyStack() const
{
    return(stackTop == NULL);
} //end isEmptyStack

template <class Type>
bool linkedStackType<Type>::isFullStack() const
{
    return false;
} //end isFullStack
```

Recall that in the linked implementation of stacks, the function `isFullStack` does not apply because logically the stack is never full. However, you must provide its definition because it is included as an abstract function in the parent `class stackADT`.

Initialize Stack

The operation `initializeStack` reinitializes the stack to an empty state. Because the stack might contain some elements and we are using a linked implementation of a stack, we must deallocate the memory occupied by the stack elements and set `stackTop` to `NULL`. The definition of this function is as follows:

```
template <class Type>
void linkedStackType<Type>:: initializeStack()
{
    nodeType<Type> *temp; //pointer to delete the node

    while (stackTop != NULL)   //while there are elements in
                               //the stack
    {
        temp = stackTop;        //set temp to point to the
                                //current node
        stackTop = stackTop->link;   //advance stackTop to the
                                     //next node
        delete temp;      //deallocate memory occupied by temp
    }
} //end initializeStack
```

Next, we consider the push, top, and pop operations. From Figure 7-10(b), it is clear that the newElement will be added (in the case of push) at the beginning of the linked list pointed to by stackTop. In the case of pop, the node pointed to by stackTop will be removed. In both cases, the value of the pointer stackTop is updated. The operation top returns the info of the node to which stackTop is pointing.

Push

Consider the stack shown in Figure 7-11.

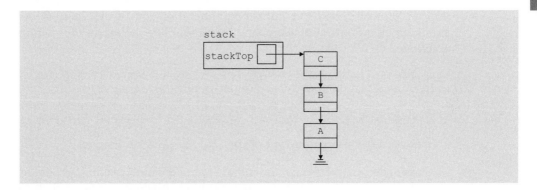

FIGURE 7-11   Stack before the push operation

Figure 7-12 shows the steps of the `push` operation. (Assume that the new element to be pushed is `'D'`.)

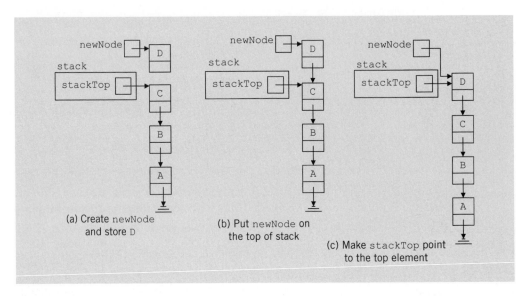

FIGURE 7-12 Push operation

As shown in Figure 7-12, to push `'D'` into the stack, first we create a new node and store `'D'` into it. Next, we put the new node on top of the stack. Finally, we make `stackTop` point to the top element of the stack. The definition of the function `push` is as follows:

```
template <class Type>
void linkedStackType<Type>::push(const Type& newElement)
{
    nodeType<Type> *newNode;  //pointer to create the new node

    newNode = new nodeType<Type>; //create the node

    newNode->info = newElement; //store newElement in the node
    newNode->link = stackTop; //insert newNode before stackTop
    stackTop = newNode;        //set stackTop to point to the
                               //top node
} //end push
```

We do not need to check whether the stack is full before we push an element onto the stack because in this implementation, logically, the stack is never full.

Return the Top Element

The operation to return the top element of the stack is quite straightforward. Its definition is as follows:

```
template <class Type>
Type linkedStackType<Type>::top() const
{
    assert(stackTop != NULL); //if stack is empty,
                              //terminate the program
    return stackTop->info;    //return the top element
}//end top
```

Pop

Now we consider the pop operation, which removes the top element of the stack. Consider the stack shown in Figure 7-13.

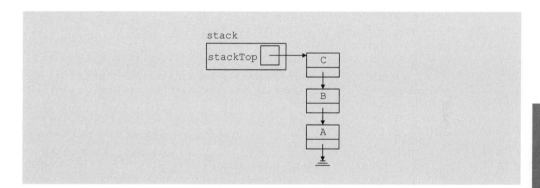

FIGURE 7-13 Stack before the pop operation

Figure 7-14 shows the pop operation.

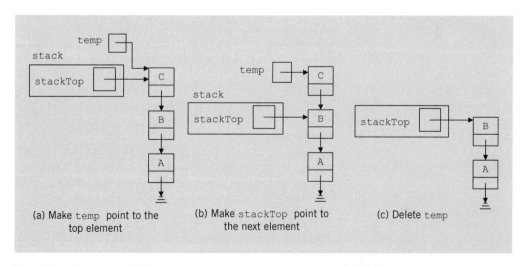

(a) Make temp point to the
    top element

(b) Make stackTop point to
    the next element

(c) Delete temp

FIGURE 7-14 Pop operation

As shown in Figure 7-14, first we make a pointer temp point to the top of the stack. Next we make stackTop point to the next element of the stack, which will become the top element of the stack. Finally, we delete temp. The definition of the function pop is as follows:

```
template <class Type>
void linkedStackType<Type>::pop()
{
    nodeType<Type> *temp;    //pointer to deallocate memory

    if (stackTop != NULL)
    {
        temp = stackTop;  //set temp to point to the top node

        stackTop = stackTop->link;  //advance stackTop to the
                                    //next node
        delete temp;     //delete the top node
    }
    else
        cout << "Cannot remove from an empty stack." << endl;
}//end pop
```

Copy Stack

The function copyStack makes an identical copy of a stack. Its definition is similar to the definition of copyList for linked lists, given in Chapter 5. The definition of the function copyStack is as follows:

```
template  <class Type>
void linkedStackType<Type>::copyStack
                    (const linkedStackType<Type>& otherStack)
{
    nodeType<Type> *newNode, *current, *last;

    if (stackTop != NULL) //if stack is nonempty, make it empty
        initializeStack();

    if (otherStack.stackTop == NULL)
        stackTop = NULL;
    else
    {
        current = otherStack.stackTop;  //set current to point
                                        //to the stack to be copied

            //copy the stackTop element of the stack
        stackTop = new nodeType<Type>;  //create the node

        stackTop->info = current->info; //copy the info
        stackTop->link = NULL;  //set the link field to NULL
        last = stackTop;        //set last to point to the node
        current = current->link; //set current to point to the
                                 //next node
```

```
        //copy the remaining stack
    while (current != NULL)
    {
        newNode = new nodeType<Type>;

        newNode->info = current->info;
        newNode->link = NULL;
        last->link = newNode;
        last = newNode;
        current = current->link;
    }//end while
}//end else
} //end copyStack
```

Constructors and Destructors

We have already discussed the default constructor. To complete the implementation of the stack operations, next we give the definitions of the functions to implement the copy constructor and the destructor, and to overload the assignment operator. (These functions are similar to those discussed for linked lists in Chapter 5.)

```
    //copy constructor
template <class Type>
linkedStackType<Type>::linkedStackType(
                    const linkedStackType<Type>& otherStack)
{
    stackTop = NULL;
    copyStack(otherStack);
}//end copy constructor

    //destructor
template  <class Type>
linkedStackType<Type>::~linkedStackType()
{
    initializeStack();
}//end destructor
```

Overloading the Assignment Operator (=)

The definition of the function to overload the assignment operator for the class linkedStackType is as follows:

```
template <class Type>
const linkedStackType<Type>& linkedStackType<Type>::operator=
                    (const linkedStackType<Type>& otherStack)
{
    if (this != &otherStack) //avoid self-copy
        copyStack(otherStack);

    return *this;
}//end operator=
```

Table 7-2 summarizes the time complexity of the operations to implement a linked stack.

TABLE 7-2 Time complexity of the operations of the `class linkedStackType` on a stack with *n* elements

Function	Time complexity
`isEmptyStack`	$O(1)$
`isFullStack`	$O(1)$
`initializeStack`	$O(n)$
constructor	$O(1)$
`top`	$O(1)$
`push`	$O(1)$
`pop`	$O(1)$
`copyStack`	$O(n)$
destructor	$O(n)$
copy constructor	$O(n)$
Overloading the assignment operator	$O(n)$

The definition of a stack, and the functions to implement the stack operations discussed previously, are generic. Also, as in the case of an array representation of a stack, in the linked representation of a stack, we put the definition of the stack and the functions to implement the stack operations together in a (header) file. A client's program can include this header file via the `include` statement.

The program in Example 7-3 illustrates how a `linkedStack` object is used in a program.

EXAMPLE 7-3

We assume that the definition of the `class linkedStackType` and the functions to implement the stack operations are included in the header file `"linkedStack.h"`.

```
//************************************************************
// Author: D.S. Malik
//
// This program tests various operations of a linked stack.
//************************************************************
```

```cpp
#include <iostream>
#include "linkedStack.h"

using namespace std;

void testCopy(linkedStackType<int> OStack);

int main()
{
    linkedStackType<int> stack;
    linkedStackType<int> otherStack;
    linkedStackType<int> newStack;

        //Add elements into stack
    stack.push(34);
    stack.push(43);
    stack.push(27);

        //Use the assignment operator to copy the elements
        //of stack into newStack
    newStack = stack;

    cout << "After the assignment operator, newStack: "
         << endl;

        //Output the elements of newStack
    while (!newStack.isEmptyStack())
    {
        cout << newStack.top() << endl;
        newStack.pop();
    }

        //Use the assignment operator to copy the elements
        //of stack into otherStack
    otherStack = stack;

    cout << "Testing the copy constructor." << endl;

    testCopy(otherStack);

    cout << "After the copy constructor, otherStack: " << endl;

    while (!otherStack.isEmptyStack())
    {
        cout << otherStack.top() << endl;
        otherStack.pop();
    }

    return 0;
}
```

7

```
    //Function to test the copy constructor
void testCopy(linkedStackType<int> OStack)
{
    cout << "Stack in the function testCopy:" << endl;

    while (!OStack.isEmptyStack())
    {
        cout << OStack.top() << endl;
        OStack.pop();
    }
}
```

Sample Run:

```
After the assignment operator, newStack:
27
43
34
Testing the copy constructor.
Stack in the function testCopy:
27
43
34
After the copy constructor, otherStack:
27
43
34
```

Stack as Derived from the `class unorderedLinkedList`

If we compare the push function of the stack with the `insertFirst` function discussed for general lists in Chapter 5, we see that the algorithms to implement these operations are similar. A comparison of other functions, such as `initializeStack` and `initializeList`, `isEmptyList` and `isEmptyStack`, and so on, suggests that the `class linkedStackType` can be derived from the `class linkedListType`. Moreover, the functions `pop` and `isFullStack` can be implemented as in the previous section. Note that the `class linkedListType` is an abstract class and does not implement all the operations. However, the `class unorderedLinkedList` is derived from the the `class linkedListType` and provides the definitions of the abstract functions of the `class linkedListType`. Therefore, we can derive the `class linkedStackType` from the `class unorderedLinkedList`.

Next, we define the `class linkedStackType` that is derived from the `class unorderedLinkedList`. The definitions of the functions to implement the stack operations are also given.

```
#include <iostream>
#include "unorderedLinkedList.h"
```

```cpp
using namespace std;

template <class Type>
class linkedStackType: public unorderedLinkedList<Type>
{
public:
    void initializeStack();
    bool isEmptyStack() const;
    bool isFullStack() const;
    void push(const Type& newItem);
    Type top() const;
    void pop();
};

template <class Type>
void linkedStackType<Type>::initializeStack()
{
    unorderedLinkedList<Type>::initializeList();
}

template <class Type>
bool linkedStackType<Type>::isEmptyStack() const
{
    return unorderedLinkedList<Type>::isEmptyList();
}

template <class Type>
bool linkedStackType<Type>::isFullStack() const
{
    return false;
}

template <class Type>
void linkedStackType<Type>::push(const Type& newElement)
{
    unorderedLinkedList<Type>::insertFirst(newElement);
}

template <class Type>
Type linkedStackType<Type>::top() const
{
    return unorderedLinkedList<Type>::front();
}

template <class Type>
void linkedStackType<Type>::pop()
{
    nodeType<Type> *temp;

    temp = first;
    first = first->link;
    delete temp;
}
```

7

Application of Stacks: Postfix Expressions Calculator

The usual notation for writing arithmetic expressions (the notation we learned in elementary school) is called **infix** notation, in which the operator is written between the operands. For example, in the expression $a + b$, the operator $+$ is between the operands a and b. In infix notation, the operators have precedence. That is, we must evaluate expressions from left to right, and multiplication and division have higher precedence than addition and subtraction. If we want to evaluate the expression in a different order, we must include parentheses. For example, in the expression $a + b \star c$, we first evaluate $\star$ using the operands b and c, and then we evaluate $+$ using the operand a and the result of $b \star c$.

In the early 1920s, the Polish mathematician Jan Lukasiewicz discovered that if operators were written before the operands (**prefix** or **Polish** notation; for example, $+ \ a \ b$), the parentheses can be omitted. In the late 1950s, the Australian philosopher and early computer scientist Charles L. Hamblin proposed a scheme in which the operators *follow* the operands (postfix operators), resulting in the **Reverse Polish** notation. This has the advantage that the operators appear in the order required for computation.

For example, the expression:

$a + b \star c$

in a postfix expression is:

$a \ b \ c \star +$

The following example shows various infix expressions and their equivalent postfix expressions.

EXAMPLE 7-4

Infix expression	Equivalent postfix expression
$a + b$	$a \ b +$
$a + b * c$	$a \ b \ c * +$
$a * b + c$	$a \ b * c +$
$(a + b) * c$	$a \ b + c *$
$(a - b) * (c + d)$	$a \ b - c \ d + *$
$(a + b) * (c - d / e) + f$	$a \ b + c \ d \ e / - * f +$

Shortly after Lukasiewicz's discovery, it was realized that postfix notation had important applications in computer science. In fact, many compilers use stacks to first translate infix expressions into some form of postfix notation and then translate this postfix expression into machine code. Postfix expressions can be evaluated using the following algorithm:

Scan the expression from left to right. When an operator is found, back up to get the required number of operands, perform the operation, and continue.

Consider the following postfix expression:

```
6 3 + 2 * =
```

Let us evaluate this expression using a stack and the previous algorithm. Figure 7-15 shows how this expression gets evaluated.

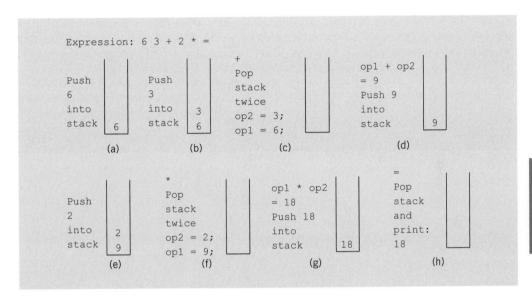

FIGURE 7-15   Evaluating the postfix expression: 6 3 + 2 * =

Read the first symbol, 6, which is a number. Push the number onto the stack; see Figure 7-15(a). Read the next symbol, 3, which is a number. Push the number onto the stack; see Figure 7-15(b). Read the next symbol, +, which is an operator. Because an operator requires two operands to be evaluated, pop the stack twice; see Figure 7-15(c). Perform the operation and put the result back onto the stack; see Figure 7-15(d).

Read the next symbol, 2, which is a number. Push the number onto the stack; see Figure 7-15(e). Read the next symbol, *, which is an operator. Because an operator requires two operands to be evaluated, pop the stack twice; see Figure 7-15(f). Perform the operation and put the result back onto the stack; see Figure 7-15(g).

Scan the next symbol, =, which is the equal sign, indicating the end of the expression. Therefore, print the result. The result of the expression is in the stack, so pop and print; see Figure 7-15(h).

The value of the expression 6 3 + 2 * = 18.

From this discussion, it is clear that when we read a symbol other than a number, the following cases arise:

1. The symbol we read is one of the following: +, -, *, /, or =.

    a. If the symbol is +, -, *, or /, the symbol is an operator and so we must evaluate it. Because an operator requires two operands, the stack must have at least two elements; otherwise, the expression has an error.

    b. If the symbol is = (an equal sign), the expression ends and we must print the answer. At this step, the stack must contain exactly one element; otherwise, the expression has an error.

2. The symbol we read is something other than +, -, *, /, or =. In this case, the expression contains an illegal operator.

It is also clear that when an operand (number) is encountered in an expression, it is pushed onto the stack because the operator comes after the operands.

Consider the following expressions:

   i.   7 6 + 3 ; 6 - =

  ii.   14 + 2 3 * =

 iii.   14 2 3 + =

Expression (i) has an illegal operator, expression (ii) does not have enough operands for +, and expression (iii) has too many operands. In the case of expression (iii), when we encounter the equal sign (=), the stack will have two elements and this error cannot be discovered until we are ready to print the value of the expression.

To make the input easier to read, we assume that the postfix expressions are in the following form:

#6 #3 + #2 * =

The symbol # precedes each number in the expression. If the symbol scanned is #, the next input is a number (that is, an operand). If the symbol scanned is not #, it is either an operator (might be illegal) or an equal sign (indicating the end of the expression). Furthermore, we assume that each expression contains only the +, -, *, and / operators.

This program outputs the entire postfix expression together with the answer. If the expression has an error, the expression is discarded. In this case, the program outputs the expression together with an appropriate error message. Because an expression might contain an error, we must clear the stack before processing the next expression. Also, the stack must be initialized; that is, the stack must be empty.

MAIN ALGORITHM

Pursuant to the previous discussion, the main algorithm in pseudocode is as follows:

```
Read the first character
while not the end of input data
{
    a. initialize the stack
    b. process the expression
    c. output result
    d. get the next expression
}
```

To simplify the complexity of the function main, we write four functions—evaluateExpression, evaluateOpr, discardExp, and printResult. The function evaluateExpression, if possible, evaluates the expression and leaves the result in the stack. If the postfix expression is error free, the function printResult outputs the result. The function evaluateOpr evaluates an operator, and the function discardExp discards the current expression if there is any error in the expression.

FUNCTION evaluateExpression

The function evaluateExpression evaluates each postfix expression. Each expression ends with the symbol =. The general algorithm in pseudocode is as follows:

```
while (ch is not = '=') //process each expression
                        //= marks the end of an expression
{
    switch (ch)
    {
    case '#':
        read a number
        output the number;
        push the number onto the stack;
        break;
     default:
        assume that ch is an operation
        evaluate the operation;
    } //end switch

    if no error was found, then
    {
        read next ch;
        output ch;
    }
    else
        Discard the expression
} //end while
```

From this algorithm, it follows that this method has five parameters—a parameter to access the input file, a parameter to access the output file, a parameter to access the stack, a parameter to pass a character of the expression, and a parameter to indicate whether there is an error in the expression. The definition of this function is as follows:

```
void evaluateExpression(ifstream& inpF, ofstream& outF,
                    stackType<double>& stack,
                    char& ch, bool& isExpOk)
```

```
{
    double num;
    outF << ch;

    while (ch != '=')
    {
        switch (ch)
        {
        case '#':
            inpF >> num;
            outF << num << " ";
            if (!stack.isFullStack())
                stack.push(num);
            else
            {
                cout << "Stack overflow. "
                     << "Program terminates!" << endl;
                exit(0);   //terminate the program
            }

            break;

        default:
            evaluateOpr(outF, stack, ch, isExpOk);
        }//end switch

        if (isExpOk) //if no error
        {
            inpF >> ch;
            outF << ch;

            if (ch != '#')
                outF << " ";
        }
        else
            discardExp(inpF, outF, ch);
    } //end while (!= '=')
} //end evaluateExpression
```

Note that the funtion `exit` terminates the program.

FUNCTION `evaluateOpr`

This function (if possible) evaluates an expression. Two operands are needed to evaluate an operation and operands are saved in the stack. Therefore, the stack must contain at least two numbers. If the stack contains fewer than two numbers, the expression has an error. In this case, the entire expression is discarded and an appropriate message is printed. This function also checks for any illegal operations. In pseudocode, this function is as follows:

```
if stack is empty
{
    error in the expression
    set expressionOk to false
}
else
{
    retrieve the top element of stack into op2
    pop stack
    if stack is empty
    {
        error in the expression
        set expressionOk to false
    }
    else
    {
        retrieve the top element of stack into op1
        pop stack

          //If the operation is legal, perform the operation and
          //push the result onto the stack;
          //otherwise, report the error.
        switch (ch)
        {
        case '+': //add the operands: op1 + op2
            stack.push(op1 + op2);
            break;
        case '-': //subtract the operands: op1 - op2
            stack.push(op1 - op2);
            break;
        case '*': //multiply the operands: op1 * op2
            stack.push(op1 * op2);
            break;
        case '/': //If (op2 != 0), op1 / op2
            stack.push(op1 / op2);
            break;
        otherwise operation is illegal
            {
                output an appropriate message;
                set expressionOk to false
            }
        } //end switch
}
```

Following this pseudocode, the definition of the function evaluateOpr is as follows:

```
void evaluateOpr(ofstream& out, stackType<double>& stack,
                 char& ch, bool& isExpOk)
{
    double op1, op2;
```

```cpp
        if (stack.isEmptyStack())
        {
            out << " (Not enough operands)";
            isExpOk = false;
        }
        else
        {
            op2 = stack.top();
            stack.pop();

            if (stack.isEmptyStack())
            {
                out << " (Not enough operands)";
                isExpOk = false;
            }
            else
            {
                op1 = stack.top();
                stack.pop();

                switch (ch)
                {
                case '+':
                    stack.push(op1 + op2);
                    break;

                case '-':
                    stack.push(op1 - op2);
                    break;

                case '*':
                    stack.push(op1 * op2);
                    break;

                case '/':
                    if (op2 != 0)
                        stack.push(op1 / op2);
                    else
                    {
                        out << " (Division by 0)";
                        isExpOk = false;
                    }
                    break;

                default:
                    out << " (Illegal operator)";
                    isExpOk = false;
                }//end switch
            } //end else
        } //end else
} //end evaluateOpr
```

FUNCTION `discardExp`

This function is called whenever an error is discovered in the expression. It reads and writes the input data only until the input is `'='`, the end of the expression. The definiton of this function is as follows:

```
void discardExp(ifstream& in, ofstream& out, char& ch)
{
    while (ch != '=')
    {
        in.get(ch);
        out << ch;
    }
} //end discardExp
```

FUNCTION `printResult`

If the postfix expression contains no errors, the function `printResult` prints the result; otherwise, it outputs an appropriate message. The result of the expression is in the stack and the output is sent to a file. Therefore, this function must have access to the stack and the output file. Suppose that no errors were encountered by the method `evaluateExpression`. If the stack has only one element, the expression is error free and the top element of the stack is printed. If either the stack is empty or it has more than one element, there is an error in the postfix expression. In this case, this method outputs an appropriate error message. The definition of this method is as follows:

```
void printResult(ofstream& outF, stackType<double>& stack,
                 bool isExpOk)
{
    double result;

    if (isExpOk) //if no error, print the result
    {
        if (!stack.isEmptyStack())
        {
            result = stack.top();
            stack.pop();

            if (stack.isEmptyStack())
                outF << result << endl;
            else
                outF << " (Error: Too many operands)" << endl;
        } //end if
        else
            outF << " (Error in the expression)" << endl;
    }
    else
        outF << " (Error in the expression)" << endl;

    outF << "_____"
         << endl << endl;
} //end printResult
```

PROGRAM LISTING

```
//*************************************************************
// Author: D.S. Malik
//
// This program uses a stack to evaluate postfix expressions.
//*************************************************************

#include <iostream>
#include <iomanip>
#include <fstream>
#include "mystack.h"

using namespace std;

void evaluateExpression(ifstream& inpF, ofstream& outF,
                        stackType<double>& stack,
                        char& ch, bool& isExpOk);
void evaluateOpr(ofstream& out, stackType<double>& stack,
                 char& ch, bool& isExpOk);
void discardExp(ifstream& in, ofstream& out, char& ch);
void printResult(ofstream& outF, stackType<double>& stack,
                 bool isExpOk);

int main()
{
    bool expressionOk;
    char ch;
    stackType<double> stack(100);
    ifstream infile;
    ofstream outfile;

    infile.open("RpnData.txt");

    if (!infile)
    {
        cout << "Cannot open the input file. "
             << "Program terminates!" << endl;
        return 1;
    }

    outfile.open("RpnOutput.txt");

    outfile << fixed << showpoint;
    outfile << setprecision(2);

    infile >> ch;
    while (infile)
    {
        stack.initializeStack();
        expressionOk = true;
        outfile << ch;
```

```
            evaluateExpression(infile, outfile, stack, ch,
                               expressionOk);
            printResult(outfile, stack, expressionOk);
            infile >> ch; //begin processing the next expression
    } //end while

    infile.close();
    outfile.close();

    return 0;

} //end main
```

```
//Place the definitions of the function evaluateExpression,
//evaluateOpr, discardExp, and printResult as described
//previously here.
```

Sample Run:

Input File

```
#35 #27 + #3 * =
#26 #28 + #32 #2 ; - #5 / =
#23 #30 #15 * / =
#2 #3 #4 + =
#20 #29 #9 * ; =
#25 #23 - + =
#34 #24 #12 #7 / * + #23 - =
```

Output

#35.00 #27.00 + #3.00 * = 186.00

_____

#26.00 #28.00 + #32.00 #2.00 ; (Illegal operator) - #5 / = (Error in the expression)

_____

#23.00 #30.00 #15.00 * / = 0.05

_____

#2.00 #3.00 #4.00 + = (Error: Too many operands)

_____

#20.00 #29.00 #9.00 * ; (Illegal operator) = (Error in the expression)

_____

#25.00 #23.00 - + (Not enough operands) = (Error in the expression)

_____

#34.00 #24.00 #12.00 #7.00 / * + #23.00 - = 52.14

_____

7

Removing Recursion: Nonrecursive Algorithm to Print a Linked List Backward

In Chapter 6, we used recursion to print a linked list backward. In this section, you will learn how a stack can be used to design a nonrecursive algorithm to print a linked list backward.

Consider the linked list shown in Figure 7-16.

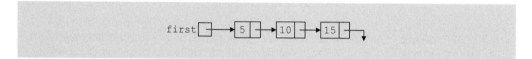

FIGURE 7-16 Linked list

To print the list backward, first we need to get to the last node of the list, which we can do by traversing the linked list starting at the first node. However, once we are at the last node, how do we get back to the previous node, especially given that links go in only one direction? You can again traverse the linked list with the appropriate loop termination condition, but this approach might waste a considerable amount of computer time, especially if the list is very large. Moreover, if we do this for every node in the list, the program might execute very slowly. Next, we show how to use a stack effectively to print the list backward.

After printing the `info` of a particular node, we need to move to the node immediately behind this node. For example, after printing 15, we need to move to the node with `info` 10. Thus, while initially traversing the list to move to the last node, we must save a pointer to each node. For example, for the list in Figure 7-16, we must save a pointer to each of the nodes with `info` 5 and 10. After printing 15, we go back to the node with `info` 10; after printing 10, we go back to the node with `info` 5. From this, it follows that we must save pointers to each node in a stack, so as to implement the Last In First Out principle.

Because the number of nodes in a linked list is usually not known, we will use the linked implementation of a stack. Suppose that `stack` is an object of type `linkedListType`, and `current` is a pointer of the same type as the pointer `first`. Consider the following statements:

```
current = first;                   //Line 1

while (current != NULL)            //Line 2
{                                  //Line 3
    stack.push(current);           //Line 4
    current = current->link;       //Line 5
}                                  //Line 6
```

After the statement in Line 1 executes, current points to the first node. (See Figure 7-17)

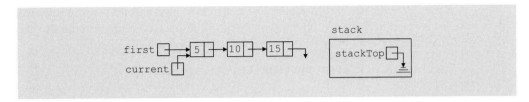

FIGURE 7-17 List after the statement current = first; executes

Because current is not NULL, the statements in Lines 4 and 5 execute. (See Figure 7-18.)

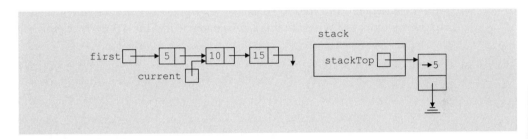

FIGURE 7-18 List and stack after the statements stack.push(current); and current = current->link; execute

Because current is not NULL, statements in Lines 4 and 5 execute. In fact, statements in Lines 4 and 5 execute until current beomes NULL. When current is NULL, Figure 7-19 results.

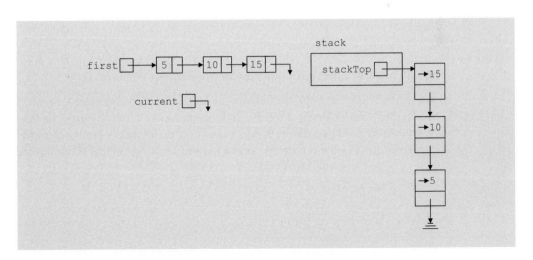

FIGURE 7-19 List and stack after the while statement executes

After the statement in Line 4 executes, the loop condition, in Line 2, is evaluated again. Because `current` is `NULL`, the loop condition evaluates to `false` and the `while` loop, in Line 2, terminates. From Figure 7-19, it follows that a pointer to each node in the linked list is saved in the stack. The top element of the stack contains a pointer to the last node in the list, and so on. Let us now execute the following statements:

```
while (!stack.isEmptyStack())          //Line 7
{                                      //Line 8
    current = stack.top();             //Line 9
    stack.pop();                       //Line 10
    cout << current->info << " ";      //Line 11
}                                      //Line 12
```

The loop condition in Line 7 evaluates to `true` because the stack is nonempty. Therefore, the statements in Lines 9, 10, and 11 execute. After the statement in Line 9 executes, `current` points to the last node. The statement in Line 10 removes the top element of the stack; see Figure 7-20.

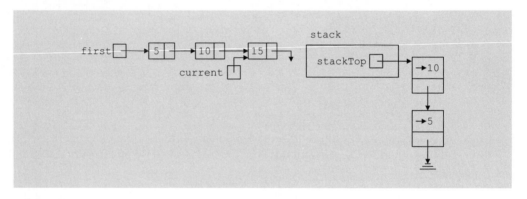

FIGURE 7-20 List and stack after the statements `current = stack.top();` and `stack.pop();` execute

The statement in Line 11 outputs `current->info`, which is 15.

Because `stack` is nonempty, the body of the `while` loop executes again. In fact, for the linked list in Figure 7-20, the body of the `while` loop executes two more times; the first time it prints 10, and the second time it prints 5. Ater printing 5, the `stack` becomes empty and the `while` loop terminates. It follows that the `while` loop in Line 7 produces the following output:

```
15 10 5
```

STL class stack

The previous sections discussed the data structure `stack` in detail. Because a stack is an important data structure, the Standard Template Library (STL) provides a class to implement a stack in a program. The name of the class defining a stack is `stack`; the name of the header file containing the definition of the class stack is stack. The implementation of the class stack provided by the STL is similar to the one described in this chapter. Table 7-3 defines the various operations supported by the stack container class.

TABLE 7-3 Operations on a stack object

Operation	Effect
size	Returns the actual number of elements in the stack.
empty	Returns true if the stack is empty, and false otherwise.
push(item)	Inserts a copy of item into the stack.
top	Returns the top element of the stack, but does not remove the top element from the stack. This operation is implemented as a value-returning function.
pop	Removes the top element of the stack.

In addition to the operations size, empty, push, top, and pop, the stack container class provides relational operators to compare two stacks. For example, the relational operator == can be used to determine whether two stacks are identical.

The program in Example 7-5 illustrates how to use the stack container class.

EXAMPLE 7-5

```
//************************************************************
// Author: D.S. Malik
//
// This program illustrates how to use the STL class stack in
// a program.
//************************************************************

#include <iostream>                              //Line 1
#include <stack>                                 //Line 2

using namespace std;                             //Line 3

int main()                                       //Line 4
{                                                //Line 5
    stack<int>  intStack;                        //Line 6
```

```
intStack.push(16);                                     //Line 7
intStack.push(8);                                      //Line 8
intStack.push(20);                                     //Line 9
intStack.push(3);                                      //Line 10

cout << "Line 11: The top element of intStack: "
     << intStack.top() << endl;                        //Line 11

intStack.pop();                                        //Line 12

cout << "Line 13: After the pop operation, the "
     << " top element of intStack: "
     << intStack.top() << endl;                        //Line 13

cout << "Line 14: intStack elements: ";               //Line 14

while (!intStack.empty())                              //Line 15
{                                                      //Line 16
    cout << intStack.top() << " ";                    //Line 17
    intStack.pop();                                    //Line 18
}                                                      //Line 19

cout << endl;                                          //Line 20

return 0;                                              //Line 21
}                                                      //Line 22
```

Sample Run:

```
Line 11: The top element of intStack: 3
Line 13: After the pop operation, the top element of intStack: 20
Line 14: intStack elements: 20 8 16
```

The preceding output is self-explanatory. The details are left as an exercise for you.

QUICK REVIEW

1. A stack is a data structure in which the items are added and deleted from one end only.

2. A stack is a Last In First Out (LIFO) data structure.

3. The basic operations on a stack are as follows: Push an item onto the stack, pop an item from the stack, retrieve the top element of the stack, initialize the stack, check whether the stack is empty, and check whether the stack is full.

4. A stack can be implemented as an array or a linked list.

5. The middle elements of a stack should not be accessed directly.

6. Stacks are restricted versions of arrays and linked lists.

7. Postfix notation does not require the use of parentheses to enforce operator precedence.

8. In postfix notation, the operators are written after the operands.

9. Postfix expressions are evaluated according to the following rules:

   a. Scan the expression from left to right.

   b. If an operator is found, back up to get the required number of operands, evaluate the operator, and continue.

10. The STL class `stack` can be used to implement a stack in a program.

EXERCISES

1. Consider the following statements:

   ```
   stackType<int> stack;
   int x, y;
   ```

   Show what is output by the following segment of code:

   ```
   x = 4;
   y = 0;
   stack.push(7);
   stack.push(x);
   stack.push(x + 5);
   y = stack.top();
   stack.pop();
   stack.push(x + y);
   stack.push(y - 2);
   stack.push(3);
   x = stack.top();
   stack.pop();

   cout << "x = " << x << endl;
   cout << "y = " << y << endl;

   while (!stack.isEmptyStack())
   {
       cout << stack.top() << endl;
       stack.pop();
   }
   ```

2. Consider the following statements:

   ```
   stackType<int> stack;
   int x;
   ```

   Suppose that the input is:

   ```
   14 45 34 23 10 5 -999
   ```

   Show what is output by the following segment of code:

```
stack.push(5);

cin >> x;

while (x != -999)
{
    if (x % 2 == 0)
    {
        if (!stack.isFullStack())
            stack.push(x);
    }
    else
        cout << "x = " << x << endl;
    cin >> x;
}

cout << "Stack Elements: ";

while (!stack.isEmptyStack())
{
    cout << " " << stack.top();
    stack.pop();
}
cout << endl;
```

3. Evaluate the following postfix expressions:

   a.   8 2 + 3 * 16 4 / - =

   b.   12 25 5 1 / / * 8 7 + - =

   c.   70 14 4 5 15 3 / * - - / 6 + =

   d.   3 5 6 * + 13 - 18 2 / + =

4. Convert the following infix expressions to postfix notations:

   a.   (A + B) * (C + D) - E

   b.   A - (B + C) * D + E / F

   c.   ((A + B) / (C - D) + E) * F - G

   d.   A + B * (C + D) - E / F * G + H

5. Write the equivalent infix expression for the following postfix expressions:

   a.   A B * C +

   b.   A B + C D - *

   c.   A B - C - D *

6. What is the output of the following program?

```
#include <iostream>
#include <string>
#include "myStack.h"

using namespace std;
```

```
template <class Type>
void mystery(stackType<Type>& s, stackType<Type>& t);

int main()
{
    stackType<string> s1;
    stackType<string> s2;

    string list[] = {"Winter", "Spring", "Summer", "Fall",
                     "Cold", "Warm", "Hot"};

    for (int i = 0; i < 7; i++)
        s1.push(list[i]);

    mystery(s1, s2);

    while (!s2.isEmptyStack())
    {
        cout << s2.top() << " ";
        s2.pop();
    }
    cout << endl;
}

template <class Type>
void mystery(stackType<Type>& s, stackType<Type>& t)
{
    while (!s.isEmptyStack())
    {
        t.push(s.top());
        s.pop();
    }
}
```

7. What is the effect of the following statements? If a statement is invalid, explain why it is invalid. The classes stackADT, stackType, and linkedStackType are as defined in this chapter.

   a. `stackADT<int> newStack;`

   b. `stackType<double> sales(-10);`

   c. `stackType<string> names;`

   d. `linkedStackType<int> numStack(50);`

8. What is the output of the following program?

```
#include <iostream>
#include <string>
#include "myStack.h"

using namespace std;

void mystery(stackType<int>& s, stackType<int>& t);
```

```
int main()
{
    int list[] = {5, 10, 15, 20, 25};

    stackType<int> s1;
    stackType<int> s2;

    for (int i = 0; i < 5; i++)
        s1.push(list[i]);

    mystery(s1, s2);

    while (!s2.isEmptyStack())
    {
        cout << s2.top() << " ";
        s2.pop();
    }
    cout << endl;
}

void mystery(stackType<int>& s, stackType<int>& t)
{
    while (!s.isEmptyStack())
    {
        t.push(2 * s.top());
        s.pop();
    }
}
```

9. What is the output of the following program segment?

```
linkedStackType<int> myStack;

myStack.push(10);
myStack.push(20);
myStack.pop();
cout << myStack.top() << endl;
myStack.push(25);
myStack.push(2 * myStack.top());
myStack.push(-10);
myStack.pop();

linkedStackType<int> tempStack;

tempStack = myStack;

while (!tempStack.isEmptyStack())
{
    cout << tempStack.top() << " ";
    tempStack.pop();
}

cout << endl;

cout << myStack.top() << endl;
```

10. Write the definition of the function template `printListReverse` that uses a stack to print a linked list in reverse order. Assume that this function is a member of the `class linkedListType`, designed in Chapter 5.

11. Write the definition of the function template `second` that takes as a parameter a stack object and returns the second element of the stack. The original stack remains unchanged.

12. Draw the UML class diagram of the `class linkedStackType`.

13. Write the definition of the function template `clear` that takes as a parameter a stack object of the type `stack` (STL class) and removes all the elements from the stack.

PROGRAMMING EXERCISES

1. Two stacks of the same type are the same if they have the same number of elements and their elements at the corresponding positions are the same. Overload the relational operator `==` for the `class stackType` that returns `true` if two stacks of the same type are the same, `false` otherwise. Also, write the definition of the function template to overload this operator.

2. Repeat Exercise 1 for the `class linkedStackType`.

3. a. Add the following operation to the `class stackType`:

   ```
   void reverseStack(stackType<Type> &otherStack);
   ```

   This operation copies the elements of a stack in reverse order onto another stack.

   Consider the following statements:

   ```
   stackType<int> stack1;
   stackType<int> stack2;
   ```

   The statement

   ```
   stack1.reverseStack(stack2);
   ```

   copies the elements of `stack1` onto `stack2` in reverse order. That is, the top element of `stack1` is the bottom element of `stack2`, and so on. The old contents of `stack2` are destroyed and `stack1` is unchanged.

   b. Write the definition of the function `template` to implement the operation `reverseStack`.

4. Repeat Exercises 3a and 3b for the `class linkedStackType`.

5. Write a program that takes as input an arithmetic expression. The program outputs whether the expression contains matching grouping symbols. For example, the arithmetic expressions {25 + (3 − 6) * 8} and 7 + 8 * 2 contains matching grouping symbols. However, the expression 5 + { (13 + 7) / 8 − 2 * 9 does not contain matching grouping symbols.

6. Write a program that uses a stack to print the prime factors of a positive integer in descending order.

7. **(Converting a Number from Binary to Decimal)** The language of a computer, called machine language, is a sequence of 0s and 1s. When you press the key A on the keyboard, 01000001 is stored in the computer. Also, the collating sequence of A in the ASCII character set is 65. In fact, the binary representation of A is 01000001 and the decimal representation of A is 65.

The numbering system we use is called the decimal system, or base 10 system. The numbering system that the computer uses is called the **binary system**, or **base 2 system**. The purpose of this exercise is to write a function to convert a number from base 2 to base 10.

To convert a number from base 2 to base 10, we first find the weight of each bit in the binary number. The weight of each bit in the binary number is assigned from right to left. The weight of the rightmost bit is 0. The weight of the bit immediately to the left of the rightmost bit is 1, the weight of the bit immediately to the left of it is 2, and so on. Consider the binary number 1001101. The weight of each bit is as follows:

weight   6 5 4 3 2 1 0
        1 0 0 1 1 0 1

We use the weight of each bit to find the equivalent decimal number. For each bit, we multiply the bit by 2 to the power of its weight, and then we add all of the numbers. For the binary number 1001101, the equivalent decimal number is

$$1 \times 2^6 + 0 \times 2^5 + 0 \times 2^4 + 1 \times 2^3 + 1 \times 2^2 + 0 \times 2^1 + 1 \times 2^0$$
$$= 64 + 0 + 0 + 8 + 4 + 0 + 1 = 77$$

To write a program that converts a binary number into the equivalent decimal number, we note two things: (1) The weight of each bit in the binary number must be known, and (2) the weight is assigned from right to left. Because we do not know in advance how many bits are in the binary number, we must process the bits from right to left. After processing a bit, we can add 1 to its weight, giving the weight of the bit immediately to its left. Also, each bit must be extracted from the binary number and multiplied by 2 to the power of its weight. To extract a bit, you can use the mod operator. Write a program that uses a stack to convert a binary number into an equivalent decimal number and test your function for the following values: 11000101, 10101010, 11111111, 10000000, 1111100000.

8. Chapter 6 described how to use recursion to convert a decimal number into an equivalent binary number. Write a program that uses a stack to convert a decimal number into an equivalent binary number.

9. **(Infix to Postfix)** Write a program that converts an infix expression into an equivalent postfix expression.

The rules to convert an infix expression into an equivalent postfix expression are as follows:

Suppose `infx` represents the infix expression and `pfx` represents the postfix expression. The rules to convert `infx` into `pfx` are as follows:

a. Initialize `pfx` to an empty expression and also initialize the stack.

b. Get the next symbol, `sym`, from `infx`.

   b.1. If `sym` is an operand, append `sym` to `pfx`.

   b.2. If `sym` is (, push `sym` into the stack.

   b.3. If `sym` is), pop and append all the symbols from the stack until the most recent left parenthesis. Pop and discard the left parenthesis.

   b.4. If `sym` is an operator:

      b.4.1. Pop and append all the operators from the stack to `pfx` that are above the most recent left parenthesis and have precedence greater than or equal to `sym`.

      b.4.2. Push `sym` onto the stack.

c. After processing `infx`, some operators might be left in the stack. Pop and append to `pfx` everything from the stack.

In this program, you will consider the following (binary) arithmetic operators: +, −, *, and /. You may assume that the expressions you will process are error free.

Design a class that stores the infix and postfix strings. The class must include the following operations:

- **getInfix**—Stores the infix expression
- **showInfix**—Outputs the infix expression
- **showPostfix**—Outputs the postfix expression

Some other operations that you might need are the following:

- **convertToPostfix**—Converts the infix expression into a postfix expression. The resulting postfix expression is stored in `pfx`.
- **precedence**—Determines the precedence between two operators. If the first operator is of higher or equal precedence than the second operator, it returns the value `true`; otherwise, it returns the value `false`.

Include the constructors and destructors for automatic initialization and dynamic memory deallocation.

7

Test your program on the following five expressions:

```
A + B - C;
(A + B ) * C;
(A + B) * (C - D);
A + ((B + C) * (E - F) - G) / (H - I);
A + B * (C + D ) - E / F * G + H;
```

For each expression, your answer must be in the following form:

```
Infix Expression: A + B - C;
Postfix Expression: A B + C -
```

10. Redo the program in the section "Application of Stacks: Postfix Expressions Calculator" of this chapter so that it uses the STL class stack to evaluate the postfix expressions.

11. Redo Programming Exercise 9 so that it uses the STL class stack to convert the infix expressions to postfix expressions.

CHAPTER 8

QUEUES

IN THIS CHAPTER, YOU WILL:

- · Learn about queues
- · Examine various queue operations
- · Learn how to implement a queue as an array
- · Learn how to implement a queue as a linked list
- · Discover queue applications
- · Become aware of the STL `class queue`

This chapter discusses another important data structure, called a **queue**. The notion of a queue in computer science is the same as the notion of the queues to which you are accustomed in everyday life. There are queues of customers in a bank or in a grocery store and queues of cars waiting to pass through a tollbooth. Similarly, because a computer can send a print request faster than a printer can print, a queue of documents is often waiting to be printed at a printer. The general rule to process elements in a queue is that the customer at the front of the queue is served next and that when a new customer arrives, he or she stands at the end of the queue. That is, a queue is a First In First Out data structure.

Queues have numerous applications in computer science. Whenever a system is modeled on the First In First Out principle, queues are used. At the end of this section, we will discuss one of the most widely used applications of queues, computer simulation. First, however, we need to develop the tools necessary to implement a queue. The next few sections discuss how to design classes to implement queues as an ADT.

A queue is a set of elements of the same type in which the elements are added at one end, called the **back** or **rear**, and deleted from the other end, called the **front**. For example, consider a line of customers in a bank, wherein the customers are waiting to withdraw/deposit money or to conduct some other business. Each new customer gets in the line at the rear. Whenever a teller is ready for a new customer, the customer at the front of the line is served.

The rear of the queue is accessed whenever a new element is added to the queue, and the front of the queue is accessed whenever an element is deleted from the queue. As in a stack, the middle elements of the queue are inaccessible, even if the queue elements are stored in an array.

Queue: A data structure in which the elements are added at one end, called the rear, and deleted from the other end, called the front; a First In First Out (FIFO) data structure.

Queue Operations

From the definition of queues, we see that the two key operations are add and delete. We call the add operation **addQueue** and the delete operation **deleteQueue**. Because elements can be neither deleted from an empty queue nor added to a full queue, we need two more operations to successfully implement the addQueue and **deleteQueue** operations: **isEmptyQueue** (checks whether the queue is empty) and **isFullQueue** (checks whether a queue is full).

We also need an operation, **initializeQueue**, to initialize the queue to an empty state. Moreover, to retrieve the first and last elements of the queue, we include the operations **front** and **back** as described in the following list. Some of the queue operations are as follows:

- **initializeQueue**—Initializes the queue to an empty state.
- **isEmptyQueue**—Determines whether the queue is empty. If the queue is empty, it returns the value true; otherwise, it returns the value false.

- `isFullQueue`—Determines whether the queue is full. If the queue is full, it returns the value `true`; otherwise, it returns the value `false`.
- `front`—Returns the front, that is, the first element of the queue. Prior to this operation, the queue must exist and must not be empty.
- `back`—Returns the last element of the queue. Prior to this operation, the queue must exist and must not be empty.
- **addQueue**—Adds a new element to the rear of the queue. Prior to this operation, the queue must exist and must not be full.
- **deleteQueue**—Removes the front element from the queue. Prior to this operation, the queue must exist and must not be empty.

As in the case of a stack, a queue can be stored in an array or in a linked structure. We will consider both implementations. Because elements are added at one end and removed from the other end, we need two pointers to keep track of the front and rear of the queue, called **queueFront** and **queueRear**.

The following abstract `class queueADT` defines these operations as an ADT:

```
//************************************************************
// Author: D.S. Malik
//
// This class specifies the basic operations on a queue.
//************************************************************

template <class Type>
class queueADT
{
public:
    virtual bool isEmptyQueue() const = 0;
      //Function to determine whether the queue is empty.
      //Postcondition: Returns true if the queue is empty,
      //      otherwise returns false.

    virtual bool isFullQueue() const = 0;
      //Function to determine whether the queue is full.
      //Postcondition: Returns true if the queue is full,
      //      otherwise returns false.

    virtual void initializeQueue() = 0;
      //Function to initialize the queue to an empty state.
      //Postcondition: The queue is empty.

    virtual Type front() const = 0;
      //Function to return the first element of the queue.
      //Precondition: The queue exists and is not empty.
      //Postcondition: If the queue is empty, the program
      //      terminates; otherwise, the first element of the queue
      //      is returned.
```

8

```
        virtual Type back() const = 0;
          //Function to return the last element of the queue.
          //Precondition: The queue exists and is not empty.
          //Postcondition: If the queue is empty, the program
          //    terminates; otherwise, the last element of the queue
          //    is returned.

        virtual void addQueue(const Type& queueElement) = 0;
          //Function to add queueElement to the queue.
          //Precondition: The queue exists and is not full.
          //Postcondition: The queue is changed and queueElement is
          //    added to the queue.

        virtual void deleteQueue() = 0;
          //Function to remove the first element of the queue.
          //Precondition: The queue exists and is not empty.
          //Postcondition: The queue is changed and the first element
          //    is removed from the queue.
};
```

We leave it as an exercise for you to draw the UML diagram of the class queueADT.

Implementation of Queues as Arrays

Before giving the definition of the class to implement a queue as an ADT, we need to decide how many member variables are needed to implement the queue. Of course, we need an array to store the queue elements, the variables queueFront and queueRear to keep track of the first and last elements of the queue, and the variable maxQueueSize to specify the maximum size of the queue. Thus, we need at least four member variables.

Before writing the algorithms to implement the queue operations, we need to decide how to use queueFront and queueRear to access the queue elements. How do queueFront and queueRear indicate that the queue is empty or full? Suppose that queueFront gives the index of the first element of the queue, and queueRear gives the index of the last element of the queue. To add an element to the queue, first we advance queueRear to the next array position and then add the element to the position that queueRear is pointing to. To delete an element from the queue, first we retrieve the element that queueFront is pointing to and then advance queueFront to the next element of the queue. Thus, queueFront changes after each deleteQueue operation and queueRear changes after each addQueue operation.

Let us see what happens when queueFront changes after a deleteQueue operation and queueRear changes after an addQueue operation. Assume that the array to hold the queue elements is of size 100.

Initially, the queue is empty. After the operation:

```
addQueue(Queue,'A');
```

the array is as shown in Figure 8-1.

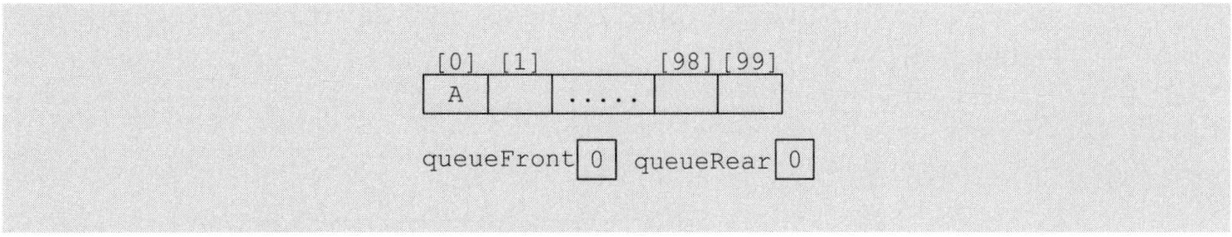

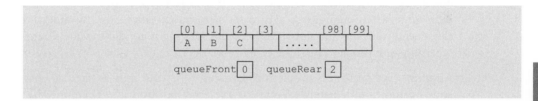

FIGURE 8-1 Queue after the first `addQueue` operation

After two more **addQueue** operations:

```
addQueue(Queue,'B');
addQueue(Queue,'C');
```

the array is as shown in Figure 8-2.

FIGURE 8-2 Queue after two more `addQueue` operations

8

Now consider the **deleteQueue** operation:

```
deleteQueue();
```

After this operation, the array containing the queue is as shown in Figure 8-3.

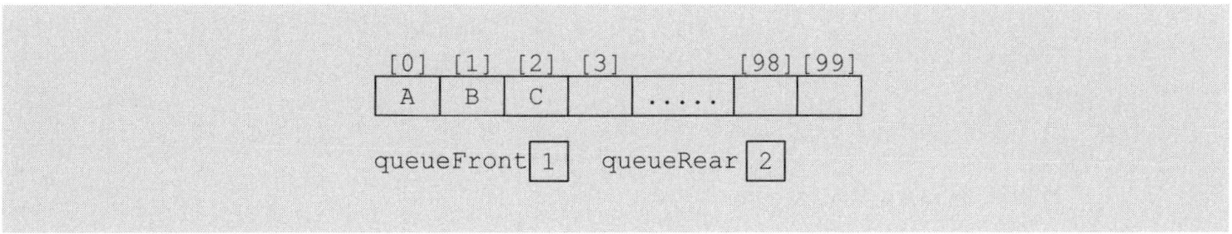

FIGURE 8-3 Queue after the `deleteQueue` operation

Will this queue design work? Suppose A stands for adding (that is, **addQueue**) an element to the queue, and D stands for deleting (that is, **deleteQueue**) an element from the queue. Consider the following sequence of operations:

AAADADADADADADADA...

This sequence of operations would eventually set the index `queueRear` to point to the last array position, giving the impression that the queue is full. However, the queue has only two or three elements and the front of the array is empty. (See Figure 8-4.)

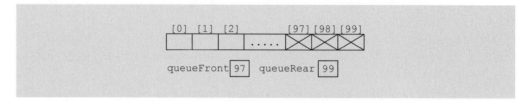

FIGURE 8-4   Queue after the sequence of operations AAADADADADADA...

One solution to this problem is that when the queue overflows to the rear (that is, `queueRear` points to the last array position), we can check the value of the index `queueFront`. If the value of `queueFront` indicates that there is room in the front of the array, then when `queueRear` gets to the last array position, we can slide all of the queue elements toward the first array position. This solution is good if the queue size is very small; otherwise, the program might execute more slowly.

Another solution to this problem is to assume that the array is circular—that is, the first array position immediately follows the last array position. (See Figure 8-5.)

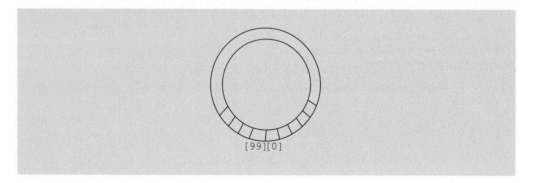

FIGURE 8-5   Circular queue

We will consider the array containing the queue to be circular, although we will draw the figures of the array holding the queue elements as before.

Suppose that we have the queue as shown in Figure 8-6(a).

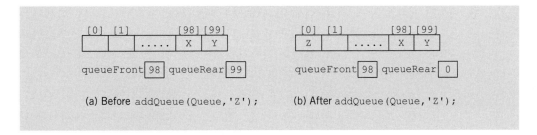

FIGURE 8-6 Queue before and after the add operation

After the operation `addQueue(Queue,'Z');`, the queue is as shown in Figure 8-6(b).

Because the array containing the queue is circular, we can use the following statement to advance `queueRear` (`queueFront`) to the next array position:

```
queueRear = (queueRear + 1) % maxQueueSize;
```

If `queueRear < maxQueueSize - 1`, then `queueRear + 1 <= maxQueueSize - 1`, so `(queueRear + 1) % maxQueueSize = queueRear + 1`. If `queueRear == maxQueueSize - 1` (that is, `queueRear` points to the last array position), `queueRear + 1 == maxQueueSize`, so `(queueRear + 1) % maxQueueSize = 0`. In this case, `queueRear` will be set to 0, which is the first array position.

This queue design seems to work well. Before we write the algorithms to implement the queue operations, consider the following two cases.

Case 1: Suppose that after certain operations, the array containing the queue is as shown in Figure 8-7(a).

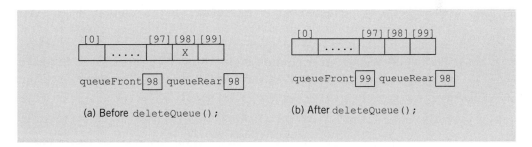

FIGURE 8-7 Queue before and after the delete operation

After the operation `deleteQueue();`, the resulting array is as shown in Figure 8-7(b).

Case 2: Let us now consider the queue shown in Figure 8-8(a).

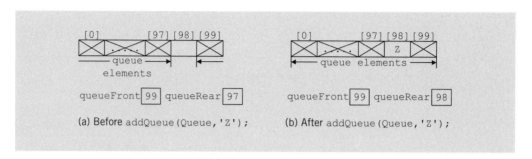

(a) Before addQueue(Queue,'Z'); (b) After addQueue(Queue,'Z');

FIGURE 8-8 Queue before and after the add operation

After the operation addQueue (Queue, 'Z');, the resulting array is as shown in Figure 8-8(b).

The arrays in Figures 8-7(b) and 8-8(b) have identical values for queueFront and queueRear. However, the resulting array in Figure 8-7(b) represents an empty queue, whereas the resulting array in Figure 8-8(b) represents a full queue. This latest queue design has brought up another problem of distinguishing between an empty and a full queue.

This problem has several solutions. One solution is to keep a count. In addition to the member variables queueFront and queueRear, we need another variable, count, to implement the queue. The value of count is incremented whenever a new element is added to the queue, and it is decremented whenever an element is removed from the queue. In this case, the function initializeQueue initializes count to 0. This solution is very useful if the user of the queue frequently needs to know the number of elements in the queue.

Another solution is to let queueFront indicate the index of the array position *preceding* the first element of the queue, rather than the index of the (actual) first element itself. In this case, assuming queueRear still indicates the index of the last element in the queue, the queue is empty if queueFront == queueRear. In this solution, the slot indicated by the index queueFront (that is, the slot preceding the first true element) is reserved. The queue will be full if the next available space is the special reserved slot indicated by queueFront. Finally, because the array position indicated by queueFront is to be kept empty, if the array size is, say, 100, then 99 elements can be stored in the queue. (See Figure 8-9.)

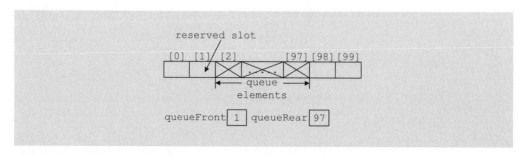

FIGURE 8-9 Array to store the queue elements with a reserved slot

Let us implement the queue using the first solution. That is, we use the variable count to indicate whether the queue is empty or full.

The following class implements the functions of the abstract class queueADT. Because arrays can be allocated dynamically, we will leave it for the user to specify the size of the array to implement the queue. The default size of the array is 100.

```
//****************************************************************
// Author: D.S. Malik
//
// This class specifies the basic operation on a queue as an
// array.
//****************************************************************

template <class Type>
class queueType: public queueADT<Type>
{
public:
    const queueType<Type>& operator=(const queueType<Type>&);
        //Overload the assignment operator.

    bool isEmptyQueue() const;
        //Function to determine whether the queue is empty.
        //Postcondition: Returns true if the queue is empty,
        //    otherwise returns false.

    bool isFullQueue() const;
        //Function to determine whether the queue is full.
        //Postcondition: Returns true if the queue is full,
        //    otherwise returns false.

    void initializeQueue();
        //Function to initialize the queue to an empty state.
        //Postcondition: The queue is empty.

    Type front() const;
        //Function to return the first element of the queue.
        //Precondition: The queue exists and is not empty.
        //Postcondition: If the queue is empty, the program
        //    terminates; otherwise, the first element of the
        //    queue is returned.

    Type back() const;
        //Function to return the last element of the queue.
        //Precondition: The queue exists and is not empty.
        //Postcondition: If the queue is empty, the program
        //    terminates; otherwise, the last element of the queue
        //    is returned.

    void addQueue(const Type& queueElement);
        //Function to add queueElement to the queue.
        //Precondition: The queue exists and is not full.
```

8

```
        //Postcondition: The queue is changed and queueElement is
        //    added to the queue.

    void deleteQueue();
        //Function to remove the first element of the queue.
        //Precondition: The queue exists and is not empty.
        //Postcondition: The queue is changed and the first element
        //    is removed from the queue.

    queueType(int queueSize = 100);
        //Constructor

    queueType(const queueType<Type>& otherQueue);
        //Copy constructor

    ~queueType();
        //Destructor

private:
    int maxQueueSize; //variable to store the maximum queue size
    int count;        //variable to store the number of
                      //elements in the queue
    int queueFront;   //variable to point to the first
                      //element of the queue
    int queueRear;    //variable to point to the last
                      //element of the queue
    Type *list;       //pointer to the array that holds
                      //the queue elements
};
```

We leave the UML diagram of the class queueType as an exercise for you. (See Exercise 15 at the end of this chapter.)

Next, we consider the implementation of the queue operations.

Empty Queue and Full Queue

As discussed earlier, the queue is empty if count == 0, and the queue is full if count == maxQueueSize. So the functions to implement these operations are as follows:

```
template <class Type>
bool queueType<Type>::isEmptyQueue() const
{
    return (count == 0);
} //end isEmptyQueue

template <class Type>
bool queueType<Type>::isFullQueue() const
{
    return (count == maxQueueSize);
} //end isFullQueue
```

Initialize Queue

This operation initializes a queue to an empty state. The first element is added at the first array position. Therefore, we initialize queueFront to 0, queueRear to maxQueueSize – 1, and count to 0. See Figure 8-10.

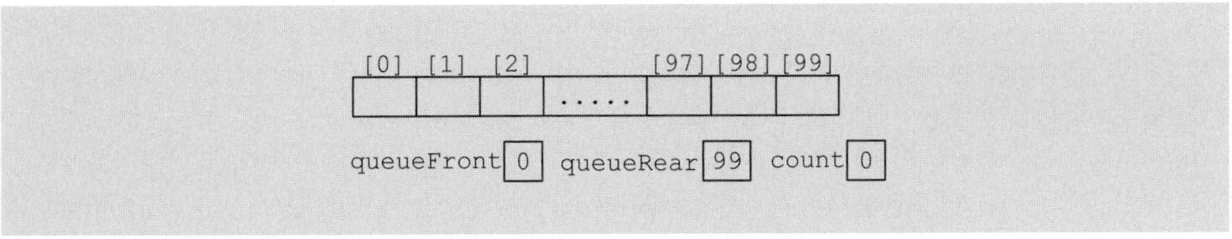

FIGURE 8-10 Empty queue

The definition of the function initializeQueue is as follows:

```
template <class Type>
void queueType<Type>::initializeQueue()
{
    queueFront = 0;
    queueRear = maxQueueSize - 1;
    count = 0;
} //end initializeQueue
```

Front

This operation returns the first element of the queue. If the queue is nonempty, the element of the queue indicated by the index queueFront is returned; otherwise, the program terminates.

```
template <class Type>
Type queueType<Type>::front() const
{
    assert(!isEmptyQueue());
    return list[queueFront];
} //end front
```

Back

This operation returns the last element of the queue. If the queue is nonempty, the element of the queue indicated by the index queueRear is returned; otherwise, the program terminates.

```
template <class Type>
Type queueType<Type>::back() const
{
    assert(!isEmptyQueue());
    return list[queueRear];
} //end back
```

Add Queue

Next, we implement the addQueue operation. Because queueRear points to the last element of the queue, to add a new element to the queue, we first advance queueRear to the next array position, and then add the new element to the array position indicated by queueRear. We also increment count by 1. So the function addQueue is as follows:

```
template <class Type>
void queueType<Type>::addQueue(const Type& newElement)
{
    if (!isFullQueue())
    {
        queueRear = (queueRear + 1) % maxQueueSize; //use the
                            //mod operator to advance queueRear
                            //because the array is circular
        count++;
        list[queueRear] = newElement;
    }
    else
        cout << "Cannot add to a full queue." << endl;
} //end addQueue
```

Delete Queue

To implement the deleteQueue operation, we access the index queueFront. Because queueFront points to the array position containing the first element of the queue, to remove the first queue element, we decrement count by 1 and advance queueFront to the next queue element. So the function deleteQueue is as follows:

```
template <class Type>
void queueType<Type>::deleteQueue()
{
    if (!isEmptyQueue())
    {
        count--;
        queueFront = (queueFront + 1) % maxQueueSize; //use the
                            //mod operator to advance queueFront
                            //because the array is circular
    }
    else
        cout << "Cannot remove from an empty queue" << endl;
} //end deleteQueue
```

Constructors and Destructors

To complete the implementation of the queue operations, we next consider the implementation of the constructor and the destructor. The constructor gets the maxQueueSize from the user, sets the variable maxQueueSize to the value specified by the user, and creates an array of size maxQueueSize. If the user does not specify the queue size, the constructor uses the default value, which is 100, to create an array of size 100. The constructor also initializes `queueFront` and `queueRear` to indicate that the queue is empty. The definition of the function to implement the constructor is as follows:

```
template <class Type>
queueType<Type>::queueType(int queueSize)
{
    if (queueSize <= 0)
    {
        cout << "Size of the array to hold the queue must "
             << "be positive." << endl;
        cout << "Creating an array of size 100." << endl;

        maxQueueSize = 100;
    }
    else
        maxQueueSize = queueSize;        //set maxQueueSize to
                                         //queueSize

    queueFront = 0;                      //initialize queueFront
    queueRear = maxQueueSize - 1;        //initialize queueRear
    count = 0;
    list = new Type[maxQueueSize];       //create the array to
                                         //hold the queue elements
} //end constructor
```

The array to store the queue elements is created dynamically. Therefore, when the queue object goes out of scope, the destructor simply deallocates the memory occupied by the array that stores the queue elements. The definition of the function to implement the destructor is as follows:

```
template <class Type>
queueType<Type>::~queueType()
{
    delete [] list;
}
```

The implementation of the copy constructor and overloading the assignment operator are left as exercises for you, (see Programming Exercise 1 at the end of this chapter). (The definitions of these functions are similar to those discussed for array-based lists and stacks.)

Linked Implementation of Queues

Because the size of the array to store the queue elements is fixed, only a finite number of queue elements can be stored in the array. Also, the array implementation of the queue requires the array to be treated in a special way together with the values of the indices `queueFront` and `queueRear`. The linked implementation of a queue simplifies many of the special cases of the array implementation and, because the memory to store a queue element is allocated dynamically, the queue is never full. This section discusses the linked implementation of a queue.

Because elements are added at one end, queueRear, and removed from the other end, queueFront, we need to know the front of the queue and the rear of the queue. Thus, we need two pointers, **queueFront** and **queueRear**, to maintain the queue. The following class implements the functions of the abstract class queueADT:

```
//***************************************************************
// Author: D.S. Malik
//
// This class specifies the basic operations on a queue as a
// linked list.
//***************************************************************

//Definition of the node
template <class Type>
struct nodeType
{
    Type info;
    nodeType<Type> *link;
};

template <class Type>
class linkedQueueType: public queueADT<Type>
{
public:
    const linkedQueueType<Type>& operator=
                    (const linkedQueueType<Type>&);
      //Overload the assignment operator.

    bool isEmptyQueue() const;
      //Function to determine whether the queue is empty.
      //Postcondition: Returns true if the queue is empty,
      //    otherwise returns false.

    bool isFullQueue() const;
      //Function to determine whether the queue is full.
      //Postcondition: Returns true if the queue is full,
      //    otherwise returns false.

    void initializeQueue();
      //Function to initialize the queue to an empty state.
      //Postcondition: queueFront = NULL; queueRear = NULL

    Type front() const;
      //Function to return the first element of the queue.
      //Precondition: The queue exists and is not empty.
      //Postcondition: If the queue is empty, the program
      //    terminates; otherwise, the first element of the
      //    queue is returned.

    Type back() const;
      //Function to return the last element of the queue.
      //Precondition: The queue exists and is not empty.
```

```
    //Postcondition: If the queue is empty, the program
    //     terminates; otherwise, the last element of the
    //     queue is returned.

 void addQueue(const Type& queueElement);
    //Function to add queueElement to the queue.
    //Precondition: The queue exists and is not full.
    //Postcondition: The queue is changed and queueElement is
    //     added to the queue.

 void deleteQueue();
    //Function to remove the first element of the queue.
    //Precondition: The queue exists and is not empty.
    //Postcondition: The queue is changed and the first element
    //     is removed from the queue.

 linkedQueueType();
    //Default constructor

 linkedQueueType(const linkedQueueType<Type>& otherQueue);
    //Copy constructor

 ~linkedQueueType();
    //Destructor

private:
    nodeType<Type> *queueFront; //pointer to the front of the queue
    nodeType<Type> *queueRear;  //pointer to the rear of the queue
};
```

The UML diagram of the class linkedQueueType is left as an exercise for you. (See Exercise 16 at the end of this chapter.)

Next, we write the definitions of the functions of the class linkedQueueType.

Empty and Full Queue

The queue is empty if queueFront is NULL. Memory to store the queue elements is allocated dynamically. Therefore, the queue is never full and so the function to implement the isFullQueue operation returns the value false. (The queue is full only if the program runs out of memory.)

```
template <class Type>
bool linkedQueueType<Type>::isEmptyQueue() const
{
    return(queueFront == NULL);
} //end

template <class Type>
bool linkedQueueType<Type>::isFullQueue() const
{
    return false;
} //end isFullQueue
```

Note that in reality, in the linked implementation of queues, the function `isFullQueue` does not apply because logically the queue is never full. However, you must provide its definition because it is included as an abstract function in the parent `class queueADT`.

Initialize Queue

The operation `initializeQueue` initializes the queue to an empty state. The queue is empty if there are no elements in the queue. Note that the constructor initializes the queue when the queue object is declared. So this operation must remove all the elements, if any, from the queue. Therefore, this operation traverses the list containing the queue starting at the first node, and it deallocates the memory occupied by the queue elements. The definition of this function is as follows:

```
template <class Type>
void linkedQueueType<Type>::initializeQueue()
{
    nodeType<Type> *temp;

    while (queueFront!= NULL)   //while there are elements left
                               //in the queue
    {
        temp = queueFront;   //set temp to point to the current node
        queueFront = queueFront->link;   //advance first to
                                        //the next node
        delete temp;     //deallocate memory occupied by temp
    }

    queueRear = NULL;   //set rear to NULL
} //end initializeQueue
```

`addQueue`, `front`, `back`, and `deleteQueue` Operations

The `addQueue` operation adds a new element at the end of the queue. To implement this operation, we access the pointer `queueRear`.

If the queue is nonempty, the operation `front` returns the first element of the queue and so the element of the queue indicated by the pointer `queueFront` is returned. If the queue is empty, the function `front` terminates the program.

If the queue is nonempty, the operation `back` returns the last element of the queue and so the element of the queue indicated by the pointer `queueRear` is returned. If the queue is empty, the function `back` terminates the program. Similarly, if the queue is nonempty, the operation `deleteQueue` removes the first element of the queue, and so we access the pointer `queueFront`.

The definitions of the functions to implement these operations are as follows:

```
template <class Type>
void linkedQueueType<Type>::addQueue(const Type& newElement)
```

```cpp
{
    nodeType<Type> *newNode;

    newNode = new nodeType<Type>;    //create the node

    newNode->info = newElement; //store the info
    newNode->link = NULL;   //initialize the link field to NULL

    if (queueFront == NULL) //if initially the queue is empty
    {
        queueFront = newNode;
        queueRear = newNode;
    }
    else            //add newNode at the end
    {
        queueRear->link = newNode;
        queueRear = queueRear->link;
    }
}//end addQueue

template <class Type>
Type linkedQueueType<Type>::front() const
{
    assert(queueFront != NULL);
    return queueFront->info;
} //end front

template <class Type>
Type linkedQueueType<Type>::back() const
{
    assert(queueRear!= NULL);
    return queueRear->info;
} //end back

template <class Type>
void linkedQueueType<Type>::deleteQueue()
{
    nodeType<Type> *temp;

    if (!isEmptyQueue())
    {
        temp = queueFront;  //make temp point to the first node
        queueFront = queueFront->link; //advance queueFront

        delete temp;    //delete the first node

        if (queueFront == NULL) //if after deletion the
                                //queue is empty
            queueRear = NULL;   //set queueRear to NULL
    }
    else
        cout << "Cannot remove from an empty queue" << endl;
}//end deleteQueue
```

8

The definition of the default constructor is as follows:

```
template<class Type>
linkedQueueType<Type>::linkedQueueType()
{
    queueFront = NULL; //set front to null
    queueRear = NULL;  //set rear to null
} //end default constructor
```

When the queue object goes out of scope, the destructor destroys the queue; that is, it deallocates the memory occupied by the elements of the queue. The definition of the function to implement the destructor is similar to the definition of the function `initializeQueue`. Also, the functions to implement the copy constructor and overload the assignment operators are similar to the corresponding functions for stacks. Implementing these operations is left as an exercise for you, (see Programming Exercise 2 at the end of this chapter).

EXAMPLE 8-1

The following program tests various operations on a queue. It uses the `class` `linkedQueueType` to implement a queue.

```
//*************************************************************
// Author: D.S. Malik
//
// This program illustrates how to use the class linkedQueueType
// in a program.
//*************************************************************

#include <iostream>
#include "linkedQueue.h"

using namespace std;

int main()
{
    linkedQueueType<int> queue;
    int x, y;

    queue.initializeQueue();
    x = 4;
    y = 5;
    queue.addQueue(x);
    queue.addQueue(y);
    x = queue.front();
    queue.deleteQueue();
    queue.addQueue(x + 5);
    queue.addQueue(16);
    queue.addQueue(x);
    queue.addQueue(y - 3);

    cout << "Queue Elements: ";
```

```
    while (!queue.isEmptyQueue())
    {
        cout << queue.front() << " ";
        queue.deleteQueue();
    }

    cout << endl;

    return 0;
}
```

Sample Run:

```
Queue Elements: 5 9 16 4 2
```

Queue Derived from the `class unorderedLinkedList`

From the definitions of the functions to implement the queue operations, it is clear that the linked implementation of a queue is similar to the implementation of a linked list created in a forward manner (see Chapter 5). The `addQueue` operation is similar to the operation `insertFirst`. Likewise, the operations `initializeQueue` and `initializeList`, `isEmptyQueue`, and `isEmptyList` are similar. The `deleteQueue` operation can be implemented as before. The pointer `queueFront` is the same as the pointer `first`, and the pointer `queueRear` is the same as the pointer `last`. This correspondence suggests that we can derive the class to implement the queue from the `class linkedListType` (see Chapter 5). Note that the `class linkedListType` is an abstract and does not implement all the operations. However, the `class unorderedLinkedList` is derived from the the `class linkedListType` and provides the definitions of the abstract functions of the the `class linkedListType`. Therefore, we can derive the `class linkedQueueType` from the `class unorderedLinkedList`.

We leave it as an exercise for you to write the definition of the `class linkedQueueType` that is derived from the `class unorderedLinkedList` (see Programming Exercise 7 at the end of this chapter).

STL `class queue` (Queue Container Adapter)

The preceding sections discussed the data structure queue in detail. Because a queue is an important data structure, the Standard Template Library (STL) provides a class to implement queues in a program. The name of the class defining the queue is `queue`, and the name of the header file containing the definition of the `class queue` is `queue`. The `class queue` provided by the STL is implemented similar to the classes discussed in this chapter. Table 8-1 defines various operations supported by the queue container class.

TABLE 8-1 Operations on a `queue` object

Operation	Effect
size	Returns the actual number of elements in the queue.
empty	Returns **true** if the queue is empty, and **false** otherwise.
push(item)	Inserts a copy of item into the queue.
front	Returns the next—that is, first—element in the queue, but does not remove the element from the queue. This operation is implemented as a value-returning function.
back	Returns the last element in the queue, but does not remove the element from the queue. This operation is implemented as a value-returning function.
pop	Removes the next element in the queue.

In addition to the operations `size`, `empty`, `push`, `front`, `back`, and `pop`, the queue container class provides relational operators to compare two queues. For example, the relational operator `==` can be used to determine whether two queues are identical.

The program in Example 8-2 illustrates how to use the queue container class.

EXAMPLE 8-2

```
//**************************************************************
// Author: D.S. Malik
//
// This program illustrates how to use the STL class queue in a
// program.
//**************************************************************

#include <iostream>                              //Line 1
#include <queue>                                 //Line 2

using namespace std;                             //Line 3

int main()                                       //Line 4
{                                                //Line 5
    queue<int> intQueue;                         //Line 6

    intQueue.push(26);                           //Line 7
    intQueue.push(18);                           //Line 8
    intQueue.push(50);                           //Line 9
    intQueue.push(33);                           //Line 10
```

```
    cout << "Line 11: The front element of intQueue: "
        << intQueue.front() << endl;                    //Line 11

    cout << "Line 12: The last element of intQueue: "
        << intQueue.back() << endl;                     //Line 12

    intQueue.pop();                                     //Line 13

    cout << "Line 14: After the pop operation, the "
        << "front element of intQueue: "
        << intQueue.front() << endl;                    //Line 14

    cout << "Line 15: intQueue elements: ";             //Line 15

    while (!intQueue.empty())                           //Line 16
    {                                                   //Line 17
        cout << intQueue.front() << " ";                //Line 18
        intQueue.pop();                                 //Line 19
    }                                                   //Line 20

    cout << endl;                                       //Line 21

    return 0;                                           //Line 22
}                                                       //Line 23
```

Sample Run:

```
Line 11: The front element of intQueue: 26
Line 12: The last element of intQueue: 33
Line 14: After the pop operation, the front element of intQueue: 18
Line 15: intQueue elements: 18 50 33
```

The preceding output is self-explanatory. The details are left as an exercise for you.

Priority Queues

The preceding sections describe how to implement a queue in a program. The use of a queue structure ensures that the items are processed in the order they are received. For example, in a banking environment, the customers who arrive first are served first. However, there are certain situations when this First In First Out rule needs to be relaxed somewhat. In a hospital environment, patients are, usually, seen in the order they arrive. Therefore, you could use a queue to ensure that the patients are seen in the order they arrive. However, if a patient arrives with severe or life-threatening symptoms, they are treated first. In other words, these patients take priority over the patients who can wait to be seen, such as those awaiting their routine annual checkup. For another example, in a shared environment, when print requests are sent to the printer, interactive programs take priority over batch-processing programs.

There are many other situations where some priority is assigned to the customers. To implement such a data structure in a program, we use a special type of queue, called **priority queues**. In a priority queue, customers or jobs with higher priority are pushed to the front of the queue.

One way to implement a priority queue is to use an ordinary linked list, which keeps the items in order from the highest to lowest priority. However, an effective way to implement a priority queue is to use a treelike structure. In Chapter 10, we discuss a special type of sorting algorithm, called the *heapsort*, which uses a treelike structure to sort a list. After describing this algorithm, we discuss how to effectively implement a priority queue.

STL class `priority_queue`

The STL provides the `class` template `priority_queue<elemType>`, where the data type of the queue elements is specified by `elemType`. This class template is contained in the STL header file `queue`. You can specify the priority of the elements of a priority queue in various ways. The default priority criteria for the queue elements uses the less-than operator, <. For example, a program that implements a priority queue of numbers could use the operator < to assign the priority to the numbers so that larger numbers are always at the front of the queue. If you design your own class to implement the queue elements, you can specify your priority rule by overloading the less-than operator, <, to compare the elements. You could also define a comparison function to specify the priority. The implementation of comparison functions is discussed in Chapter 13.

Application of Queues: Simulation

A technique in which one system models the behavior of another system is called **simulation**. For example, physical simulators include wind tunnels used to experiment with the design of car bodies and flight simulators are used to train airline pilots. Simulation techniques are used when it is too expensive or dangerous to experiment with real systems. You can also design computer models to study the behavior of real systems. (We will describe some real systems modeled by computers shortly.) Simulating the behavior of an expensive or dangerous experiment using a computer model is usually less expensive than using the real system, and a good way to gain insight without putting human life in danger. Moreover, computer simulations are particularly useful for complex systems where it is difficult to construct a mathematical model. For such systems, computer models can retain descriptive accuracy. In mathematical simulations, the steps of a program are used to model the behavior of a real system. Let us consider one such problem.

The manager of a local movie theater is hearing complaints from customers about the time they have to wait in line to buy tickets. The theater currently has only one cashier. Another theater is preparing to open in the neighborhood and the manager is afraid of losing customers. The manager wants to hire enough cashiers so that a customer does not have to wait too long to buy a ticket, but does not want to hire extra cashiers on a trial basis and potentially waste time and money. One thing that the manager would like to know is the average time a customer has to wait for service. The manager wants someone to write a program to simulate the behavior of the theater.

In computer simulation, the objects being studied are usually represented as data. For the theater problem, some of the objects are the customers and the cashier. The cashier serves the customers and we want to determine a customer's average waiting time. Actions are implemented by writing algorithms, which in a programming language are implemented with the help of functions. Thus, functions are used to implement the actions of the objects. In C++, we can combine the data and the operations on that data into a single unit with the help of classes. Thus, objects can be represented as classes. The member variables of the class describe the properties of the objects, and the function members describe the actions on that data. This change in simulation results can also occur if we change the values of the data or modify the definitions of the functions (that is, modify the algorithms implementing the actions). The main goal of a computer simulation is to either generate results showing the performance of an existing system or predict the performance of a proposed system.

In the theater problem, when the cashier is serving a customer, the other customers must wait. Because customers are served on a first-come, first-served basis and queues are an effective way to implement a First In First Out system, queues are important data structures for use in computer simulations. This section examines computer simulations in which queues are the basic data structure. These simulations model the behavior of systems, called **queuing systems**, in which queues of objects are waiting to be served by various servers. In other words, a queuing system consists of servers and queues of objects waiting to be served. We deal with a variety of queuing systems on a daily basis. For example, a grocery store and a banking system are both queuing systems. Furthermore, when you send a print request to a networked printer that is shared by many people, your print request goes in a queue. Print requests that arrived before your print request are usually completed before yours. Thus, the printer acts as the server when a queue of documents is waiting to be printed.

Designing a Queuing System

In this section, we describe a queuing system that can be used in a variety of applications, such as a bank, grocery store, movie theater, printer, or mainframe environment in which several people are trying to use the same processors to execute their programs. To describe a queuing system, we use the term **server** for the object that provides the service. For example, in a bank, a teller is a server; in a grocery store or movie theater, a cashier is a server. We will call the object receiving the service the **customer**, and the service time— the time it takes to serve a customer—the **transaction time**.

Because a queuing system consists of servers and a queue of waiting objects, we will model a system that consists of a list of servers and a waiting queue holding the customers to be served. The customer at the front of the queue waits for the next available server. When a server becomes free, the customer at the front of the queue moves to the free server to be served.

When the first customer arrives, all servers are free and the customer moves to the first server. When the next customer arrives, if a server is available, the customer immediately moves to the available server; otherwise, the customer waits in the queue. To model a queuing system, we need to know the number of servers, the expected arrival time of a customer, the time between the arrivals of customers, and the number of events affecting the system.

Let us again consider the movie theater system. The performance of the system depends on how many servers are available, how long it takes to serve a customer, and how often a customer arrives. If it takes too long to serve a customer and customers arrive frequently, then more servers are needed. This system can be modeled as a time-driven simulation. In a **time-driven simulation**, the clock is implemented as a counter and the passage of, say, 1 minute can be implemented by incrementing the counter by 1. The simulation is run for a fixed amount of time. If the simulation needs to be run for 100 minutes, the counter starts at 1 and goes up to 100, which can be implemented by using a loop.

For the simulation described in this section, we want to determine the average wait time for a customer. To calculate the average wait time for a customer, we need to add the waiting time of each customer, and then divide the sum by the number of customers who have arrived. When a customer arrives, he or she goes to the end of the queue and the customer's waiting time starts. If the queue is empty and a server is free, the customer is served immediately and so this customer's waiting time is zero. On the other hand, if when the customer arrives and either the queue is nonempty or all the servers are busy, the customer must wait for the next available server and, therefore, this customer's waiting time starts. We can keep track of the customer's waiting time by using a timer for each customer. When a customer arrives, the timer is set to 0, which is incremented after each clock unit.

Suppose that, on average, it takes five minutes for a server to serve a customer. When a server becomes free and the waiting customer's queue is nonempty, the customer at the front of the queue proceeds to begin the transaction. Thus, we must keep track of the time a customer is with a server. When the customer arrives at a server, the transaction time is set to five and is decremented after each clock unit. When the transaction time becomes zero, the server is marked free. Hence, the two objects needed to implement a time-driven computer simulation of a queuing system are the customer and the server.

Before designing the main algorithm to implement the simulation, we design classes to implement each of the two objects: *customer* and *server*.

Customer

Every customer has a customer number, arrival time, waiting time, transaction time, and departure time. If we know the arrival time, waiting time, and transaction time, we can determine the departure time by adding these three times. Let us call the class to implement the customer object `customerType`. It follows that the `class customerType` has four member variables: the `customerNumber`, `arrivalTime`, `waitingTime`, and `transactionTime`, each of type int. The basic operations that must be performed on an object of type customerType are as follows: Set the customer's number, arrival time, and waiting time; increment the waiting time by one clock unit; return the waiting time; return the arrival time; return the transaction time; and return the customer number. The following class, customerType, implements the customer as an ADT:

```
//**********************************************************
// Author: D.S. Malik
//
// class customerType
// This class specifies the members to implement a customer.
//**********************************************************

class customerType
{
public:
    customerType(int cN = 0, int arrvTime = 0, int wTime = 0,
                int tTime = 0);
      //Constructor to initialize the instance variables
      //according to the parameters
      //If no value is specified in the object declaration,
      //the default values are assigned.
      //Postcondition: customerNumber = cN; arrivalTime = arrvTime;
      //    waitingTime = wTime; transactionTime = tTime

    void setCustomerInfo(int cN = 0, int inTime = 0,
                        int wTime = 0, int tTime = 0);
      //Function to initialize the instance variables.
      //Instance variables are set according to the parameters.
      //Postcondition: customerNumber = cN; arrivalTime = arrvTime;
      //    waitingTime = wTime; transactionTime = tTime;

    int getWaitingTime() const;
      //Function to return the waiting time of a customer.
      //Postcondition: The value of waitingTime is returned.

    void setWaitingTime(int time);
      //Function to set the waiting time of a customer.
      //Postcondition: waitingTime = time;

    void incrementWaitingTime();
      //Function to increment the waiting time by one time unit.
      //Postcondition: waitingTime++;

    int getArrivalTime() const;
      //Function to return the arrival time of a customer.
      //Postcondition: The value of arrivalTime is returned.

    int getTransactionTime() const;
      //Function to return the transaction time of a customer.
      //Postcondition: The value of transactionTime is returned.
```

8

```
    int getCustomerNumber() const;
      //Function to return the customer number.
      //Postcondition: The value of customerNumber is returned.

private:
    int customerNumber;
    int arrivalTime;
    int waitingTime;
    int transactionTime;
};
```

Figure 8-11 shows the UML diagram of the class customerType.

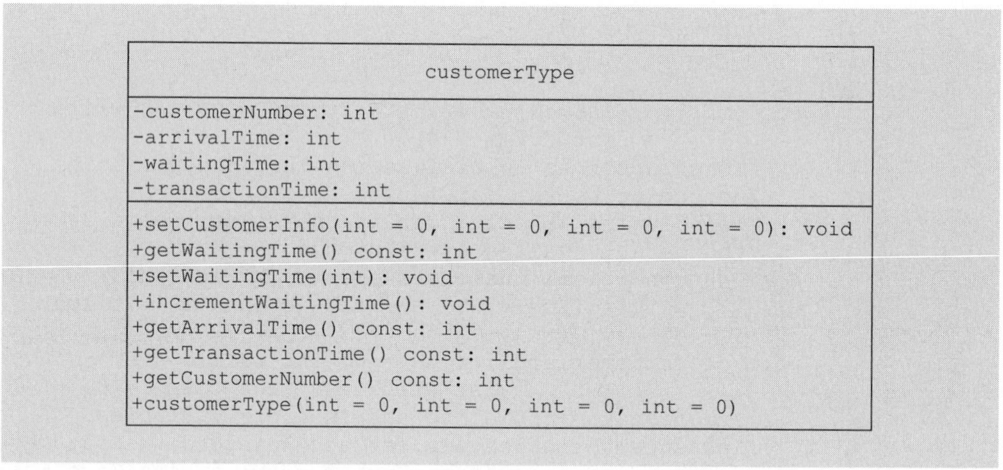

FIGURE 8-11 UML diagram of the class customerType

The definitions of the member functions of the class customerType follow easily from their descriptions. Next, we give the definitions of the member functions of the class customerType.

The function setCustomerInfo uses the values of the parameters to initialize customerNumber, arrivalTime, waitingTime, and transactionTime. Its definition is as follows:

```
void customerType::setCustomerInfo(int cN, int arrvTime,
                                   int wTime, int tTime)
{
    customerNumber = cN;
    arrivalTime = arrvTime;
    waitingTime = wTime;
    transactionTime = tTime;
}
```

The definition of the constructor is similar to the definition of the function setCustomerInfo. It uses the values of the parameters to initialize customerNumber, arrivalTime, waitingTime, and transactionTime. To make debugging easier, we use the function setCustomerInfo to write the definition of the constructor, which is given next.

```
customerType::customerType(int cN, int arrvTime,
                           int wTime, int tTime)
{
    setCustomerInfo(cN, arrvTime, wTime, tTime);
}
```

The function getWaitingTime returns the current waiting time. The definition of the function getWaitingTime is as follows:

```
int customerType::getWaitingTime() const
{
    return waitingTime;
}
```

The function incrementWaitingTime increments the value of waitingTime. Its definition is as follows:

```
void customerType::incrementWaitingTime()
{
    waitingTime++;
}
```

The definitions of the functions setWaitingTime, getArrivalTime, getTransactionTime, and getCustomerNumber are left as an exercise for you, (see Programming Exercise 8 a the end of this chapter).

Server

At any given time unit, the server is either busy serving a customer or is free. We use a string variable to set the status of the server. Every server has a timer and because the program might need to know which customer is served by which server, the server also stores the information of the customer being served. Thus, three member variables are associated with a server: the status, the transactionTime, and the currentCustomer. Some of the basic operations that must be performed on a server are as follows: Check whether the server is free; set the server as free; set the server as busy; set the transaction time (that is, how long it takes to serve the customer); return the remaining transaction time (to determine whether the server should be set to free); if the server is busy after each time unit, decrement the transaction time by one time unit; and so on. The following class, serverType, implements the server as an ADT:

```
//*************************************************************
// Author: D.S. Malik
//
// class serverType
// This class specifies the members to implement a server.
//*************************************************************
```

```
class serverType
{
public:
    serverType();
      //Default constructor
      //Sets the values of the instance variables to their default
      //values.
      //Postcondition: currentCustomer is initialized by its
      //    default constructor; status = "free"; and the
      //    transaction time is initialized to 0.

    bool isFree() const;
      //Function to determine if the server is free.
      //Postcondition: Returns true if the server is free,
      //    otherwise returns false.

    void setBusy();
      //Function to set the status of the server to busy.
      //Postcondition: status = "busy";

    void setFree();
      //Function to set the status of the server to "free."
      //Postcondition: status = "free";

    void setTransactionTime(int t);
      //Function to set the transaction time according to the
      //parameter t.
      //Postcondition: transactionTime = t;

    void setTransactionTime();
      //Function to set the transaction time according to
      //the transaction time of the current customer.
      //Postcondition:
      //    transactionTime = currentCustomer.transactionTime;

    int getRemainingTransactionTime() const;
      //Function to return the remaining transaction time.
      //Postcondition: The value of transactionTime is returned.

    void decreaseTransactionTime();
      //Function to decrease the transactionTime by 1 unit.
      //Postcondition: transactionTime--;

    void setCurrentCustomer(customerType cCustomer);
      //Function to set the info of the current customer
      //according to the parameter cCustomer.
      //Postcondition: currentCustomer = cCustomer;

    int getCurrentCustomerNumber() const;
      //Function to return the customer number of the current
      //customer.
      //Postcondition: The value of customerNumber of the
      //    current customer is returned.
```

```
    int getCurrentCustomerArrivalTime() const;
      //Function to return the arrival time of the current
      //customer.
      //Postcondition: The value of arrivalTime of the current
      //    customer is returned.

    int getCurrentCustomerWaitingTime() const;
      //Function to return the current waiting time of the
      //current customer.
      //Postcondition: The value of transactionTime is returned.

    int getCurrentCustomerTransactionTime() const;
      //Function to return the transaction time of the
      //current customer.
      //Postcondition: The value of transactionTime of the
      //    current customer is returned.

private:
    customerType currentCustomer;
    string status;
    int transactionTime;
};
```

Figure 8-12 shows the UML diagram of the class serverType.

```
                    serverType
 ─────────────────────────────────────────────────
 -currentCustomer: customerType
 -status: string
 -transactionTime: int
 ─────────────────────────────────────────────────
 +isFree() const: bool
 +setBusy(): void
 +setFree(): void
 +setTransactionTime(int): void
 +setTransactionTime(): void
 +getRemainingTransactionTime() const: int
 +decreaseTransactionTime(): void
 +setCurrentCustomer(customerType): void
 +getCurrentCustomerNumber() const: int
 +getCurrentCustomerArrivalTime() const: int
 +getCurrentCustomerWaitingTime() const: int
 +getCurrentCustomerTransactionTime() const: int
 +serverType()
```

FIGURE 8-12 UML diagram of the class serverType

The definitions of some of the member functions of the **class** serverType are as follows:

```
serverType::serverType()
{
    status = "free";
    transactionTime = 0;
}

bool serverType::isFree() const
{
    return (status == "free");
}

void serverType::setBusy()
{
    status = "busy";
}

void serverType::setFree()
{
    status = "free";
}

void serverType::setTransactionTime(int t)
{
    transactionTime = t;
}

void serverType::setTransactionTime()
{
    int time;

    time = currentCustomer.getTransactionTime();

    transactionTime = time;
}

void serverType::decreaseTransactionTime()
{
    transactionTime--;
}
```

We leave the definitions of the functions getRemainingTransactionTime, setCurrentCustomer, getCurrentCustomerNumber, getCurrentCustomerArrivalTime, getCurrentCustomerWaitingTime, and getCurrentCustomerTransactionTime as an exercise for you, (see Programming Exercise 8 at the end of this chapter).

Because we are designing a simulation program that can be used in a variety of applications, we need to design two more classes: a class to create and process a list of servers and a class to create and process a queue of waiting customers. The next two sections describe each of these classes.

Server List

A server list is a set of servers. At any given time, a server is either free or busy. For the customer at the front of the queue, we need to find a server in the list that is free. If all the servers are busy, the customer must wait until one of the servers becomes free. Thus, the class that implements a list of servers has two member variables: one to store the number of servers and one to maintain a list of servers. Using dynamic arrays, depending on the number of servers specified by the user, a list of servers is created during program execution. Some of the operations that must be performed on a server list are as follows: Return the server number of a free server; when a customer gets ready to do business and a server is available, set the server to busy; when the simulation ends, some of the servers might still be busy, so return the number of busy servers; after each time unit, reduce the `transactionTime` of each busy server by one time unit; and if the `transactionTime` of a server becomes zero, set the server to free. The following class, `serverListType`, implements the list of servers as an ADT:

```
//***********************************************************
// Author: D.S. Malik
//
// class serverListType
// This class specifies the members to implement a list of
// servers.
//***********************************************************

class serverListType
{
public:
    serverListType(int num = 1);
      //Constructor to initialize a list of servers
      //Postcondition: numOfServers = num
      //     A list of servers, specified by num, is created and
      //     each server is initialized to "free".

    ~serverListType();
      //Destructor
      //Postcondition: The list of servers is destroyed.

    int getFreeServerID() const;
      //Function to search the list of servers.
      //Postcondition: If a free server is found, returns its ID;
      //     otherwise, returns -1.

    int getNumberOfBusyServers() const;
      //Function to return the number of busy servers.
      //Postcondition: The number of busy servers is returned.

    void setServerBusy(int serverID, customerType cCustomer,
                       int tTime);
      //Function to set a server busy.
```

8

```
    //Postcondition: The server specified by serverID is set to
    //    "busy", to serve the customer specified by cCustomer,
    //    and the transaction time is set according to the
    //    parameter tTime.

  void setServerBusy(int serverID, customerType cCustomer);
    //Function to set a server busy.
    //Postcondition: The server specified by serverID is set to
    //    "busy", to serve the customer specified by cCustomer.

  void updateServers(ostream& outFile);
    //Function to update the status of a server.
    //Postcondition: The transaction time of each busy server
    //    is decremented by one unit. If the transaction time of
    //    a busy server is reduced to zero, the server is set to
    //    "free". Moreover, if the actual parameter corresponding
    //    to outFile is cout, a message indicating which customer
    //    has been served is printed on the screen, together with the
    //    customer's departing time. Otherwise, the output is sent
    //    to a file specified by the user.

private:
    int numOfServers;
    serverType *servers;
};
```

Figure 8-13 shows the UML diagram of the class serverListType.

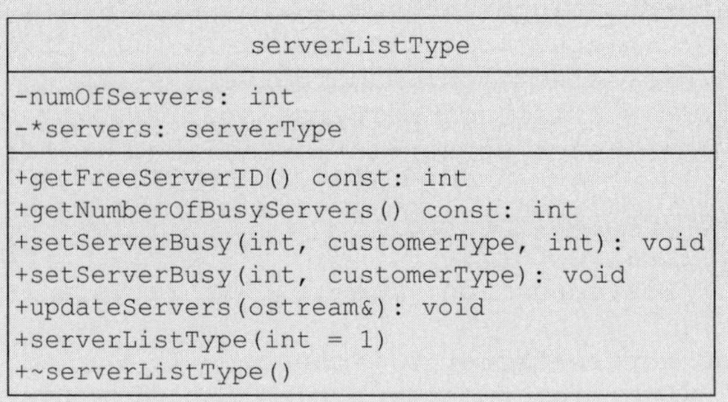

FIGURE 8-13 UML diagram of the class serverListType

Following are the definitions of the member functions of the class serverListType. The definitions of the constructor and destructor are straightforward.

```
serverListType::serverListType(int num)
{
    numOfServers = num;
    servers = new serverType[num];
}
```

```
serverListType::~serverListType()
{
    delete [] servers;
}
```

The function `getFreeServerID` searches the list of servers. If a free server is found, it returns the server's ID; otherwise, the value -1 is returned, which indicates that all the servers are busy. The definition of this function is as follows:

```
int serverListType::getFreeServerID() const
{
    int serverID = -1;

    for (int i = 0; i < numOfServers; i++)
        if (servers[i].isFree())
        {
            serverID = i;
            break;
        }

    return serverID;
}
```

The function `getNumberOfBusyServers` searches the list of servers and determines the number of busy servers. The number of busy servers is returned. The definition of this function is as follows:

```
int serverListType::getNumberOfBusyServers() const
{
    int busyServers = 0;

    for (int i = 0; i < numOfServers; i++)
        if (!servers[i].isFree())
            busyServers++;

    return busyServers;
}
```

The function `setServerBusy` sets a server to busy. This function is overloaded. The `serverID` of the server that is set to busy is passed as a parameter to this function. One function sets the server's transaction time according to the parameter `tTime`; the other function sets it by using the transaction time stored in the object `cCustomer`. The transaction time is later needed to determine the average waiting time. The definitions of these functions are as follows:

```
void serverListType::setServerBusy(int serverID,
                        customerType cCustomer, int tTime)
{
    servers[serverID].setBusy();
    servers[serverID].setTransactionTime(tTime);
    servers[serverID].setCurrentCustomer(cCustomer);
}
```

```
void serverListType::setServerBusy(int serverID,
                                   customerType cCustomer)
{
    int time = cCustomer.getTransactionTime();

    servers[serverID].setBusy();
    servers[serverID].setTransactionTime(time);
    servers[serverID].setCurrentCustomer(cCustomer);
}
```

The definition of the function `updateServers` is quite straightforward. Starting at the first server, it searches the list of servers for busy servers. When a busy server is found, its `transactionTime` is decremented by 1. If the `transactionTime` reduces to zero, the server is set to free. If the `transactionTime` of a busy server reduces to zero, the transaction of the customer being served by the server is complete. If the actual parameter corresponding to `outFile` is cout, a message indicating which customer has been served is printed on the screen, together with the customer's departing time. Otherwise, the output is sent to a file specified by the user. The definition of this function is as follows:

```
void serverListType::updateServers(ostream& outF)
{
    for (int i = 0; i < numOfServers; i++)
        if (!servers[i].isFree())
        {
            servers[i].decreaseTransactionTime();

            if (servers[i].getRemainingTransactionTime() == 0)
            {
                outF << "From server number " << (i + 1)
                     << " customer number "
                     << servers[i].getCurrentCustomerNumber()
                     << "\n      departed at clock unit "
                     << servers[i].getCurrentCustomerArrivalTime()
                     + servers[i].getCurrentCustomerWaitingTime()
                     + servers[i].getCurrentCustomerTransactionTime()
                     << endl;
                servers[i].setFree();
            }
        }
}
```

Waiting Customers Queue

When a customer arrives, he or she goes to the end of the queue. When a server becomes available, the customer at the front of the queue leaves to conduct the transaction. After each time unit, the waiting time of each customer in the queue is incremented by 1. The ADT `queueType` designed in this chapter has all the operations needed to implement a queue, except the operation of incrementing the waiting time of each customer in the queue by one time unit. We will derive a class, `waitingCustomerQueueType`, from the class `queueType` and add the additional operations to implement the customer queue. The definition of the class `waitingCustomerQueueType` is as follows:

```
//*********************************************************
// Author: D.S. Malik
//
// class waitingCustomerQueueType
// This class extends the class queueType to implement a list
// of waiting customers.
//*********************************************************

class waitingCustomerQueueType: public queueType<customerType>
{
public:
    waitingCustomerQueueType(int size = 100);
      //Constructor
      //Postcondition: The queue is initialized according to the
      //      parameter size. The value of size is passed to the
      //      constructor of queueType.

    void updateWaitingQueue();
      //Function to increment the waiting time of each
      //customer in the queue by one time unit.
};
```

 NOTE Notice that the class `waitingCustomerQueueType` is derived from the `class queueType`, which implements the queue in an array. You can also derive it from the class `linkedQueueType`, which implements the queue in a linked list. We leave the details as an exercise for you.

The definitions of the member functions are given next. The definition of the constructor is as follows:

```
waitingCustomerQueueType::waitingCustomerQueueType(int size)
                         :queueType<customerType>(size)
{
}
```

The function `updateWaitingQueue` increments the waiting time of each customer in the queue by one time unit. The class `waitingCustomerQueueType` is derived from the `class queueType`. Because the member variables of `queueType` are `private`, the function `updateWaitingQueue` cannot directly access the elements of the queue. The only way to access the elements of the queue is to use the `deleteQueue` operation. After incrementing the waiting time, the element can be put back into the queue by using the `addQueue` operation.

The `addQueue` operation inserts the element at the end of the queue. If we perform the `deleteQueue` operation followed by the `addQueue` operation for each element of the queue, eventually the front element again becomes the front element. Given that each `deleteQueue` operation is followed by an `addQueue` operation, how do we determine that all the elements of the queue have been processed? We cannot use the `isEmptyQueue` or `isFullQueue` operations on the queue because the queue will never be empty or full.

One solution to this problem is to create a temporary queue. Every element of the original queue is removed, processed, and inserted into the temporary queue. When the original queue becomes empty, all of the elements in the queue are processed. We can then copy the elements from the temporary queue back into the original queue. However, this solution requires us to use extra memory space, which could be significant. Also, if the queue is large, extra computer time is needed to copy the elements from the temporary queue back into the original queue. Let us look into another solution.

In the second solution, before starting to update the elements of the queue, we can insert a dummy customer with a waiting time of, say -1. During the update process, when we arrive at the customer with the waiting time of -1, we can stop the update process without processing the customer with the waiting time of -1. If we do not process the customer with the waiting time -1, this customer is removed from the queue and after processing all the elements of the queue, the queue will contain no extra elements. This solution does not require us to create a temporary queue, so we do not need extra computer time to copy the elements back into the original queue. We will use this solution to update the queue. Therefore, the definition of the function updateWaitingQueue is as follows:

```
void waitingCustomerQueueType::updateWaitingQueue()
{
    customerType cust;

    cust.setWaitingTime(-1);
    int wTime = 0;

    addQueue(cust);

    while (wTime != -1)
    {
        cust = front();
        deleteQueue();

        wTime = cust.getWaitingTime();
        if (wTime == -1)
            break;
        cust.incrementWaitingTime();
        addQueue(cust);
    }
}
```

Main Program

To run the simulation, we first need to get the following information:

- The number of time units the simulation should run. Assume that each time unit is one minute.
- The number of servers.
- The amount of time it takes to serve a customer—that is, the transaction time.
- The approximate time between customer arrivals.

These pieces of information are called simulation parameters. By changing the values of these parameters, we can observe the changes in the performance of the system. We can write a function, setSimulationParameters, to prompt the user to specify these values. The definition of this function is as follows:

```
void setSimulationParameters(int& sTime, int& numOfServers,
                             int& transTime, int& tBetweenCArrival)
{
    cout << "Enter the simulation time: ";
    cin >> sTime;
    cout << endl;

    cout << "Enter the number of servers: ";
    cin >> numOfServers;
    cout << endl;

    cout << "Enter the transaction time: ";
    cin >> transTime;
    cout << endl;

    cout << "Enter the time between customers arrival: ";
    cin >> tBetweenCArrival;
    cout << endl;
}
```

When a server becomes free and the customer queue is nonempty, we can move the customer at the front of the queue to the free server to be served. Moreover, when a customer starts the transaction, the waiting time ends. The waiting time of the customer is added to the total waiting time. The general algorithm to start the transaction (supposing that serverID denotes the ID of the free server) is as follows:

1. Remove the customer from the front of the queue.

   ```
   customer = customerQueue.front();
   customerQueue.deleteQueue();
   ```

2. Update the total waiting time by adding the current customer's waiting time to the previous total waiting time.

   ```
   totalWait = totalWait + customer.getWaitingTime();
   ```

3. Set the free server to begin the transaction.

   ```
   serverList.setServerBusy(serverID, customer, transTime);
   ```

To run the simulation, we need to know the number of customers arriving at a given time unit and how long it takes to serve the customer. We use the Poisson distribution from statistics, which says that the probability of y events occurring at a given time is given by the formula:

$$P(y) = \frac{\lambda^y e^{-\lambda}}{y!}, y = 0, 1, 2, \ldots,$$

where λ is the expected value that y events occur at that time. Suppose that, on average, a customer arrives every four minutes. During this four-minute period, the customer can arrive at any one of the four minutes. Assuming an equal likelihood of each of the four minutes, the expected value that a customer arrives in each of the four minutes is, therefore, $1 / 4 = 0.25$. Next, we need to determine whether the customer actually arrives at a given minute.

Now $P(0) = e^{-\lambda}$ is the probability that no event occurs at a given time. One of the basic assumptions of the Poisson distribution is that the probability of more than one outcome occurring in a short time interval is negligible. For simplicity, we assume that only one customer arrives at a given time unit. Thus, we use $e^{-\lambda}$ as the cutoff point to determine whether a customer arrives at a given time unit. Suppose that, on average, a customer arrives every four minutes. Then $\lambda = 0.25$. We can use an algorithm to generate a number between 0 and 1. If the value of the number generated is $> e^{-0.25}$, we can assume that the customer arrived at a particular time unit. For example, suppose that $rNum$ is a random number such that $0 \leq rNum \leq 1$. If $rNum > e^{-0.25}$, the customer arrived at the given time unit.

We now describe the function `runSimulation` to implement the simulation. Suppose that we run the simulation for 100 time units and customers arrive at time units 93, 96, and 100. The average transaction time is 5 minutes—that is, 5 time units. For simplicity, assume that we have only one server and the server becomes free at time unit 97, and that all customers arriving before time unit 93 have been served. When the server becomes free at time unit 97, the customer arriving at time unit 93 starts the transaction. Because the transaction of the customer arriving at time unit 93 starts at time unit 97 and it takes 5 minutes to complete a transaction, when the simulation loop ends, the customer arriving at time unit 93 is still at the server. Moreover, customers arriving at time units 96 and 100 are in the queue. For simplicity, we assume that when the simulation loop ends, the customers at the servers are considered served. The general algorithm for this function is as follows:

1. Declare and initialize the variables such as the simulation parameters, customer number, clock, total and average waiting times, number of customers arrived, number of customers served, number of customers left in the waiting queue, number of customers left with the servers, `waitingCustomersQueue`, and a list of servers.

2. The main loop is as follows:

```
for (clock = 1; clock <= simulationTime; clock++)
{
```

2.1. Update the server list to decrement the transaction time of each busy server by one time unit.

2.2. If the customer's queue is nonempty, increment the waiting time of each customer by one time unit.

2.3. If a customer arrives, increment the number of customers by 1 and add the new customer to the queue.

2.4. If a server is free and the customer's queue is nonempty, remove a customer from the front of the queue and send the customer to the free server.

```
}
```

3. Print the appropriate results. Your results must include the number of customers left in the queue, the number of customers still with servers, the number of customers arrived, and the number of customers who actually completed a transaction.

Once you have designed the function runSimulation, the definition of the function main is simple and straightforward because the function main calls only the function runSimulation. (See Programming Exercise 8 at the end of this chapter.)

When we tested our version of the simulation program, we generated the following results. We assumed that the average transaction time is 5 minutes and that on average a customer arrives every 4 minutes, and we used a random number generator to generate a number between 0 and 1 to decide whether a customer arrived at a given time unit.

Sample Run:

```
Customer number 1 arrived at time unit 4
Customer number 2 arrived at time unit 8
From server number 1 customer number 1
     departed at clock unit 9
Customer number 3 arrived at time unit 9
Customer number 4 arrived at time unit 12
From server number 1 customer number 2
     departed at clock unit 14
From server number 1 customer number 3
     departed at clock unit 19
Customer number 5 arrived at time unit 21
From server number 1 customer number 4
     departed at clock unit 24
From server number 1 customer number 5
     departed at clock unit 29
Customer number 6 arrived at time unit 37
Customer number 7 arrived at time unit 38
Customer number 8 arrived at time unit 41
From server number 1 customer number 6
     departed at clock unit 42
Customer number 9 arrived at time unit 43
Customer number 10 arrived at time unit 44
From server number 1 customer number 7
     departed at clock unit 47
Customer number 11 arrived at time unit 49
Customer number 12 arrived at time unit 51
From server number 1 customer number 8
     departed at clock unit 52
Customer number 13 arrived at time unit 52
Customer number 14 arrived at time unit 53
Customer number 15 arrived at time unit 54
From server number 1 customer number 9
     departed at clock unit 57
Customer number 16 arrived at time unit 59
From server number 1 customer number 10
     departed at clock unit 62
```

8

```
Customer number 17 arrived at time unit 66
From server number 1 customer number 11
     departed at clock unit 67
Customer number 18 arrived at time unit 71
From server number 1 customer number 12
     departed at clock unit 72
From server number 1 customer number 13
     departed at clock unit 77
Customer number 19 arrived at time unit 78
From server number 1 customer number 14
     departed at clock unit 82
From server number 1 customer number 15
     departed at clock unit 87
Customer number 20 arrived at time unit 90
From server number 1 customer number 16
     departed at clock unit 92
Customer number 21 arrived at time unit 92
From server number 1 customer number 17
     departed at clock unit 97

The simulation ran for 100 time units
Number of servers: 1
Average transaction time: 5
Average arrival time difference between customers: 4
Total waiting time: 269
Number of customers that completed a transaction: 17
Number of customers left in the servers: 1
The number of customers left in queue: 3
Average waiting time: 12.81
************** END SIMULATION *************
```

QUICK REVIEW

1. A queue is a data structure in which the items are added at one end and removed from the other end.

2. A queue is a First In First Out (FIFO) data structure.

3. The basic operations on a queue are as follows: Add an item to the queue, remove an item from the queue, retrieve the first and last element of the queue, initialize the queue, check whether the queue is empty, and check whether the queue is full.

4. A queue can be implemented as an array or a linked list.

5. The middle elements of a queue should not be accessed directly.

6. If the queue is nonempty, the function `front` returns the front element of the queue and the function `back` returns the last element in the queue.

7. Queues are restricted versions of arrays and linked lists.

EXERCISES

1. Consider the following statements:

```
queueType<int> queue;
int x, y;
```

Show what is output by the following segment of code:

```
x = 4;
y = 5;
queue.addQueue(x);
queue.addQueue(y);
x = queue.front();
queue.deleteQueue();
queue.addQueue(x + 5);
queue.addQueue(16);
queue.addQueue(x);
queue.addQueue(y - 3);

cout << "Queue Elements: ";
while (!queue.isEmptyQueue())
{
    cout << queue.front() << " ";
    queue.deleteQueue();
}
cout << endl;
```

2. Consider the following statements:

```
stackType<int> stack;
queueType<int> queue;
int x;
```

Suppose the input is:

```
15 28 14 22 64 35 19 32 7 11 13 30 -999
```

Show what is written by the following segment of code:

```
stack.push(0);
queue.addQueue(0);
cin >> x;

while (x != -999)
{
    switch (x % 4)
    {
    case 0:
        stack.push(x);
        break;
    case 1:
        if (!stack.isEmptyStack())
        {
            cout << "Stack Element = " << stack.top()
                << endl;
            stack.pop();
        }
```

8

```
                    else
                        cout << "Sorry, the stack is empty." << endl;
                        break;
                case 2:
                    queue.addQueue(x);
                    break;
                case 3:
                    if (!queue.isEmptyQueue())
                    {
                        cout << "Queue Element = " << queue.front()
                            << endl;
                        queue.deleteQueue();
                    }
                    else
                        cout << "Sorry, the queue is empty." << endl;
                    break;
            } //end switch

        cin >> x;
    } //end while

    cout << "Stack Elements: ";
    while (!stack.isEmptyStack())
    {
        cout << stack.top() << " ";
        stack.pop();
    }

    cout << endl;

    cout << "Queue Elements: ";
    while (!queue.isEmptyQueue())
    {
        cout << queue.front() << " ";
        queue.deleteQueue();
    }
    cout << endl;
```

3. What does the following function do?

```
    void mystery(queueType<int>& q)
    {
        stackType<int> s;

        while (!q.isEmptyQueue())
        {
            s.push(q.front());
            q.deleteQueue();
        }

        while (!s.isEmptyStack())
        {
            q.addQueue(2 * s.top());
            s.pop();
        }
    }
```

4. What is the effect of the following statements? If a statement is invalid, explain why it is invalid. The classes `queueADT`, `queueType`, and `linkedQueueType` are as defined in this chapter.

   a. `queueADT<int> newQueue;`

   b. `queueType <double> sales(-10);`

   c. `queueType <string> names;`

   d. `linkedQueueType <int> numQueue(50);`

5. What is the output of the following program segment?

   ```
   linkedQueueType<int> queue;

   queue.addQueue(10);
   queue.addQueue(20);
   cout << queue.front() << endl;
   queue.deleteQueue();
   queue.addQueue(2 * queue.back());
   queue.addQueue(queue.front());
   queue.addQueue(5);
   queue.addQueue(queue.back() - 2);

   linkedQueueType<int> tempQueue;

   tempQueue = queue;

   while (!tempQueue.isEmptyQueue())
   {
       cout << tempQueue.front() << " ";
       tempQueue.deleteQueue();
   }

   cout << endl;

   cout << queue.front() << " " << queue.back() << endl;
   ```

6. Suppose that `queue` is a `queueType` object and the size of the array implementing queue is 100. Also, suppose that the value of `queueFront` is 50 and the value of `queueRear` is 99.

   a. What are the values of `queueFront` and `queueRear` after adding an element to queue?

   b. What are the values of `queueFront` and `queueRear` after removing an element from queue?

7. Suppose that `queue` is a `queueType` object and the size of the array implementing queue is 100. Also, suppose that the value of `queueFront` is 99 and the value of `queueRear` is 25.

a. What are the values of `queueFront` and `queueRear` after adding an element to `queue`?

b. What are the values of `queueFront` and `queueRear` after removing an element from `queue`?

8. Suppose that `queue` is a `queueType` object and the size of the array implementing `queue` is 100. Also, suppose that the value of `queueFront` is 25 and the value of `queueRear` is 75.

a. What are the values of `queueFront` and `queueRear` after adding an element to `queue`?

b. What are the values of `queueFront` and `queueRear` after removing an element from `queue`?

9. Suppose that `queue` is a `queueType` object and the size of the array implementing `queue` is 100. Also, suppose that the value of `queueFront` is 99 and the value of `queueRear` is 99.

a. What are the values of `queueFront` and `queueRear` after adding an element to `queue`?

b. What are the values of `queueFront` and `queueRear` after removing an element from `queue`?

10. Suppose that `queue` is implemented as an array with the special reserved slot, as described in this chapter. Also, suppose that the size of the array implementing `queue` is 100. If the value of `queueFront` is 50, what is the position of the first queue element?

11. Suppose that `queue` is implemented as an array with the special reserved slot, as described in this chapter. Suppose that the size of the array implementing `queue` is 100. Also, suppose that the value of `queueFront` is 74 and the value of `queueRear` is 99.

a. What are the values of `queueFront` and `queueRear` after adding an element to `queue`?

b. What are the values of `queueFront` and `queueRear` after removing an element from `queue`? Also, what is the position of the removed queue element?

12. Write a function template, `reverseQueue`, that takes as a parameter a queue object and uses a stack object to reverse the elements of the queue.

13. Add the operation `queueCount` to the `class queueType` (the array implementation of queues), which returns the number of elements in the queue. Write the definition of the function template to implement this operation.

14. Draw the UML diagram of the `class queueADT`.

15. Draw the UML diagram of the `class queueType`.

16. Draw the UML diagram of the `class linkedQueueType`.

PROGRAMMING EXERCISES

1. Write the definitions of the functions to overload the assignment operator and copy constructor for the class queueType. Also, write a program to test these operations.

2. Write the definitions of the functions to overload the assignment operator and copy constructor for the class linkedQueueType. Also, write a program to test these operations.

3. This chapter described the array implementation of queues that use a special array slot, called the reserved slot, to distinguish between an empty and a full queue. Write the definition of the class and the definitions of the function members of this queue design. Also, write a test program to test various operations on a queue.

4. Write the definition of the function moveNthFront that takes as a parameter a positive integer, n. The function moves the nth element of the queue to the front. The order of the remaining elements remains unchanged. For example, suppose

    queue = {5, 11, 34, 67, 43, 55} and n = 3.

    After a call to the function moveNthFront,

    queue = {34, 5, 11, 67, 43, 55}.

    Add this function to the class queueType. Also write a program to test your method.

5. Write a program that reads a line of text, changes each uppercase letter to lowercase, and places each letter both in a queue and onto a stack. The program should then verify whether the line of text is a palindrome (a set of letters or numbers that is the same whether read forward or backward).

6. The implementation of a queue in an array, as given in this chapter, uses the variable count to determine whether the queue is empty or full. You can also use the variable count to return the number of elements in the queue. (See Exercise 13.) On the other hand, class linkedQueueType does not use such a variable to keep track of the number of elements in the queue. Redefine the class linkedQueueType by addding the variable count to keep track of the number of elements in the queue. Modify the definitions of the functions addQueue and deleteQueue as necessary. Add the function queueCount to return the number of elements in the queue. Also, write a program to test various operations of the class you defined.

7. Write the definition of the class linkedQueueType, which is derived from the class unorderedLinkedList, as explained in this chapter. Also write a program to test various operations of this class.

8

8. a. Write the definitions of the functions `setWaitingTime`, `getArrivalTime`, `getTransactionTime`, and `getCustomerNumber` of the class `customerType` defined in the section, "Application of Queues: Simulation."

  b. Write the definitions of the functions `getRemainingTransactionTime`, `setCurrentCustomer`, `getCurrentCustomerNumber`, `getCurrentCustomerArrivalTime`, `getCurrentCustomerWaitingTime`, and `getCurrentCustomerTransactionTime` of the class `serverType` defined in the section, "Application of Queues: Simulation."

  c. Write the definition of the function `runSimulation` to complete the design of the computer simulation program (see the section, "Application of Queues: Simulation"). Test run your program for a variety of data. Moreover, use a random number generator to decide whether a customer arrived at a given time unit.

9. Redo the simulation program of this chapter so that it uses the STL `class` `queue` to maintain the list of waiting customers.

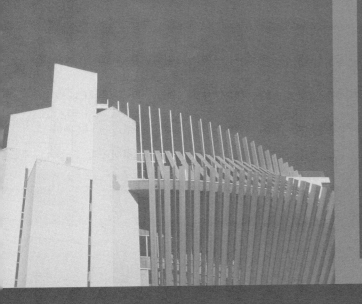

CHAPTER

9

SEARCHING AND HASHING ALGORITHMS

IN THIS CHAPTER, YOU WILL:

- Learn the various search algorithms
- Explore how to implement the sequential and binary search algorithms
- Discover how the sequential and binary search algorithms perform
- Become aware of the lower bound on comparison-based search algorithms
- Learn about hashing

Chapter 3 described how to organize data into computer memory using an array and how to perform basic operations on that data. Chapter 5 then described how to organize data using linked lists. The most important operation performed on a list is the search algorithm. Using the search algorithm, you can do the following:

- Determine whether a particular item is in the list.
- If the data is specially organized (for example, sorted), find the location in the list where a new item can be inserted.
- Find the location of an item to be deleted.

The search algorithm's performance, therefore, is crucial. If the search is slow, it takes a large amount of computer time to accomplish your task; if the search is fast, you can accomplish your task quickly.

Search Algorithms

Chapters 3 and 5 described how to implement the sequential search algorithm. This chapter discusses other search algorithms and analyzes them. The analysis of algorithms enables programmers to decide which algorithm to use for a specific application. Before describing these algorithms, let us make the following observations.

Associated with each item in a data set is a special member that uniquely identifies the item in the data set. For example, if you have a data set consisting of student records, then the student ID uniquely identifies each student in a particular school. This unique member of the item is called the **key** of the item. The keys of the items in the data set are used in such operations as searching, sorting, insertion, and deletion. For instance, when we search the data set for a particular item, we compare the key of the item for which we are searching with the keys of the items in the data set.

As previously remarked, in addition to describing searching algorithms, this chapter analyzes these algorithms. In the analysis of an algorithm, the key comparisons refer to comparing the key of the search item with the key of an item in the list. Moreover, the number of key comparisons refers to the number of times the key of the item (in algorithms such as searching and sorting) is compared with the keys of the items in the list.

In Chapter 3, we designed and implemented the `class arrayListType` to implement a list and the basic operations in an array. Because this chapter refers to this class, for easy reference we give its definition, without documentation to save space, here:

```
template <class elemType>
class arrayListType
{
public:
    const arrayListType<elemType>& operator=
                    (const arrayListType<elemType>&);
```

```
    bool isEmpty() const;
    bool isFull() const;
    int listSize() const;
    int maxListSize() const;
    void print() const;
    bool isItemAtEqual(int location, const elemType& item) const;
    void insertAt(int location, const elemType& insertItem);
    void insertEnd(const elemType& insertItem);
    void removeAt(int location);
    void retrieveAt(int location, elemType& retItem) const;
    void replaceAt(int location, const elemType& repItem);
    void clearList();
    int seqSearch(const elemType& item) const;
    void insert(const elemType& insertItem);
    void remove(const elemType& removeItem);

    arrayListType(int size = 100);

    arrayListType(const arrayListType<elemType>& otherList);

    ~arrayListType();

protected:
    elemType *list;   //array to hold the list elements
    int length;       //to store the length of the list
    int maxSize;      //to store the maximum size of the list
};
```

Sequential Search

The sequential search (also called linear search) on array-based lists was described in Chapter 3, and the sequential search on linked lists was covered in Chapter 5. The sequential search works the same for both array-based and linked lists. The search always starts at the first element in the list and continues until either the item is found in the list or the entire list is searched.

Because we are interested in the performance of the sequential search (that is, the analysis of this type of search), for easy reference and for the sake of completeness, we give the sequential search algorithm for array-based lists (as described in Chapter 3). If the search item is found, its index (that is, its location in the array) is returned. If the search is unsuccessful, –1 is returned. Note that the following sequential search does not require the list elements to be in any particular order.

```
template <class elemType>
int arrayListType<elemType>::seqSearch(const elemType& item) const
{
    int loc;
    bool found = false;

    for (loc = 0; loc < length; loc++)
        if (list[loc] == item)
```

```
        {
            found = true;
            break;
        }

    if (found)
        return loc;
    else
        return -1;
} //end seqSearch
```

> **NOTE** You can also write a recursive algorithm to implement the sequential search algorithm. (See Programming Exercise 1 at the end of this chapter.)

SEQUENTIAL SEARCH ANALYSIS

This section analyzes the performance of the sequential search algorithm in both the worst case and the average case.

The statements before and after the loop are executed only once and, hence, require very little computer time. The statements in the `for` loop are the ones that are repeated several times. For each iteration of the loop, the search item is compared with an element in the list, and a few other statements are executed, including some other comparisons. Clearly, the loop terminates as soon as the search item is found in the list. Therefore, the execution of the other statements in the loop is directly related to the outcome of the key comparison. Also, different programmers might implement the same algorithm differently, although the number of key comparisons would typically be the same. The speed of a computer can also easily affect the time an algorithm takes to perform, but not the number of key comparisons.

Therefore, when analyzing a search algorithm, we count the number of key comparisons because this number gives us the most useful information. Furthermore, the criteria for counting the number of key comparisons can be applied equally well to other search algorithms.

Suppose that L is list of length n. We want to determine the number of key comparisons made by the sequential search when the L is searched for a given item.

If the search item is not in the list, we then compare the search item with every element in the list, making n comparisons. This is an unsuccessful case.

Suppose that the search item is in the list. Then the number of key comparisons depends on where in the list the search item is located. If the search item is the first element of L, we make only one key comparison. This is the best case. On the other hand, if the search item is the last element in the list, the algorithm makes n comparisons. This is the worst case. The best and worst cases are not likely to occur every time we apply the sequential search on L, so it would be more helpful if we could determine the average behavior of the algorithm. That is, we need to determine the average number of key comparisons the sequential search algorithm makes in the successful case.

To determine the average number of comparisons in the successful case of the sequential search algorithm:

1. Consider all possible cases.
2. Find the number of comparisons for each case.
3. Add the number of comparisons and divide by the number of cases.

If the search item, called the **target**, is the first element in the list, one comparison is required. If the target is the second element in the list, two comparisons are required. Similarly, if the target is the kth element in the list, k comparisons are required. We assume that the target can be any element in the list; that is, all list elements are equally likely to be the target. Suppose that there are n elements in the list. The following expression gives the average number of comparisons:

$$\frac{1 + 2 + \ldots + n}{n}$$

It is known that

$$1 + 2 + \cdots + n = \frac{n(n + 1)}{2}$$

Therefore, the following expression gives the average number of comparisons made by the sequential search in the successful case:

$$\frac{1 + 2 + \ldots + n}{n} = \frac{1}{n}\frac{n(n + 1)}{2} = \frac{n + 1}{2}$$

This expression shows that, on average, the sequential search searches half the list. It, thus, follows that if the list size is 1,000,000, on average, the sequential search makes 500,000 comparisons. As a result, the sequential search is not efficient for large lists.

Ordered Lists

A list is ordered if its elements are ordered according to some criteria. The elements of a list are usually in ascending order. Several operations that can be performed on an ordered list are similar to the operations performed on an arbitrary list. For example, determining whether the list is empty or full, determining the length of the list, printing the list, and clearing the list for an ordered list are the same operations as those on an unordered list. Therefore, to define an ordered list as an abstract data type (ADT), by using the mechanism of inheritance, we can derive the class to implement the ordered lists from the `class arrayListType` discussed in the previous section. Depending on whether a specific application of a list can be stored in either an array or a linked list, we define two classes.

The following class, orderedArrayListType, defines an ordered list stored in an array as an ADT:

```
template <class elemType>
class orderedArrayListType: public arrayListType<elemType>
{
public:
    orderedArrayListType(int size = 100);
        //constructor

    ...
        //We will add the necessary members as needed.

private:
        //We will add the necessary members as needed.
}
```

Chapter 5 defined the following class to implement ordered linked lists:

```
template <class elemType>
class orderedLinkedListType: public linkedListType<elemType>
{
public:
    ...
}
```

Binary Search

As you can see, the sequential search is not efficient for large lists because, on average, the sequential search searches half the list. We therefore describe another search algorithm, called the binary search, which is very fast. However, a binary search can be performed only on ordered lists. We, therefore, assume that the list is ordered. In the next chapter, we describe several sorting algorithms.

The binary search algorithm uses the divide-and-conquer technique to search the list. First, the search item is compared with the middle element of the list. If the search item is found, the search terminates. If the search item is less than the middle element of the list, we restrict the search to the first half of the list; otherwise, we search the second half of the list.

Consider the sorted list of length = 12 in Figure 9-1.

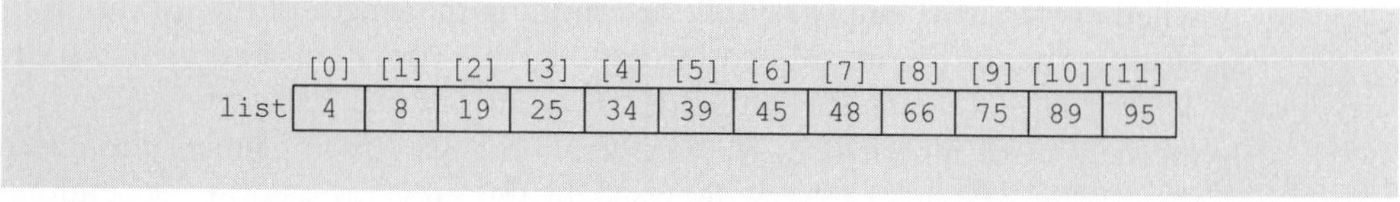

	[0]	[1]	[2]	[3]	[4]	[5]	[6]	[7]	[8]	[9]	[10]	[11]
list	4	8	19	25	34	39	45	48	66	75	89	95

FIGURE 9-1   List of length 12

Suppose that we want to determine whether 75 is in the list. Initially, the entire list is the search list (see Figure 9-2).

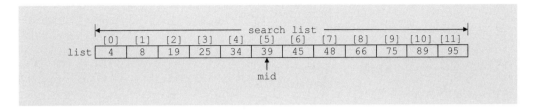

FIGURE 9-2 Search list, `list[0]...list[11]`

First, we compare 75 with the middle element in this list, `list[5]` (which is 39). Because 75 ≠ `list[5]` and 75 > `list[5]`, we restrict our search to the list `list[6]...list[11]`, as shown in Figure 9-3.

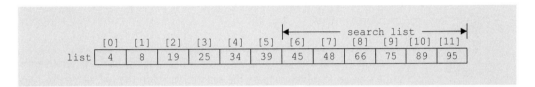

FIGURE 9-3 Search list, `list[6]...list[11]`

This process is now repeated on the list `list[6]...list[11]`, which is a list of length = 6.

Because we need to determine the middle element of the list frequently, the binary search algorithm is typically implemented for array-based lists. To determine the middle element of the list, we add the starting index, `first`, and the ending index, `last`, of the search list and then divide by 2 to calculate its index. That is, `mid = (first + last) / 2`.

Initially, `first = 0` and `last = length - 1` (this is because an array index in C++ starts at 0 and `length` denotes the number of elements in the list).

The following C++ function implements the binary search algorithm. If the item is found in the list, its location is returned; if the search item is not in the list, –1 is returned.

```
template<class elemType>
int orderedArrayListType<elemType>::binarySearch
                            (const elemType& item) const
{
    int first = 0;
    int last = length - 1;
    int mid;

    bool found = false;
```

```
    while (first <= last && !found)
    {
        mid = (first + last) / 2;

        if (list[mid] == item)
            found = true;
        else if (list[mid] > item)
            last = mid - 1;
        else
            first = mid + 1;
    }

    if (found)
        return mid;
    else
        return -1;
}//end binarySearch
```

In the binary search algorithm, each time through the loop we make two key comparisons. The only exception is in the successful case; the last time through the loop only one key comparison is made.

NOTE   The binary search algorithm, as given in this chapter, uses an iterative control structure (the `while` loop) to compare the search item with the list elements. You can also write a recursive algorithm to implement the binary search algorithm. (See Programming Exercise 2 at the end of this chapter.)

Example 9-1 further illustrates how the binary search algorithm works.

EXAMPLE 9-1

Consider the list given in Figure 9-4.

	[0]	[1]	[2]	[3]	[4]	[5]	[6]	[7]	[8]	[9]	[10]	[11]
list	4	8	19	25	34	39	45	48	66	75	89	95

FIGURE 9-4 Sorted list for a binary search

The number of elements in this list is 12, so `length` = 12. Suppose that we are searching for item 89. Table 9-1 shows the values of `first`, `last`, and `mid` each time through the loop. It also shows the number of times the item is compared with an element in the list each time through the loop.

TABLE 9-1 Values of `first`, `last`, and `mid` and the number of comparisons for search item 89

Iteration	first	last	Mid	list[mid]	Number of comparisons
1	0	11	5	39	2
2	6	11	8	66	2
3	9	11	10	89	1(found is true)

The item is found at `location` 10, and the total number of comparisons is 5.

Next, let us search the list for item 34. Table 9-2 shows the values of **first**, **last**, and mid each time through the loop. It also shows the number of times the item is compared with an element in the list each time through the loop.

TABLE 9-2 Values of `first`, `last`, and `mid` and the number of comparisons for search item 34

Iteration	first	last	mid	list[mid]	Number of comparisons
1	0	11	5	39	2
2	0	4	2	19	2
3	3	4	3	25	2
4	4	4	4	34	1 (found is true)

The item is found at `location` 4, and the total number of comparisons is 7.

Let us now search for item 22, as shown in Table 9-3.

TABLE 9-3 Values of `first`, `last`, and `mid` and the number of comparisons for search item 22

Iteration	first	last	mid	list[mid]	Number of comparisons
1	0	11	5	39	2
2	0	4	2	19	2
3	3	4	3	25	2
4	3	2	The loop stops (because `first` > `last`)		

This is an unsuccessful search. The total number of comparisons is 6.

9

PERFORMANCE OF BINARY SEARCH

Suppose that L is a sorted list of size 1024 and we want to determine if an item x is in L. From the binary search algorithm, it follows that every iteration of the **while** loop cuts the size of the search list by half. (For example, see Figures 9-2 and 9-3.) Because $1024 = 2^{10}$, the **while** loop will have, at most, 11 iterations to determine whether x is in L. Because every iteration of the **while** loop makes two item (key) comparisons, that is, x is compared twice with the elements of L, the binary search will make, at most, 22 comparisons to determine whether x is in L. On the other hand, recall that a sequential search on average will make 512 comparisons to determine whether x is in L.

To better understand how fast binary search is compared with sequential search, suppose that L is of size 1048576. Because $1048576 = 2^{20}$, it follows that the **while** loop in a binary search will have at most 21 iterations to determine whether an element is in L. Every iteration of the **while** loop makes two key (that is, item) comparisons. Therefore, to determine whether an element is in L, a binary search makes at most 42 item comparisons.

Note that $40 = 2 \star 20 = 2 \star \log_2 2^{20} = 2 \star \log_2(1048576)$.

In general, suppose that L is a sorted list of size n. Moreover, suppose that n is a power of 2, that is, $n = 2^m$, for some nonnegative integer m. After each iteration of the **for** loop, about half the elements are left to search, that is, the search sublist for the next iteration is half the size of the current sublist. For example, after the *first* iteration, the search sublist is of size about $n/2 = 2^{m-1}$. It is easy to see that the maximum number of the iteration of the **for** loop is about $m + 1$. Also $m = \log_2 n$. Each iteration makes 2 key comparisons. Thus, the maximum number of comparisons to determine whether an element x is in L is $2(m + 1) = 2(\log_2 n + 1) = 2\log_2 n + 2$.

In the case of a successful search, it can be shown that for a list of length n, on average, a binary search makes $2\log_2 n - 3$ key comparisons. In the case of an unsuccessful search, it can be shown that for a list of length n, a binary search makes approximately $2\log_2(n+1)$ key comparisons.

Now that we know how to effectively search an ordered list stored in an array, let us discuss how to insert an item into an ordered list.

Insertion into an Ordered List

Suppose that you have an ordered list and want to insert an item in the list. After insertion, the resulting list must also be ordered. Chapter 5 described how to insert an item into an ordered linked list. This section describes how to insert an item into an ordered list stored in an array.

To store the item in the ordered list, first we must find the place in the list where the item is to be inserted. Then we slide the list elements one array position down to make room for the item to be inserted, and then we insert the item. Because the list is sorted and stored in an array, we can use an algorithm similar to the binary search algorithm to find the place in the list where the item is to be inserted. We can then use the function insertAt (of the class arrayListType) to insert the item. (Note that we cannot use the binary search algorithm as designed previously because it returns −1 if the item is not in the list. Of course, we can write another function using the binary search technique to find the position in the array where the item is to be inserted.) Therefore, the algorithm to insert the item is: (The special cases, such as inserting an item in an empty list or in a full list, are handled separately.)

1.   Use an algorithm similar to the binary search algorithm to find the place where the item is to be inserted.

2.   if the item is already in this list
           output an appropriate message
       else
           use the function insertAt to insert the item in the list.

The following function, insertOrd, implements this algorithm.

```
template <class elemType>
void orderedArrayListType<elemType>::insertOrd(const elemType& item)
{
    int first = 0;
    int last = length - 1;
    int mid;

    bool found = false;

    if (length == 0)     //the list is empty
    {
        list[0] = item;
        length++;
    }
    else if (length == maxSize)
        cerr << "Cannot insert into a full list." << endl;
    else
    {
        while (first <= last && !found)
        {
            mid = (first + last) / 2;

            if (list[mid] == item)
                found = true;
            else if (list[mid] > item)
                last = mid - 1;
            else
                first = mid + 1;
        }//end while

        if (found)
            cerr << "The insert item is already in the list. "
                 << "Duplicates are not allowed." << endl;
        else
```

```
        {
            if (list[mid] < item)
                mid++;

            insertAt(mid, item);
        }
    }
}//end insertOrd
```

Similarly, you can write a function to remove an element from an ordered list; see Programming Exercise 6 at the end of this chapter.

If we add the binary search algorithm and the `insertOrd` algorithm to the `class` `orderedArrayListType`, the definition of this class is as follows:

```
template <class elemType>
class orderedArrayListType: public arrayListType<elemType>
{
public:
    void insertOrd(const elemType&);
    int binarySearch(const elemType& item) const;
    orderedArrayListType(int size = 100);
};
```

Because the `class orderedArrayListType` is derived from the `class arrayListType`, and the list elements of an `orderedArrayListType` are ordered, we must override the functions `insertAt` and `insertEnd` of the `class arrayListType` in the `class` `orderedArrayListType`. We do this so that if these functions are used by an object of type `orderedArrayListType`, then after using these functions, the list elements of the object are still in order. We leave the details of these functions as an exercise for you. Furthermore, you can also override the function `seqSearch` so that while performing a sequential search on an ordered list, it takes into account that the elements are in order. We leave the details of this function also as an exercise.

Table 9-4 summarizes the algorithm analysis of the search algorithms discussed earlier.

TABLE 9-4 Number of comparisons for a list of length n

Algorithm	Successful search	Unsuccessful search
Sequential search	$(n + 1) / 2 = O(n)$	$n = O(n)$
Binary search	$2\log_2 n - 3 = O(\log_2 n)$	$2\log_2(n+1) = O(\log_2 n)$

Lower Bound on Comparison-Based Search Algorithms

Sequential and binary search algorithms search the list by comparing the target element with the list elements. For this reason, these algorithms are called **comparison-based search algorithms**. Earlier sections of this chapter showed that a sequential search is of the order n, and a binary search is of the order $\log_2 n$, where n is the size of the list. The obvious question is: Can we devise a search algorithm that has an order less than $\log_2 n$? Before we answer this question, first we obtain the lower bound on the number of comparisons for the comparison-based search algorithms.

Theorem: Let L be a list of size $n > 1$. Suppose that the elements of L are sorted. If $\mathrm{SRH}(n)$ denotes the minimum number of comparisons needed, in the worst case, by using a comparison-based algorithm to recognize whether an element x is in L, then $\mathrm{SRH}(n) \geq \log_2 (n + 1)$.

Corollary: The binary search algorithm is the optimal worst-case algorithm for solving search problems by the comparison method.

From these results, it follows that if we want to design a search algorithm that is of an order less than $\log_2 n$, it cannot be comparison based.

Hashing

Previous sections of this chapter discussed two search algorithms: sequential and binary. In a binary search, the data must be sorted; in a sequential search, the data does not need to be in any particular order. We also analyzed both these algorithms and showed that a sequential search is of order n, and a binary search is of order $\log_2 n$, where n is the length of the list. The obvious question is: Can we construct a search algorithm that is of order less than $\log_2 n$? Recall that both search algorithms, sequential and binary, are comparison-based algorithms. We obtained a lower bound on comparison-based search algorithms, which shows that comparison-based search algorithms are at least of order $\log_2 n$. Therefore, if we want to construct a search algorithm that is of order less than $\log_2 n$, it cannot be comparison based. This section describes an algorithm that, on average, is of order 1.

The previous section showed that for comparison-based algorithms, a binary search achieves the lower bound. However, a binary search requires the data to be specially organized, that is, the data must be sorted. The search algorithm that we now describe, called **hashing**, also requires the data to be specially organized.

In hashing, the data is organized with the help of a table, called the **hash table**, denoted by *HT*, and the hash table is stored in an array. To determine whether a particular item with a key, say X, is in the table, we apply a function h, called the **hash function**, to the key X; that is, we compute $h(X)$, read as h of X. The function h is typically an arithmetic function and $h(X)$ gives the address of the item in the hash table. Suppose that the size of the hash table, *HT*, is m. Then $0 \leq h(X) < m$. Thus, to determine whether the item with key X is in the table, we look at the entry $HT[h(X)]$ in the hash table. Because the address of an item is computed with the help of a function, it follows that the items are stored in no particular order. Before continuing with this discussion, let us consider the following questions:

- How do we choose a hash function?
- How do we organize the data with the help of the hash table?

First, we discuss how to organize the data in the hash table.

There are two ways that data is organized with the help of the hash table. In the first approach, the data is stored within the hash table, that is, in an array. In the second approach, the data is stored in linked lists and the hash table is an array of pointers to those linked lists. Each approach has its own advantages and disadvantages, and we discuss both approaches in detail. However, first we introduce some more terminology that is used in this section.

The hash table HT is, usually, divided into, say b buckets $HT[0]$, $HT[1]$, ..., $HT[b-1]$. Each bucket is capable of holding, say r items. Thus, it follows that $br = m$, where m is the size of HT. Generally, $r = 1$ and so each bucket can hold one item.

The hash function h maps the key X onto an integer t, that is, $h(X) = t$, such that $0 \leq h(X) \leq b - 1$.

EXAMPLE 9-2

Suppose there are six students a_1, a_2, a_3, a_4, a_5, a_6 in the Data Structures class and their IDs are a_1: 197354863; a_2: 933185952; a_3: 132489973; a_4: 134152056; a_5: 216500306; and a_6: 106500306.

Let $k_1 = 197354863$, $k_2 = 933185952$, $k_3 = 132489973$, $k_4 = 134152056$, $k_5 = 216500306$, and $k_6 = 106500306$.

Suppose that HT denotes the hash table and HT is of size 13 indexed 0, 1, 2, ..., 12.

Define the function h: $\{k_1, k_2, k_3, k_4, k_5, k_6\} \rightarrow \{0, 1, 2, ..., 12\}$ by $h(k_i) = k_i \% 13$. (Note that % denotes the mod operator.)

Now

$h(k_1) = h(197354863) = 197354863 \% 13 = 4$	$h(k_4) = h(134152056) = 134152056 \% 13 = 12$
$h(k_2) = h(933185952) = 933185952 \% 13 = 10$	$h(k_5) = h(216500306) = 216500306 \% 13 = 9$
$h(k_3) = h(132489973) = 132489973 \% 13 = 5$	$h(k_6) = h(106500306) = 106500306 \% 13 = 3$

Suppose $HT[b] \leftarrow a$ means "store the data of the student with ID a into $HT[b]$." Then

$HT[4] \leftarrow 197354863$	$HT[5] \leftarrow 132489973$	$HT[9] \leftarrow 216500306$
$HT[10] \leftarrow 933185952$	$HT[12] \leftarrow 134152056$	$HT[3] \leftarrow 106500306$

We consider now a slight variation of Example 9-2.

EXAMPLE 9-3

Suppose there are eight students in the class in a college and their IDs are 197354864, 933185952, 132489973, 134152056, 216500306, 106500306, 216510306, and 197354865. We want to store each student's data into HT in this order.

Let k_1 = 197354864, k_2 = 933185952, k_3 = 132489973, k_4 = 134152056, k_5 = 216500306, k_6 = 106500306, k_7 = 216510306, and k_8 = 197354865.

Suppose that HT denotes the hash table and HT is of size 13 indexed 0, 1, 2, ..., 12.

Define the function h: $\{k_1, k_2, k_3, k_4, k_5, k_6, k_7, k_8\} \rightarrow \{0, 1, 2, ..., 12\}$ by $h(k_i) = k_i \% 13$. Now

$h(k_1)$ = 197354864 % 13 = 5	$h(k_4)$ = 134152056 % 13 = 12	$h(k_7)$ = 216510306 % 13 = 12
$h(k_2)$ = 933185952 % 13 = 10	$h(k_5)$ = 216500306 % 13 = 9	$h(k_8)$ = 197354865 % 13 = 6
$h(k_3)$ = 132489973 % 13 = 5	$h(k_6)$ = 106500306 % 13 = 3	

As before, suppose $HT[b] \leftarrow a$ means "store the data of the student with ID a into $HT[b]$." Then

$HT[5] \leftarrow$ 197354864	$HT[12] \leftarrow$ 134152056	$HT[12] \leftarrow$ 216510306
$HT[10] \leftarrow$ 933185952	$HT[9] \leftarrow$ 216500306	$HT[6] \leftarrow$ 197354865
$HT[5] \leftarrow$ 132489973	$HT[3] \leftarrow$ 106500306	

It follows that the data of the student with ID 132489973 is to be stored in $HT[5]$. However, $HT[5]$ is already occupied by the data of the student with ID 197354864. In such a situation, we say that a *collision* has occurred. Later in this section, we discuss some ways to handle collisions.

Two keys, X_1 and X_2, such that $X_1 \neq X_2$, are called **synonyms** if $h(X_1) = h(X_2)$. Let X be a key and $h(X) = t$. If bucket t is full, we say that an **overflow** occurs. Let X_1 and X_2 be two nonidentical keys. If $h(X_1) = h(X_2)$, we say that a **collision** occurs. If $r = 1$, that is, the bucket size is 1, an overflow and a collision occur at the same time.

When choosing a hash function, the main objectives are to:

- Choose a hash function that is easy to compute.
- Minimize the number of collisions.

Next, we consider some examples of hash functions.

Suppose that *HTSize* denotes the size of the hash table, that is, the size of the array holding the hash table. We assume that the bucket size is 1. Thus, each bucket can hold one item and, therefore, overflow and collision occur simultaneously.

Hash Functions: Some Examples

Several hash functions are described in the literature. Here we describe some of the commonly used hash functions.

Mid-Square: In this method, the hash function, h, is computed by squaring the identifier, and then using the appropriate number of bits from the middle of the square to obtain the bucket address. Because the middle bits of a square usually depend on all the characters, it is expected that different keys will yield different hash addresses with high probability, even if some of the characters are the same.

Folding: In folding, the key X is partitioned into parts such that all the parts, except possibly the last parts, are of equal length. The parts are then added, in some convenient way, to obtain the hash address.

Division (Modular arithmetic): In this method, the key X is converted into an integer i_X. This integer is then divided by the size of the hash table to get the remainder, giving the address of X in HT. That is, (in C++)

$$h(X) = i_X \% HTSize;$$

Suppose that each *key* is a string. The following C++ function uses the division method to compute the address of the key.

```
int hashFunction(char *insertKey, int keyLength)
{
    int sum = 0;

    for (int j = 0; j < keyLength; j++)
        sum = sum + static_cast<int>(insertKey[j]);

    return (sum % HTSize);
} // end hashFunction
```

Collision Resolution

As noted previously, the hash function that we choose not only should be easy to compute, but it is most desirable that the number of collisions is minimized. However, in reality, collisions are unavoidable because usually a hash function always maps a larger domain onto a smaller range. Thus, in hashing, we must include algorithms to handle collisions. Collision resolution techniques are classified into two categories: **open addressing** (also called **closed hashing**), and **chaining** (also called **open hashing**). In open addressing, the data is stored within the hash table. In chaining, the data is organized in linked lists and the hash table is an array of pointers to the linked lists. First we discuss collision resolution by open addressing.

Open Addressing

As described previously, in open addressing, the data is stored within the hash table. Therefore, for each key X, $h(X)$ gives the index in the array where the item with key X is likely to be stored. Open addressing can be implemented in several ways. Next, we describe some of the common ways to implement it.

LINEAR PROBING

Suppose that an item with key X is to be inserted in HT. We use the hash function to compute the index $h(X)$ of this item in HT. Suppose that $h(X) = t$. Then $0 \leq h(X) \leq HTSize - 1$. If $HT[t]$ is empty, we store this item into this array slot. Suppose that $HT[t]$ is already occupied by another item; we have a collision. In linear probing, starting at location t, we search the array sequentially to find the next available array slot.

In linear probing, we assume that the array is circular so that if the lower portion of the array is full, we can continue the search in the top portion of the array. This can be easily accomplished by using the mod operator. That is, starting at t, we check the array locations t, $(t + 1)$ % $HTSize$, $(t + 2)$ % $HTSize$, ..., $(t + j)$ % $HTSize$. This is called the **probe sequence**.

The next array slot is given by

$$(h(X) + j) \text{ \% } HTSize$$

where j is the jth probe.

EXAMPLE 9-4

Consider the students' IDs and the hash function given in Example 9-3. Then we know that

$h(197354864) = 5 = h(132489973)$	$h(134152056) = 12 = h(216510306)$	$h(106500306) = 3$
$h(933185952) = 10$	$h(216500306) = 9$	$h(197354865) = 6$

Using the linear probing, the array position where each student's data is stored is:

ID	$h(\text{ID})$	$(h(\text{ID}) + 1)$ % 13	$(h(\text{ID}) + 2)$ % 13
197354864	5		
933185952	10		
132489973	5	6	
134152056	12		
216500306	9		
106500306	3		
216510306	12	0	
197354865	6	7	

As before, suppose $HT[b] \leftarrow a$ means "store the data of the student with ID a into $HT[b]$." Then

$HT[5] \leftarrow 197354864$	$HT[12] \leftarrow 134152056$	$HT[0] \leftarrow 216510306$
$HT[10] \leftarrow 933185952$	$HT[9] \leftarrow 216500306$	$HT[7] \leftarrow 197354865$
$HT[6] \leftarrow 132489973$	$HT[3] \leftarrow 106500306$	

The following C++ code implements linear probing:

```
hIndex = hashFunction(insertKey);
found = false;

while (HT[hIndex] != emptyKey && !found)
    if (HT[hIndex].key == key)
        found = true;
    else
        hIndex = (hIndex + 1) % HTSize;

if (found)
    cerr << "Duplicate items are not allowed." << endl;
else
    HT[hIndex] = newItem;
```

From the definition of linear probing, we see that linear probing is easy to implement. However, linear probing causes **clustering**; that is, more and more new keys would likely be hashed to the array slots that are already occupied. For example, consider the hash table of size 20, as shown in Figure 9-5.

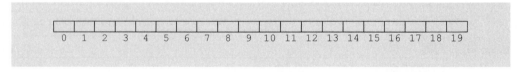

FIGURE 9-5 Hash table of size 20

Initially, all the array positions are available. Because all the array positions are available, the probability of any position being probed is (1/20). Suppose that after storing some of the items, the hash table is as shown in Figure 9-6.

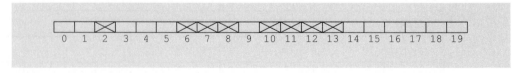

FIGURE 9-6 Hash table of size 20 with certain positions occupied

In Figure 9-6, a cross indicates that this array slot is occupied. Slot 9 will be occupied next if, for the next key, the hash address is 6, 7, 8, or 9. Thus, the probability that slot 9 will be occupied next is 4/20. Similarly, in this hash table, the probability that array position 14 will be occupied next is 5/20.

Now consider the hash table of Figure 9-7.

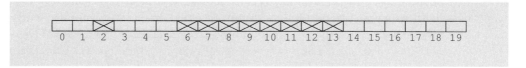

FIGURE 9-7   Hash table of size 20 with certain positions occupied

In this hash table, the probability that the array position 14 will be occupied next is 9/20, whereas the probability that the array positions 15, 16, or 17 will be occupied next is 1/20. We see that items tend to cluster, which would increase the search length. Linear probing, therefore, causes clustering. This clustering is called **primary clustering**.

One way to improve linear probing is to skip array positions by a fixed constant, say c, rather than 1. In this case, the hash address is as follows:

$(h(X) + i \star c)$ % $HTSize$

If $c = 2$ and $h(X) = 2k$, that is, $h(X)$ is even, only the even-numbered array positions are visited. Similarly, if $c = 2$ and $h(X) = 2k + 1$, that is, $h(X)$ is odd, only the odd-numbered array positions are visited. To visit all the array positions, the constant c must be relatively prime to $HTSize$.

RANDOM PROBING

This method uses a random number generator to find the next available slot. The ith slot in the probe sequence is

$(h(X) + r_i)$ % $HTSize$

where r_i is the ith value in a random permutation of the numbers 1 to $HTSize - 1$. All insertions and searches use the same sequence of random numbers.

EXAMPLE 9-5

Suppose that the size of the hash table is 101, and for the keys X_1 and X_2, $h(X_1) = 26$ and $h(X_2) = 35$. Also suppose that $r_1 = 2$, $r_2 = 5$, and $r_3 = 8$. Then the probe sequence of X_1 has the elements 26, 28, 31, and 34. Similarly, the probe sequence of X_2 has the elements 35, 37, 40, and 43.

REHASHING

In this method, if a collision occurs with the hash function h, we use a series of hash functions, $h_1, h_2, \ldots, h_s$. That is, if the collision occurs at $h(X)$, the array slots $h_i(X)$, $1 \leq h_i(X) \leq s$ are examined.

QUADRATIC PROBING

Suppose that an item with key X is hashed at t, that is, $h(X) = t$ and $0 \leq t \leq HTSize - 1$. Further suppose that position t is already occupied. In quadratic probing, starting at position t, we linearly search the array at locations $(t + 1)$ % $HTSize$, $(t + 2^2)$ % $HTSize = (t + 4)$ % $HTSize$, $(t + 3^2)$ % $HTSize = (t + 9)$ % $HTSize$, $\ldots$, $(t + i^2)$ % $HTSize$. That is, the probe sequence is: t, $(t + 1)$ % $HTSize$ $(t + 2^2)$ % $HTSize$, $(t + 3^2)$ % $HTSize$, $\ldots$, $(t + i^2)$ % $HTSize$.

EXAMPLE 9-6

Suppose that the size of the hash table is 101 and for the keys X_1, X_2, and X_3, $h(X_1) = 25$, $h(X_2) = 96$, and $h(X_3) = 34$. Then the probe sequence for X_1 is 25, 26, 29, 34, 41, and so on. The probe sequence for X_2 is 96, 97, 100, 4, 11, and so on. (Notice that $(96 + 3^2)$ % $101 = 105$ % $101 = 4$.)

The probe sequence for X_3 is 34, 35, 38, 43, 50, 59, and so on. Even though element 34 of the probe sequence of X_3 is the same as the fourth element of the probe sequence of X_1, both probe sequences after 34 are different.

Although quadratic probing reduces primary clustering, we do not know if it probes all the positions in the table. In fact, it does not probe all the positions in the table. However, when $HTSize$ is a prime, quadratic probing probes about half the table before repeating the probe sequence. Let us prove this observation.

Suppose that $HTSize$ is a prime and for $0 \leq i < j \leq HTSize$,

$$(t + i^2)\%HTSize = (t + j^2)\%HTSize.$$

This implies that $HTSize$ divides $(j^2 - i^2)$, that is, $HTSize$ divides $(j - i)$ $(j + i)$. Because $HTSize$ is a prime, we get $HTSize$ divides $(j - i)$ or $HTSize$ divides $(j + i)$.

Now because $0 < j - i < HTSize$, it follows that $HTSize$ does not divide $(j - i)$. Hence, $HTSize$ divides $(j + i)$. This implies that $j + i \geq HTSize$, so $j \geq (HTSize / 2)$.

Hence, quadratic probing probes half the table before repeating the probe sequence. Thus, it follows that if the size of $HTSize$ is a prime at least twice the number of items, we can resolve all the collisions.

Because probing half the table is already a considerable number of probes, after making these many probes we assume that the table is full and stop the insertion (and search). (This can occur when the table is actually half full; in practice, it seldom happens unless the table is nearly full.)

Next we describe how to generate the probe sequence.

Note that

$$
\begin{aligned}
2^2 &= 1 + (2 \cdot 2 - 1) \\
3^2 &= 1 + 3 + (2 \cdot 3 - 1) \\
4^2 &= 1 + 3 + 5 + (2 \cdot 4 - 1) \\
&\vdots \\
i^2 &= 1 + 3 + 5 + 7 + \ldots + (2 \cdot i - 1), \quad i \geq 1.
\end{aligned}
$$

Thus, it follows that

$$
(t + i^2) \% \, HTSize = (t + 1 + 3 + 5 + 7 + \ldots + (2 \cdot i - 1)) \% \, HTSize
$$

Consider the probe sequence t, $t + 1$, $t + 2^2$, $t + 3^2$, $\ldots$, $(t + i^2) \% HTSize$. The following C++ code computes the ith probe, that is, $(t + i^2) \% HTSize$:

```
int inc = 1;
int pCount = 0;

while (p < i)
{
    t = (t + inc) % HTSize;
    inc = inc + 2;
    pCount++;
}
```

The following pseudocode implements quadratic probing (assume that *HTSize* is a prime):

```
int pCount;
int inc;
int hIndex;

hIndex = hashFunction(insertKey);

pCount = 0;
inc = 1;

while (HT[hIndex] is not empty
       && HT[hIndex] is not the same as the insert item
       && pCount < HTSize / 2)
{
    pCount++;
    hIndex = (hIndex + inc ) % HTSize;
    inc = inc + 2;
}

if (HT[hIndex] is empty)
    HT[hIndex] = newItem;
else if (HT[hIndex] is the same as the insert item)
    cerr << "Error: No duplicates are allowed." << endl;
```

9

```
else
    cerr << "Error: The table is full. "
         << "Unable to resolve the collisions." << endl;
```

Both random and quadratic probings eliminate primary clustering. However, if two nonidentical keys, say X_1 and X_2, are hashed to the same home position, that is, $h(X_1) = h(X_2)$, then the same probe sequence is followed for both keys. The same probe sequence is used for both keys because random probing and quadratic probing are functions of the home positions, not the original key. It follows that if the hash function causes a cluster at a particular home position, the cluster remains under these probings. This is called **secondary clustering**.

One way to solve secondary clustering is to use linear probing, with the increment value a function of the key. This is called **double hashing**. In double hashing, if a collision occurs at $h(X)$, the probe sequence is generated by using the rule:

$(h(X) + i \star g(X))$ % $HTSize$

where g is the second hash function, and $i = 0, 1, 2, 3, \ldots$.

If the size of the hash table is a prime p, then we can define g as follows:

$g(k) = 1 + (k$ % $(p - 2))$

EXAMPLE 9-7

Suppose that the size of the hash table is 101 and for the keys X_1 and X_2, $h(X_1) = 35$ and $h(X_2) = 83$. Also suppose that $g(X_1) = 3$ and $g(X_2) = 6$. Then the probe sequence for X_1 is 35, 38, 41, 44, 47, and so on. The probe sequence for X_2 is 83, 89, 95, 0, 6, and so on. (Notice that $(83 + 3 \star 6)$ % $101 = 101$ % $101 = 0$.)

EXAMPLE 9-8

Suppose there are six students in the Data Structures class and their IDs are 115, 153, 586, 206, 985, and 111, respectively. We want to store each student's data in this order. Suppose HT is of the size 19 indexed 0,1,2,3, ..., 18. Consider the prime number $p = 19$. Then $p - 2 = 17$. For the ID k, we define the hashing functions:

$h(k) = k$ % 19 and $g(k) = 1 + (k$ % $(p - 2)) = 1 + (k$ % $17)$

Let $k = 115$. Now $h(115) = 115$ % $19 = 1$. So the data of the student with ID 115 is stored in $HT[1]$.

Next consider $k = 153$. Now $h(153) = 153$ % $19 = 1$. However, $HT[1]$ is already occupied. So we first calculate $g(153)$, to find the probe sequence of 153. Now $g(153) = 1 + (153$ % $17) = 1 + 0 = 1$. Thus, $h(153) = 1$ and $g(153) = 1$. Therefore, probe sequence of 153 is given by $(h(153) + i \cdot g(153))$ % $19 = (1 + i \cdot 1)$ % 19, $i = 0, 1, 2, 3, \ldots$. Hence, the probe sequence of 153 is 1, 2, 3, ... Because $HT[2]$ is empty, the data of the student with ID 153 is stored in $HT[2]$.

Consider $k = 586$. Now $h(586) = 586 \% 19 = 16$. Because $HT[16]$ is empty, we store the data of the student with ID 586 in $HT[16]$.

Consider $k = 206$. Now $h(206) = 206 \% 19 = 16$. Because $HT[16]$ is already occupied, we compute $g(206)$. Now $g(206) = 1 + (206 \% 17) = 1 + 2 = 3$. So the probe sequence of 206 is, 16, 0, 3, 6, ... Note that $(16 + 3) \% 19 = 0$. Because $HT[0]$ is empty, the data of the student with ID 206 is stored in $HT[0]$.

We apply this process and find the array position to store the data of each student. If a collision occurs for an ID, then the following table shows the probe sequence of that ID.

ID	$h(ID)$	$g(ID)$	Probe sequence	
115	1			
153	1	1	1, 2, 3, 4, 5, ...	
586	16			
206	16	3	16, 0, 3, 6, 9,	Note that $(16 + 3) \% 19 = 0$
985	16	17	16, 14, 12, 10, ...	Note that $(16 + 17) \% 19 = 14$
111	16	10	16, 7, 17, 8, ...	

As before, suppose $HT[b] \leftarrow a$ means "store the data of the student with ID a into $HT[b]$." Then

$HT[1] \leftarrow 115$	$HT[16] \leftarrow 586$	$HT[14] \leftarrow 985$
$HT[2] \leftarrow 153$	$HT[0] \leftarrow 206$	$HT[7] \leftarrow 111$

Deletion: Open Addressing

Suppose that an item, say R, is to be deleted from the hash table, HT. Clearly, we first must find the index of R in HT. To find the index of R, we apply the same criteria we applied to R when R was inserted in HT. Let us further assume that after inserting R, another item, R', was inserted in HT, and the home position of R and R' is the same. The probe sequence of R is contained in the probe sequence of R' because R' was inserted in the hash table after R. Suppose that we delete R simply by marking the array slot containing R as empty. If this array position stays empty, then while searching for R' and following its probe sequence, the search terminates at this empty array position. This gives the impression that R' is not in the table, which, of course, is incorrect. The item R cannot be deleted simply by marking its position as empty from the hash table.

One way to solve this problem is to create a special key to be stored in the key of the items to be deleted. The special key in any slot indicates that this array slot is available for a new item to be inserted. However, during the search, the search should not terminate at this location. This, unfortunately, makes the deletion algorithm slow and complicated.

Another solution is to use another array, say `indexStatusList` of int, of the same size as the hash table as follows: Initialize each position of `indexStatusList` to 0, indicating that the corresponding position in the hash table is empty. When an item is added to the hash table at position, say i, we set `indexStatusList[i]` to 1. When an item is deleted from the hash table at position, say k, we set `indexStatusList[k]` to −1. Therefore, each entry in the array `indexStatusList` is −1, 0, or 1.

For example, suppose that you have the hash table as shown in Figure 9-8.

	indexStatusList		HashTable
[0]	1	[0]	Mike
[1]	1	[1]	Gina
[2]	0	[2]	
[3]	1	[3]	Goldy
[4]	0	[4]	
[5]	1	[5]	Ravi
[6]	1	[6]	Danny
[7]	0	[7]	
[8]	1	[8]	Sheila
[9]	0	[9]	

FIGURE 9-8 Hash table and `indexStatusList`

In Figure 9-8, the hash table positions 0, 1, 3, 5, 6, and 8 are occupied. Suppose that the entries at positions 3 and 6 are removed. To remove these entries from the hash table, we store −1 at positions 3 and 6 in the array indexStatusList (see Figure 9-9).

	indexStatusList		HashTable
[0]	1	[0]	Mike
[1]	1	[1]	Gina
[2]	0	[2]	
[3]	−1	[3]	Goldy
[4]	0	[4]	
[5]	1	[5]	Ravi
[6]	−1	[6]	Danny
[7]	0	[7]	
[8]	1	[8]	Sheila
[9]	0	[9]	

FIGURE 9-9 Hash table and `indexStatusList` after removing the entries at positions 3 and 6

Hashing: Implementation Using Quadratic Probing

This section briefly describes how to design a class, as an ADT, to implement hashing using quadratic probing. To implement hashing, we use two arrays. One is used to store the data, and the other, `indexStatusList` as described in the previous section, is used to indicate whether a position in the hash table is free, occupied, or used previously. The following `class` template implements hashing as an ADT:

```
//**************************************************************
// Author: D.S. Malik
//
// This class specifies the members to implement a hash table as
// an ADT. It uses quadratic probing to resolve collisions.
//**************************************************************

template <class elemType>
class hashT
{
public:
    void insert(int hashIndex, const elemType& rec);
        //Function to insert an item in the hash table. The first
        //parameter specifies the initial hash index of the item to
        //be inserted. The item to be inserted is specified by the
        //parameter rec.
        //Postcondition: If an empty position is found in the hash
        //    table, rec is inserted and the length is incremented by
        //    one; otherwise, an appropriate error message is
        //    displayed.

    void search(int& hashIndex, const elemType& rec, bool& found) const;
        //Function to determine whether the item specified by the
        //parameter rec is in the hash table. The parameter hashIndex
        //specifies the initial hash index of rec.
        //Postcondition: If rec is found, found is set to true and
        //    hashIndex specifies the position where rec is found;
        //    otherwise, found is set to false.

    bool isItemAtEqual(int hashIndex, const elemType& rec) const;
        //Function to determine whether the item specified by the
        //parameter rec is the same as the item in the hash table
        //at position hashIndex.
        //Postcondition: Returns true if HTable[hashIndex] == rec;
        //    otherwise, returns false.

    void retrieve(int hashIndex, elemType& rec) const;
        //Function to retrieve the item at position hashIndex.
        //Postcondition: If the table has an item at position
        //    hashIndex, it is copied into rec.

    void remove(int hashIndex, const elemType& rec);
        //Function to remove an item from the hash table.
        //Postcondition: Given the initial hashIndex, if rec is found
```

9

```
//     in the table it is removed; otherwise, an appropriate
//     error message is displayed.

void print() const;
    //Function to output the data.

hashT(int size = 101);
    //constructor
    //Postcondition: Create the arrays HTTable and indexStatusList;
    //    initialize the array indexStatusList to 0; length = 0;
    //    HTSize = size; and the default array size is 101.

~hashT();
    //destructor
    //Postcondition: Array HTable and indexStatusList are deleted.

private:
    elemType *HTable;    //pointer to the hash table
    int *indexStatusList;  //pointer to the array indicating the
                            //status of a position in the hash table
    int length;      //number of items in the hash table
    int HTSize;      //maximum size of the hash table
};
```

We give the definition of only the function insert and leave the others as an exercise for you.

The definition of the function insert using quadratic probing is as follows:

```
template <class elemType>
void hashT<elemType>::insert(int hashIndex, const elemType& rec)
{
    int pCount;
    int inc;

    pCount = 0;
    inc = 1;

    while (indexStatusList[hashIndex] == 1
            && HTable[hashIndex] != rec && pCount < HTSize / 2)
    {
        pCount++;
        hashIndex = (hashIndex + inc) % HTSize;
        inc = inc + 2;
    }

    if (indexStatusList[hashIndex] != 1)
    {
        HTable[hashIndex] = rec;
        indexStatusList[hashIndex] = 1;
        length++;
    }
```

```
else if(HTable[hashIndex] == rec)
    cerr << "Error: No duplicates are allowed." << endl;
else
    cerr << "Error: The table is full. "
         << "Unable to resolve the collision." << endl;
}
```

Chaining

In chaining, the hash table, *HT*, is an array of pointers (see Figure 9-10). Therefore, for each j, where $0 \leq j \leq HTSize - 1$, $HT[j]$ is a pointer to a linked list. The size of the hash table, *HTSize*, is less than or equal to the number of items.

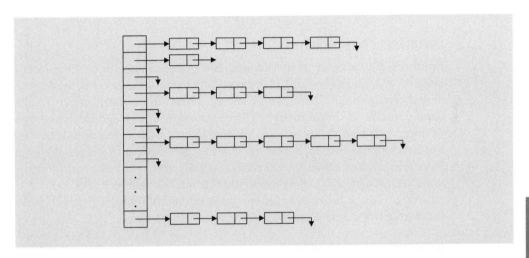

FIGURE 9-10 Linked hash table

ITEM INSERTION AND COLLISION

For each key X (in the item), we first find $h(X) = t$, where $0 \leq t \leq HTSize - 1$. The item with this key is then inserted in the linked list (which might be empty) pointed to by $HT[t]$. It then follows that for nonidentical keys X_1 and X_2, if $h(X_1) = h(X_2)$, the items with keys X_1 and X_2 are inserted in the same linked list and so collision is handled quickly and effectively. (A new item can be inserted at the beginning of the linked list because the data in a linked list is in no particular order.)

SEARCH

Suppose that we want to determine whether an item R with key X is in the hash table. As usual, first we calculate $h(X)$. Suppose $h(X) = t$. Then the linked list pointed to by $HT[t]$ is searched sequentially.

DELETION

To delete an item, say R, from the hash table, first we search the hash table to find where in a linked list R exists. We then adjust the pointers at the appropriate locations and deallocate the memory occupied by R.

OVERFLOW

Because data is stored in linked lists, overflow is no longer a concern because memory space to store the data is allocated dynamically. Furthermore, the size of the hash table no longer needs to be greater than the number of items. If the size of the hash table is less than the number of items, some of the linked lists contain more than one item. However, with a good hash function, the average length of a linked list is still small and so the search is efficient.

ADVANTAGES OF CHAINING

From the construction of the hash table using chaining, we see that item insertion and deletion are straightforward. If the hash function is efficient, few keys are hashed to the same home position. Thus, on average, a linked list is short, which results in a shorter search length. If the item size is large, it saves a considerable amount of space. For example, suppose there are 1000 items and each item requires 10 words of storage. Further suppose that each pointer requires one word of storage. We then need 1000 words for the hash table, 10,000 words for the items, and 1000 words for the link in each node. A total of 12,000 words of storage space, therefore, is required to implement chaining. On the other hand, if we use quadratic probing, if the hash table size is twice the number of items, we need 20,000 words of storage.

DISADVANTAGES OF CHAINING

If the item size is small, a considerable amount of space is wasted. For example, suppose there are 1000 items, each requiring 1 word of storage. Chaining then requires a total of 3000 words of storage. On the other hand, with quadratic probing, if the hash table size is twice the number of items, only 2000 words are required for the hash table. Also, if the table size is three times the number of items, then in quadratic probing the keys are reasonably spread out. This results in fewer collisions and so the search is fast.

Hashing Analysis

Let

$$\alpha = \frac{\text{Number of records in the table}}{HTSize}$$

The parameter α is called the **load factor**.

The average number of comparisons for a successful search and an unsuccessful search are given in Table 9-5.

TABLE 9-5 Number of comparisons in hashing

	Successful search	Unsuccessful search
Linear probing	$\dfrac{1}{2}\left\{1+\dfrac{1}{1-\alpha}\right\}$	$\dfrac{1}{2}\left\{1+\dfrac{1}{(1-\alpha)^2}\right\}$
Quadratic probing	$\dfrac{-\log_2(1-\alpha)}{\alpha}$	$\dfrac{1}{1-\alpha}$
Chaining	$1+\dfrac{\alpha}{2}$	α

QUICK REVIEW

1. A list is a set of elements of the same type.
2. The length of a list is the number of elements in the list.
3. A one-dimensional array is a convenient place to store and process lists.
4. The sequential search algorithm searches the list for a given item, starting with the first element in the list. It continues to compare the search item with the elements in the list until either the item is found or no more elements are left in the list with which it can be compared.
5. On average, the sequential search algorithm searches half the list.
6. For a list of length n, in a successful search, on average, the sequential search makes $(n + 1) / 2 = O(n)$ comparisons.
7. A sequential search is not efficient for large lists.
8. A binary search is much faster than a sequential search.
9. A binary search requires the list elements to be in order—that is, sorted.
10. For a list of length n, in a successful search, on average, the binary search makes $2 \log_2 n - 3 = O(\log_2 n)$ key comparisons.
11. Let L be a list of size $n > 1$. Suppose that the elements of L are sorted. If $SRH(n)$ is the minimum number of comparisons needed, in the worst case, by using a comparison-based algorithm to recognize whether an element x is in L, then $SRH(n) \geq \log_2(n + 1)$.
12. The binary search algorithm is the optimal worst-case algorithm for solving search problems by using the comparison method.
13. To construct a search algorithm of the order less than $\log_2 n$, it cannot be comparison based.
14. In hashing, the data is organized with the help of a table, called the hash table, denoted by HT. The hash table is stored in an array.

9

15. To determine whether a particular item with the key, say X, is in the hash table, we apply a function h, called the hash function, to the key X; that is, we compute $h(X)$, read as h of X. The function h is an arithmetic function, and $h(X)$ gives the address of the item in the hash table.

16. In hashing, because the address of an item is computed with the help of a function, it follows that the items are stored in no particular order.

17. Two keys X_1 and X_2, such that $X_1 \neq X_2$, are called synonyms if $h(X_1) = h(X_2)$.

18. Let X be a key and $h(X) = t$. If bucket t is full, we say that an overflow has occurred.

19. Let X_1 and X_2 be two nonidentical keys. If $h(X_1) = h(X_2)$, we say that a collision has occurred. If $r = 1$, that is, the bucket size is 1, an overflow and a collision occurs at the same time.

20. Collision resolution techniques are classified into two categories: open addressing (also called closed hashing) and chaining (also called open hashing).

21. In open addressing, data is stored within the hash table.

22. In chaining, the data is organized in linked lists, and the hash table is an array of pointers to the linked lists.

23. In linear probing, if a collision occurs at location t, then, starting at location t, we search the array sequentially to find the next available array slot.

24. In linear probing, we assume that the array is circular so that if the lower portion of the array is full, we can continue the search in the top portion of the array. If a collision occurs at location t, then starting at t, we check the array locations $t, t + 1, t + 2, \ldots, (t + j) \% HTSize$. This is called the probe sequence.

25. Linear probing causes clustering, called primary clustering.

26. In random probing, a random number generator is used to find the next available slot.

27. In rehashing, if a collision occurs with the hash function h, we use a series of hash functions.

28. In quadratic probing, if a collision occurs at position t, then starting at position t we linearly search the array at locations $(t + 1) \% HTSize$, $(t + 2^2) \% HTSize = (t + 4) \% HTSize$, $(t + 3^2) \% HTSize = (t + 9) \% HTSize$, $\ldots$, $(t + i^2) \% HTSize$. The probe sequence is: t, $(t + 1) \% HTSize$, $(t + 2^2) \% HTSize$, $(t + 3^2) \% HTSize$, $\ldots$, $(t + i^2) \% HTSize$.

29. Both random and quadratic probing eliminate primary clustering. However, if two nonidentical keys, say X_1 and X_2, are hashed to the same home position, that is, $h(X_1) = h(X_2)$, the same probe sequence is followed for both keys. This is because random probing and quadratic probing are functions of the home positions, not the original key. If the hash function causes a cluster at a particular home position, the cluster remains under these probings. This is called secondary clustering.

30. One way to solve secondary clustering is to use linear probing, wherein the increment value is a function of the key. This is called double hashing. In double hashing, if a collision occurs at $h(X)$, the probe sequence is generated by using the rule: $(h(X) + i \star g(X))$ % $HTSize$, where g is the second hash function.

31. In open addressing, when an item is deleted, its position in the array cannot be marked as empty.

32. In chaining, for each key X (in the item), first we find $h(X) = t$, where $0 \leq t \leq HTSize - 1$. The item with this key is then inserted in the linked list (which might be empty) pointed to by $HT[t]$.

33. In chaining, for nonidentical keys X_1 and X_2, if $h(X_1) = h(X_2)$, the items with keys X_1 and X_2 are inserted in the same linked list.

34. In chaining, to delete an item, say R, from the hash table, first we search the hash table to find where in the linked list R exists. Then we adjust the pointers at the appropriate locations and deallocate the memory occupied by R.

35. Let $\alpha = $ (Number of records in the table / $HTSize$). The parameter α is called the load factor.

36. In linear probing, the average number of comparisons in a successful search is $(1/2)\{1 + (1 / (1 - \alpha))\}$ and in an unsuccessful search is $(1/2)\{1 + (1 / (1 - \alpha)^2)\}$.

37. In quadratic probing, the average number of comparisons in a successful search is $(-\log_2(1 - \alpha)) / \alpha$ and in an unsuccessful search is $1 / (1 - \alpha)$.

38. In chaining, the average number of comparisons in a successful search is $(1 + \alpha / 2)$ and in an unsuccessful search is α.

9

EXERCISES

1. Mark the following statements as true or false.

   a. A sequential search of a list assumes that the list is in ascending order.

   b. A binary search of a list assumes that the list is sorted.

   c. A binary search is faster on ordered lists and slower on unordered lists.

   d. A binary search is faster on large lists, but a sequential search is faster on small lists.

2. Consider the following list: 63, 45, 32, 98, 46, 57, 28, 100

   Using the sequential search as described in this chapter, how many comparisons are required to find whether the following items are in the list? (Recall that by comparisons we mean item comparisons, not index comparisons.)

   a. 90

   b. 57

   c. 63

   d. 120

3. Write the definition of the class `orderedArrayListType` that implements the search algorithms for array-based lists as discussed in this chapter.

4. Consider the following list: 2, 10, 17, 45, 49, 55, 68, 85, 92, 98, 110

   Using the binary search as described in this chapter, how many comparisons are required to find whether the following items are in the list? Show the values of `first`, `last`, and `mid` and the number of comparisons after each iteration of the loop.

   a. 15

   b. 49

   c. 98

   d. 99

5. Suppose that the size of the hash table is 150 and the bucket size is 5. How many buckets are in the hash table, and how many items can a bucket hold?

6. Explain how collision is resolved using linear probing.

7. Explain how collision is resolved using quadratic probing.

8. What is double hashing?

9. Suppose that the size of the hash table is 101 and items are inserted in the table using quadratic probing. Also, suppose that a new item is to be inserted in the table and its hash address is 30. If position 30 in the hash table is occupied and the next four positions given by the probe sequence are also occupied, determine where in the table the item will be inserted.

10. Suppose that the size of the hash table is 101. Further suppose that certain keys with the indices 15, 101, 116, 0, and 217 are to be inserted in this order into an initially empty hash table. Using modular arithmetic, find the indices in the hash table if:

    a. Linear probing is used.

    b. Quadratic probing is used.

11. Suppose that 50 keys are to be inserted into an initially empty hash table using quadratic probing. What should be the size of the hash table to guarantee that all the collisions are resolved?

12. Suppose there are eight students with IDs 907354877, 193318608, 132489986, 134052069, 316500320, 106500319, 116510320, and 107354878. Suppose hash table, *HT*, is of the size 13, indexed 0,1,2, ..., 12. Show how these students' IDs, in the order given, are inserted in *HT* using the hashing function $h(k) = k \% 13$, where k is a student ID.

13. Suppose there are eight teachers with IDs 2733, 1409, 2731, 1541, 2004, 2101, 2168, and 1863. Suppose hash table, *HT*, is of the size 15, indexed 0, 1, 2, ..., 12. Show how these IDs are inserted in *HT* using the hashing function $h(k) = k \% 13$, where k is an ID.

14. Suppose there are eight students with IDs 197354883, 933185971, 132489992, 134152075, 216500325, 106500325, 216510325, 197354884. Suppose hash table, HT, is of the size 19, indexed 0, 1, 2, ..., 18. Show how these students' IDs, in the order given, are inserted in HT using the hashing function $h(k) = k \% 19$. Use linear probing to resolve collision.

15. Suppose there are six workers, in a workshop, with IDs 147, 169, 580, 216, 974, and 124. Suppose hash table, HT, is of the size 13, indexed 0, 1, 2, ..., 12. Show how these workers' IDs, in the order given, are inserted in HT using the hashing function $h(k) = k \% 13$. Use linear probing to resolve collision.

16. Suppose there are five workers, in a shop, with IDs 909, 185, 657, 116, and 150. Suppose hash table, HT, is of the size 7, indexed 0, 1, 2, ..., 6. Show how these workers' IDs, in the order given, are inserted in HT using the hashing function $h(k) = k \% 7$. Use linear probing to resolve collision.

17. Suppose there are seven students with IDs 5701, 9302, 4210, 9015, 1553, 9902, and 2104. Suppose hash table, HT, is of the size 19, indexed 0,1,2, ..., 18. Show how these students' IDs, in the order given, are inserted in HT using the hashing function $h(k) = k \% 19$. Use double hashing to resolve collision, where the second hash function is given by $g(k) = (k+1) \% 17$.

18. Suppose that an item is to be removed from a hash table that was implemented using linear or quadratic probing. Why wouldn't you mark the position of the item to be deleted as empty?

19. What are the advantages of open hashing?

20. Give a numerical example to show that collision resolution by quadratic probing is better than chaining.

21. Give a numerical example to show that collision resolution by chaining is better than quadratic probing.

22. Suppose that the size of the hash table is 1001 and the table has 850 items. What is the load factor?

23. Suppose that the size of the hash table is 1001 and the table has 750 items. On average, how many comparisons are made to determine whether an item is in the list if:

   a. Linear probing is used.

   b. Quadratic probing is used.

   c. Chaining is used.

24. Suppose that 550 items are to be stored in a hash table. If, on average, three key comparisons are needed to determine whether an item is in the table, what should be the size of the hash table if:

   a. Linear probing is used.

   b. Quadratic probing is used.

   c. Chaining is used.

9

PROGRAMMING EXERCISES

1. **(Recursive sequential search)** The sequential search algorithm given in Chapter 3 is nonrecursive. Write and implement a recursive version of the sequential search algorithm.

2. **(Recursive binary search)** The binary search algorithm given in this chapter is nonrecursive. Write and implement a recursive version of the binary search algorithm. Also, write a version of the sequential search algorithm that can be applied to sorted lists. Add this operation to the `class orderedArrayListType` for array-based lists. Moreover, write a test program to test your algorithm.

3. The sequential search algorithm as given in this chapter does not assume that the list is in order. Therefore, it usually works the same for both sorted and unsorted lists. However, if the elements of the list are sorted, you can somewhat improve the performance of the sequential search algorithm. For example, if the search item is not in the list, you can stop the search as soon as you find an element in the list that is larger than the search item. Write the function `seqOrdSearch` to implement a version of the sequential search algorithm for sorted lists. Add this function to the `class orderedArrayListType` and write a program to test it.

4. Write a program to find the number of comparisons using the binary search and sequential search algorithms as follows:

   Suppose list is an array of 1000 elements.

   a. Use a random number generator to fill list.

   b. Use any sorting algorithm to sort list. Alternatively, you can use the function `insertOrd` to initially insert all the elements in the list.

   c. Search the list for some items, as follows:

      i. Use the binary search algorithm to search the list. (You might need to modify the algorithm given in this chapter to count the number of comparisons.)

      ii. Use the binary search algorithm to search the list, switching to a sequential search when the size of the search list reduces to less than 15. (Use the sequential search algorithm for a sorted list.)

   d. Print the number of comparisons for Steps c.i and c.ii. If the item is found in the list, then print its position.

5. Write a program to test the function `insertOrd` that inserts an item into an array-based ordered list.

6. Write the function `removeOrd` that removes an item from an array-based ordered list. The item to be removed is passed as a parameter to this function. After removing the item, the resulting list must be ordered with no empty array positions between the elements. Add this function to the `class orderedArrayListType` and write a program to test it.

7. Write the definitions of the functions `search`, `isItemAtEqual`, `retrieve`, `remove`, and `print`, the constructor, and the destructor for the `class` `hashT`, as described in the section, "Hashing: Implementation Using Quadratic Probing," of this chapter. Also, write a program to test various hashing operations.

8. a. Some of the attributes of a state in the United States are its name, capital, area, year of admission to the union, and the order of admission to the union. Design the `class stateData` to keep track of the information for a state. Your class must include appropriate functions to manipulate the state's data, such as the functions `setStateInfo`, `getStateInfo`, and so on. Also, overload the relational operators to compare two states by their name. For easy input and output, overload the stream operators.

    b. Use the `class hashT` as described in the section, "Hashing: Implementation Using Quadratic Probing," which uses quadratic probing to resolve collision, to create a hash table to keep track of each state's information. Use the state's name as the key to determine the hash address. You may assume that a state's name is a string of no more than 15 characters.

    Test your program by searching for and removing certain states from the hash table.

    You may use the following hash function to determine the hash address of an item:

```
int hashFunc(string name)
{
    int i, sum;
    int len;

    i = 0;
    sum = 0;

    len = name.length();

    for (int k = 0; k < 15 - len; k++)
        name = name + ' ';   //increase the length of the name
                             //to 15 characters

    for (int k = 0; k < 5; k++)
    {
        sum = sum + static_cast<int>(name[i]) * 128 * 128
                  + static_cast<int>(name[i + 1]) * 128
                  + static_cast<int>(name[i + 2]);
        i = i + 3;
    }

    return sum % HTSize;
}
```

9

10
CHAPTER

SORTING ALGORITHMS

IN THIS CHAPTER, YOU WILL:

- Learn the various sorting algorithms
- Explore how to implement selection sort, insertion sort, Shellsort, quicksort, mergesort, and heapsort
- Discover how the sorting algorithms discussed in this chapter perform
- Learn how priority queues are implemented

Chapter 9 discussed the search algorithms on lists. A sequential search does not assume that the data is in any particular order; however, as noted, this search does not work efficiently for large lists. By contrast, a binary search is very fast for array-based lists, but it requires the data to be in order. Because a binary search requires the data to be in order and its performance is good for array-based lists, this chapter focuses on sorting algorithms.

Sorting Algorithms

There are several sorting algorithms in the literature. In this chapter, we discuss some of the most commonly used sorting algorithms. To compare the performance of these algorithms, we also provide the analysis of these algorithms. These sorting algorithms can be applied to either array-based lists or linked lists. We will specify whether the algorithm being developed is for array-based lists or linked lists.

The functions implementing these sorting algorithms are included as `public` members of the related class. (For example, for an array-based list, these are the members of the `class arrayListType`.) By doing so, the algorithms have direct access to the list elements.

Suppose that the sorting algorithm selection sort (described in the next section) is to be applied to array-based lists. The following statements show how to include selection sort as a member of the `class arrayListType`:

```
template <class elemType>
class arrayListType
{
public:
    void selectionSort();
    ...
};
```

Selection Sort: Array-Based Lists

In selection sort, a list is sorted by selecting elements in the list, one at a time, and moving them to their proper positions. This algorithm finds the location of the smallest element in the unsorted portion of the list and moves it to the top of the unsorted portion (that is, the whole list) of the list. The first time we locate the smallest item in the entire list, the second time we locate the smallest item in the list starting from the second element in the list, and so on. Selection sort described here is designed for array-based lists.

Suppose you have the list shown in Figure 10-1.

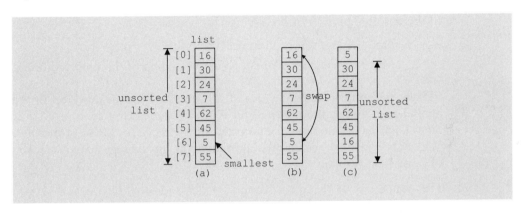

FIGURE 10-1 List of 8 elements

Figure 10-2 shows the elements of `list` in the first iteration.

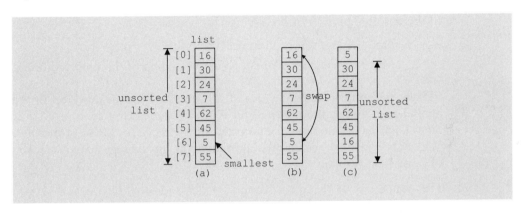

FIGURE 10-2 Elements of `list` during the first iteration

Initially, the entire list is unsorted. So we find the smallest item in the list. The smallest item is at position 6, as shown in Figure 10-2(a). Because this is the smallest item, it must be moved to position 0. So we swap 16 (that is, `list[0]`) with 5 (that is, `list[6]`), as shown in Figure 10-2(b). After swapping these elements, the resulting list is as shown in Figure 10-2(c).

Figure 10-3 shows the elements of `list` in the second iteration.

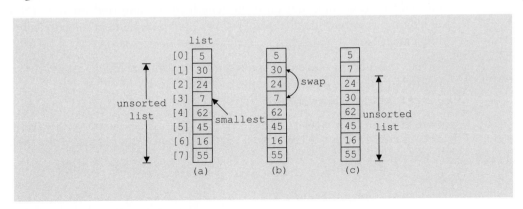

FIGURE 10-3 Elements of `list` during the second iteration

Now the unsorted list is `list[1]...list[7]`. So we find the smallest element in the unsorted list. The smallest element is at position 3, as shown in Figure 10-3(a). Because the smallest element in the unsorted list is at position 3, it must be moved to position 1. So we swap 7 (that is, `list[3]`) with 30 (that is, `list[1]`), as shown in Figure 10-3(b). After swapping `list[1]` with `list[3]`, the resulting list is as shown in Figure 10-3(c).

Now the unsorted list is `list[2]...list[7]`. So we repeat the preceding process of finding the (position of the) smallest element in the unsorted portion of the list and moving it to the beginning of the unsorted portion of the list. Selection sort, thus, involves the following steps.

In the unsorted portion of the list:

1. Find the location of the smallest element.
2. Move the smallest element to the beginning of the unsorted list.

Initially, the entire list, `list[0]...list[length-1]`, is the unsorted list. After executing Steps 1 and 2 once, the unsorted list is `list[1]...list[length-1]`. After executing Steps 1 and 2 a second time, the unsorted list is `list[2]...list[length-1]`, and so on. We can keep track of the unsorted portion of the list and repeat Steps a and b with the help of a `for` loop as follows:

```
for (index = 0; index < length - 1; index++)
{
    1. Find the location, smallestIndex, of the smallest element in
       list[index]...list[length - 1].
    2. Swap the smallest element with list[index]. That is, swap
       list[smallestIndex] with list[index].
}
```

The first time through the loop, we locate the smallest element in `list[0]...list[length-1]` and swap this smallest element with `list[0]`. The second time through the loop, we locate the smallest element in `list[1]...list[length-1]` and swap this smallest element with `list[1]`, and so on. This process continues until the length of the unsorted list is 1. (Note that a list of length 1 is sorted.) It, therefore, follows that to implement selection sort, we need to implement Steps 1 and 2.

Given the starting index, `first`, and the ending index, `last`, of the list, the following C++ function returns the index of the smallest element in `list[first]...list[last]`:

```
template <class elemType>
int arrayListType<elemType>::minLocation(int first, int last)
{
    int minIndex;

    minIndex = first;
```

```
for (int loc = first + 1; loc <= last; loc++)
    if( list[loc] < list[minIndex])
        minIndex = loc;

    return minIndex;
} //end minLocation
```

Given the locations in the list of the elements to be swapped, the following C++ function, swap, swaps those elements:

```
template <class elemType>
void arrayListType<elemType>::swap(int first, int second)
{
    elemType temp;

    temp = list[first];
    list[first] = list[second];
    list[second] = temp;
}//end swap
```

We can now complete the definition of the function selectionSort:

```
template <class elemType>
void arrayListType<elemType>::selectionSort()
{
    int minIndex;

    for (int loc = 0; loc < length - 1; loc++)
    {
        minIndex = minLocation(loc, length - 1);
        swap(loc, minIndex);
    }
}
```

You can add the functions to implement selection sort in the definition of the class arrayListType as follows:

```
template<class elemType>
class arrayListType
{
public:
    //Place the definitions of the function given earlier here.

    void selectionSort();
    ...

private:
    //Place the definitions of the members given earlier here.
    void swap(int first, int second);
    int minLocation(int first, int last);
};
```

EXAMPLE 10-1

The following program tests selection sort:

```
//****************************************************************
// Author: D.S. Malik
//
// This program illustrates how to use selection sort in a
// program.
//****************************************************************

#include <iostream>                                    //Line 1
#include "arrayListType.h"                              //Line 2

using namespace std;                                    //Line 3

int main()                                              //Line 4
{                                                       //Line 5
    arrayListType<int> list;                            //Line 6
    int num;                                            //Line 7

    cout << "Line 8: Enter numbers ending with -999"
         << endl;                                       //Line 8

    cin >> num;                                         //Line 9

    while (num != -999)                                 //Line 10
    {                                                   //Line 11
        list.insert(num);                               //Line 12
        cin >> num;                                     //Line 13
    }                                                   //Line 14

    cout << "Line 15: The list before sorting:" << endl; //Line 15
    list.print();                                       //Line 16
    cout << endl;                                       //Line 17

    list.selectionSort();                               //Line 18

    cout << "Line 19: The list after sorting:" << endl; //Line 19
    list.print();                                       //Line 20
    cout << endl;                                       //Line 21

    return 0;                                           //Line 22
}                                                       //Line 23
```

Sample Run: In this sample run, the user input is shaded.

```
Line 8: Enter numbers ending with -999
34 67 23 12 78 56 36 79 5 32 66 -999
Line 15: The list before sorting:
34 67 23 12 78 56 36 79 5 32 66
```

```
Line 19: The list after sorting:
5 12 23 32 34 36 56 66 67 78 79
```

For the most part, the preceding output is self-explanatory. Notice that the statement in Line 12 calls the function insert of the class arrayListType. Similarly, the statements in Lines 16 and 20 call the function print of the class arrayListType. The statement in Line 18 calls the function selectionSort to sort the list.

<table>
<tr><td>NOTE</td><td>

1. Selection sort can also be implemented by selecting the largest element in the (unsorted portion of the) list and moving it to the bottom of the list. You can easily implement this form of selection sort by altering the if statement in the function minLocation, and passing the appropriate parameters to the corresponding function and the function swap, when these functions are called in the function selectionSort.

2. Selection sort can also be applied to linked lists. The general algorithm is the same, and the details are left as an exercise for you. See Programming Exercise 1 at the end of this chapter.

</td></tr>
</table>

Analysis: Selection Sort

In the case of search algorithms (Chapter 9), our only concern was with the number of key (item) comparisons. A sorting algorithm makes key comparisons and also moves the data. Therefore, in analyzing the sorting algorithm, we look at the number of key comparisons as well as the number of data movements. Let us look at the performance of selection sort.

Suppose that the length of the list is n. The function swap does three item assignments and is executed $n - 1$ times. Hence, the number of item assignments is $3(n - 1)$.

The key comparisons are made by the function minLocation. For a list of length k, the function minLocation makes $k - 1$ key comparisons. Also, the function minLocation is executed $n - 1$ times (by the function selectionSort). The first time, the function minLocation finds the index of the smallest key item in the entire list and so makes $n - 1$ comparisons. The second time, the function minLocation finds the index of the smallest element in the sublist of length $n - 1$ and so makes $n - 2$ comparisons, and so on. Hence the number of key comparisons is as follows:

$$(n-1) + (n-2) + \cdots + 2 + 1 = (1/2)n(n-1) = (1/2)n^2 - (1/2)n = O(n^2)$$

Thus, it follows that if $n = 1000$, the number of key comparisons the selection sort makes is $1/2(1000^2) - 1/2(1000) = 499500 \approx 500000$.

Insertion Sort: Array-Based Lists

The previous section described and analyzed the selection sort algorithm. It was shown that if $n = 1000$, the number of key comparisons is approximately 500,000, which is quite high. This section describes the sorting algorithm called insertion sort, which tries to improve—that is, reduce—the number of key comparisons.

Insertion sort sorts the list by moving each element to its proper place. Consider the list given in Figure 10-4.

```
           [0] [1] [2] [3] [4] [5] [6] [7]
      list  10  18  25  30  23  17  45  35
```

FIGURE 10-4 `list`

The length of the list is 8. In this list, the elements `list[0]`, `list[1]`, `list[2]`, and `list[3]` are in order. That is, `list[0]...list[3]` is sorted, as shown in Figure 10-5(a).

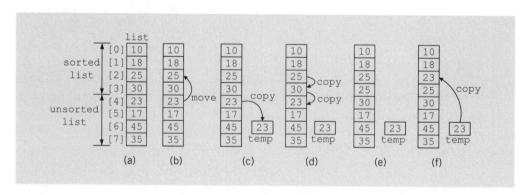

FIGURE 10-5 `list` elements while moving `list[4]` to its proper place

Next, we consider the element `list[4]`, the first element of the unsorted list. Because `list[4] < list[3]`, we need to move the element `list[4]` to its proper location. It follows that element `list[4]` should be moved to `list[2]`, as shown in Figure 10-5(b). To move `list[4]` into `list[2]`, first we copy `list[4]` into `temp`, a temporary memory space—see Figure 10-5(c).

Next, we copy `list[3]` into `list[4]`, and then `list[2]` into `list[3]`, as shown in Figure 10-5(d). After copying `list[3]` into `list[4]` and `list[2]` into `list[3]`, the list is as shown in Figure 10-5(e). Next we copy `temp` into `list[2]`. Figure 10-5(f) shows the resulting list.

Now `list[0]...list[4]` is sorted and `list[5]...list[7]` is unsorted. We repeat this process on the resulting list by moving the first element of the unsorted list into the sorted list in the proper place.

From this discussion, we see that during the sorting phase the array containing the list is divided into two sublists, upper and lower. Elements in the upper sublist are sorted; elements in the lower sublist are to be moved to the upper sublist in their proper places one at a time. We use an index—say, `firstOutOfOrder`—to point to the first element in the lower sublist; that is, `firstOutOfOrder` gives the index of the first element in the unsorted portion of the array. Initially, `firstOutOfOrder` is initialized to 1.

This discussion translates into the following pseudoalgorithm:

```
for (firstOutOfOrder = 1; firstOutOfOrder < length; firstOutOfOrder++)
  if (list[firstOutOfOrder] is less than list[firstOutOfOrder - 1])
  {
      copy list[firstOutOfOrder] into temp

      initialize location to firstOutOfOrder

      do
      {
          a. move list[location - 1] one array slot down
          b. decrement location by 1 to consider the next element
             sorted of the portion of the array
      }
      while (location > 0 && the element in the upper list at
             location - 1 is greater than temp)
  }
copy temp into list[location]
```

The length of this list is 8; that is, `length` = 8. We initialize `firstOutOfOrder` to 1 (see Figure 10-6).

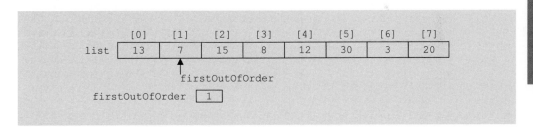

FIGURE 10-6 `firstOutOfOrder = 1`

Now `list[firstOutOfOrder]` = 7, `list[firstOutOfOrder - 1]` = 13 and 7 < 13, and the expression in the **if** statement evaluates to **true**, so we execute the body of the **if** statement.

```
temp = list[firstOutOfOrder] = 7
location = firstOutOfOrder = 1
```

Next, we execute the **do...while** loop.

```
list[1] = list[0] = 13    (copy list[0] into list[1])
location = 0              (decrement location)
```

The **do...while** loop terminates because `location = 0`. We copy `temp` into `list[location]`—that is, into `list[0]`. Figure 10-7 shows the resulting list.

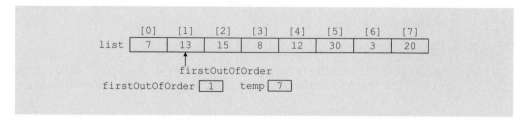

FIGURE 10-7 `list` after the first iteration of insertion sort

Now suppose that we have the list given in Figure 10-8(a).

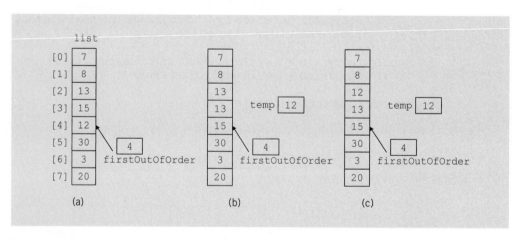

FIGURE 10-8 `list` elements while moving `list[4]` to its proper place

Here `list[0]...list[3]`, or the elements `list[0]`, `list[1]`, `list[2]`, and `list[3]`, are in order. Now `firstOutOfOrder = 4`. Because `list[4] < list[3]`, the element `list[4]`, which is 12, needs to be moved to its proper location.

As before:

```
temp = list[firstOutOfOrder] = 12
location = firstOutOfOrder = 4
```

First, we copy `list[3]` into `list[4]` and decrement `location` by 1. Then we copy `list[2]` into `list[3]` and again decrement `location` by 1. Now the value of `location` is 2. At this point, the list is as shown in Figure 10-8(b).

Next, because list[1] < temp, the **do...while** loop terminates. At this point, location is 2, so we copy temp into list[2]. That is, list[2] = temp = 12. Figure 10-8(c) shows the resulting list.

Suppose that we have the list given in Figure 10-9.

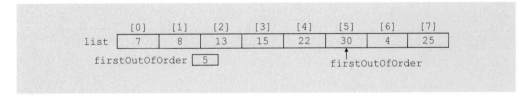

FIGURE 10-9 First out-of-order element is at position 5

Here list[0]...list[4], or the elements list[0], list[1], list[2], list[3], and list[4], are in order. Now firstOutOfOrder = 5. Because list[5] > list[4], the **if** statement evaluates to **false**. So the body of the **if** statement does not execute and the next iteration of the **for** loop, if any, takes place. Note that this is the case when the firstOutOfOrder element is already at the proper place. So we simply need to advance firstOutOfOrder to the next array element, if any.

We can repeat this process for the remaining elements of list to sort list.

The following C++ function implements the previous algorithm:

```
template <class elemType>
void arrayListType<elemType>::insertionSort()
{
    int firstOutOfOrder, location;
    elemType temp;

    for (firstOutOfOrder = 1; firstOutOfOrder < length;
                              firstOutOfOrder++)
        if (list[firstOutOfOrder] < list[firstOutOfOrder - 1])
        {
            temp = list[firstOutOfOrder];
            location = firstOutOfOrder;

            do
            {
                list[location] = list[location - 1];
                location--;
            }
            while (location > 0 && list[location - 1] > temp);

            list[location] = temp;
        }
} //end insertionSort
```

1
0

Insertion Sort: Linked List-Based Lists

Insertion sort can also be applied to linked lists. Therefore, this section describes insertion sort for linked lists. Consider the linked list shown in Figure 10-10.

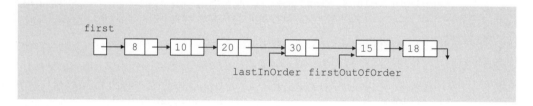

FIGURE 10-10 Linked list

In Figure 10-10, `first` is a pointer to the first node of the linked list.

If the list is stored in an array, we can traverse the list in either direction using an index variable. However, if the list is stored in a linked list, we can traverse the list in only one direction starting at the first node because the links are only in one direction, as shown in Figure 10-10. Therefore, in the case of a linked list, to find the location of the node to be inserted, we do the following. Suppose that `firstOutOfOrder` is a pointer to the node that is to be moved to its proper location, and `lastInOrder` is a pointer to the last node of the sorted portion of the list. For example, see the linked list in Figure 10-11. (We assume that the nodes are in the usual `info-link` form as described in Chapter 5.)

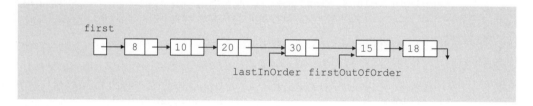

FIGURE 10-11 Linked list and pointers `lastInOrder` and `firstOutOfOrder`

First, we compare the `info` of `firstOutOfOrder` with the `info` of the first node. If the `info` of `firstOutOfOrder` is smaller than the `info` of `first`, then the node `firstOutOfOrder` is to be moved before the first node of the list; otherwise, we search the list starting at the second node to find the location where to move `firstOutOfOrder`. As usual, we search the list using two pointers, for example `current` and `trailCurrent`. The pointer `trailCurrent` points to the node just before `current`. In this case, the node `firstOutOfOrder` is to be moved between `trailCurrent` and `current`. Of course, we also handle any special cases such as an empty list, a list with only one node, or a list in which the node `firstOutOfOrder` is already in the proper place.

This discussion translates into the following algorithm:

```
if (firstOutOfOrder->info is less than first->info)
    move firstOutOfOrder before first
else
{
    set trailCurrent to first
    set current to the second node in the list first->link;

     //search the list
    while (current->info is less than firstOutOfOrder->info)
    {
        advance trailCurrent;
        advance current;
    }

    if (current is not equal to firstOutOfOrder)
    {    //insert firstOutOfOrder between current and trailCurrent
        lastInOrder->link = firstOutOfOrder->link;
        firstOutOfOrder->link = current;
        trailCurrent->link = firstOutOfOrder;
    }
    else    //firstOutOfOrder is already at the first place
        lastInOrder = lastInOrder->link;
}
```

Let us illustrate this algorithm on the list shown in Figure 10-12. We consider several cases.

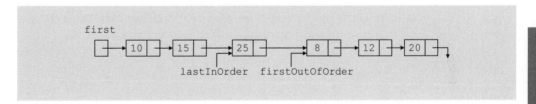

FIGURE 10-12 Linked list and pointers `lastInOrder` and `firstOutOfOrder`

Case 1: Because `firstOutOfOrder->info` is less than `first->info`, the node `firstOutOfOrder` is to be moved before `first`. So we adjust the necessary links, and Figure 10-13 shows the resulting list.

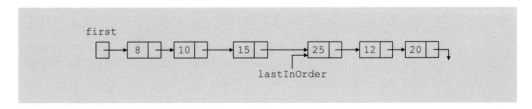

FIGURE 10-13 Linked list after moving the node with `info` 8 to the beginning

Case 2: Consider the list shown in Figure 10-14.

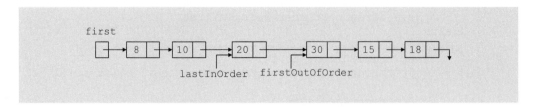

FIGURE 10-14 Linked list and pointers `lastInOrder` and `firstOutOfOrder`

Because `firstOutOfOrder->info` is greater than `first->info`, we search the list to find the place where `firstOutOfOrder` is to be moved. As explained previously, we use the pointers `trailCurrent` and `current` to traverse the list. For this list, these pointers end up at the nodes as shown in Figure 10-15.

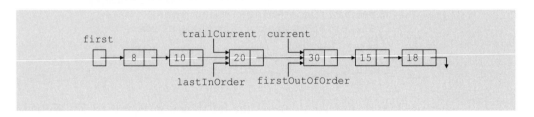

FIGURE 10-15 Linked list and pointers `trailCurrent` and `current`

Because `current` is the same as `firstOutOfOrder`, the node `firstOutOfOrder` is in the right place. So no adjustment of the links is necessary.

Case 3: Consider the list in Figure 10-16.

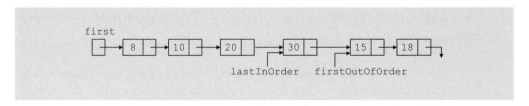

FIGURE 10-16 Linked list and pointers `lastInOrder` and `firstOutOfOrder`

Because `firstOutOfOrder->info` is greater than `first->info`, we search the list to find the place where `firstOutOfOrder` is to be moved. As in Case 2, we use the pointers `trailCurrent` and `current` to traverse the list. For this list, these pointers end up at the nodes as shown in Figure 10-17.

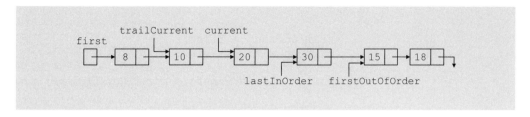

FIGURE 10-17 Linked list and pointers `trailCurrent` and `current`

Now, `firstOutOfOrder` is to be moved between `trailCurrent` and `current`. So we adjust the necessary links and obtain the list as shown in Figure 10-18.

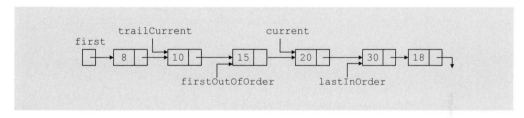

FIGURE 10-18 Linked list after moving `firstOutOfOrder` between `trailCurrent` and `current`

We now write the C++ function, `linkedInsertionSort`, to implement the previous algorithm:

```cpp
template <class elemType>
void unorderedLinkedList<elemType>::linkedInsertionSort()
{
    nodeType<elemType> *lastInOrder;
    nodeType<elemType> *firstOutOfOrder;
    nodeType<elemType> *current;
    nodeType<elemType> *trailCurrent;

    lastInOrder = first;

    if (first == NULL)
        cerr << "Cannot sort an empty list." << endl;
    else if (first->link == NULL)
        cout << "The list is of length 1. "
             << "It is already in order." << endl;
    else
        while (lastInOrder->link != NULL)
        {
            firstOutOfOrder = lastInOrder->link;

            if (firstOutOfOrder->info < first->info)
            {
                lastInOrder->link = firstOutOfOrder->link;
                firstOutOfOrder->link = first;
                first = firstOutOfOrder;
            }
```

```
        else
        {
            trailCurrent = first;
            current = first->link;

            while (current->info < firstOutOfOrder->info)
            {
                trailCurrent = current;
                current = current->link;
            }

            if (current != firstOutOfOrder)
            {
                lastInOrder->link = firstOutOfOrder->link;
                firstOutOfOrder->link = current;
                trailCurrent->link = firstOutOfOrder;
            }
            else
                lastInOrder = lastInOrder->link;
        }
    } //end while
} //end linkedInsertionSort
```

We leave it as exercise for you to write a program to test insertion sort. See Programming Exercises 2 and 3 at the end of this chapter.

Analysis: Insertion Sort

Suppose that the list is of length n. If the list is sorted, the number of comparisons is $(n - 1)$ and the number of item assignments is 0. This is the best case. (See Exercise 15 at the end of this chapter.) Now suppose that the list is sorted, but in the reverse order. In this case, it can be checked that the number of comparisons is $(1/2)(n^2 - n)$ and the number of item assignments is $(1/2)(n^2 + 3n) - 2$. This is the worst case. (See Exercise 14 at the end of this chapter.)

Table 10-1 summarizes the average-case behavior of selection and insertion sort. The proofs of the results of insertion sort are given in Appendix F.

TABLE 10-1 Average-case behavior of the selection sort and insertion sort for a list of length n

Algorithm	Number of comparisons	Number of swaps/item assignments
Selection sort	$(1/2)n(n - 1) = O(n^2)$	$3(n - 1) = O(n)$
Insertion sort	$(1/4)n^2 + O(n) = O(n^2)$	$(1/4)n^2 + O(n) = O(n^2)$

Shellsort

In the previous sections, we described selection sort and insertion sort. We noticed that selection sort makes more comparisons and less item movements than insertion sort. Selection sort makes more comparisons because it makes many redundant comparisons. The number of item movements in selection sort is less because each item is moved at most one time. In fact, the number of item movements in insertion sort is considerably more than selection sort because it moves items one position at a time, so to move an item to its final position, it might require many movements.

We can reduce the number of item movements in insertion sort by modifying it. The modified insertion sort that we present next was introduced in 1959 by D. E. Shell and is known as the Shellsort algorithm. This sort is also known as **diminishing–increment sort**.

In Shellsort, the elements of the list are viewed as sublists at a particular distance. Each sublist is sorted, so that elements that are far apart move closer to their final position. For example, suppose that you have a list of 15 elements, as shown in Figure 10-19. First we view the list as 7 sublists, that is, we sort the elements at a distance of 7. Note that several elements have moved closer to their final position. For example, 2, 19, and 60 are closer to their final position. In the next iteration, we sort the elements at a distance of 4, as shown in Figure 10-19(b). Finally, we sort the elements at a distance of 1, that is, the entire list is sorted. Figure 10-19(c) shows the elements before and after the final sorting phase.

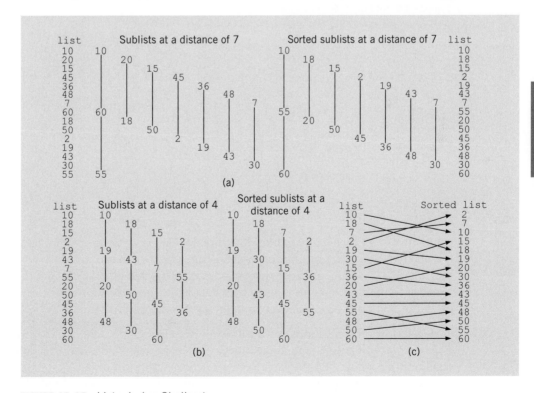

FIGURE 10-19 Lists during Shellsort

In Figure 10-19, we sorted the elements at a distance of 7, 4, and then 1. The sequence 1, 4, 7 is called the **increment sequence**. How do we choose an increment sequence? In general, this question cannot be answered satisfactorily. The literature provides a discussion of various increment sequences, and some have been found to be useful. Typically, the increment sequences are chosen to decrease roughly geometrically so that the number of increments is logarithmic in the size of the list. For example, if the number of increments is about one-half of the previous increment, then we need at most 20 increments to sort a list of 1 million elements. However, using as few increments as possible is desirable.

D. E. Knuth recommended the increment sequence 1, 4, 13, 40, 121, 364, 1093, 3280, ... The ratio between successive increments is about one-third. In fact, the ith increment = $3 \bullet (i - 1)$th increment + 1. There are many other increment sequences that could lead to more efficient sorts. However, for large lists, it is difficult to get a better performance by more than 20% than the increment sequence recommended by Knuth.

There are certain increment sequences that must be avoided. For example, the increment sequence, 1, 2, 4, 8, 16, 32, 64, 128, 256, ..., is likely to lead to a bad performance because elements at odd positions are not compared with the elements at even positions until the final pass. We will use the increment sequence suggested by Knuth in the Shellsort algorithm we implement.

This following function implements the Shellsort algorithm:

```
template <class elemType>
void arrayListType<elemType>::shellSort()
{
    int inc;

    for (inc = 1; inc < (length - 1) / 9; inc = 3 * inc + 1);

    do
    {
        for (int begin = 0; begin < inc; begin++)
            intervalInsertionSort(begin, inc);

        inc = inc / 3;
    }
    while (inc > 0);
} //end shellSort
```

In the function `shellSort`, we use the function `intervalInsertionSort`, which is a modified version of insertion sort for array-based lists, discussed earlier in this chapter. In the `intervalInsertionSort`, the sublist starts at the variable `begin`, and the increment between successive elements is given by the variable `inc` instead of 1. We leave the details of the function `intervalInsertionSort` as an exercise for you.

The analysis of the Shellsort is difficult to obtain. In fact, to date, good estimates of the number of comparisons and item movements have been obtained only under special conditions depending on the increment sequence. Empirical studies suggest that for large lists of size n, the number of moves is in the range of $n^{1.25}$ to $1.6n^{1.25}$, which is a considerable improvement over insertion sort.

Lower Bound on Comparison-Based Sort Algorithms

The previous sections discussed selection sort and insertion sort, and noted that the average-case behavior of these algorithms is $O(n^2)$. Both of these algorithms are comparison-based algorithms; that is, the lists are sorted by comparing their respective keys. Before discussing any additional sorting algorithms, let us discuss the best-case scenario for the comparison-based sorting algorithms.

We can trace the execution of a comparison-based algorithm using a graph called a **comparison tree**. Let L be a list of n distinct elements, where $n > 0$. For any j and k, where $1 \leq j, k \leq n$, either $L[j] < L[k]$ or $L[j] > L[k]$. Because each comparison of the keys has two outcomes, the comparison tree is a binary tree. While drawing this figure, we draw each comparison as a circle, called a **node**. The node is labeled as $j:k$, representing the comparison of $L[j]$ with $L[k]$. If $L[j] < L[k]$, follow the left branch; otherwise, follow the right branch. Figure 10-20 shows the comparison tree for a list of length 3. (In Figure 10-20, the rectangle, called **leaf**, represents the final ordering of the nodes.)

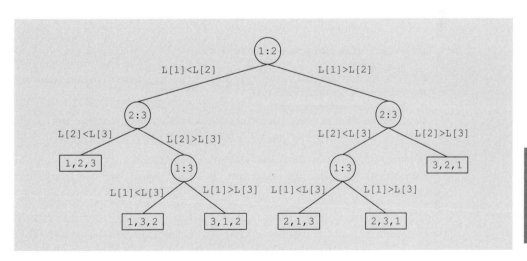

FIGURE 10-20 Comparison tree for sorting three items

We call the top node in the figure the **root** node. The straight line that connects the two nodes is called a **branch**. A sequence of branches from a node, x, to another node, y, is called a **path** from x to y.

Associated with each path from the root to a leaf is a unique permutation of the elements of L. This uniqueness follows because the sort algorithm only moves the data and makes comparisons. Furthermore, the data movement on any path from the root to a leaf is the same regardless of the initial inputs. For a list of n elements, $n > 0$, there are $n!$ different permutations. Any one of these $n!$ permutations might be the correct ordering of L. Thus, the comparison tree must have at least $n!$ leaves.

Let us consider the worst case for all comparison-based sorting algorithms. We state the following result without proof.

Theorem: Let L be a list of n distinct elements. Any sorting algorithm that sorts L by comparison of the keys only, in its worst case, makes at least $O(n\log_2 n)$ key comparisons.

As analyzed in the previous sections, both selection sort and insertion sort are of the order $O(n^2)$. The remainder of this chapter discusses sorting algorithms that, on average, are of the order $O(n\log_2 n)$.

Quicksort: Array-Based Lists

In the previous section, we noted that the lower bound on comparison-based algorithms is $O(n\log_2 n)$. The sorting algorithms selection sort and insertion sort, discussed earlier in this chapter, are $O(n^2)$. In this and the next two sections, we discuss sorting algorithms that are usually of the order $O(n\log_2 n)$. The first algorithm is quicksort.

Quicksort uses the divide-and-conquer technique to sort a list. The list is partitioned into two sublists, and the two sublists are then sorted and combined into one list in such a way so that the combined list is sorted. Thus, the general algorithm is as follows:

```
if (the list size is greater than 1)
{
    a. Partition the list into two sublists, say lowerSublist and upperSublist.
    b. Quicksort lowerSublist.
    c. Quicksort upperSublist.
    d. Combine the sorted lowerSublist and sorted upperSublist.
}
```

After partitioning the list into two sublists—`lowerSublist` and `upperSublist`—these two sublists are sorted using quicksort. In other words, we use *recursion* to implement quicksort.

Quicksort described here is for array-based lists. The algorithm for linked lists can be developed in a similar manner and is left as an exercise for you. See Programming Exercise 7 at the end of this chapter.

In quicksort, the list is partitioned in such a way that combining the sorted `lowerSublist` and `upperSublist` is trivial. Therefore, in quicksort, all the sorting work is done in partitioning the list. Because all the sorting work occurs during the partition, we first describe the partition procedure in detail.

To partition the list into two sublists, first we choose an element of the list called the **pivot**. The `pivot` is used to divide the list into two sublists: the `lowerSublist` and the `upperSublist`. The elements in the `lowerSublist` are smaller than the `pivot`, and the elements in the `upperSublist` are greater than the `pivot`. For example, consider the list in Figure 10-21.

	[0]	[1]	[2]	[3]	[4]	[5]	[6]	[7]	[8]
list	45	82	25	94	50	60	78	32	92

FIGURE 10-21 `list` before the partition

There are several ways to determine the `pivot`. However, the `pivot` is chosen so that, it is hoped, the `lowerSublist` and `upperSublist` are of nearly equal size. For illustration purposes, let us choose the middle element of the list as the `pivot`. The partition procedure that we describe partitions this list using the `pivot` as the middle element, in our case 50, as shown in Figure 10-22.

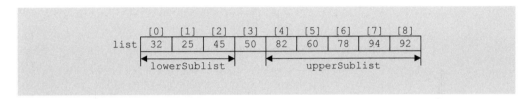

FIGURE 10-22 `list` after the partition

From Figure 10-22, it follows that after partitioning `list` into `lowerSublist` and `upperSublist`, the `pivot` is in the right place. Thus, after sorting `lowerSublist` and `upperSublist`, combining the two sorted sublists is trivial.

The partition algorithm is as follows: (We assume that `pivot` is chosen as the middle element of the list.)

1. Determine the `pivot`, and swap the `pivot` with the first element of the list.

    Suppose that the index `smallIndex` points to the last element smaller than the `pivot`. The index `smallIndex` is initialized to the first element of the list.

2. For the remaining elements in the list (starting at the second element) If the current element is smaller than the `pivot`

    a. Increment `smallIndex`.

    b. Swap the current element with the array element pointed to by `smallIndex`.

3. Swap the first element, that is, the `pivot`, with the array element pointed to by `smallIndex`.

Step 2 can be implemented using a `for` loop, with the loop starting at the second element of the list.

Step 1 determines the `pivot` and moves the `pivot` in the first array position. During the execution of Step 2, the elements of the list get arranged as shown in Figure 10-23. (Suppose the name of the array containing the list elements is `list`.)

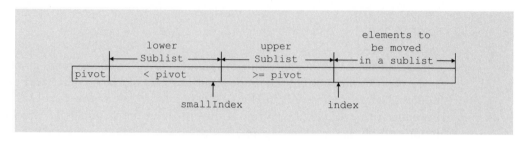

FIGURE 10-23 List during the execution of Step 2

As shown in Figure 10-23, the `pivot` is in the first array position, elements in `lowerSublist` are less than the `pivot`, and elements in the `upperSublist` are greater than or equal to the `pivot`. The variable `smallIndex` contains the index of the last element of `lowerSublist` and the variable `index` contains the index of the next element that needs to be moved either in `lowerSublist` or in `upperSublist`. As explained in Step 2, if the next element of the list (that is, `list[index]`) is less than the `pivot`, we advance `smallIndex` to the next array position and swap `list[index]` with `list[smallIndex]`. Next we illustrate Step 2.

Suppose that `list` is as given in Figure 10-24.

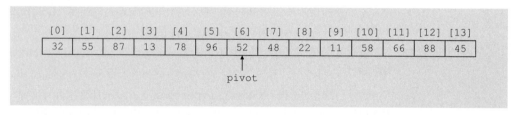

FIGURE 10-24 `list` before sorting

For the list in Figure 10-24, the `pivot` is at position 6. After moving the `pivot` at the first array position, the list is shown in Figure 10-25. (Notice that in Figure 10-25, 52 is swapped with 32.)

[0]	[1]	[2]	[3]	[4]	[5]	[6]	[7]	[8]	[9]	[10]	[11]	[12]	[13]
52	55	87	13	78	96	32	48	22	11	58	66	88	45

pivot

FIGURE 10-25 List after moving `pivot` at the first array position

Suppose that after executing Step 2 a few times, the list is as shown in Figure 10-26.

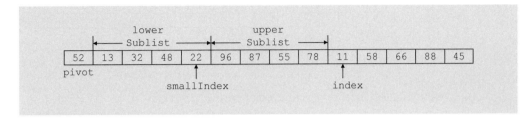

FIGURE 10-26 List after a few iterations of Step 2

As shown in Figure 10-26, the next element of the list that needs to be moved in a sublist is indicated by `index`. Because `list[index] < pivot`, we need to move the element `list[index]` in `lowerSublist`. To do so, we first advance `smallIndex` to the next array position and then swap `list[smallIndex]` with `list[index]`. The resulting list is shown in Figure 10-27. (Notice that 11 is swapped with 96.)

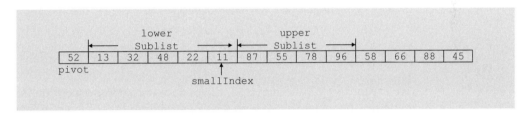

FIGURE 10-27 List after moving 11 into `lowerSublist`

Now consider the list in Figure 10-28.

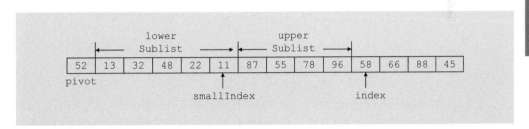

FIGURE 10-28 List before moving 58 into a sublist

For the list in Figure 10-28, `list[index]` is 58, which is greater than the `pivot`. Therefore, `list[index]` is to be moved in `upperSublist`. This is accomplished by leaving 58 at its position and increasing the size of `upperSublist`, by one, to the next array position. After moving 58 into `upperSublist`, the list is as shown in Figure 10-29.

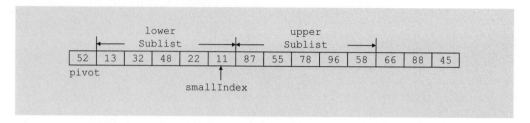

FIGURE 10-29 List after moving 58 into upperSublist

After moving the elements that are less than the pivot into lowerSublist and elements that are greater than the pivot into upperSublist (that is, after completely executing Step 2), the resulting list is as shown in Figure 10-30.

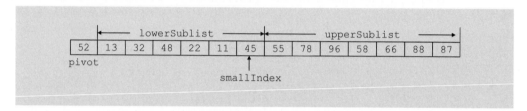

FIGURE 10-30 List elements after arranging into lowerSublist and upperSublist

Next, we execute Step 3 and move 52, the pivot, to the proper position in the list. This is accomplished by swapping 52 with 45. The resulting list is shown in Figure 10-31.

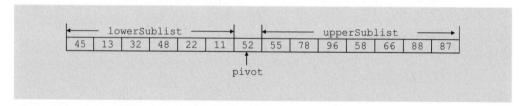

FIGURE 10-31 List after swapping 52 with 45

As shown in Figure 10-31, the preceding algorithm, Steps 1, 2, and 3, partitions the list into two sublists such that the elements less than the pivot are in lowerSublist and elements greater than or equal to the pivot are in upperSublist.

To partition the list into the lower and upper sublists, we only need to keep track of the last element of the lowerSublist and the next element of the list that needs to be moved either in lowerSublist or in upperSublist. In fact, upperSublist is between the two indices smallIndex and index.

We now write the function, partition, to implement the preceding partition algorithm. After rearranging the elements of the list, the function returns the location of the pivot so that we can determine the starting and ending locations of the sublists. Also, because the function partition will be a member of the class, it has direct access to the array containing the list. Thus, to partition a list, we need to pass only the starting and ending indices of the list.

```
template <class elemType>
int arrayListType<elemType>::partition(int first, int last)
{
    elemType pivot;

    int index, smallIndex;

    swap(first, (first + last) / 2);

    pivot = list[first];
    smallIndex = first;

    for (index = first + 1; index <= last; index++)
        if (list[index] < pivot)
        {
            smallIndex++;
            swap(smallIndex, index);
        }

    swap(first, smallIndex);

    return smallIndex;
}
```

As you can see from the definition of the function partition, certain elements of the list need to be swapped. The following function, swap, accomplishes this task:

```
template <class elemType>
void arrayListType<elemType>::swap(int first, int second)
{
    elemType temp;

    temp = list[first];
    list[first] = list[second];
    list[second] = temp;
}
```

Once the list is partitioned into lowerSublist and upperSublist, we again apply the quicksort method to sort the two sublists. Because both sublists are sorted using the same quicksort algorithm, the easiest way to implement this algorithm is to use recursion. Therefore, this section gives the recursive version of quicksort. As explained previously, after rearranging the elements of the list, the function partition returns the index of the pivot so that the starting and ending indices of the sublists can be determined.

Given the starting and ending indices of a list, the following function, recQuickSort, implements the recursive version of quicksort:

```
template <class elemType>
void arrayListType<elemType>::recQuickSort(int first, int last)
{
    int pivotLocation;

    if (first < last)
    {
        pivotLocation = partition(first, last);
        recQuickSort(first, pivotLocation - 1);
        recQuickSort(pivotLocation + 1, last);
    }
}
```

Finally, we write the quicksort function, `quickSort`, that calls the function recQuickSort of the original list:

```
template <class elemType>
void arrayListType<elemType>::quickSort()
{
    recQuickSort(0, length -1);
}
```

We leave it as an exercise for you to write a program to test quicksort. See Programming Exercise 7 at the end of this chapter.

Analysis: Quicksort

Table 10-2 summarizes the behavior of quicksort for a list of length n. (The proofs of these results are given in Appendix F.)

TABLE 10-2 Analysis of quicksort for a list of length n

	Number of comparisons	Number of swaps
Average case	$1.39n\log_2 n + O(n) = O(n\log_2 n)$	$0.69n\log_2 n + O(n) = O(n\log_2 n)$
Worst case	$(1/2)(n^2 - n) = O(n^2)$	$(1/2)n^2 + (3/2)n - 2 = O(n^2)$

Mergesort: Linked List-Based Lists

In the previous section, we described quicksort and stated that the average-case behavior of quicksort is $O(n\log_2 n)$. However, the worst-case behavior of quicksort is $O(n^2)$. This section describes a sorting algorithm whose behavior is always $O(n\log_2 n)$.

Like quicksort, mergesort uses the divide-and-conquer technique to sort a list. Mergesort also partitions the list into two sublists, sorts the sublists, and then combines the sorted sublists into one sorted list. This section describes mergesort for linked list-based lists.

We leave it for you to develop mergesort for array-based lists, which can be done by using the techniques described for linked lists.

Mergesort and quicksort differ in how they partition the list. As discussed earlier, quicksort first selects an element in the list, called `pivot`, and then partitions the list so that the elements in one sublist are less than `pivot` and the elements in the other sublist are greater than or equal to `pivot`. By contrast, mergesort divides the list into two sublists of nearly equal size. For example, consider the list whose elements are as follows:

`list: 35  28  18  45  62  48  30  38`

Mergesort partitions this list into two sublists as follows:

`first sublist: 35  28  18  45`
`second sublist: 62  48  30  38`

The two sublists are sorted using the same algorithm (that is, mergesort) used on the original list. Suppose that we have sorted the two sublists. That is, suppose that the lists are now as follows:

`first sublist: 18  28  35  45`
`second sublist: 30  38  48  62`

Next, mergesort combines, that is, merges, the two sorted sublists into one sorted list.

Figure 10-32 further illustrates the mergesort process.

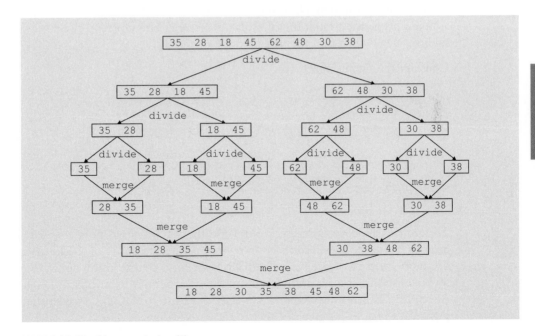

FIGURE 10-32 Mergesort algorithm

From Figure 10-32, it is clear that in mergesort, most of the sorting work is done in merging the sorted sublists.

The general algorithm for mergesort is as follows:

```
if the list is of a size greater than 1
{
    1. Divide the list into two sublists.
    2. Mergesort the first sublist.
    3. Mergesort the second sublist.
    4. Merge the first sublist and the second sublist.
}
```

As remarked previously, after dividing the list into two sublists—the first sublist and the second sublist—these two sublists are sorted using mergesort. In other words, we use recursion to implement mergesort.

We next describe the necessary algorithm to:

- Divide the list into two sublists of nearly equal size.
- Mergesort both sublists.
- Merge the sorted sublists.

Divide

Because data is stored in a linked list, we do not know the length of the list. Furthermore, a linked list is not a random access data structure. Therefore, to divide the list into two sublists, we need to find the middle node of the list.

Consider the list in Figure 10-33.

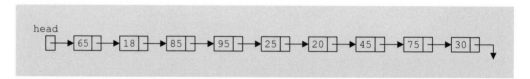

FIGURE 10-33 Unsorted linked list

To find the middle of the list, we traverse the list with two pointers—say, `middle` and `current`. The pointer `middle` is initialized to the first node of the list. Because this list has more than two nodes, we initialize `current` to the third node. (Recall that we sort the list only if it has more than one element because a list of size 1 is already sorted. Also, if the list has only two nodes, we set `current` to `NULL`.) Consider the list shown in Figure 10-34.

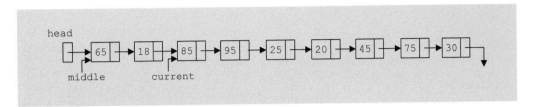

FIGURE 10-34 `middle` and `current` before traversing the list

Every time we advance `middle` by one node, we advance `current` by one node. After advancing `current` by one node, if `current` is not NULL, we again advance `current` by one node. That is, for the most part, every time `middle` advances by one node, `current` advances by two nodes. Eventually, `current` becomes NULL and `middle` points to the last node of the first sublist. For example, for the list in Figure 10-34, when `current` becomes NULL, `middle` points to the node with `info` 25 (see Figure 10-35).

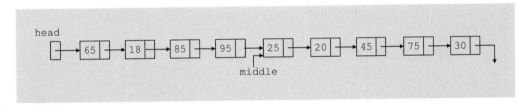

FIGURE 10-35 `middle` after traversing the list

It is now easy to divide the list into two sublists. First, using the link of `middle`, we assign a pointer to the node following `middle`. Then we set the link of `middle` to NULL. Figure 10-36 shows the resulting sublists.

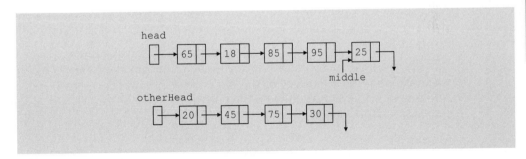

FIGURE 10-36 List after dividing it into two lists

This discussion translates into the following C++ function, `divideList`:

```
template <class Type>
void unorderedLinkedList<Type>::
              divideList(nodeType<Type>* first1,
                    nodeType<Type>* &first2)
```

```
{
    nodeType<Type>* middle;
    nodeType<Type>* current;

    if (first1 == NULL)    //list is empty
        first2 = NULL;
    else if (first1->link == NULL)   //list has only one node
        first2 = NULL;
    else
    {
        middle = first1;
        current = first1->link;

        if (current != NULL)     //list has more than two nodes
            current = current->link;
        while (current != NULL)
        {
            middle = middle->link;
            current = current->link;
            if (current != NULL)
                current = current->link;
        } //end while

        first2 = middle->link;  //first2 points to the first
                                //node of the second sublist
        middle->link = NULL;    //set the link of the last node
                                //of the first sublist to NULL
    } //end else
} //end divideList
```

Now that we know how to divide a list into two sublists of nearly equal size, next we focus on merging the sorted sublists. Recall that, in mergesort, most of the sorting work is done in merging the sorted sublists.

Merge

Once the sublists are sorted, the next step in mergesort is to merge the sorted sublists. Sorted sublists are merged into a sorted list by comparing the elements of the sublists, and then adjusting the references of the nodes with the smaller info. Let us illustrate this procedure on the sublists shown in Figure 10-37. Suppose that first1 points to the first node of the first sublist, and first2 points to the first node of the second sublist.

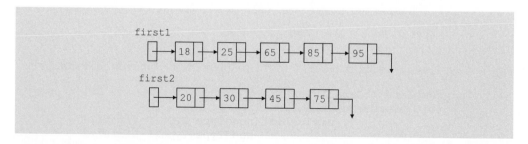

FIGURE 10-37 Sublists before merging

We first compare the info of the first node of each of the two sublists to determine the first node of the merged list. We set newHead to point to the first node of the merged list. We also use the pointer lastMerged to keep track of the last node of the merged list. The pointer of the first node of the sublist with the smaller node then advances to the next node of that sublist. Figure 10-38 shows the sublist of Figure 10-37 after setting newHead and lastMerged and advancing first1.

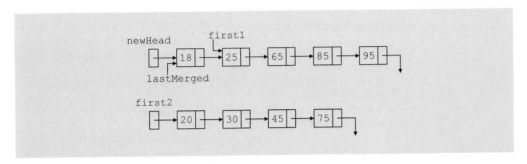

FIGURE 10-38   Sublists after setting newHead and lastMerged and advancing first1

In Figure 10-38, first1 points to the first node of the first sublist that is yet to be merged with the second sublist. So we again compare the nodes pointed to by first1 and first2, and adjust the link of the smaller node and the last node of the merged list so as to move the smaller node to the end of the merged list. For the sublists shown in Figure 10-38, after adjusting the necessary links, we have Figure 10-39.

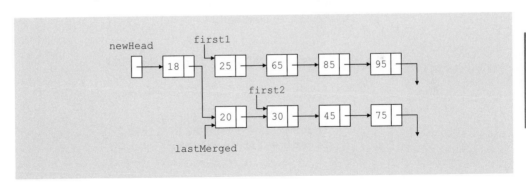

FIGURE 10-39   Merged list after putting the node with info 20 at the end of the merged list

We continue this process for the remaining elements of both sublists. Every time we move a node to the merged list, we advance either first1 or first2 to the next node. Eventually, either first1 or first2 becomes NULL. If first1 becomes NULL, the first sublist is exhausted first, so we attach the remaining nodes of the second sublist at the end of the partially merged list. If first2 becomes NULL, the second sublist is exhausted first, so we attach the remaining nodes of the first sublist at the end of the partially merged list.

Following this discussion, we can now write the C++ function, `mergeList`, to merge the two sorted sublists. The references (that is, addresses) of the first nodes of the sublists are passed as parameters to the function `mergeList`.

```
template <class Type>
nodeType<Type>* unorderedLinkedList<Type>::
                    mergeList(nodeType<Type>* first1,
                              nodeType<Type>* first2)
{
    nodeType<Type> *lastSmall; //pointer to the last node of
                               //the merged list
    nodeType<Type> *newHead;    //pointer to the merged list

    if (first1 == NULL)    //the first sublist is empty
        return first2;
    else if (first2 == NULL)    //the second sublist is empty
        return first1;
    else
    {
        if (first1->info < first2->info) //compare the first nodes
        {
            newHead = first1;
            first1 = first1->link;
            lastSmall = newHead;
        }
        else
        {
            newHead = first2;
            first2 = first2->link;
            lastSmall = newHead;
        }

        while (first1 != NULL && first2 != NULL)
        {
            if (first1->info < first2->info)
            {
                lastSmall->link = first1;
                lastSmall = lastSmall->link;
                first1 = first1->link;
            }
            else
            {
                lastSmall->link = first2;
                lastSmall = lastSmall->link;
                first2 = first2->link;
            }
        } //end while

        if (first1 == NULL) //first sublist is exhausted first
            lastSmall->link = first2;
```

```
        else                    //second sublist is exhausted first
            lastSmall->link = first1;

        return newHead;
    }
}//end mergeList
```

Finally, we write the recursive mergesort function, recMergeSort, which uses the divideList and mergeList functions to sort a list. The reference of the first node of the list to be sorted is passed as a parameter to the function recMergeSort.

```
template <class Type>
void unorderedLinkedList<Type>::recMergeSort(nodeType<Type>* &head)
{
    nodeType<Type> *otherHead;

    if (head != NULL)  //if the list is not empty
        if (head->link != NULL) //if the list has more than one node
        {
            divideList(head, otherHead);
            recMergeSort(head);
            recMergeSort(otherHead);
            head = mergeList(head, otherHead);
        }
} //end recMergeSort
```

We can now give the definition of the function mergeSort, which should be included as a public member of the class unorderedLinkedList. (Note that the functions divideList, merge, and recMergeSort can be included as private members of the class unorderedLinkedList because these functions are used only to implement the function mergeSort.) The function mergeSort calls the function recMergeSort and passes first to this function. It also sets last to point to the last node of the list. The definition of the function mergeSort is as follows:

```
template<class Type>
void unorderedLinkedList<Type>::mergeSort()
{
    recMergeSort(first);

    if (first == NULL)
        last = NULL;
    else
    {
        last = first;
        while (last->link != NULL)
            last = last->link;
    }
} //end mergeSort
```

We leave it as an exercise for you to write a program to test mergesort. See Programming Exercise 10 at the end of this chapter.

Analysis: Mergesort

Suppose that L is a list of n elements, where $n > 0$. Suppose that n is a power of 2, that is, $n = 2^m$ for some nonnegative integer m, so that we can divide the list into two sublists, each of size $n / 2 = 2^m / 2 = 2^{m-1}$. Moreover, each sublist can also be divided into two sublists of the same size. Each call to the function `recMergeSort` makes two recursive calls to the function `recMergeSort` and each call divides the sublist into two sublists of the same size. Suppose that $m = 3$, that is, $n = 2^3 = 8$. So the length of the original list is 8. The first call to the function `recMergeSort` divides the original list into two sublists, each of size 4. The first call then makes two recursive calls to the function `recMergeSort`. Each of these recursive calls divides each sublist, of size 4, into two sublists, each of size 2. We now have 4 sublists, each of size 2. The next set of recursive calls divides each sublist, of size 2, into sublists of size 1. So we now have 8 sublists, each of size 1. It follows that the exponent 3 in 2^3 indicates the level of the recursion, as shown in Figure 10-40.

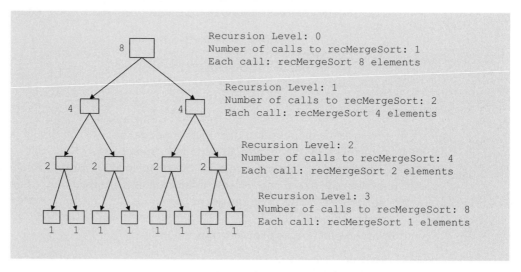

```
Recursion Level: 0
Number of calls to recMergeSort: 1
Each call: recMergeSort 8 elements

Recursion Level: 1
Number of calls to recMergeSort: 2
Each call: recMergeSort 4 elements

Recursion Level: 2
Number of calls to recMergeSort: 4
Each call: recMergeSort 2 elements

Recursion Level: 3
Number of calls to recMergeSort: 8
Each call: recMergeSort 1 elements
```

FIGURE 10-40 Levels of recursion levels to `recMergeSort` for a list of length 8

Let us consider the general case when $n = 2^m$. Note that the number of recursion levels is m. Also, note that to merge a sorted list of size s with a sorted list of size t, the maximum number of comparisons is $s + t - 1$.

Consider the function `mergeList`, which merges two sorted lists into a sorted list. Note that this is where the actual work, comparisons and assignments, is done. The initial call to the function `recMergeSort`, at level 0, produces two sublists, each of size $n / 2$. To merge these two lists, after they are sorted, the maximum number of comparisons is $n / 2 + n / 2 - 1 = n - 1 = O(n)$. At level 1, we merge two sets of sorted lists, where each sublist is of size $n / 4$. To merge two sorted sublists, each of size $n / 4$, we need at most $n / 4 + n / 4 - 1 = n / 2 - 1$ comparisons. Thus, at level 1 of the recursion, the number of comparisons is $2(n / 2 - 1) = n - 2 = O(n)$. In general, at level k of the recursion, there are a total of 2^k calls to the function `mergeList`. Each of these calls merge two sublists, each of size $n / 2^{k+1}$, which requires a maximum of $n / 2^k - 1$ comparisons. Thus, at level k of the recursion, the maximum number of comparisons is $2^k (n / 2^k - 1) = n - 2^k = O(n)$. It now follows that the maximum number of comparisons at each level of the recursion is $O(n)$. Because the number of levels of the recursion is m, the maximum number of comparisons made by mergesort is $O(nm)$. Now $n = 2^m$ implies that $m = \log_2 n$. Hence, the maximum number of comparisons made by mergesort is $O(n \log_2 n)$.

If $W(n)$ denotes the number of key comparisons in the worst case to sort L, then $W(n) = O(n \log_2 n)$.

Let $A(n)$ denote the number of key comparisons in the average case. In the average case, during the merge process one of the sublists will exhaust before the other list. From this, it follows that on average merging of two sorted sublists of combined size n, the number of comparisons will be less than $n - 1$. On average, it can be shown that the number of comparisons for mergesort is given by the following equation: If n is a power of 2, $A(n) = n \log_2 n - 1.25n = O(n \log_2 n)$. This is also a good approximation when n is not a power of 2.

> **NOTE** We can also obtain an analysis of mergesort by constructing and solving certain equations as follows. As noted before, in mergesort, all the comparisons are made in the method `mergeList`, which merges two sorted sublists. If one sublist is of size s and the other sublist is of size t, merging these lists would require at most $s + t - 1$ comparisons in the worst case. Hence,
>
> $$W(n) = W(s) + W(t) + s + t - 1$$
>
> Note that $s = n / 2$ and $t = n / 2$. Suppose that $n = 2^m$. Then $s = 2^{m-1}$ and $t = 2^{m-1}$. It follows that $s + t = n$. Hence,
>
> $$W(n) = W(n / 2) + W(n / 2) + n - 1 = 2\,W(n / 2) + n - 1, \; n > 0$$
>
> Also,
>
> $$W(1) = 0$$
>
> It is known that when n is a power of 2, $W(n)$ is given by the following equation:
>
> $$W(n) = n \log_2 n - (n - 1) = O(n \log_2 n)$$

Heapsort: Array-Based Lists

In an earlier section, we described the quicksort algorithm for contiguous lists, that is, array-based lists. We remarked that, on average, quicksort is of the order $O(n \log_2 n)$. However, in the worst case, quicksort is of the order $O(n^2)$. This section describes another algorithm, the **heapsort**, for array-based lists. This algorithm is of order $O(n \log_2 n)$ even in the worst case, therefore overcoming the worst case of the quicksort.

Definition: A **heap** is a list in which each element contains a key, such that the key in the element at position k in the list is at least as large as the key in the element at position $2k + 1$ (if it exists) and $2k + 2$ (if it exists).

Recall that, in C++ the array index starts at 0. Therefore, the element at position k is in fact the $k + 1th$ element of the list.

Consider the list in Figure 10-41.

[0]	[1]	[2]	[3]	[4]	[5]	[6]	[7]	[8]	[9]	[10]	[11]	[12]
85	70	80	50	40	75	30	20	10	35	15	62	58

FIGURE 10-41 A heap

It can be checked that the list in Figure 10-41 is in a heap. For example, consider `list[3]`, which is 50. The elements at position `list[7]` and `list[8]` are 20 and 10, respectively. Clearly, `list[3]` is larger than `list[7]` and `list[8]`.

In heapsort, elements at position k, $2k + 1$, and $2k + 2$, if they exist, are accessed frequently. Therefore, to facilitate the discussion of heapsort, we typically view data in the form of a complete binary tree as described next. For example, the data given in Figure 10-41 can be viewed in a complete binary tree, as shown in Figure 10-42.

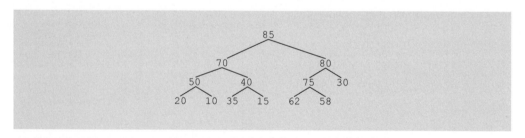

FIGURE 10-42 Complete binary tree corresponding to the list in Figure 10-41

In Figure 10-42, the first element of the list, which is 85, is the *root* node of the tree. The second element of the list, which is 70, is the *left child* of the root node; the third element of the list, which is 80, is the *right child* of the root node. Thus, in general, for the node k, which is the $k - 1th$ element of the list, its left child is the $2kth$ (if it exists) element of the list, which is at position $2k - 1$ in the list, and the right child is the $2k + 1st$ (if it exists) element of the list, which is at position $2k$ in the list. Note that Figure 10-42 clearly shows that the list in Figure 10-41 is in a heap. Also note that in Figure 10-42, the elements 20, 10, 35, 15, 62, 58, and 30 are called *leaves* as they have no children.

As remarked earlier, to demonstrate the heapsort algorithm, we will draw the complete binary tree corresponding to a list. Note that even though we will draw a complete binary tree to illustrate heapsort, the data gets manipulated in an array. We now describe heapsort.

The first step in heapsort is to convert the list into a heap, called `buildHeap`. After we convert the array into a heap, the sorting phase begins.

Build Heap

This section describes the build heap algorithm.

The general algorithm is as follows: Suppose `length` denotes the length of the list. Let `index = length / 2 - 1`. Then `list[index]` is the last element in the list which is not a leaf; that is, this element has at least one child. Thus, elements `list[index + 1]` `...list[length - 1]` are leaves.

First, we convert the subtree with the root node `list[index]` into a heap. Note that this subtree has at most three nodes. We then convert the subtree with the root node `list[index - 1]` into a heap, and so on.

To convert a subtree into a heap, we perform the following steps: Suppose that `list[a]` is the root node of the subtree, `list[b]` is the left child, and `list[c]`, if it exists, is the right child of `list[a]`.

Compare `list[b]` with `list[c]` to determine the larger child. If `list[c]` does not exist, then `list[b]` is the larger child. Suppose that `largerIndex` indicates the larger child. (Notice that, `largerIndex` is either b or c.)

Compare `list[a]` with `list[largerIndex]`. If `list[a] < list[largerIndex]`, then swap `list[a]` with `list[largerIndex]`; otherwise, the subtree with root node `list[a]` is already in a heap.

Suppose that `list[a] < list[largerIndex]` and we swap the elements `list[a]` with `list[largerIndex]`. After making this swap, the subtree with root node `list[largerIndex]` might not be in a heap. If this is the case, then we repeat Steps 1 and 2 at the subtree with root node `list[largerIndex]` and continue this process until either the heap in the subtrees is restored or we arrive at an empty subtree. This step is implemented using a loop, which will be described when we write the algorithm.

Consider the list in Figure 10-43. Let us call this `list`.

	[0]	[1]	[2]	[3]	[4]	[5]	[6]	[7]	[8]	[9]	[10]
list	15	60	72	70	56	32	62	92	45	30	65

FIGURE 10-43 Array `list`

Figure 10-44 shows the complete binary tree corresponding to the list in Figure 10-43.

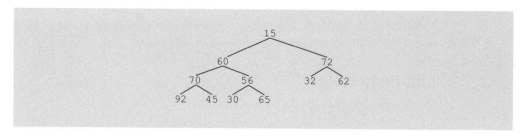

FIGURE 10-44 Complete binary tree corresponding to the list in Figure 10-43

To facilitate this discussion, when we say node **56**, we mean the node with info **56**.

This list has **11** elements, so the length of the list is **11**. To convert the array into a heap, we start at the list element n/2 – 1 = 11/2 – 1 = 5 – 1 = 4, which is the fifth element of the list.

Now `list[4]` = **56**. The children of `list[4]` are `list[4 * 2 + 1]` and `list[4 * 2 + 2]`, that is, `list[9]` and `list[10]`. In the previous list, both `list[9]` and `list[10]` exist. To convert the tree with root node `list[4]`, we perform the previous hree steps:

1. Find the larger of `list[9]` and `list[10]`, that is, the largest child of `list[4]`. In this case, `list[10]` is larger than `list[9]`.

2. Compare the larger child with the parent node. If the larger child is larger than the parent, swap the larger child with the parent. Because `list[4] < list[10]`, we swap `list[4]` with `list[10]`.

3. Because `list[10]` does not have a subtree, Step 3 does not execute.

Figure 10-45(a) shows the resulting binary tree.

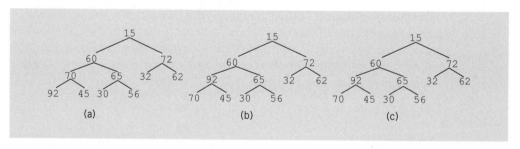

FIGURE 10-45 Binary tree while building heaps at `list[4]`, `list[3]`, and `list[2]`

Next, we consider the subtree with root node `list[3]`, that is, **70** and repeat the three steps given earlier, to obtain the complete binary tree as given in Figure 10-45(b). (Notice that Step 3 does not execute here either.)

Now we consider the subtree with the root node `list[2]`, that is, **72**, and apply the three steps given earlier. Figure 10-45(c) shows the resulting binary tree. (Note that in this case, because the parent is larger than both children, this subtree is already in a heap.)

Next, we consider the subtree with the root node list[1], that is, 60, see 10-45(c). First, we apply Steps 1 and 2. Because list[1] = 60 < list[3] = 92 (the larger child), we swap list[1] with list[3], to obtain the tree as given in Figure 10-46(a).

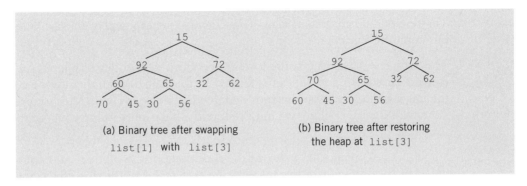

(a) Binary tree after swapping
list[1] with list[3]

(b) Binary tree after restoring
the heap at list[3]

FIGURE 10-46 Binary tree while building heap at list[1]

However, after swapping list[1] with list[3], the subtree with the root node list[3], that is, 60, is no longer a heap. Thus, we must restore the heap in this subtree. To do this, we apply Step 3 and find the larger child of 60 and swap it with 60. We then obtain the binary tree as given in Figure 10-46(b).

Once again, the subtree with the root node list[1], that is, 92, is in a heap (see Figure 10-46(b)).

Finally, we consider the tree with the root node list[0], that is, 15. We repeat the previous three steps to obtain the binary tree as given in Figure 10-47(a).

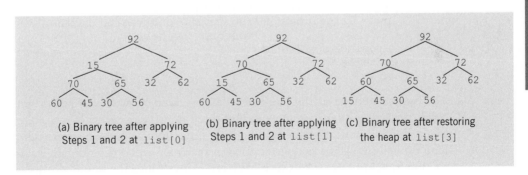

(a) Binary tree after applying
Steps 1 and 2 at list[0]

(b) Binary tree after applying
Steps 1 and 2 at list[1]

(c) Binary tree after restoring
the heap at list[3]

FIGURE 10-47 Binary tree while building heap at list[0]

We see that the subtree with the root node list[1], that is, 15, is no longer in a heap. So we must apply Step 3 to restore the heap in this subtree. (This requires us to repeat Steps 1 and 2 at the subtree with root node list[1].) We swap list[1] with the larger child, which is list[3] (that is, 70). We then get the binary tree of Figure 10-47(b).

The subtree with the root node list[3] = 15 is not in a heap, and so we must restore the heap in this subtree. To do so, we apply Steps 1 and 2 at the subtree with root node list[3]. We swap list[3] with the larger child, which is list[7] (that is, 60). Figure 10-47(c) shows the resulting binary tree.

The resulting binary tree in Figure 10-47(c) is in a heap, and so the list corresponding to this complete binary tree is in a heap.

Thus, in general, starting at the lowest level from right to left, we look at a subtree and convert the subtree into a heap as follows: If the root node of the subtree is smaller than the larger child, we swap the root node with the larger child. After swapping the root node with the larger child, we must restore the heap in the subtree whose root node was swapped.

Suppose low contains the index of the root node of the subtree and high contains the index of the last item in the list. The heap is to be restored in the subtree rooted at list[low]. The preceding discussion translates into the following C++ algorithm:

```
int largeIndex = 2 * low + 1;    //index of the left child

while (largeIndex <= high)
{
   if ( largeIndex < high)
       if (list[largeIndex] < list[largeIndex + 1])
           largeIndex = largeIndex + 1;   //index of the larger child
   if (list[low] > list[largeIndex])    //the subtree is already in
                                         //a heap
       break;
   else
   {
       swap(list[low], list[largeIndex]);    //Line swap**
       low = largeIndex;   //go to the subtree to further
                           //restore the heap
       largeIndex = 2 * low + 1;
   } //end else
}//end while
```

The swap statement at the line marked Line swap** swaps the parent with the larger child. Because a swap statement makes three item assignments to swap the contents of two variables, each time through the loop three item assignments are made. The while loop moves the parent node to a place in the tree so that the resulting subtree with the root node list[low] is in a heap. We can easily reduce the number of assignments each time through the loop from three to one by first storing the root node in a temporary location, say temp. Then each time through the loop, the larger child is compared with temp. If the larger child is larger than temp, we move the larger child to the root node of the subtree under consideration.

Next, we describe the function heapify, which restores the heap in a subtree by making one item assignment each time through the loop. The index of the root node of the list and the index of the last element of the list are passed as parameters to this function.

```
template<class elemType>
void arrayListType<elemType>::heapify(int low, int high)
{
    int largeIndex;

    elemType temp = list[low]; //copy the root node of the subtree

    largeIndex = 2 * low + 1;   //index of the left child

    while (largeIndex <= high)
    {
        if (largeIndex < high)
            if (list[largeIndex] < list[largeIndex + 1])
                largeIndex = largeIndex + 1; //index of the largest
                                             //child

        if (temp > list[largeIndex]) //subtree is already in a heap
            break;
        else
        {
            list[low] = list[largeIndex]; //move the larger child
                                          //to the root
            low = largeIndex; //go to the subtree to restore the heap
            largeIndex = 2 * low + 1;
        }
    }//end while


    list[low] = temp; //insert temp into the tree, that is, list

} //end heapify
```

Next, we use the function `heapify` to implement the `buildHeap` function to convert the list into a heap.

```
template <class elemType>
void arrayListType<elemType>::buildHeap()
{
    for (int index = length / 2 - 1; index >= 0; index--)
        heapify(index, length - 1);
}
```

We now describe heapsort.

Suppose the list is in a heap. Consider the complete binary tree representing the list as given in Figure 10-48(a).

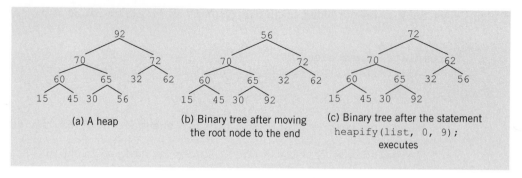

(a) A heap

(b) Binary tree after moving
the root node to the end

(c) Binary tree after the statement
heapify(list, 0, 9);
executes

FIGURE 10-48 Heapsort

Because this is a heap, the root node is the largest element of the tree, that is, the largest element of the list. So it must be moved to the end of the list. We swap the root node of the tree, that is, the first element of the list, with the last node in the tree (which is the last element of the list). We then obtain the binary tree as shown in Figure 10-48(b).

Because the largest element is now in its proper place, we consider the remaining elements of the list, that is, elements list[0]...list[9]. The complete binary tree representing this list is no longer a heap, and so we must restore the heap in this portion of the complete binary tree. We use the function heapify to restore the heap. A call to this function is as follows:

```
heapify(list, 0, 9);
```

We thus obtain the binary tree as shown in Figure 10-48(c).

We repeat this process for the complete binary tree corresponding to the list elements list[0]...list[9]. We swap list[0] with list[9] and then restore the heap in the complete binary tree corresponding to the list elements list[0]...list[8]. We continue this process.

The following C++ function describes this algorithm:

```cpp
template <class elemType>
void arrayListType<elemType>::heapSort()
{
    elemType temp;

    buildHeap();

    for (int lastOutOfOrder = length - 1; lastOutOfOrder >= 0;
                                          lastOutOfOrder--)
    {
        temp = list[lastOutOfOrder];
        list[lastOutOfOrder] = list[0];
        list[0] = temp;
        heapify(0, lastOutOfOrder - 1);
    }//end for
}//end heapSort
```

We leave as an exercise for you to write a program to test heapsort; see Programming Exercise 11 at the end of this chapter.

Analysis: Heapsort

Suppose that L is a list of n elements, where $n > 0$. In the worst case, the number of key comparisons in heapsort to sort L (the number of comparisons in `heapSort` and the number of comparisons in `buildHeap`) is $2n\log_2 n + O(n)$. Also, in the worst case, the number of item assignments in heapsort to sort L is $n\log_2 n + O(n)$. On average, the number of comparisons made by heapsort to sort L is of $O(n\log_2 n)$.

In the average case of quicksort, the number of key comparisons is $1.39n\log_2 n + O(n)$ and the number of swaps is $0.69n\log_2 n + O(n)$. Because each swap is three assignments, the number of item assignments in the average case of quicksort is at least $1.39n\log_2 n + O(n)$. It now follows that for the key comparisons, the average case of quicksort is somewhat better than the worst case of heapsort. On the other hand, for the item assignments, the average case of quicksort is somewhat poorer than the worst case of heapsort. However, the worst case of quicksort is of $O(n^2)$. Empirical studies have shown that heapsort usually takes twice as long as quicksort, but avoids the slight possibility of poor performance.

Priority Queues (Revisited)

Chapter 8 introduced priority queues. Recall that in a priority queue, customers or jobs with higher priorities are pushed to the front of the queue. Chapter 8 stated that we would discuss the implementation of priority queues after describing heapsort. For simplicity, we assume that the priority of the queue elements is assigned using the relational operators.

In a heap, the largest element of the list is always the first element of the list. After removing the largest element of the list, the function `heapify` restores the heap in the list. To ensure that the largest element of the priority queue is always the first element of the queue, we can implement priority queues as heaps. We can write algorithms similar to the ones used in the function `heapify` to insert an element in the priority queue (addQueue operation), and remove an element from the queue (deleteQueue operation). The next two sections describe these algorithms.

INSERT AN ELEMENT IN THE PRIORITY QUEUE

Assuming the priority queue is implemented as a heap, we perform the following steps:

1. Insert the new element in the first available position in the list. (This ensures that the array holding the list is a complete binary tree.)

2. After inserting the new element in the heap, the list might no longer be a heap. So to restore the heap:

```
while (the parent of the new entry is smaller than the new entry)
    swap the parent with the new entry.
```

Notice that restoring the heap might result in moving the new entry to the root node.

REMOVE AN ELEMENT FROM THE PRIORITY QUEUE

Assuming the priority queue is implemented as a heap, to remove the first element of the priority queue, we perform the following steps:

1. Copy the last element of the list into the first array position.
2. Reduce the length of the list by 1.
3. Restore the heap in the list.

The other operations for priority queues can be implemented in the same way as implemented for queues. We leave the implementation of the priority queues as an exercise for you; see Programming Exercise 12 at the end of this chapter.

PROGRAMMING EXAMPLE: Election Results

The presidential election for the student council of your local university is about to be held. The chair of the election committee wants to computerize the voting and has asked you to write a program to analyze the data and report the winner.

The university has four major divisions, and each division has several departments. For the election, the four divisions are labeled as region 1, region 2, region 3, and region 4. Each department in each division handles its own voting and reports the votes received by each candidate to the election committee. The voting is reported in the following form:

```
firstName lastName regionNumber numberOfVotes
```

The election committee wants the output in the following tabular form:

```
--------------------Election Results--------------------

                                      Votes
Candidate Name      Region1  Region2  Region3  Region4   Total
--------------------  -------  -------  -------  -------  ------
Sheila    Bower          23       70      133      267     493
Danny     Dillion        25       71      156       97     349
Lisa      Fisher        110      158        0        0     268
Greg      Goldy          75       34      134        0     243
Peter     Lamba         285       56        0       46     387
Mickey    Miller        112      141      156       67     476

Winner: Sheila Bower, Votes Received: 493

Total votes polled: 2216
```

The names of the candidates must be in alphabetical order in the output.

For this program, we assume that six candidates are seeking the student council's president post. This program can be enhanced to handle any number of candidates.

The data are provided in two files. One file, candData.txt, consists of the names of the candidates seeking the president's post. The names of the candidates in this file are in no particular order. In the second file, voteData.txt, each line consists of the voting results in the following form:

```
firstName lastName regionNumber numberOfVotes
```

Each line in the file voteData.txt consists of the candidate's name, the region number, and the number of votes received by the candidate in that region. There is one entry per line. For example, the input file containing the voting data looks like the following:

```
Greg Goldy 2 34
Mickey Miller 1 56
Lisa Fisher 2 56
.
.
.
```

The first line indicates that Greg Goldy received 34 votes from region 2.

Input   Two files: one containing the candidates' names and the other containing the voting data as described previously.

Output   The election results in a tabular form, as described previously, and the winner.

PROBLEM ANALYSIS AND ALGORITHM DESIGN

From the output, it is clear that the program must organize the voting data by region and calculate the total votes both received by each candidate and polled for the election. Furthermore, the names of the candidates must appear in alphabetical order.

The main component of this program is a candidate. Therefore, first we design a class candidateType to implement a candidate object. Every candidate has a name and receives votes. Because there are four regions, we can use an array of four components. In Example 1-12 (Chapter 1), we designed the class personType to implement the name of a person. Recall that an object of the type personType can store the first name and the last name. Now that we have discussed operator overloading (see Chapter 2), we can redesign the class personType and define the relational operators so that the names of two people can be compared. We can also overload the assignment operator for easy assignment, and use the stream insertion and extraction operators for input/output. Because every candidate is a person, we derive the class candidateType from the class personType.

personType

The class personType implements the first name and last name of a person. Therefore, the class personType has two data members: a data member, firstName, to store the first name and a data member, lastName, to store the last name. We declare these as protected so that the definition of the class personType can be easily extended to accommodate the requirements of a specific application needed to implement a person's name. The definition of the class personType is given next:

```cpp
//************************************************************
// Author: D.S. Malik
//
// This class specifies the members to implement a person's
// name.
//************************************************************

#include <iostream>
#include <string>

using namespace std;

class personType
{
        //Overload the stream insertion and extraction operators.
    friend istream& operator>>(istream&, personType&);
    friend ostream& operator<<(ostream&, const personType&);

public:
    const personType& operator=(const personType&);
      //Overload the assignment operator.

    void setName(string first, string last);
      //Function to set firstName and lastName according to
      //the parameters.
      //Postcondition: firstName = first; lastName = last

    string getFirstName() const;
      //Function to return the first name.
      //Postcondition: The value of firstName is returned.

    string getLastName() const;
      //Function to return the last name.
      //Postcondition: The value of lastName is returned.

    personType(string first = "", string last = "");
      //constructor with parameters
      //Set firstName and lastName according to the parameters.
      //Postcondition: firstName = first; lastName = last

        //Overload the relational operators.
    bool operator==(const personType& right) const;
    bool operator!=(const personType& right) const;
    bool operator<=(const personType& right) const;
```

```
        bool operator<(const personType& right) const;
        bool operator>=(const personType& right) const;
        bool operator>(const personType& right) const;

protected:
        string firstName; //variable to store the first name
        string lastName;  //variable to store the last name
};
```

We only give the definitions of the functions to overload the operators == and >> and leave others as an exercise for you; see Programming Exercise 13 at the end of this chapter.

```
        //overload the operator ==
bool personType::operator==(const personType& right) const
{
    return (firstName == right.firstName
            && lastName == right.lastName);
}


        //overload the stream insertion operator
istream& operator>>(istream& isObject, personType& pName)
{
        isObject >> pName.firstName >> pName.lastName;

        return isObject;
}
```

candidateType The main component of this program is the candidate, which is described and implemented in this section. Every candidate has a first and a last name, and receives votes. Because there are four regions, we declare an array of four components to keep track of the votes for each region. We also need a data member to store the total number of votes received by each candidate. Because every candidate is a person and we have designed a class to implement the first and last name, we derive the class candidateType from the class personType. Because the data members of the class personType are protected, these data members can be accessed directly in the class candidateType.

There are six candidates. Therefore, we declare a list of six candidates of type candidateType. This chapter discussed sorting algorithms and added these algorithms to the class arrayListType. In Chapter 9, we derived the class orderedArrayList from the class arrayListType and included the binary search algorithm. We will use this class to maintain the list of candidates. This list of candidates will be sorted and searched. Therefore, we must define (that is, overload) the assignment and relational operators for the class candidateType because these operators are used by the searching and sorting algorithms.

Data in the file containing the candidates' data consists of only the names of the candidates. Therefore, in addition to overloading the assignment operator so that the value of one object can be assigned to another object, we also overload the assignment operator for the `class candidateType`, so that only the name (of the `personType`) of the candidate can be assigned to a candidate object. That is, we overload the assignment operator twice: once for objects of the type `candidateType`, and another for objects of the types `candidateType` and `personType`.

```
//*************************************************************
// Author: D.S. Malik
//
// This class specifies the members to implement a candidate.
//*************************************************************

#include <string>
#include "personType.h"

using namespace std;

const int NO_OF_REGIONS = 4;

class candidateType: public personType
{
public:
    const candidateType& operator=(const candidateType&);
        //Overload the assignment operator for objects of the
        //type candidateType

    const candidateType& operator=(const personType&);
        //Overload the assignment operator for objects so that
        //the value of an object of type personType can be
        //assigned to an object of type candidateType

    void updateVotesByRegion(int region, int votes);
        //Function to update the votes of a candidate for a
        //particular region.
        //Postcondition: Votes for the region specified by the
        //    parameter are updated by adding the votes specified
        //    by the parameter votes.

    void setVotes(int region, int votes);
        //Function to set the votes of a candidate for a
        //particular region.
        //Postcondition: Votes for the region specified by the
        //    parameter are set to the votes specified by the
        //    parameter votes.

    void calculateTotalVotes();
        //Function to calculate the total votes received by a
        //candidate.
        //Postcondition: The votes in each region are added and
        //    assigned to totalVotes.
```

```
        int getTotalVotes() const;
          //Function to return the total votes received by a
          //candidate.
          //Postcondition: The value of totalVotes is returned.

        void printData() const;
          //Function to output the candidate's name, the votes
          //received in each region, and the total votes received.

        candidateType();
          //Default constructor.
          //Postcondition: Candidate's name is initialized to blanks,
          //    the number of votes in each region, and the total
          //    votes are initialized to 0.

          //Overload the relational operators.
        bool operator==(const candidateType& right) const;
        bool operator!=(const candidateType& right) const;
        bool operator<=(const candidateType& right) const;
        bool operator<(const candidateType& right) const;
        bool operator>=(const candidateType& right) const;
        bool operator>(const candidateType& right) const;

private:
        int votesByRegion[NO_OF_REGIONS];    //array to store the votes
                                // received in each region
        int totalVotes; //variable to store the total votes
};
```

The definitions of the member functions of the class candidateType are given next.

To set the votes of a particular region, the region number and the number of votes are passed as parameters to the function setVotes. Because an array index starts at 0, region 1 corresponds to the array component at position 0, and so on. Therefore, to set the value of the correct array component, 1 is subtracted from the region. The definition of the function setVotes is as follows:

```
void candidateType::setVotes(int region, int votes)
{
    votesByRegion[region - 1] = votes;
}
```

To update the votes for a particular region, the region number and the number of votes for that region are passed as parameters. The votes are then added to the region's previous value. The definition of the function updateVotesByRegion is as follows:

```
void candidateType::updateVotesByRegion(int region, int votes)
{
    votesByRegion[region - 1] = votesByRegion[region - 1] + votes;
}
```

The definitions of the functions `calculateTotalVotes`, `getTotalVotes`, `printData`, the default constructor, and `getName` are given next:

```
void candidateType::calculateTotalVotes()
{
    totalVotes = 0;

    for (int i = 0; i < NO_OF_REGIONS; i++)
        totalVotes += votesByRegion[i];
}

int candidateType::getTotalVotes() const
{
    return totalVotes;
}

void candidateType::printData() const
{
    cout << left
         << setw(10) << firstName << " "
         << setw(10) << lastName << " ";

    cout << right;

    for (int i = 0; i < NO_OF_REGIONS; i++)
        cout << setw(7) << votesByRegion[i] << "   ";
    cout << setw(7) << totalVotes << endl;
}

candidateType::candidateType()
{
    for (int i = 0; i < NO_OF_REGIONS; i++)
        votesByRegion[i] = 0;

    totalVotes = 0;
}
```

To overload the relational operators for the `class candidateType`, the names of the candidates are compared. For example, two candidates are the same if they have the same name. The definitions of these functions are similar to the definitions of the functions to overload the relational operators for the `class personType`. We only give the definition of the function to overload the operator `==` and leave others as an exercise for you; see Programming Exercise 13.

```
bool candidateType::operator==(const candidateType& right) const
{
    return (firstName == right.firstName
            && lastName == right.lastName);
}
```

The definitions of the functions to overload the assignment operators for the `class candidateType` are also left as an exercise for you; see Programming Exercise 13.

MAIN
PROGRAM

Now that the **class candidateType** has been designed, we focus on designing the main program.

Because there are six candidates, we create a list, **candidateList**, containing six components of the type **candidateType**. The first thing that the program should do is read each candidate's name from the file **candData.txt** into the list **candidateList**. Next, we sort **candidateList**.

The next step is to process the voting data from the file **voteData.txt**, which holds the voting data. After processing the voting data, the program should calculate the total votes received by each candidate and then print the data as shown previously. Thus, the general algorithm is as follows:

1. Read each candidate's name into **candidateList**.
2. Sort **candidateList**.
3. Process the voting data.
4. Calculate the total votes received by each candidate.
5. Print the results.

The following statement creates the object **candidateList** of type **orderedArrayListType**.

orderedArrayListType<candidateType> candidateList(NO_OF_CANDIDATES);

Figure 10-49 shows the object **candidateList**. Every component of the array **list** is an object of the type **candidateType**.

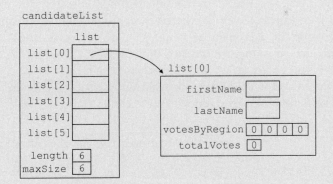

FIGURE 10-49 candidateList

In Figure 10-49, the array **votesByRegion** and the variable **totalVotes** are initialized to 0 by the default constructor of the **class candidateType**. To save space, whenever needed, we will draw the object `candidateList` as shown in Figure 10-50.

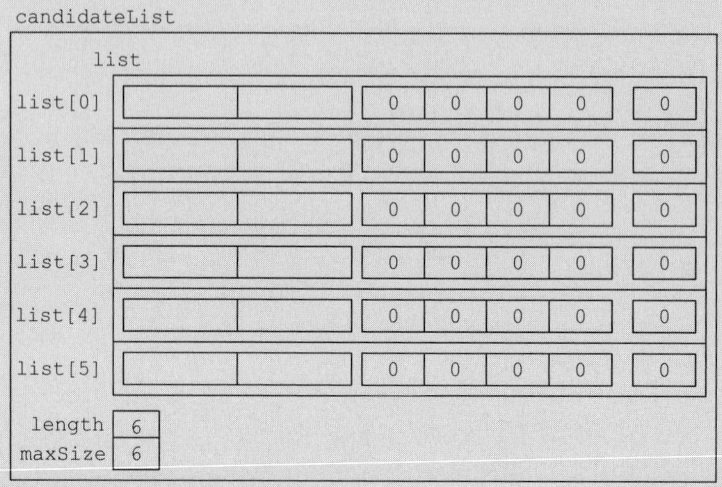

FIGURE 10-50 Object `candidateList`

fillNames   The first thing that the program must do is to read the candidates' names into `candidateList`. Therefore, we write a function to accomplish this task. The file `candData.txt` is opened in the function `main`. The name of the input file and `candidateList` are therefore passed as parameters to the function `fillNames`. Because the data member `list` of the object `candidateList` is a protected data member, it cannot be accessed directly. We, therefore, create an object, `temp`, of the type `candidateType`, to store the candidates' names, and use the function `insertAt` (of `list`) to store each candidate's name in the object `candidateList`. The definition of the function `fillNames` is as follows:

```
void fillNames(ifstream& inFile,
               orderedArrayListType<candidateType>& cList)
{
    string firstN;
    string lastN;

    candidateType temp;
```

```
        for (int i = 0; i < NO_OF_CANDIDATES; i++)
        {
            inFile >> firstN >> lastN;
            temp.setName(firstN, lastN);
            cList.insertAt(i, temp);
        }
}
```

After a call to the function `fillNames`, Figure 10-51 shows the object `candidateList`.

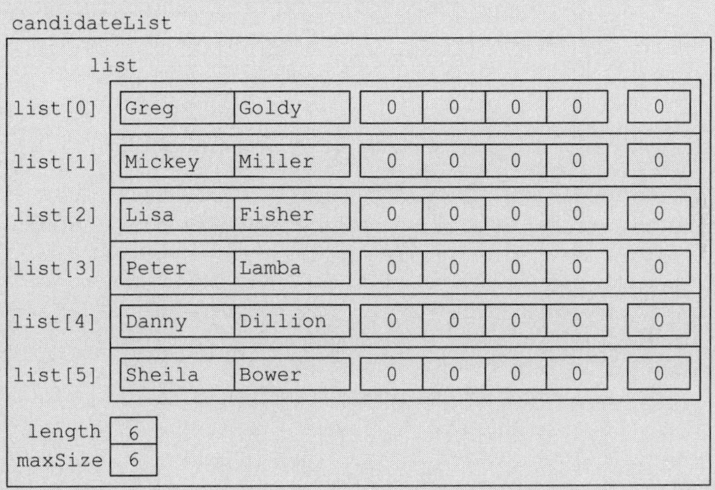

FIGURE 10-51 Object `candidateList` after a call to the function `fillNames`

Sort Names After reading the candidates' names, next we sort the array `list` of the object `candidateList` using any of the (array-based) sorting algorithms discussed in this chapter. Because `candidateList` is an object of the type `orderedArrayListType`, all sorting algorithms discussed in this chapter are available to it. For illustration purposes, we use a selection sort. The following statement accomplishes this task:

`candidateList.selectionSort();`

After this statement executes, `candidateList` is as shown in Figure 10-52.

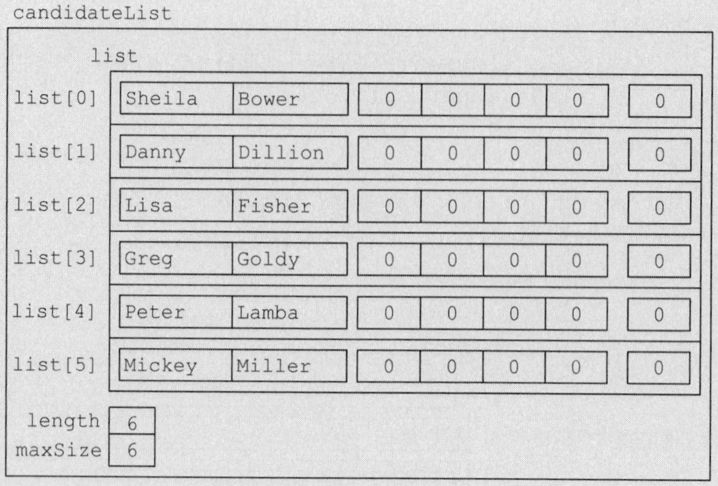

candidateList

list							
list[0]	Sheila	Bower	0	0	0	0	0
list[1]	Danny	Dillion	0	0	0	0	0
list[2]	Lisa	Fisher	0	0	0	0	0
list[3]	Greg	Goldy	0	0	0	0	0
list[4]	Peter	Lamba	0	0	0	0	0
list[5]	Mickey	Miller	0	0	0	0	0

length 6
maxSize 6

FIGURE 10-52 Object `candidateList` after the statement `candidateList.selectionSort();` executes

Process Voting Data

We now discuss how to process the voting data. Each entry in the file `voteData.txt` is of the form

```
firstName lastName regionNumber numberOfVotes
```

After reading an entry from the file `voteData.txt`, we locate the row in the array `list` (of the object `candidateList`) corresponding to the specific candidate, and update the entry specified by `regionNumber`.

The component `votesByRegion` is a `private` data member of each component of the array `list`. Moreover, `list` is a `private` data member of `candidateList`. The only way that we can update the votes of a candidate is to make a copy of that candidate's record into a temporary object, update the object, and then copy the temporary object back into `list` by replacing the old value with the new value of the temporary object. We can use the member function `retrieveAt` to make a copy of the candidate whose votes need to be updated. After updating the temporary object, we can use the member function `replaceAt` to copy the temporary object back into the list. Suppose the next entry read is

```
Lisa Fisher 2 35
```

This entry says that `Lisa Fisher` received 35 votes from region 2. Suppose that before processing this entry, `candidateList` is as shown in Figure 10-53.

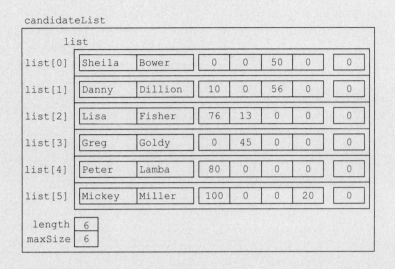

FIGURE 10-53 Object `candidateList` before processing the entry `Lisa Fisher 2 35`

We make a copy of the row corresponding to **Lisa Fisher** (see Figure 10-54).

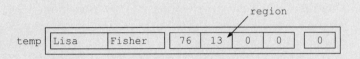

FIGURE 10-54 Object `temp`

Next, the following statement updates the voting data for region 2. (Here **region** = 2 and **votes** = 35.)

`temp.updateVotesByRegion(region, votes);`

After this statement executes, the object **temp** is as shown in Figure 10-55.

FIGURE 10-55 Object `temp` after the statement `temp.updateVotesByRegion(region, votes);` executes

Now we copy the object `temp` into `list` (see Figure 10-56).

FIGURE 10-56 candidateList after copying temp

Because the member `list` of `candidateList` is sorted, we can use the binary search algorithm to find the row position in `list` corresponding to the candidate whose votes need to be updated. Also, the function `binarySearch` is a member of the class `orderedArrayListType`, so we can use this function to search the array `list`. We leave the definition of the function `processVotes` to process the voting data as an exercise for you; see Programming Exercise 13 at the end of this chapter.

Add Votes   After processing the voting data, the next step is to find the total votes received by each candidate. This is done by adding the votes received in each region. Now `votesByRegion` is a `private` data member of `candidateType` and `list` is a `protected` data member of `candidateList`. Therefore, to add the votes for each candidate, we use the `retrieveAt` function to make a temporary copy of each candidate's data, add the votes in the temporary object, and then copy the temporary object back into `candidateList`. The following function does this:

```
void addVotes(orderedArrayListType<candidateType>& cList)
{
    candidateType temp;

    for (int i = 0; i < NO_OF_CANDIDATES; i++)
```

```
    {
        cList.retrieveAt(i, temp);
        temp.calculateTotalVotes();
        cList.replaceAt(i, temp);
    }
}
```

Figure 10-57 shows `candidateList` after adding the votes for each candidate—that is, after a call to the function `addVotes`.

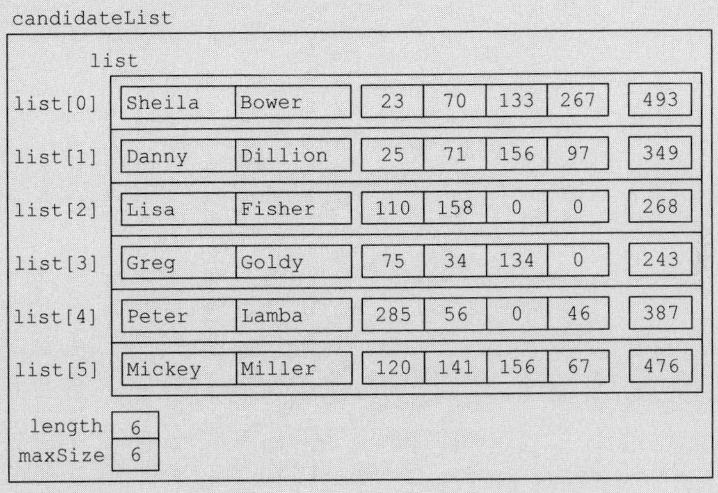

FIGURE 10-57 `candidateList` after a call to the function `addVotes`

Print Heading and Print Results
To complete the program, we include a function to print the heading, the first four lines of the output. The following function accomplishes this task:

```
void printHeading()
{
    cout << "          --------------------Election Results---------"
         << "-----------" << endl << endl;
    cout << "                                         Votes" << endl;
    cout << "     Candidate Name       Region1  Region2  Region3  "
         <<"Region4   Total" << endl;
    cout << "---------------------  -------  -------  "
         << "-------  -------  -----" << endl;
}
```

We now describe the function printResults, which prints the results. Suppose that the variable sumVotes holds the total votes polled for the election, the variable largestVotes holds the largest number of votes received by a candidate, and the variable winLoc holds the index of the winning candidate in the array list. Further suppose that temp is an object of the type candidateType. The algorithm for this function is as follows:

1. Initialize sumVotes, largestVotes, and winLoc to 0.

2. For each candidate

   a. Retrieve the candidate's data into temp.

   b. Print the candidate's name and relevant data.

   c. Retrieve the total votes received by the candidate and update sumVotes.

```
if (largestVotes < temp.getTotalVotes())
{
    largestVotes = temp.getTotalVotes();
    winLoc = i; //this is the ith candidate
}
```

3. Output the final lines of the output.

We leave the definition of the function printResults to print the results as an exercise for you; see Programming Exercise 13 at the end of this chapter.

PROGRAM LISTING (MAIN PROGRAM)

```
//****************************************************************
// Author: D.S. Malik
//
// Program: Election Results
// Given candidates' voting this program determines the winner
// of the election. The program outputs the votes received by
// each candidate and the winner.
//****************************************************************

#include <iostream>
#include <string>
#include <fstream>
#include "candidateType.h"
#include "orderedArrayListType.h"

using namespace std;

const int NO_OF_CANDIDATES = 6;
```

```
void fillNames(ifstream& inFile,
               orderedArrayListType<candidateType>& cList);
void processVotes(ifstream& inFile,
                  orderedArrayListType<candidateType>& cList);
void addVotes(orderedArrayListType<candidateType>& cList);

void printHeading();

void printResults(orderedArrayListType<candidateType>& cList);

int main()
{
    orderedArrayListType<candidateType>
            candidateList(NO_OF_CANDIDATES);

    ifstream inFile;

    inFile.open("candData.txt");

    fillNames(inFile, candidateList);

    candidateList.selectionSort();

    inFile.close();

    inFile.open("voteData.txt");

    processVotes(inFile, candidateList);

    addVotes(candidateList);

    printHeading();

    printResults(candidateList);

    return 0;
}

//Place the definitions of the functions fillNames, addVotes,
//printHeading here. Also write and place the definitions
//of the functions processVotes and printResults here.
```

Sample Output (After you have written the definitions of the functions of the classes personType and candidateType, and the definitions of the function processVotes and printResults, and run your program, it should produce the following output; see Programming Exercise 13.)

```
--------------------Election Results--------------------

                                        Votes
     Candidate Name      Region1   Region2   Region3   Region4    Total
    -----------------    -------   -------   -------   -------   ------
     Sheila   Bower         23        70       133       267       493
     Danny    Dillion       25        71       156        97       349
     Lisa     Fisher       110       158         0         0       268
     Greg     Goldy         75        34       134         0       243
     Peter    Lamba        285        56         0        46       387
     Mickey   Miller       112       141       156        67       476
```

Winner: Sheila Bower, Votes Received: 493

Total votes polled: 2216

Input Files

candData.txt

```
Greg Goldy
Mickey Miller
Lisa Fisher
Peter Lamba
Danny Dillion
Sheila Bower
```

voteData.txt

```
Greg Goldy 2 34
Mickey Miller 1 56
Lisa Fisher 2 56
Peter Lamba 1 78
Danny Dillion 4 29
Sheila Bower 4 78
Mickey Miller 2 63
Lisa Fisher 1 23
Peter Lamba 2 56
Danny Dillion 1 25
Sheila Bower 2 70
Peter Lamba 4 23
Danny Dillion 4 12
Greg Goldy 3 134
Sheila Bower 4 100
Mickey Miller 3 67
Lisa Fisher 2 67
Danny Dillion 3 67
Sheila Bower 1 23
Mickey Miller 1 56
Lisa Fisher 2 35
Sheila Bower 3 78
Peter Lamba 1 27
```

```
Danny Dillion 2 34
Greg Goldy 1 75
Peter Lamba 4 23
Sheila Bower 3 55
Mickey Miller 4 67
Peter Lamba 1 23
Danny Dillion 3 89
Mickey Miller 3 89
Peter Lamba 1 67
Danny Dillion 2 37
Sheila Bower 4 89
Mickey Miller 2 78
Lisa Fisher 1 87
Peter Lamba 1 90
Danny Dillion 4 56
```

QUICK REVIEW

1. Selection sort sorts a list by finding the smallest (or equivalently, the largest) element in the list, and moving it to the beginning (or the end) of the list.

2. For a list of length n, where $n > 0$, selection sort makes $(1/2)n(n-1)$ key comparisons and $3(n-1)$ item assignments.

3. For a list of length n, where $n > 0$, on average, insertion sort makes $(1/4)n^2 + O(n) = O(n^2)$ key comparisons and $(1/4)n^2 + O(n) = O(n^2)$ item assignments.

4. Empirical studies suggest that for large lists of size n, the number of moves in Shellsort is in the range of $n^{1.25}$ to $1.6n^{1.25}$.

5. Let L be a list of n distinct elements. Any sorting algorithm that sorts L by comparison of the keys only, in its worst case, makes at least $O(n\log_2 n)$ key comparisons.

6. Both quicksort and mergesort sort a list by partitioning the list.

7. To partition a list, quicksort first selects an item from the list, called the pivot. The algorithm then rearranges the elements so that the elements in one of the sublists are less than the pivot, and the elements in the second sublist are greater than or equal to the pivot.

8. In a quicksort, the sorting work is done in partitioning the list.

9. On average, the number of key comparisons in quicksort is $O(n\log_2 n)$. In the worst case, the number of key comparisons in quicksort is $O(n^2)$.

10. Mergesort partitions the list by dividing it in the middle.

11. In mergesort, the sorting work is done in merging the list.

12. The number of key comparisons in mergesort is $O(n\log_2 n)$.

10

13. A heap is a list in which each element contains a key, such that the key in the element at position k in the list is at least as large as the key in the element at position $2k + 1$ (if it exists) and $2k + 2$ (if it exists).

14. The first step in the heapsort algorithm is to convert the list into a heap, called `buildHeap`. After we convert the array into a heap, the sorting phase begins.

15. Suppose that L is a list of n elements, where $n > 0$. In the worst case, the number of key comparisons in heapsort to sort L is $2n\log_2 n + O(n)$. Also, in the worst case, the number of item assignments in heapsort to sort L is $n\log_2 n + O(n)$.

EXERCISES

1. Sort the following list using selection sort as discussed in this chapter. Show the list after each iteration of the outer **for** loop.

   26, 45, 17, 65, 33, 55, 12, 18

2. Sort the following list using selection sort as discussed in this chapter. Show the list after each iteration of the outer **for** loop.

   36, 55, 17, 35, 63, 85, 12, 48, 3, 66

3. Assume the following list of keys: 5, 18, 21, 10, 55, 20
   The first three keys are in order. To move 10 to its proper position using insertion sort as described in this chapter, exactly how many key comparisons are executed?

4. Assume the following list of keys: 7, 28, 31, 40, 5, 20

   The first four keys are in order. To move 5 to its proper position using insertion sort as described in this chapter, exactly how many key comparisons are executed?

5. Assume the following list of keys: 28, 18, 21, 10, 25, 30, 12, 71, 32, 58, 15
   This list is to be sorted using insertion sort as described in this chapter for array-based lists. Show the resulting list after six passes of the sorting phase—that is, after six iterations of the **for** loop.

6. Recall insertion sort for array-based lists as discussed in this chapter. Assume the following list of keys: 18, 8, 11, 9, 15, 20, 32, 61, 22, 48, 75, 83, 35, 3

   Exactly how many key comparisons are executed to sort this list using insertion sort?

7. Explain why the number of item movements in Shellsort is less than the number of item movements in insertion sort.

8. Consider the following list of keys: 80, 57, 65, 30, 45, 77, 27, 4, 90, 54, 45, 2, 63, 38, 81, 28, 62. Suppose that this list is to be sorted using Shellsort. Show the list during each increment, as in this chapter.

a. Use the increment sequence 1, 3, 5

b. Use the increment sequence 1, 4, 7.

9. Both mergesort and quicksort sort a list by partitioning the list. Explain how mergesort differs from quicksort in partitioning the list.

10. Assume the following list of keys: 16, 38, 54, 80, 22, 65, 55, 48, 64, 95, 5, 100, 58, 25, 36

   This list is to be sorted using quicksort as discussed in this chapter. Use pivot as the middle element of the list.

   a. Give the resulting list after one call to the partition procedure.

   b. Give the resulting list after two calls to the partition procedure.

11. Assume the following list of keys: 18, 40, 16, 82, 64, 67, 57, 50, 37, 47, 72, 14, 17, 27, 35

   This list is to be sorted using quicksort as discussed in this chapter. Use pivot as the median of the first, last, and middle elements of the list.

   a. What is the pivot?

   b. Give the resulting list after one call to the partition procedure.

12. Using the function buildHeap as given in this chapter, convert the following array into a heap. Show the final form of the array.

   47, 78, 81, 52, 50, 82, 58, 42, 65, 80, 92, 53, 63, 87, 95, 59, 34, 37, 7, 20

13. Suppose that the following list was created by the function buildHeap during the heap creation phase of heapsort.

   100, 85, 94, 47, 72, 82, 76, 30, 20, 60, 65, 50, 45, 17, 35, 14, 28, 5

   Show the resulting array after two passes of heapsort. (Use the heapify procedure as given in this chapter.) Exactly how many key comparisons are executed during the first pass?

14. Suppose that L is a list is of length n and it is sorted using insertion sort. If L is already sorted in the reverse order, show that the number of comparisons is $(1/2)(n^2 - n)$ and the number of item assignments is $(1/2)(n^2 + 3n) - 2$.

15. Suppose that L is a list is of length n and it is sorted using insertion sort. If L is already sorted, show that the number of comparisons is $(n - 1)$ and the number of item assignments is 0.

16. Write the definition of the class arrayListType that implements the sorting algorithms for array-based lists as discussed in this chapter.

17. Write the definition of the class unorderedLinkedList that implements the searching (described in Chapter 5) and sorting algorithms for linked lists as discussed in this chapter.

10

PROGRAMMING EXERCISES

1. Write and test a version of selection sort for linked lists.

2. Write a program to test insertion sort for array-based lists as given in this chapter.

3. Write a program to test insertion sort for linked lists as given in this chapter.

4. Write the definition of the function `intervalInsertionSort` described in Shellsort. Also write a program to test Shellsort given in this chapter.

5. Write a program to sort an array as follows.

   a. Use insertion sort to sort the array. Print the number of comparisons and the number of item movements.

   b. Use Shellsort to sort the array using the function `shellSort` given in this chapter. Print the number of comparisons and the number of item movements.

   c. Test your program on a list of 1,000 elements and on a list of 10,000 elements.

6. Write a program to test quicksort for array-based lists as given in this chapter.

7. Write and test a version of quicksort for linked lists.

8. (**C. A. R. Hoare**) Let L be a list of size n. Quicksort can be used to find the kth smallest item in L, where $0 \leq k \leq n - 1$, without completely sorting L. Write and implement a C++ function, `kThSmallestItem`, that uses a version of quicksort to determine the kth smallest item in L without completely sorting L.

9. Sort an array of 10,000 elements using quicksort as follows:

   a. Sort the array using `pivot` as the middle element of the array.

   b. Sort the array using `pivot` as the median of the first, last, and middle elements of the array.

   c. Sort the array using `pivot` as the middle element of the array. However, when the size of any sublist reduces to less than 20, sort the sublist using insertion sort.

   d. Sort the array using `pivot` as the median of the first, last, and middle elements of the array. When the size of any sublist reduces to less than 20, sort the sublist using insertion sort.

   e. Calculate and print the CPU time for each of the preceding four steps.

10. Write a program to test mergesort for linked lists as given in this chapter.

11. Write a program to test heapsort for array-based lists as given in this chapter.

12. a. Write the definition of the class template to define the priority queues, as discussed in this chapter as an abstract data type (ADT).

b. Write the definitions of the function templates to implement the operations of the priority queues as defined in part (a).

c. Write a program to test various operations of the priority queues.

13. a. Write the definitions of the functions of the `class personType`, of the Programming Example Election Results, not given in the programming example.

b. Write the definitions of the functions of the `class candidateType`, of the Programming Example Election Results, not given in the programming example.

c. Write the definitions of the function `processVotes` and `printResults`, of the Programming Example Election Results.

d. After completing parts a, b, and c, write a program to produce the output shown in the Sample Run of the Programming Example Election Results.

14. In the Programming Example Election Results, the `class candidateType` contains the function `calculateTotalVotes`. After processing the voting data, this function calculates the total number of votes received by a candidate. The function `updateVotesByRegion` (of the `class candidateType`) updates only the number of votes for a particular region. Modify the definition of this function so that it also updates the total number of votes received by the candidate. By doing so, the function `addVotes` in the main program is no longer needed. Modify and run your program with the modified definition of the function `updateVotesByRegion`.

15. In the Programming Example Election Results, the object `candidateList` of the type `orderedArrayListType` is declared to process the voting data. The operations of inserting a candidate's data and updating and retrieving the votes were somewhat complicated. To update the candidate's votes, we copied each candidate's data from `candidateList` into a temporary object of the type `candidateType`, updated the temporary object, and then replaced the candidate's data with the temporary object. This is because the data member's `list` is a `protected` member of `candidateList`, and each component of `list` is a `private` data member. In this exercise, you are to modify the Programming Example Election Results to simplify the accessing of a candidate's data as follows: Derive a `class candidateListType` from the `class orderedArrayListType`.

```
class candidateListType: public orderedArrayListType<candidateType>
{
public:
  candidateListType();
   //default constructor
  candidateListType(int size);
   //constructor
```

1
0

```
    void processVotes(string fName, string lName, int region,
              int votes);
    //Function to update the number of votes for a
    //particular candidate for a particular region.
    //Postcondition: The name of the candidate, the region,
    //and the number of votes are passed as parameters.
    void addVotes();
    //Function to find the total number of votes received by
    //each candidate.
    void printResult() const;
    //Function to output the voting data.
};
```

Because the class candidateListType is derived from the class orderedArrayListType, and list is a protected data member of the class orderedArrayListType (inherited from the class arrayListType), list can be directly accessed by a member of the class candidateListType.

Write the definitions of the member functions of the class candidateListType. Rewrite and run your program using the class candidateListType.

11 CHAPTER

BINARY TREES AND B-TREES

IN THIS CHAPTER, YOU WILL:

- Learn about binary trees
- Explore various binary tree traversal algorithms
- Learn how to organize data in a binary search tree
- Discover how to insert and delete items in a binary search tree
- Explore nonrecursive binary tree traversal algorithms
- Learn about AVL (height-balanced) trees
- Learn about B-trees

When data is being organized, a programmer's highest priority is to organize it in such a way that item insertion, deletion, and lookups (searches) are fast. You have already seen how to store and process data in an array. Because an array is a random access data structure, if the data is properly organized (for example, sorted), we can use a search algorithm, such as a binary search, to effectively find and retrieve an item from the list. However, we know that storing data in an array has its limitations. For example, item insertion (especially if the array is sorted) and item deletion can be very time consuming, especially if the list size is very large, because each of these operations requires data movement. To speed up item insertion and deletion, we can use linked lists. Item insertion and deletion in a linked list do not require any data movement; we simply adjust some of the pointers in the list. However, one of the drawbacks of linked lists is that they must be processed sequentially. That is, to insert or delete an item, or simply search the list for a particular item, we must begin our search at the first node in the list. As you know, a sequential search is good only for very small lists because the average search length of a sequential search is half the size of the list.

Binary Trees

This chapter discusses how to dynamically organize data so that item insertion, deletion, and lookups are more efficient.

We first introduce some definitions to facilitate our discussion.

Definition: A **binary tree**, T, is either empty or such that

    i. T has a special node called the **root** node.

    ii. T has two sets of nodes, L_T and R_T, called the **left subtree** and **right subtree** of T, respectively.

    iii. L_T and R_T are binary trees.

A binary tree can be shown pictorially. Suppose that T is a binary tree with a root node A. Let L_A denote the left subtree of A and R_A denote the right subtree of A. Now L_A and R_A are binary trees. Suppose that B is the root node of L_A and C is the root node of R_A. B is called the **left child** of A; C is called the **right child** of A. Furthermore, A is called the **parent** of B and C.

In the diagram of a binary tree, each node of the binary tree is represented as a circle and the circle is labeled by the node. The root node of the binary tree is drawn at the top. The left child of the root node (if any) is drawn below and to the left of the root node. Similarly, the right child of the root node (if any) is drawn below and to the right of the root node. Children are connected to the parent by an *arrow* from the parent to the child. An arrow is usually called a **directed edge** or a **directed branch** (or simply a **branch**). Because the root node, B, of L_A is already drawn, we apply the same procedure to draw the remaining parts of L_A. R_A is drawn similarly. If a node has no left child, for example, when we draw an arrow from the node to the left child, we end the arrow with three lines. That is, three lines at the end of an arrow indicate that the subtree is empty.

The diagram in Figure 11-1 is an example of a binary tree. The root node of this binary tree is A. The left subtree of the root node, which we denoted by L_A, is the set $L_A = \{B, D, E, G\}$ and the right subtree of the root node, which we denote by R_A, is the set $R_A = \{C, F, H\}$. The root node of the left subtree of A—that is, the root node of L_A—is node B. The root node of R_A is C, and so on. Clearly, L_A and R_A are binary trees. Because three lines at the end of an arrow mean that the subtree is empty, it follows that the left subtree of D is empty.

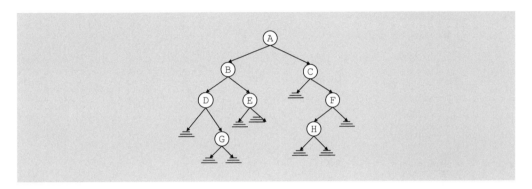

FIGURE 11-1 Binary tree

In Figure 11-1, the left child of A is B and the right child of A is C. Similarly, for node F, the left child is H and node F has no right child.

Example 11-1 shows nonempty binary trees.

EXAMPLE 11-1

Figure 11-2 shows binary trees with one, two, or three nodes.

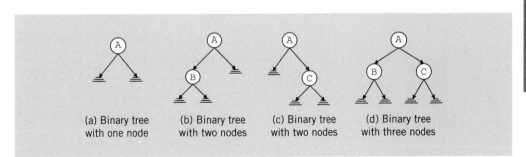

(a) Binary tree with one node

(b) Binary tree with two nodes

(c) Binary tree with two nodes

(d) Binary tree with three nodes

FIGURE 11-2 Binary tree with one, two, or three nodes

In the binary tree of Figure 11-2(a), the root node is A, L_A = empty, and R_A = empty.

In the binary tree of Figure 11-2(b), the root node is A, $L_A = \{B\}$, and R_A = empty. The root node of $L_A = B$, L_B = empty, and R_B = empty.

In the binary tree of Figure 11-2(c), the root node is A, L_A = empty, $R_A = \{C\}$. The root node of $R_A = C$, L_C = empty, and R_C = empty.

In the binary tree of Figure 11-2(d), the root node is A, $L_A = \{B\}$, $R_A = \{C\}$. The root node of $L_A = B$, L_B = empty, R_B = empty. The root node of $R_A = C$, L_C = empty, R_C = empty.

EXAMPLE 11-2

This example shows other cases of nonempty binary trees with three nodes. See Figure 11-3.

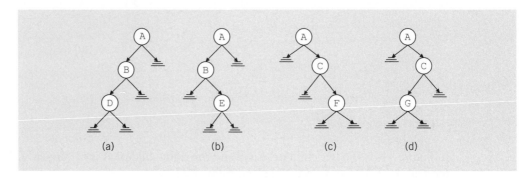

FIGURE 11-3 Various binary trees with three nodes

As you can see from the preceding examples, every node in a binary tree has at most two children. Thus, every node, other than storing its own information, must keep track of its left subtree and right subtree. This implies that every node has two pointers, `llink` and `rlink`. The pointer `llink` points to the root node of the left subtree; the pointer `rlink` points to the root node of the right subtree.

The following `struct` defines the node of a binary tree:

```
template <class elemType>
struct binaryTreeNode
{
    elemType info;
    binaryTreeNode<elemType> *llink;
    binaryTreeNode<elemType> *rlink;
};
```

From the definition of the node, it is clear that for each node,

- The data is stored in `info`.
- A pointer to the left child is stored in `llink`.
- A pointer to the right child is stored in `rlink`.

Furthermore, a pointer to the root node of the binary tree is stored outside the binary tree in a pointer variable, usually called the **root**, of type `binaryTreeNode`. Thus, in general, a binary tree looks like the diagram in Figure 11-4.

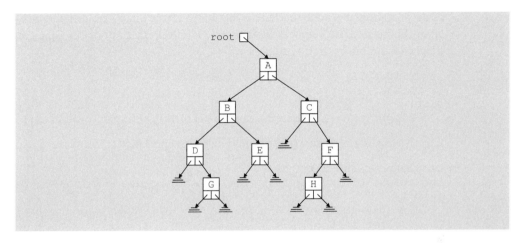

FIGURE 11-4 Binary tree

For simplicity, we will continue to draw binary trees as before. That is, we use circles to represent nodes, and left and right arrows to represent links. As before, three lines at the end of an arrow mean that the subtree is empty.

Before we leave this section, let us define a few more terms.

A node in the binary tree is called a **leaf** if it has no left and right children. Let U and V be two nodes in the binary tree T. U is called a **parent** of V if there is a branch from U to V. A **path** from a node X to a node Y in the binary tree is a sequence of nodes $X_0, X_1, \ldots, X_n$ such that

   i. $X = X_0$, $X_n = Y$
   ii. X_{i-1} is the parent of X_i for all $i = 1, 2, \ldots, n$. That is, there is a branch from X_0 to X_1, X_1 to $X_2, \ldots, X_{i-1}$ to $X_i, \ldots, X_{n-1}$ to X_n.

Because the branches go only from a parent to its children, from the previous discussion it is clear that in a binary tree, there is a unique path from the root to every node in the binary tree.

Definition: The **level of a node** in a binary tree is the number of branches on the path from the root to the node.

Clearly, the level of the root node of a binary tree is 0, and the level of the children of the root node is 1.

Definition: The **height of a binary tree** is the number of nodes on the longest path from the root to a leaf.

Suppose that a pointer p to the root node of a binary tree is given. We next describe the C++ function height to find the height of the binary tree. The pointer to the root node is passed as a parameter to the function height.

If the binary tree is empty, the height is 0. Suppose that the binary tree is nonempty. To find the height of the binary tree, we first find the height of the left subtree and the height of the right subtree. We then take the maximum of these two heights and add 1 to find the height of the binary tree. To find the height of the left (right) subtree, we apply the same procedure because the left (right) subtree is a binary tree. Therefore, the general algorithm to find the height of a binary tree is as follows. Suppose `height(p)` denotes the height of the binary tree with root p.

```
if (p is NULL)
    height(p) =  0
else
    height(p) = 1 + max(height(p->llink), height(p->rlink))
```

Clearly, this is a recursive algorithm. The following function implements this algorithm:

```
template <class elemType>
int height(binaryTreeNode<elemType> *p) const
{
    if (p == NULL)
        return 0;
    else
        return 1 + max(height(p->llink), height(p->rlink));
}
```

The definition of the function height uses the function `max` to determine the larger of two integers. The function `max` can be easily implemented.

Similarly, we can implement algorithms to find the number of nodes and number of leaves in a binary tree.

Copy Tree

One useful operation on binary trees is to make an identical copy of a binary tree. A binary tree is a dynamic data structure; that is, memory for its nodes is allocated and deallocated during program execution. Therefore, if we use just the value of the pointer of the root node to make a copy of a binary tree, we get a shallow copy of the data. To make an identical copy of a binary tree, we need to create as many nodes as there are in the binary tree to be copied. Moreover, in the copied tree, these nodes must appear in the same order as they are in the original binary tree.

Given a pointer to the root node of a binary tree, we next describe the function `copyTree`, which makes a copy of a given binary tree. This function is also useful in implementing the copy constructor and overloading the assignment operator, as described later in this chapter (see the section, "Implementing Binary Trees").

```
template <class elemType>
void copyTree(binaryTreeNode<elemType>* &copiedTreeRoot,
              binaryTreeNode<elemType>* otherTreeRoot)
{
    if (otherTreeRoot == NULL)
        copiedTreeRoot = NULL;
```

```
    else
    {
        copiedTreeRoot = new binaryTreeNode<elemType>;
        copiedTreeRoot->info = otherTreeRoot->info;
        copyTree(copiedTreeRoot->llink, otherTreeRoot->llink);
        copyTree(copiedTreeRoot->rlink, otherTreeRoot->rlink);
    }
}//end copyTree
```

Binary Tree Traversal

The item insertion, deletion, and lookup operations require that the binary tree be traversed. Thus, the most common operation performed on a binary tree is to traverse the binary tree, or visit each node of the binary tree. As you can see from the diagram of a binary tree, the traversal must start at the root node because there is a pointer to the root node. For each node, we have two choices:

- Visit the node first.
- Visit the subtrees first.

These choices lead to three different traversals of a binary tree—Inorder, preorder, and postorder.

Inorder Traversal

In an inorder traversal, the binary tree is traversed as follows:

1. Traverse the left subtree.
2. Visit the node.
3. Traverse the right subtree.

Preorder Traversal

In a preorder traversal, the binary tree is traversed as follows:

1. Visit the node.
2. Traverse the left subtree.
3. Traverse the right subtree.

Postorder Traversal

In a postorder traversal, the binary tree is traversed as follows:

1. Traverse the left subtree.
2. Traverse the right subtree.
3. Visit the node.

Clearly, each of these traversal algorithms is recursive.

The listing of the nodes produced by the inorder traversal of a binary tree is called the **inorder sequence**. The listing of the nodes produced by the preorder traversal of a binary tree is called the **preorder sequence**. The listing of the nodes produced by the postorder traversal of a binary tree is called the **postorder sequence**.

Before giving the C++ code for each of these traversals, let us illustrate the inorder traversal of the binary tree in Figure 11-5. For simplicity, we assume that visiting a node means to output the data stored in the node. The section, "Binary Tree Traversal and Functions as Parameters," located later in this chapter, explains how to modify the binary tree traversal algorithms so that by using a function, the user can specify the action to be performed on a node when the node is visited.

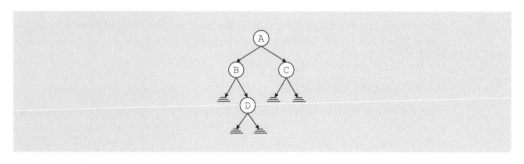

FIGURE 11-5 Binary tree for an inorder traversal

A pointer to the binary tree in Figure 11-5 is stored in the pointer variable `root` (which points to the node with info A). Therefore, we start the traversal at A.

1. Traverse the left subtree of A; that is, traverse $L_A = \{B, D\}$.
2. Visit A.
3. Traverse the right subtree of A; that is, traverse $R_A = \{C\}$.

Now, we cannot do Step 2 until we have finished Step 1.

1. Traverse the left subtree of A; that is, traverse $L_A = \{B, D\}$. Now L_A is a binary tree with the root node B. Because L_A is a binary tree, we apply the inorder traversal criteria to L_A.

   1.1. Traverse the left subtree of B; that is, traverse $L_B = $ empty.
   1.2. Visit B.
   1.3. Traverse the right subtree of B; that is, traverse $R_B = \{D\}$.

As before, first we complete Step 1.1 before going to Step 1.2.

   1.1. Because the left subtree of B is empty, there is nothing to traverse. Step 1.1 is completed, so we proceed to Step 1.2.
   1.2. Visit B. That is, output B on an output device. Clearly, the first node printed is B. This completes Step 1.2, so we proceed to Step 1.3.

1.3. Traverse the right subtree of B; that is, traverse $R_B = \{D\}$. Now R_B is a binary tree with the root node D. Because R_B is a binary tree, we apply the inorder traversal criteria to R_B.

    1.3.1. Traverse the left subtree of D; that is, traverse $L_D =$ empty.

    1.3.2. Visit D.

    1.3.3. Traverse the right subtree of D; that is, traverse $R_D =$ empty.

    1.3.1. Because the left subtree of D is empty, there is nothing to traverse. Step 1.3.1 is completed, so we proceed to Step 1.3.2.

    1.3.2. Visit D. That is, output D on an output device. This completes Step 1.3.2, so we proceed to Step 1.3.3.

    1.3.3. Because the right subtree of D is empty, there is nothing to traverse. Step 1.3.3 is completed.

This completes Step 1.3. Because Steps 1.1, 1.2, and 1.3 are completed, Step 1 is completed, and so we go to Step 2.

2. Visit A. That is, output A on an output device. This completes Step 2, so we proceed to Step 3.

3. Traverse the right subtree of A; that is, traverse $R_A = \{C\}$. Now R_A is a binary tree with the root node C. Because R_A is a binary tree, we apply the inorder traversal criteria to R_A.

    3.1. Traverse the left subtree of C; that is, traverse $L_C =$ empty.

    3.2. Visit C.

    3.3. Traverse the right subtree of C; that is, traverse $R_C =$ empty.

    3.1. Because the left subtree of C is empty, there is nothing to traverse. Step 3.1 is completed.

    3.2. Visit C. That is, output C on an output device. This completes Step 3.2, so we proceed to Step 3.3.

    3.3. Because the right subtree of C is empty, there is nothing to traverse. Step 3.3 is completed.

This completes Step 3, which in turn completes the traversal of the binary tree.

Clearly, the inorder traversal of the previous binary tree outputs the nodes in the following order:

Inorder sequence: $B\ D\ A\ C$

Similarly, the preorder and postorder traversals output the nodes in the following order:

Preorder sequence: $A\ B\ D\ C$

Postorder sequence: $D\ B\ C\ A$

As you can see from the walk-through of the inorder traversal, after visiting the left subtree of a node we must come back to the node itself. The links are only in one direction; that is, the parent node points to the left and right children, but there is no pointer from each child to the parent. Therefore, before going to a child, we must somehow save a pointer to the parent node. A convenient way to do this is to write a recursive inorder function because in a recursive call after completing a particular call, the control goes back to the caller. (Later we discuss how to write nonrecursive traversal functions.) The recursive definition of the function to implement the inorder traversal algorithms is as follows:

```
template <class elemType>
void inorder(binaryTreeNode<elemType> *p) const
{
    if (p != NULL)
    {
        inorder(p->llink);
        cout << p->info << " ";
        inorder(p->rlink);
    }
}
```

To do the inorder traversal of a binary tree, the root node of the binary tree is passed as a parameter to the function inorder. For example, if the root points to the root node of the binary tree, a call to the function inorder is as follows:

```
inorder(root);
```

Similarly, we can write the functions to implement the preorder and postorder traversals. The definitions of these functions are given next.

```
template <class elemType>
void preorder(binaryTreeNode<elemType> *p) const
{
    if (p != NULL)
    {
        cout << p->info << " ";
        preorder(p->llink);
        preorder(p->rlink);
    }
}

template <class elemType>
void postorder(binaryTreeNode<elemType> *p) const
{
    if (p != NULL)
    {
        postorder(p->llink);
        postorder(p->rlink);
        cout << p->info << " ";
    }
}
```

Implementing Binary Trees

The previous sections described various operations that can be performed on a binary tree, as well as the functions to implement these operations. This section describes binary trees as an abstract data type (ADT). Before designing the class to implement a binary tree as an ADT, let us list various operations that are typically performed on a binary tree:

- Determine whether the binary tree is empty.
- Search the binary tree for a particular item.
- Insert an item in the binary tree.
- Delete an item from the binary tree.
- Find the height of the binary tree.
- Find the number of nodes in the binary tree.
- Find the number of leaves in the binary tree.
- Traverse the binary tree.
- Copy the binary tree.

The item search, insertion, and deletion operations all require the binary tree to be traversed. However, because the nodes of a binary tree are in no particular order, these algorithms are not very efficient on arbitrary binary trees. That is, no criteria exist to guide the search on these binary trees, as we will see in the next section. Therefore, we will discuss these algorithms when we discuss special binary trees.

Other than for the search, insertion, and deletion operations, the following class defines binary trees as an ADT. The definition of the node is the same as before. However, for the sake of completeness and easy reference, we give the definition of the node followed by the definition of the class.

```
//****************************************************************
// Author: D.S. Malik
//
// class binaryTreeType
// This class specifies the basic operations to implement a
// binary tree.
//****************************************************************

    //Definition of the node
template <class elemType>
struct binaryTreeNode
{
    elemType info;
    binaryTreeNode<elemType> *llink;
    binaryTreeNode<elemType> *rlink;
};

    //Definition of the class
template <class elemType>
class binaryTreeType
```

```
{
public:
    const binaryTreeType<elemType>& operator=
                   (const binaryTreeType<elemType>&);
      //Overload the assignment operator.
    bool isEmpty() const;
      //Returns true if the binary tree is empty;
      //otherwise, returns false.
    void inorderTraversal() const;
      //Function to do an inorder traversal of the binary tree.
    void preorderTraversal() const;
      //Function to do a preorder traversal of the binary tree.
    void postorderTraversal() const;
      //Function to do a postorder traversal of the binary tree.

    int treeHeight() const;
      //Returns the height of the binary tree.
    int treeNodeCount() const;
      //Returns the number of nodes in the binary tree.
    int treeLeavesCount() const;
      //Returns the number of leaves in the binary tree.
    void destroyTree();
      //Deallocates the memory space occupied by the binary tree.
      //Postcondition: root = NULL;

    binaryTreeType(const binaryTreeType<elemType>& otherTree);
      //copy constructor

    binaryTreeType();
      //default constructor

    ~binaryTreeType();
      //destructor

protected:
    binaryTreeNode<elemType>  *root;

private:
    void copyTree(binaryTreeNode<elemType>* &copiedTreeRoot,
                  binaryTreeNode<elemType>* otherTreeRoot);
      //Makes a copy of the binary tree to which
      //otherTreeRoot points. The pointer copiedTreeRoot
      //points to the root of the copied binary tree.

    void destroy(binaryTreeNode<elemType>* &p);
      //Function to destroy the binary tree to which p points.
      //Postcondition: p = NULL

    void inorder(binaryTreeNode<elemType> *p) const;
      //Function to do an inorder traversal of the binary
      //tree to which p points.
```

```
        void preorder(binaryTreeNode<elemType> *p) const;
          //Function to do a preorder traversal of the binary
          //tree to which p points.
        void postorder(binaryTreeNode<elemType> *p) const;
          //Function to do a postorder traversal of the binary
          //tree to which p points.

        int height(binaryTreeNode<elemType> *p) const;
          //Function to return the height of the binary tree
          //to which p points.
        int max(int x, int y) const;
          //Returns the larger of x and y.
        int nodeCount(binaryTreeNode<elemType> *p) const;
          //Function to return the number of nodes in the binary
          //tree to which p points
        int leavesCount(binaryTreeNode<elemType> *p) const;
          //Function to return the number of leaves in the binary
          //tree to which p points
};
```

Notice that the definition of the `class binaryTreeType` contains the statement to overload the assignment operator, copy constructor, and destructor. This is because the `class binaryTreeType` contains pointer data members. Recall that for classes with pointer data members, the three things that we must do are explicitly overload the assignment operator, include the copy constructor, and include the destructor.

The definition of the `class binaryTreeType` contains several member functions that are `private` members of the class. These functions are used to implement the `public` member functions of the class and the user need not know their existence. For example, to do an inorder traversal, the function `inorderTraversal` calls the function `inorder` and passes the pointer `root` as a parameter to this function. Suppose that you have the following statement:

`binaryTreeType<int> myTree;`

The following statement does an inorder traversal of `myTree`:

`myTree.inorder();`

Also, note that in the definition of the `class binaryTreeType`, the pointer `root` is declared as a `protected` member so that we can later derive special binary trees.

Next, we give the definitions of the member functions of the `class binaryTreeType`.

The binary tree is empty if `root` is `NULL`. So the definition of the function `isEmpty` is as follows:

```
template <class elemType>
bool binaryTreeType<elemType>::isEmpty() const
{
    return (root == NULL);
}
```

11

The default constructor initializes the binary tree to an empty state; that is, it sets the pointer `root` to NULL. Therefore, the definition of the default constructor is as follows:

```
template <class elemType>
binaryTreeType<elemType>::binaryTreeType()
{
    root = NULL;
}
```

The definitions of the other functions are as follows:

```
template <class elemType>
void binaryTreeType<elemType>::inorderTraversal() const
{
    inorder(root);
}
```

```
template <class elemType>
void binaryTreeType<elemType>::preorderTraversal() const
{
    preorder(root);
}
```

```
template <class elemType>
void binaryTreeType<elemType>::postorderTraversal() const
{
    postorder(root);
}
```

```
template <class elemType>
int binaryTreeType<elemType>::treeHeight() const
{
    return height(root);
}
```

```
template <class elemType>
int binaryTreeType<elemType>::treeNodeCount() const
{
    return nodeCount(root);
}
```

```
template <class elemType>
int binaryTreeType<elemType>::treeLeavesCount() const
{
    return leavesCount(root);
}
```

```
template <class elemType>
void binaryTreeType<elemType>::
                    inorder(binaryTreeNode<elemType> *p) const
```

```
{
    if (p != NULL)
    {
        inorder(p->llink);
        cout << p->info << " ";
        inorder(p->rlink);
    }
}

template <class elemType>
void binaryTreeType<elemType>::
                    preorder(binaryTreeNode<elemType> *p) const
{
    if (p != NULL)
    {
        cout << p->info << " ";
        preorder(p->llink);
        preorder(p->rlink);
    }
}

template <class elemType>
void binaryTreeType<elemType>::
                    postorder(binaryTreeNode<elemType> *p) const
{
    if (p != NULL)
    {
        postorder(p->llink);
        postorder(p->rlink);
        cout << p->info << " ";
    }
}

template <class elemType>
int binaryTreeType<elemType>::
                    height(binaryTreeNode<elemType> *p) const
{
    if (p == NULL)
        return 0;
    else
        return 1 + max(height(p->llink), height(p->rlink));
}

template <class elemType>
int binaryTreeType<elemType>::max(int x, int y) const
{
    if (x >= y)
        return x;
    else
        return y;
}
```

The definitions of the functions nodeCount and leavesCount are left as exercises for you. See Programming Exercises 1 and 2 at the end of this chapter.

Next, we give the definitions of the functions `copyTree`, `destroy`, and `destroyTree`, as well as the definitions of the copy constructor and the destructor, and overload the assignment operator.

The definition of the function `copyTree` is the same as before; here this function is a member of the `class binaryTreeType`:

```
template <class elemType>
void binaryTreeType<elemType>::copyTree
                        (binaryTreeNode<elemType>* &copiedTreeRoot,
                         binaryTreeNode<elemType>* otherTreeRoot)
{
    if (otherTreeRoot == NULL)
        copiedTreeRoot = NULL;
    else
    {
        copiedTreeRoot = new binaryTreeNode<elemType>;
        copiedTreeRoot->info = otherTreeRoot->info;
        copyTree(copiedTreeRoot->llink, otherTreeRoot->llink);
        copyTree(copiedTreeRoot->rlink, otherTreeRoot->rlink);
    }
} //end copyTree
```

To destroy a binary tree, for each node, first we destroy its left subtree, then its right subtree, and then the node itself. We must use the operator `delete` to deallocate the memory occupied by each node. The definition of the function `destroy` is as follows:

```
template <class elemType>
void binaryTreeType<elemType>::destroy(binaryTreeNode<elemType>* &p)
{
    if (p != NULL)
    {
        destroy(p->llink);
        destroy(p->rlink);
        delete p;
        p = NULL;
    }
}
```

To implement the function `destroyTree`, we use the function `destroy` and pass the root node of the binary tree to the function `destroy`. The definition of the function `destroyTree` is as follows:

```
template <class elemType>
void binaryTreeType<elemType>::destroyTree()
{
    destroy(root);
}
```

Recall that when a class object is passed by value, the copy constructor copies the value of the actual parameters into the formal parameters. Because the `class binaryTreeType` has pointer data members, which creates dynamic memory, we must provide the definition of the copy constructor to avoid the shallow copying of data. The definition of the copy constructor, given next, uses the function `copyTree` to make an identical copy of the binary tree that is passed as a parameter.

```
    //copy constructor
template <class elemType>
binaryTreeType<elemType>::binaryTreeType
              (const binaryTreeType<elemType>& otherTree)
{
    if (otherTree.root == NULL) //otherTree is empty
        root = NULL;
    else
        copyTree(root, otherTree.root);
}
```

The definition of the destructor is quite straightforward. When an object of type `binaryTreeType` goes out of scope, the destructor deallocates the memory occupied by the nodes of the binary tree. The definition of the destructor uses the function `destroy` to accomplish this task.

```
    //destructor
template <class elemType>
binaryTreeType<elemType>::~binaryTreeType()
{
    destroy(root);
}
```

Next, we discuss the function to overload the assignment operator. To assign the value of one binary tree to another binary tree, we make an identical copy of the binary tree to be assigned by using the function `copyTree`. The definition of the function to overload the assignment operator is as follows:

```
    //overloading the assignment operator
template <class elemType>
const binaryTreeType<elemType>& binaryTreeType<elemType>::operator=
                  (const binaryTreeType<elemType>& otherTree)
{
    if (this != &otherTree) //avoid self-copy
    {
        if (root != NULL)   //if the binary tree is not empty,
                            //destroy the binary tree
            destroy(root);

        if (otherTree.root == NULL) //otherTree is empty
            root = NULL;
        else
            copyTree(root, otherTree.root);
    }//end else

    return *this;
}
```

11

Binary Search Trees

Now that you know the basic operations on a binary tree, this section discusses a special type of binary tree, called a binary search tree.

Consider the binary tree in Figure 11-6.

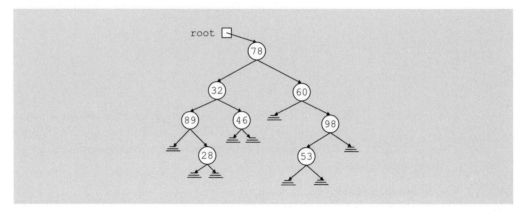

FIGURE 11-6 Arbitrary binary tree

Suppose that we want to determine whether 50 is in the binary tree. To do so, we can use any of the previous traversal algorithms to visit each node and compare the search item with the data stored in the node. However, this could require us to traverse a large part of the binary tree, so the search would be slow. We need to visit each node in the binary tree until either the item is found or we have traversed the entire binary tree because no criteria exist to guide our search. This case is like an arbitrary linked list where we must start our search at the first node, and continue looking at each node until either the item is found or the entire list is searched.

On the other hand, consider the binary tree in Figure 11-7.

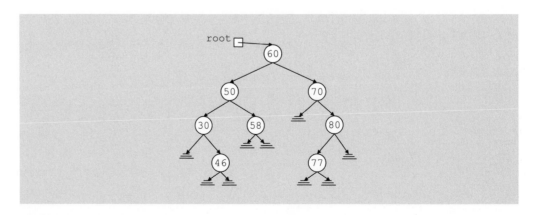

FIGURE 11-7 Binary search tree

In the binary tree in Figure 11-7, the data in each node is

- Larger than the data in its left subtree
- Smaller than the data in its right subtree

The binary tree in Figure 11-7 has some structure. Suppose that we want to determine whether 58 is in this binary tree. As before, we must start our search at the root node. We compare 58 with the data in the root node; that is, we compare 58 with 60. Because 58 ≠ 60 and 58 < 60, it is guaranteed that 58 will not be in the right subtree of the root node. Therefore, if 58 is in the binary tree, it must be in the left subtree of the root node. We follow the left pointer of the root node and go to the node with info 50. We now apply the same criteria at this node. Because 58 > 50, we must follow the right pointer of this node and go to the node with info 58. At this node we find item 58.

This example shows that every time we move down to a child, we eliminate one of the subtrees of the node from our search. If the binary tree is nicely constructed, the search is very similar to the binary search on arrays.

The binary tree given in Figure 11-7 is a special type of binary tree, called a binary search tree. (In the following definition, by the term *key of the node* we mean the key of the data item that uniquely identifies the item.)

Definition: A binary search tree, T, is either empty or the following is true:

   i. T has a special node called the **root** node.

   ii. T has two sets of nodes, L_T and R_T, called the left subtree and right subtree of T, respectively.

   iii.   The key in the root node is larger than every key in the left subtree and smaller than every key in the right subtree.

   iv. L_T and R_T are binary search trees.

The following operations are typically performed on a binary search tree:

- Search the binary search tree for a particular item.
- Insert an item in the binary search tree.
- Delete an item from the binary search tree.
- Find the height of the binary search tree.
- Find the number of nodes in the binary search tree.
- Find the number of leaves in the binary search tree.
- Traverse the binary search tree.
- Copy the binary search tree.

Clearly, every binary search tree is a binary tree. The height of a binary search tree is determined the same way as the height of a binary tree. Similarly, the operations to find the number of nodes, to find the number of leaves, and to do inorder, preorder, and postorder traversals of a binary search tree are the same as those for a binary tree. Therefore, we can inherit all of these operations from the binary tree. That is, we can extend the definition of the binary tree by using the principle of inheritance and, hence, define the binary search tree.

The following class defines a binary search tree as an ADT by extending the definition of the binary tree:

```cpp
//*************************************************************
// Author: D.S. Malik
//
// This class specifies the basic operations to implement a
// binary search tree.
//*************************************************************

template <class elemType>
class bSearchTreeType: public binaryTreeType<elemType>
{
public:
    bool search(const elemType& searchItem) const;
        //Function to determine if searchItem is in the binary
        //search tree.
        //Postcondition: Returns true if searchItem is found in the
        //    binary search tree; otherwise, returns false.

    void insert(const elemType& insertItem);
        //Function to insert insertItem in the binary search tree.
        //Postcondition: If no node in the binary search tree has the
        //    same info as insertItem, a node with the info insertItem
        //    is created and inserted in the binary search tree.

    void deleteNode(const elemType& deleteItem);
        //Function to delete deleteItem from the binary search tree.
        //Postcondition: If a node with the same info as deleteItem
        //    is found, it is deleted from the binary search tree.

private:
    void deleteFromTree(binaryTreeNode<elemType>* &p);
        //Function to delete the node to which p points is deleted
        //from the binary search tree.
        //Postcondition: The node to which p points is deleted from
        //    the binary search tree.
};
```

Next, we describe each of these operations.

Search

The function search searches the binary search tree for a given item. If the item is found in the binary search tree, it returns true; otherwise, it returns false. Because the pointer root points to the root node of the binary search tree, we must begin our search at the root node. Furthermore, because root must always point to the root node, we need a pointer, say current, to traverse the binary search tree. The pointer current is initialized to root.

If the binary search tree is nonempty, we first compare the search item with the info in the root node. If they are the same, we stop the search and return `true`. Otherwise, if the search item is smaller than the info in the node, we follow `llink` to go to the left subtree; otherwise, we follow `rlink` to go to the right subtree. We repeat this process for the next node. If the search item is in the binary search tree, our search ends at the node containing the search item; otherwise, the search ends at an empty subtree. Thus, the general algorithm is as follows:

```
if root is NULL
    Cannot search an empty tree, returns false.
else
{
    current = root;
    while (current is not NULL and not found)
        if (current->info is the same as the search item)
            set found to true;
        else if(current->info is greater than the search item)
            follow the llink of current
        else
            follow the rlink of current
}
```

This pseudocode algorithm translates into the following C++ function:

```cpp
template <class elemType>
bool bSearchTreeType<elemType>::
                    search(const elemType& searchItem) const
{
    binaryTreeNode<elemType> *current;
    bool found = false;

    if (root == NULL)
        cerr << "Cannot search the empty tree." << endl;
    else
    {
        current = root;

        while (current != NULL && !found)
        {
            if (current->info == searchItem)
                found = true;
            else if (current->info > searchItem)
                current = current->llink;
            else
                current = current->rlink;
        }//end while
    }//end else

    return found;
}//end search
```

1
1

Insert

After inserting an item in a binary search tree, the resulting binary tree must also be a binary search tree. To insert a new item, first we search the binary search tree and find the place where the new item is to be inserted. The search algorithm is similar to the search algorithm of the function `search`. Here we traverse the binary search tree with two pointers—a pointer, say `current`, to check the current node and a pointer, say `trailCurrent`, pointing to the parent of current. Because duplicate items are not allowed, our search must end at an empty subtree. We can then use the pointer `trailCurrent` to insert the new item at the proper place. The item to be inserted, `insertItem`, is passed as a parameter to the function `insert`. The general algorithm is as follows:

a. Create a new node and copy `insertItem` into the new node. Also set `llink` and `rlink` of the new node to NULL.

b. if the root is NULL, the tree is empty so make `root` point to the new node.
   else
   {

```
        current = root;
        while (current is not NULL)    //search the binary tree
        {
                trailCurrent = current;
                if (current->info is the same as the insertItem)
                        Error: Cannot insert duplicate
                        exit
                else if(current->info > insertItem)
                        Follow llink of current
                else
                        Follow rlink of current
        }

        //insert the new node in the binary tree

        if (trailCurrent->info > insertItem)
                make the new node the left child of trailCurrent
        else
                make the new node the right child of trailCurrent
   }
```

This pseudocode algorithm translates into the following C++ function:

```cpp
template <class elemType>
void bSearchTreeType<elemType>::insert(const elemType& insertItem)
{
    binaryTreeNode<elemType> *current;  //pointer to traverse the tree
    binaryTreeNode<elemType> *trailCurrent; //pointer behind current
    binaryTreeNode<elemType> *newNode;  //pointer to create the node
```

```
    newNode = new binaryTreeNode<elemType>;
    assert(newNode != NULL);
    newNode->info = insertItem;
    newNode->llink = NULL;
    newNode->rlink = NULL;

    if (root == NULL)
        root = newNode;
    else
    {
        current = root;

        while (current != NULL)
        {
            trailCurrent = current;

            if (current->info == insertItem)
            {
                cerr << "The insert item is already in the list-";
                cerr << "duplicates are not allowed."
                    << insertItem << endl;
                return;
            }
            else if (current->info > insertItem)
                current = current->llink;
            else
                current = current->rlink;
        }//end while

        if (trailCurrent->info > insertItem)
            trailCurrent->llink = newNode;
        else
            trailCurrent->rlink = newNode;
    }
}//end insert
```

Delete

As before, first we search the binary search tree to find the node to be deleted. To help you better understand the delete operation, before describing the function to delete an item from the binary search tree, let us consider the binary search tree given in Figure 11-8.

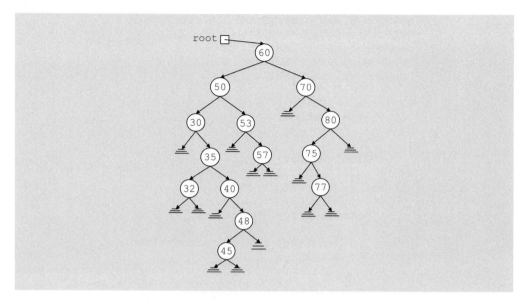

FIGURE 11-8 Binary search tree before deleting a node

After deleting the desired item (if it exists in the binary search tree), the resulting tree must be a binary search tree. The delete operation has four cases, as follows:

Case 1: The node to be deleted has no left and right subtrees; that is, the node to be deleted is a leaf. For example, the node with `info 45` is a leaf.

Case 2: The node to be deleted has no left subtree; that is, the left subtree is empty, but it has a nonempty right subtree. For example, the left subtree of node with `info 40` is empty and its right subtree is nonempty.

Case 3: The node to be deleted has no right subtree; that is, the right subtree is empty, but it has a nonempty left subtree. For example, the left subtree of node with `info 80` is empty and its right subtree is nonempty.

Case 4: The node to be deleted has nonempty left and right subtrees. For example, the left and the right subtrees of node with `info 50` are nonempty.

Figure 11-9 illustrates these four cases.

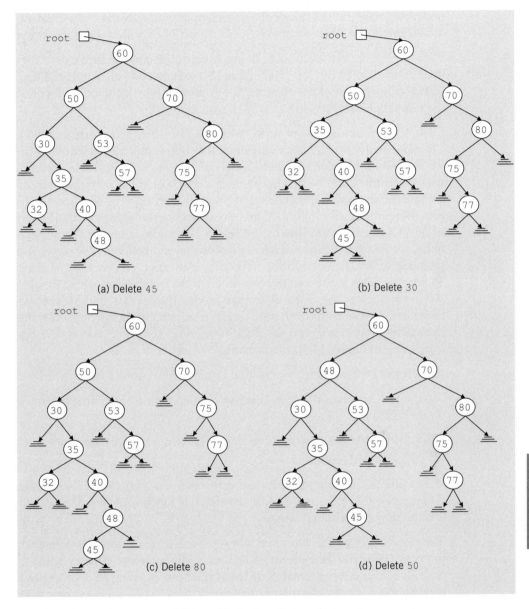

(a) Delete 45

(b) Delete 30

(c) Delete 80

(d) Delete 50

FIGURE 11-9 The binary tree of Figure 11-8 after deleting various items

Case 1: Suppose that we want to delete 45 from the binary search tree in Figure 11-8. We search the binary tree and arrive at the node containing 45. Because this node is a leaf and is the left child of its parent, we can simply set the llink of the parent node to NULL and deallocate the memory occupied by this node. After deleting this node, Figure 11-9(a) shows the resulting binary search tree.

Case 2: Suppose that we want to delete 30 from the binary search tree in Figure 11-8. In this case, the node to be deleted has no left subtree. Because 30 is the left child of its parent node, we make the `llink` of the parent node point to the right child of 30 and then deallocate the memory occupied by 30. Figure 11-9(b) shows the resulting binary tree.

Case 3: Suppose that we want to delete 80 from the binary search tree of Figure 11-8. The node containing 80 has no right child and is the right child of its parent. Thus, we make the `rlink` of the parent of 80—that is, 70—point to the left child of 80. Figure 11-9(c) shows the resulting binary tree.

Case 4: Suppose that we want to delete 50 from the binary search tree in Figure 11-8. The node with `info` 50 has a nonempty left subtree and a nonempty right subtree. Here, we first reduce this case to either Case 2 or Case 3 as follows. To be specific, suppose that we reduce it to Case 3—that is, the node to be deleted has no right subtree. For this case, we find the immediate predecessor of 50 in this binary tree, which is 48. This is done by first going to the left child of 50 and then locating the rightmost node of the left subtree of 50. To do so, we follow the `rlink` of the nodes. Because the binary search tree is finite, we eventually arrive at a node that has no right subtree. Next, we swap the info in the node to be deleted with the info of its immediate predecessor. In this case, we swap 48 with 50. This reduces to the case wherein the node to be deleted has no right subtree. We now apply Case 3 to delete the node. (Note that because we will delete the immediate predecessor from the binary tree, we, in fact, copy only the info of the immediate predecessor into the node to be deleted.) After deleting 50 from the binary search tree in Figure 11-8, the resulting binary tree is as shown in Figure 11-9(d).

In each case, we see that the resulting binary tree is again a binary search tree.

From this discussion, it follows that to delete an item from a binary search tree, we must do the following:

1. Find the node containing the item (if any) to be deleted.
2. Delete the node.

We accomplish the second step by a separate function, which we will call `deleteFromTree`. Given a pointer to the node to be deleted, this function deletes the node by taking into account the previous four cases.

The preceding examples show that whenever we delete a node from a binary tree, we adjust one of the pointers of the parent node. Because the adjustment has to be made in the parent node, we must call the function `deleteFromTree` by using an appropriate pointer of the parent node. For example, suppose that the node to be deleted is 35, which is the right child of its parent node. Further suppose that `trailCurrent` points to the node containing 30, the parent node of 35. A call to the function `deleteFromTree` is as follows:

```
deleteFromTree(trailCurrent->rlink);
```

Of course, if the node to be deleted is the root node, then the call to the function `deleteFromTree` is as follows:

```
deleteFromTree(root);
```

We now define the C++ function deleteFromTree:

```cpp
template <class elemType>
void bSearchTreeType<elemType>::deleteFromTree
                            (binaryTreeNode<elemType>* &p)
{
    binaryTreeNode<elemType> *current;//pointer to traverse the tree
    binaryTreeNode<elemType> *trailCurrent; //pointer behind current
    binaryTreeNode<elemType> *temp;     //pointer to delete the node

    if (p == NULL)
        cerr << "Error: The node to be deleted is NULL." << endl;
    else if(p->llink == NULL && p->rlink == NULL)
    {
        temp = p;
        p = NULL;
        delete temp;
    }
    else if(p->llink == NULL)
    {
        temp = p;
        p = temp->rlink;
        delete temp;
    }
    else if(p->rlink == NULL)
    {
        temp = p;
        p = temp->llink;
        delete temp;
    }
    else
    {
        current = p->llink;
        trailCurrent = NULL;

        while (current->rlink != NULL)
        {
            trailCurrent = current;
            current = current->rlink;
        }//end while

        p->info = current->info;

        if (trailCurrent == NULL) //current did not move;
                                  //current == p->llink; adjust p
            p->llink = current->llink;
        else
            trailCurrent->rlink = current->llink;

        delete current;
    }//end else
}//end deleteFromTree
```

1
1

Next, we describe the function deleteNode. The function deleteNode first searches the binary search tree to find the node containing the item to be deleted. The item to be deleted, deleteItem, is passed as a parameter to the function. If the node containing deleteItem is found in the binary search tree, the function deleteNode calls the function deleteFromTree to delete the node. The definition of the function deleteNode is given next.

```
template <class elemType>
void bSearchTreeType<elemType>::deleteNode(const elemType& deleteItem)
{
    binaryTreeNode<elemType> *current; //pointer to traverse the tree
    binaryTreeNode<elemType> *trailCurrent; //pointer behind current
    bool found = false;

    if (root == NULL)
        cout << "Cannot delete from the empty tree." << endl;
    else
    {
        current = root;
        trailCurrent = root;

        while (current != NULL && !found)
        {
            if (current->info == deleteItem)
                found = true;
            else
            {
                trailCurrent = current;

                if (current->info > deleteItem)
                    current = current->llink;
                else
                    current = current->rlink;
            }
        }//end while

        if (current == NULL)
            cout << "The delete item is not in the tree." << endl;
        else if (found)
        {
            if (current == root)
                deleteFromTree(root);
            else if (trailCurrent->info > deleteItem)
                deleteFromTree(trailCurrent->llink);
            else
                deleteFromTree(trailCurrent->rlink);
        }//end if
    }
}//end deleteNode
```

Binary Search Tree: Analysis

This section provides an analysis of the performance of binary search trees. Let T be a binary search tree with n nodes, where $n > 0$. Suppose that we want to determine whether an item, x, is in T. The performance of the search algorithm depends on the shape of T. Let us first consider the worst case. In the worst case, T is linear. That is, T is one of the forms shown in Figure 11-10.

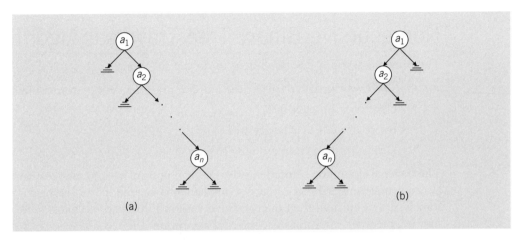

FIGURE 11-10 Linear binary trees

Because T is linear, the performance of the search algorithm on T is the same as its performance on a linear list. Therefore, in the successful case, on average, the search algorithm makes $(n + 1) / 2$ key comparisons. In the unsuccessful case, it makes n comparisons.

Let us now consider the average-case behavior. In the successful case, the search would end at a node. Because there are n items, there are $n!$ possible orderings of the keys. We assume that all $n!$ orderings of the keys are possible. Let $S(n)$ denote the number of comparisons in the average successful case, and $U(n)$ denote the number of comparisons in the average unsuccessful case.

The number of comparisons required to determine whether x is in T is one more than the number of comparisons required to insert x in T. Furthermore, the number of comparisons required to insert x in T is the same as the number of comparisons made in the unsuccessful search, reflecting that x is not in T. From this, it follows that

$$S(n) = 1 + \frac{U(0) + U(1) + \ldots + U(n - 1)}{n}$$

(Equation 11-1)

It is also known that

$$S(n) = \left(1 + \frac{1}{n}\right) U(n) - 3$$

(Equation 11-2)

Solving Equations (11-1) and (11-2), it can be shown that $U(n) \approx 2.77\log_2 n$ and $S(n) \approx 1.39\log_2 n$.

We can now formulate the following result.

Theorem: Let T be a binary search tree with n nodes, where $n > 0$. The average number of nodes visited in a search of T is approximately $1.39\log_2 n = O(\log_2 n)$ and the number of key comparisons is approximately $2.77 \log_2 n = O(\log_2 n)$.

Nonrecursive Binary Tree Traversal Algorithms

The previous sections described how to do the following:

- Traverse a binary tree using the inorder, preorder, and postorder methods.
- Construct a binary tree.
- Insert an item in a binary tree.
- Delete an item from a binary tree.

The traversal algorithms—inorder, preorder, and postorder—discussed earlier are recursive. Because traversing a binary tree is a fundamental operation and recursive functions are somewhat less efficient then their iterative versions, this section discusses the nonrecursive inorder, preorder, and postorder traversal algorithms.

Nonrecursive Inorder Traversal

In the inorder traversal of a binary tree, for each node, the left subtree is visited first, then the node, and then the right subtree. It follows that in an inorder traversal, the first node visited is the leftmost node of the binary tree. For example, in the binary tree in Figure 11-11, the leftmost node is the node with `info 28`.

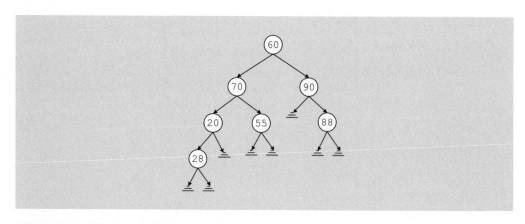

FIGURE 11-11 Binary tree; leftmost node is 28

To get to the leftmost node of the binary tree, we start by traversing the binary tree at the root node and then follow the left link of each node until the left link of a node becomes null. We then back up to the parent node, visit the node, and then move to the right node. Because links go in only one direction, to get back to a node, we must save a pointer to the node before moving to the child node. Moreover, the nodes must be backtracked in the order they were traversed. It follows that while backtracking, the nodes must be visited in a last-in, first-out manner. This can be done by using a stack. We, therefore, save a pointer to a node in a stack. The general algorithm is as follows:

1. `current = root;` `//start traversing the binary tree at the root node`

2. `while (current` is not NULL `or stack` is nonempty)
   `if (current` is not NULL)
   ```
   {
       push current into the stack;
       current = current->llink;
   }
   else
   {
   ```
   `    pop stack into current;`
   `    visit current;`   `//visit the node`
   `    current = current->rlink;`   `//move to the right child`
   ```
   }
   ```

The following function implements the nonrecursive inorder traversal of a binary tree:

```
template <class elemType>
void binaryTreeType<elemType>::nonRecursiveInTraversal() const
{
    stackType<binaryTreeNode<elemType>* > stack;
    binaryTreeNode<elemType> *current;
    current = root;

    while ((current != NULL) || (!stack.isEmptyStack()))
        if (current != NULL)
        {
            stack.push(current);
            current = current->llink;
        }
        else
        {
            current = stack.top();
            stack.pop();
            cout << current->info << " ";
            current = current->rlink;
        }

    cout << endl;
}
```

Nonrecursive Preorder Traversal

In a preorder traversal of a binary tree, for each node, first the node is visited, then the left subtree is visited, and then the right subtree is visited. As in the case of an inorder traversal, after visiting a node and before moving to the left subtree, we must save a pointer to the node so that after visiting the left subtree, we can visit the right subtree. The general algorithm is as follows:

1. `current = root;`   `//start the traversal at the root node`
2. `while (current is not NULL or stack is nonempty)`
   `if (current is not NULL)`
   `{`
       `visit current node;`
       `push current into stack;`
       `current = current->llink;`
   `}`
   `else`
   `{`
       `pop stack into current;`
       `current = current->rlink; //prepare to visit the`
                                  `//right subtree`
   `}`

The following function implements the nonrecursive preorder traversal algorithm:

```
template <class elemType>
void binaryTreeType<elemType>::nonRecursivePreTraversal() const
{
    stackType<binaryTreeNode<elemType>*> stack;
    binaryTreeNode<elemType> *current;

    current = root;

    while ((current != NULL) || (!stack.isEmptyStack()))
        if (current != NULL)
        {
            cout << current->info << " ";
            stack.push(current);
            current = current->llink;
        }
        else
        {
            current = stack.top();
            stack.pop();
            current = current->rlink;
        }

    cout << endl;
}
```

Nonrecursive Postorder Traversal

In a postorder traversal of a binary tree, for each node, first the left subtree is visited, then the right subtree is visited, and then the node is visited. As in the case of an inorder traversal, in a postorder traversal, the first node visited is the leftmost node of the binary tree. Because—for each node—the left and right subtrees are visited before visiting the node, we must indicate to the node whether the left and right subtrees have been visited. After visiting the left subtree of a node and before visiting the node, we must visit its right subtree. Therefore, after returning from a left subtree, we must tell the node that the right subtree needs to be visited, and after visiting the right subtree we must tell the node that it can now be visited. To do this, other than saving a pointer to the node (to get back to the right subtree and to the node itself), we also save an integer value of 1 before moving to the left subtree and an integer value of 2 before moving to the right subtree. Whenever the stack is popped, the integer value associated with that pointer is popped as well. This integer value tells whether the left and right subtrees of a node have been visited.

The general algorithm is as follows:

1. `current = root;` //start the traversal at the root node
2. `v = 0;`
3. `if (current is NULL)`
   the binary tree is empty
4. `if (current is not NULL)`
   a. `push current into stack;`
   b. `push 1 into stack;`
   c. `current = current->llink;`
   d. `while (stack is not empty)`

```
        if (current is not NULL and v is 0)
        {
            push current and 1 into stack;
            current = current->llink;
        }
        else
        {
            pop stack into current and v;
            if (v == 1)
            {
                push current and 2 into stack;
                current = current->rlink;
                v = 0;
            }
            else
                visit current;
        }
```

We use two (parallel) stacks: one to save a pointer to a node and another to save the integer value (1 or 2) associated with this pointer. We leave it as an exercise for you write the definition of a C++ function to implement the preceding postorder traversal algorithm; see Programming Exercise 6 at the end of this chapter.

Binary Tree Traversal and Functions as Parameters

Suppose that you have stored employee data in a binary search tree, and at the end of the year pay increases or bonuses are to be awarded to each employee. This task requires that each node in the binary search tree be visited and that the salary of each employee be updated. The preceding sections discussed various ways to traverse a binary tree. However, in these traversal algorithms—inorder, preorder, and postorder—whenever we visited a node, for simplicity and for illustration purposes, we only output the data contained in each node. How do we use a traversal algorithm to visit each node and update the data in each node? One way to do so is to first create another binary search tree in which the data in each node is the updated data of the original binary search tree, and then destroy the old binary search tree. This would require extra computer time and perhaps extra memory, and, therefore, is not efficient. Another solution is to write separate traversal algorithms to update the data. This solution requires you to frequently modify the definition of the class implementing the binary search tree. However, if the user can write an appropriate function to update the data of each employee and then pass this function as a parameter to the traversal algorithms, we can considerably enhance the program's flexibility. This section describes how to pass functions as parameters to other functions.

In C++, a function name without any parentheses is considered a pointer to the function. To specify a function as a formal parameter to another function, we specify the function type, followed by the function name as a pointer, followed by the parameter types of the function. For example, consider the following statements:

```
void fParamFunc1(void (*visit) (int));         //Line 1
void fParamFunc2(void (*visit) (elemType&));   //Line 2
```

The statement in Line 1 declares `fParamFunc1` to be a function that takes as a parameter any `void` function that has one value parameter of type `int`. The statement in Line 2 declares `fParamFunc2` to be a function that takes as a parameter any `void` function that has one reference parameter of type `elemType`.

We can now rewrite the inorder traversal function of the `class binaryTreeType`. Alternatively, we can overload the existing inorder traversal functions. To further illustrate function overloading, we will overload the inorder traversal functions. Therefore, we include the following statements in the definition of the `class binaryTreeType`:

```
void inorderTraversal(void (*visit) (elemType&));
  //Function to do an inorder traversal of the binary tree.
  //The parameter visit, which is a function, specifies the
  //action to be taken at each node.
```

```
void inorder(binaryTreeNode<elemType> *p, void (*visit) (elemType&));
    //Function to do an inorder traversal of the binary
    //tree, starting at the node specified by the parameter p.
    //The parameter visit, which is a function, specifies the
    //action to be taken at each node.
```

The definitions of these functions are as follows:

```
template <class elemType>
void binaryTreeType<elemType>::inorderTraversal
                            (void (*visit) (elemType& item))
{
    inorder(root, *visit);
}

template <class elemType>
void binaryTreeType<elemType>::inorder(binaryTreeNode<elemType>* p,
                            void (*visit) (elemType& item))
{
    if (p != NULL)
    {
        inorder(p->llink, *visit);
        (*visit)(p->info);
        inorder(p->rlink, *visit);
    }
}
```

The statement

```
(*visit)(p->info);
```

in the definition of the function `inorder` makes a call to the function with one reference parameter of the type `elemType` pointed to by the pointer `visit`.

Example 11-3 further illustrates how functions are passed as parameters to other functions.

EXAMPLE 11-3

This example shows how to pass a user-defined function as a parameter to the binary tree traversal algorithms. For illustration purposes, we show how to use only the inorder traversal function.

The following program uses the class `bSearchTreeType`, which is derived from the class `binaryTreeType`, to build the binary tree. The traversal functions are included in the class `binaryTreeType`, which are then inherited by the class `bSearchTreeType`.

```
//***************************************************************
// Author: D.S. Malik
//
// This program illustrates how to pass a user-defined function
// as a parameter to the binary tree traversal algorithms.
//***************************************************************
```

```cpp
#include <iostream>                                      //Line 1
#include "binarySearchTree.h"                            //Line 2

using namespace std;                                     //Line 3

void print(int& x);                                      //Line 4
void update(int& x);                                     //Line 5

int main()                                               //Line 6
{                                                        //Line 7
    bSearchTreeType<int>  treeRoot;                      //Line 8

    int num;                                             //Line 9

    cout << "Line 10: Enter numbers ending with -999"
         << endl;                                        //Line 10
    cin >> num;                                          //Line 11

    while (num != -999)                                  //Line 12
    {                                                    //Line 13
        treeRoot.insert(num);                            //Line 14
        cin >> num;                                      //Line 15
    }                                                    //Line 16

    cout << endl << "Line 17: Tree nodes in inorder: ";  //Line 17
    treeRoot.inorderTraversal(print);                    //Line 18
    cout << endl << "Line 19: Tree Height: "
         << treeRoot.treeHeight()
         << endl << endl;                                //Line 19

    cout << "Line 20: ******* Update Nodes *******"
         << endl;                                        //Line 20
    treeRoot.inorderTraversal(update);                   //Line 21

    cout << "Line 22: Tree nodes in inorder after "
         << "the update: " << endl << "            ";    //Line 22
    treeRoot.inorderTraversal(print);                    //Line 23
    cout << endl <<"Line 24: Tree Height: "
         << treeRoot.treeHeight() << endl;               //Line 24

    return 0;                                            //Line 25
}                                                        //Line 26

void print(int& x)                                       //Line 27
{                                                        //Line 28
    cout << x << " ";                                    //Line 29
}                                                        //Line 30

void update(int& x)                                      //Line 31
{                                                        //Line 32
    x = 2 * x;                                           //Line 33
}                                                        //Line 34
```

Sample Run: In this sample run, the user input is shaded.

```
Line 10: Enter numbers ending with -999
56 87 23 65 34 45 12 90 66 -999

Line 17: Tree nodes in inorder: 12 23 34 45 56 65 66 87 90
Line 19: Tree Height: 4

Line 20: ******* Update Notes *******
Line 22: Tree nodes in inorder after the update:
         24 46 68 90 112 130 132 174 180
Line 24: Tree Height: 4
```

This program works as follows. The statement in Line 8 declares `treeRoot` to be a binary search tree object, in which the data in each node is of type `int`. The statements in Lines 11 through 16 build the binary search tree. The statement in Line 18 uses the member function `inorderTraversal` of `treeRoot` to traverse the binary search tree `treeRoot`. The parameter to the function `inorderTraversal`, in Line 18, is the function `print` (defined at Line 27). Because the function `print` outputs the value of its argument, the statement in Line 18 outputs the data of the nodes of the binary search tree `treeNode`. The statement in Line 19 outputs the height of the binary search tree.

The statement in Line 21 uses the member function `inorderTraversal` to traverse the binary search tree `treeRoot`. In Line 21, the actual parameter of the function `inorderTraversal` is the function `update` (defined at Line 31). The function `update` doubles the value of its argument. Therefore, the statement in Line 21 updates the data of each node of the binary search tree by doubling the value. The statements in Lines 23 and 24 output the nodes and the height of the binary search tree.

AVL (Height-Balanced) Trees

In the previous sections, you learned how to build and manipulate a binary search tree. The performance of the search algorithm on a binary search tree depends on how the binary tree is built. The shape of the binary search tree depends on the data set. If the data set is sorted, the binary search tree is linear and so the search algorithm would not be efficient. On the other hand, if the tree is nicely built, the search would be fast. In fact, the smaller the height of the tree, the faster the search. Therefore, we want the height of the binary search tree to be as small as possible. This section describes a special type of binary search tree, called the **AVL tree** (also called the **height-balanced tree**) in which the resulting binary search is nearly balanced. AVL trees are due to the mathematicians G. M. Adelson-Velskii and E. M. Landis and are so named in their honor. The methods of building such binary trees were given by them in 1962.

We begin by defining the following terms.

Definition: A **perfectly balanced** binary tree is a binary tree such that

   i.   The heights of the left and right subtrees of the root are equal.

   ii.   The left and right subtrees of the root are perfectly balanced binary trees.

Figure 11-12 shows a perfectly balanced binary tree.

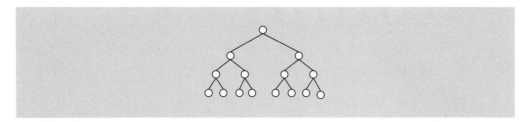

FIGURE 11-12 Perfectly balanced binary tree

Let T be a binary tree and x be a node in T. If T is perfectly balanced, then from the definition of the perfectly balanced tree, it follows that the height of the left subtree of x is the same as the height of the right subtree of x.

It can be proved that, if T is a perfectly balanced binary tree of height h, then the number of nodes in T is $2^h - 1$. From this, it follows that if the number of items in the data set is not equal to $2^h - 1$ for some nonnegative integer h, then we cannot construct a perfectly balanced binary tree. Moreover, perfectly balanced binary trees are a too stringent refinement.

Definition: An **AVL tree** (or **height-balanced tree**) is a binary search tree such that

    i.   The heights of the left and right subtrees of the root differ by at most 1.

    ii.   The left and right subtrees of the root are AVL trees.

Figure 11-13 gives examples of AVL and non–AVL trees.

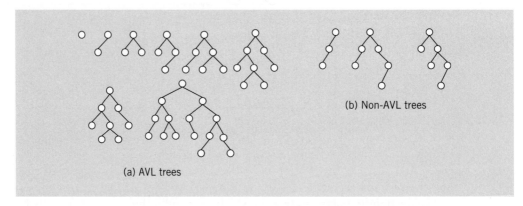

FIGURE 11-13 AVL and non-AVL trees

Let x be a node in a binary tree. Let x_l denote the height of the left subtree of x, and x_h denote the height of the right subtree of x.

Proposition: Let T be an AVL tree and x be a node in T. Then $|x_h - x_l| \leq 1$, where $|x_h - x_l|$ denotes the absolute value of $x_h - x_l$.

Let x be a node in the AVL tree T.

1. If $x_l > x_h$, we say that x is **left high**. In this case, $x_l = x_h + 1$.
2. If $x_l = x_h$, we say that x is **equal high**.
3. If $x_h > x_l$, we say that x is **right high**. In this case, $x_h = x_l + 1$.

Definition: The **balance factor** of x, written $bf(x)$, is defined by $bf(x) = x_h - x_l$.

Let x be a node in the AVL tree T. Then,

1. If x is left high, $bf(x) = -1$.
2. If x is equal high, $bf(x) = 0$.
3. If x is right high, $bf(x) = 1$.

Definition: Let x be a node in a binary tree. We say that the node x **violates the balance criteria** if $|x_h - x_l| > 1$, that is, the heights of the left and right subtrees of x differ by more than 1.

From the preceding discussion, it follows that in addition to the data and pointers to the left and right subtrees, one more thing is associated with each node x in the AVL tree T, which is the balance factor of x. Thus, every node must keep track of its balance factor. To make the algorithms efficient, we store the balance factor of each node in the node itself. Hence, the definition of a node in the AVL tree is as follows:

```
template<class elemType>
struct AVLNode
{
    elemType info;
    int bfactor;  //balance factor
    AVLNode<elemType> *llink;
    AVLNode<elemType> *rlink;
};
```

Because an AVL tree is a binary search tree, the search algorithm for an AVL tree is the same as the search algorithm for a binary search tree. Other operations, such as finding the height, determining the number of nodes, checking whether the tree is empty, tree traversal, and so on, on AVL trees can be implemented exactly the same way they are implemented on binary trees. However, item insertion and deletion operations on AVL trees are somewhat different from the ones discussed for binary search trees. This is because after inserting (or deleting) a node from an AVL tree, the resulting binary tree must be an AVL tree. Next, we describe these operations.

Insertion

To insert an item in an AVL tree, first we search the tree and find the place where the new item is to be inserted. Because an AVL tree is a binary search tree, to find the place for the new item we can search the AVL tree using a search algorithm similar to the search algorithm designed for binary search trees. If the item to be inserted is already in the tree, the search ends at a nonempty subtree. Because duplicates are not allowed, in this case we can output an appropriate error message. Suppose that the item to be inserted is not in the AVL tree. Then, the search ends at an empty subtree and we insert the item in that subtree. After inserting the new item in the tree, the resulting tree might not be an AVL tree. Thus, we must restore the tree's balance criteria. This is accomplished by traveling the same path, back to the root node, which was followed when the new item was inserted in the AVL tree. The nodes on this path (back to the root node) are visited and either their balance factor is changed, or we might have to reconstruct part of the tree. We illustrate these cases with the help of the following examples.

> **NOTE** In Figures 11-14 to 11-17, for each node, we show only the data stored in the node. Furthermore, an equal sign, =, on the top of a node indicates that the balance factor of this node is 0, the less-than sign, <, indicates that the balance factor of this node is −1, and the greater-than sign, >, indicates that the balance factor of this node is 1.

Consider the AVL tree of Figure 11-14 (a). Let us insert 90 into this AVL tree.

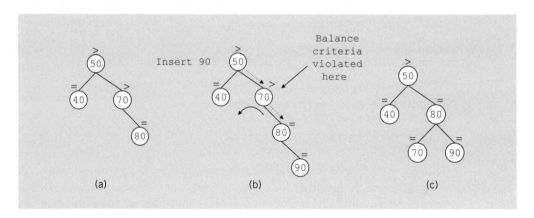

FIGURE 11-14 AVL tree before and after inserting 90

We search the tree starting at the root node to find the place for 90. The dotted arrow shows the path. We insert a node with `info` 90 and obtain the tree of Figure 11-14(b). The binary tree of Figure 11-14(b) is not an AVL tree. So we backtrack and go to node 80. Prior to insertion, `bf(80)` was 0. Because the new node was inserted into the (empty) right subtree of 80, we change its balance factor to 1 (not shown in the figure). Now we go back to node 70. Prior to insertion, `bf(70)` was 1. Because after insertion the height of the right subtree of 70 is increased, we see that the subtree with root node

70 is not an AVL tree. In this case, we reconstruct this subtree (this is called rotating the tree at root node 70). Therefore, we obtain the tree shown in Figure 11-14(c). The binary tree of Figure 11-14 is an AVL tree.

Now consider the AVL tree of Figure 11-15(a). Let us insert 75 into the AVL tree of Figure 11-15(a).

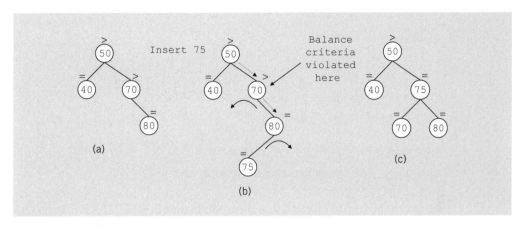

FIGURE 11-15 AVL tree before and after inserting 75

As before, we search the tree starting at the root node. The dotted arrows show the path traversed. After inserting 75, the resulting tree is shown in Figure 11-15(b). After inserting 75, we backtrack. First we go to node 80 and change its balance factor to –1. The subtree with root node 80 is an AVL tree. Now we go back to 70. Clearly, the subtree with root node 70 is not an AVL tree. So we construct this subtree. In this case, we first reconstruct the subtree at root node 80, and then reconstruct the subtree at root node 70 to obtain the tree shown in Figure 11-15(c). (These constructions, that is, rotations, are explained in the next section, "AVL Tree Rotations.")

Notice that in Figures 11-14(c) and 11-15(c), after reconstructing the subtree at the node, the subtree no longer grew in height. At this point, we usually send the message that overall the tree did not gain any height to the remaining nodes on the path back to the root node of the tree, and so the remaining nodes on the path do not need to do anything.

Next, consider the AVL tree of Figure 11-16. Let us insert 95 into this AVL tree.

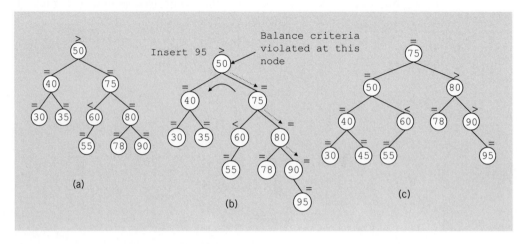

FIGURE 11-16 AVL tree before and after inserting 95

We search the tree and insert 95, as shown in Figure 11-16(b). After inserting 95, we see that the subtrees with root nodes 90, 80, and 75 are still AVL trees. When backtracking the path, we simply adjust the balance factor of these nodes (if needed). However, when we backtrack to the root node, we discover that the tree at this node is no longer an AVL tree. Prior to insertion, bf(50) was 1, that is, its right subtree was higher than its left subtree. After insertion, the subtree grew in height, thus violating the balance criteria at 50. So we construct the tree at node 50. In this case, the tree will be reconstructed as shown in Figure 11-16(c).

Before discussing the general algorithms for reconstructing (rotating) a subtree, let us consider one more case. Consider the AVL tree as shown in Figure 11-17(a). Let us insert 88 in this tree.

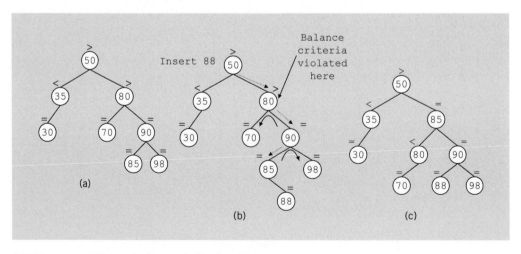

FIGURE 11-17 AVL tree before and after inserting 88

Following the insertion procedure as described previously, we obtain the tree as shown in Figure 11-17(b). As before, we now backtrack to the root node. We adjust the balance factor of nodes 85 and 90. When we visit node 80, we discover that at this node we need to reconstruct the subtree. In this case, the subtree is reconstructed as shown in Figure 11-17(c). As before, after reconstructing the subtree, the entire tree is balanced. So for the remaining nodes on the path back to the root node, we would not do anything.

The examples described previously indicate that if part of the tree requires reconstruction, then after reconstructing that part of the tree, we can ignore the remaining nodes on the path back to the root node. (This is, indeed, the case.) Also, after inserting the node, the reconstruction can occur at any node on the path back to the root node.

AVL Tree Rotations

We now describe the reconstruction procedure, called **rotating** the tree. There are two types of rotations: **left rotation** and **right rotation**. Suppose the rotation occurs at a node x. If it is a left rotation, then certain nodes from the right subtree of x move to its left subtree; the root of the right subtree of x becomes the new root of the reconstructed subtree. Similarly, if it is a right rotation at x, certain nodes from the left subtree of x move to its right subtree; the root of the left subtree of x becomes the new root of the reconstructed subtree.

Case 1: Consider Figure 11-18.

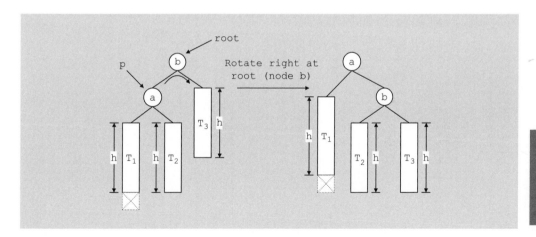

FIGURE 11-18 Right rotation at b

In Figure 11-18, subtrees T_1, T_2, and T_3 are of equal height, say h. The dotted rectangle shows an item insertion in T_1, causing the height of the subtree T_1 to increase by 1. The subtree at node a is still an AVL tree, but the balance criteria is violated at the root node. We note the following in this tree. Because the tree is a binary search tree,

- Every key in subtree T_1 is smaller than the key in node a.
- Every key in subtree T_2 is larger than the key in node a.
- Every key in subtree T_2 is smaller than the key in node b.

Therefore,

1. We make T_2 (the right subtree of node a) the left subtree of node b.
2. We make node b the right child of node a.
3. Node a becomes the root of the reconstructed tree, as shown in Figure 11-18.

Case 2: This case is a mirror image of Case 1. See Figure 11-19.

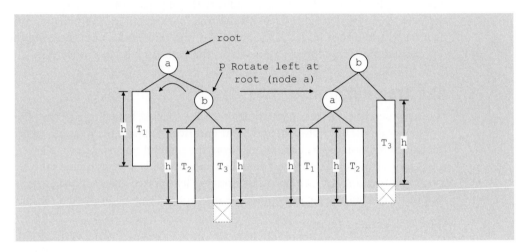

FIGURE 11-19 Left rotation at *a*

Case 3: Consider Figure 11-20.

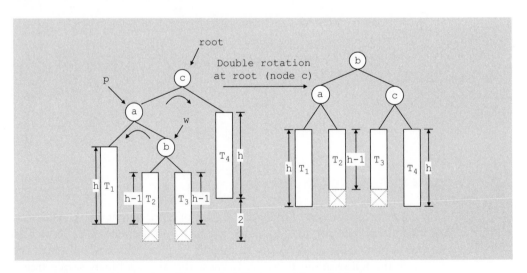

FIGURE 11-20 Double rotation: First rotate left at *a* and then right at *c*

In Figure 11-20, the tree on the left is the tree prior to the reconstruction. The heights of the subtrees are shown in the figure. The dotted rectangle shows that a new item is inserted in the subtree, causing the subtree to grow in height. The new item is inserted either in T_2 or T_3. We note the following (in the tree prior to reconstruction):

- All keys in T_3 are smaller than the key in node c.
- All keys in T_3 are larger than the key in node b.
- All keys in T_2 are smaller than the key in node b.
- All keys in T_2 are larger than the key in node a.
- After insertion, the subtrees with root nodes a and b are still AVL trees.
- The balance criteria is violated at the root node, c, of the tree.
- The balance factors of node c, $bf(c) = -1$, and node a, $bf(a) = 1$ are opposite.

This is an example of double rotation. One rotation is required at node a, and another rotation is required at node c. If the balance factor of the node, where the tree is to be reconstructed, and the balance factor of the higher subtree are opposite, that node requires a double rotation. First, we rotate the tree at node a and then at node c. Now the tree at node a is right high and so we make a left rotation at a. Next, because the tree at node c is left high, we make a right rotation at c. Figure 11-20 shows the resulting tree (which is to the right of the tree after insertion). Figure 11-21, however, shows both rotations in sequence.

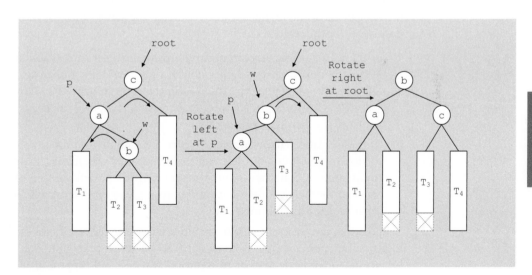

FIGURE 11-21 Left rotation at *a* followed by a right rotation at *c*

Case 4: This is a mirror image of Case 3. We illustrate this with the help of Figure 11-22.

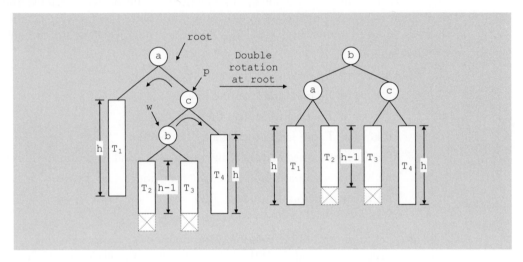

FIGURE 11-22 Double rotation: First rotate right at *c*, then rotate left at *a*

Using these four cases, we now describe what type of rotation might be required at a node.

Suppose that the tree is to be reconstructed, by rotation, at node x. Then, the subtree with root node x requires either a single or a double rotation.

1.   Suppose that the balance factor of the node x and the balance factor of the root node of the higher subtree of x have the same sign, that is, both positive or both negative.

   a.   If these balance factors are positive, make a single *left* rotation at x. (Prior to insertion, the right subtree of x was higher than its left subtree. The new item was inserted in the right subtree of x, causing the height of the right subtree to increase in height, which in turn violated the balance criteria at x.)

   b.   If these balance factors are negative, make a single *right* rotation at x. (Prior to insertion, the left right subtree of x was higher than its right subtree. The new item was inserted in the left subtree of x, causing the height of the left subtree to increase in height, which in turn violated the balance criteria at x.)

2.   Suppose that the balance factor of the node x and the balance factor of the higher subtree of x are opposite in sign. To be specific, suppose that the balance factor of node x prior to insertion was -1 and suppose that y is the root node of the left subtree of x. After insertion, the balance factor of node y is 1. That is, after insertion, the right subtree of node y grew in height. In this case, we require a *double* rotation at x. First, we make a left rotation at y (because y is right high). Then, we make a right rotation at x. The other case, which is a mirror image of this case, is handled similarly.

The following C++ functions implement the left and right rotations of a node. The pointer of the node requiring the rotation is passed as a parameter to the function.

```cpp
template <class elemT>
void rotateToLeft(AVLNode<elemT>* &root)
{
    AVLNode<elemT> *p;   //pointer to the root of the
                         //right subtree of root
    if (root == NULL)
        cerr << "Error in the tree" << endl;
    else if (root->rlink == NULL)
        cerr << "Error in the tree:"
            <<" No right subtree to rotate." << endl;
    else
    {
        p = root->rlink;
        root->rlink = p->llink; //the left subtree of p becomes
                                //the right subtree of root
        p->llink = root;
        root = p;   //make p the new root node
    }
}//rotateLeft

template <class elemT>
void rotateToRight(AVLNode<elemT>* &root)
{
    AVLNode<elemT> *p;   //pointer to the root of
                         //the left subtree of root

    if (root == NULL)
        cerr << "Error in the tree" << endl;
    else if (root->llink == NULL)
        cerr << "Error in the tree:"
            << " No left subtree to rotate." << endl;
    else
    {
        p = root->llink;
        root->llink = p->rlink; //the right subtree of p becomes
                                //the left subtree of root
        p->rlink = root;
        root = p;   //make p the new root node
    }
}//end rotateRight
```

Now that we know how to implement both rotations, we next write the C++ functions, `balanceFromLeft` and `balanceFromRight`, which are used to reconstruct the tree at a particular node. The pointer of the node where reconstruction occurs is passed as a parameter to this function. These functions use the functions `rotateToLeft` and `rotateToRight` to reconstruct the tree, and also adjust the balance factors of the nodes affected by the reconstruction. The function `balanceFromLeft` is called when the subtree is left double high and certain nodes need to be moved to the right subtree. The function balanceFromRight has similar conventions.

```cpp
template <class elemT>
void balanceFromLeft(AVLNode<elemT>* &root)
{
    AVLNode<elemT> *p;
    AVLNode<elemT> *w;

    p = root->llink;    //p points to the left subtree of root

    switch (p->bfactor)
    {
    case -1:
        root->bfactor = 0;
        p->bfactor = 0;
        rotateToRight(root);
        break;

    case 0:
        cerr << "Error: Cannot balance from the left." << endl;
        break;

    case 1:
        w = p->rlink;
        switch (w->bfactor)  //adjust the balance factors
        {
        case -1:
            root->bfactor = 1;
            p->bfactor = 0;
            break;

        case 0:
            root->bfactor = 0;
            p->bfactor = 0;
            break;

        case 1:
            root->bfactor = 0;
            p->bfactor = -1;
        }//end switch

        w->bfactor = 0;
        rotateToLeft(p);
        root->llink = p;
        rotateToRight(root);
    }//end switch;
}//end balanceFromLeft
```

For the sake of completeness, we also give the definition of the function `balanceFromRight`:

```cpp
template <class elemT>
void balanceFromRight(AVLNode<elemT>* &root)
{
    AVLNode<elemT> *p;
    AVLNode<elemT> *w;

    p = root->rlink;    //p points to the left subtree of root

    switch (p->bfactor)
    {
    case -1:
        w = p->llink;
        switch (w->bfactor)  //adjust the balance factors
        {
        case -1:
            root->bfactor = 0;
            p->bfactor = 1;
            break;

        case 0:
            root->bfactor = 0;
            p->bfactor = 0;
            break;

        case 1:
            root->bfactor = -1;
            p->bfactor = 0;
        }//end switch

        w->bfactor = 0;
        rotateToRight(p);
        root->rlink = p;
        rotateToLeft(root);
        break;

    case 0:
        cerr << "Error: Cannot balance from the left." << endl;
        break;

    case 1:
        root->bfactor = 0;
        p->bfactor = 0;
        rotateToLeft(root);
    }//end switch;
}//end balanceFromRight
```

We now focus our attention on the function `insertIntoAVL`. The function `insertIntoAVL` inserts the new item in the AVL tree. The item to be inserted and the pointer of the root node of the AVL tree are passed as parameters to this function.

The following steps describe the function `insertIntoAVL`:

1. Create a node and copy the item to be inserted into the newly created node.
2. Search the tree and find the place for the new node in the tree.
3. Insert the new node in the tree.
4. Backtrack the path, which was constructed to find the place for the new node in the tree, to the root node. If necessary, adjust the balance factors of the nodes, or reconstruct the tree at a node on the path.

Because Step 4 requires us to backtrack the path to the root node, and in the binary tree we have links only from the parent to the children, the easiest way to implement the function `insertIntoAVL` is to use recursion. (Recall that recursion automatically takes care of the backtracking.) This is exactly what we do. The function `insertIntoAVL` also uses a reference `bool` parameter, `isTaller`, to indicate to the parent whether the subtree grew in height or not.

```
template <class elemT>
void insertIntoAVL(AVLNode<elemT>* &root,
                   AVLNode<elemT>  *newNode, bool& isTaller)
{
    if (root == NULL)
    {
        root = newNode;
        isTaller = true;
    }
    else if (root->info == newNode->info)
        cerr << "No duplicates are allowed." << endl;
    else if (root->info > newNode->info) //newItem goes in
                                         //the left subtree
    {
        insertIntoAVL(root->llink, newNode, isTaller);

        if (isTaller) //after insertion, the subtree grew in height
            switch (root->bfactor)
            {
            case -1:
                balanceFromLeft(root);
                isTaller = false;
                break;

            case 0:
                root->bfactor = -1;
                isTaller = true;
                break;
```

```
            case 1:
                root->bfactor = 0;
                isTaller = false;
            }//end switch
        }//end if

    else
    {
        insertIntoAVL(root->rlink, newNode, isTaller);

        if (isTaller) //after insertion, the subtree grew in
                            //height
            switch (root->bfactor)
            {
            case -1:
                root->bfactor = 0;
                isTaller = false;
                break;

            case 0:
                root->bfactor = 1;
                isTaller = true;
                break;

            case 1:
                balanceFromRight(root);
                isTaller = false;
            }//end switch
    }//end else
}//insertIntoAVL
```

Next, we illustrate the `insertIntoAVL` function and build an AVL tree from scratch. Initially the tree is empty. Each figure shows the item to be inserted as well as the balance factor of each node. An equal sign, =, on the top of a node indicates that the balance factor of this node is 0, the less-than sign, <, indicates that the balance factor of this node is −1, and the greater-than sign, >, indicates that the balance factor of this node is 1.

Figure 11-23 shows how items are inserted into an initially empty AVL tree.

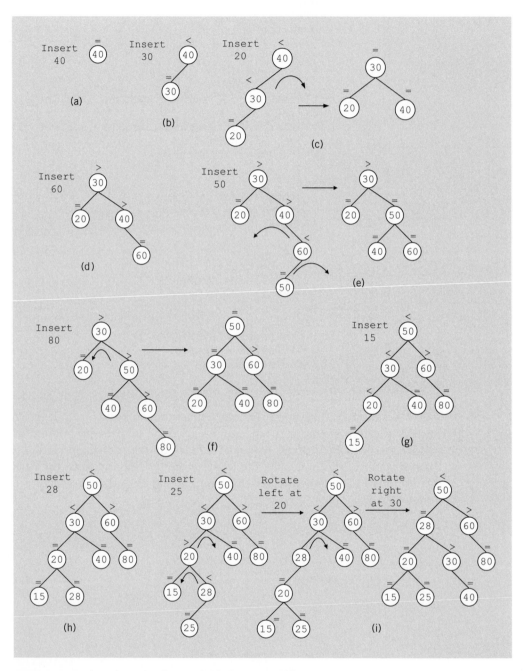

FIGURE 11-23 Item insertion into an initially empty AVL tree

First, we insert 40; see Figure 11-23(a). Next, we insert 30 into the AVL tree. Item 30 is inserted into the left subtree of node 40, causing the left subtree of 40 to grow in height. After insertion, the balance factor of node 40 is -1; see Figure 11-23(b).

Next, we insert 20 into the AVL tree. See Figure 11-23(c). The insertion of 20 violates the balance criteria at node 40. The tree is reconstructed at node 40 by making a single right rotation.

Next, we insert 60 into the AVL tree. See Figure 11-23(d). The insertion of 60 does not require reconstruction; only the balance factor is adjusted at nodes 40 and 30.

Next, we insert 50. See Figure 11-23(e). The insertion of 50 requires the tree to be reconstructed at 40. Notice that a double rotation is made at node 40.

Next, we insert 80; see Figure 11-23(f). The insertion of 80 requires the tree to be reconstructed at node 30.

Next, we insert 15; see Figure 11-23(g). The insertion of node 15 does not require any part of the tree to be reconstructed. We need to only adjust the balance factor of nodes 20, 30, and 50.

Next, we insert 28; see Figure 11-23(h). The insertion of node 28 also does not require any part of the tree to be reconstructed. We need only to adjust the balance factor of node 20.

Next, we insert 25. The insertion of 25 requires a double rotation at node 30. Figure 11-23(i) shows both rotations in sequence. In Figure 11-23(i), the tree is first rotated left at node 20 and then right at node 30.

The following function creates a node, stores the info in the node, and calls the function `insertIntoAVL` to insert the new node in the AVL tree:

```
template <class elemT>
void insert(const elemT &newItem)
{
    bool isTaller = false;
    AVLNode<elemT>  *newNode;

    newNode = new AVLNode<elemT>;
    newNode->info = newItem;
    newNode->bfactor = 0;
    newNode->llink = NULL;
    newNode->rlink = NULL;

    insertIntoAVL(root, newNode, isTaller);
}
```

We leave it as an exercise for you to design the class to implement AVL trees as an ADT. (Notice that because the structure of the node of an AVL tree is different from the structure of the node of a binary tree discussed in the beginning of this chapter, you cannot use inheritance to derive the class to implement AVL trees from the class `binaryTreeType`.)

11

Deletion from AVL Trees

To delete an item from an AVL tree, first we find the node containing the item to be deleted. The following four cases arise:

Case 1: The node to be deleted is a leaf.

Case 2: The node to be deleted has no right child, that is, its right subtree is empty.

Case 3: The node to be deleted has no left child, that is, its left subtree is empty.

Case 4: The node to be deleted has a left child and a right child.

Cases 1–3 are easier to handle than Case 4. Let us first discuss Case 4.

Suppose that the node to be deleted, say x, has a left and a right child. As in the case of deletion from a binary search tree, we reduce Case 4 to Case 2. That is, we find the immediate predecessor, say y of x. Then, the data of y is copied into x and now the node to be deleted is y. Clearly, y has no right child.

To delete the node, we adjust one of the pointers of the parent node. After deleting the node, the resulting tree might no longer be an AVL tree. As in the case of insertion into an AVL tree, we traverse the path (from the parent node) back to the root node. For each node on this path, sometimes we need to change only the balance factor, while other times the tree at a particular node is reconstructed. The following steps describe what to do to a node on the path back to the root node. (As in the case of insertion, we use the `bool` variable `shorter` to indicate whether the height of the subtree is reduced.) Let p be a node on the path back to the root node. We look at the current balance factor of p.

1. If the current balance factor of p is equal high, the balance factor of p is changed according to if the left subtree of p was shortened or the right subtree of p was shortened. The variable `shorter` is set to `false`.

2. Suppose that the balance factor of p is not equal and the taller subtree of p is shortened. The balance factor of p is changed to equal high, and the variable `shorter` is left as `true`.

3. Suppose that the balance factor of p is not equal and the shorter subtree of p is shortened. Further suppose that q points to the root of the taller subtree of p.

    a. If the balance factor of q is equal, a single rotation is required at p and `shorter` is set to `false`.

    b. If the balance factor of q is the same as p, a single rotation is required at p and `shorter` is set to `true`.

    c. Suppose that the balance factors of p and q are opposite. A double rotation is required at p (a single rotation at q and then a single rotation at p). We adjust the balance factors and set `shorter` to `true`.

Analysis: AVL Trees

Consider all possible AVL trees of height h. Let T_h be an AVL tree of height h such that T_h has the fewest number of nodes. Let T_{hl} denote the left subtree of T_h and T_{hr} denote the right subtree of T_h. Then

$$|T_h| = |T_{hl}| + |T_{hr}| + 1,$$

where $|T_h|$ denotes the number of nodes in T_h.

Because T_h is an AVL tree of height h such that T_h has the fewest number of nodes, it follows that one of the subtrees of T_h is of height $h - 1$ and the other is of height $h - 2$. To be specific, suppose T_{hl} is of height $h - 1$ and T_{hr} is of height $h - 2$. From the definition of T_h, it follows that T_{hl} is an AVL tree of height $h - 1$ such that T_{hl} has the fewest number of nodes among all AVL trees of height $h - 1$. Similarly, T_{hr} is an AVL tree of height $h - 2$ that has the fewest number of nodes among all AVL trees of height $h - 2$. Thus, T_{hl} is of the form T_{h-1} and T_{hr} is of the form T_{h-2}. Hence,

$$|T_h| = |T_{h-1}| + |T_{h-2}| + 1.$$

Clearly,

$$|T_0| = 1$$
$$|T_1| = 2$$

Let $F_{h+2} = |T_h| + 1$. Then,

$$F_{h+2} = F_{h+1} + F_h$$
$$F_2 \quad = 2$$
$$F_3 \quad = 3.$$

This is called a Fibonacci sequence. The solution to F_h is given by

$$F_h \approx \frac{\phi^h}{\sqrt{5}}, \quad \text{where } \phi = \frac{1 + \sqrt{5}}{2}.$$

Hence,

$$|T_h| \approx \frac{\phi^{h+2}}{\sqrt{5}} = \frac{1}{\sqrt{5}} \left[\frac{1 + \sqrt{5}}{2} \right]^{h+2}.$$

From this, it can be concluded that

$$h \approx (1.44) \log_2 |T_h|.$$

11

This implies that, in the worst case, the height of an AVL tree with n nodes is approximately $(1.44)\log_2 n$. Because the height of a perfectly balanced binary tree with n nodes is $\log_2 n$, it follows that, in the worst case, the time to manipulate an AVL tree is no more than 44% of the optimum time. However, in general, AVL trees are not as sparse as in the worst case. It can be shown that the average search time of an AVL tree is about 4% more than the optimum.

PROGRAMMING EXAMPLE: Video Store (Revisited)

In Chapter 5, we designed a program to help a video store to automate its video rental process. That program used an (unordered) linked list to keep track of the video inventory in the store. Because the search algorithm on a linked list is sequential and the list is fairly large, the search could be time consuming. In this chapter, you learned how to organize data into a binary tree. If the binary tree is nicely constructed (that is, it is not linear), the search algorithm can be improved considerably. Moreover, in general, item insertion and deletion in a binary search tree is faster than in a linked list. We will, therefore, redesign the video store program so that the video inventory can be maintained in a binary tree. As in Chapter 5, we leave the design of the customer list in a binary tree as an exercise for you.

VIDEO OBJECT In Chapter 5, a linked list was used to maintain a list of videos in the store. Because the linked list was unordered, to see whether a particular video was in stock, the sequential search algorithm used the equality operator for comparison. However, in the case of a binary tree, we need other relational operators for the search, insertion, and deletion operations. We, therefore, overload all of the relational operators. Other than this difference, the `class videoType` is the same as before. However, we give its definition, without the documentation, here for easy reference and for the sake of completeness.

```
#include <iostream>
#include <string>

using namespace std;

class videoType
{
    friend ostream& operator<<(ostream&, const videoType&);

public:
    void setVideoInfo(string title, string star1,
                    string star2, string producer,
                    string director, string productionCo,
                    int setInStock);
```

```
        int getNoOfCopiesInStock() const;
        void checkOut();
        void checkIn();
        void printTitle() const;
        void printInfo() const;
        bool checkTitle(string title);
        void updateInStock(int num);
        void setCopiesInStock(int num);
        string getTitle();
        videoType(string title = "", string star1 = "",
                  string star2 = "", string producer = "",
                  string director = "", string productionCo = "",
                  int setInStock = 0);

        bool operator==(const videoType&) const;
        bool operator!=(const videoType&) const;
        bool operator<(const videoType&) const;
        bool operator<=(const videoType&) const;
        bool operator>(const videoType&) const;
        bool operator>=(const videoType&) const;

private:
    string videoTitle;
    string movieStar1;
    string movieStar2;
    string movieProducer;
    string movieDirector;
    string movieProductionCo;
    int copiesInStock;
};
```

The definitions of the member functions of the class videoType are the same as in Chapter 5. Because here we are overloading all of the relational operators, we give only the definitions of these member functions.

```
    //Overload the relational operators.
bool videoType::operator==(const videoType& right) const
{
    return (videoTitle == right.videoTitle);
}

bool videoType::operator!=(const videoType& right) const
{
    return (videoTitle != right.videoTitle);
}

bool videoType::operator <(const videoType& right) const
{
    return (videoTitle < right.videoTitle);
}
```

```
bool videoType::operator <=(const videoType& right) const
{
    return (videoTitle <= right.videoTitle);
}

bool videoType::operator >(const videoType& right) const
{
    return (videoTitle > right.videoTitle);
}

bool videoType::operator >=(const videoType& right) const
{
    return (videoTitle >= right.videoTitle);
}
```

VIDEO LIST   The video list is maintained in a binary search tree. Therefore, we derive the `class videoBinaryTree` from the `class bSearchTreeType`. The definition of the `class videoBinaryTree` is as follows:

```cpp
#include <iostream>
#include <string>
#include "binarySearchTree.h"
#include "videoType.h"

using namespace std;

class videoBinaryTree:public bSearchTreeType<videoType>
{
public:
    bool videoSearch(string title);
      //Function to search the list to see whether a particular
      //title, specified by the parameter title, is in stock.
      //Postcondition: Returns true if the title is found,
      //     false otherwise.
    bool isVideoAvailable(string title);
      //Function to determine whether at least one copy of a
      //particular video is in stock.
      //Postcondition: Returns true if at least one copy is in
      //     stock, false otherwise.
    void videoCheckOut(string title);
      //Function to check out a video, that is, rent a video.
      //Postcondition: copiesInStock is decremented by 1.
    void videoCheckIn(string title);
      //Function to check in a video returned by a customer.
      //Postcondition: copiesInStock is incremented by 1.
    bool videoCheckTitle(string title);
      //Function to determine whether a particular video is in
      //stock.
      //Postcondition: Returns true if the video is in stock,
      //     false otherwise.
```

```
    void videoUpdateInStock(string title, int num);
      //Function to update the number of copies of a video by
      //adding the value of the parameter num. The parameter title
      //specifies the name of the video for which the number of
      //copies is to be updated.
      //Postcondition: copiesInStock = copiesInStock + num

    void videoSetCopiesInStock(string title, int num);
      //Function to reset the number of copies of a video. The
      //parameter title specifies the name of the video for which
      //the number of copies is to be reset; the parameter num
      //specifies the number of copies.
      //Postcondition: copiesInStock = num

    void videoPrintTitle();
      //Function to print the titles of all the videos in stock.

private:
    void searchVideoList(string title, bool& found,
                          binaryTreeNode<videoType>* &current);
      //Function to search the video list for a particular video,
      //specified by the parameter title.
      //Postcondition: If the video is found, the parameter found
      //    is set to true, false otherwise. The parameter current
      //    points to the node containing the video.

    void inorderTitle(binaryTreeNode<videoType> *p);
      //Function to print the titles of all the videos in stock.
};
```

The definitions of the member functions of the class videoBinaryTree are similar to the ones given in Chapter 5. We only give the definitions of the functions searchVideoList, inorderTitle, and videoPrintTitle. (See Programming Exercise 12 at the end of the chapter.)

The function searchVideoList uses a search algorithm similar to the search algorithm for a binary search tree given earlier in this chapter. It returns true if the search item is found in the list. It also returns a pointer to the node containing the search item. Note that the function searchVideoList is a private member of the class videoBinaryTree. So the user cannot directly use this function in a program. Therefore, even though this function returns a pointer to a node in the tree, the user cannot directly access the node. The function searchVideoList is used only to implement other functions of the class videoBinaryTree. The definition of this function is as follows:

```
void videoBinaryTree::searchVideoList(string title, bool& found,
                          binaryTreeNode<videoType>* &current)
{
    found = false;

    videoType temp;
```

```
        temp.setVideoInfo(title, "", "", "", "", "", 0);

        if (root == NULL)  //the tree is empty
            cout << "Cannot search an empty list. " << endl;
        else
        {
            current = root; //set current point to the root node
                            //of the binary tree
            found = false;  //set found to false

            while (!found && current != NULL) //search the tree
                if (current->info == temp)    //the item is found
                    found = true;
                else if (current->info > temp)
                    current = current->llink;
                else
                    current = current->rlink;
        } //end else
}
```

Given a pointer to the root node of the binary tree containing the videos, the function `inorderTitle` uses the inorder traversal algorithm to print the titles of the videos. Notice that this function outputs only the video titles. The definition of this function is as follows:

```
void videoBinaryTree::inorderTitle(binaryTreeNode<videoType> *p)
{
    if (p != NULL)
    {
        inorderTitle(p->llink);
        p->info.printTitle();
        inorderTitle(p->rlink);
    }
}
```

The function `videoPrintTitle` uses the function `inorderTitle` to print the titles of all the videos in the store. The definition of this function is as follows:

```
void videoBinaryTree::videoPrintTitle()
{
    inorderTitle(root);
}
```

MAIN PROGRAM

The main program is the same as before. Here we give only the listing of this program. We assume that the name of the header file containing the definition of the class `videoBinaryTree` is `videoBinaryTree.h`, and so on.

```
//******************************************************************
// Author: D.S. Malik
//
// This program illustrates how to use the classes videoType
// and videoBinaryTree to create and process a list of videos.
//******************************************************************

#include <iostream>
#include <fstream>
#include <string>
#include "binarySearchTree.h"
#include "videoType.h"
#include "videoBinaryTree.h"

using namespace std;

void createVideoList(ifstream& infile,
                     videoBinaryTree& videoList);
void displayMenu();

int main()
{
    videoBinaryTree  videoList;
    int choice;
    char ch;
    string title;

    ifstream infile;

    infile.open("videoDat.txt");

    if (!infile)
    {
        cout << "The input file does not exist" << endl;
        return 1;
    }

    createVideoList(infile, videoList);
    infile.close();

    displayMenu();
    cout << "Enter your choice: ";
    cin >> choice;     //get the request
    cin.get(ch);
    cout << endl;

        //process the request
    while (choice != 9)
```

```cpp
{
    switch(choice)
    {
    case 1:
        cout << "Enter the title: ";
        getline(cin, title);
        cout << endl;
        if (videoList.videoSearch(title))
            cout << "Title found." << endl;
        else
            cout << "The store does not carry this title."
                 << endl;
        break;

    case 2:
        cout << "Enter the title: ";
        getline(cin, title);
        cout << endl;
        if (videoList.videoSearch(title))
        {
            if (videoList.isVideoAvailable(title))
            {
                videoList.videoCheckOut(title);
                cout << "Enjoy your movie: " << title << endl;
            }
            else
                cout << "The video is currently out of stock."
                     << endl;
        }
        else
            cout << "The video is not in the store." << endl;
        break;

    case 3:
        cout << "Enter the title: ";
        getline(cin, title);
        cout << endl;
        if (videoList.videoSearch(title))
        {
            videoList.videoCheckIn(title);
            cout << "Thanks for returning " << title << endl;
        }
        else
            cout << "This video is not from our store." << endl;
        break;

    case 4:
        cout << "Enter the title: ";
        getline(cin, title);
        cout << endl;
```

```
               if (videoList.videoSearch(title))
               {
                   if (videoList.isVideoAvailable(title))
                       cout << "The video is currently in stock."
                            << endl;
                   else
                       cout << "The video is out of stock." << endl;
               }
               else
                   cout << "The video is not in the store." << endl;
               break;

           case 5:
               videoList.videoPrintTitle();
                break;

           case 6:
               videoList.inorderTraversal();
               break;

           default: cout << "Invalid selection." << endl;
           }//end switch

           displayMenu();
           cout << "Enter your choice: ";
           cin >> choice;   //get the next request
           cin.get(ch);
           cout << endl;
       }//end while

       return 0;
}

void createVideoList(ifstream& infile, videoBinaryTree& videoList)
{
    string title;
    string star1;
    string star2;
    string producer;
    string director;
    string productionCo;
    char    ch;
    int     inStock;

    videoType newVideo;

    getline(infile, title);
    while (infile)
    {
        getline(infile, star1);
        getline(infile, star2);
        getline(infile, producer);
```

```
                    getline(infile, director);
                    getline(infile, productionCo);
                    infile >> inStock;
                    infile.get(ch);
                    newVideo.setVideoInfo(title, star1, star2, producer,
                                     director, productionCo, inStock);
                    videoList.insert(newVideo);

                    getline(infile, title);
            }//end while
      }//end createVideoList

      void displayMenu()
      {
            cout << "Select one of the following: " << endl;
            cout << "1: To check whether a particular video is in "
                 << "the store" << endl;
            cout << "2: To check out a video" << endl;
            cout << "3: To check in a video" << endl;
            cout << "4: To see whether a particular video is in stock"
                 << endl;
            cout << "5: To print the titles of all the videos" << endl;
            cout << "6: To print a list of all the videos" << endl;
            cout << "9: To exit" << endl;
      }
```

B-Trees

In the previous sections of this chapter, we discussed how to build binary search trees and in particular AVL trees to effectively organize data dynamically and effectively search the data. However, the performance of the search depends on the height of the tree. In this section, we discuss B-trees in which the leaves are on the same level and are not too far from the root.

Definition: (*m*-way search tree) An ***m*-way search tree** is a tree in which each node has at most *m* children, and if the tree is nonempty, it has the following properties:

1. Each node has the following form:

n	P_0	K_1	P_1	K_2	K_2	$\ldots$	K_n	P_n

where $P_0, P_1, P_2, \ldots, P_n$ are pointers to the subtrees of the node, $K_1, K_2, \ldots, K_n$ are keys such that $K_1 < K_2 < \ldots < K_n$, and $n \leq m - 1$.

2. All keys, if any, in the node to which P_i points are less than K_{i+1}.

3. All keys, if any, in the node to which P_i points are greater than K_i.

4. The subtrees, if any, to which each P_i points are *m*-way search trees.

Figure 11-24 shows a 5-way search tree.

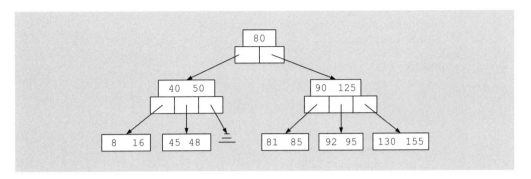

FIGURE 11-24   A 5-way search tree

Definition: **(B-tree of order *m*)** A **B-tree of order *m*** is an *m*-way search tree that is either empty, or has the following properties:

1.   All leaves are on the same level.
2.   All internal nodes except the root have at most *m* (nonempty) children and at least ⌈*m*/2⌉ children. (Note that ⌈*m*/2⌉ denotes the ceiling of *m*/2.)
3.   The root has at least 2 children if it is not a leaf, and at most *m* children.

Figure 11-25 shows a B-tree of order 5.

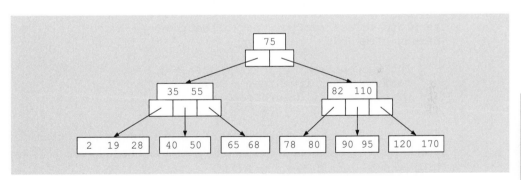

FIGURE 11-25   A B-tree of order 5

Note that the 5-way search tree in Figure 11-24 is not a B-tree of order 5.

The basic operations performed on a B-tree are search the tree, insert an item in the tree, delete an item from the tree, and traverse the tree. In the remainder of this section, we discuss how to implement some of these operations.

Before discussing these properties and describing the structure of a node and the class to implement the properties of a B-tree, we note the following: Until now, we have passed only data types as parameters to templates. Just like types (data types), constant expressions can also be passed as parameters to templates. For example, consider the following `class template`:

```
template<class elemType, int size>
class listType
{
public:
    .
    .
    .
private:
    int maxSize;
    int length;
    elemType listElem[size];
};
```

This `class template` contains an array data member. The array element type and the size of the array are passed as parameters to the `class template`. To create a list of 100 components of `int` elements, we use the following statement:

```
listType<int, 100> intList;
```

Next, we give the definitions of the B-tree node and the class that implements the properties of a B-tree.

Each node should store the number of keys in the node, the records, and the pointer to subtrees. We use an array to store the records and an array to store the pointers to the subtrees. Thus, the definition of a B-tree node is as follows:

```
template <class recType, int bTreeOrder>
struct bTreeNode
{
    int recCount;
    recType list[bTreeOrder - 1];
    bTreeNode *children[bTreeOrder];
};
```

The class implementing the properties of a B-tree must, among others, implement the search, traversal, insertion, and deletion algorithms. The following class implements the basic properties of a B-tree as an ADT:

```
//************************************************************
// Author: D.S. Malik
//
// class bTree
// This class specifies the basic operations to implement a
// B-tree.
//************************************************************

template <class recType, int bTreeOrder>
class bTree
```

```
{
public:
    bool search(const recType& searchItem);
      //Function to determine if searchItem is in the B-tree.
      //Postcondition: Returns true if searchItem is found in the
      //     B-tree; otherwise, returns false.

    void insert(const recType& insertItem);
      //Function to insert insertItem in the B-tree.
      //Postcondition: If insertItem is not in the the B-tree, it
      //     is inserted in the B-tree.

    void inOrder();
      //Function to do an inorder traversal of the B-tree.

    bTree();
      //constructor

    //Add additional members as needed.

protected:
    bTreeNode<recType, bTreeOrder> *root;
};
```

Search

The function **search** searches the binary search tree for a given item. If the item is found in the binary search tree, it returns **true**; otherwise, it returns **false**. The search must start at the root node. Because, usually, there is more than one item in a node, we must search the array containing the data. Therefore, in addition to the function **search**, we also write the function **searchNode** that searches a node sequentially. If **item** is found, the function **searchNode** returns **true** and the location in the array where **item** is found. If **item** is not in the node, the function returns **false** and **location** points to either the first item that is larger than the search item or one past the last item in the node. The definitions of these functions are as follows:

```
template <class recType, int bTreeOrder>
void bTree<recType, bTreeOrder>::searchNode
                    (bTreeNode<recType, bTreeOrder> *current,
                     const recType& item,
                     bool& found, int& location)
{
    location = 0;

    while (location < current->recCount
            && item > current->list[location])
        location++;

    if (location < current->recCount
            && item == current->list[location])
        found = true;
    else
        found = false;
} //end searchNode
```

```
template <class recType, int bTreeOrder>
bool bTree<recType, bTreeOrder>::search(const recType& searchItem)
{
    bool found = false;
    int location;

    bTreeNode<recType, bTreeOrder> *current;

    current = root;

    while (current != NULL && !found)
    {
        searchNode(current, item, found, location);

        if (!found)
            current = current->children[location];
    }

    return found;
} //end search
```

Note that the function searchNode searches the node sequentially. However, because the data in the node is ordered, we can also use a binary search algorithm to search the node. We leave it as an exercise for you to modify the definition of the function searchNode so that it uses a binary search algorithm to search the node; see Programming Exercise 16 at the end of this chapter.

Traversing a B-Tree

As in the case of a binary tree, a B-tree can be traversed in three ways: inorder, preorder, and postorder. We only discuss the inorder traversal algorithm and leave the others as an exercise.

```
template <class recType, int bTreeOrder>
void bTree<recType, bTreeOrder>::inOrder()
{
    recInorder(root);
} // end inOrder

template <class recType, int bTreeOrder>
void bTree<recType, bTreeOrder>::recInorder
                    (bTreeNode<recType, bTreeOrder> *current)
{
    if (current != NULL)
    {
        recInorder(current->children[0]);
```

```
        for (int i = 0; i < current->recCount; i++)
        {
            cout << current->list[i] << " ";

            recInorder(current->children[i + 1]);
        }
    }
} //end recInorder
```

Insertion into a B-Tree

The general algorithm to insert an item in a B-tree is as follows.

Insert Algorithm: Search the tree to see if the key is already in the tree. If the key is already in the tree, output an error messsage. If the key is not in the tree, the search terminates at a leaf. The record is inserted into the leaf if there is room. If the leaf is full, split the node into two nodes and the median key is moved to the parent node. (Note that the median is determined by considering all the keys in the node and the new key to be inserted.) The splitting can propogate upward even as far as the root, causing the tree to increase in height.

Next, we illustrate how the insert algorithm works.

Figures 11-26 to 11-29 shows the insertion of items into an initially empty B-tree of order 5.

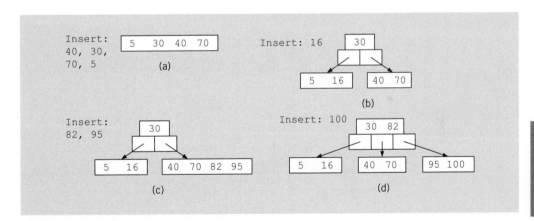

FIGURE 11-26 Item insertion into a B-tree of order 5

The insertion of 40, 30, 70, and 5 is shown in Figure 11-26(a). The insertion of 16 requires to split the root node, causing the height of the tree to increase; see Figure 11-26(b). The insertion of 82 and 95 is shown in Figure 11-26(c). The next item inserted is 100; see Figure 11-26(d). The item 100 is to be inserted in the right child of the root node. However, the right child of the root node is full. So we split this node and move the median key, which is 82, to the parent node. Because the parent node is not full, we can insert 82 in the parent node; see Figure 11-26(d).

Figure 11-27 shows the insertion of 73, 54, 98, and 37.

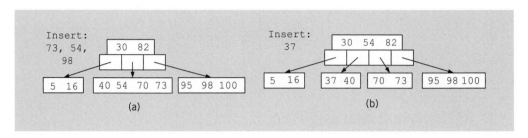

FIGURE 11-27 Insertion of 73, 54, 98, and 37

Note that 73, 54, and 98 are inserted without splitting any node; see Figure 11-27(a). However, the insertion of 37 requires the splitting of a node. The item 37 is to be inserted in the right child of 30. However, the right child of 30 is full, as shown in Figure 11-27(a). So we split the right child of 30, insert 37, and move the median key, which is 54, to the parent node. Because the parent node is not full, the median key 54 is inserted into the parent node; see Figure 11-27(b).

Figure 11-28 shows the insertion of 25, 62, 81, 150, and 79 into the B-tree of Figure 11-27(b).

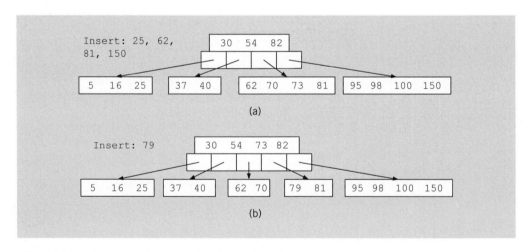

FIGURE 11-28 Insertion of 25, 62, 81, 150, and 79

Note that 25, 62, 81, and 150 are inserted without splitting any node; see Figure 11-28(a). However, the insertion of 79 requires the splitting of a node. The item 79 is to be inserted in the right child of 54. However, the right child of 54 is full; see Figure 11-28(a). So we split the right child of 54, insert 79, and move the median key, which is 73, to the parent node. Because the parent node is not full, the median key 73 is inserted into the parent node; see Figure 11-28(b).

Next, we insert 200, as shown in Figure 11-29.

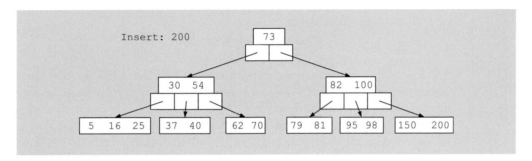

FIGURE 11-29 Insertion of 200

The item 200 is to be inserted in the right child of 82; see Figure 11-28(b). However, the right child of 82 is full. So we split the right child of 82, insert 200 in the node, and move the median key, which is 100, to the parent node. However, the parent node, which is the root node in Figure 11-28(b), is also full. So we split the parent node and move the median key, which is 73, to the new root node; see Figure 11-29. From Figure 11-29, it is clear that the height of the B-tree is increased.

From the previous discussion, it follows that to implement the insertion algorithm, we need algorithms to split a node, insert an item into a node, and move the median key to the parent node. Furthermore, because the insertion of an item might require the splitting of a node and moving the median key to the parent node, the simplest way to implement the insertion algorithm is to use recursion. To trigger the recursion, we will write another function, `insertBTree`. The definition of the function `insert`, which uses the function `insertBTree`, is as follows:

```
template <class recType, int bTreeOrder>
void bTree<recType, bTreeOrder>::insert(const recType& insertItem)
{
    bool isTaller = false;
    recType median;

    bTreeNode<recType, bTreeOrder> *rightChild;

    insertBTree(root, insertItem, median,
                rightChild, isTaller);

    if (isTaller) //the tree is initially empty or the root
                  //was split by the function insertBTree
    {
        bTreeNode<recType, bTreeOrder> *tempRoot;
        tempRoot = new bTreeNode<recType, bTreeOrder>;
        tempRoot->recCount = 1;
        tempRoot->list[0] = median;
```

11

```
            tempRoot->children[0] = root;
            tempRoot->children[1] = rightChild;

            root = tempRoot;
        }
} //insert
```

The function `insertBTree` recursively inserts an item into a B-tree. After inserting an item, it returns `true` if the height of the tree is to be increased. If the root node is to be split, this function splits the root node, sets `isTaller` to `true`, and sends the median key, `median`, and a pointer, `rightChild`, of the right child of `median` to the function `insert`. The function `insert` adjusts the root of the B-tree. This function has five parameters: `current`—a pointer to the B-tree in which to insert an item, `insertItem`—item to be inserted in the B-tree, `median`—to return the median key, `rightChild`—pointer to the right child of `median`, and `isTaller`—to indicate if the height of a B-tree is to be increased. In pseudocode, the algorithm is as follows:

```
if (current is NULL)
{
    Either the B-tree is empty or the search ends at an empty subtree.
    Set median to insertItem
    Set rightChild to NULL
    Set isTaller to true
}
else
{
    Call function searchNode to search the current node

    if insertItem is in the node
        output an error message
    else
    {
        call the function insertBTree with appropriate parameters
        if isTaller is true
            if current node is not full
                insert item into current node
            else
                call the function splitNode to split the node
    }
}
```

We leave it as an exercise for you to write the definition of the function `insertBTree`; see Programming Exercise 15 at the end of this chapter.

The function `insertNode` inserts an item in the node. Because the keys in the node are in order, the algorithm to insert a new item is similar to the `insertAt` function discussed in Chapter 3. The function has four parameters: `current`—a pointer to the node in which to insert the new item, `insertItem`—the item to be inserted, `rightChild`—a pointer to the right subtree of the item to be inserted, and `insertPosition`—the position in the array where to insert the item. The definition of this function is as follows:

```
template <class recType, int bTreeOrder>
void bTree<recType, bTreeOrder>::insertNode
                    (bTreeNode<recType, bTreeOrder> *current,
                     const recType& insertItem,
                     bTreeNode<recType, bTreeOrder>* &rightChild,
                     int insertPosition)
{
    int index;

    for (index = current->recCount; index > insertPosition;
                                    index--)
    {
        current->list[index] = current->list[index - 1];
        current->children[index + 1] = current->children[index];
    }

    current->list[index] = insertItem;
    current->children[index + 1] = rightChild;
    current->recCount++;
} //end insertNode
```

The function `splitNode` splits a node into two nodes and inserts the new item in the relevant node. It returns the median key and a pointer to the second half of the node. The parameter `current` points to the node to be split, `insertItem` is the item to be inserted, `newChild` is a pointer to the right child of the item to be inserted, `insertPosition` specifies the position where to insert the new item, after splitting the node the parameter `rightNode` returns a pointer to the right half of the node, and `median` returns the median key of the node.

```
template <class recType, int bTreeOrder>
void bTree<recType, bTreeOrder>::splitNode
                    (bTreeNode<recType, bTreeOrder> *current,
                     const recType& insertItem,
                     bTreeNode<recType, bTreeOrder>* rightChild,
                     int insertPosition,
                     bTreeNode<recType, bTreeOrder>* &rightNode,
                     recType &median)
{
    rightNode = new bTreeNode<recType, bTreeOrder>;

    int mid = (bTreeOrder - 1)  / 2;

    if (insertPosition <= mid) //new item goes in the first
                               //half of the node
    {
        int index = 0;
        int i = mid;
```

11

```
        while (i < bTreeOrder - 1)
        {
            rightNode->list[index] = current->list[i];
            rightNode->children[index + 1] =
                                current->children[i + 1];
            index++;
            i++;
        }

        current->recCount = mid;
        insertNode(current, insertItem, rightChild,
                    insertPosition);
        (current->recCount)--;

        median = current->list[current->recCount];

        rightNode->recCount = index;
        rightNode->children[0] =
                current->children[current->recCount + 1];
    }
    else  //new item goes in the second half of the node
    {
        int i = mid + 1;
        int index = 0;

        while (i < bTreeOrder - 1)
        {
            rightNode->list[index] = current->list[i];
            rightNode->children[index + 1] =
                                current->children[i + 1];
            index++;
            i++;
        }

        current->recCount = mid;
        rightNode->recCount = index;

        median = current->list[mid];
        insertNode(rightNode, insertItem, rightChild,
                    insertPosition - mid - 1);
        rightNode->children[0] =
                current->children[current->recCount + 1];
    }
} //splitNode
```

We leave it as an exercise for you to include the functions to insert an item in a B-tree and the functions to search and traverse a B-tree in the class BTree, and write a program to perform these operations on a B-tree; see Programming Exercise 15 at the end of this chapter.

Deletion from a B-Tree

To delete an item from a B-tree, we search the tree for the item to be deleted, say deleteItem. The following cases arise:

1. If `deleteItem` is not in the tree, output an appropriate error message.

2. If `deleteItem` is in the tree, find the node containing the `deleteItem`. If the node containing the `deleteItem` is not a leaf, its immediate predecessor (or successor) is in a leaf. So we can swap the immediate predecessor (or successor) with the `deleteItem` to move the `deleteItem` into a leaf. We consider the cases to delete an item from a leaf.

   a. If the leaf contains more than the minimum number of keys, delete the `deleteItem` from the leaf. (In this case, no further action is required.)

   b. If the leaf contains only the minimum number of keys, look at the sibling nodes that are adjacent to the leaf. (Note that the sibling nodes and the leaf have the same parent node.)

      i. If one of the sibling nodes has more than the minimum number of keys, move one of the keys from that sibling node to the parent and one key from the parent to the leaf, and then delete `deleteItem`.

      ii. If the adjacent siblings have only the minimum number of keys, then combine one of the siblings with the leaf and the median key from the parent. If this action does not leave the minimum number of keys in the parent node, this process of combining the nodes propogates upward, possibly as far as the root node, which could result in reducing the height of the B-tree.

Next, we illustrate how the deletion process works. Consider the B-tree of order 5 shown in Figure 11-30.

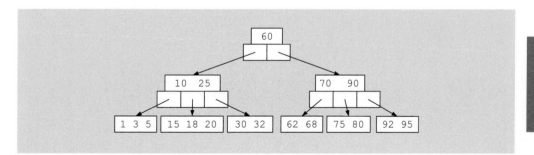

FIGURE 11-30 A B-tree of order 5

Let us delete 18 from this B-tree. Because 18 is in a leaf and the leaf has more than the minimum number of keys, we simply delete 18 from the leaf; see Figure 11-31.

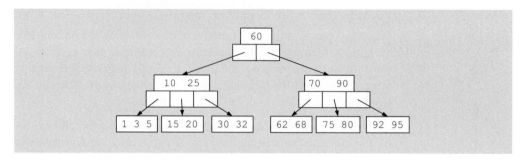

FIGURE 11-31 Deleting 18 from a B-tree of order 5

Next, let us delete 30. Figure 11-32 shows the B-tree before and after deleting 30.

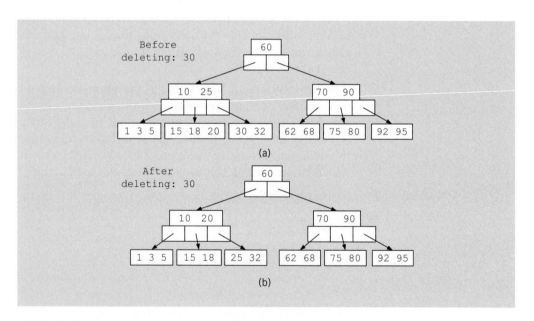

FIGURE 11-32 B-tree before and after deleting 30

The leaf containing 30 has only the minimum number of keys. However, its adjacent sibling has more than the minimum number of keys. So we move 20 from the adjacent sibling to the parent node and then move 25 from the parent node to the leaf; see Figure 11-32(b).

Next, let us delete 70. Figure 11-33 shows the process of deleting 70.

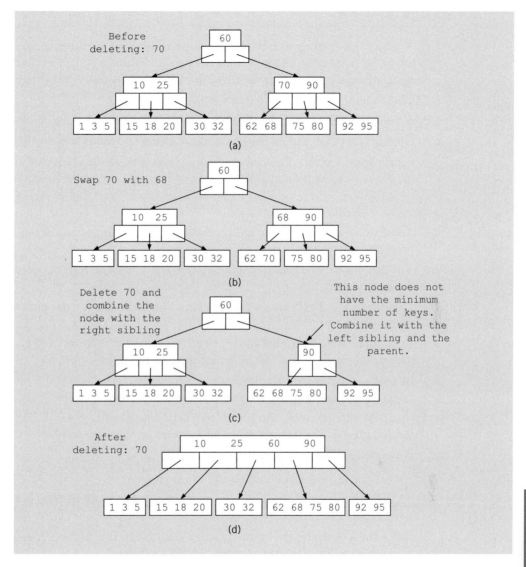

FIGURE 11-33 Deletion of 70 from the B-tree

The node containing 70 is not a leaf. So we swap 70 with its immediate predecessor, which is 68; see Figure 11-33(b). After deleting 70 from the leaf, because the leaf does not have the minimum number of keys, it is combined with its adjacent sibling; see Figure 11-33(c). However, this process does not leave the minimum number of keys in the parent node, which is 90. So we combine this node with its left sibling and their parent, which in this case is the root node; see Figure 11-33(d). Note that the deletion of 70 resulted in reducing the height of the B-tree.

We leave it as an exercise for you to develop the necessary algorithms to delete a record from a B-tree.

QUICK REVIEW

1. A binary tree is either empty or it has a special node called the root node. If the tree is nonempty, the root node has two sets of nodes, called the left and right subtrees, such that the left and right subtrees are also binary trees.

2. The node of a binary tree has two links in it.

3. A node in a binary tree is called a leaf if it has no left and right children.

4. A node U is called the parent of a node V if there is a branch from U to V.

5. A path from a node X to a node Y in a binary tree is a sequence of nodes $X_0, X_1, \ldots, X_n$ such that (a) $X = X_0$, $X_n = Y$ and (b) X_{i-1} is the parent of X_i for all $i = 1, 2, \ldots, n$. That is, there is a branch from X_0 to X_1, X_1 to $X_2, \ldots, X_{i-1}$ to $X_i, \ldots, X_{n-1}$ to X_n.

6. The level of a node in a binary tree is the number of branches on the path from the root to the node.

7. The level of the root node of a binary tree is 0; the level of the children of the root node is 1.

8. The height of a binary tree is the number of nodes on the longest path from the root to a leaf.

9. In an inorder traversal, the binary tree is traversed as follows: (a) Traverse the left subtree; (b) visit the node; (c) traverse the right subtree.

10. In a preorder traversal, the binary tree is traversed as follows: (a) Visit the node; (b) traverse the left subtree; (c) traverse the right subtree.

11. In a postorder traversal, the binary tree is traversed as follows: (a) Traverse the left subtree; (b) traverse the right subtree; (c) visit the node.

12. A binary search tree T is either empty or

    i. T has a special node called the *root* node.

    ii. T has two sets of nodes, L_T and R_T, called the left subtree and the right subtree of T, respectively.

    iii. The key in the root node is larger than every key in the left subtree and smaller than every key in the right subtree.

    iv. L_T and R_T are binary search trees.

13. To delete a node from a binary search tree that has both left and right nonempty subtrees, first its immediate predecessor is located, then the predecessor's `info` is copied into the node, and finally the predecessor is deleted.

14. A perfectly balanced binary tree is a binary tree such that

    i. The heights of the left and right subtrees of the root are equal.

    ii. The left and right subtrees of the root are perfectly balanced binary trees.

15. An AVL (or height-balanced) tree is a binary search tree such that

 i. The heights of the left and right subtrees of the root differ by at most 1.

 ii. The left and right subtrees of the root are AVL trees.

16. Let x be a node in a binary tree. x_l denotes the height of the left subtree of x; x_h denotes the height of the right subtree of x.

17. Let T be an AVL tree and x be a node in T. Then $|x_h - x_l| \leq 1$, where $|x_h - x_l|$ denotes the absolute value of $x_h - x_l$.

18. Let x be a node in the AVL tree T.

 a. If $x_l > x_h$, we say the x is left high. In this case, $x_l = x_h + 1$.

 b. If $x_l = x_h$, we say the x is equal high.

 c. If $x_h > x_l$, we say the x is right high. In this case, $x_h = x_l + 1$.

19. The balance factor of x, written $bf(x)$, is defined as $bf(x) = x_h - x_l$.

20. Let x be a node in the AVL tree T. Then,

 a. If x is left high, $bf(x) = -1$.

 b. If x is equal high, $bf(x) = 0$.

 c. If x is right high, $bf(x) = 1$.

21. Let x be a node in a binary tree. We say that node x violates the balance criteria if $|x_h - x_l| > 1$, that is, the heights of the left and right subtrees of x differ by more than 1.

22. Every node x in the AVL tree T, in addition to the data and pointers to the left and right subtrees, must keep track of its balance factor.

23. In an AVL tree, there are two types of rotations: left rotation and right rotation. Suppose that the rotation occurs at node, say x. If it is a left rotation, certain nodes from the right subtree of x move to its left subtree; the root of the right subtree of x becomes the new root of the reconstructed subtree. Similarly, if it is a right rotation at x, certain nodes from the left subtree of x move to its right subtree; the root of the left subtree of x becomes the new root of the reconstructed subtree.

24. A B-tree of order m is an m-way search tree that is either empty, or has the following properties: (1) All leaves are on the same level; (2) All internal nodes except the root have at most m (nonempty) children and at least $\lceil m/2 \rceil$ children. (Note that $\lceil m/2 \rceil$ denotes the ceiling of $m/2$.); (3) The root has at least 2 children if it is not a leaf, and at most m children.

25. To insert an item into a B-tree, search the tree to see if the record is already in the tree. If the record is already in the tree, output an error messsage. If the record is not in the tree, the search terminates at a leaf. The record is inserted into the leaf if there is room. If the leaf is full, split the node into two nodes and the median record is moved to the parent node. The splitting can propogate upward even as far as the root, causing the tree to increase in height.

11

EXERCISES

1. Mark the following statements as true or false.

   a. A binary tree must be nonempty.

   b. The level of the root node is 0.

   c. If a tree has only one node, the height of this tree is 0 because the number of levels is 0.

   d. The inorder traversal of a binary tree always outputs the data in ascending order.

2. There are 14 different binary trees with four nodes. Draw all of them.

The binary tree of Figure 11-34 is to be used for Exercises 3 through 8.

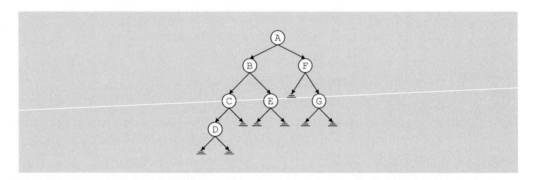

FIGURE 11-34 Binary tree for Exercises 3 through 8

3. Find L_A, the node in the left subtree of A.

4. Find R_A, the node in the right subtree of A.

5. Find R_B, the node in the right subtree of B.

6. List the nodes of this binary tree in an inorder sequence.

7. List the nodes of this binary tree in a preorder sequence.

8. List the nodes of this binary tree in a postorder sequence.

The binary tree of Figure 11-35 is to be used for Exercises 9 through 13.

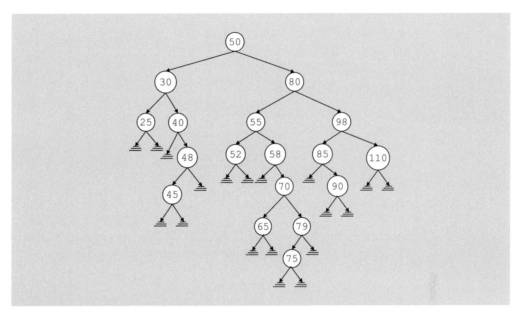

FIGURE 11-35 Binary tree for Exercises 9 through 13

9. List the path from the node with `info` 80 to the node with `info` 79.

10. A node with `info` 35 is to be inserted in the tree. List the nodes that are visited by the function `insert` to insert 35. Redraw the tree after inserting 35.

11. Delete node 52 and redraw the binary tree.

12. Delete node 40 and redraw the binary tree.

13. Delete nodes 80 and 58 in that order. Redraw the binary tree after each deletion.

14. Suppose that you are given two sequences of elements corresponding to the inorder sequence and the preorder sequence. Prove that it is possible to reconstruct a unique binary tree.

15. The nodes in a binary tree in preorder and inorder sequences are as follows:

    ```
    preorder:   ABCDEFGHIJKLM
    inorder:    CEDFBAHJIKGML
    ```

    Draw the binary tree.

16. Given the preorder sequence and the postorder sequence, show that it might not be possible to reconstruct the binary tree.

1
1

17. Insert 100 in the AVL tree of Figure 11–36. The resulting tree must be an AVL tree. What is the balance factor at the root node after the insertion?

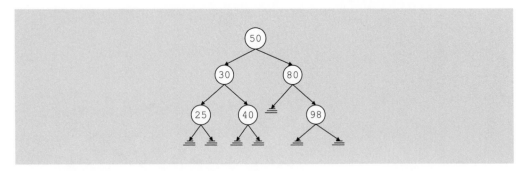

FIGURE 11-36 AVL tree for Exercise 17

18. Insert 45 in the AVL tree of Figure 11–37. The resulting tree must be an AVL tree. What is the balance factor at the root node after the insertion?

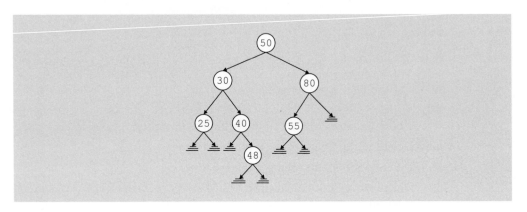

FIGURE 11-37 AVL tree for Exercise 18

19. Insert 42 in the AVL tree of Figure 11–38. The resulting tree must be an AVL tree. What is the balance factor at the root node after the insertion?

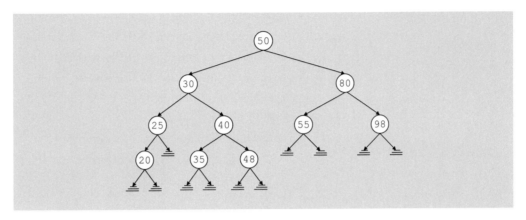

FIGURE 11-38 AVL tree for Exercise 19

20. The keys 24, 39, 31, 46, 48, 34, 19, 5, and 29 are inserted (in the order given) into an initially empty AVL tree. Show the AVL tree after each insertion.

The binary tree of Figure 11-39 is to be used for Exercises 21 to 23.

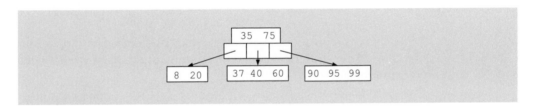

FIGURE 11-39 B-tree of order 5 for Exercises 21 to 23

21. Insert the keys 72, 30, and 50, in this order, into the B-tree of order 5 of Figure 11-39. Show the resulting tree.

22. Insert the keys 38, 45, 55, 80, and 85 into the B-tree of order 5 of Figure 11-39. Show the resulting tree.

23. Insert the keys 2, 30, 42, 10, 96, 15, 50, 82, and 98 into the B-tree of order 5 of Figure 11-39. Show the resulting tree.

The binary tree of Figure 11-40 is to be used for Exercises 24 to 27.

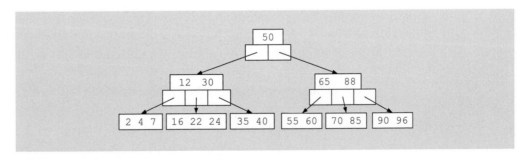

FIGURE 11-40 B-tree of order 5 for Exercises 24 to 27

24. Delete 7 from the B-tree of order 5 of Figure 11-40. Show the resulting tree.

25. Delete 40 from the B-tree of order 5 of Figure 11-40. Show the resulting tree.

26. Delete 88 from the B-tree of order 5 of Figure 11-40. Show the resulting tree.

27. Delete 12 from the B-tree of order 5 of Figure 11-40. Show the resulting tree.

28. Suppose that you have the keys 40, 30, 70, 5, 16, 82, 95, 100, 73, 54, 98, 37, 25, 62, 81, 150, 79, and 87.

    a. Insert these keys into an initially empty B-tree of order 5.

    b. Insert these keys into an initially empty B-tree of order 6.

PROGRAMMING EXERCISES

1. Write the definition of the function, `nodeCount`, that returns the number of nodes in a binary tree. Add this function to the `class binaryTreeType` and create a program to test this function.

2. Write the definition of the function, `leavesCount`, that takes as a parameter a pointer to the root node of a binary tree and returns the number of leaves in a binary tree. Add this function to the `class binaryTreeType` and create a program to test this function.

3. Write a function, `swapSubtrees`, that swaps all of the left and right subtrees of a binary tree. Add this function to the `class binaryTreeType` and create a program to test this function.

4. Write a function, `singleParent`, that returns the number of nodes in a binary tree that have only one child. Add this function to the `class binaryTreeType` and create a program to test this function. (Note: First create a binary search tree.)

5. Write a program to test various operations on a binary search tree.

6. a. Write the definition of the function to implement the nonrecursive postorder traversal algorithm.

    b. Write a program to test the nonrecursive inorder, preorder, and postorder traversal algorithms. (Note: First create a binary search tree.)

7. Write a version of the preorder traversal algorithm in which a user-defined function can be passed as a parameter to specify the visiting criteria at a node.

8. Write a version of the postorder traversal algorithm in which a user-defined function can be passed as a parameter to specify the visiting criteria at a node.

9. a. Write the definition of the class template that implements an AVL tree as an ADT. (You do not need to implement the delete operation.)

    b. Write the definitions of the member functions of the class that you defined in (a).

    c. Write a program to test various operations of an AVL tree.

10. Write a function that inserts the nodes of a binary tree into an ordered linked list. Also write a program to test your function.

11. Write a program to do the following:

    a. Build a binary search tree, T_1.

    b. Do a postorder traversal of T_1 and while doing the postorder traversal, insert the nodes into a second binary search tree T_2.

    c. Do a preorder traversal of T_2 and while doing the preorder traversal, insert the node into a third binary search tree T_3.

    d. Do an inorder traversal of T_3.

    e. Output the heights and the number of leafs in each of the three binary search trees.

12. Write the definitions of the functions of the `class videoBinaryTree` not given in the Programming Example Video Store. Also write a program to test the video store program.

13. (**Video Store Program**) In Programming Exercise 14 in Chapter 5, you were asked to design and implement a class to maintain customer data in a linked list. Because the search on a linked list is sequential and, therefore, can be time consuming, design and implement the `class customerBTreeType` so that this customer data can be stored in a binary search tree. The `class customerBTreeType` must be derived from the `class bSearchTreeType` as designed in this chapter.

14. (**Video Store Program**) Using classes to implement the video data, video list data, customer data, and customer list data, as designed in this chapter and in Programming Exercises 12 and 13, design and complete the program to put the video store into operation.

15. Write the definition of the function `insertBTree` to recursively insert a record into a B-tree. Also write a program to test various operations on a B-tree.

16. Rewrite the definition of the function `searchNode` of the class B-tree so that it uses a binary search to search the node. Also write a program to test various operations on a B-tree.

1
1

CHAPTER 12

GRAPHS

IN THIS CHAPTER, YOU WILL:

· Learn about graphs

· Become familiar with the basic terminology of graph theory

· Discover how to represent graphs in computer memory

· Examine and implement various graph traversal algorithms

· Learn how to implement a shortest path algorithm

· Examine and implement the minimum spanning tree algorithm

· Explore topological sort

· Learn how to find Euler circuits in a graph

In previous chapters, you learned various ways to represent and manipulate data. This chapter discusses how to implement and manipulate graphs, which have numerous applications in computer science.

Introduction

In 1736, the following problem was posed. In the town of Königsberg (now called Kaliningrad), the river Pregel (Pregolya) flows around the island Kneiphof and then divides into two. See Figure 12-1.

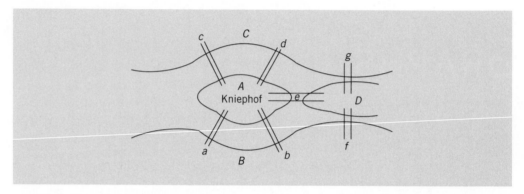

FIGURE 12-1 The Königsberg bridge problem

The river has four land areas (*A, B, C, D*), as shown in the figure. These land areas are connected using seven bridges, as shown in Figure 12-1. The bridges are labeled *a, b, c, d, e, f,* and *g*. The Königsberg bridge problem is as follows: Starting at one land area, is it possible to walk across all the bridges exactly once and return to the starting land area? In 1736, Euler represented the Königsberg bridge problem as a graph, as shown in Figure 12-2, and answered the question in the negative. This marked (as recorded) the birth of graph theory.

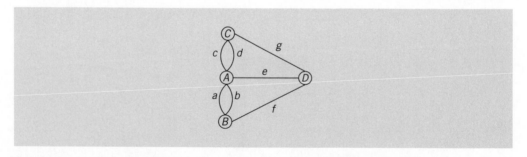

FIGURE 12-2 Graph representation of the Königsberg bridge problem

Over the past 200 years, graph theory has been applied to a variety of applications. Graphs are used to model electrical circuits, chemical compounds, highway maps, and so on. They are also used in the analysis of electrical circuits, finding the shortest route, project planning, linguistics, genetics, social science, and so forth. In this chapter, you learn about graphs and their applications in computer science.

Graph Definitions and Notations

To facilitate and simplify our discussion, we borrow a few definitions and terminology from set theory. Let X be a set. If a is an element of X, we write $a \in X$. (The symbol "$\in$" means "belongs to.") A set Y is called a **subset** of X if every element of Y is also an element of X. If Y is a subset of X, we write $Y \subseteq X$. (The symbol "$\subseteq$" means "is a subset of.") The **intersection** of sets A and B, written $A \cap B$, is the set of all elements that are in A and B; that is, $A \cap B = \{x \mid x \in A$ and $x \in B\}$. (The symbol "$\cap$" means "intersection.") The **union** of sets A and B, written $A \cup B$, is the set of all elements that are in A or in B; that is, $A \cup B = \{x \mid x \in A$ or $x \in B\}$. (The symbol "$\cup$" means "union.") For sets A and B, the set $A \times B$ is the set of all ordered pairs of elements of A and B; that is, $A \times B = \{(a, b) \mid a \in A, b \in B\}$. (The symbol "$\times$" means "**Cartesian product**.")

A **graph** G is a pair, $G = (V, E)$, where V is a finite nonempty set, called the set of **vertices** of G and $E \subseteq V \times V$. That is, the elements of E are pairs of elements of V. E is called the set of **edges** of G. G is called **trivial** if it has only one vertex.

Let $V(G)$ denote the set of vertices, and $E(G)$ denote the set of edges of a graph G. If the elements of E are ordered pairs, G is called a **directed graph** or **digraph**; otherwise, G is called an **undirected graph**. In an undirected graph, the pairs (u, v) and (v, u) represent the same edge.

Let G be a graph. A graph H is called a **subgraph** of G if $V(H) \subseteq V(G)$ and $E(H) \subseteq E(G)$; that is, every vertex of H is a vertex of G, and every edge in H is an edge in G.

A graph can be shown pictorially. The vertices are drawn as circles, and a label inside the circle represents the vertex. In an undirected graph, the edges are drawn using lines. In a directed graph, the edges are drawn using arrows.

1
2

EXAMPLE 12-1

Figure 12-3 shows some examples of undirected graphs.

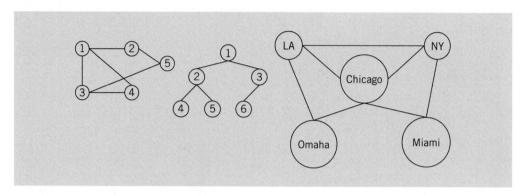

FIGURE 12-3 Various undirected graphs

EXAMPLE 12-2

Figure 12-4 shows some examples of directed graphs.

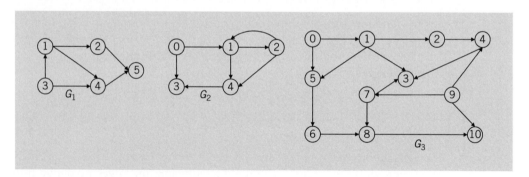

FIGURE 12-4 Various directed graphs

For the graphs of Figure 12-4, we have

$V(G_1) = \{1, 2, 3, 4, 5\}$ $E(G_1) = \{(1, 2), (1, 4), (2, 5), (3, 1), (3, 4), (4, 5)\}$

$V(G_2) = \{0, 1, 2, 3, 4\}$ $E(G_2) = \{(0, 1), (0, 3), (1, 2), (1, 4), (2, 1), (2, 4), (4, 3)\}$

$V(G_3) = \{0, 1, 2, 3, 4, 5, 6, 7, 8, 9, 10\}$ $E(G_3) = \{(0, 1), (0, 5), (1, 2), (1, 3), (1, 5), (2, 4), (4, 3),$
$(5, 6), (6, 8), (7, 3), (7, 8), (8, 10), (9, 4),$
$(9, 7), (9, 10)\}$

Let G be an undirected graph. Let u and v be two vertices in G. Then u and v are called **adjacent** if there is an edge from one to the other; that is, $(u, v) \in E$. An edge incident on a single vertex is called a **loop**. If two edges, e_1 and e_2, are associated with the same pair of vertices $\{u, v\}$, then e_1 and e_2 are called **parallel edges**. A graph is called a **simple graph** if it has no loops and no parallel edges. Let $e = (u, v)$ be an edge in G. We then say that edge e is **incident** on the vertices u and v. The degree of u, written $\deg(u)$ or $d(u)$, is the number of edges incident with u. We make the convention that each loop on a vertex u contributes 2 to the degree of u. u is called an **even (odd) degree** vertex if the degree of u is even (odd). There is a **path** from u to v if there is a sequence of vertices $u_1, u_2, \ldots, u_n$ such that $u = u_1$, $u_n = v$ and (u_i, u_{i+1}) is an edge for all $i = 1, 2, \ldots, n - 1$. Vertices u and v are called **connected** if there is a path from u to v. A **simple path** is a path in which all the vertices, except possibly the first and last vertices, are distinct. A **cycle** in G is a simple path in which the first and last vertices are the same. G is called **connected** if there is a path from any vertex to any other vertex. A maximal subset of connected vertices is called a **component** of G.

Let G be a directed graph, and let u and v be two vertices in G. If there is an edge from u to v, that is, $(u, v) \in E$, we say that u is **adjacent to** v and v is **adjacent from** u. The definitions of the paths and cycles in G are similar to those for undirected graphs. G is called **strongly connected** if any two vertices in G are connected.

Consider the directed graphs of Figure 12-4. In G_1, 1–4–5 is a path from vertex 1 to vertex 5. There are no cycles in G_1. In G_2, 1–2–1 is a cycle. In G_3, 0–1–2–4–3 is a path from vertex 0 to vertex 3; 1–5–6–8–10 is a path from vertex 1 to vertex 10. There are no cycles in G_3.

Graph Representation

To write programs that process and manipulate graphs, the graphs must be stored—that is, represented—in computer memory. A graph can be represented (in computer memory) in several ways. We now discuss two commonly used ways: adjacency matrices and adjacency lists.

Adjacency Matrices

Let G be a graph with n vertices, where $n > 0$. Let $V(G) = \{v_1, v_2, \ldots, v_n\}$. The adjacency matrix A_G is a two-dimensional $n \times n$ matrix such that the (i, j)th entry of A_G is 1 if there is an edge from v_i to v_j; otherwise, the (i, j)th entry is 0. That is,

$$A_G(i,j) = \begin{cases} 1 & \text{if } (v_i, v_j) \in E(G) \\ 0 & \text{otherwise} \end{cases}$$

In an undirected graph, if $(v_i, v_j) \in E(G)$, then $(v_j, v_i) \in E(G)$, so $A_G(i, j) = 1 = A_G(j, i)$. It follows that the adjacency matrix of an undirected graph is symmetric.

EXAMPLE 12-3

Consider the directed graphs of Figure 12-4. The adjacency matrices of the directed graphs G_1 and G_2 are as follows:

$$A_{G_1} = \begin{bmatrix} 0 & 1 & 0 & 1 & 0 \\ 0 & 0 & 0 & 0 & 1 \\ 1 & 0 & 0 & 1 & 0 \\ 0 & 0 & 0 & 0 & 1 \\ 0 & 0 & 0 & 0 & 0 \end{bmatrix}, \; A_{G_2} = \begin{bmatrix} 0 & 1 & 0 & 1 & 0 \\ 0 & 0 & 1 & 0 & 1 \\ 0 & 1 & 0 & 0 & 1 \\ 0 & 0 & 0 & 0 & 0 \\ 0 & 0 & 0 & 1 & 0 \end{bmatrix}.$$

Adjacency Lists

Let G be a graph with n vertices, where $n > 0$. Let $V(G) = \{v_1, v_2, \ldots, v_n\}$. In the adjacency list representation, corresponding to each vertex, v, there is a linked list such that each node of the linked list contains the vertex, u, such that $(v, u) \in E(G)$. Because there are n nodes, we use an array, A, of size n, such that $A[i]$ is a reference variable pointing to the first node of the linked list containing the vertices to which v_i is adjacent. Clearly, each node has two components, say `vertex` and `link`. The component `vertex` contains the index of the vertex adjacent to vertex i.

EXAMPLE 12-4

Consider the directed graphs of Figure 12-4. Figure 12-5 shows the adjacency list of the directed graph G_2.

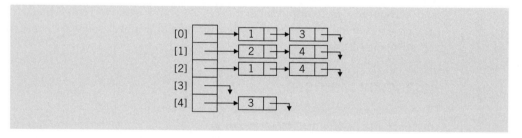

FIGURE 12-5 Adjacency list of graph G_2 of Figure 12-4

Figure 12-6 shows the adjacency list of the directed graph G_3.

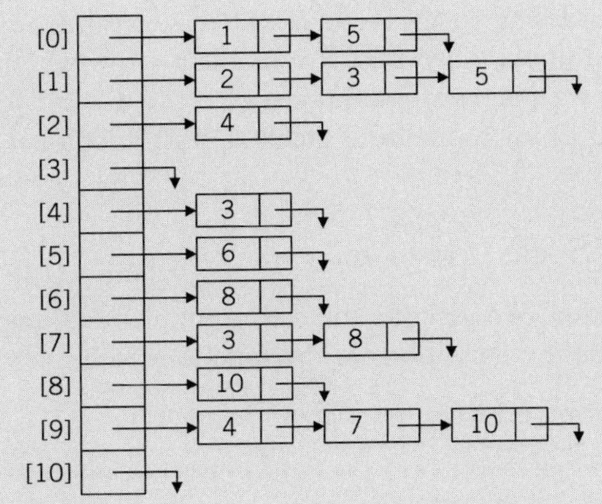

FIGURE 12-6 Adjacency list of graph G_3 of Figure 12-4

Operations on Graphs

Now that you know how to represent graphs in computer memory, the next obvious step is to learn the basic operations on a graph. The operations commonly performed on a graph are as follows:

1. Create the graph. That is, store the graph in computer memory using a particular graph representation.
2. Clear the graph. This operation makes the graph empty.
3. Determine whether the graph is empty.
4. Traverse the graph.
5. Print the graph.

We will add more operations on a graph when we discuss a specific application or a particular graph later in this chapter.

How a graph is represented in computer memory depends on the specific application. For illustration purposes, we use the adjacency list (linked list) representation of graphs. Therefore, for each vertex v the vertices adjacent to v (in a directed graph, also called the **immediate successors**) are stored in the linked list associated with v.

To manage the data in a linked list, we use the `class unorderedLinkedList`, discussed in Chapter 5.

The labeling of the vertices of a graph depends on a specific application. If you are dealing with the graph of cities, you could label the vertices by the names of the cities. However, to write algorithms to manipulate a graph as well as to simplify the algorithm, there must be some ordering to the vertices. That is, we must specify the first vertex, the second vertex, and so on. Therefore, for simplicity, throughout this chapter we assume that the n vertices of the graphs are numbered 0, 1, ..., $n - 1$. Moreover, it follows that the class we will design to implement the graph algorithm will *not* be a template.

Graphs as ADTs

In this section, we describe the class to implement graphs as an abstract data type (ADT) and provide the definitions of the functions to implement the operations on a graph.

The following class defines a graph as an ADT:

```
//*************************************************************
// Author: D.S. Malik
//
// class graphType
// This class specifies the basic operations to implement a graph.
//*************************************************************

class graphType
{
public:
    bool isEmpty() const;
    //Function to determine whether the graph is empty.
    //Postcondition: Returns true if the graph is empty;
    //    otherwise, returns false.

    void createGraph();
    //Function to create a graph.
    //Postcondition: The graph is created using the
    //    adjacency list representation.

    void clearGraph();
    //Function to clear graph.
    //Postcondition: The memory occupied by each vertex
    //    is deallocated.

    void printGraph() const;
    //Function to print graph.
    //Postcondition: The graph is printed.

    void depthFirstTraversal();
    //Function to perform the depth first traversal of
    //the entire graph.
    //Postcondition: The vertices of the graph are printed
    //    using the depth first traversal algorithm.
```

```
    void dftAtVertex(int vertex);
      //Function to perform the depth first traversal of
      //the graph at a node specified by the parameter vertex.
      //Postcondition: Starting at vertex, the vertices are
      //      printed using the depth first traversal algorithm.

    void breadthFirstTraversal();
      //Function to perform the breadth first traversal of
      //the entire graph.
      //Postcondition: The vertices of the graph are printed
      //      using the breadth first traversal algorithm.

    graphType(int size = 0);
      //Constructor
      //Postcondition: gSize = 0; maxSize = size;
      //      graph is an array of pointers to linked lists.

    ~graphType();
      //Destructor
      //The storage occupied by the vertices is deallocated.

protected:
    int maxSize;      //maximum number of vertices
    int gSize;        //current number of vertices
    unorderedLinkedList<int> *graph; //array to create
                                     //adjacency lists

private:
    void dft(int v, bool visited[]);
      //Function to perform the depth first traversal of
      //the graph at a node specified by the parameter vertex.
      //This function is used by the public member functions
      //depthFirstTraversal and dftAtVertex.
      //Postcondition: Starting at vertex, the vertices are
      //      printed using the depth first traversal algorithm.
};
```

We leave the UML class diagram of the class graphType as an exercise.

The definitions of the functions of the class graphType are discussed next.

A graph is empty if the number of vertices is 0—that is, if gSize is 0. Therefore, the definition of the function isEmpty is as follows:

```
bool graphType::isEmpty() const
{
    return (gSize == 0);
}
```

The definition of the function createGraph depends on how the data is input into the program. For illustration purposes, we assume that the data to the program is input from a file. The user is prompted for the input file. The data in the file appears in the following form:

```
5
0  2  4  ...  -999
1  3  6  8  ...  -999
...
```

The first line of input specifies the number of vertices in the graph. The first entry in the remaining lines specifies the vertex, and all of the remaining entries in the line (except the last) specify the vertices that are adjacent to the vertex. Each line ends with the number −999.

Using these conventions, the definition of the function createGraph is as follows:

```
void graphType::createGraph()
{
    ifstream infile;
    char fileName[50];

    int vertex;
    int adjacentVertex;

    if (gSize != 0)   //if the graph is not empty, make it empty
        clearGraph();

    cout << "Enter input file name: ";
    cin >> fileName;
    cout << endl;

    infile.open(fileName);

    if (!infile)
    {
        cout << "Cannot open input file." << endl;
        return;
    }

    infile >> gSize;     //get the number of vertices

    for (int index = 0; index < gSize; index++)
    {
        infile >> vertex;
        infile >> adjacentVertex;

        while (adjacentVertex != -999)
        {
            graph[vertex].insertLast(adjacentVertex);
            infile >> adjacentVertex;
        } //end while
    } // end for

    infile.close();
} //end createGraph
```

The function clearGraph empties the graph by deallocating the storage occupied by each linked list and then setting the number of vertices to 0.

```
void graphType::clearGraph()
{
    for (int index = 0; index < gSize; index++)
        graph[index].destroyList();

    gSize = 0;
} //end clearGraph
```

The definition of the function `printGraph` is given next:

```
void graphType::printGraph() const
{
    for (int index = 0; index < gSize; index++)
    {
        cout << index << " ";
        graph[index].print();
        cout << endl;
    }

    cout << endl;
} //end printGraph
```

The definitions of the constructor and the destructor are as follows:

```
    //Constructor
graphType::graphType(int size)
{
    maxSize = size;
    gSize = 0;
    graph = new unorderedLinkedList<int>[size];
}

    //Destructor
graphType::~graphType()
{
    clearGraph();
}
```

Graph Traversals

Processing a graph requires the ability to traverse the graph. This section discusses the graph traversal algorithms.

Traversing a graph is similar to traversing a binary tree, except that traversing a graph is a bit more complicated. Now a binary tree has no cycles and starting at the root node we can traverse the entire tree. On the other hand, a graph might have cycles and we might not be able to traverse the entire graph from a single vertex (for example, if the graph is not connected). Therefore, we must keep track of the vertices that have been visited. We must also traverse the graph from each vertex (that has not been visited) of the graph. This ensures that the entire graph is traversed.

The two most common graph traversal algorithms are the **depth-first traversal** and **breadth-first traversal**, which are described next. For simplicity, we assume that when a vertex is visited, its index is output. Moreover, each vertex is visited only once. We use the `bool` array `visited` to keep track of the visited vertices.

Depth-First Traversal

The **depth-first traversal** is similar to the preorder traversal of a binary tree. The general algorithm is as follows:

```
for each vertex, v, in the graph
    if v is not visited
        start the depth first traversal at v
```

Consider the graph G_3 of Figure 12-4. It is shown here again as Figure 12-7 for easy reference.

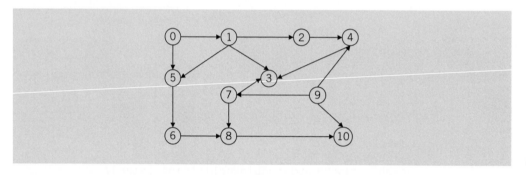

FIGURE 12-7 Directed graph G_3

The depth-first ordering of the vertices of graph G_3 in Figure 12-7 is as follows:

```
0 1 2 4 3 5 6 8 10 7 9
```

For the graph of Figure 12-7, the depth-first search starts at the vertex 0. After visiting all the vertices that can be reached starting at the vertex 0, the depth-first search starts at the next vertex that is not visited. There is a path from the vertex 0 to every other vertex except the vertices 7 and 9. Therefore, when the depth-first search starts at the vertex 0, all the vertices except 7 and 9 are visited before these vertices. After completing the depth-first search that started at the vertex 0, the depth-first search starts at the vertex 7 and then at the vertex 9. Note that there is no path from the vertex 7 to the vertex 9. Therefore, after completing the depth-first search that started at the vertex 7, the depth-first search starts at the vertex 9. The general algorithm to do a depth-first traversal *at a given node*, *v*, is as follows:

1. mark node v as visited

2. visit the node

3. for each vertex u adjacent to v
        if u is not visited
            start the depth first traversal at u

Clearly, this is a recursive algorithm. We use a recursive function, `dft`, to implement this algorithm. The vertex at which the depth-first traversal is to be started, and the `bool` array `visited`, are passed as parameters to this function.

```cpp
void graphType::dft(int v, bool visited[])
{
    visited[v] = true;
    cout << " " << v << " ";  //visit the vertex

    linkedListIterator<int> graphIt;

        //for each vertex adjacent to v
    for (graphIt = graph[v].begin(); graphIt != graph[v].end();
                                    ++graphIt)
    {
        int w = *graphIt;
        if (!visited[w])
            dft(w, visited);
    } //end while
} //end dft
```

In the preceding code, note that the statement

```cpp
linkedListIterator<int> graphIt;
```

declares `graphIt` to be an iterator. In the `for` loop, we use it to traverse a linked list (adjacency list) to which the pointer `graph[v]` points. Next, let us look at the statement

```cpp
int w = *graphIt;
```

The expression `*graphIt` returns the label of the vertex, adjacent to the vertex `v`, to which `graphIt` points.

Next, we give the definition of the function `depthFirstTraversal` to implement the depth-first traversal of the graph.

```cpp
void graphType::depthFirstTraversal()
{
    bool *visited; //pointer to create the array to keep
                   //track of the visited vertices
    visited = new bool[gSize];

    for (int index = 0; index < gSize; index++)
        visited[index] = false;

        //For each vertex that is not visited, do a depth
        //first traverssal
    for (int index = 0; index < gSize; index++)
        if (!visited[index])
            dft(index,visited);
    delete [] visited;
} //end depthFirstTraversal
```

The function `depthFirstTraversal` performs a depth-first traversal of the entire graph. The definition of the function `dftAtVertex`, which performs a depth-first traversal at a given vertex, is as follows:

```
void graphType::dftAtVertex(int vertex)
{
    bool *visited;

    visited = new bool[gSize];

    for (int index = 0; index < gSize; index++)
        visited[index] = false;

    dft(vertex, visited);

    delete [] visited;
} // end dftAtVertex
```

Breadth-First Traversal

The **breadth-first traversal** of a graph is similar to traversing a binary tree level-by-level (the nodes at each level are visited from left to right). All the nodes at any level, i, are visited before visiting the nodes at level $i + 1$.

The breadth-first ordering of the vertices of the graph G_3 in Figure 12-7 is as follows:

```
0  1  5  2  3  6  4  8  10  7  9
```

For the graph G_3, we start the breadth traversal at vertex 0. After visiting the vertex 0, we visit the vertices that are directly connected to it and are not visited, which are 1 and 5. Next, we visit the vertices that are directly connected to 1 and are not visited, which are 2 and 3. After this, we visit the vertices that are directly connected to 5 and are not visited, which is 6. After this, we visit the vertices that are directly connected to 2 and are not visited, and so on.

As in the case of the depth-first traversal, because it might not be possible to traverse the entire graph from a single vertex, the breadth-first traversal also traverses the graph from each vertex that is not visited. Starting at the first vertex, the graph is traversed as much as possible; we then go to the next vertex that has not been visited. To implement the breadth-first search algorithm, we use a queue. The general algorithm is as follows:

1. for each vertex v in the graph
        if v is not visited
            add v to the queue //start the breadth first search at v

2. Mark v as visited

3. while the queue is not empty

    3.1. Remove vertex u from the queue

    3.2. Retrieve the vertices adjacent to u

    3.3.   for each vertex w that is adjacent to u
             if w is not visited

             3.3.1.   Add w to the queue

             3.3.2.   Mark w as visited

The following C++ function, breadthFirstTraversal, implements this algorithm:

```cpp
void graphType::breadthFirstTraversal()
{
    linkedQueueType<int> queue;

    bool *visited;
    visited = new bool[gSize];

    for (int ind = 0; ind < gSize; ind++)
        visited[ind] = false;    //initialize the array
                                 //visited to false

    linkedListIterator<int> graphIt;

    for (int index = 0; index < gSize; index++)
        if (!visited[index])
        {
            queue.addQueue(index);
            visited[index] = true;
            cout << " " << index << " ";

            while (!queue.isEmptyQueue())
            {
                int u = queue.front();
                queue.deleteQueue();

                for (graphIt = graph[u].begin();
                     graphIt != graph[u].end(); ++graphIt)
                {
                    int w = *graphIt;
                    if (!visited[w])
                    {
                        queue.addQueue(w);
                        visited[w] = true;
                        cout << " " << w << " ";
                    }
                }
            } //end while
        }

    delete [] visited;
} //end breadthFirstTraversal
```

As we continue to discuss graph algorithms, we will be writing C++ functions to implement specific algorithms, and so we will derive (using inheritance) new classes from the class graphType.

Shortest Path Algorithm

Graph theory has many applications. For example, we can use graphs to show how different chemicals are related or to show airline routes. Graphs also be used to show the highway structure of a city, state, or country. The edges connecting two vertices can be assigned a nonnegative real number, called the **weight of the edge**. If the graph represents a highway structure, the weight can represent the distance between two places or the travel time from one place to another. Such graphs are called **weighted graphs**.

Let G be a weighted graph. Let u and v be two vertices in G, and let P be a path in G from u to v. The **weight of the path** P is the sum of the weights of all the edges on the path P, which is also called the **weight** of v from u via P.

Let G be a weighted graph representing a highway structure. Suppose that the weight of an edge represents the travel time. For example, to plan monthly business trips, a salesperson wants to find the **shortest path** (that is, the path with the smallest weight) from her or his city to every other city in the graph. Many such problems exist in which we want to find the shortest path from a given vertex, called the **source**, to every other vertex in the graph.

This section describes the **shortest path algorithm**, also called a **greedy algorithm**, developed by Dijkstra.

Let G be a graph with n vertices, where $n \geq 0$. Let $V(G) = \{v_1, v_2, \ldots, v_n\}$. Let W be a two-dimensional $n \times n$ matrix such that

$$W(i,j) = \begin{cases} w_{ij} & \text{if}\,(v_i, v_j) \text{ is an edge in } G \text{ and } w_{ij} \text{ is the weight of the edge } (v_i, v_j) \\ \infty & \text{if there is no edge from } v_i \text{ to } v_j \end{cases}$$

The input to the program is the graph and the weight matrix associated with the graph. To make inputting the data easier, we extend the definition of the `class graphType` (using inheritance), and add the function `createWeightedGraph` to create the graph and the weight matrix associated with the graph. Let us call this `class weightedGraphType`. The functions to implement the shortest path algorithm will also be added to this class.

```
///******************************************************************
// Author: D.S. Malik
//
// class weightedGraphType
// This class specifies the operations to find the weight of the
// shortest path from a given vertex to every other vertex in a
// graph.
///******************************************************************

class weightedGraphType: public graphType
{
public:
    void createWeightedGraph();
        //Function to create the graph and the weight matrix.
        //Postcondition: The graph using adjacency lists and
        //    its weight matrix is created.
```

```
    void shortestPath(int vertex);
      //Function to determine the weight of a shortest path
      //from vertex, that is, source, to every other vertex
      //in the graph.
      //Postcondition: The weight of the shortest path from vertex
      //    to every other vertex in the graph is determined.

    void printShortestDistance(int vertex);
      //Function to print the shortest weight from the vertex
      //specified by the parameter vertex to every other vertex in
      //the graph.
      //Postcondition: The weight of the shortest path from vertex
      //    to every other vertex in the graph is printed.

    weightedGraphType(int size = 0);
      //Constructor
      //Postcondition: gSize = 0; maxSize = size;
      //    graph is an array of pointers to linked lists.
      //    weights is a two-dimensional array to store the weights
      //        of the edges.
      //    smallestWeight is an array to store the smallest weight
      //        from source to vertices.

    ~weightedGraphType();
      //Destructor
      //The storage occupied by the vertices and the arrays
      //weights and smallestWeight is deallocated.

protected:
    double **weights;    //pointer to create weight matrix
    double *smallestWeight; //pointer to create the array to store
                    //the smallest weight from source to vertices
};
```

We leave the UML class diagram of the class `weightedGraphType` and the inheritance hierarchy as an exercise. The definition of the function `createWeightedGraph` is also left as an exercise for you. Next, we describe the shortest path algorithm.

Shortest Path

Given a vertex, say `vertex` (that is, a source), this section describes the shortest path algorithm. The general algorithm is as follows:

1. Initialize the array `smallestWeight` so that

   `smallestWeight[u] = weights[vertex, u]`

2. Set `smallestWeight[vertex] = 0`.

3. Find the vertex `v` that is closest to `vertex` for which the shortest path has not been determined.

4. Mark `v` as the (next) vertex for which the smallest weight is found.

5. For each vertex w in G, such that the shortest path from **vertex** to w has not been determined and an edge (v, w) exists, if the weight of the path to w via v is smaller than its current weight, update the weight of w to the weight of v + the weight of the edge (v, w).

Because there are *n* vertices, Steps 3 through 5 are repeated *n* − 1 times. Example 12-5 illustrates the shortest path algorithm. (We use the Boolean array **weightFound** to keep track of the vertices for which the smallest weight from the source vertex has been found. If the smallest weight for a vertex, from the source, has been found, then this vertex's corresponding entry in the array **weightFound** is set to **true**; otherwise the corresponding entry is **false**.)

EXAMPLE 12-5

Let G be the graph shown in Figure 12-8.

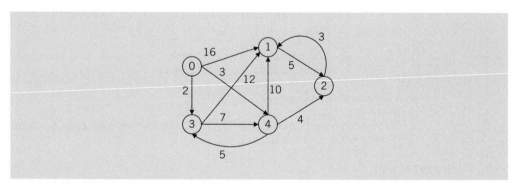

FIGURE 12-8 Weighted graph *G*

Suppose that the source vertex of G is 0. The graph shows the weight of each edge. After Steps 1 and 2 execute, the resulting graph is as shown in Figure 12-9.

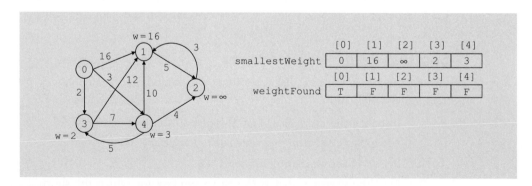

FIGURE 12-9 Graph after Steps 1 and 2 execute

Iteration 1 of Steps 3 through 5: At Step 3, we select a vertex that is closest to the vertex 0 and for which the shortest path has not been found. We do this by finding a vertex in the array

smallestWeight that has the smallest weight and its corresponding entry in the array
weightFound is false. Therefore, in this iteration, we select the vertex 3. At Step 4, we
mark weightFound[3] as true. Next at Step 5, we consider vertices 1 and 4 because these
are the vertices for which there is an edge from the vertex 3 and the shortest path from 0 to
these vertices has not been found. We then check if the path from the vertex 0 to the vertices
1 and 4 via the vertex 3 can be improved. The weight of the path 0-3-1 from 0 to 1 is less
than the weight of the path 0-1. So we update smallestWeight[1] to 14. The weight of
the path 0-3-4, which is 2 + 7 = 9, is greater than the weight of the path 0-4, which is 3. So
we do not update the weight of the vertex 4. Figure 12-10 shows the resulting graph. (The
dotted arrow shows the shortest path from the source—that is, from 0—to the vertex.)

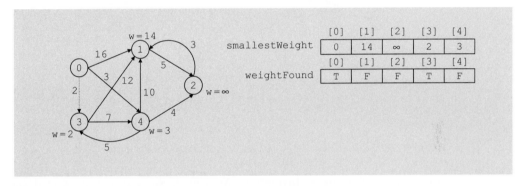

FIGURE 12-10 Graph after the first iteration of Steps 3 to 5

Iteration 2 of Steps 3 through 5: At Step 3, we select vertex 4 because this is the vertex in
the array smallestWeight that has the smallest weight and its corresponding entry in the
array weightFound is false. Next we execute Steps 4 and 5. At Step 4, we set
weightFound[4] to true. At Step 5, we consider vertices 1 and 2 because these are the
vertices for which there is an edge from the vertex 4 and the shortest path from 0 to these
vertices has not been found. We then check if the path from the vertex 0 to the vertices 1 and
2 via the vertex 4 can be improved. Clearly, the weight of the path 0-4-1, which is 13, is
smaller than the current weight of 1, which is 14. So we update smallestWeight[1].
Similarly, we update smallestWeight[2]. Figure 12-11 shows the resulting graph.

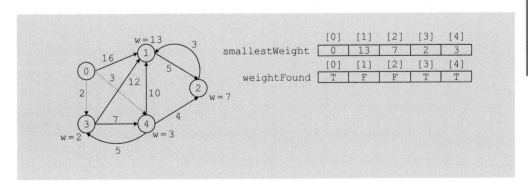

FIGURE 12-11 Graph after the second iteration of Steps 3 to 5

Iteration 3 of Steps 3 through 5: At Step 3, the vertex selected is 2. At Step 4, we set `weightFound[2]` to true. Next at Step 5, we consider the vertex 1 because this is the vertex for which there is an edge from the vertex 2 and the shortest path from 0 to this vertex has not been found. We then check if the path from the vertex 0 to the vertex 1 via the vertex 2 can be improved. Clearly, the weight of the path `0-4-2-1`, which is 10, from 0 to 1 is smaller than the current weight of 1 (which is 13). So we update `smallestWeight[1]`. Figure 12-12 shows the resulting graph.

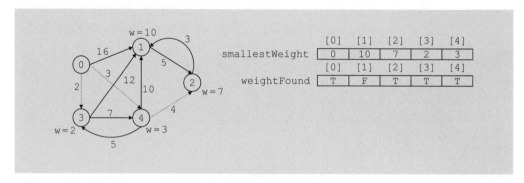

FIGURE 12-12 Graph after the third iteration of Steps 3 to 5

Iteration 4 of Steps 3 through 5: At Step 3, the vertex 1 is selected and at Step 4, `weightFound[1]` is set to true. In this iteration, the action of Step 5 is null because the shortest path from the vertex 0 to every other vertex in the graph has been determined. Figure 12-13 shows the final graph.

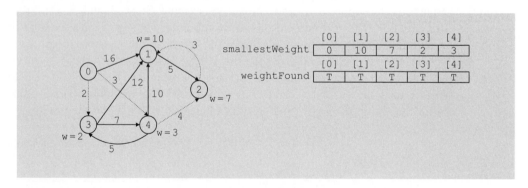

FIGURE 12-13 Graph after the fourth iteration of Steps 3 through 5

The following C++ function, `shortestPath`, implements the previous algorithm:

```cpp
void weightedGraphType::shortestPath(int vertex)
{
    for (int j = 0; j < gSize; j++)
        smallestWeight[j] = weights[vertex][j];
```

```
    bool *weightFound;
    weightFound = new bool[gSize];

    for (int j = 0; j < gSize; j++)
        weightFound[j] = false;

    weightFound[vertex] = true;
    smallestWeight[vertex] = 0;

    for (int i = 0; i < gSize - 1; i++)
    {
        double minWeight = DBL_MAX;
        int v;

        for (int j = 0; j < gSize; j++)
            if (!weightFound[j])
                if (smallestWeight[j] < minWeight)
                {
                    v = j;
                    minWeight = smallestWeight[v];
                }

        weightFound[v] = true;

        for (int j = 0; j < gSize; j++)
            if (!weightFound[j])
                if (minWeight + weights[v][j] < smallestWeight[j])
                    smallestWeight[j] = minWeight + weights[v][j];
    } //end for
} //end shortestPath
```

Note that the function shortestPath records only the weight of the shortest path from the source to a vertex. We leave it for you to modify this function so that the shortest path from the source to a vertex is also recorded. Moreover, this function uses the named constant DBL_MAX, which is defined in the header file cfloat.

Let G be a graph with n vertices. In the function shortestPath, the first for loop executes n times and the second for loop also executes n times. The third for loop executes $n - 1$ times. The body of the third for loop contains two for loops, in sequence, and each of these for loops executes n times. Thus, the total number of iterations of the for loops is $n + n + (n - 1)(n + n) = 2n + 2n(n - 1) = O(n^2)$. Hence, the function shortestPath, that is, the shortest path algorithm is of order $O(n^2)$.

The definitions of the function printShortestDistance and the constructor and destructor are as follows:

```
void weightedGraphType::printShortestDistance(int vertex)
{
    cout << "Source Vertex: " << vertex << endl;
    cout << "Shortest distance from source to each vertex."
         << endl;
    cout << "Vertex  Shortest_Distance" << endl;
```

```
    for (int j = 0; j < gSize; j++)
        cout << setw(4) << j << setw(12) << smallestWeight[j]
            << endl;
    cout << endl;
} //end printShortestDistance

    //Constructor
weightedGraphType::weightedGraphType(int size)
                    :graphType(size)
{
    weights = new double*[size];

    for (int i = 0; i < size; i++)
        weights[i] = new double[size];

    smallestWeight = new double[size];
}

    //Destructor
weightedGraphType::~weightedGraphType()
{
    for (int i = 0; i < gSize; i++)
        delete [] weights[i];

    delete [] weights;
    delete smallestWeight;
}
```

Minimum Spanning Tree

Consider the graph of Figure 12-14, which represents the airline connections of a company, between seven cities. The number on each edge represents some cost factor of maintaining the connection between cities.

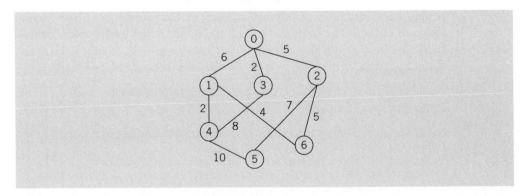

FIGURE 12-14 Airline connections between cities and the cost factor of maintaining the connections

Due to financial hardship, the company needs to shut down the maximum number of connections and still be able to fly (may be not directly) from one city to another. The graphs of Figure 12-15(a), (b), and (c) show three different solutions.

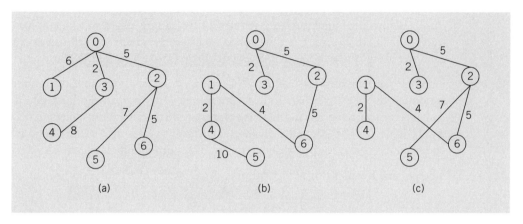

FIGURE 12-15 Possible solutions to the graph of Figure 12-14

The total cost factor of maintaining the remaining connections in Figure 12-15(a) is 33, in Figure 12-15(b) it is 28, and in Figure 12-15(c) it is 25. Out of these three solutions, obviously, the desired solution is the one shown by the graph of Figure 12-15(c) because it gives the lowest cost factor. Graphs of Figure 12-15 are called spanning trees of the graph of Figure 12-14.

Let us note the following from the graphs of Figure 12-15. Each of the graphs of Figure 12-15 is a subgraph of the graph of Figure 12-14, and there is a unique path from a node to any other node. Such graphs are called trees. There are many other situations, where given a weighted graph, we need to determine a graph such as in Figure 12-15 with the smallest weight. In this section, we give an algorithm to determine such graphs. However, first we introduce some terminology.

A (**free**) **tree** T is a simple graph such that if u and v are two vertices in T, there is a unique path from u to v. A tree in which a particular vertex is designated as a root is called a **rooted tree**. If a weight is assigned to the edges in T, T is called a **weighted tree**. If T is a weighted tree, the **weight** of T, denoted by $W(T)$, is the sum of the weights of all the edges in T.

A tree T is called a **spanning tree** of graph G if T is a subgraph of G such that $V(T) = V(G)$, that is, all the vertices of G are in T.

Suppose G denotes the graph of Figure 12-14. Then the graphs of Figure 12-15 show three spanning trees of G. Let us note the following theorem.

Theorem 12-1: A graph G has a spanning tree if and only if G is connected.

From this theorem, it follows that to determine a spanning tree of a graph, the graph must be connected.

Definition: Let G be a weighted graph. A **minimum (minimal) spanning tree** of G is a spanning tree with the minimum weight.

There are two well-known algorithms, Prim's algorithm and Kruskal's algorithm, for finding a minimum spanning tree of a graph. This section discusses Prim's algorithm to find a minimum spanning tree. If interested, you can find Kruskal's algorithm in the discrete structures book or a data structures book listed in Appendix H.

Prim's algorithm builds the tree iteratively by adding edges until a minimum spanning tree is obtained. We start with a designated vertex, which we call the source vertex. At each iteration, a new edge that does not form a cycle is added to the tree.

Let G be a weighted graph such that $V(G) = \{v_0, v_1, \ldots, v_{n-1}\}$, where n, the number of vertices, is nonnegative. Let v_0 be the source vertex. Let T be the partially built tree. Initially $V(T)$ contains the source vertex and $E(T)$ is empty. At the next iteration, a new vertex that is not in $V(T)$ is added to $V(T)$, such that an edge exists from a vertex in T to the new vertex so that the corresponding edge has the smallest weight. The corresponding edge is added to $E(T)$.

The general form of Prim's algorithm is as follows. (Let n be the number of vertices in G.)

1. Set V(T) = {source}
2. Set E(T) = empty
3. for i = 1 to n

    3.1. minWeight = infinity;

    3.2. for j = 1 to n
```
            if vⱼ is in V(T)
               for k = 1 to n
                  if vₖ is not in T and weight[vⱼ, vₖ] < minWeight
                  {
                      endVertex = vₖ;
                      edge = (vⱼ, vₖ);
                      minWeight = weight[vⱼ, vₖ];
                  }
```

    3.3. V(T) = V(T) ∪ {endVertex};

    3.4. E(T) = E(T) ∪ {edge};

Let us illustrate Prim's algorithm using the graph G of Figure 12-16 (which is same as the graph of Figure 12-14).

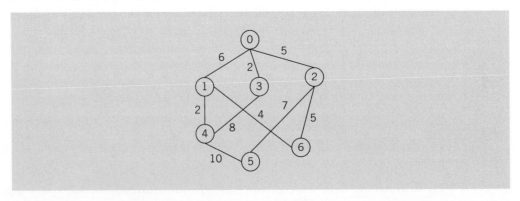

FIGURE 12-16 Weighted graph G

Let N denote the set of vertices of G that are not in T. Suppose that the source vertex is 0. Figure 12-17 shows how Prim's algorithm works.

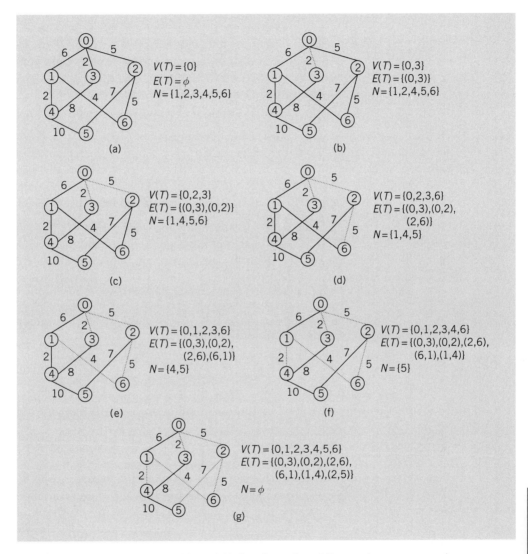

FIGURE 12-17 Graph G, $V(T)$, $E(T)$, and N after Steps 1 and 2 execute

After Steps 1 and 2 execute, $V(T)$, $E(T)$, and N are as shown in Figure 12-17(a). Step 3 checks the following edges: (0,1), (0,2), and (0,3). The weight of the edge (0,1) is 6, the weight of the edge (0,2) is 5, and the weight of the edge (0,3) is 2. Clearly, the edge (0,3) has the smallest weight; see Figure 12-17(b). Therefore, vertex 3 is added to $V(T)$ and the edge (0,3) is added to $E(T)$. Figure 12-17(b) shows the resulting graph, $V(T)$, $E(T)$, and N. (The dotted line shows the edge in T.)

Next, Step 3 checks the following edges: (0,1), (0,2), and (3,4). The weight of the edge (0,1) is 6, the weight of the edge (0,2) is 5, and the weight of the edge (3,4) is 8. Clearly, the edge (0,2) has the smallest weight. Therefore, vertex 2 is added to $V(T)$ and the edge (0,2) is added to $E(T)$. Figure 12-17(c) shows the resulting graph, $V(T)$, $E(T)$, and N.

At the next iteration, Step 3 checks the following edges: (0,1), (2,5), (2,6), and (3,4). The weight of the edge (0,1) is 6, the weight of the edge (2,5) is 7, the weight of the edge (2,6) is 5, and the weight of the edge (3,4) is 8. Clearly, the edge (2,6) has the smallest weight. Therefore, vertex 6 is added to $V(T)$ and the edge (2,6) is added to $E(T)$. Figure 12-17(d) shows the resulting graph, $V(T)$, $E(T)$, and N. (The dotted lines show the edges in T.)

At the next iteration, Step 3 checks the following edges: (0,1), (2,5), (3,4), and (6,1). The weight of the edge (0,1) is 6, the weight of the edge (2,5) is 7, the weight of the edge (3,4) is 8, and the weight of the edge (6,1) is 4. Clearly, the edge (6,1) has the smallest weight. Therefore, vertex 1 is added to $V(T)$ and the edge (6,1) is added to $E(T)$. Figure 12-17(e) shows the resulting graph, $V(T)$, $E(T)$, and N. (The dotted lines show the edges in T.)

At the next iteration, Step 3 checks the following edges: (1,4), (2,5), and (3,4). The weight of the edge (1,4) is 2, the weight of the edge (2,5) is 7, and the weight of the edge (3,4) is 8. Clearly, the edge (1,4) has the smallest weight. Therefore, vertex 4 is added to $V(T)$ and the edge (1,4) is added to $E(T)$. Figure 12-17(f) shows the resulting graph, $V(T)$, $E(T)$, and N. (The dotted lines show the edges in T.)

At the next iteration, Step 3 checks the following edges: (2,5) and (4,5). The weight of the edge (2,5) is 7 and the weight of the edge (4,5) is 10. Clearly, the edge (2,5) has the smallest weight. Therefore, vertex 5 is added to $V(T)$ and the edge (2,5) is added to $E(T)$. Figure 12-17(g) shows the resulting graph, $V(T)$, $E(T)$, and N. (The dotted lines show the edges in T.)

In Figure 12-17(g), the dotted lines show a minimum spanning tree of G of weight 25.

Before we give the definition of the function to implement Prim's algorithm, let us first define a spanning tree as an ADT.

Let `mstv` be a `bool` array such that `mstv[j]` is true if the vertex v_i is in T, and false otherwise. Let `edges` be an array such that `edges[j] = k`, if there is an edge connecting vertices v_j and v_k. Suppose that the edge (v_i, v_j) is in the minimum spanning tree. Let `edgeWeights` be an array such that `edgeWeights[j]` is the weight of the edge (v_i, v_j).

Using these conventions, the following class defines a spanning tree as an ADT:

```
//**************************************************************
// Author: D.S. Malik
//
// class msTreeType
// This class specifies the operations to find a minimum
// spanning tree in a graph.
//**************************************************************
```

```
class msTreeType: public graphType
{
public:
    void createSpanningGraph();
        //Function to create the graph and the weight matrix.
        //Postcondition: The graph using adjacency lists and
        //    its weight matrix is created.

    void minimumSpanning(int sVertex);
        //Function to create a minimum spanning tree with
        //root as sVertex.
        // Postcondition: A minimum spanning tree is created.
        //      The weight of the edges is also saved in the array
        //      edgeWeights.

    void printTreeAndWeight();
        //Function to output the edges of the minimum spanning tree
        //and the weight of the minimum spanning tree.
        //Postcondition: The edges of a minimum spanning tree
        //    and their weights are printed.

    msTreeType(int size = 0);
        //Constructor
        //Postcondition: gSize = 0; maxSize = size;
        //      graph is an array of pointers to linked lists.
        //      weights is a two-dimensional array to store the weights
        //        of the edges.
        //      edges is an array to store the edges of a minimum
        //        spanning tree.
        //      edgeWeights is an array to store the weights of the
        //        edges of a minimum spanning tree.

    ~msTreeType();
        //Destructor
        //The storage occupied by the vertices and the arrays
        //weights, edges, and edgeWeights is deallocated.

protected:
    int source;
    double **weights;
    int *edges;
    double *edgeWeights;
};
```

We leave the UML class diagram of the class msTreeType and the inheritance hierarchy as an exercise. The definition of the function createSpanningGraph is also left as an exercise for you. This function creates the graph and the weight matrix associated with the graph.

The following C++ function, minimumSpanning, implements Prim's algorithm, as described previously:

```cpp
void msTreeType::minimumSpanning(int sVertex)
{
    int startVertex, endVertex;
    double minWeight;

    source = sVertex;

    bool *mstv;
    mstv = new bool[gSize];

    for (int j = 0; j < gSize; j++)
    {
        mstv[j] = false;
        edges[j] = source;
        edgeWeights[j] = weights[source][j];
    }

    mstv[source] = true;
    edgeWeights[source] = 0;

    for (int i = 0; i < gSize - 1; i++)
    {
        minWeight = DBL_MAX;

        for (int j = 0; j < gSize; j++)
            if (mstv[j])
                for (int k = 0; k < gSize; k++)
                    if (!mstv[k] && weights[j][k] < minWeight)
                    {
                        endVertex = k;
                        startVertex = j;
                        minWeight = weights[j][k];
                    }

        mstv[endVertex] = true;
        edges[endVertex] = startVertex;
        edgeWeights[endVertex] = minWeight;
    } //end for
} //end minimumSpanning
```

The definition of the function `minimumSpanning` contains three nested `for` loops. Therefore, in the worst case, Prim's algorithm given in this section is of the order $O(n^3)$. It is possible to design Prim's algorithm so that it is of the order $O(n^2)$; Programming Exercise 5 at the end of this chapter asks you to do this.

The definition of the function `printTreeAndWeight` is as follows:

```cpp
void msTreeType::printTreeAndWeight()
{
    double treeWeight = 0;

    cout << "Source Vertex: " << source << endl;
    cout << "Edges    Weight" << endl;
```

```
    for (int j = 0; j < gSize; j++)
    {
        if (edges[j] != j)
        {
            treeWeight = treeWeight + edgeWeights[j];
            cout << "("<<edges[j] << ", " << j << ")      "
                << edgeWeights[j] << endl;
        }
    }

    cout << endl;
    cout << "Minimum spanning Tree Weight: "
        << treeWeight << endl;
} //end printTreeAndWeight
```

The definitions of the constructor and the destructor are as follows:

```
msTreeType::msTreeType(int size)
        :graphType(size)
{
    weights = new double*[size];

    for (int i = 0; i < size; i++)
        weights[i] = new double[size];

    edges  = new int[size];

    edgeWeights = new double[size];
}

    //Destructor
msTreeType::~msTreeType()
{
    for (int i = 0; i < gSize; i++)
        delete [] weights[i];

    delete [] weights;
    delete [] edges;
    delete edgeWeights;
}
```

Topological Order

In college, before taking a particular course, students, usually, must take all its prerequisite courses, if any. For example, before taking the Programming II course, the student must take the Programming I course. However, certain courses can be taken independent of each other. The courses within a department can be represented as a directed graph. A directed edge from, say vertex u to vertex v means the course represented by the vertex u is a prerequisite of the course represented by the vertex v. It would be helpful for the students to know, before starting a major, the sequence in which they can take the courses so that before taking a course they take all its prerequisite courses and fulfill the graduation requirements on time. In this section, we describe an algorithm that can be used to output the vertices of a directed graph in such a sequence. Let us first introduce some terminology.

Let G be a directed graph and $V(G) = \{v_1, v_2, \ldots, v_n\}$, where $n \geq 0$. A **topological ordering** of $V(G)$ is a linear ordering $v_{i1}, v_{i2}, \ldots, v_{in}$ of the vertices such that, if v_{ij} is a predecessor of $v_{ik}, j \neq k, 1 \leq j \leq n, 1 \leq k \leq n$, then v_{ij} precedes v_{ik}, that is, $j < k$ in this linear ordering.

In this section, we describe an algorithm, topological order, which outputs the vertices of a directed graph in topological order. We assume that the graph has no cycles. We leave it as an exercise for you to modify the algorithm for the graphs that have cycles.

Because the graph has no cycles, the following is true:

- There exists a vertex v in G such that v has no successor.
- There exists a vertex u in G such that u has no predecessor.

Suppose that the array topologicalOrder (of size n, the number of vertices) is used to store the vertices of G in topological order. Thus, if a vertex, say u, is a successor of the vertex v and topologicalOrder[j] = v and topologicalOrder[k] = u, then $j < k$.

The topological sort algorithm can be implemented either using the depth-first traversal or the breadth-first traversal. This section discusses how to implement topological ordering using the breadth-first traversal. Programming Exercise 7 at the end of this chapter describes how to implement the topological sort using the depth-first traversal.

We extend the definition of the class graphType (using inheritance) to implement the breadth-first topological ordering algorithm. Let us call this class topologicalOrderType. Next, we give the definition of the class that includes the functions to implement the topological ordering algorithm.

```
//*****************************************************************
// Author: D.S. Malik
//
// class topologicalOrderType
// This class specifies the operations to find a topological
// ordering of a graph.
//*****************************************************************

class topologicalOrderType: public graphType
{
public:
    void bfTopOrder();
        //Function to perform breadth first topological ordering of
        //a graph.
        //Postcondition: The vertices are output in a breadth first
        //topological order.
```

```
        topologicalOrderType(int size = 0);
          //Constructor
          //Postcondition: gSize = 0; maxSize = size;
          //      graph is an array of pointers to linked lists.
};
```

Next, we discuss how to implement the function `bfTopOrder`.

Breadth-First Topological Ordering

Recall that the breadth-first traversal algorithm is similar to traversing a binary tree level-by-level, and so the root node (which has no predecessor) is visited first. Therefore, in the breadth-first topological ordering, we first find a vertex that has no predecessor vertex and place it first in the topological ordering. We next find the vertex, say v, all of whose predecessors have been placed in the topological ordering and place v next in the topological ordering. To keep track of the number of vertices of a vertex, we use the array `predCount`. Initially, `predCount[j]` is the number of predecessors of the vertex v_j. The queue used to guide the breadth-first traversal is initialized to those vertices v_k such that `predCount[k]` is 0. In essence, the general algorithm is as follows:

1. Create the array `predCount` and initialize it so that `predCount[i]` is the number of predecessors of the vertex v_i.

2. Initialize the queue, say `queue`, to all those vertices v_k so that `predCount[k]` is 0. (Clearly, `queue` is not empty because the graph has no cycles.)

3. `while` the queue is not empty

    3.1.   Remove the front element, u, of the queue.

    3.2.   Put u in the next available position, say `topologicalOrder[topIndex]`, and increment `topIndex`.

    3.3.   For all the immediate successors w of u,

        3.3.1.   Decrement the predecessor count of w by 1.

        3.3.2.   `if` the predecessor count of w is 0, add w to `queue`.

The graph G_3 of Figure 12-7 has no cycles. The vertices of G_3 in breadth-first topological ordering are as follows:

`Breadth First Topological order: 0 9 1 7 2 5 4 6 3 8 10`

Next, we illustrate the breadth-first topological ordering of the graph G_3.

1
2

After Steps 1 and 2 execute, the arrays predCount, topologicalOrder, and queue are as shown in Figure 12-18. (Notice that for simplicity, we show only the elements of the queue.)

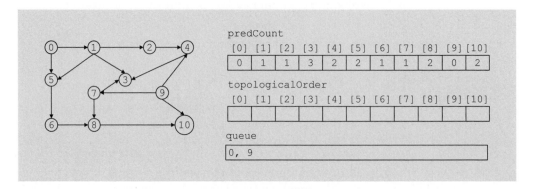

FIGURE 12-18 Arrays predCount, topologicalOrder, and queue after Steps 1 and 2 execute

Step 3 executes as long as the queue is nonempty.

Iteration 1 of Step 3: After Step 3.1 executes, the value of u is 0. Step 3.2 stores the value of u, which is 0, in the next available position in the array topologicalOrder. Notice that 0 is stored at position 0 in this array. Step 3.3 reduces the predecessor count of all the successors of 0 by 1, and if the predecessor count of any successor node of 0 reduces to 0, that node is pushed into queue. The successor nodes of the node 0 are the nodes 1 and 5. The predecessor count of the node 1 reduces to 0, and the predecessor count of the node 5 reduces to 1. The node 1 is pushed into queue. After the first iteration of Step 3, the arrays predCount, topologicalOrder, and queue are as shown in Figure 12-19.

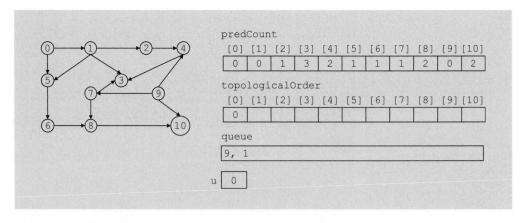

FIGURE 12-19 Arrays predCount, topologicalOrder, and queue after the first iteration of Step 3

Iteration 2 of Step 3: The queue is nonempty. After Step 3.1 executes, the value of u is 9. Step 3.2 stores the value of u, which is 9, in the next available position in the array topologicalOrder. Notice that 9 is stored at position 1 in this array. Step 3.3 reduces the predecessor count of all the successors of 9 by 1, and if the predecessor count of any successor node of 9 reduces to 0, that node is pushed into queue. The successor nodes of the node 9 are the nodes 4, 7, and 10. The predecessor count of the node 7 reduces to 0 and the predecessor count of the nodes 4 and 10 reduces to 1. The node 7 is pushed into queue. After the second iteration of Step 3, the arrays predCount, topologicalOrder, and queue are as shown in Figure 12-20.

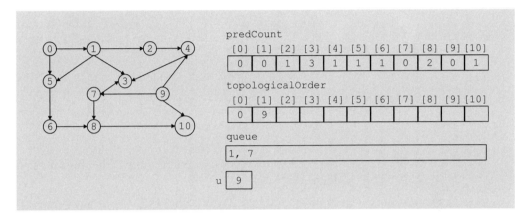

FIGURE 12-20 Arrays predCount, topologicalOrder, and queue after the second iteration of Step 3

Iteration 3 of Step 3: The queue is nonempty. After Step 3.1 executes, the value of u is 1. Step 3.2 stores the value of u, which is 1, in the next available position in the array topologicalOrder. Notice that 1 is stored at position 2 in this array. Step 3.3 reduces the predecessor count of all the successors of 1 by 1 and if the predecessor count of any successor node of 1 reduces to 0, that node is pushed into queue. The successor nodes of the node 1 are the nodes 2, 3, and 5. The predecessor count of the nodes 2 and 5 reduces to 0 and the predecessor count of the node 3 reduces to 2. The nodes 2 and 5, in this order, are pushed into the queue. After the third iteration of Step 3, the arrays predCount, topologicalOrder, and queue are as shown in Figure 12-21.

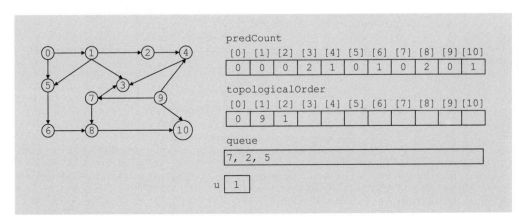

FIGURE 12-21 Arrays predCount, topologicalOrder, and queue after the third iteration of Step 3

If you repeat Step 3 eight more times, the arrays predCount, topologicalOrder, and queue are as shown in Figure 12-22.

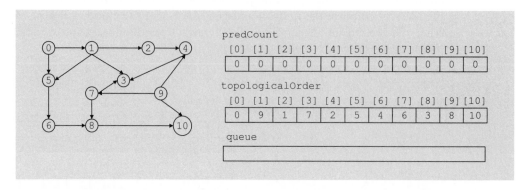

predCount

[0]	[1]	[2]	[3]	[4]	[5]	[6]	[7]	[8]	[9]	[10]
0	0	0	0	0	0	0	0	0	0	0

topologicalOrder

[0]	[1]	[2]	[3]	[4]	[5]	[6]	[7]	[8]	[9]	[10]
0	9	1	7	2	5	4	6	3	8	10

queue

FIGURE 12-22 Arrays predCount, topologicalOrder, and queue after Step 3 executes

In Figure 12-22, the array topologicalOrder shows the breadth-first topological ordering of the nodes of the graph G_3.

The following C++ function implements this breadth-first topological ordering algorithm:

```cpp
void topologicalOrderType::bfTopOrder()
{
    linkedQueueType<int> queue;

    int *topologicalOrder; //pointer to the array to store
                           //breadth first topological ordering
    topologicalOrder = new int[gSize];

    int topIndex = 0;

    linkedListIterator<int> graphIt; //iterator to traverse a
                                     //linked list

    int *predCount;     //pointer to the array to store the
                        //predecessor count of a vertex.
    predCount = new int[gSize];

    for (int ind = 0; ind < gSize; ind++)
        predCount[ind] = 0;

        //Determine the predecessor count of all the vertices.
    for (int ind = 0; ind < gSize; ind++)
    {
        for (graphIt = graph[ind].begin();
             graphIt != graph[ind].end(); ++graphIt)
        {
            int w = *graphIt;
            predCount[w]++;
        }
    }
```

```
            //Initialize queue: If the predecessor count of
            //vertex is 0, put this node into the queue.
    for (int ind = 0; ind < gSize; ind++)
        if (predCount[ind] == 0)
            queue.addQueue(ind);

    while (!queue.isEmptyQueue())
    {
        int u = queue.front();
        queue.deleteQueue();
        topologicalOrder[topIndex++] = u;

            //Reduce the predecessor count of all the successors
            //of u by 1. If the predecessor count of a vertex
            //becomes 0, put this vertex into the queue.
        for (graphIt = graph[u].begin();
            graphIt != graph[u].end(); ++graphIt)
        {
            int w = *graphIt;
            predCount[w]--;
            if (predCount[w] == 0)
                queue.addQueue(w);
        }
    }//end while

        //output the vertices in breadth first topological order
    for (int ind = 0; ind < gSize; ind++)
        cout << topologicalOrder[ind] << " ";

    cout << endl;

    delete [] topologicalOrder;
    delete [] predCount;
}//bfTopOrder
```

We leave the definition of the constructor as an exercise. (See Programming Exercise 6 at the end of this chapter.)

Euler Circuits

Let us consider the Königsberg bridge problem stated at the beginning of the chapter. The problem is to determine whether it is possible to take a walk that crosses each bridge exactly once before returning to the starting point; see Figure 12-1. As remarked earlier, Euler converted this problem into a graph theory problem as follows: Each of the islands *A*, *B*, *C*, and *D* is considered as a vertex of a graph and the bridges are considered as edges, as shown in Figure 12-2. Now the problem reduces to finding a circuit in the graph of Figure 12-2, such that it contains all the edges. In this section, we further describe properties of graphs, which will help us answer this question.

Definition: A **circuit** is a path of nonzero length from a vertex u to u with no repeated edges.

Definition: A circuit in a graph that includes all the edges of the graph is called an **Euler circuit**.

Definition: A graph G is said to be **Eulerian** if either G is a trivial graph or G has an Euler circuit.

Notice that the graph of Figure 12-2 is a connected graph and this graph has odd degree vertices as well as even degree vertices.

Let us consider a connected graph with more than one vertex such that every vertex has odd degree. For example, consider the graph of Figure 12-23. This is a connected graph and every vertex of this graph is odd degree. This graph has no circuit and so has no circuit that contains all the edges.

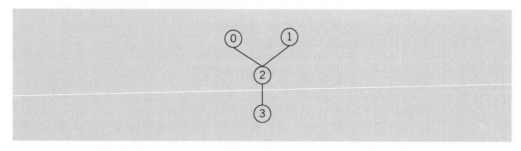

FIGURE 12-23   A graph with all vertices of odd degree

Next consider the connected graph G of Figure 12-24 such that every vertex has even degree.

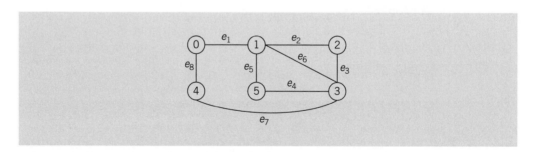

FIGURE 12-24   A graph with all vertices of even degree

The graph of Figure 12-24 has an Euler circuit. For example, $(0, e_1, 1, e_2, 2, e_3, 3, e_4, 5, e_5, 1, e_6, 3, e_7, 4, e_8, 0)$ is an Euler circuit in the graph of Figure 12-24.

The following theorems give necessary and sufficient conditions for a connected graph to have an Euler circuit.

Theorem 12-2: If a connected graph G is Eulerian, then every vertex of G has even degree.

Theorem 12-3: Let G be a connected graph such that every vertex of G is of even degree. Then G has an Euler circuit.

We can effectively use this theorem to determine whether a connected graph G has an Euler circuit by checking whether all of its vertices are of even degree.

Let us again consider the Königsberg bridge problem. Notice that the graph corresponding to this problem is a connected graph but has vertices of odd degree; see Figure 12-2. Hence, by Theorem 12-2, the graph of Figure 12-2 has no Euler circuit. In other words, starting at one land area, it is not possible to walk across all the bridges exactly once and return to the starting land area.

After 1736, two additional bridges have been constructed on the Pregel river—one is between the regions B and C and the other is between A and D. The graph with the additional two bridges is shown in Figure 12-25.

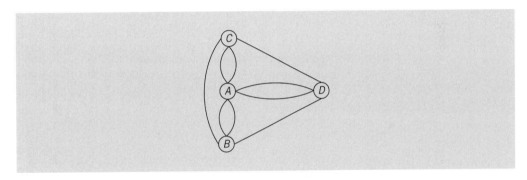

FIGURE 12-25 Graph of the Königsberg bridge problem with two additional bridges

By Theorem 12-3, every connected graph with only even degree vertices has an Euler circuit. Next, we describe an algorithm, known as Fleury's algorithm, which can be used to construct an Euler circuit in a connected graph with vertices of even degrees.

Fleury's Algorithm

Step 1. Choose a vertex v as the starting vertex for the circuit and choose an edge e with v as one of the end vertices.

Step 2. If the other end vertex u of the edge e is also v, go to Step 3. Otherwise, choose an edge e_1 different from e with u as one of the end vertices. If the other vertex u_1 of e_1 is v, go to Step 3; otherwise, choose an edge e_2 different from e and e_1 with u_1 as one of the end vertices and repeat Step 2.

Step 3. If the circuit T_1 obtained in Step 2 contains all the edges, then stop. Otherwise, choose an edge e_j different from the edges of T_1 such that one of the end vertices of e_j, say, w is a member of the circuit T_1.

Step 4. Construct a circuit T_2 with starting vertex w, as in Steps 1 and 2, such that all the edges of T_2 are different from the edges in the circuit T_1.

Step 5. Construct the circuit T_3 by inserting the circuit T_2 at w of the circuit T_1. Now go to Step 3 and repeat Step 3 with the circuit T_3.

Next, we illustrate how Fleury's algorithm works. Consider the graph of Figure 12-26.

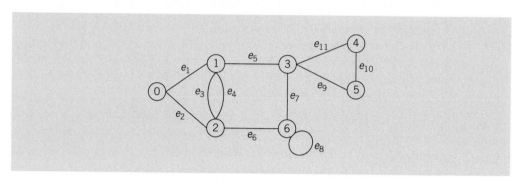

FIGURE 12-26 A graph with all vertices of even degree

Let us apply Fleury's algorithm to find an Eulerian circuit.

First, select vertex 0 and form the circuit: T_1: (0, e_1, 1, e_3, 2, e_2, 0).

Next, select vertex 1 and edge e_4. Construct the circuit: C_1: (1, e_4, 2, e_6, 6, e_7, 3, e_5, 1).

Then form the circuit: T_2: (0, e_1, C_1, e_3, 2, e_2, 0).

Circuit T_2 does not contain all the edges of the given graph. Now choose vertex 6 and edge e_8 and form the circuit: C_2: (6, e_8, 6).

Now construct the circuit: T_3: (0, e_1, 1, e_4, 2, e_6, C_2, e_7, 3, e_5, 1, e_3, 2, e_2, 0).

This circuit also does not contain all the edges. Select now vertex 3 and edge e_{11}. Form the circuit: C_3: (3, e_{11}, 4, e_{10}, 5, e_9, 3).

Next, construct the circuit: T_4: (0, e_1,1, e_4, 2, e_6, C_2, e_7, C_3, e_5, 1, e_3, 2, e_2, 0).

Circuit T_4 contains all the vertices and all the edges of the given graph and, hence, it is an Euler circuit.

We leave it as an exercise for you to write a program to implement Fleury's algorithm. (See Programming Exercise 8 at the end of this chapter.)

QUICK REVIEW

1. A graph G is a pair, $G = (V, E)$, where V is a finite nonempty set, called the set of vertices of G and $E \subseteq V \times V$, called the set of edges.

2. In an *undirected* graph $G = (V, E)$, the elements of E are unordered pairs.

3. In a directed graph $G = (V, E)$, the elements of E are ordered pairs.

4. Let G be a graph. A graph H is called a subgraph of G if every vertex of H is a vertex of G and every edge in H is an edge in G.

5. Two vertices u and v in an undirected graph are called adjacent if there is an edge from one to the other.

6. An edge incident on a single vertex is called a loop.

7. In an undirected graph, if two edges e_1 and e_2 are associated with the same pair of vertices $\{u, v\}$, then e_1 and e_2 are called parallel edges.

8. A graph is called a simple graph if it has no loops and no parallel edges.

9. Let $e = (u, v)$ be an edge in an undirected graph G. The edge e is said to be incident on the vertices u and v.

10. A path from a vertex u to a vertex v is a sequence of vertices $u_1, u_2, \ldots, u_n$ such that $u = u_1, u_n = v$, and (u_i, u_{i+1}) is an edge for all $i = 1, 2, \ldots, n - 1$.

11. The vertices u and v are called connected if there is a path from u to v.

12. A simple path is a path in which all the vertices, except possibly the first and last vertices, are distinct.

13. A cycle in G is a simple path in which the first and last vertices are the same.

14. An undirected graph G is called connected if there is a path from any vertex to any other vertex.

15. A maximal subset of connected vertices is called a component of G.

16. Suppose that u and v are vertices in a directed graph G. If there is an edge from u to v, that is, $(u, v) \in E$, we say that u is adjacent to v and v is adjacent from u.

17. A directed graph G is called strongly connected if any two vertices in G are connected.

18. Let G be a graph with n vertices, where $n > 0$. Let $V(G) = \{v_1, v_2, \ldots, v_n\}$. The adjacency matrix A_G is a two-dimensional $n \times n$ matrix such that the (i, j)th entry of A_G is 1 if there is an edge from v_i to v_j; otherwise, the (i, j)th entry is 0.

19. In an adjacency list representation, corresponding to each vertex v is a linked list such that each node of the linked list contains the vertex u and $(v, u) \in E(G)$.

20. The depth-first traversal of a graph is similar to the preorder traversal of a binary tree.

21. The breadth-first traversal of a graph is similar to the level-by-level traversal of a binary tree.

22. The shortest path algorithm gives the shortest distance for a given node to every other node in the graph.

23. In a weighted graph, every edge has a nonnegative weight.

24. The weight of the path P is the sum of the weights of all the edges on the path P, which is also called the weight of v from u via P.

25. A (free) tree T is a simple graph such that if u and v are two vertices in T, there is a unique path from u to v.

26. A tree in which a particular vertex is designated as a root is called a rooted tree.

27. Suppose T is a tree. If a weight is assigned to the edges in T, T is called a weighted tree.

28. If T is a weighted tree, the weight of T, denoted by $W(T)$, is the sum of the weights of all the edges in T.

29. A tree T is called a spanning tree of graph G if T is a subgraph of G such that $V(T) = V(G)$—that is, if all the vertices of G are in T.

30. Let G be a graph and $V(G) = \{v_1, v_2, \ldots, v_n\}$, where $n \geq 0$. A topological ordering of $V(G)$ is a linear ordering $v_{i1}, v_{i2}, \ldots, v_{in}$ of the vertices such that if v_{ij} is a predecessor of v_{ik}, $j \neq k$, $1 \leq j, k \leq n$, then v_{ij} precedes v_{ik}, that is, $j < k$ in this linear ordering.

31. A circuit is a path of nonzero length from a vertex u to u with no repeated edges.

32. A circuit in a graph that includes all the edges of the graph is called an Euler circuit.

33. A graph G is said to be Eulerian if either G is a trivial graph or G has an Euler circuit.

EXERCISES

Use the graph in Figure 12-27 for Exercises 1 through 4.

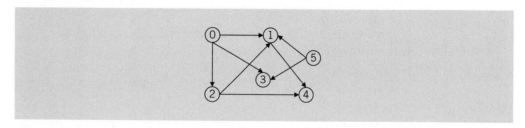

FIGURE 12-27 Graph for Exercises 1 through 4

1. Find the adjacency matrix of the graph.
2. Draw the adjacency list of the graph.
3. List the nodes of the graph in a depth-first traversal.
4. List the nodes of the graph in a breadth-first traversal.

5. Find the weight matrix of the graph in Figure 12-28.

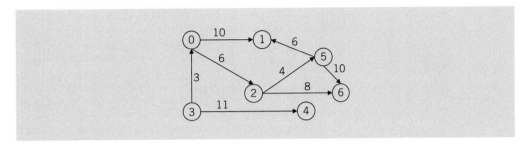

FIGURE 12-28 Graph for Exercise 5

6. Consider the graph in Figure 12-29. Find the shortest distance from node 0 to every other node in the graph.

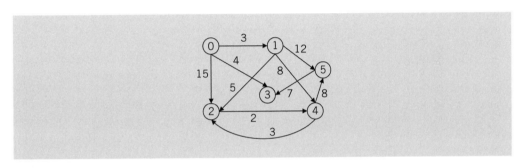

FIGURE 12-29 Graph for Exercise 6

7. Find a spanning tree in the graph in Figure 12-30.

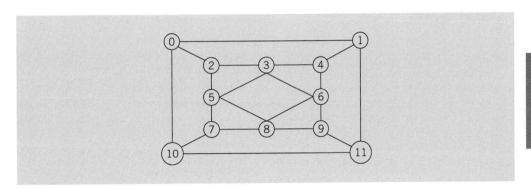

FIGURE 12-30 Graph for Exercise 7

8. Find a spanning tree in the graph in Figure 12-31.

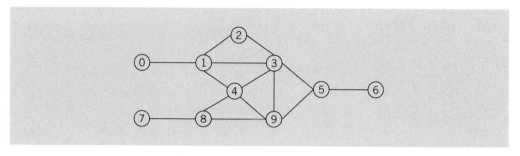

FIGURE 12-31 Graph for Exercise 8

9. Find the minimum spanning tree for the graph in Figure 12-32 using the algorithm given in this chapter.

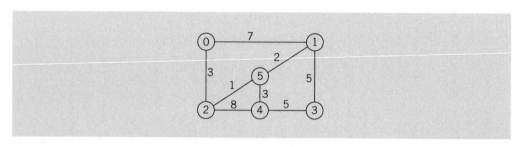

FIGURE 12-32 Graph for Exercise 9

10. List the nodes of the graph of Figure 12-33 in a breadth-first topological ordering.

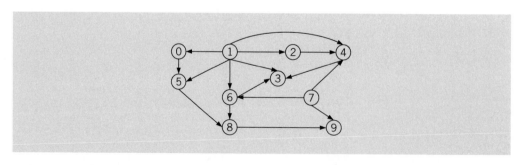

FIGURE 12-33 Graph for Exercise 10

11. Describe whether the graph in Figure 12-34 has an Euler circuit. If the graph has an Euler circuit, find one such circuit.

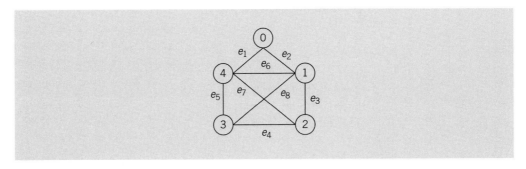

FIGURE 12-34 Graph for Exercise 11

12. Describe whether the graph in Figure 12-35 has an Euler circuit. If the graph has an Euler circuit, find one such circuit.

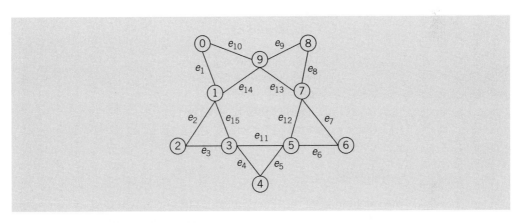

FIGURE 12-35 Graph for Exercise 12

PROGRAMMING EXERCISES

1. Write a program that outputs the nodes of a graph in a depth-first traversal.

2. Write a program that outputs the nodes of a graph in a breadth-first traversal.

3. Write a program that outputs the shortest distance from a given node to every other node in the graph.

4. Write a program that outputs the minimum spanning tree for a given graph.

5. The algorithm to determine the minimum spanning tree given in this chapter is of the order $O(n^3)$. The following is an alternative to Prim's algorithm that is of the order $O(n^2)$.

Input: A connected weighted graph $G = (V, E)$ of n vertices, numbered 0, 1, ..., $n - 1$; starting with vertex s, with a weight matrix of W.

Output: The minimum spanning tree.

```
Prim2(G, W, n, s)
Let T = (V, E), where E = ϕ.
for (j = 0; j < n; j++)
{
    edgeWeight[j] = W(s,j);
    edges[j] = s;
    visited[s] = false;
}
edgeWeight[s] = 0;
visited[s] = true;
while(not all nodes are visited)
{
    Choose the node that is not visited and has the smallest weight, and
    call it k.
    visited[k] = true;
    E = E ∪ {(k, edges[k])}
    V = V ∪ {k}
    for each node j that is not visited
        if(W(k,j) < edgeWeight[k])
        {
            edgeWeight[k] = W(k,j);
            edges[j] = k;
        }
}
return T.
```

Write a definition of the function `Prim2` to implement this algorithm, and also add this function to the `class msTreeType`. Furthermore, write a program to test this version of Prim's algorithm.

6. Write a program to test the breadth-first topological ordering algorithm.

7. Let G be a graph and $V(G) = \{v_1, v_2, ..., v_n\}$, where $n \geq 0$. Recall that a topological ordering of $V(G)$ is a linear ordering $v_{i1}, v_{i2}, ..., v_{in}$ of the vertices such that if v_{ij} is a predecessor of v_{ik}, $j \neq k$, $1 \leq j \leq n$, $1 \leq k \leq n$, then v_{ij} precedes v_{ik}, that is, $j < k$ in this linear ordering. Suppose that G has no cycles. The following algorithm, a depth-first topological ordering, lists the nodes of the graph in a topological ordering.

In a depth-first topological ordering, we start with finding a vertex that has no successors (such a vertex exists because the graph has no cycles), and place it last in the topological order. After we have placed all the successors of a vertex in topological order, we place the vertex in the topological order before any of its successors. Clearly, in the depth-first topological ordering, first we find the vertex to be placed in `topologicalOrder[n-1]`, then `topologicalOrder[n-2]`, and so on.

Write the definitions of the C++ functions to implement the depth-first topological ordering. Add these functions to the class `topologicalOrderType`, which is derived from the class `graphType`. Also, write a program to test your depth-first topological ordering.

8. Write a program to implement Fleury's algorithm as described in this chapter.

CHAPTER 13

STANDARD TEMPLATE LIBRARY (STL) II

IN THIS CHAPTER, YOU WILL:

- · Learn more about the Standard Template Library (STL)
- · Become familiar with associative containers
- · Explore how associative containers are used to manipulate data in a program
- · Learn about various generic algorithms

Chapter 4 introduced the Standard Template Library (STL). Recall that the basic components of the STL are containers, iterators, and algorithms. The three categories of containers are sequence containers, associative containers, and container adapters. Chapter 4 described the sequence containers `vector` and `deque`; Chapter 5 described the sequence container `list`. The container adapter `stack` is described in Chapter 7, and the container adapters `queue` and `priority_queue` are described in Chapter 8. Chapter 4 discussed iterators. This chapter discusses the components of the STL not discussed in the previous chapters, specifically, the associative containers and algorithms.

Before discussing the associative containers, first we discuss the `class pair`, which is used by some of the associative containers.

Class pair

With the help of the `class pair`, two values can be combined into a single unit and, therefore, can be treated as one unit. Thus, a function can return two values by using the `class pair`. This class is used in several other places in the STL. For example, the `classes map` and `multimap`, described later in this chapter, also use the `class pair` to manage their elements.

The definition of the `class pair` is contained in the header file `utility`. Thus, to use the `class pair` in a program, the program must include the following statement:

```
#include <utility>
```

The `class pair` has two constructors: the default constructor and a constructor with two parameters. Thus, the general syntax to declare an object of type `pair` is as follows:

```
pair<Type1, Type2>  pElement;
```

or

```
pair<Type1, Type2>  pElement(expr1, expr2);
```

where `expr1` is of type `Type1` and `expr2` is of type `Type2`.

Every object of type `pair` has two data members, `first` and `second`, and these two data members are `public`. Because the data members of an object of type `pair` are `public`, each object of type `pair` can directly access these data members in a program.

Example 13-1 illustrates the use of the `class pair`.

EXAMPLE 13-1

Consider the following statements.

```
pair<int, double>  x;                 //Line 1
pair<int, double>  y(13, 45.9);       //Line 2
```

```
pair<int, int>    z(10, 20);                          //Line 3
pair<string, string>    name("Bill", "Brown");        //Line 4
pair<string, double>    employee("John Smith", 45678.50);  //Line 5
```

The statement in Line 1 declares x to be an object of type pair. The first component of x is of type int; the second component is of type double. Because no values are specified in the declaration of x, the default constructor of the class pair executes and the data members, first and second, are initialized to their default value, which in this case is 0.

The statement in Line 2 declares y to be an object of type pair. The first component of y is of type int; the second component is of type double. The first component of y, that is, first, is initialized to 13; the second component, that is, second, is initialized to 45.9.

The statement in Line 3 declares z to be an object of type pair. Both components of z are of type int. The first component of z, that is, first, is initialized to 10; the second component, that is, second, is initialized to 20.

The statement in Line 4 declares name to be an object of type pair. Both components of name are of type string. The first component of name, that is, first, is initialized to "Bill"; the second component, that is, second, is initialized to "Brown".

The statement in Line 5 declares employee to be an object of type pair. The first component of employee is of type string; the second component is of type double. The first component of employee, that is, first, is initialized to "John Smith"; the second component, that is, second, is initialized to 45678.50.

The statement

```
x.first = 50;
```

assigns 50 to the data member first of x. Similarly, the statement

```
name.second = "Calvert";
```

assigns "Calvert" to the data member second of name.

The following statements show how to output the value of an object of type pair. Assume that we have the declarations of Lines 1 through 5.

Statement	Effect
`cout << y.first << " " << y.second << endl;`	Outputs: 13 45.9
`cout << name.first << " "` `    << name.second << endl;`	Outputs: Bill Brown
`cout << employee.first << " "` `    << employee.second << endl;`	Outputs: John Smith 45678.50

1
3

Comparing Objects of Type `pair`

The relational operators have been overloaded for the `class pair`. Similar objects of the `pair` type are compared as follows.

Suppose `x` and `y` are objects of type `pair`, and the corresponding data members of `x` and `y` are of the same type. (If the data members of `x` and `y` are not of the built-in type, the relational operators must be properly defined on the data members.) Table 13-1 describes how the relational operators are defined for the `class pair`.

TABLE 13-1 Relational operators for the `class pair`

Comparison	Description
`x == y`	`if (x.first == y.first)` and `(x.second == y.second)`
`x < y`	`if (x.first < y.first)` or `((x.first >= y.first)` and `(x.second < y.second))`
`x <= y`	`if (x < y)` or `(x == y)`
`x > y`	`if not(x <= y)`
`x >= y`	`if not(x < y)`
`x != y`	`if not(x == y)`

Type `pair` and Function `make_pair`

The header file `utility` also contains the definition of the function template `make_pair`. With the help of the function `make_pair`, we can create pairs without explicitly specifying the type `pair`. The definition of the function template `make_pair` is similar to the following:

```
template <class T1, class T2>
pair<T1, T2> make_pair(const T1& X, const T2& Y)
{
    return (pair<T1, T2>(X, Y));
}
```

From the definition of the function template `make_pair`, it is clear that the function template `make_pair` is a value-returning function and returns a value of type `pair`. The components of the value returned by the function template `make_pair` are passed as parameters to the function template `make_pair`.

The expression

```
make_pair(75, 'A')
```

returns a value of type `pair`. The value of the first component is 75; the value of the second component is the character `'A'`.

The function make_pair is especially useful if a pair is to be passed as an argument to a function. Example 13-2 illustrates the use of make_pair.

EXAMPLE 13-2

```
//****************************************************************
// Author: D.S. Malik
//
// This program illustrates how to use the functions pair and
// make_pair.
//****************************************************************

#include <algorithm>                              //Line 1
#include <iostream>                               //Line 2
#include <utility>                                //Line 3
#include <string>                                 //Line 4

using namespace std;                              //Line 5

void funcExp(pair<int,int>);                      //Line 6
void funcExp1(pair<int, char>);                   //Line 7
void funcExp2(pair<int, string> x);               //Line 8
void funcExp3(pair<int, char *> x);               //Line 9

int main()                                        //Line 10
{                                                 //Line 11
    pair<int, double> x(50, 87.67);               //Line 12
    pair<string, string> name("John", "Johnson"); //Line 13

    cout << "Line 14: " << x.first << " " << x.second
         << endl;                                 //Line 14
    cout << "Line 15: " << name.first << " "
         << name.second << endl;                  //Line 15

    pair<int, int> y;                             //Line 16
    cout << "Line 17: " << y.first << " " << y.second
         << endl;                                 //Line 17

    pair<string, string> name2;                   //Line 18
    cout << "Line 19: " << name2.first << "***"
         << name2.second << endl;                 //Line 19
    funcExp(make_pair(75, 80));                   //Line 20
    funcExp1(make_pair(87, 'H'));                 //Line 21
    funcExp1(pair<int, char>(198, 'K'));          //Line 22
    funcExp2(pair<int, string>(250, "Hello"));    //Line 23
    funcExp2(make_pair(65,string("Hello There"))); //Line 24
    funcExp3(pair<int, char *>(35, "Hello World")); //Line 25
    funcExp3(make_pair(22, (char *)("Sunny")));   //Line 26

    return 0;                                     //Line 27
}                                                 //Line 28
```

1
3

```
void funcExp(pair<int, int> x)                          //Line 29
{                                                       //Line 30
    cout << "Line 31: " << "In funcExp: " << x.first
         << " " << x.second << endl;                    //Line 31
}                                                       //Line 32

void funcExp1(pair<int, char> x)                        //Line 33
{                                                       //Line 34
    cout << "Line 36: " << "In funcExp1: " << x.first   //Line 35
         << " " << x.second << endl;                    //Line 36
}                                                       //Line 37

void funcExp2(pair<int, string> x)                      //Line 38
{                                                       //Line 39
    cout << "Line 40: " << "In funcExp2: " << x.first
         << " " << x.second << endl;                    //Line 40
}                                                       //Line 41
void funcExp3(pair<int, char *> x)                      //Line 42
{                                                       //Line 43
    cout << "Line 44: " << "In funcExp3: " << x.first
         << " " << x.second << endl;                    //Line 44
}                                                       //Line 45
```

Sample Run:

```
Line 14: 50 87.67
Line 15: John Johnson
Line 17: 0 0
Line 19: ***
Line 31: In funcExp: 75 80
Line 36: In funcExp1: 87 H
Line 36: In funcExp1: 198 K
Line 40: In funcExp2: 250 Hello
Line 40: In funcExp2: 65 Hello There
Line 44: In funcExp3: 35 Hello World
Line 44: In funcExp3: 22 Sunny
```

Associative Containers

Elements in an associative container are automatically sorted according to some ordering criteria. The default ordering criterion is the relational operator < (less than). Users also have the option of specifying their own ordering criterion.

Because elements in an associative container are sorted automatically, when a new element is inserted in the container, it is inserted at the proper place. A convenient and fast way to implement this type of data structure is to use a binary search tree. This is, in fact, how associative containers are implemented. Thus, every element in the container has a parent node (except the root node) and at most two children. For each element, the key in the parent node is larger than the key in the left child and smaller than the key in the right child.

The predefined associative containers in the STL are sets, multisets, maps, and multimaps.

The following sections describe these containers.

Associative Containers: set and multiset

As described earlier, both the containers set and multiset automatically sort their elements according to some sort criteria. The default sorting criterion is the relational operator < (less than); that is, the elements are arranged in ascending order. The user can also specify other sorting criteria. For user-defined data types, such as classes, the relational operators must be properly overloaded.

The only difference between the containers set and multiset is that the container multiset allows duplicates, whereas the container set does not.

The name of the class defining the container set is set; the name of the class defining the container multiset is multiset. The name of the header file containing the definitions of the classes set and multiset, and the definitions of the functions to implement various operations on these containers, is set. Thus, to use any of these containers, the program must include the following statement:

#include <set>

DECLARING set OR multiset ASSOCIATIVE CONTAINERS

The classes set and multiset contain several constructors to declare and initialize containers of these types. This section discusses the various ways that these types of associative containers are declared and initialized. Table 13-2 describes how a set/multiset container of a specific type can be declared and initialized.

TABLE 13-2   Various ways to declare a set/multiset container

Statement	Effect
ctType<elmType> ct;	Creates an empty set/multiset container, ct. The sort criterion is <.
ctType<elmType, sortOp> ct;	Creates an empty set/multiset container, ct. The sort criterion is specified by sortOp.
ctType<elmType> ct(otherCt);	Creates a set/multiset container, ct. The elements of otherCt are copied into ct. The sort criterion is <. Both ct and otherCt are of the same type.

1
3

TABLE 13-2 Various ways to declare a `set/multiset` container (continued)

Statement	Effect
`ctType<elmType, sortOp> ct(otherCt);`	Creates a `set/multiset` container, `ct`. The elements of `otherCt` are copied into `ct`. The sort criterion is specified by `sortOp`. Both `ct` and `otherCt` are of the same type. Note that the sort criteria of `ct` and `otherCt` must be the same.
`ctType<elmType> ct(beg, end);`	Creates a `set/multiset` container, `ct`. The elements starting at the position `beg` until the position `end-1` are copied into `ct`. Both `beg` and `end` are iterators.
`ctType<elmType, sortOp> ct(beg, end);`	Creates a `set/multiset` container, `ct`. The elements starting at the position `beg` until the position `end-1` are copied into `ct`. Both `beg` and `end` are iterators. The sort criterion is specified by `sortOp`.

If you want to use a sort criterion other than the default, you must specify this option when the container is declared. For example, consider the following statements:

```
set<int> intSet;                                        //Line 1
set<int, greater<int> >  otherIntSet;                   //Line 2
multiset<string>  stringMultiSet;                       //Line 3
multiset<string, greater<string> >  otherStringMultiSet; //Line 4
```

The statement in Line 1 declares `intSet` to be an empty `set` container, the element type is `int`, and the sort criterion is the default sort criterion. The statement in Line 2 declares `otherIntSet` to be an empty `set` container, the element type is `int`, and the sort criterion is greater than (that is, the elements in the container `otherIntSet` will be arranged in descending order). The statements in Lines 3 and 4 have similar conventions. The statements in Lines 2 and 4 illustrate how to specify the descending sorting criterion.

NOTE In the statements in Lines 2 and 4, note the space between the two >—that is, the space between `greater<int>` and `>`. This space is important because `>>` is also a shift operator in C++.

ITEM INSERTION AND DELETION FROM `set/multiset`

Suppose that `ct` is of type either `set` or `multiset`. Table 13-3 describes the operations that can be used to insert or delete elements from a set. Table 13-3 also illustrates how to use these operations. The name of the function is shown in bold.

TABLE 13-3 Operations to insert or delete elements from a set

Expression	Effect
`ct.insert(elem)`	Inserts a copy of `elem` into `ct`. In the case of sets, it also returns whether the insert operation succeeded.
`ct.insert(position, elem)`	Inserts a copy of `elem` into `ct`. The position where `elem` is inserted is returned. The first parameter, `position`, hints at where to begin the search for insert. The parameter `position` is an iterator.
`ct.insert(beg, end);`	Inserts a copy of all the elements into `ct` starting at the position `beg` until `end-1`. Both `beg` and `end` are iterators.
`ct.erase(elem);`	Deletes all the elements with the value `elem`. The number of deleted elements is returned.
`ct.erase(position);`	Deletes the element at the position specified by the iterator `position`. No value is returned.
`ct.erase(beg, end);`	Deletes all the elements starting at the position `beg` until the position `end-1`. Both `beg` and `end` are iterators. No value is returned.
`ct.clear();`	Deletes all the elements from the container `ct`. After this operation, the container `ct` is empty.

Example 13-3 illustrates various operations on a `set/multiset` container.

EXAMPLE 13-3

```
//*********************************************************
// Author: D.S. Malik
//
// This program illustrates how the operations on a set/multiset
// container work.
//*********************************************************
```

```
#include <iostream>                                      //Line 1
#include <set>                                           //Line 2
#include <string>                                        //Line 3
#include <iterator>                                      //Line 4
#include <algorithm>                                     //Line 5

using namespace std;                                     //Line 6

int main()                                               //Line 7
{                                                        //Line 8
    set<int> intSet;                                     //Line 9
    set<int, greater<int> > intSetA;                     //Line 10

    set<int, greater<int> >::iterator intGtIt;           //Line 11

    ostream_iterator<int> screen(cout, " ");             //Line 12

    intSet.insert(16);                                   //Line 13
    intSet.insert(8);                                    //Line 14
    intSet.insert(20);                                   //Line 15
    intSet.insert(3);                                    //Line 16

    cout << "Line 17: intSet: ";                         //Line 17
    copy(intSet.begin(), intSet.end(), screen);          //Line 18
    cout << endl;                                        //Line 19

    intSetA.insert(36);                                  //Line 20
    intSetA.insert(30);                                  //Line 21
    intSetA.insert(39);                                  //Line 22
    intSetA.insert(59);                                  //Line 23
    intSetA.insert(156);                                 //Line 24

    cout << "Line 25: intSetA: ";                        //Line 25
    copy(intSetA.begin(), intSetA.end(), screen);        //Line 26
    cout << endl;                                        //Line 27

    intSetA.erase(59);                                   //Line 28

    cout << "Line 29: After removing 59, intSetA: ";     //Line 29
    copy(intSetA.begin(), intSetA.end(), screen);        //Line 30
    cout << endl;                                        //Line 31

    intGtIt = intSetA.begin();                           //Line 32
    ++intGtIt;                                           //Line 33

    intSetA.erase(intGtIt);                              //Line 34

    cout << "Line 35: After removing the second "
         << "element, intSetA: ";                        //Line 35
    copy(intSetA.begin(), intSetA.end(), screen);        //Line 36
    cout << endl;                                        //Line 37

    multiset<string, greater<string> > namesMultiSet;    //Line 38
    multiset<string, greater<string> >::iterator iter;   //Line 39
```

```
        ostream_iterator<string> pScreen(cout, " ");      //Line 40

        namesMultiSet.insert("Donny");                     //Line 41
        namesMultiSet.insert("Zippy");                     //Line 42
        namesMultiSet.insert("Ronny");                     //Line 43
        namesMultiSet.insert("Hungry");                    //Line 44
        namesMultiSet.insert("Ronny");                     //Line 45

        cout << "Line 46: namesMultiSet: ";                //Line 46
        copy(namesMultiSet.begin(), namesMultiSet.end(),
            pScreen);                                      //Line 47
        cout << endl;                                      //Line 48

        return 0;                                          //Line 49
}                                                          //Line 50
```

Sample Run:

```
Line 17: intSet: 3 8 16 20
Line 25: intSetA: 156 59 39 36 30
Line 29: After removing 59, intSetA: 156 39 36 30
Line 35: After removing the second element, intSetA: 156 36 30
Line 46: namesMultiSet: Zippy Ronny Ronny Hungry Donny
```

The statement in Line 9 declares `intSet` to be a set container. The statement in Line 10 declares `intSetA` to be a set container whose elements are to be arranged in descending order. The statement in Line 11 declares `intGtIt` to be a `set` iterator. The iterator `intGtIt` can process the elements of any set container whose elements are of type `int` and arranged in descending order. The statement in Line 12 declares `screen` to be an `ostream` iterator that outputs the elements of any container whose elements are of type `int`.

The statements in Lines 13 through 16 insert 16, 8, 20, and 3 into `intSet`; the statement in Line 18 outputs the elements of `intSet`. In the output, see the line marked Line 17, which contains the output of the statements in Lines 17 through 19 of the program.

The statements in Lines 20 through 24 insert 36, 30, 39, 59, and 156 into `intSetA`; the statement in Line 26 outputs the elements of `intSetA`. In the output, see the line marked Line 25, which contains the output of the statements in Lines 25 through 27 of the program. Notice that the elements of `intSetA` appear in descending order.

The statement in Line 28 removes 59 from `intSetA`. After the statement in Line 32 executes, `intGtIt` points to the first element of `intSetA`. After the statement in Line 32 executes, `intGtIt` points to the second element of `intSetA`. The statement in Line 33 removes the element of `intSetA` to which `intGtIt` points. The statement in Line 36 outputs the elements of `intSetA`.

The statement in Line 38 declares `namesMultiSet` to be a container of type `multiset`. The elements in `namesMultiSet` are of type `string` and are arranged in descending order. The statement in Line 39 declares `iter` to be a `multiset` iterator.

The statements in Lines 41 through 45 insert `Donny`, `Zippy`, `Ronny`, `Hungry`, and `Ronny` into `namesMultiSet`. The statement in Line 47 outputs the elements of `namesMultiSet`.

1
3

Associative Containers: `map` and `multimap`

The containers `map` and `multimap` manage their elements in the form key/pair. The elements are automatically sorted according to some sort criteria applied on the key. The default sorting criterion is the relational operator < (less than); that is, the elements are arranged in ascending order. The user can also specify other sorting criteria. For user-defined data types, such as classes, the relational operators must be properly overloaded.

The only difference between the containers `map` and `multimap` is that the container `multimap` allows duplicates, whereas the container `map` does not.

The name of the class defining the container `map` is `map`; the name of the `class` defining the container `multimap` is also `multimap`. The name of the header file containing the definitions of the `classes map` and `multimap`, and the definitions of the functions to implement various operations on these containers, is `map`. Therefore, to use any of these containers, the program must include the following statement:

```
#include <map>
```

DECLARING `map` OR `multimap` ASSOCIATIVE CONTAINERS

The `classes map` and `multimap` contain several constructors to declare and initialize containers of these types. This section discusses the various ways that these types of associative containers are declared and initialized. Table 13-4 describes how a `map`/`multimap` container of a specific type can be declared and initialized. (In Table 13-4, `ctType` is either a `map` or a `multimap`.)

TABLE 13-4 Various ways to declare a `map`/`multimap` container

Statement	Effect
`ctType<key, elmType> ct;`	Creates an empty `map`/`multimap` container, ct. The sort criterion is <.
`ctType<key, elmType, sortOp> ct;`	Creates an empty `map`/`multimap` container, ct. The sort criterion is specified by sortOp.
`ctType<key, elmType> ct(otherCt);`	Creates a `map`/`multimap` container, ct. The elements of otherCt are copied into ct. The sort criterion is <. Both ct and otherCt are of the same type.
`ctType<key, elmType, sortOp> ct(otherCt);`	Creates a `map`/`multimap` container, ct. The elements of otherCt are copied into ct. The sort criterion is specified by sortOp. Both ct and otherCt are of the same type. Note that the sort criteria of ct and otherCt must be the same.

TABLE 13-4 Various ways to declare a `map`/`multimap` container (continued)

Statement	Effect
`ctType<key, elmType> ct(beg, end);`	Creates a `map`/`multimap` container, `ct`. The elements starting at the position `beg` until the position `end-1` are copied into `ct`. Both `beg` and `end` are iterators.
`ctType<key, elmType, sortOp> ct(beg, end);`	Creates a `map`/`multimap` container, `ct`. The elements starting at the position `beg` until the position `end-1` are copied into `ct`. Both `beg` and `end` are iterators. The sort criterion is specified by `sortOp`.

If you want to use a sort criterion other than the default, you must specify this option when the container is declared. For example, consider the following statements:

```
map<int, int>  intMap;                                   //Line 1
map<int, int, greater<int> >  otherIntMap;               //Line 2
multimap<int, string>  stringMultiMap;                   //Line 3
multimap<int, string, greater<string> >  otherStringMultiMap; //Line 4
```

The statement in Line 1 declares `intMap` to be an empty `map` container, the key type and the element type are `int`, and the sort criterion is the default sort criterion. The statement in Line 2 declares `otherIntMap` to be an empty `map` container, the key type and the element type are `int`, and the sort criterion is greater than. That is, the elements in the container `otherIntMap` will be arranged in descending order. The statements in Lines 3 and 4 have similar conventions. The statements in Lines 2 and 4 illustrate how to specify the descending sorting criterion.

> **NOTE** In the statements in Lines 2 and 4, note the space between the two >—that is, the space between `greater<int>` and >. This space is important because >> is also a shift operator in C++.

ITEM INSERTION AND DELETION FROM `map`/`multimap`

Suppose that `ct` is of type either `map` or `multimap`. Table 13-5 describes the operations that can be used to insert or delete elements from a set. Table 13-5 also illustrates how to use these operations. The name of the function is shown in bold. In this table, `ct` is either a `map` or `multimap` container.

TABLE 13-5 Operations to insert or delete elements from a `map` or `multimap`

Expression	Effect
`ct.insert(elem)`	Inserts a copy of `elem` into `ct`. In the case of sets, it also returns whether the insert operation succeeded.
`ct.insert(position, elem)`	Inserts a copy of `elem` into `ct`. The position where `elem` is inserted is returned. The first parameter, `position`, hints at where to begin the search for insert. The parameter `position` is an iterator.
`ct.insert(beg, end);`	Inserts a copy of all the elements into `ct` starting at the position `beg` until `end-1`. Both `beg` and `end` are iterators.
`ct.erase(elem);`	Deletes all the elements with the value `elem`. The number of deleted elements is returned.
`ct.erase(position);`	Deletes the element at the position specified by the iterator `position`. No value is returned.
`ct.erase(beg, end);`	Deletes all the elements starting at the position `beg` until the position `end-1`. Both `beg` and `end` are iterators. No value is returned.
`ct.clear();`	Deletes all the elements from the container `ct`. After this operation, the container `ct` is empty.

Example 13-4 illustrates various operations on a map/multimap container.

EXAMPLE 13-4

```
//**************************************************************
// Author: D.S. Malik
//
// This program illustrates how the operations on a map/multimap
// container work.
//**************************************************************

#include <iostream>                                      //Line 1
#include <map>                                           //Line 2
#include <utility>                                       //Line 3
#include <string>                                        //Line 4
#include <iterator>                                      //Line 5
```

```
using namespace std;                                    //Line 6

int main()                                              //Line 7
{                                                       //Line 8
    map<int, int>  intMap;                              //Line 9
    map<int, int>::iterator  mapItr;                    //Line 10

    intMap.insert(make_pair(1, 16));                    //Line 11
    intMap.insert(make_pair(2, 8));                     //Line 12
    intMap.insert(make_pair(4, 20));                    //Line 13
    intMap.insert(make_pair(3, 3));                     //Line 14
    intMap.insert(make_pair(1, 23));                    //Line 15
    intMap.insert(make_pair(20, 18));                   //Line 16
    intMap.insert(make_pair(8, 28));                    //Line 17
    intMap.insert(make_pair(15, 60));                   //Line 18
    intMap.insert(make_pair(6, 43));                    //Line 19
    intMap.insert(pair<int, int>(12, 16));              //Line 20

    cout << "Line 21: The elements of intMap" << endl;  //Line 21
    for (mapItr = intMap.begin();
            mapItr != intMap.end(); mapItr++)           //Line 22
        cout << mapItr->first << "\t"
             << mapItr->second << endl;                 //Line 23
    cout << endl;                                       //Line 24

    intMap.erase(12);                                   //Line 25

    mapItr = intMap.begin();                            //Line 26
    ++mapItr;                                           //Line 27
    ++mapItr;                                           //Line 28
    intMap.erase(mapItr);                               //Line 29

    cout << "Line 30: After deleting, elements of "
         << "intMap" << endl;                           //Line 30
    for (mapItr = intMap.begin();
            mapItr != intMap.end(); mapItr++)           //Line 31
        cout << mapItr->first << "\t"
             << mapItr->second << endl;                 //Line 32
    cout << endl;                                       //Line 33

    multimap<string, string> namesMultiMap;             //Line 34
    multimap<string, string>::iterator nameItr;         //Line 35

    namesMultiMap.insert(make_pair("A1", "Donny"));     //Line 36
    namesMultiMap.insert(make_pair("B1", "Zippy"));     //Line 37
    namesMultiMap.insert(make_pair("K1", "Ronny"));     //Line 38
    namesMultiMap.insert(make_pair("A2", "Hungry"));    //Line 39
    namesMultiMap.insert(make_pair("D1", "Ronny"));     //Line 40
    namesMultiMap.insert(make_pair("A1", "Dumpy"));     //Line 41

    cout << "Line 42: namesMultiMap: " << endl;         //Line 42
    for (nameItr = namesMultiMap.begin();
            nameItr != namesMultiMap.end(); nameItr++)  //Line 43
```

```
        cout << nameItr->first << "\t"
              << nameItr->second << endl;            //Line 44
    cout << endl;                                    //Line 45

    return 0;                                        //Line 46
}                                                    //Line 47
```

Sample Run:

```
Line 21: The elements of intMap
1        16
2        8
3        3
4        20
6        43
8        28
12       16
15       60
20       18


Line 30: After deleting, elements of intMap
1        16
2        8
4        20
6        43
8        28
15       60
20       18


Line 42: namesMultiMap:
A1       Donny
A1       Dumpy
A2       Hungry
B1       Zippy
D1       Ronny
K1       Ronny
```

The statement in Line 9 declares `intMap` to be a `map` container. The statement in Line 10 declares `mapItr` to be a `map` iterator. The iterator `intGtIt` can process the elements of any `map` container whose elements have the key type and the element type `int`.

The statements in Lines 11 through 20 insert the elements with their keys. For example, 16 is inserted with the key 1. The statements in Lines 11 through 19 use the function `make_pair` to insert the elements; the statement in Line 20 uses the `class pair` as the cast operator to insert the element.

The `for` loop in Line 22 outputs the elements of the container `intMap`.

The statement in Line 25 removes the element with key 12 from `intMap`. The statement in Line 26 initializes `mapItr` to the first element in the container `intMap`. The statements in Line 27 and 28 each advance `mapItr` to the next element in `intMap`. After the statement in Line 28 executes, `mapItr` points to the third element of `intMap`. The statement in Lines 29 removes the element of `intMap` to which `mapItr` points. The `for` loop in Line 31 outputs the elements of the container `intMap`.

The statement in Line 34 declares `namesMultiMap` to be a container of type `multimap`. The elements and their keys in `namesMultiMap` are of type `string`. The statement in Line 35 declares `nameItr` to be a `multimap` iterator.

The statements in Lines 36 through 41 insert the elements into `namesMultiMap`. The `for` loop in Line 43 outputs the elements of the container `namesMultiMap`.

Containers, Associated Header Files, and Iterator Support

Chapters 4 and 5 and the previous sections discussed various types of containers. Recall that every container is a class. The definition of the class implementing a specific container is contained in the header file. Table 13-6 describes the container, its associated header file, and the type of iterator supported by the container.

TABLE 13-6 Containers, their associated header files, and the type of iterator supported by each container

Sequence containers	Associated header file	Type of iterator support
vector	`<vector>`	Random access
deque	`<deque>`	Random access
list	`<list>`	Bidirectional
Associative containers	**Associated header file**	**Type of iterator support**
map	`<map>`	Bidirectional
multimap	`<map>`	Bidirectional
set	`<set>`	Bidirectional
multiset	`<set>`	Bidirectional
Adapters	**Associated header file**	**Type of iterator support**
stack	`<stack>`	No iterator support
queue	`<queue>`	No iterator support
priority_queue	`<queue>`	No iterator support

1
3

Algorithms

Several operations can be defined for a container. Some of the operations are very specific to a container and, therefore, are provided as part of the container definition (that is, as member functions of the class implementing the container). However, several operations—such as `find`, `sort`, and `merge`—are common to all containers. These operations are provided as generic algorithms and can be applied to all containers as well as the built-in array type. The algorithms are bound to a particular container through an iterator pair.

The generic algorithms are contained in the header file `algorithm`. This section describes several of these algorithms and shows how to use them in a program. Because algorithms are implemented with the help of functions, in the following sections, the terms *function* and *algorithm* mean the same thing.

STL Algorithm Classification

In earlier sections, you applied various operations on the sequence container, such as `clear`, `sort`, `merge`, and so on. However, those algorithms were tied to a specific container as members of a specific class. All those algorithms and a few more are also available in more general forms, called **generic algorithms**, and can be applied in a variety of situations. This section discusses some of these generic algorithms.

The STL contains algorithms that only look at the elements in a container and that move the elements of a container. It also has algorithms that can perform specific calculations, such as finding the sum of the elements of a numeric container. In addition, the STL contains algorithms for basic set theory operations, such as set union and intersection. You have already encountered some of the generic algorithms such as the `copy` algorithm, which copies the elements from a given range of elements to another place such as another container or the screen. The algorithms in the STL can be classified into the following categories:

- Nonmodifying algorithms
- Modifying algorithms
- Numeric algorithms
- Heap algorithms

The next four sections describe these algorithms. Most of the generic algorithms are contained in the header file `algorithm`. Certain algorithms, such as the numeric algorithms, are contained in the header file `numeric`.

Nonmodifying Algorithms

Nonmodifying algorithms do not modify the elements of the container; they merely investigate the elements. Table 13-7 lists the nonmodifying algorithms.

TABLE 13-7 Nonmodifying algorithms

adjacent_find	find_end	max_element
binary_search	find_first_of	min
count	find_if	min_element
count_if	for_each	mismatch
equal	includes	search
equal_range	lower_bound	search_n
find	max	upper_bound

Modifying Algorithms

Modifying algorithms, as the name implies, modify the elements of the container by rearranging, removing, or changing the values of the elements. Table 13-8 lists the modifying algorithms.

TABLE 13-8 Modifying algorithms

copy	prev_permutation	rotate_copy
copy_backward	random_shuffle	set_difference
fill	remove	set_intersection
fill_n	remove_copy	set_symmetric_difference
generate	remove_copy_if	set_union
generate_n	remove_if	sort
inplace_merge	replace	stable_partition
iter_swap	replace_copy	stable_sort
merge	replace_copy_if	swap
next_permutation	replace_if	swap_ranges
nth_element	reverse	transform
partial_sort	reverse_copy	unique
partial_sort_copy	rotate	unique_copy
partition		

1
3

Modifying algorithms that change the order of the elements, not their values, are also called **mutating algorithms**. For example, `next_permutation`, `partition`, `prev_permutation`, `random_shuffle`, `reverse`, `reverse_copy`, `rotate`, `rotate_copy`, and `stable_partition` are mutating algorithms.

Numeric Algorithms

Numeric algorithms are designed to perform numeric calculations on the elements of a container. Table 13-9 lists these algorithms.

TABLE 13-9   Numeric algorithms

`accumulate`	`inner_product`
`adjacent_difference`	`partial_sum`

Heap Algorithms

Chapter 10 described the heapsort algorithm. Recall that in the heapsort algorithm, the array containing the data is viewed as a binary tree. Therefore, a heap is a form of binary tree represented as an array. In a heap, the first element is the largest element, and the *i*th element (if it exists) is larger than the elements at positions $2i$ and $2i + 1$ (if they exist). In the heapsort algorithm, first the array containing the data is converted into a heap, and then the array is sorted using a special type of sorting algorithm. Table 13-10 lists the algorithms provided by the STL to implement the heap sort algorithm.

TABLE 13-10   Heap algorithms

`make_heap`	`push_heap`
`pop_heap`	`sort_heap`

Most of the STL algorithms are explained toward the end of this section. For the most part, the function prototypes of these algorithms are given along with a brief explanation of what each algorithm does. You then learn how to use these algorithms with the help of a C++ program. The STL algorithms are very powerful and accomplish wonderful results. Furthermore, they have been made general, in the sense that other than using the natural operations to manipulate containers, they allow the user to specify the manipulating criteria. For example, the natural sorting order is ascending, but the user can specify criteria to sort the container in descending order. Thus, every algorithm is typically implemented with the help of overloaded functions. Before starting to describe these algorithms, we discuss **function objects**, which allow the user to specify the manipulating criteria.

Function Objects

To make the generic algorithms flexible, the STL usually provides two forms of an algorithm using the mechanism of function overloading. The first form of an algorithm uses the natural operation to accomplish this goal. In the second form, the user can specify the criteria based on which the algorithm processes the elements. For example, the algorithm `adjacent_find` searches the container and returns the position of the first two elements that are equal. In the second form of this algorithm, we can specify criteria (say, less than) to look for the first two elements such that the second element is less than the first element. These criteria are passed as a function object. More formally, a **function object** contains a function that can be treated as a function using the function call operator, `()`. In fact, a function object is a class template that overloads the function call operator, `()`.

In addition to allowing you to create your own function objects, the STL provides arithmetic, relational, and logical function objects, which are described in Table 13-11. The STL's function objects are contained in the header file `functional`.

TABLE 13-11 Arithmetic STL function objects

Function object name	Description
plus<Type>	plus<int> addNum; int sum = addNum(12, 35); The value of sum is 47.
minus<Type>	minus<int> subtractNum; int difference = subtractNum(56, 35); The value of difference is 21.
multiplies<Type>	multiplies<int> multiplyNum; int product = multiplyNum(6, 3); The value of product is 18.
divides<Type>	divides<int> divideNum; int quotient = divideNum(16, 3); The value of quotient is 5.
modulus<Type>	modulus<int> remainder; int rem = remainder(16, 7); The value of rem is 2.
negate<Type>	negate<int> opposite; int num = opposite(-25); The value of opposite is 25.

1
3

Example 13-5 illustrates how to use the STL's arithmetic function objects.

EXAMPLE 13-5

```
//*************************************************************
// Author: D.S. Malik
//
// This program shows how STL arithmetic function objects work.
//*************************************************************

#include <iostream>                                          //Line 1
#include <string>                                            //Line 2
#include <algorithm>                                         //Line 3
#include <numeric>                                           //Line 4
#include <iterator>                                          //Line 5
#include <vector>                                            //Line 6
#include <functional>                                        //Line 7

using namespace std;                                         //Line 8

int funcAdd(plus<int>, int, int);                            //Line 9

int main()                                                   //Line 10
{                                                            //Line 11
    plus<int> addNum;                                        //Line 12
    int num = addNum(34, 56);                                //Line 13

    cout << "Line 14: num = " << num << endl;                //Line 14

    plus<string> joinString;                                 //Line 15

    string str1 = "Hello ";                                  //Line 16
    string str2 = "There";                                   //Line 17

    string str = joinString(str1, str2);                     //Line 18

    cout << "Line 19: str = " << str << endl;                //Line 19
    cout << "Line 20: Sum of 34 and 26 = "
         << funcAdd(addNum, 34, 26) << endl;                 //Line 20

    int list[8] = {1, 2, 3, 4, 5, 6, 7, 8};                  //Line 21

    vector<int> intList(list, list + 8);                     //Line 22
    ostream_iterator<int> screenOut(cout, " ");              //Line 23

    cout << "Line 24: intList: ";                            //Line 24
    copy(intList.begin(), intList.end(), screenOut);         //Line 25
    cout << endl;                                            //Line 26

        //accumulate
    int sum = accumulate(intList.begin(),
                         intList.end(), 0);                  //Line 27
```

```
    cout << "Line 28: Sum of the elements of intList = "
         << sum << endl;                                      //Line 28

    int product = accumulate(intList.begin(), intList.end(),
                        1, multiplies<int>());                //Line 29

    cout << "Line 30: Product of the elements of intList = "
         << product << endl;                                  //Line 30

    return 0;                                                 //Line 31
}                                                             //Line 32

int funcAdd(plus<int> sum, int x, int y)                      //Line 33
{                                                             //Line 34
    return sum(x, y);                                         //Line 35
}                                                             //Line 36
```

Sample Run:

```
Line 14: num = 90
Line 19: str = Hello There
Line 20: Sum of 34 and 26 = 60
Line 24: intList: 1 2 3 4 5 6 7 8
Line 28: Sum of the elements of intList = 36
Line 30: Product of the elements of intList = 40320
```

Table 13-12 describes the relational STL function objects.

TABLE 13-12 Relational STL function objects

Function object name	Description

equal_to<Type>	Returns true if the two arguments are equal, and false otherwise. For example,
	`equal_to<int> compare;`
	`bool isEqual = compare(5, 5);`
	The value of isEqual is true.

not_equal_to<Type>	Returns true if the two arguments are not equal, and false otherwise. For example,
	`not_equal_to<int> compare;`
	`bool isNotEqual = compare(5, 6);`
	The value of isNotEqual is true.

greater<Type>	Returns true if the first argument is greater than the second argument, and false otherwise. For example,
	`greater<int> compare;`
	`bool isGreater = compare(8, 5);`
	The value of isGreater is true.

1
3

TABLE 13-12 Relational STL function objects (continued)

Function object name	Description

greater_equal<Type>	Returns `true` if the first argument is greater than or equal to the second argument, and `false` otherwise. For example,
	 `greater_equal<int> compare;`
	 `bool isGreaterEqual = compare(8, 5);`
	 The value of `isGreaterEqual` is `true`.

less<Type>	Returns `true` if the first argument is less than the second argument, and `false` otherwise. For example,
	 `less<int> compare;`
	 `bool isLess = compare(3, 5);`
	 The value of `isLess` is `true`.

less_equal<Type>	Returns `true` if the first argument is less than or equal to the second argument, and `false` otherwise. For example,
	 `less_equal<int> compare;`
	 `bool isLessEqual = compare(8, 15);`
	 The value of `isLessEqual` is `true`.

The STL relational function objects can also be applied to containers, as shown next. The STL algorithm `adjacent_find` searches a container and returns the position in the container where the two elements are equal. This algorithm has a second form that allows the user to specify the comparison criteria. For example, consider the following vector, `vecList`:

```
vecList = {2, 3, 4, 5, 1, 7, 8, 9};
```

The elements of `vecList` are supposed to be in ascending order. To see if the elements are out of order, we can use the algorithm `adjacent_find` as follows:

```
intItr = adjacent_find(vecList.begin(), vecList.end(),
                       greater<int>());
```

where `intItr` is an iterator of type `vector`. The function `adjacent_find` starts at the position `vecList.begin()`—that is, at the first element of `vecList`—and looks for the first set of consecutive elements such that the first element is greater than the second. The function returns a pointer to element 5, which is stored in `intItr`.

The program in Example 13-6 further illustrates how to use the relational function objects.

EXAMPLE 13-6

```
//***********************************************************
// Author: D.S. Malik
// This program shows how STL relational function objects work.
//***********************************************************
```

```
#include <iostream>                                       //Line 1
#include <string>                                         //Line 2
#include <algorithm>                                      //Line 3
#include <iterator>                                       //Line 4
#include <vector>                                         //Line 5
#include <functional>                                     //Line 6

using namespace std;                                      //Line 7

int main()                                                //Line 8
{                                                         //Line 9
    equal_to<int> compare;                                //Line 10
    bool isEqual = compare(6, 6);                         //Line 11

    cout << "Line 12: isEqual = " << isEqual << endl;     //Line 12

    greater<string> greaterStr;                           //Line 13

    string str1 = "Hello";                                //Line 14
    string str2 = "There";                                //Line 15

    if (greaterStr(str1, str2))                           //Line 16
        cout << "Line 17: \"" << str1 << "\" is greater "
             << "than \"" << str2 << "\"" << endl;        //Line 17
    else                                                  //Line 18
        cout << "Line 19: \"" << str1 << "\" is not "
             << "greater than \"" << str2 << "\""
             << endl;                                     //Line 19

    int temp[8] = {2, 3, 4, 5, 1, 7, 8, 9};               //Line 20

    vector<int> vecList(temp, temp + 8);                  //Line 21
    vector<int>::iterator intItr1, intItr2;               //Line 22
    ostream_iterator<int> screen(cout, " ");              //Line 23

    cout << "Line 24: vecList: ";                         //Line 24
    copy(vecList.begin(), vecList.end(), screen);         //Line 25
    cout << endl;                                         //Line 26

    intItr1 = adjacent_find(vecList.begin(),
                  vecList.end(), greater<int>());         //Line 27
    intItr2 = intItr1 + 1;                                //Line 28

    cout << "Line 29: In vecList, the first set of "
         << "out of order elements are: " << *intItr1
         << " " << *intItr2 << endl;                      //Line 29
    cout << "Line 30: In vecList, the first out of "
         << "order element is at position: "
         << vecList.end() - intItr2 << endl;              //Line 30

    return 0;                                             //Line 31
}                                                         //Line 32
```

13

Sample Run:

```
Line 12: isEqual = 1
Line 19: "Hello" is not greater than "There"
Line 24: vecList: 2 3 4 5 1 7 8 9
Line 29: In vecList, the first set of out of order elements are: 5 1
Line 30: In vecList, the first out of order element is at position: 4
```

Table 13-13 describes the logical STL function objects.

TABLE 13-13 Logical STL function objects

Function object name	Effect
logical_not<Type>	Returns true if its operand evaluates to false, and false otherwise. This is a unary function object.
logical_and<Type>	Returns true if both of its operands evaluate to true, and false otherwise. This is a binary function object.
logical_or<Type>	Returns true if at least one of its operands evaluates to true, and false otherwise. This is a binary function object.

Predicates

Predicates are special types of function objects that return Boolean values. There are two types of predicates—unary and binary. Unary predicates check a specific property for a single argument; binary predicates check a specific property for a pair—that is, two—of arguments. Predicates are typically used to specify searching or sorting criteria. In the STL, a predicate must always return the same result for the same value. Therefore, the functions that modify their internal states *cannot* be considered predicates.

INSERT ITERATOR

Consider the following statements:

```
int list[5] = {1, 3, 6, 9, 12};   //Line 1
vector<int> vList;                 //Line 2
```

The statement in Line 1 declares and initializes list to be an array of 5 components; the statement in Line 2 declares vList to be a vector. Because no size is specified for vList, no memory space is reserved for the elements of vList. Now suppose that we want to copy the elements of list into vList. The statement

```
copy(list, list + 8, vList.begin());
```

will not work because no memory space is allocated for the elements of vList, and the copy function uses the assignment operator to copy the elements from the source to the destination.

One solution to this problem is to use a for loop to step through the elements of list and use the function push_back of vList to copy the elements of list. However, there is a better solution, which is convenient and applicable whenever no memory space is allocated at the destination. The STL provides three iterators, called **insert iterators**, to insert the elements at the destination: back_inserter, front_inserter, and inserter.

back_inserter: This inserter uses the push_back operation of the container in place of the assignment operator. The argument to this iterator is the container itself. For example, for the preceding problem, we can copy the elements of list into vList by using back_inserter as follows:

```
copy(list, list + 5, back_inserter(vList));
```

front_inserter: This inserter uses the push_front operation of the container in place of the assignment operator. The argument to this iterator is the container itself. Because the vector class does not support the push_front operation, this iterator cannot be used for the vector container.

inserter: This inserter uses the container's insert operation in place of the assignment operator. This iterator has two arguments: The first argument is the container itself; the second argument is an iterator to the container specifying the position at which the insertion should begin.

The program in Example 13-7 illustrates the effect of inserters on a container.

EXAMPLE 13-7

```
//************************************************************
// Author: D.S. Malik
//
// This program shows how STL inserters work.
//************************************************************

#include <iostream>                                    //Line 1
#include <algorithm>                                   //Line 2
#include <iterator>                                    //Line 3
#include <vector>                                      //Line 4
#include <list>                                        //Line 5

using namespace std;                                   //Line 6

int main()                                             //Line 7
{                                                      //Line 8
    int temp[8] = {1, 2, 3, 4, 5, 6, 7, 8};            //Line 9

    vector<int> vecList1;                              //Line 10
    vector<int> vecList2;                              //Line 11

    ostream_iterator<int> screenOut(cout, " ");        //Line 12

    copy(temp, temp + 8, back_inserter(vecList1));     //Line 13
```

1
3

```
    cout << "Line 14: vecList1: ";                          //Line 14
    copy(vecList1.begin(), vecList1.end(), screenOut);      //Line 15
    cout << endl;                                           //Line 16

    copy(vecList1.begin(), vecList1.end(),
         inserter(vecList2, vecList2.begin()));             //Line 17

    cout << "Line 18: vecList2: ";                          //Line 18
    copy(vecList2.begin(), vecList2.end(), screenOut);      //Line 19
    cout << endl;                                           //Line 20

    list<int> tempList;                                     //Line 21

    copy(vecList2.begin(), vecList2.end(),
         front_inserter(tempList));                         //Line 22

    cout << "Line 23: tempList: ";                          //Line 23
    copy(tempList.begin(), tempList.end(), screenOut);      //Line 24
    cout << endl;                                           //Line 25

    return 0;                                               //Line 26
}                                                           //Line 27
```

Sample Run:

```
Line 14: vecList1: 1 2 3 4 5 6 7 8
Line 18: vecList2: 1 2 3 4 5 6 7 8
Line 23: tempList: 8 7 6 5 4 3 2 1
```

STL Algorithms

This section describes most of the STL algorithms. Each algorithm also includes the function prototypes, a brief description of what the algorithm does, and a program showing how to use it. In the function prototypes, the parameter types indicate for which type of container the algorithm is applicable. For example, if a parameter is of type `randomAccessIterator`, then the algorithm is applicable only for random access type containers such as vectors. Throughout, we use abbreviations such as `outputItr` to mean output iterator, `inputItr` to mean input iterator, `forwardItr` to mean forward iterator, and so on.

Functions `fill` and `fill_n`

The function `fill` is used to fill a container with elements; the function `fill_n` is used to fill in the next n elements. The element that is used as a filling element is passed as a parameter to these functions. Both of these functions are defined in the header file `algorithm`. The prototypes of these functions are as follows:

```
template <class forwardItr, class Type>
void fill(forwardItr first, forwardItr last, const Type& value);

template <class forwardItr, class size, class Type>
void fill_n(forwardItr first, size n, const Type& value);
```

The first two parameters of the function `fill` are forward iterators specifying the starting and ending positions of the container; the third parameter is the filling element. The first parameter of the function `fill_n` is a forward iterator that specifies the starting position of the container, the second parameter specifies the number of elements to be filled, and the third parameter specifies the filling element. The program in Example 13-8 illustrates how to use these functions.

EXAMPLE 13-8

```cpp
//************************************************************
// Author: D.S. Malik
//
// This program shows how the STL functions fill and fill_n
// work.
//************************************************************

#include <iostream>                                        //Line 1
#include <algorithm>                                       //Line 2
#include <iterator>                                        //Line 3
#include <vector>                                          //Line 4

using namespace std;                                       //Line 5

int main()                                                 //Line 6
{                                                          //Line 7
    vector<int> vecList(8);                                //Line 8
    ostream_iterator<int> screen(cout, " ");               //Line 9

    fill(vecList.begin(), vecList.end(), 2);               //Line 10

    cout << "Line 11: After filling vecList with 2's: ";   //Line 11
    copy(vecList.begin(), vecList.end(), screen);          //Line 12
    cout << endl;                                          //Line 13

    fill_n(vecList.begin(), 3, 5);                         //Line 14

    cout << "Line 15: After filling the first three "
         << "elements with 5's: " << endl << "      "; //Line 15
    copy(vecList.begin(), vecList.end(), screen);          //Line 16
    cout << endl;                                          //Line 17

    return 0;                                              //Line 18
}                                                          //Line 19
```

1
3

Sample Run:

```
Line 11: After filling vecList with 2's: 2 2 2 2 2 2 2 2
Line 15: After filling the first three elements with 5's:
         5 5 5 2 2 2 2 2
```

The statements in Lines 8 and 9 declare `vecList` to be a sequence container of size 8, and `screen` to be an `ostream` iterator initialized to `cout` with the delimit character space. The statement in Line 10 uses the function `fill` to fill `vecList` with 2; that is, all eight elements of `vecList` are set to 2. Recall that `vecList.begin()` returns an iterator to the first element of `vecList`, and `vecList.end()` returns an iterator to the last element of `vecList`. The statement in Line 12 outputs the elements of `vecList` using the `copy` function. The statement in Line 14 uses the function `fill_n` to store 5 in the elements of `vecList`. The first parameter of `fill_n` is `vecList.begin()`, which specifies the starting position of where to begin copying. The second parameter of `fill_n` is 3, which specifies the number of elements to be filled. The third parameter, 5, specifies the filling character. Therefore, 5 is copied into the first three elements of `vecList`. The statement in Line 16 outputs the elements of `vecList`.

Functions `generate` and `generate_n`

The functions `generate` and `generate_n` are used to generate elements and fill a sequence. These functions are defined in the header file `algorithm`. The prototypes of these functions follow:

```
template <class forwardItr, class function>
void generate(forwardItr first, forwardItr last, function gen);

template <class forwardItr, class size, class function>
void generate_n(forwardItr first, size n, function gen);
```

The function `generate` fills a sequence in the range `first...last-1`, with successive calls to the function `gen()`. The function `generate_n` fills a sequence in the range `first...first+n-1`—that is, starting at position `first`, with n successive calls to the function `gen()`. Note that `gen` can also be a pointer to a function. Moreover, if `gen` is a function, it must be a value-returning function without parameters. The program in Example 13-9 illustrates how to use these functions.

EXAMPLE 13-9

```
//**********************************************************
// Author: D.S. Malik
//
// This program shows how the STL functions generate and
// generate_n work.
//**********************************************************
```

```
#include <iostream>                                         //Line 1
#include <algorithm>                                        //Line 2
#include <iterator>                                         //Line 3
#include <vector>                                           //Line 4

using namespace std;                                        //Line 5

int nextNum();                                              //Line 6

int main()                                                  //Line 7
{                                                           //Line 8
    vector<int> vecList(8);                                 //Line 9
    ostream_iterator<int> screen(cout, " ");                //Line 10

    generate(vecList.begin(), vecList.end(), nextNum);      //Line 11

    cout << "Line 12: vecList after filling with "
         << "numbers: ";                                    //Line 12

    copy(vecList.begin(), vecList.end(), screen);           //Line 13
    cout << endl;                                           //Line 14

    generate_n(vecList.begin(), 3, nextNum);                //Line 15

    cout << "Line 16: vecList, after filling the first "
         << "three elements " << endl
         << "          with the next number: ";             //Line 16
    copy(vecList.begin(), vecList.end(), screen);           //Line 17
    cout << endl;                                           //Line 18

    return 0;                                               //Line 19
}                                                           //Line 20

int nextNum()                                               //Line 21
{                                                           //Line 22
    static int n = 1;                                       //Line 23

    return n++;                                             //Line 24
}                                                           //Line 25
```

Sample Run:

```
Line 12: vecList after filling with numbers: 1 2 3 4 5 6 7 8
Line 16: vecList, after filling the first three elements
          with the next number: 9 10 11 4 5 6 7 8
```

This program contains a value-returning function nextNum, which contains a static variable n initialized to 1. A call to this function returns the current value of n and then increments the value of n. Therefore, the first call of nextNum returns 1, the second call returns 2, and so on.

The statements in Lines 9 and 10 declare vecList to be a sequence container of size 8, and screen to be an ostream iterator initialized to cout with the delimit character space. The statement in Line 11 uses the function `generate` to fill `vecList` by successively calling the function `nextNum`. Notice that after the statement in Line 11 executes, the value of the static variable n of `nextNum` is 9. The statement in Line 13 outputs the elements of `vecList`. The statement in Line 15 calls the function `generate_n` to fill the first three elements of `vecList` by calling the function `nextNum` three times. The starting position is `vecList.begin()`, which is the first element of `vecList`, and the number of elements to be filled is 3, given by the second parameter of `generate_n` (see Line 15). The statement in Line 17 outputs the elements of `vecList`.

Functions `find`, `find_if`, `find_end`, and `find_first_of`

The functions `find`, `find_if`, `find_end`, and `find_first_of` are used to find the elements in a given range. These functions are defined in the header file `algorithm`. The prototypes of the functions `find` and `find_if` are as follows:

```
template <class inputItr, class size, class Type>
inputItr find(inputItr first, inputItr last,
              const Type& searchValue);

template <class inputItr, class unaryPredicate>
inputItr find_if(inputItr first, inputItr last, unaryPredicate op);
```

The function `find` searches the range of elements `first...last-1` for the element `searchValue`. If `searchValue` is found in the range, the function returns the position in the range where `searchValue` is found; otherwise, it returns `last`. The function `find_if` searches the range of elements `first...last-1` for the element for which `op(rangeElement)` is true. If an element satisfying `op(rangeElement)` is true is found, it returns the position in the given range where such an element is found; otherwise, it returns `last`.

Example 13-10 illustrates how to use the functions `find` and `find_if`.

EXAMPLE 13-10

Consider the following statements.

```
char cList[10] = {'a', 'i', 'C', 'd', 'e', 'f',
                  'o', 'H', 'u', 'j'};               //Line 1
vector<char> charList(cList, cList + 10);            //Line 2
vector<char>::iterator position;                     //Line 3
```

After the statement in Line 2 executes, the vector container `charList` is as follows:

```
charList = {'a', 'i', 'C', 'd', 'e', 'f', 'o', 'H', 'u', 'j'};
```

Consider the following statement:

```
position = find(charList.begin(), charList.end(), 'd');
```

This statement searches `charList` for the first occurrence of `'d'` and returns an iterator, which is stored in `position`. Because `'d'` is the fourth character in `charList`, its position is 3. Therefore, `position` points to the element at position 3 in `charList`.

Now consider the following statement:

```
position = find_if(charList.begin(), charList.end(), isupper);
```

This statement uses the function `find_if` to find the first uppercase character in `charList`. Note that the function `isupper` from the header file `cctype` is passed as the third parameter to the function `find_if`. The first uppercase character in `charList` is the third element. Therefore, after this statement executes, `position` points to the third element of `charList`.

We leave it as an exercise for you to write a program that test the functions `find` and `find_if`; see Programming Exercise 1 at the end of this chapter.

Next, we describe the functions `find_end` and `find_first_of`. Both of these functions have two forms. The prototypes of the function `find_end` are as follows:

```
template <class forwardItr1, class forwardItr2>
forwardItr1 find_end(forwardItr1 first1, forwardItr1 last1,
                     forwardItr2 first2, forwardItr2 last2);

template <class forwardItr1, class forwardItr2,
          class binaryPredicate>
forwardItr1 find_end(forwardItr1 first1, forwardItr1 last1,
                     forwardItr2 first2, forwardItr2 last2,
                     binaryPredicate op);
```

Both forms of the function `find_end` search the range `first1...last1-1` for the last occurrence of the range `first2...last2-1`. If the search is successful, the function returns the position in `first1..last1-1` where the match occurs; otherwise, it returns `last1`. That is, the function `find_end` returns the position of the last element in the range `first1...last1-1` where the range `first2...last2-1` is a subrange of `first1...last1-1`. In the first form, the elements are compared for equality; in the second form, the comparison `op(elementFirstRange, elementSecondRange)` must be `true`.

The prototypes of the function `find_first_of` are as follows:

```
template <class forwardItr1, class forwardItr2>
forwardItr1 find_first_of(forwardItr1 first1, forwardItr1 last1,
                          forwardItr2 first2, forwardItr2 last2);

template <class forwardItr1, class forwardItr2,
          class binaryPredicate>
forwardItr1 find_first_of(forwardItr1 first1, forwardItr1 last1,
                          forwardItr2 first2, forwardItr2 last2,
                          binaryPredicate op);
```

The first form returns the position, within the range `first1...last1-1`, of the first element of `first2...last2-1` that is also in the range `first1...last1-1`. The second form returns the position, within the range `first1...last1-1`, of the first element of `first2...last2-1` for which `op(elemRange1, elemRange2)` is `true`. If no match is found, both forms return `last1-1`.

Example 13-11 illustrates how to use the functions `find_end` and `find_first_of`.

EXAMPLE 13-11

Suppose that you have the following statements:

```
int list1[10] = {12, 34, 56, 21, 34, 78, 34, 56, 12, 25};
int list2[2] = {34, 56};
int list3[5] = {33, 48, 21, 34, 73};
vector<int>::iterator location;
```

Consider the following statement:

```
location = find_end(list1, list1 + 10, list2, list2 + 2);
```

This statement uses the function `find_end` to find the last occurrence of `list2`, as a subsequence, within `list1`. The last occurrence of `list2` in `list1` starts at position 6 (that is, at the seventh element). Therefore, after this statement executes, `location` points to the element at position 6, in `list1`, which is the seventh element of `list1`.

Now consider the following statement:

```
location = find_first_of(list1, list1 + 10, list3, list3 + 5);
```

This statement uses the function `find_first_of` to find the position in `list1` where the first element of `list3` is also an element of `list1`. The first element of `list3`, which is also an element of `list1`, is 34 and its position in `list1` is 1, the second element of `list1`. Therefore, after this statement executes, `location` points to the element at position 1, in `list1`, which is the second element of `list1`.

We leave it as an exercise for you to write a program that tests the functions `find_end` and `find_first_of`; see Programming Exercise 2 at the end of this chapter.

Functions `remove`, `remove_if`, `remove_copy`, and `remove_copy_if`

The function `remove` is used to remove certain elements from a sequence; the function `remove_if` is used to remove the elements from a sequence by using some criteria. The function `remove_copy` copies the elements of a sequence into another sequence by excluding certain elements of the first sequence. Similarly, the function `remove_copy_if` copies the elements of a sequence into another sequence by excluding certain elements, using some criteria, of the first sequence. These functions are defined in the header file `algorithm`.

The prototypes of the functions `remove` and `remove_if` are as follows:

```
template <class forwardItr, class Type>
forwardItr remove(forwardItr first, forwardItr last,
                  const Type& value);

template <class forwardItr, class unaryPredicate>
forwardItr remove_if(forwardItr first, forwardItr last,
                  unaryPredicate op);
```

The function `remove` removes each occurrence of a given element in the range `first...last-1`. The element to be removed is passed as the third parameter to this function. The function `remove_if` removes those elements, in the range `first...last-1`, for which the predicate `op(element)` is `true`. Both of these functions return `forwardItr`, which points to the position after the last element of the new range of elements. These functions do not modify the size of the container; in fact, the elements are moved to the beginning of the container. For example, if the sequence is {3, 7, 2, 5, 7, 9} and the element to be removed is 7, then after removing 7, the resulting sequence is {3, 2, 5, 9, 9}. The function returns a pointer to element 9 (which is after 5).

The program in Example 13-12 further illustrates the importance of this returned `forwardItr`. (See Lines 17, 19, 21, and 23.)

Let us now look at the prototypes of the functions `remove_copy` and `remove_copy_if`:

```
template <class inputItr, class outputItr, class Type>
outputItr remove_copy(inputItr first1, inputItr last1,
                  outputItr destFirst, const Type& value);

template <class inputItr, class outputItr, class unaryPredicate>
outputItr remove_copy_if(inputItr first1, inputItr last1,
                  outputItr destFirst,
                  unaryPredicate op);
```

The function `remove_copy` copies all the elements in the range `first1...last1-1`, except the elements specified by `value`, into the sequence starting at the position `destFirst`. Similarly, the function `remove_copy_if` copies all the elements in the range `first1...last1-1`, except the elements for which `op(element)` is `true`, into the sequence starting at the position `destFirst`. Both of these functions return an `outputItr`, which points to the position after the last element copied.

The program in Example 13-12 shows how to use the functions `remove`, `remove_if`, `remove_copy`, and `remove_copy_if`.

1
3

EXAMPLE 13-12

```
//********************************************************
// Author: D.S. Malik
//
// This program shows how the STL functions remove, remove_if,
// remove_copy, and remove_copy_if works.
//********************************************************
```

```
#include <iostream>                                          //Line 1
#include <cctype>                                            //Line 2
#include <algorithm>                                         //Line 3
#include <iterator>                                          //Line 4
#include <vector>                                            //Line 5

using namespace std;                                         //Line 6

bool lessThanEqualTo50(int num);                             //Line 7

int main()                                                   //Line 8
{                                                            //Line 9
    char cList[10] = {'A', 'a', 'A', 'B', 'A',
                      'c', 'D', 'e', 'F', 'A'};              //Line 10

    vector<char> charList(cList, cList + 10);                //Line 11
    vector<char>::iterator lastElem, newLastElem;            //Line 12

    ostream_iterator<char> screen(cout, " ");                //Line 13

    cout << "Line 14: Character list: ";                     //Line 14
    copy(charList.begin(), charList.end(), screen);          //Line 15
    cout <<  endl;                                           //Line 16

        //remove
    lastElem = remove(charList.begin(),
                    charList.end(), 'A');                    //Line 17

    cout << "Line 18: Character list after removing A: "; //Line 18
    copy(charList.begin(), lastElem, screen);                //Line 19
    cout << endl;                                            //Line 20

        //remove_if
    newLastElem = remove_if (charList.begin(),
                        lastElem, isupper);                  //Line 21
    cout << "Line 22: Character list after removing "
        << "the uppercase letters: " << endl;                //Line 22
    copy(charList.begin(), newLastElem, screen);             //Line 23
    cout << endl << endl;                                    //Line 24


    int list[10] = {12, 34, 56, 21, 34, 78, 34, 55, 12,
                25};                                         //Line 25

    vector<int> intList(list, list + 10);                    //Line 26
    vector<int>::iterator  endElement;                       //Line 27

    ostream_iterator<int> screenOut(cout, " ");              //Line 28

    cout << "Line 29: intList: ";                            //Line 29
    copy(intList.begin(), intList.end(), screenOut);         //Line 30
    cout << endl;                                            //Line 31
```

```
        vector<int> temp1(10);                                  //Line 32

            //remove_copy
        endElement = remove_copy(intList.begin(), intList.end(),
                            temp1.begin(), 34);                  //Line 33

        cout << "Line 34: temp1 after copying all the "
             << "elements of intList except 34: " << endl;      //Line 34
        copy(temp1.begin(), endElement, screenOut);             //Line 35
        cout << endl;                                           //Line 36

        vector<int> temp2(10, 0);                               //Line 37

            //remove_copy_if
        remove_copy_if (intList.begin(), intList.end(),
                    temp2.begin(), lessThanEqualTo50);          //Line 38

        cout << "Line 39: temp2 after copying all the elements of "
             << "intList except \nnumbers less than 50: ";      //Line 39
        copy(temp2.begin(), temp2.end(), screenOut);            //Line 40
        cout << endl;                                           //Line 41

        return 0;                                               //Line 42
}                                                               //Line 43

bool lessThanEqualTo50(int num)                                 //Line 44
{                                                               //Line 45
    return (num <= 50);                                         //Line 46
}                                                               //Line 47
```

Sample Run:

```
Line 14: Character list: A a A B A c D e F A
Line 18: Character list after removing A: a B c D e F
Line 22: Character list after removing the uppercase letters:
a c e

Line 29: intList: 12 34 56 21 34 78 34 55 12 25
Line 34: temp1 list after copying all the elements of intList except 34:
12 56 21 78 55 12 25
Line 39: temp2 after copying all the elements of intList except
numbers less than 50: 56 78 55 0 0 0 0 0 0 0
```

The statement in Line 11 creates a vector list, charList, of type char, and initializes charList using the array cList created in Line 10. The statement in Line 12 declares two vector iterators, lastElem and newLastElem. The statement in Line 13 declares an ostream iterator, screen. The statement in Line 15 outputs the value of charList. The statement in Line 17 uses the function remove to remove all the occurrences of 'A' from charList. The function returns a pointer to one past the last element of the new range, which is stored in lastElem. The statement in Line 19 outputs the elements in the new range. (Note that the statement in Line 19 outputs the elements in the range `charList.begin()...lastElem-1`.) The statement in Line 21 uses the function `remove_if` to remove the uppercase letters from the list `charList` and stores the pointer returned by the function `remove_if` in `newLastElem`. The statement in Line 23 outputs the elements in the new range.

The statement in Line 26 creates a vector, `intList`, of type `int` and initializes `intList` using the array `list`, created in Line 25. The statement in Line 30 outputs the elements of `intList`. The statement in Line 33 copies all the elements, except the occurrences of 34, of `intList` into `temp1`. The list `intList` is not modified. The statement in Line 35 outputs the elements of `temp1`. The statement in Line 37 creates a vector, `temp2`, of type `int` of 10 components and initializes all the elements of `temp2` to 0. The statement in Line 38 uses the function `remove_copy_if` to copy those elements of `intList` that are less than 50. The statement in Line 40 outputs the elements of `temp2`.

Functions `replace`, `replace_if`, `replace_copy`, and `replace_copy_if`

The function `replace` is used to replace all the occurrences, within a given range, of a given element with a new value. The function `replace_if` is used to replace the values of the elements, within a given range, satisfying certain criteria with a new value. The prototypes of these functions are as follows:

```
template <class forwardItr, class Type>
void replace(forwardItr first, forwardItr last,
    const Type& oldValue, const Type& newValue);

template <class forwardItr, class unaryPredicate, class Type>
void replace_if(forwardItr first, forwardItr last,
                unaryPredicate op, const Type& newValue);
```

The function `replace` replaces all the elements in the range `first...last-1` whose values are equal to `oldValue` with the value specified by `newValue`. The function `replace_if` replaces all the elements in the range `first...last-1`, for which `op(element)` is `true`, with the value specified by `newValue`.

The function `replace_copy` is a combination of `replace` and `copy`. Similarly, the function `replace_copy_if` is a combination of `replace_if` and `copy`. Let us first look at the prototypes of the functions `replace_copy` and `replace_copy_if`:

```
template <class inputItr, class outputItr, class Type>
outputItr replace_copy(forwardItr first, forwardItr last,
                       outputItr destFirst,
                       const Type& oldValue,
                       const Type& newValue);

template <class forwardItr, class outputItr,
          class unaryPredicate, class Type>
```

```
outputItr replace_copy_if(forwardItr first, forwardItr last,
                          outputItr destFirst,
                          unaryPredicate op,
                          const Type& newValue);
```

The function `replace_copy` copies all the elements in the range `first...last-1` into the container starting at `destFirst`. If the value of an element in this range is equal to `oldValue`, it is replaced by `newValue`. The function `replace_copy_if` copies all the elements in the range `first...last-1` into the container starting at `destFirst`. If for any element in this range `op(element)` is `true`, at the destination its value is replaced by `newValue`. Both of these functions return an `outputItr` (a pointer) positioned one past the last element copied at the destination.

Example 13-13 illustrates how to use the functions `replace`, `replace_if`, `replace_copy`, and `replace_copy_if`.

EXAMPLE 13-13

Consider the following statements:

```
char cList[10] = {'A', 'a', 'A', 'B', 'A',
                  'c', 'D', 'e', 'F', 'A'};         //Line 1
vector<char> charList(cList, cList + 10);           //Line 2
```

After the statement in Line 2 executes, the vector container `charList` is as follows:

```
charList = {'A', 'a', 'A', 'B', 'A', 'c',
            'D', 'e', 'F', 'A'}                     //Line 3
```

Now consider the following statement:

```
replace(charList.begin(), charList.end(), 'A', 'Z'); //Line 4
```

This statement uses the function `replace` to replace all the occurrences of `'A'` with `'Z'` in `charList`. After this statement executes, `charList` is as follows:

```
charList ={'Z', 'a', 'Z', 'B', 'Z', 'c', 'D',
           'e', 'F', 'Z'}                           //Line 5
```

Now consider the following statement:

```
replace_if(charList.begin(), charList.end(), isupper, '*'); //Line 6
```

This statement uses the function `replace_if` to replace the uppercase letters with `'*'` in the list `charList`. After this statement executes, `charList` is as follows:

```
charList ={'*', 'a', '*', '*', '*', 'c', '*',
           'e', '*', '*'}                           //Line 7
```

Next suppose that you have the following statements:

```
int list[10] = {12, 34, 56, 21, 34, 78, 34, 55, 12, 25}; //Line 8
vector<int> intList(list, list + 10);                    //Line 9
vector<int> temp(10);                                    //Line 10
```

1
3

The statement in Line 9 creates a vector, `intList`, of type `int` and initializes `intList` using the array `list`, created in Line 8. After the statement in Line 9 executes, `intList` is as follows:

`intList = {12, 34, 56, 21, 34, 78, 34, 55, 12, 25}`

The statement in Line 10 declares a vector `temp` of type `int`. Next consider the following statement:

```
replace_copy(intList.begin(), intList.end(),
             temp1.begin(), 34, 0);                        //Line 11
```

This statement copies all the elements of `intList` and replaces 34 with 0. The list `intList` is not modified. After this statement executes, `temp` is as follows:

`temp = {12, 0, 56, 21, 0, 78, 0, 55, 12, 25}`

Next, suppose that you have the following function definition:

```
bool lessThanEqualTo50(int num)                           //Line 12
{
    return (num <= 50);
}
```

The function `lessThanEqualTo50` returns `true` if `num` is less than or equal to 50, otherwise it returns `false`. Consider the following statement:

```
replace_copy_if(intList.begin(), intList.end(),
                temp.begin(), lessThanEqualTo50, 50);     //Line 13
```

This statement uses the function `replace_copy_if` to copy the elements of `intList` into `temp` and replaces all the elements less than 50 with 50. Notice that the fourth parameter of the function `replace_copy_if` is the function `lessThanEqualTo50`. After the statement in Line 13 executes, `temp` is as follows:

`temp = {50, 50, 56, 50, 50, 78, 50, 55, 50, 50}`

We leave it as an exercise for you to write a program that further illustrates how to use the functions `replace`, `replace_if`, `replace_copy`, and `replace_copy_if`; see Programming Exercise 3 at the end of this chapter.

Functions `swap`, `iter_swap`, and `swap_ranges`

The functions `swap`, `iter_swap`, and `swap_ranges` are used to swap elements. These functions are defined in the header file `algorithm`. The prototypes of these functions are as follows:

```
template <class Type>
void swap(Type& object1, Type& object2);

template <class forwardItr1, class forwardItr2>
void iter_swap(forwardItr1 first, forwardItr2 second);
```

```
template <class forwardItr1, class forwardItr2>
forwardItr2 swap_ranges(forwardItr1 first1, forwardItr1 last1,
                        forwardItr2 first2);
```

The function `swap` swaps the values of `object1` and `object2`. The function `iter_swap` swaps the values to which the iterators `first` and `second` point.

The function `swap_ranges` swaps the elements of the range `first1...last1-1` with the consecutive elements starting at position `first2`. It returns the iterator of the second range positioned one past the last element swapped. The program in Example 13-14 illustrates how to use these functions.

EXAMPLE 13-14

```
//***************************************************************
// Author: D.S. Malik
//
// This program shows how the STL functions swap, iter_swap,
// and swap_ranges work.
//***************************************************************

#include <iostream>                                    //Line 1
#include <algorithm>                                   //Line 2
#include <vector>                                       //Line 3
#include <iterator>                                     //Line 4

using namespace std;                                    //Line 5

int main()                                              //Line 6
{                                                       //Line 7
    char cList[10] = {'A', 'B', 'C', 'D', 'F',
                      'G', 'H', 'I', 'J', 'K'};          //Line 8

    vector<char> charList(cList, cList + 10);           //Line 9
    vector<char>::iterator  charItr;                    //Line 10

    ostream_iterator<char> screen(cout, " ");           //Line 11

    cout << "Line 12: Character list: ";                //Line 12
    copy(charList.begin(), charList.end(), screen);     //Line 13
    cout << endl;                                        //Line 14
        //swap
    swap(charList[0], charList[1]);                     //Line 15

    cout << "Line 16: Character list after swapping the "
         << "first and second elements: " << endl;       //Line 16
    copy(charList.begin(), charList.end(), screen);     //Line 17
    cout << endl;                                        //Line 18

        //iter_swap
    iter_swap(charList.begin() + 2,
              charList.begin() + 3);                    //Line 19
```

1
3

```
        cout << "Line 20: Character list after swapping the "
             << "third and fourth elements: " << endl;      //Line 20
        copy(charList.begin(), charList.end(), screen);      //Line 21
        cout << endl;                                        //Line 22

        charItr = charList.begin() + 4;                      //Line 23
        iter_swap(charItr, charItr + 1);                     //Line 24

        cout << "Line 25: Character list after swapping the "
             << "fifth and sixth elements: " << endl;        //Line 25
        copy(charList.begin(), charList.end(), screen);      //Line 26
        cout << endl << endl;                                //Line 27

        int list[10] = {1, 2, 3, 4, 5, 6, 7, 8, 9, 10};      //Line 28

        vector<int> intList(list, list + 10);                //Line 29

        ostream_iterator<int> screenOut(cout, " ");          //Line 30

        cout << "Line 31: intList: ";                        //Line 31
        copy(intList.begin(), intList.end(), screenOut);     //Line 32
        cout << endl;                                        //Line 33

            //swap_ranges
        swap_ranges(intList.begin(), intList.begin() + 4,
                    intList.begin() + 5);                    //Line 34

        cout << "Line 35: intList after swapping the first "
             << "four elements with the \n        four elements "
             << "starting at the sixth element of intList: "
             << endl;                                        //Line 35
        copy(intList.begin(), intList.end(), screenOut);     //Line 36
        cout << endl;                                        //Line 37

        return 0;                                            //Line 38
}                                                            //Line 39
```

Sample Run:

```
Line 12: Character list: A B C D F G H I J K
Line 16: Character list after swapping the first and second elements:
B A C D F G H I J K
Line 20: Character list after swapping the third and fourth elements:
B A D C F G H I J K
Line 25: Character list after swapping the fifth and sixth elements:
B A D C G F H I J K

Line 31: intList: 1 2 3 4 5 6 7 8 9 10
Line 35: intList after swapping the first four elements with
        four elements starting at the sixth element of intList:
6 7 8 9 5 1 2 3 4 10
```

The statement in Line 9 creates the vector `charList` and initializes it using the array `cList` declared in Line 8. The statement in Line 13 outputs the values of `charList`. The statement in Line 15 swaps the first and second elements of `charList`. The statement in Line 19, using the function `iter_swap`, swaps the third and fourth elements of `charList`. (Recall that the position of the first element in `charList` is 0.) After the statement in Line 23 executes, `charItr` points to the fifth element of `charList`. The statement in Line 24 uses the iterator `charItr` to swap the fifth and sixth elements of `charList`. The statement in Line 26 outputs the values of the elements of `charList`. (In the output, the line marked Line 25 contains the output of Lines 25 through 27 of the program.)

The statement in Line 29 creates the vector `intList` and initializes it using the array declared in Line 28. The statement in Line 32 outputs the values of the elements of `intList`. The statement in Line 34 uses the function `swap_ranges` to swap the first four elements of `intList` with the four elements of `intList` starting at the sixth element of `intList`. The statement in Line 36 outputs the elements of `intList`. (In the output, the line marked Line 35 contains the output of Lines 35 through 37 of the program.)

Functions `search`, `search_n`, `sort`, and `binary_search`

The functions `search`, `search_n`, `sort`, and `binary_search` are used to search elements. These functions are defined in the header file `algorithm`.

The prototypes of the function `search` are as follows:

```
template <class forwardItr1, class forwardItr2>
forwardItr1 search(forwardItr1 first1, forwardItr1 last1,
                   forwardItr2 first2, forwardItr2 last2);

template <class forwardItr1, class forwardItr2,
          class binaryPredicate>
forwardItr1 search(forwardItr1 first1, forwardItr1 last1,
                   forwardItr2 first2, forwardItr2 last2,
                   binaryPredicate op);
```

Given two ranges of elements, `first1...last1-1` and `first2...last2-1`, the function `search` searches the first element in the range `first1...last1-1` where the range `first2...last2-1` occurs as a subrange of `first1...last1-1`. The first form makes the equality comparison between the elements of the two ranges. For the second form, the comparison `op(elemFirstRange, elemSecondRange)` must be `true`. If a match is found, the function returns the position in the range `first1...last1-1` where the match occurs; otherwise, the function returns `last1`.

The prototypes of the function `search_n` are as follows:

```
template <class forwardItr, class size, class Type>
forwardItr search_n(forwardItr first, forwardItr last,
                    size count, const Type& value);
```

1
3

```
template <class forwardItr, class size, class Type,
         class binaryPredicate>
forwardItr search_n(forwardItr first, forwardItr last,
                    size count, const Type& value,
                    binaryPredicate op);
```

Given a range of elements first...last-1, the function search_n searches count for any consecutive occurrences of value. The first form returns the position in the range first...last-1 where a subsequence of count consecutive elements have values equal to value. The second form returns the position in the range first...last-1 where a subsequence of count consecutive elements exists for which op(elemRange, value) is true. If no match is found, both forms return last.

The prototypes of the function sort are as follows:

```
template <class randomAccessItr>
void sort(randomAccessItr first, randomAccessItr last);
```

```
template <class randomAccessItr, class compare>
void sort(randomAccessItr first, randomAccessItr last,
         compare op);
```

The first form of the sort function reorders the elements in the range first...last-1 in ascending order. The second form reorders the elements according to the criteria specified by op.

The prototypes of the function binary_search are as follows:

```
template <class forwardItr, class Type>
bool binary_search(forwardItr first, forwardItr last,
                   const Type& searchValue);
```

```
template <class forwardItr, class Type, class compare>
bool binary_search(forwardItr first, forwardItr last,
                   const Type& searchValue, compare op);
```

The first form returns true if searchValue is found in the range first...last-1, and false otherwise. The second form uses a function object, op, that specifies the search criteria.

Example 13-15 illustrates how to use these searching and sorting functions.

EXAMPLE 13-15

```
//*************************************************************
// Author: D.S. Malik
//
// This program shows how the STL functions search, search_n,
// sort, and binary_search work.
//*************************************************************
```

```cpp
#include <iostream>                                      //Line 1
#include <algorithm>                                     //Line 2
#include <iterator>                                      //Line 3
#include <vector>                                        //Line 4

using namespace std;                                     //Line 5

int main()                                               //Line 6
{                                                        //Line 7
    int intList[15] = {12, 34, 56, 34, 34, 78, 38, 43,
                       12, 25, 34, 56, 62, 5, 49};       //Line 8

    vector<int> vecList(intList, intList + 15);          //Line 9
    int list[2] = {34, 56};                              //Line 10

    vector<int>::iterator location;                      //Line 11

    ostream_iterator<int> screenOut(cout, " ");          //Line 12

    cout << "Line 13: vecList: ";                        //Line 13
    copy(vecList.begin(), vecList.end(), screenOut);     //Line 14
    cout << endl;                                        //Line 15

    cout << "Line 16: list: ";                           //Line 16
    copy(list, list + 2, screenOut);                     //Line 17
    cout << endl;                                        //Line 18

        //search
    location = search(vecList.begin(), vecList.end(),
                      list, list + 2);                   //Line 19

    if (location != vecList.end())                       //Line 20
       cout << "Line 21: list found in vecList. The "
            << "first occurrence of \n    list in vecList "
            << "is at position: "
            << (location - vecList.begin()) << endl;     //Line 21
    else                                                 //Line 22
        cout << "Line 23: list is not in vecList"
             << endl;                                    //Line 23

        //search_n
    location = search_n(vecList.begin(), vecList.end(),
                        2, 34);                           //Line 24

    if (location != vecList.end())                       //Line 25
        cout << "Line 26: Two consecutive occurrences of "
             << "34 found in \n    vecList at position: "
             << (location - vecList.begin()) << endl;    //Line 26
    else                                                 //Line 27
        cout << "Line 28: Two consecutive occurrences "
             << "of 34 not in vecList" << endl;          //Line 28
```

13

```
        //sort
    sort(vecList.begin(), vecList.end());                   //Line 29

    cout << "Line 30: vecList after sorting:"
           << endl << "      ";                              //Line 30
    copy(vecList.begin(), vecList.end(), screenOut);         //Line 31
    cout << endl;                                            //Line 32

        //binary_search
    bool found;                                              //Line 33

    found = binary_search(vecList.begin(),
                          vecList.end(), 78);                //Line 34

    if (found)                                               //Line 35
        cout << "Line 36: 43 found in vecList " << endl;     //Line 36
    else                                                     //Line 37
        cout << "Line 38: 43 is not in vecList" << endl;     //Line 38

    return 0;                                                //Line 39
}                                                            //Line 40
```

Sample Run:

```
Line 13: vecList: 12 34 56 34 34 78 38 43 12 25 34 56 62 5 49
Line 16: list: 34 56
Line 21: list found in vecList. The first occurrence of
    list in vecList is at position: 1
Line 26: Two consecutive occurrences of 34 found in
    vecList at position: 3
Line 30: vecList after sorting:
    5 12 12 25 34 34 34 34 38 43 49 56 56 62 78
Line 36: 43 found in vecList
```

The statement in Line 9 creates a vector, vecList, and initializes it using the array intList created in Line 8. The statement in Line 10 creates an array, list, of two components and initializes list. The statement in Line 14 outputs vecList. The statement in Line 19 uses the function search and searches vecList to find the position (of the first occurrence) in vecList where list occurs as a subsequence. The statements in Lines 20 through 23 output the result of the search; see the line marked Line 21 in the output.

The statement in Line 24 uses the function search_n to find the position in vecList where two consecutive instances of 34 occur. The statements in Lines 25 through 28 output the result of the search.

The statement in Line 29 uses the function sort to sort vecList. The statement in Line 31 outputs vecList. In the output, the line marked Line 30 contains the output of the statements in Lines 30 through 32 of the program.

The statement in Line 34 uses the function binary_search to search vecList. The statements in Lines 35 through 38 output the search result.

Functions `adjacent_find`, `merge`, and `inplace_merge`

The algorithm `adjacent_find` is used to find the first occurrence of consecutive elements that meet certain criteria. The prototypes of the functions implementing this algorithm are as follows:

```
template <class forwardItr>
forwardItr adjacent_find(forwardItr first, forwardItr last);

template <class forwardItr, class binaryPredicate>
forwardItr adjacent_find(forwardItr first, forwardItr last,
                         binaryPredicate op);
```

The first form of `adjacent_find` uses the equality criteria; that is, it looks for the first consecutive occurrence of the same element. In the second form, the algorithm returns an iterator to the element in the range `first...last-1` for which `op(elem, nextElem)` is `true`, where `elem` is an element in the range `first...last-1` and `nextElem` is an element in this range next to `elem`. If no matching elements are found, both algorithms return `last`.

Suppose that `intList` is a list container of type `int`. Further assume that `intList` is as follows:

```
intList = {0, 1, 1, 2, 3, 4, 4, 5, 6, 6};    //Line 1
```

Consider the following statements:

```
list<int>::iterator listItr;                            //Line 2
listItr = adjacent_find(intList.begin(), intList.end());//Line 3
```

The statement in Line 2 declares `listItr` to be a `list` iterator that can point to any `list` container of type `int`. The statement in Line 3 uses the function `adjacent_find` to find the position of the (first set of) consecutive identical elements. The function returns a pointer to the first set of consecutive elements, which is stored in `listItr`. After the statement in Line 3 executes, `listItr` points to the second element of `intList`.

Now suppose that `vecList` is a `vector` container of type `int`. Further assume that `vecList` is as follows:

```
vecList = {1, 3, 5, 7, 9, 0, 2, 4, 6, 8};    //Line 4
```

Consider the following statements:

```
vector<int>::iterator intItr;                   //Line 5
intItr = adjacent_find(vecList.begin(), vecList.end(),
                       greater<int>());         //Line 6
```

The statement in Line 5 declares `intItr` to be a `vector` iterator that can point to any `vector` container of type `int`. The statement in Line 6 uses the second form of the function `adjacent_find` to find the first element of `vecList` that is greater than the following element of `vecList`. Notice that the third parameter of the function `adjacent_find` is the binary predicate `greater`, which returns the position in `vecList` where the first element is greater than the second element. The returned position is stored in the iterator `intItr`. After the statement in Line 6 executes, `intItr` points to the element 9.

Next we discuss the algorithm merge. The algorithm merge merges the sorted lists. The result is a sorted list. Both lists must be sorted according to the same criteria. For example, both lists should be in either ascending or descending order. The prototypes of the functions to implement the merge algorithms are as follows:

```
template <class inputItr1, class inputItr2,
        class outputItr>
outputItr merge(inputItr1 first1, inputItr1 last1,
            inputItr2 first2, inputItr2 last2,
            outputItr destFirst);

template <class inputItr1, class inputItr2,
        class outputItr, class binaryPredicate>
outputItr merge(inputItr1 first1, inputItr1 last1,
            inputItr2 first2, inputItr2 last2,
            outputItr destFirst, binaryPredicate op);
```

Both forms of the algorithm merge merge the elements of the sorted ranges first1...last1-1 and first2...last2-1. The destination range beginning with the iterator destFirst contains the merged elements. The first form uses the less-than operator, <, for ordering the elements. The second form uses the binary predicate op to order the elements; that is, op(elemRange1, elemRange2) must be true. Both forms return the position after the last copied element in the destination range. Moreover, the source ranges are not modified and the destination range should not overlap with the source ranges.

Consider the following statements:

```
int list1[5] = {0, 2, 4, 6, 8};          //Line 7
int list2[5] = {1, 3, 5, 7, 9};          //Line 8

list<int> intList;                       //Line 9
merge(list1, list1 + 5, list2, list2 + 5,
      back_inserter(intList));            //Line 10
```

The statements in Lines 7 and 8 create the sorted arrays list1 and list2. The statement in Line 9 declares intList to be a list container of type int. The statement in Line 10 uses the function merge to merge list1 and list2. The third parameter of the function merge, in Line 10, is a call to back_inserter, which places the merged list into intList. After the statement in Line 10 executes, intList contains the merged list, that is,

```
intList = {0, 1, 2, 3, 4, 5, 6, 7, 8, 9}
```

The algorithm inplace_merge is used to combine the sorted consecutive sequence. The prototypes of the functions implementing this algorithm are as follows:

```
template <class biDirectionalItr>
void inplace_merge(biDirectionalItr first,
            biDirectionalItr middle,
            biDirectionalItr last);
```

```
template <class biDirectionalItr, class binaryPredicate>
void inplace_merge(biDirectionalItr first,
                   biDirectionalItr middle,
                   biDirectionalItr last,
                   binaryPredicate op);
```

Both forms merge the sorted consecutive sequences `first...middle-1` and `middle...last-1`. The merged elements overwrite the two ranges beginning at `first`. The first form uses the less-than criterion to merge the two consecutive sequences. The second form uses the binary predicate `op` to merge the sequences; that is, for the elements of the two sequences, `op(elemSeq1, elemSeq2)` must be `true`. For example, suppose that

`vecList = {1, 3, 5, 7, 9, 2, 4, 6, 8}`

where `vecList` is a vector container. Further suppose that `vecItr` is a vector iterator pointing to element 2. Then, after the execution of the statement

`inplace_merge(vecList.begin(), vecItr, vecList.end());`

the elements in `vecList` are in the following order:

`vecList = {1, 2, 3, 4, 5, 6, 7, 8, 9}`

We leave it as an exercise for you to write a program that further illustrates how to use the functions `adjacent_find`, `merge`, and `inplace_merge`; see Programming Exercise 4 at the end of this chapter.

Functions `reverse`, `reverse_copy`, `rotate`, and `rotate_copy`

The algorithm `reverse` reverses the order of the elements in a given range. The prototype of the function to implement the algorithm `reverse` is as follows:

```
template <class biDirectionalItr>
void reverse(biDirectionalItr first, biDirectionalItr last);
```

The elements in the range `first...last-1` are reversed. For example, if `vecList = {1, 2, 5, 3, 4}`, then the elements in reverse order are `vecList = {4, 3, 5, 2, 1}`.

The algorithm `reverse_copy` reverses the elements of a given range while copying into a destination range. The source is not modified. The prototype of the function implementing the `reverse_copy` algorithm is as follows:

```
template <class biDirectionalItr, class outputItr>
outputItr reverse_copy(biDirectionalItr first,
                       biDirectionalItr last,
                       outputItr destFirst);
```

The elements in the range `first...last-1` are copied in reverse order at the destination beginning with `destFirst`. The function also returns the position one past the last element copied at the destination.

The algorithm `rotate` rotates the elements of a given range. Its prototype is as follows:

```
template <class forwardItr>
void rotate(forwardItr first, forwardItr newFirst,
            forwardItr last);
```

The elements in the range `first...newFirst-1` are moved to the end of the range. The element specified by `newFirst` becomes the first element of the range. For example, suppose that

```
vecList = {3, 5, 4, 0, 7, 8, 2, 5}
```

and the iterator `vecItr` points to 0. Then, after the statement

```
rotate(vecList.begin(), vecItr, vecList.end());
```

executes, `vecList` is as follows:

```
vecList = {0, 7, 8, 2, 5, 3, 5, 4}
```

The algorithm `rotate_copy` is a combination of `rotate` and `copy`. That is, the elements of the source are copied at the destination in a rotated order. The source is not modified. The prototype of the function implementing this algorithm is as follows:

```
template <class forwardItr, class outputItr>
outputItr rotate_copy(forwardItr first, forwardItr middle,
                      forwardItr last,
                      outputItr destFirst);
```

The elements in the range `first...last-1` are copied into the destination range beginning with `destFirst` in the rotated order so that the element specified by `middle` in the range `first...last-1` becomes the first element of the destination. The function also returns the position one past the last element copied at the destination.

The algorithms `reverse`, `reverse_copy`, `rotate`, and `rotate_copy` are contained in the header file `algorithm`. The program in Example 13-16 illustrates how to use these algorithms.

EXAMPLE 13-16

```
//************************************************************
// Author: D.S. Malik
//
// This program shows how the STL functions reverse,
// reverse_copy, rotate, and rotate_copy work.
//************************************************************

#include <iostream>                                    //Line 1
#include <algorithm>                                   //Line 2
#include <iterator>                                    //Line 3
#include <list>                                        //Line 4
```

```
using namespace std;                                    //Line 5

int main()                                              //Line 6
{                                                       //Line 7
    int temp[10] = {1, 3, 5, 7, 9, 0, 2, 4, 6, 8};      //Line 8

    list<int> intList(temp, temp + 10);                 //Line 9
    list<int> resultList;                               //List 10
    list<int>::iterator listItr;                        //Line 11

    ostream_iterator<int> screen(cout, " ");            //Line 12

    cout << "Line 13: intList: ";                       //Line 13
    copy(intList.begin(), intList.end(), screen);       //Line 14
    cout << endl;                                        //Line 15

    reverse(intList.begin(), intList.end());      //reverse Line 16

    cout << "Line 17: intList after reversal: ";        //Line 17
    copy(intList.begin(), intList.end(), screen);       //Line 18
    cout << endl;                                        //Line 19

    reverse_copy(intList.begin(), intList.end(),
            back_inserter(resultList)); //reverse_copy Line 20

    cout << "Line 21: resultList: ";                    //Line 21
    copy(resultList.begin(), resultList.end(), screen); //Line 22
    cout << endl;                                        //Line 23

    listItr = intList.begin();                          //Line 24
    listItr++;                                           //Line 25
    listItr++;                                           //Line 26

    cout << "Line 27: intList before rotating: ";       //Line 27
    copy(intList.begin(), intList.end(), screen);       //Line 28
    cout << endl;                                        //Line 29

    rotate(intList.begin(), listItr, intList.end());    //Line 30

    cout << "Line 31: intList after rotating: ";        //Line 31
    copy(intList.begin(), intList.end(), screen);       //Line 32
    cout << endl;                                        //Line 33

    resultList.clear();                                 //Line 34

    rotate_copy(intList.begin(), listItr, intList.end(),
            back_inserter(resultList)); //rotate_copy Line 35

    cout << "Line 36: intList after rotating and "
        << "copying: ";                                 //Line 36
    copy(intList.begin(), intList.end(), screen);       //Line 37
    cout << endl;                                        //Line 38
```

1
3

```
    cout << "Line 39: resultList after rotating and "
         << "copying: ";                                 //Line 39
    copy(resultList.begin(), resultList.end(), screen);  //Line 40
    cout << endl;                                         //Line 41

    resultList.clear();                                   //Line 42

    rotate_copy(intList.begin(),
                find(intList.begin(),
                intList.end(), 6), intList.end(),
                back_inserter(resultList));               //Line 43

    cout << "Line 44: resultList after rotating and "
         << "copying: ";                                  //Line 44
    copy(resultList.begin(), resultList.end(),
         screen);                                         //Line 45
    cout << endl;                                         //Line 46

    return 0;                                             //Line 47
}                                                         //Line 48
```

Sample Run:

```
Line 13: intList: 1 3 5 7 9 0 2 4 6 8
Line 17: intList after reversal: 8 6 4 2 0 9 7 5 3 1
Line 21: resultList: 1 3 5 7 9 0 2 4 6 8
Line 27: intList before rotating: 8 6 4 2 0 9 7 5 3 1
Line 31: intList after rotating: 4 2 0 9 7 5 3 1 8 6
Line 36: intList after rotating and copying: 4 2 0 9 7 5 3 1 8 6
Line 39: resultList after rotating and copying: 0 9 7 5 3 1 8 6 4 2
Line 44: resultList after rotating and copying: 6 4 2 0 9 7 5 3 1 8
```

The preceding output is self-explanatory. The details are left as an exercise for you.

Functions `count`, `count_if`, `max_element`, `min_element`, and `random_shuffle`

The algorithm `count` counts the occurrences of a given value in a given range. The prototype of the function implementing this algorithm is as follows:

```
template <class inputItr, class type>
iterator_traits<inputItr>:: difference_type
    count(inputItr first, inputItr last, const Type& value);
```

The function count returns the number of times the value specified by the parameter value occurs in the range `first...last-1`.

The algorithm `count_if` counts the occurrences of a given value in a given range satisfying a certain criterion. The prototype of the function implementing this algorithm is as follows:

```
template <class inputItr, class unaryPredicate>
iterator_traits<inputItr>::difference_type
    count_if(inputItr first, inputItr last, unaryPredicate op);
```

The function count_if returns the number of elements in the range first...last-1 for which op(elemRange) is true.

The algorithm max is used to determine the maximum of two values. It has two forms, as shown by the following prototypes:

```
template <class Type>
const Type& max(const Type& aVal, const Type& bVal);

template <class Type, class compare>
const Type& max(const Type& aVal, const Type& bVal, compare comp);
```

In the first form, the greater-than operator associated with Type is used. In the second form, the comparison operation specified by comp is used.

The algorithm max_element is used to determine the largest element in a given range. This algorithm has two forms, as shown by the following prototypes:

```
template <class forwardItr>
forwardItr max_element(forwardItr first, forwardItr last);

template <class forwardItr, class compare>
forwardItr max_element(forwardItr first, forwardItr last,
                       compare comp);
```

The first form uses the greater-than operator associated with the data type of the elements in the range first...last-1. In the second form, the comparison operation specified by comp is used. Both forms return an iterator to the element containing the largest value in the range first...last-1.

The algorithm min is used to determine the minimum of two values. It has two forms, as shown by the following prototypes:

```
template <class Type>
const Type& min(const Type& aVal, const Type& bVal);

template <class Type, class compare>
const Type& min(const Type& aVal, const Type& bVal, compare comp);
```

In the first form, the less-than operator associated with Type is used. In the second form, the comparison operation specified by comp is used.

The algorithm min_element is used to determine the smallest element in a given range. This algorithm has two forms, as shown by the following prototypes:

```
template <class forwardItr>
forwardItr min_element(forwardItr first, forwardItr last);

template <class forwardItr, class compare>
forwardItr min_element(forwardItr first, forwardItr last,
                       compare comp);
```

1
3

The first form uses the less-than operator associated with the data type of the elements in the range `first...last-1`. In the second form, the comparison operation specified by `comp` is used. Both forms return an iterator to the element containing the smallest value in the range `first...last-1`.

The algorithm `random_shuffle` is used to randomly order the elements in a given range. There are two forms of this algorithm, as shown by the following prototypes:

```
template <class randomAccessItr>
void random_shuffle(randomAccessItr first,
                    randomAccessItr last);

template <class randomAccessItr, class randomAccessGenerator>
void random_shuffle(randomAccessItr first,
                    randomAccessItr last,
                    randomAccessGenerator rand);
```

The first form reorders the elements in the range `first...last-1` using a uniform distribution random number generator. The second form reorders the elements in the range `first...last-1` using a random number-generating function object or a pointer to a function.

Example 13-17 illustrates how to use these functions.

EXAMPLE 13-17

```
//************************************************************
// Author: D.S. Malik
//
// This program shows how the STL functions count, count_if,
// max_element, min_element, and random_shuffle work.
//************************************************************

#include <iostream>                                      //Line 1
#include <cctype>                                         //Line 2
#include <algorithm>                                      //Line 3
#include <iterator>                                       //Line 4
#include <vector>                                         //Line 5

using namespace std;                                      //Line 6

int main()                                                //Line 7
{                                                         //Line 8
    char cList[10] = {'Z', 'a', 'Z', 'B', 'Z',
                      'c', 'D', 'e', 'F', 'Z'};           //Line 9

    vector<char> charList(cList, cList + 10);             //Line 10

    ostream_iterator<char> screen(cout, " ");             //Line 11

    cout << "Line 12: charList: ";                        //Line 12
    copy(charList.begin(), charList.end(), screen);       //Line 13
    cout << endl;                                         //Line 14
```

```
    int noOfZs = count(charList.begin(), charList.end(),
                       'Z');                            //count; Line 15

    cout << "Line 16: Number of Z\'s in charList:"
         << noOfZs << endl;                             //Line 16

    int noOfUpper = count_if (charList.begin(), charList.end(),
                       isupper);                 //count_if; Line 17

    cout << "Line 18: Number of uppercase letters in "
         << "charList: " << noOfUpper << endl;          //Line 18

    int list[10] = {12, 34, 56, 21, 34,
                    78, 34, 55, 12, 25};                //Line 19

    ostream_iterator<int> screenOut(cout, " ");         //Line 20

    cout << "Line 21: list: ";                          //Line 21
    copy(list, list + 10, screenOut);                   //Line 22
    cout << endl;                                       //Line 23

    int *maxLoc = max_element(list,
                         list + 10);  //max_element; Line 24

    cout << "Line 25: Largest element in list: "
         << *maxLoc << endl;                            //Line 25

    int *minLoc = min_element(list,
                         list + 10); //min_element; Line 26

    cout << "Line 27: Smallest element in list: "
         << *minLoc << endl;                            //Line 27

    random_shuffle(list, list + 10);     //random_shuffle; Line 28

    cout << "Line 29: list after random shuffle: ";     //Line 29
    copy(list, list + 10, screenOut);                   //Line 30
    cout << endl;                                       //Line 31

    return 0;                                           //Line 32
}                                                       //Line 33
```

Sample Run:

```
Line 12: charList: Z a Z B Z c D e F Z
Line 16: Number of Z's in charList:4
Line 18: Number of uppercase letters in charList: 7
Line 21: list: 12 34 56 21 34 78 34 55 12 25
Line 25: Largest element in list: 78
Line 27: Smallest element in list: 12
Line 29: list after random shuffle: 12 34 25 56 12 78 55 21 34 34
```

The preceding output is self-explanatory. The details are left as an exercise for you.

Functions `for_each` and `transform`

The algorithm `for_each` is used to access and process each element in a given range by applying a function, which is passed as a parameter. The prototype of the function implementing this algorithm is as follows:

```
template <class inputItr, class function>
function for_each(inputItr first, inputItr last, function func);
```

The function specified by the parameter `func` is applied to each element in the range `first...last-1`. The function `func` can modify the element. The returned value of the function `for_each` is usually ignored.

The algorithm `transform` has two forms. The prototypes of the functions implementing this algorithm are as follows:

```
template <class inputItr, class outputItr,
          class unaryOperation>
outputItr transform(inputItr first, inputItr last,
                    outputItr destFirst,
                    unaryOperation op);

template <class inputItr1, class inputItr2,
          class outputItr, class binaryOperation>
outputItr transform(inputItr1 first1, inputItr1 last,
                    inputItr2 first2,
                    outputItr destFirst,
                    binaryOperation bOp);
```

The first form of the function `transform` has four parameters. This function creates a sequence of elements at the destination, beginning with `destFirst`, by applying the unary operation `op` to each element in the range `first1...last-1`. This function returns the position one past the last element copied at the destination.

The second form of the function `transform` has five parameters. The function creates a sequence of elements by applying the binary operation `bOp`—that is `bOp(elemRange1, elemRange2)`—to the corresponding elements in the range `first1...last1-1` and the range beginning with `first2`. The resulting sequence is placed at the destination beginning with `destFirst`. The function returns the position one element past the last element copied at the destination.

Example 13-18 illustrates how to use these functions.

EXAMPLE 13-18

```
//*****************************************************************
// Author: D.S. Malik
//
// This program shows how the STL functions for_each and
// transform work.
//*****************************************************************
```

```
#include <iostream>                                      //Line 1
#include <cctype>                                        //Line 2
#include <algorithm>                                     //Line 3
#include <iterator>                                      //Line 4
#include <vector>                                        //Line 5

using namespace std;                                     //Line 6

void doubleNum(int& num);                                //Line 7

int main()                                               //Line 8
{                                                        //Line 9
    char cList[5] = {'a', 'b', 'c', 'd', 'e'};           //Line 10

    vector<char> charList(cList, cList + 5);             //Line 11

    ostream_iterator<char> screen(cout, " ");            //Line 12

    cout << "Line 13: charList: ";                       //Line 13
    copy(charList.begin(), charList.end(), screen);      //Line 14
    cout << endl;                                        //Line 15

    transform(charList.begin(), charList.end(),
              charList.begin(), toupper);                //Line 16

    cout << "Line 17: charList after changing all lowercase"
         << " letters to \n          uppercase: ";       //Line 17
    copy(charList.begin(), charList.end(), screen);      //Line 18
    cout << endl;                                        //Line 19

    int list[7] = {2, 8, 5, 1, 7, 11, 3};                //Line 20

    ostream_iterator<int> screenOut(cout, " ");          //Line 21

    cout << "Line 22: list: ";                           //Line 22
    copy(list, list + 7, screenOut);                     //Line 23
    cout << endl;                                        //Line 24

    cout << "Line 25: The effect of the for_each "
         << "function: ";                                //Line 25
    for_each(list, list + 7, doubleNum);                 //Line 26
    cout << endl;                                        //Line 27

    cout << "Line 28: list after a call to the for_each "
         << "function: ";                                //Line 28
    copy(list, list + 7, screenOut);                     //Line 29
    cout << endl;                                        //Line 30

    return 0;                                            //Line 31
}                                                        //Line 32
```

```
void doubleNum(int& num)                                    //Line 33
{                                                           //Line 34
    num = 2 * num;                                          //Line 35
    cout << num << " ";                                     //Line 36
}                                                           //Line 37
```

Sample Run:

```
Line 13: cList: a b c d e
Line 17: cList after changing all lowercase letters to
         uppercase: A B C D E
Line 22: list: 2 8 5 1 7 11 3
Line 25: The effect of the for_each function: 4 16 10 2 14 22 6
Line 28: list after a call to the for_each function: 4 16 10 2 14 22 6
```

The statement in Line 16 uses the function `transform` to change every lowercase letter of `cList` into its uppercase counterpart. In the output, the line marked Line 17 contains the output of the statements in Lines 17 through 19 in the program. Notice that the fourth parameter of the function `transform` (in Line 16) is the function `toupper` from the header file `cctype`.

The statement in Line 26 calls the function `for_each` to process each element in the list using the function `doubleNum`. The function `doubleNum` has a reference parameter, `num`, of type `int`. Moreover, this function doubles the value of `num` and then outputs the value of `num`. Because `num` is a reference parameter, the value of the actual parameter is changed. In the output, the line marked Line 25 contains the output produced by the `cout` statement in the function `doubleNum`, which is passed as the third parameter of the function `for_each` (see Line 26). The statement in Line 29 outputs the values of the elements of `list`. In the output, Line 28 contains the output of the statements in Lines 28 through 29 of the program.

Functions `includes`, `set_intersection`, `set_union`, `set_difference`, and `set_symmetric_difference`

This section describes the set theory operations `includes` (subset), `set_intersection`, `set_union`, `set_difference`, and `set_symmetric_difference`. These algorithms assume that the elements within each given range are already sorted.

The algorithm `includes` determines whether the elements in one range appear in another range. This function has two forms, as shown by the following prototypes:

```
template <class inputItr1, class inputItr2>
bool includes(inputItr1 first1, inputItr1 last1,
              inputItr2 first2, inputItr2 last2);

template <class inputItr1, class inputItr2,
          class binaryPredicate>
bool includes(inputItr1 first1, inputItr1 last1,
              inputItr2 first2, inputItr2 last2,
              binaryPredicate op);
```

Both forms of the function `includes` assume that the elements in the ranges `first1...last1-1` and `first2...last2-1` are sorted according to the same sorting criterion. The function returns `true` if all the elements in the range `first2...last2-1` are also in `first1...last1-1`. In other words, the function returns `true` if `first1...last1-1` contains all the elements in the range `first2...last2-1`. The first form assumes that the elements in both ranges are in ascending order. The second form uses the operation `op` to determine the ordering of the elements.

Example 13-19 illustrates how the function `includes` works.

EXAMPLE 13-19

```cpp
//***************************************************************
// Author: D.S. Malik
//
// This program shows how the STL function includes works.
// This function assumes that the elements in the given ranges
// are ordered according to some sorting criterion.
//***************************************************************

#include <iostream>                                          //Line 1
#include <algorithm>                                         //Line 2

using namespace std;                                         //Line 3

int main()                                                   //Line 4
{                                                            //Line 5
    char setA[5] = {'A', 'B', 'C', 'D', 'E'};                //Line 6
    char setB[10] = {'A', 'B', 'C', 'D', 'E',
                     'F', 'I', 'J', 'K', 'L'};               //Line 7
    char setC[5] = {'A', 'E', 'I', 'O', 'U'};                //Line 8

    ostream_iterator<char> screen(cout, " ");                //Line 9

    cout << "Line 10: setA: ";                               //Line 10
    copy(setA, setA + 5, screen);                            //Line 11
    cout << endl;                                            //Line 12

    cout << "Line 13: setB: ";                               //Line 13
    copy(setB, setB + 10, screen);                           //Line 14
    cout << endl;                                            //Line 15

    cout << "Line 16: setC: ";                               //Line 16
    copy(setC, setC + 5, screen);                            //Line 17
    cout << endl;                                            //Line 18

    if (includes(setB, setB + 10, setA, setA + 5))           //Line 19
        cout << "Line 20: setA is a subset of setB"
             << endl;                                        //Line 20
```

```
        else                                                    //Line 21
            cout << "Line 22: setA is not a subset of setB"
                    << endl;                                     //Line 22

        if (includes(setB, setB + 10, setC, setC + 5))          //Line 23
            cout << "Line 24: setC is a subset of setB"
                    << endl;                                     //Line 24
        else                                                    //Line 25
            cout << "Line 26: setC is not a subset of setB"
                    << endl;                                     //Line 26

        return 0;                                               //Line 27
}                                                               //Line 28
```

Sample Run:

```
Line 10: setA: A B C D E
Line 13: setB: A B C D E F I J K L
Line 16: setC: A E I O U
Line 20: setA is a subset of setB
Line 26: setC is not a subset of setB
```

The preceding output is self-explanatory. The details are left as exercise for you.

The algorithm `set_intersection` is used to find the elements that are common to two ranges of elements. This algorithm has two forms, as shown by the following prototypes:

```
template <class inputItr1, class inputItr2,
        class outputItr>
outputItr set_intersection(inputItr1 first1, inputItr1 last1,
                            inputItr2 first2, inputItr2 last2,
                            outputItr destFirst);

template <class inputItr1, class inputItr2,
        class outputItr, class binaryPredicate>
outputItr set_intersection(inputItr1 first1, inputItr1 last1,
                            inputItr2 first2, inputItr2 last2,
                            outputItr destFirst,
                            binaryPredicate op);
```

Both forms create a sequence of sorted elements that are common to two sorted ranges, `first1...last1-1` and `first2...last2-1`. The created sequence is placed in the container beginning with `destFirst`. Both forms return an iterator positioned one past the last element copied at the destination range. The first form assumes that the elements are in ascending order. The second form assumes that both ranges are sorted using the operation specified by op. The elements in the source ranges are not modified.

Suppose that

```
setA[5] = {2, 4, 5, 7, 8};
setB[7] = {1, 2, 3, 4, 5, 6, 7};
setC[5] = {2, 5, 8, 8, 15};
```

```
setD[6] = {1, 4, 4, 6, 7, 12};
setE[7] = {2, 3, 4, 4, 5, 6, 10};
```

Then

```
AintersectB = {2, 4, 5, 7}
AintersectC = {2, 5, 8}
DintersectE = {4, 4, 6}
```

Notice that because 8 appears only once in setA, 8 appears only once in AintersectC, even though 8 appears twice in setC. However, because 4 appears twice in both setD and setE, 4 also appears twice in DintersectE.

The algorithm set_union is used to find the elements that are contained in two ranges of elements. This algorithm has two forms, as shown by the following prototypes:

```
template <class inputItr1, class inputItr2,
        class outputItr>
outputItr set_union(inputItr1 first1, inputItr1 last1,
                inputItr2 first2, inputItr2 last2,
                outputItr destFirst);

template <class inputItr1, class inputItr2,
        class outputItr, class binaryPredicate>
outputItr set_union(inputItr1 first1, inputItr1 last1,
                inputItr2 first2, inputItr2 last2,
                outputItr result,
                binaryPredicate op);
```

Both forms create a sequence of sorted elements that appear in either two sorted ranges, first1...last1 - 1 or first2...last2 - 1. The created sequence is placed in the container beginning with destFirst. Both forms return an iterator positioned one past the last element copied at the destination range. The first form assumes that the elements are in ascending order. The second form assumes that both ranges are sorted using the operation specified by op. The elements in the source ranges are not modified.

Suppose that you have setA, setB, setC, setD, and setE as defined previously. Then

```
AunionB = {1, 2, 3, 4, 5, 6, 7, 8}
AunionC = {2, 4, 5, 7, 8, 8, 15}
BunionD = {1, 2, 3, 4, 4, 5, 6, 7, 12}
DunionE = {1, 2, 3, 4, 4, 5, 6, 7, 10, 12}
```

Notice that because 8 appears twice in setC, it appears twice in AunionC. Because 4 appears twice in setD and in setE, 4 appears twice in DunionE.

We leave it as an exercise for you to write a program that further illustrates how to use the functions set_union and set_intersection; see Programming Exercise 5 at the end of this chapter.

The algorithm set_difference is used to find the elements in one range of elements that do not appear in another range of elements. This algorithm has two forms, as shown by the following prototypes:

1
3

```
template <class inputItr1, class inputItr2,
          class outputItr>
outputItr set_difference(inputItr1 first1, inputItr1 last1,
                         inputItr2 first2, inputItr2 last2,
                         outputItr destFirst);

template <class inputItr1, class inputItr2,
          class outputItr, class binaryPredicate>
outputItr set_difference(inputItr1 first1, inputItr1 last1,
                         inputItr2 first2, inputItr2 last2,
                         outputItr destFirst,
                         binaryPredicate op);
```

Both forms create a sequence of sorted elements that are in the sorted range `first1...last1-1`, but not in the sorted range `first2...last2-1`. The created sequence is placed in the container beginning with `destFirst`. Both forms return an iterator positioned one past the last element copied at the destination range. The first form assumes that the elements are in ascending order. The second form assumes that both ranges are sorted using the operation specified by `op`. The elements in the source ranges are not modified.

Suppose that

```
setA = {2, 4, 5, 7, 8}
setC = {1, 5, 6, 8, 15}
setD = {2, 5, 5, 6, 9}
setE = {1, 5, 7, 9, 12}
```

Then

```
AdifferenceC = {2, 4, 7}
DdifferenceE = {2, 5, 6}
```

Because 5 appears twice in `setD` but only once in `setE`, 5 appears once in `DdifferenceE`.

The algorithm `set_symmetric_difference` has two forms, as shown by the following prototypes:

```
template <class inputItr1, class inputItr2, class outputItr>
outputItr set_symmetric_difference(inputItr1 first1,
                                   inputItr1 last1,
                                   inputItr2 first2,
                                   inputItr2 last2,
                                   outputItr destFirst);

template <class inputItr1, class inputItr2,
          class outputItr, class binaryPredicate>
outputItr set_symmetric_difference(inputItr1 first1,
                                   inputItr1 last1,
                                   inputItr2 first2,
                                   inputItr2 last2,
                                   outputItr destFirst,
                                   binaryPredicate op);
```

Both forms create a sequence of sorted elements that are in the sorted range `first1...last1-1` but not in `first2...last2-1`, or elements that are in the sorted range `first2...last2-1` but not in `first1...last1-1`. In other words, the sequence of elements created by `set_symmetric_difference` contains the elements that are in `range1_difference_range2` union `range2_difference_range1`. The created sequence is placed in the container beginning with `destFirst`. Both forms return an iterator positioned one past the last element copied at the destination range. The first form assumes that the elements are in ascending order. The second form assumes that both ranges are sorted using the operation specified by `op`. The elements in the source ranges are not modified. It can be shown that the sequence created by `set_symmetric_difference` contains elements that are in `range1_union_range2`, but not in `range1_intersection_range2`.

Suppose that

```
setB = {3, 4, 5, 6, 7, 8, 10}
setC = {1, 5, 6, 8, 15}
setD = {2, 5, 5, 6, 9}
```

Notice that `BdifferenceC = {3, 4, 7, 10}` and `CdifferenceB = {1, 15}`. Therefore,

```
BsymDiffC = {1, 3, 4, 7, 10, 15}
```

Now `DdifferenceC = {2, 5, 9, 15}` and `CdifferenceD = {1, 8, 15}`. Therefore,

```
DsymDiffC = {1, 2, 5, 8, 9, 15}
```

Example 13-20 further illustrates how the functions `set_difference` and `set_symmetric_difference` work.

EXAMPLE 13-20

Suppose that we have the following statements:

```
int setA[5] = {2, 4, 5, 7, 8};            //Line 1
int setB[7] = {3, 4, 5, 6, 7, 8, 10};     //Line 2
int setC[5] = {1, 5, 6, 8, 15};           //Line 3

int AdifferenceC[5];                      //Line 4
int BsymDiffC[10];                        //Line 5
```

Consider the following statement:

```
set_difference(setA, setA + 5, setC, setC + 5, AdifferenceC);  //Line 6
```

After this statement executes, `AdifferenceC` contains the elements that are in `setA` and not in `setC`, that is,

```
AdifferenceC = {2, 4, 7}                  //Line 7
```

Now consider the following statement:

```
set_symmetric_difference(setB, setB + 7, setC, setC + 5,
                         BsymDiffC);      //Line 8
```

1
3

After this statement executes, `BsymDiffC` contains the elements that are in `setB`, but not in `setC` or the elements that are in `setC`, but not in `setB`, that is,

```
BsymDiffC = {1, 3, 4, 7, 10, 15}                        //Line 9
```

We leave it as an exercise for you to write a program that further illustrates how to use the functions `set_difference` and `set_symmetric_difference`; see Programming Exercise 6 at the end of this chapter.

Functions `accumulate`, `adjacent_difference`, `inner_product`, and `partial_sum`

The algorithms `accumulate`, `adjacent_difference`, `inner_product`, and `partial_sum` are numerical functions and, thus, manipulate numeric data. Each of these functions has two forms. The first form uses the natural operation to manipulate the data. For example, the algorithm `accumulate` finds the sum of all the elements in a given range. In the second form, we can specify the operation to be applied to the elements of the range. For example, rather than add the elements of a given range, we can specify the multiplication operation to the algorithm `accumulate` to multiply the elements of the range. Next, as usual, we give the prototype of each of these algorithms followed by a brief explanation. The algorithms are contained in the header file `numeric`.

```
template <class inputItr, class Type>
Type accumulate(inputItr first, inputItr last, Type init);
```

```
template <class inputItr, class Type, class binaryOperation>
Type accumulate(inputItr first, inputItr last,
                Type init, binaryOperation op);
```

The first form of the algorithm `accumulate` adds all the elements to an initial value specified by the parameter `init`, in the range `first...last-1`. For example, if the value of `init` is `0`, the algorithm returns the sum of all the elements. In the second form, we can specify a binary operation, such as multiplication, to be applied to the elements of the range. For example, if the value of `init` is `1` and the binary operation is multiplication, the algorithm returns the products of the elements in the range.

Next, we describe the algorithm `adjacent_difference`. Its prototypes are as follows:

```
template <class inputItr, class outputItr>
outputItr adjacent_difference(inputItr first, inputItr last,
                              outputItr destFirst);
```

```
template <class inputItr, class outputItr,
          class binaryOperation>
outputItr adjacent_difference(inputItr first, inputItr last,
                              outputItr destFirst,
                              binaryOperation op);
```

The first form creates a sequence of elements in which the first element is the same as the first element in the range `first...last-1`, and all the other elements are the differences of the current and previous elements. For example, if the range of elements is

`{2, 5, 6, 8, 3, 7}`

then the sequence created by the function `adjacent_difference` is

`{2, 3, 1, 2, -5, 4}`

The first element is the same as the first element in the original range. The second element is equal to the second element in the original range minus the first element in the original range. Similarly, the third element is equal to the third element in the original range minus the second element in the original range, and so on.

In the second form of `adjacent_difference`, the binary operation op is applied to the elements in the range. The resulting sequence is copied at the destination specified by `destFirst`. For example, if the sequence is {2, 5, 6, 8, 3, 7} and the operation is multiplication, the resulting sequence is {2, 10, 30, 48, 24, 21}.

Both forms return an iterator positioned one past the last element copied at the destination.

Example 13-21 illustrates how the functions **accumulate** and `adjacent_difference` work.

EXAMPLE 13-21

```
//************************************************************
// Author: D.S. Malik
//
// This program shows how the STL numeric algorithms accumulate
// and adjacent_difference works.
//************************************************************

#include <iostream>                              //Line 1
#include <algorithm>                             //Line 2
#include <numeric>                               //Line 3
#include <iterator>                              //Line 4
#include <vector>                                //Line 5
#include <functional>                            //Line 6

using namespace std;                             //Line 7

void print(vector<int> vList);                   //Line 8

int main()                                       //Line 9
{                                                //Line 10
    int list[8] = {1, 2, 3, 4, 5, 6, 7, 8};      //Line 11

    vector<int> vecList(list, list + 8);         //Line 12
    vector<int> newVList(8);                     //Line 13
```

13

```
    cout << "Line 14: vecList: ";                        //Line 14
    print(vecList);                                      //Line 15

    int sum = accumulate(vecList.begin(),
                    vecList.end(), 0); //accumulate; Line 16

    cout << "Line 17: Sum of the elements of vecList = "
         << sum << endl;                                 //Line 17

    int product = accumulate(vecList.begin(), vecList.end(),
                    1, multiplies<int>());      //Line 18

    cout << "Line 19: Product of the elements of "
         << "vecList = " << product << endl;             //Line 19

    adjacent_difference(vecList.begin(), vecList.end(),
            newVList.begin()); //adjacent_difference; Line 20

    cout << "Line 21: newVList: ";                       //Line 21
    print(newVList);                                     //Line 22

    adjacent_difference(vecList.begin(), vecList.end(),
            newVList.begin(), multiplies<int>()); //Line 23

    cout << "Line 24: newVList: ";                       //Line 24
    print(newVList);                                     //Line 25

    return 0;                                            //Line 26
}                                                        //Line 27

void print(vector<int> vList)                            //Line 28
{                                                        //Line 29
    ostream_iterator<int> screenOut(cout, " ");          //Line 30

    copy(vList.begin(), vList.end(), screenOut);         //Line 31
    cout << endl;                                        //Line 32
}                                                        //Line 33
```

Sample Run:

```
Line 14: vecList: 1 2 3 4 5 6 7 8
Line 17: Sum of the elements of vecList = 36
Line 19: Product of the elements of vecList = 40320
Line 21: newVList: 1 1 1 1 1 1 1 1
Line 24: newVList: 1 2 6 12 20 30 42 56
```

The preceding output is self-explanatory. The details are left as an exercise for you.

The algorithm `inner_product` is used to manipulate the elements of two ranges. The prototypes of this algorithm are as follows:

```
template <class inputItr1, class inputItr2, class Type>
Type inner_product(inputItr1 first1, inputItr1 last,
                inputItr2 first2, Type init);
```

```
template <class inputItr1, class inputItr2, class Type,
        class binaryOperation1, class binaryOperation2>
Type inner_product(inputItr1 first1, inputItr1 last,
                inputItr2 first2, Type init,
                binaryOperation1 op1, binaryOperation2 op2);
```

The first form multiplies the corresponding elements in the range `first1...last - 1` and the range of elements starting with `first2`, and the products of the elements are added to the value specified by the parameter `init`. To be specific, suppose that `elem1` ranges over the first range and `elem2` ranges over the second range starting with `first2`. The first form computes

```
init = init + elem1 * elem2
```

for all the corresponding elements. For example, suppose that the two ranges are {2, 4, 7, 8} and {1, 4, 6, 9}, and that `init` is 0. The function computes and returns

```
0 + 2 * 1 + 4 * 4 + 7 * 6 + 8 * 9 = 132
```

In the second form, the default addition can be replaced by the operation specified by `op1`, and the default multiplication can be replaced by the operation specified by `op2`. This form, in fact, computes

```
init = init op1 (elem1 op2 elem2);
```

The algorithm `partial_sum` has two forms, as shown by the following prototypes:

```
template <class inputItr, class outputItr>
outputItr partial_sum(inputItr first, inputItr last,
                outputItr destFirst);

template <class inputItr, class randomAccessItr,
        class binaryOperation>
outputItr partial_sum(inputItr first, inputItr last,
                outputItr destFirst, binaryOperation op);
```

The first form creates a sequence of elements in which each element is the sum of all the previous elements in the range `first...last-1` up to the position of the element. For example, the first element of the new sequence is the same as the first element in the range `first...last-1`, the second element is the sum of the first two elements in the range `first...last-1`, the third element of the new sequence is the sum of the first three elements in the range `first...last-1`, and so on. For example, for the sequence of elements

```
{1, 3, 4, 6}
```

the function `partial_sum` generates the following sequence:

```
{1, 4, 8, 14}
```

In the second form, the default addition can be replaced by the operation specified by `op`. For example, if the sequence is

```
{1, 3, 4, 6}
```

and the operation is multiplication, the function `partial_sum` generates the following sequence:

{1, 3, 12, 72}

The created sequence is copied at the destination specified by `destFirst`, and returns an iterator positioned one past the last copied element at the destination.

Example 13-22 further illustrates how the functions `inner_product` and `partial_sum` work.

EXAMPLE 13-22

Suppose that you have the following statement:

```
int list1[8] = {1, 2, 3, 4, 5, 6, 7, 8};        //Line 1
int list2[8] = {2, 4, 5, 7, -9, 11, 12, 14};    //Line 2


vector<int> vecList(list1, list1 + 8);          //Line 3
vector<int> newVList(list2, list2 + 8);         //Line 4

int sum;                                         //Line 5
```

After the statements in Lines 3 and 4 execute,

```
vecList = {1, 2, 3, 4, 5, 6, 7, 8}              //Line 6
newVList = {2, 4, 5, 7, -9, 11, 12, 14}         //Line 7
```

Now consider the following statement:

```
sum = inner_product(vecList.begin(), vecList.end(),
                    newVList.begin(), 0);        //Line 8
```

This statement calculates the inner product of `vecList` and `newVList` and the result is stored in `sum`, that is,

```
sum = 0 + 1 * 2 + 2 * 4 + 3 * 5 + 4 * 7 + 5 * (-9)
        + 6 * 11 + 7 * 12 + 8 * 14
    = 270
```

Now consider the following statement:

```
sum = inner_product(vecList.begin(), vecList.end(),
                    newVList.begin(), 0,
                    plus<int>(), minus<int>());  //Line 9
```

This statement calculates the inner product of `vecList` and `newVList`. The multiplication, `*`, is replaced with minus, `-`, and the result is stored in `sum`, that is,

```
sum = 0 + (1 - 2) + (2 - 4) + (3 - 5) + (4 - 7) + (5 - (-9))
        + (6 - 11) + (7 - 12) + (8 - 14)
    = -10
```

Next consider the following statement:

```
partial_sum(vecList.begin(), vecList.end(),
            newVList.begin());                          //Line 10
```

This statement uses the function `partial_sum` to generate the sequence of elements 1, 3, 6, 10, 15, 21, 28, 36. These elements are assigned to `newVList`, that is,

```
newVList = {1, 3, 6, 10, 15, 21, 28, 36}
```

Next consider the following statement:

```
partial_sum(vecList.begin(), vecList.end(),
            newVList.begin(), multiplies<int>());   //Line 11
```

This statement uses the function `partial_sum` to generate the sequence of elements 1, 2, 6, 24, 120, 720, 5040, 40320. Notice that the statement in Line 11 calculates the partial multiplication of the elements of `vecList` by replacing plus with multiplication. These elements are assigned to `newVList`, that is,

```
newVList = {1, 2, 6, 24, 120, 720, 5040, 40320}
```

We leave it as an exercise for you to write a program that further illustrates how to use the functions `inner_product` and `partial_sum`; see Programming Exercise 7 at the end of this chapter.

QUICK REVIEW

1. The STL provides class templates that process lists, stacks, and queues.
2. The three main components of the STL are containers, iterators, and algorithms.
3. Algorithms are used to manipulate the elements in a container.
4. The main categories of containers are sequence containers, associative containers, and container adapters.
5. The `class pair` allows you to combine two values into a single unit. A function can return two values by using the `class pair`. The `classes map` and `multimap` use the `class pair` to manage their elements.
6. The definition of the `class pair` is contained in the header file `utility`.
7. The function `make_pair` allows you to create pairs without explicitly specifying the type `pair`. The definition of the function `make_pair` is contained in the header file `utility`.
8. Elements in an associative container are automatically sorted according to some ordering criterion. The default ordering criterion is the relational operator less than, <.
9. The predefined associative containers in the STL are `sets`, `multisets`, `maps`, and `multimaps`.

10. Containers of type `set` do not allow duplicates.

11. Containers of type `multiset` allow duplicates.

12. The name of the class defining the container `set` is `set`.

13. The name of the class defining the container `multiset` is `multiset`.

14. The name of the header file containing the definition of the `classes set` and `multiset`, and the definitions of the functions to implement various operations on these containers, is `set`.

15. The operations `insert`, `erase`, and `clear` can be used to insert or delete elements from sets.

16. The containers `map` and `multimap` manage their elements in the form key/value. The elements are automatically sorted according to some sort criteria applied on the key.

17. The default sorting criterion for the key of the containers `map` and `multimap` is the relational operator < (less than). The user can also specify other sorting criteria. For userdefined data types, such as classes, the relational operators must be properly overloaded.

18. The only difference between the containers `map` and `multimap` is that the container `multimap` allows duplicates, whereas the container `map` does not.

19. The name of the class defining the container `map` is `map`.

20. The name of the class defining the container `multimap` is `multimap`.

21. The name of the header file containing the definitions of the `classes map` and `multimap`, and the definitions of the functions to implement various operations on these containers, is `map`.

22. Most of the generic algorithms are contained in the header file `algorithm`.

23. The main categories of STL algorithms are nonmodifying, modifying, numeric, and heap.

24. Nonmodifying algorithms do not modify the elements of the container.

25. Modifying algorithms modify the elements of the container by rearranging, removing, and/or changing the values of the elements.

26. Modifying algorithms that change the order of the elements, not their values, are also called mutating algorithms.

27. Numeric algorithms are designed to perform numeric calculations on the elements of a container.

28. A function object is a class template that overloads the function call operator, `operator()`.

29. The predefined arithmetic function objects are `plus`, `minus`, `multiplies`, `divides`, `modulus`, and `negate`.

30. The predefined relational function objects are `equal_to`, `not_equal_to`, `greater`, `greater_equal`, `less`, and `less_equal`.

31. The predefined logical function objects are `logical_not`, `logical_and`, and `logical_or`.

32. Predicates are special types of function objects that return Boolean values.

33. Unary predicates check a specific property for a single argument; binary predicates check a specific property for a pair—that is, two—of arguments.

34. Predicates are typically used to specify a searching or sorting criterion.

35. In the STL, a predicate must always return the same result for the same value.

36. The functions that modify their internal states cannot be considered predicates.

37. The STL provides three iterators—`back_inserter`, `front_inserter`, and `inserter`—called insert iterators, to insert the elements at the destination.

38. The `back_inserter` uses the `push_back` operation of the container in place of the assignment operator.

39. The `front_inserter` uses the `push_front` operation of the container in place of the assignment operator.

40. Because the `class vector` does not support the `push_front` operation, this iterator cannot be used for the vector container.

41. The `inserter` iterator uses the container's `insert` operation in place of the assignment operator.

42. The function `fill` is used to fill a container with elements; the function `fill_n` is used to fill in the next n elements.

43. The functions `generate` and `generate_n` are used to generate elements and fill a sequence.

44. The functions `find`, `find_if`, `find_end`, and `find_first_of` are used to find the elements in a given range.

45. The function `remove` is used to remove certain elements from a sequence.

46. The function `remove_if` is used to remove elements from a sequence using some criterion.

47. The function `remove_copy` copies the elements in a sequence into another sequence by excluding certain elements from the first sequence.

48. The function `remove_copy_if` copies the elements in a sequence into another sequence by excluding certain elements, using some criterion, from the first sequence.

49. The functions `swap`, `iter_swap`, and `swap_ranges` are used to swap elements.

50. The functions `search`, `search_n`, `sort`, and `binary_search` are used to search elements.

51. The function `adjacent_find` is used to find the first occurrence of consecutive elements satisfying a certain criterion.

1
3

52. The algorithm `merge` merges two sorted lists.

53. The algorithm `inplace_merge` is used to combine two sorted, consecutive sequences.

54. The algorithm `reverse` reverses the order of the elements in a given range.

55. The algorithm `reverse_copy` reverses the elements in a given range while copying into a destination range. The source is not modified.

56. The algorithm `rotate` rotates the elements in a given range.

57. The algorithm `rotate_copy` copies the elements of the source at the destination in a rotated order.

58. The algorithm `count` counts the occurrences of a given value in a given range.

59. The algorithm `count_if` counts the occurrences of a given value in a given range satisfying a certain criterion.

60. The algorithm `max` is used to determine the maximum of two values.

61. The algorithm `max_element` is used to determine the largest element in a given range.

62. The algorithm `min` is used to determine the minimum of two values.

63. The algorithm `min_element` is used to determine the smallest element in a given range.

64. The algorithm `random_shuffle` is used to randomly order the elements in a given range.

65. The algorithm `for_each` is used to access and process each element in a given range by applying a function, which is passed as a parameter.

66. The function `transform` creates a sequence of elements by applying certain operations to each element in a given range.

67. The algorithm `includes` determines whether the elements of one range appear in another range.

68. The algorithm `set_intersection` is used to find the elements that are common to two ranges of elements.

69. The algorithm `set_union` is used to find the elements that are contained in two ranges of elements.

70. The algorithm `set_difference` is used to find the elements in one range of elements that do not appear in another range of elements.

71. Given two ranges of elements, the algorithm `set_symmetric_difference` determines the elements that are in the first range but not the second range, or the elements that are in the second range but not the first range.

72. The algorithms `accumulate`, `adjacent_difference`, `inner_product`, and `partial_sum` are numerical functions and manipulate numeric data.

EXERCISES

1. What is the difference between an STL container and an STL algorithm?

2. Suppose that you have the following statement:

   ```
   pair<int, string> temp;
   ```

   a. Write a C++ statement that stores the pair (1, "Hello") into temp.

   b. Write a C++ statement that outputs the pair stored in temp onto the standard output device.

3. Suppose that you have the following statement:

   ```
   pair<string, string> name;
   ```

   What is the output, if any, of the following statements?

   ```
   name = make_pair("Duckey", "Donald");
   cout << name.first << " " << name.second << endl;
   ```

4. Explain how a set container differs from a map container.

5. a. Declare the map container stateDataMap to store pairs of the form (stateName, capitalName), where stateName and capitalName are variables of type string.

   b. Write C++ statements that add the following pairs to stateDataMap: (Nebraska, Lincoln), (New York, Albany), (Ohio, Columbus), (California, Sacramento), (Massachusetts, Boston), and (Texas, Austin).

   c. Write a C++ statement that outputs the data stored in stateDataMap.

   d. Write a C++ statement that changes the capital of California to Los Angeles.

6. What is the difference between a set and a multiset?

7. What is an STL function object?

8. Suppose that charList is a vector container and:

   ```
   charList = {a, A, B, b, c, d, A, e, f, K}
   ```

   Further suppose that:

   ```
   lastElem = remove_if(charList.begin(), charList.end(), islower);
   ostream_iterator<char> screen(cout, " ");
   ```

   where lastElem is a vector iterator into a vector container of type char. What is the output of the following statement?

   ```
   copy(charList.begin(), lastElem, screen);
   ```

9. Suppose that intList is a vector container and:

   ```
   intList = {18, 24, 24, 5, 11, 56, 27, 24, 2, 24}
   ```

Furthermore, suppose that:

```
vector<int>::iterator lastElem;
ostream_iterator<int> screen(cout, " ");
vector<int> otherList(10);
lastElem = remove_copy(intList.begin(), intList.end(),
                       otherList.begin(), 24);
```

What is the output of the following statement?

```
copy(otherList.begin(), lastElem, screenOut);
```

10. Suppose that `intList` is a `vector` container and:

```
intList = {2, 4, 6, 8, 10, 12, 14, 16}
```

What is the value of `result` after the following statement executes?

```
result = accumulate(intList.begin(), intList.end(), 0);
```

11. Suppose that `intList` is a `vector` container and:

```
intList = {2, 4, 6, 8, 10, 12, 14, 16}
```

What is the value of `result` after the following statement executes?

```
result = accumulate(intList.begin(), intList.end(),
                    0, multiplies<int>());
```

12. Suppose that `setA`, `setB`, `setC`, and `setD` are defined as follows:

```
int setA[] = {3, 4, 5, 8, 9, 12, 14};
int setB[] = {2, 3, 4, 5, 6, 7, 8};
int setC[] = {2, 5, 5, 9};
int setD[] = {4, 4, 4, 6, 7, 12};
```

Further suppose that you have the following declarations:

```
int AunionB[10];
int AunionC[9];
int BunionD[10];
int AintersectB[4];
int AintersectC[2];
```

What is stored in `AunionB`, `AunionC`, `BunionD`, `AintersectB`, and `AintersectC` after the following statements execute?

```
set_union(setA, setA + 7, setB, setB + 7, AunionB);
set_union(setA, setA + 7, setC, setC + 4, AunionC);
```

PROGRAMMING EXERCISES

1. Write a program that illustrates how to use the functions `find` and `find_if`.

2. Write a program that illustrates how to use the functions `find_end` and `find_first_of`.

3. Write a program that illustrates how to use the functions `replace`, `replace_if`, `replace_copy`, and `replace_copy_if`. Your program must use the function `lessThanEqualTo50`, as shown in Example 13-13.

4. Write a program that illustrates how to use the functions `adjacent_find`, `merge`, and `inplace_merge`.

5. Write a program that illustrates how to use the functions `set_union` and `set_intersection`.

6. Write a program that illustrates how to use the functions `set_difference` and `set_symmetric_difference`.

7. Write a program that illustrates how to use the functions `inner_product` and `partial_sum`.

8. **(Stock Market Revisited)** In Programming Exercise 8 of Chapter 4, you are asked to design a program that analyzes the performance of the stocks managed by a local stock trading company and at the end of each day produce a listing of those stocks ordered by the stock symbol. The company's investors also would like see another listing of the stocks, which is ordered by the percent gained by eack stock.

   Because the company also requires you to produce the list ordered by the percent gain/loss, you need to sort the stock list by this component. However, you are not to physically sort the list by the component percent gain/loss; instead, you will provide a logical ordering with respect to this component.

   To do so, add a data member, a vector, to hold the indices of the stock list ordered by the component percent gain/loss. Call this vector `indexByGain`. When printing the list ordered by the component percent gain/loss, use the array `indexByGain` to print the list. The elements of the array `indexByGain` will tell which component of the stock list to print next.

9. Redo the Programming Example Video Store of Chapter 5 so that it uses the STL `class set` to process a list of videos.

10. Redo Programming Exercise 14 of Chapter 5 so that it uses the STL `class set` to process the list of videos rented by the customer and the list of store members.

11. Redo Programming Exercise 15 of Chapter 5 so that it uses the STL `class set` to process the list of videos owned by the store, the list of videos rented by the customer, and the list of store members.

12. Write a program to play Card Guessing Game. You program must give the user the following choices:

   a. Guess only the face value of the card.
   b. Guess only the suit of the card.
   c. Guess both the face value and suit of the card.

   Before the start of the game, create a deck of cards. Before each guess, use the function `random_shuffle` to randomly shuffle the deck.

1
3

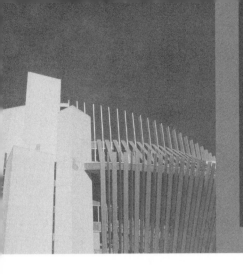

and	and_eq	asm	auto
bitand	bitor	bool	break
case	catch	char	class
compl	const	const_cast	continue
default	delete	do	double
dynamic_cast	else	enum	explicit
export	extern	false	float
for	friend	goto	if
include	inline	int	long
mutable	namespace	new	not
not_eq	operator	or	or_eq
private	protected	public	register
reinterpret_cast	return	short	signed
sizeof	static	static_cast	struct
switch	template	this	throw
true	try	typedef	typeid
typename	union	unsigned	using
virtual	void	volatile	wchar_t
while	xor	xor_eq	

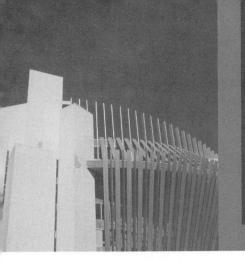

The following table shows the precedence (highest to lowest) and associativity of the operators in C++.

Operator	Associativity
:: (binary scope resolution)	Left to right
:: (unary scope resolution)	Right to left
()	Left to right
[] -> .	Left to right
++ -- (as postfix operators)	Right to left
typeid dynamic_cast	Right to left
static_cast const_cast	Right to left
reinterpret_cast	Right to left
++ -- (as prefix operators) ! + (unary) - (unary)	Right to left
~ & (address of) * (dereference)	Right to left
new delete sizeof	Right to left
->* -- .*	Left to right
* / %	Left to right
+ -	Left to right
<< >>	Left to right
< <= > >=	Left to right
== !=	Left to right
&	Left to right
^	Left to right

Operator	Associativity
|	Left to right
&&	Left to right
||	Left to right
?:	Right to left
= += -= *= /= %=	Right to left
<<= >>= &= |= ^=	Right to left
throw	Right to left
, (the sequencing operator)	Left to right

CHARACTER SETS

ASCII (American Standard Code for Information Interchange)

The following table shows the ASCII character set.

ASCII										
	0	1	2	3	4	5	6	7	8	9
0	nul	soh	stx	etx	eot	enq	ack	bel	bs	ht
1	lf	vt	ff	cr	so	si	dle	dc1	dc2	dc3
2	dc4	nak	syn	etb	can	em	sub	esc	fs	gs
3	rs	us	b	!	"	#	$	%	&	'
4	(	)	*	+	,	-	.	/	0	1
5	2	3	4	5	6	7	8	9	:	;
6	<	=	>	?	@	A	B	C	D	E
7	F	G	H	I	J	K	L	M	N	O
8	P	Q	R	S	T	U	V	W	X	Y
9	Z	[	\	]	^	_	`	a	b	c
10	d	e	f	g	h	i	j	k	l	m
11	n	o	p	q	r	s	t	u	v	w
12	x	y	z	{	|	}	~	del		

The numbers 0-12 in the first column specify the left digit(s), and the numbers 0-9 in the second row specify the right digit of each character in the ASCII data set. For example, the character in the row marked 6 (the number in the first column) and the column marked 5 (the number in the second row) is A. Therefore, the character at position 65 (which is the 66th character) is A. Moreover, the character <u>b</u> at position 32 represents the space character.

The first 32 characters, that is, the characters at positions 00–31 and at position 127 are nonprintable characters. The following table shows the abbreviations and meanings of these characters.

nul	null character	ff	form feed	can	cancel
soh	start of header	cr	carriage return	em	end of medium
stx	start of text	so	shift out	sub	substitute
etx	end of text	si	shift in	esc	escape
eot	end of transmission	dle	data link escape	fs	file separator
enq	enquiry	dc1	device control 1	gs	group separator
ack	acknowledge	dc2	device control 2	rs	record separator
bel	bell	dc3	device control 3	us	unit separator
bs	back space	dc4	device control 4	<u>b</u>	space
ht	horizontal tab	nak	negative acknowledge	del	delete
lf	line feed	syn	synchronous idle		
vt	vertical tab	etb	end of transmitted block		

EBCDIC (Extended Binary Coded Decimal Interchange Code)

The following table shows some of the characters in the EBCDIC character set.

EBCDIC									
	0	1	2	3	4	5	6	7	8	9
6					<u>b</u>					
7						.	<	(	+	|
8	&									
9	!	$	*	)	;	¬	-	/		
10								,	%	_

EBCDIC	0	1	2	3	4	5	6	7	8	9
11	>	?								
12		`	:	#	@	'	=	"		a
13	b	c	d	e	f	g	h	i		
14						j	k	l	m	n
15	o	p	q	r						
16		~	s	t	u	v	w	x	y	z
17										
18	[	]								
19				A	B	C	D	E	F	G
20	H	I								J
21	K	L	M	N	O	P	Q	R		
22							S	T	U	V
23	W	X	Y	Z						
24	0	1	2	3	4	5	6	7	8	9

The numbers 6-24 in the first column specify the left digit(s), and the numbers 0-9 in the second row specify the right digits of the characters in the EBCDIC data set. For example, the character in the row marked 19 (the number in the first column) and the column marked 3 (the number in the second row) is A. Therefore, the character at position 193 (which is the 194th character) is A. Moreover, the character b at position 64 represents the space character. The preceding table does not show all the characters in the EBCDIC character set. In fact, the characters at positions 00-63 and 250-255 are nonprintable control characters.

The following table lists the operators that can be overloaded.

Operators that can be overloaded							
+	–	*	/	%	^	&	|
!	&&	||	=	==	<	<=	>
>=	!=	+=	-=	*=	/=	%=	^=
|=	&=	<<	>>	>>=	<<=	++	–
->*	,	->	[]	()	~	new	delete

The following table lists the operators that cannot be overloaded.

Operators that cannot be overloaded				
.	.*	::	?:	sizeof

HEADER FILES

The C++ standard library contains many predefined functions, named constants, and specialized data types. This appendix discusses some of the most widely used library routines (and several named constants). For additional explanation and information on functions, named constants, and so on, check your system documentation.

Header File cassert

The following table describes the function assert. Its specification is contained in the header file cassert.

assert(expression)	expression is any int expression; expression is usually a logical expression	• If the value of expression is nonzero (true), the program continues to execute. • If the value of expression is 0 (false), execution of the program terminates immediately. The expression, the name of the file containing the source code, and the line number in the source code are displayed.

NOTE To disable all the assert statements, place the preprocessor directive #define NDEBUG before the directive #include <cassert>.

Header File `cctype`

The following table shows various functions from the header file `cctype`.

Function Name and Parameters	Parameter(s) Types	Function Return Value
`isalnum(ch)`	ch is a `char` value	Function returns an `int` value as follows: • If ch is a letter or a digit character, that is (`'A'-'Z'`, `'a'-'z'`, `'0'-'9'`), it returns a nonzero value (`true`) • 0 (`false`), otherwise
`iscntrl(ch)`	ch is a `char` value	Function returns an `int` value as follows: • If ch is a control character (in ASCII, a character value 0–31 or 127), it returns a nonzero value (`true`) • 0 (`false`), otherwise
`isdigit(ch)`	ch is a `char` value	Function returns an `int` value as follows: • If ch is a digit (`'0'-'9'`), it returns a nonzero value (`true`) • 0 (`false`), otherwise
`islower(ch)`	ch is a `char` value	Function returns an `int` value as follows: • If ch is lowercase (`'a'-'z'`), it returns a nonzero value (`true`) • 0 (`false`), otherwise
`isprint(ch)`	ch is a `char` value	Function returns an `int` value as follows: • If ch is a printable character, including blank (in ASCII, `' '` through `'~'`), it returns a nonzero value (`true`) • 0 (`false`), otherwise
`ispunct(ch)`	ch is a `char` value	Function returns an `int` value as follows: • If ch is a punctuation character, it returns a nonzero value (`true`) • 0 (`false`), otherwise
`isspace(ch)`	ch is a `char` value	Function returns an `int` value as follows: • If ch is a white space character (blank, newline, tab, carriage return, form feed), it returns a nonzero value (`true`) • 0 (`false`), otherwise

Function Name and Parameters	Parameter(s) Types	Function Return Value
`isupper(ch)`	ch is a `char` value	Function returns an `int` value as follows: • If ch is an uppercase letter (`'A'-'Z'`), it returns a nonzero value (`true`) • 0 (`false`), otherwise
`tolower(ch)`	ch is a `char` value	Function returns an `int` value as follows: • If ch is an uppercase letter, it returns the ASCII value of the lowercase equivalent of ch • ASCII value of ch, otherwise
`toupper(ch)`	ch is a `char` value	Function returns an `int` value as follows: • If ch is a lowercase letter, it returns the ASCII value of the uppercase equivalent of ch • ASCII value of ch, otherwise

Header File `cfloat`

The header file `cfloat` contains many named constants. The following table lists some of these constants.

Named Constant	Description
`FLT_DIG`	Approximate number of significant digits in a `float` value
`FLT_MAX`	Maximum positive `float` value
`FLT_MIN`	Minimum positive `float` value
`DBL_DIG`	Approximate number of significant digits in a `double` value
`DBL_MAX`	Maximum positive `double` value
`DBL_MIN`	Minimum positive `double` value
`LDBL_DIG`	Approximate number of significant digits in a `long double` value
`LDBL_MAX`	Maximum positive `long double` value
`LDBL_MIN`	Minimum positive `long double` value

Header File `climits`

The header file `climits` contains many named constants. The following table lists some of these constants.

Named Constant	Description
CHAR_BIT	Number of bits in a byte
CHAR_MAX	Maximum `char` value
CHAR_MIN	Minimum `char` value
SHRT_MAX	Maximum `short` value
SHRT_MIN	Minimum `short` value
INT_MAX	Maximum `int` value
INT_MIN	Minimum `int` value
LONG_MAX	Maximum `long` value
LONG_MIN	Minimum `long` value
UCHAR_MAX	Maximum `unsigned char` value
USHRT_MAX	Maximum `unsigned short` value
UINT_MAX	Maximum `unsigned int` value
ULONG_MAX	Maximum `unsigned long` value

Header File `cmath`

The following table shows various math functions.

Function Name and Parameters	Parameter(s) Type	Function Return Value
`acos(x)`	x is a floating-point expression, $-1.0 \leq x \leq 1.0$	Arc cosine of x, a value between 0.0 and π
`asin(x)`	x is a floating-point expression, $-1.0 \leq x \leq 1.0$	Arc sine of x, a value between $-\pi/2$ and $\pi/2$

Function Name and Parameters	Parameter(s) Type	Function Return Value
atan(x)	x is a floating-point expression	Arc tan of x, a value between $-\pi/2$ and $\pi/2$
ceil(x)	x is a floating-point expression	The smallest whole number $\geq$ x, ("ceiling" of x)
cos(x)	x is a floating-point expression, x is measured in radians	Trigonometric cosine of the angle
cosh(x)	x is a floating-point expression	Hyperbolic cosine of x
exp(x)	x is a floating-point expression	The value e raised to the power of x; (e = 2.718...)
fabs(x)	x is a floating-point expression	Absolute value of x
floor(x)	x is a floating-point expression	The largest whole number $\leq$ x; ("floor" of x)
log(x)	x is a floating-point expression, where x > 0.0	Natural logarithm (base e) of x
log10(x)	x is a floating-point expression, where x > 0.0	Common logarithm (base 10) of x
pow(x,y)	x and y are floating-point expressions. If x = 0.0, y must be positive; if x $\leq$ 0.0, y must be a whole number.	x raised to the power of y
sin(x)	x is a floating-point expression; x is measured in radians	Trigonometric sine of the angle
sinh(x)	x is a floating-point expression	Hyperbolic sine of x
sqrt(x)	x is a floating-point expression, where x $\geq$ 0.0	Square root of x
tan(x)	x is a floating-point expression; x is measured in radians	Trigonometric tangent of the angle
tanh(x)	x is a floating-point expression	Hyperbolic tangent of x

Header File `cstddef`

Among others, this header file contains the definition of the following symbolic constant:

NULL: The system–dependent null pointer (usually 0)

Header File `cstring`

The following table shows various string functions.

Function Name and Parameters	Parameter(s) Type	Function Return Value
`strcat(destStr, srcStr)`	`destStr` and `srcStr` are null-terminated `char` arrays; `destStr` must be large enough to hold the result	The base address of `destStr` is returned; `srcStr`, including the null character, is concatenated to the end of `destStr`
`strcmp(str1, str2)`	`str1` and `str2` are null terminated `char` arrays	The returned value is as follows: • An `int` value < 0, if `str1` < `str2` • An `int` value 0, if `str1` = `str2` • An `int` value > 0, if `str1` > `str2`
`strcpy(destStr, srcStr)`	`destStr` and `srcStr` are null-terminated `char` arrays	The base address of `destStr` is returned; `srcStr` is copied into `destStr`
`strlen(str)`	`str` is a null-terminated `char` array	An integer value ≥ 0 specifying the length of the `str` (excluding the `'\0'`) is returned

HEADER FILE `string`

This header file—not to be confused with the header file `cstring`—supplies a programmer-defined data type named `string`. Associated with the `string` type are a data type `string::size_type` and a named constant `string::npos`. These are defined as follows:

`string::size_type`	An unsigned integer type
`string::npos`	The maximum value of type `string::size_type`

Several functions are associated with the `string` type. The following table shows some of these functions. Unless stated otherwise, `str`, `str1`, and `str2` are variables (objects) of type `string`. The position of the first character in a `string` variable (such as `str`) is 0, the second character is 1, and so on.

Function Name and Parameters	Parameter(s) Type	Function Return Value
`str.c_str()`	None	The base address of a null-terminated C-string corresponding to the characters in `str`.
`getline(istreamVar,str)`	`istreamVar` is an input stream variable (of type `istream` or `ifstream`). `str` is a `string` object (variable).	Characters until the newline character are input from `istreamVar` and stored in `str`. (The newline character is read but not stored into `str`.) The value returned by this function is usually ignored.
`str.empty()`	None	Returns `true` if `str` is empty, that is, the number of characters in `str` is zero, `false` otherwise.
`str.length()`	None	A value of type `string::size_type` giving the number of characters in the string.
`str.size()`	None	A value of type `string::size_type` giving the number of characters in the string.
`str.find(strExp)`	`str` is a string object and `strExp` is a string expression evaluating to a string. The string expression, `strExp`, can also be a character.	The `find` function searches `str` to find the first occurrence of the string or the character specified by `strExp`. If the search is successful, the function `find` returns the position in `str` where the match begins. If the search is unsuccessful, the function returns the special value `string::npos`.

Function Name and Parameters	Parameter(s) Type	Function Return Value
`str.substr(pos, len)`	Two unsigned integers, `pos` and `len`. `pos`, represent the starting position (of the substring in `str`), and `len` represents the length (of the substring). The value of `pos` must be less than `str.length()`.	A temporary string object that holds a substring of `str` starting at `pos`. The length of the substring is, at most, `len` characters. If `len` is too large, it means "to the end" of the string in `str`.
`str1.swap(str2);`	One parameter of type `string`. `str1` and `str2` are `string` variables.	The contents of `str1` and `str2` are swapped.
`str.clear();`	None	Removes all the characters from `str`.
`str.erase();`	None	Removes all the characters from `str`.
`str.erase(m);`	One parameter of type `string::size_type`.	Removes all the characters from `str` starting at index m.
`str.erase(m, n);`	Two parameters of type `int`.	Starting at index m, removes the next n characters from `str`. If n > length of `str`, removes all the characters starting at the mth.
`str.insert(m, n, c);`	Parameters m and n are of type `string::size_type`; c is a character.	Inserts n occurrences of the character c at index m into `str`.
`str1.insert(m, str2);`	Parameter m is of type `string::size_type`.	Inserts all the characters of `str2` at index m into `str1`.
`str1.replace(m, n, str2);`	Parameters m and n are of type `string::size_type`.	Starting at index m, replaces the next n characters of `str1` with all the characters of `str2`. If n > length of `str1`, then all the characters until the end of `str1` are replaced.

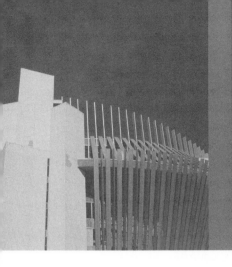

ADDITIONAL C++ TOPICS

Analysis: Insertion Sort

Let L be a list of n elements. Consider the kth entry in the list. If the kth entry is moved, it could go to any of the first $k - 1$ positions in the list. And, if the kth entry is not moved, it stays at its current position. Thus, there are a total of k possibilities for the kth entry: $(k - 1)$ possibilities to move and one possibility of not moving. Assume all possibilities are equally likely. Then, the probability of not moving is $1/k$ and the probability of moving the kth entry is $(k - 1) / k$.

If the kth entry is not moved, the number of key comparisons is one and the number of item assignments is zero.

Suppose that the kth entry is moved. Then, the average number of key comparisons (executed by the loop) to move the kth entry is

$$\frac{1 + 2 + 3 + \ldots + (k - 1)}{k - 1} = \frac{k(k - 1)}{2(k - 1)} = \frac{k}{2}.$$

Now one key comparison is made before the loop, one item assignment is done before the loop, and one item assignment is done after the loop. It now follows that, if the kth entry is moved, on average it requires $(k / 2) + 1$ key comparisons and $(k / 2) + 2$ item assignments.

Because the probability of moving the kth entry is $(k - 1) / k$ and not moving is $1/k$, the average number of key comparisons for the kth entry is

$$\left(\frac{k - 1}{k}\right)\left(\frac{k}{2} + 1\right) + \frac{1}{k}1 = \left(\frac{k - 1}{k}\right)\left(\frac{k + 2}{2}\right) + \frac{1}{k} = \frac{(k - 1)(k + 2) + 2}{2k}$$

$$= \frac{k(k + 1)}{2k} \qquad\qquad = \frac{k + 1}{2}$$

$$= \frac{1}{2}k + \frac{1}{2}.$$

Similarly, the average number of assignments for the kth entry is

$$\left(\frac{k-1}{k}\right)\left(\frac{k}{2}+2\right)+\frac{1}{k}0 = \left(\frac{k-1}{k}\right)\left(\frac{k+4}{2}\right) = \frac{(k-1)(k+4)}{2k}$$

$$= \frac{k^2+3k-4}{2k} \qquad = \frac{k^2}{2k}+\frac{3k}{2k}-\frac{4}{2k}$$

$$= \frac{1}{2}k+\frac{3}{2}-\frac{2}{k} \qquad = \frac{1}{2}k+O(1).$$

Note that the average number of key comparisons and the average number of item assignments for the kth entry are similar.

To find the average number of key comparisons made by insertion sort, we add the average number of key comparisons made by list entries 2 through n. (Note that the `for` loop starts at the second entry of the list.) Thus, the average number of key comparisons is

$$\sum_{k=2}^{n}\left[\frac{1}{2}k+\frac{1}{2}\right] = \frac{1}{2}\sum_{k=2}^{n}k+\sum_{k=2}^{n}\frac{1}{2} \qquad = \frac{1}{2}\sum_{k=2}^{n}k+\frac{n-1}{2}$$

$$= \frac{1}{2}\sum_{k=1}^{n}k+\frac{n-1}{2}-\frac{1}{2} \qquad = \frac{1}{2}\frac{n(n+1)}{2}+\frac{n-1}{2}-\frac{1}{2}$$

$$= \frac{n(n+1)+2(n-1)-2}{4} = \frac{n^2+n+2n-4}{4}$$

$$= \frac{1}{4}\left(n^2+3n-4\right) \qquad = O(n^2).$$

In a similar manner, we can show that the average number of item assignments made by insertion sort is $O(n^2)$.

Analysis: Quicksort

Let L be a list of n elements. Let $C(n)$ denote the number of key comparisons and $S(n)$ denote the number of swaps of entries in L, $n = 1, 2, 3, \ldots$.

Clearly,

$$C(1) = C(0) = 0,$$
$$S(2) = 3.$$

The `partition` function compares the `pivot` with every key in the list. Thus, the `pivot` is compared $n-1$ times for a list of length n. Suppose the `pivot` position in the list is r. Then

$$C(n) = (n-1) + C(r) + C(n-r-1) \qquad \text{(Equation 1)}$$

for all $n = 1, 2, 3, \ldots$. Clearly, the definition of $C(n)$ as given in Equation 1 is recursive. Equation 1 is also called a recurrence relation.

Worst-Case Analysis

In the worst case, r in Equation 1 will always be zero. Thus,

$$C(n) = (n-1) + C(0) + C(n - 0 - 1) = (n - 1) + C(n - 1). \qquad \text{(Equation 2)}$$

Substitute $n = 2, 3,$ and 4, respectively, in Equation 2 to get

$$C(2) = 1 + C(1) = 1 + 0 = 1,$$
$$C(3) = 2 + C(2) = 2 + 1 = 3,$$
$$C(4) = 3 + C(3) = 3 + 3 = 6.$$

We now solve Equation 1. Now

$$
\begin{aligned}
C(n) &= (n - 1) + C(n - 1) \\
&= (n - 1) + (n - 2) + C(n - 2) \text{ because } C(n - 1) = (n - 2) + C(n - 2) \\
&= (n - 1) + (n - 2) + (n - 3) + C(n - 3) \text{ because } C(n - 2) = (n - 3) + C(n - 3) \\
&\;\;\vdots \\
&= (n - 1) + (n - 2) + (n - 3) + \ldots + 2 + C(2) \\
&= (n - 1) + (n - 2) + (n - 3) + \ldots + 2 + 1 \\
&= n(n - 1)/2 \\
&= (1/2)n^2 - (1/2)n \\
&= O(n^2).
\end{aligned}
$$

We now look at the number of swaps in the worst case. In the worst case, the `pivot` is the largest key, so the function `partition` will make $n + 1$ swaps for a list of length n (one swap before the loop, $n - 1$ swaps within the loop, and one swap after the loop). Hence,

$$S(n) = (n + 1) + S(n - 1) \qquad \text{(Equation 3)}$$

for all $n = 1, 2, 3, \ldots$. Substitute $n = 3$ and 4, respectively, in Equation 3 to get,

$$S(3) = (3 + 1) + S(2) = 4 + 3 = 7,$$
$$S(4) = (4 + 1) + S(3) = 5 + 7 = 12.$$

Next, we solve Equation 3. Now

$$
\begin{aligned}
S(n) &= (n+1) + S(n-1) \\
&= (n+1) + n + S(n-2) \text{ because } S(n-1) = n + S(n-2) \\
&= (n+1) + n + (n-1) + S(n-3) \text{ because } S(n-2) = (n-1) + S(n-3) \\
&\vdots \\
&= (n+1) + n + (n-1) + \ldots + 4 + S(2) \\
&= (n+1) + n + (n-1) + \ldots + 4 + 3 \\
&= (n+1) + n + (n-1) + \ldots + 4 + 3 + 2 + 1 - 2 - 1 \\
&= (n+2)(n+1)/2 - 3 \\
&= (n^2 + 3n + 2)/2 - 3 \\
&= (1/2)n^2 + (3/2)n - 2 \\
&= O(n^2).
\end{aligned}
$$

Average-Case Analysis

Let us now see the performance of quicksort in the average case.

Let $S(n, p)$ denote the number of swaps for a list of length n such that the `pivot` is the pth key, $p = 1, 2, \ldots, n$. Now, if the `pivot` is the pth key, then

$$
S(n, p) = (p+1) + S(p-1) + S(n-p).
$$

From this, it follows that if the `pivot` is the first key,

$$
S(n, 1) = (1+1) + S(1-1) + S(n-1) = 2 + S(0) + S(n-1).
$$

Similarly,

$$
S(n, 2) = 3 + S(1) + S(n-2),
$$

$$
\vdots
$$

$$
S(n, p) = (p+1) + S(p-1) + S(n-p),
$$

$$
\vdots
$$

$$
S(n, n) = (n+1) + S(n-1) + S(0).
$$

Assume that the `pivot` can occur at any position, that is, all positions are equally likely. Then, the average number of swaps for a list of length n is as follows:

$$S(n) = \frac{S(n, 1) + S(n, 2) + \ldots + S(n, n)}{n}$$

$$= \frac{2 + 3 + \ldots + (n + 1) + 2(S(0) + S(1) + \ldots + S(n - 1))}{n}$$

$$= \frac{(1 + 2 + \ldots + (n + 1)) - 1}{n} + \frac{2(S(0) + S(1) + \ldots + S(n - 1))}{n}$$

$$= \frac{(n + 1)(n + 2)}{2n} - \frac{1}{n} + \frac{2(S(0) + S(1) + \ldots + S(n - 1))}{n}$$

$$= \frac{n^2 + 3n + 2}{2n} - \frac{1}{n} + \frac{2(S(0) + S(1) + \ldots + S(n - 1))}{n}$$

$$= \frac{n}{2} + \frac{3}{2} + \frac{2(S(0) + S(1) + \ldots + S(n - 1))}{n}.$$

From this, it follows that

$$S(n - 1) = \frac{n - 1}{2} + \frac{3}{2} + \frac{2(S(0) + S(1) + \ldots + S(n - 2))}{n - 1}.$$

This implies that

$$nS(n) - (n - 1)S(n - 1) = \frac{n^2 + 3n}{2} + 2(S(0) + S(1) + \ldots + S(n - 1)) -$$

$$\left\{ \frac{(n - 1)^2}{2} + \frac{3(n - 1)}{2} + 2(S(0) + S(1) + \ldots + S(n - 2)) \right\}$$

$$= (n + 1) + 2(S(n - 1).$$

Thus,

$$nS(n) = (n + 1) + (n + 1)S(n - 1).$$

Divide both sides by $n(n + 1)$ to obtain

$$\frac{S(n)}{n + 1} = \frac{1}{n} + \frac{S(n - 1)}{n}.$$

This implies that

$$\frac{S(n-1)}{n} = \frac{1}{n-1} + \frac{S(n-2)}{n-1},$$

$$\frac{S(n-2)}{n-1} = \frac{1}{n-2} + \frac{S(n-3)}{n-2},$$

$$\vdots$$

$$\frac{S(3)}{4} = \frac{1}{3} + \frac{S(2)}{3},$$

$$\frac{S(2)}{3} = \frac{1}{2} + \frac{S(1)}{2}.$$

Hence,

$$\frac{S(n)}{n+1} = \frac{1}{n} + \frac{1}{n-1} + \ldots + \frac{1}{3} + \frac{1}{2} + \frac{S(1)}{2}.$$

It can be shown that

$$\frac{1}{n} + \frac{1}{n-1} + \ldots + \frac{1}{3} + \frac{1}{2} + 1 = \ln(n) + O(1).$$

It follows that

$$\frac{S(n)}{n+1} = \ln(n) + O(1).$$

Hence,

$$S(n) = n\ln(n) + O(n).$$

Also, because

$$\ln(n) = \ln(2)\log_2(n) = 0.69 \log_2(n)$$

it follows that

$$S(n) = 0.69 \, n \log_2(n) + O(n) = O(n \log_2(n)).$$

Next, we derive a formula for $C(n)$ for the average case of quicksort.

Suppose the `pivot` is the pth key in the list. Let $C(n, p)$ denote the number of comparisons made by the `partition` function when the `pivot` is the pth key. Then

$$C(n, p) = (n-1) + C(p-1) + C(n-p).$$

Because all positions in the list for the `pivot` are equally likely, we have

$$C(n) = \frac{C(n,1) + C(n,2) + \ldots + C(n,n)}{n}.$$

Now,

$$C(n,1) = (n-1) + C(0) + C(n-1),$$
$$C(n,2) = (n-1) + C(1) + C(n-2),$$
$$C(n,3) = (n-1) + C(2) + C(n-3),$$

$$\vdots$$

$$C(n,p) = (n-1) + C(p-1) + C(n-p),$$

$$\vdots$$

$$C(n,n) = (n-1) + C(n-1) + C(0).$$

This implies that

$$C(n) = \frac{n(n-1) + 2(C(0) + C(1) + \cdots + C(n-1))}{n}$$
$$= (n-1) + \frac{2(C(0) + C(1) + \cdots + C(n-1))}{n}.$$

Change n to n-1 to get

$$C(n-1) = (n-2) + \frac{2(C(0) + C(1) + \cdots + C(n-2))}{n-1}.$$

Thus,

$$nC(n) - (n-1)C(n-1) = n(n-1) - (n-1)(n-2) + 2C(n-1)$$
$$= 2(n+1) + 2C(n-1).$$

This implies that

$$nC(n) = 2(n+1) + (n+1)C(n-1).$$

Divide both sides by $n(n+1)$, to get

$$\frac{C(n)}{n+1} = \frac{2}{n} + \frac{C(n-1)}{n}.$$

We now solve this equation.

Change n to $n - 1$, to get

$$\frac{C(n-1)}{n} = \frac{2}{n-1} + \frac{C(n-2)}{n-1}.$$

Thus,

$$\begin{aligned}
\frac{C(n)}{n+1} &= \frac{2}{n} + \frac{2}{n-1} + \frac{2}{n-2} + \ldots + \frac{2}{3} + \frac{2}{2} + \frac{C(1)}{2} \\
&= \frac{2}{n} + \frac{2}{n-1} + \frac{2}{n-2} + \ldots + \frac{2}{3} + \frac{2}{2} + \frac{1}{2} \\
&= 2\left(\frac{1}{n} + \frac{1}{n-1} + \frac{1}{n-2} + \ldots + \frac{1}{3} + \frac{1}{2}\right) + \frac{1}{2} \\
&= 2\left(\frac{1}{n} + \frac{1}{n-1} + \frac{1}{n-2} + \ldots + \frac{1}{3} + \frac{1}{2} + 1\right) + \frac{1}{2} - 2 \\
&= 2\ln(n) + O(1).
\end{aligned}$$

This implies that

$$\begin{aligned}
C(n) &= 2(n+1)\ln(n) + O(n) \\
&= 2n\ln(n) + O(n) \\
&\approx (1.39)n\log_2 n + O(n).
\end{aligned}$$

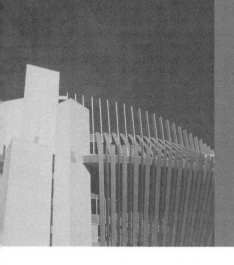

This book assumes that you are familiar with the basic elements of C++, such as data types, assignment statements, input/output, control structures, functions and parameter passing, the namespace mechanism, and arrays. However, to help you, this appendix quickly reviews these basic elements of C++. Moreover, if you have taken Java as a first programming language, this appendix helps familiarize you with the basic elements of C++. In addition to describing the basic elements of C++, we also compare various features of C++ with Java.

For more details about the C++ language, refer to the book, *C++ Programming: From Problem Analysis to Program Design, Fourth Edition* by the author and listed in the references ([6], Appendix H).

Data Types

C++ data types fall into three categories—simple data types, structured data types, and pointers. Chapter 1 describes the user-defined classes, which fall into the category of structured data types. Chapter 3 describes pointers. This section discusses the simple data types. Moreover, later in this appendix, we briefly discuss arrays, a structured data type, in C++.

C++'s simple data type is similar to Java's primitive data type. There are three categories of simple data—integral, floating-point, and enumeration type.

Like Java, C++'s integral data types have several categories. Some of the integral data types are char, bool, short, int, long, and unsigned int. Table G-1 defines the range of values belonging to some of these data types.

TABLE G-1 Values and memory allocation for three simple data types

Data type	Values	Storage (in bytes)
int	−2147483648 to 2147483647	4
bool	true and false	1
char	−128 to 127	1

NOTE **Use this table only as a guide.** Different compilers may allow different ranges of values. Check your compiler's documentation.

The data type int in C++ works the same way as the data type int works in Java.

Notice that the data type char in C++ is a set of 256 values, whereas the data type char in Java is a set of 65,536 values. In addition to dealing with small numbers, the char data type is used to represent characters—that is, letters, digits, and special symbols. Typically, C++ uses the ASCII characters, a set of 128 characters and described in Appendix C, to deal with characters.

The data type bool has only two values: true and false. Also, true and false are called the **logical (Boolean) values**. An expression that evaluates to true or false is called a **logical (Boolean) expression**.

To deal with decimal numbers, C++ provides the floating-point data type. C++ provides the data types float and double. As in the case of integral data types, the data types float and double differ in their sets of values. The data types float and double in C++ work the same way as they work in Java.

Arithmetic Operators and Expressions

The arithmetic operators— +, -, *, and /—in C++ work the same way as in Java. The operator % in C++ is used with integral data types to find the remainder in ordinary division. Furthermore, arithmetic expressions in C++ are formed and evaluated the same as they are in Java. In addition, the increment operator, ++; the decrement operator, --; and the compound assignment operators, +=, =, *=, /=, and %= in C++ work the same way as in Java.

The cast operator in C++ takes the following form:

```
static_cast<dataType> expression
```

You can also use the following C-like cast operator:

```
dataType expression
```

Named Constants, Variables, and Assignment Statements

Named constants in C++ are declared using the reserved word const. The general syntax of declaring a named constant is as follows:

```
const dataType identifier = value;
```

For example, the following statement declares CONVERSION to be a named constant of type double and assigns the value 2.54 to it:

```
const double CONVERSION = 2.54;
```

In C++, variables are declared the same way as they are declared in Java, and the syntax of the assignment statement in both languages is the same.

The general syntax for declaring one variable or multiple variables is as follows:

```
dataType identifier, identifier, . . .;
```

For example, the following statements declare amountDue to be a variable of type double and counter to be a variable of type int:

```
double amountDue;
int counter;
```

The syntax of the assignment statement is as follows:

```
variable = expression;
```

In an assignment statement, the value of the expression should match the data type of the variable. The expression on the right side is evaluated, and its value is assigned to the variable on the left side. For example, suppose that amountDue is a variable of type double and quantity is a variable of type int. If the value of quantity is 20, the following statement assigns 150.00 to amountDue:

```
amountDue = quantity * 7.50;
```

C++ Library: Preprocessor Directives

Only a small number of operations, such as arithmetic and assignment operations, are explicitly defined in C++. Many of the functions and symbols needed to run a C++ program are provided as a collection of libraries. Every library has a name and is referred to as a **header file**. For example, the descriptions of the functions needed to perform input/output (I/O) are contained in the header file iostream. Similarly, the descriptions of some very useful mathematical functions, such as power, absolute, and sine, are contained in the header file cmath. If you want to use I/O or math functions, you need to tell the computer where to find the necessary code. You use preprocessor directives and the names of the header files to tell the computer the locations of the code provided in the libraries. Preprocessor directives are processed by a program called a **preprocessor**.

Preprocessor directives are commands supplied to the preprocessor that cause the preprocessor to modify the text of a C++ program before it is complied. All preprocessor commands begin with #. There are no semicolons at the end of preprocessor commands because they are not C++ commands. To use a header file in a C++ program, use the preprocessor directive include.

The general syntax to include a system-provided header file in a C++ program is as follows:

```
#include <headerFileName>
```

For example, the following statement includes the header file `iostream` in a C++ program:

```
#include <iostream>
```

Preprocessor directives that include the header files are placed as the first lines of a program so that the identifiers declared in those header files can be used throughout the program. (In C++, identifiers must be declared before they can be used.)

Certain header files are provided as part of C++. Appendix E describes some of the commonly used header files.

C++ Program

Every C++ program has two parts: preprocessor directives and the program. The preprocessor directives are commands that direct the preprocessor to modify the C++ program before compilation. The program contains statements that accomplish some meaningful results. Taken together, the preprocessor directives and program statements constitute the C++ **source code**. To be useful, this source code must be saved in a file that has the file extension `.cpp`.

When the program is compiled, the compiler generates the object code, which is saved in a file with the file extension `.obj`. When the object code is linked with system resources, the executable code is produced and saved in a file with the file extension `.exe`. The name of the file containing the object code, and the name of the file containing the executable code, are the same as the name of the file containing the source code. For example, if the source code is located in a file named `firstProg.cpp`, the name of the file containing the object code is `firstProg.obj`, and the name of the file containing the executable code is `firstProg.exe`.

The extensions as given in the preceding paragraph—that is, `.cpp`, `.obj`, and `.exe`—are system dependent. To be absolutely sure, check your system's or integrated development environment's (IDE's) documentation.

A C++ program is a collection of functions and one of the functions is the function `main`. Therefore, every C++ program must have the function `main`. The basic parts of the function `main` are the heading and the body of the function. The heading has the following form:

```
functionType main(argument list)
```

For example, the statement:

```
int main()
```

means that the function `main` returns a value of the `int` data type, and it has no arguments.

The following is an example of a C++ program:

```
#include <iostream>

using namespace std;

int main()
{
    int num1, num2;

    num1 = 10;
    num2 = 2 * num1;

    cout << "num1 = " << num1 << ", and num2 = " << num2 << endl;

    return 0;
}
```

The next section discusses input and output (I/O) in detail.

Input and Output

Inputting data and outputting the results of a program is fundamental to any programming language. Because I/O differs quite significantly in C++ and Java, this section describes I/O in C++ in detail.

Input

Inputting data into variables from the standard input device is accomplished via the use of `cin` and the operator `>>`. The syntax of `cin` together with `>>` is as follows:

```
cin >> variable >> variable. . .;
```

This is called an **input (read)** statement. Sometimes this is also called a `cin` statement. In C++, `>>` is called the **stream extraction operator** or simply the **extraction operator**.

The input (or `cin`) statement works as follows. Suppose `miles` is a variable of the data type `double`. The statement

```
cin >> miles;
```

causes the computer to get a value from the standard input device of the data type `double` and place it in the memory cell named `miles`.

By using more than one variable with `cin`, more than one value can be read at a time. Suppose `feet` and `inch` are variables of type `int`. A statement such as

```
cin >> feet >> inch;
```

gets two integers from the keyboard and places them in the memory locations `feet` and `inch`, respectively.

> **NOTE** The extraction operator >> is defined only for putting data into variables of simple data types. Therefore, the right-side operand of the extraction operator >> is a variable of the simple data type.

How does the extraction operator >> work? When scanning for the next input, >> skips all the white space characters. **White space characters** consist of blanks and certain nonprintable characters, such as tabs and the newline character. Thus, whether you separate the input data by lines or blanks, the extraction operator >> simply finds the next input data in the input stream. For example, suppose that `payRate` and `hoursWorked` are variables of type `double`. Consider the following input statement:

```
cin >> payRate >> hoursWorked;
```

Whether the input is

```
15.50 48.30
```

or

```
15.50    48.30
```

or

```
15.50
48.30
```

the preceding input statement would store 15.50 in `payRate` and 48.30 in `hoursWorked`. Note that the first input is separated by a blank, the second input is separated by a tab, and the third input is separated by a line.

Now suppose that the input is 2. How does the extraction operator >> distinguish between the character 2 and the number 2? The right-side operand of the extraction operator >> makes this distinction. If the right-side operand is a variable of type `char`, the input 2 is treated as the character 2 and, in this case, the ASCII value of 2 is stored. If the right-side operand is a variable of type `int` or `double`, the input 2 is treated as the number 2.

Next, consider the input 25 and the statement

```
cin >> a;
```

where `a` is a variable of some simple data type. If `a` is of type `char`, only the single character 2 is stored in `a`. If `a` is of type `int`, 25 is stored in `a`. If `a` is of type `double`, the input 25 is converted to the decimal number 25.0. Table G-2 summarizes this discussion by showing the valid input for a variable of the simple data type.

TABLE G-2 Valid input for a variable of the simple data type

Data type of `a`	Valid input for `a`
`char`	One printable character except the blank.
`int`	An integer, possibly preceded by a (+ or −) sign.
`double`	A decimal number, possibly preceded by a (+ or −) sign. If the actual data input is an integer, the input is converted to a decimal number with the zero decimal part.

When reading data into a `char` variable, after skipping any leading white space characters, the extraction operator >> finds and stores only the next character; reading stops after a single character. To read data into an `int` or `double` variable, after skipping all the leading white space characters and reading the plus or minus sign (if any), the extraction operator >> reads the digits of the number, including the decimal point for floating-point variables, and stops when it finds a white space character or a character other than a digit.

Input Failure

Many things can go wrong during program execution. A program that is syntactically correct might produce incorrect results. For example, suppose that a part-time employee's paycheck is calculated by using the following formula:

```
wages = payRate * hoursWorked;
```

If you accidentally type a + in place of *, the calculated wages would be incorrect, even though the statement containing the + is syntactically correct.

What about an attempt to read invalid data? For example, what would happen if you tried to input a letter into an `int` variable? If the input data did not match the corresponding variables, the program would run into problems. For example, trying to read a letter into an `int` or `double` variable would result in an **input failure**. Consider the following statements:

```
int a, b, c;
double x;
```

If the input is:

```
W 54
```

then the statement:

```
cin >> a >> b;
```

would result in an input failure because you are trying to input the character `'W'` into the int variable a. If the input were:

```
35 67.93 48 78
```

then the input statement:

```
cin >> a >> x >> b;
```

would result in storing 35 in a, 67.93 in x, and 48 in b.

Now consider the following read statement with the previous input (the input with three values):

```
cin >> a >> b >> c;
```

This statement stores 35 in a and 67 in b. The reading stops at . (the decimal point). Because the next variable c is of the data type int, the computer tries to read . into c, which is an error. The input stream then enters a state called the **fail state**.

What actually happens when the input stream enters the fail state? Once an input stream enters a fail state, all further I/O statements using that stream are ignored. Unfortunately, the program quietly continues to execute with whatever values are stored in the variables and produce incorrect results.

Output

In C++, output on the standard output device is accomplished via the use of cout and the operator <<. The syntax of cout together with << is as follows:

```
cout << expression or manipulator << expression or manipulator...;
```

This is called an **output statement**. Sometimes this is also called a cout statement. In C++, << is called the **stream insertion operator** or simply the **insertion operator**.

Generating output with the cout statements follows two rules:

1. The expression is evaluated, and its value is printed at the current insertion point on the output device. (On the screen, the insertion point is where the cursor is.)

2. A manipulator is used to format the output. The simplest manipulator is endl(the last character is the letter el), which causes the insertion point to move to the beginning of the next line.

Example G-1 illustrates how cout statements work. In a cout statement, a string or an expression involving only one variable or a single value evaluates to itself.

EXAMPLE G-1

Consider the following statements. The output is shown to the right of each statement.

Statement	Output
`cout << 29 / 4 << endl;`	`7`
`cout << "Hello there. " << endl;`	`Hello there.`
`cout << 12 << endl;`	`12`
`cout << "4 + 7" << endl;`	`4 + 7`
`cout << 4 + 7 << endl;`	`11`
`cout << 'A' << endl;`	`A`
`cout << "4 + 7 = " << 4 + 7 << endl;`	`4 + 7 = 11`
`cout << 2 + 3 * 5 << endl;`	`17`
`cout << "Hello \nthere. " << endl;`	`Hello`
	`there.`

setprecision

You use the manipulator `setprecision` to control the output of floating-point numbers. The default output of floating-point numbers is scientific notation. Some IDEs might use a maximum of six decimal places for the default output of floating-point numbers. However, when an employee's paycheck is printed, the desired output is a maximum of two decimal places. To print floating-point output to two decimal places, you use the `setprecision` manipulator to set the precision to 2.

The general syntax of the `setprecision` manipulator is as follows:

```
setprecision(n)
```

where n is the number of decimal places.

You use the `setprecision` manipulator with `cout` and the extraction operator. For example, the statement

```
cout << setprecision(2);
```

formats the output of the decimal numbers to two decimal places, until a similar subsequent statement changes the precision. Notice that the number of decimal places, or the precision value, is passed as an argument to `setprecision`.

To use the manipulator `setprecision`, the program must include the header file `iomanip`. Thus, the following include statement is required:

```
#include <iomanip>
```

fixed

To further control the output of floating-point numbers, you can use other manipulators. To output floating-point numbers in a fixed decimal format, you use the manipulator `fixed`. The following statement sets the output of floating-point numbers in a fixed decimal format on the standard output device:

```
cout << fixed;
```

After the preceding statement executes, all floating-point numbers are displayed in the fixed-decimal format.

The manipulator `scientific` is used to output floating-point numbers in scientific format.

showpoint

Suppose that the decimal part of a decimal number is 0. In this case, when you instruct the computer to output the decimal number in a fixed decimal format, the output might not show the decimal point and the decimal part. To force the output to show the decimal point and trailing zeros, you use the manipulator `showpoint`. The following statement sets the output of decimal numbers with the decimal point and trailing zeros on the standard output device:

```
cout << showpoint;
```

Of course, the following statement sets the output of floating-point numbers in a fixed decimal format with the decimal point and trailing zeros on the standard output device:

```
cout << fixed << showpoint;
```

setw

The manipulator `setw` is used to output the value of an expression in specific columns. The value of the expression can be either a string or a number. The statement `setw(n)` outputs the value of the next expression in n columns. The output is right-justified. Thus, if you specify the number of columns to be 8, for example, and the output requires only 4 columns, the first four columns are left blank. Furthermore, if the number of columns specified is less than the number of columns required by the output, the output automatically expands to the required number of columns; the output is not truncated. For example, if `x` is an `int` variable, the following statement outputs the value of `x` in five columns on the standard output device:

```
cout << setw(5) << x << endl;
```

To use the manipulator `setw`, the program must include the header file `iomanip`. Thus, the following `include` statement is required:

```
#include <iomanip>
```

Unlike `setprecision`, which controls the output of all floating-point numbers until it is reset, `setw` controls the output of only the next expression.

`left` and `right` Manipulators

Recall that if the number of columns specified by the `setw` manipulator exceeds the number of columns required by the next expression, the output is right-justified. Sometimes you might want the output to be left-justified. To left-justify the output, you use the manipulator `left`.

The syntax to set the manipulator `left` is as follows:

```
ostreamVar << left;
```

where `ostreamVar` is an output stream variable. For example, the following statement sets the output to be left-justified on the standard output device:

```
cout << left;
```

The syntax to set the manipulator `right` is as follows:

```
ostreamVar << right;
```

where `ostreamVar` is an output stream variable. For example, the following statement sets the output to be right-justified on the standard output device:

```
cout << right;
```

File Input/Output

The previous sections discussed how to get input from the keyboard (standard input device) and send output to the screen (standard output device). This section discusses how to obtain data from other input devices, such as a flash memory (that is, secondary storage), and how to save the output to a flash memory. C++ allows a program to get data directly from, and save output directly to, secondary storage. A program can use the file I/O and read data from or write data to a file. Formally, a file is defined as follows:

File: An area in secondary storage used to hold information.

The standard I/O header file, `iostream`, contains data types and variables that are used only for input from the standard input device and output to the standard output device. In addition, C++ provides a header file called `fstream`, which is used for file I/O. Among other things, the `fstream` header file contains the definitions of two data types: `ifstream`, which means input file stream and is similar to `istream`; and `ofstream`, which means output file stream and is similar to `ostream`.

The variables `cin` and `cout` are already defined and associated with the standard input/output devices. In addition, `>>` can be used with `cin`; `<<`, and the manipulators described in the preceding section, can be used with `cout`. These same operators are also available for file I/O, but the header file `fstream` does not declare variables to use them. You must declare variables called **file stream objects**, which include `ifstream` variables for input and `ofstream` variables for output. You then use these variables together with `>>`

and << for I/O. Remember that C++ does not automatically initialize user-defined variables. Once you declare the `fstream` objects, you must associate these objects with the input/output sources.

File I/O is a five-step process:

1. Include the header file `fstream` in the program.
2. Declare file stream objects.
3. Associate the file stream objects with the input/output sources.
4. Use the file stream objects with >>, <<, or other input/output functions.
5. Close the files.

We now describe these five steps in detail. A skeleton program then shows how the steps might appear in a program.

Step 1 requires that the header file `fstream` be included in the program. The following statement accomplishes this task:

```
#include <fstream>
```

Step 2 requires you to declare file stream objects. Consider the following statements:

```
ifstream inData;
ofstream outData;
```

The first statement declares `inData` to be an `ifstream` object. The second statement declares `outData` to be an `ofstream` object.

Step 3 requires you to associate the file stream objects with the input/output sources. This step is called **opening the files**. The stream member function `open` is used to open the files. The general syntax for opening a file is as follows:

```
fileStreamVariable.open(sourceName);
```

Here `fileStreamVariable` is a file stream object, and `sourceName` is the name of the input/output file.

Suppose you include the declaration from Step 2 in a program. Further suppose that the input data is stored in a file called `prog.dat`. The following statements associate `inData` with `prog.dat` and `outData` with `prog.out`. That is, the file `prog.dat` is opened for inputting data and the file `prog.out` is opened for outputting data.

```
inData.open("prog.dat");   //open the input file;  Line 1
outData.open("prog.out");  //open the output file; Line 2
```

NOTE   IDEs such as Visual Studio .NET manage programs in the form of projects. That is, first
you create a project and then add source files to the project. The statement in Line 1
assumes that the file prog.dat is in the same directory (subdirectory) as your project.
However, if this is in a different directory (subdirectory), you must specify the path where
the file is located, along with the name of the file. For example, suppose that the file
prog.dat is on a flash memory in drive H. Then, the statement in Line 1 should be
modified as follows:

```
inData.open ("h:\\prog.dat");
```

Note that there are two \ after h:. In C++, \ is the escape character. Therefore, to
produce a \ within a string, you need \\. (To be absolutely sure about specifying the
source where the input file is stored, such as the drive h:\\, check your system's
documentation.)

Similar conventions for the statement in Line 2.

Step 4 typically works as follows. You use the file stream objects with >>, <<, or other
input/output functions. The syntax for using >> or << with file stream objects is exactly
the same as the syntax for using cin and cout. Instead of using cin and cout, however,
you use the file stream object names that were declared. For example, the statement

```
inData >> payRate;
```

reads the data from the file prog.dat and stores it in the variable payRate. The
statement

```
outData << "The paycheck is: $" << pay << endl;
```

stores the output— The paycheck is: $565.78—in the file prog.out. This statement
assumes that the pay was calculated as 565.78.

Once the I/O is complete, Step 5 requires closing the files. Closing a file means that the
file stream variables are disassociated from the storage area, and the file stream objects are
freed. Once these variables are freed, they can be reused for other file I/O. Moreover,
closing an output file ensures that the entire output is sent to the file, that is, the buffer is
emptied. You close the files by using the stream function close. For example, assuming
the program includes the declarations listed in Steps 2 and 3, the statements for closing the
files are as follows:

```
inData.close();
outData.close();
```

NOTE   On some systems, it is not necessary to close the files. When the program terminates, the
files are closed automatically. Nevertheless, it is a good practice to close the files
yourself. Also, if you want to use the same file stream variable to open another file, you
must close the first file opened with that file stream variable.

In skeleton form, a program that uses file I/O is usually of the following form:

```
#include <fstream>
//Add any additional header files that you use
using namespace std;

int main()
{
        //Declare file stream variables such as the following
    ifstream inData;
    ofstream outData;

        //Additional variable declaration

        //Open files
    inData.open("prog.dat"); //open the input file
    outData.open("prog.out"); //open the output file

        //Code for data manipulation

        //Close files
    inData.close();
    outData.close();

    return 0;
}
```

Step 3 requires the file to be opened for file I/O. Opening a file associates a file stream variable declared in the program with a physical file at the source, such as a flash memory. In the case of an input file, the file must exist before the open statement executes. If the file does not exist, the open statement fails and the input stream enters the fail state. An output file does not have to exist before it is opened; if the output file does not exist, the computer prepares an empty file for output. If the designated output file already exists, by default the old contents are erased when the file is opened.

Control Structures

C++ and Java have the same six relational operators— ==, !=, <, <=, >, and >=; and they work the same way in both the languages. The control structures in C++ and Java are the same. For example, the selection control structures are if, if...else, and switch; and the looping control structures are while, for, and do ... while. The syntax for these control structures is the same in both the languages. However, there are some differences.

In C++, any nonzero value is treated as true and the value 0 is treated as false. The reserved word true is initialized to 1 and the false is initialized to 0. Logical expressions in C++ evaluate to 0 or 1. On the other hand, logical expressions in Java evaluate to true or false. Moreover, the data type boolean in Java cannot be typecasted to a numeric type, so its values true and false cannot be typecasted to numeric values.

In C++, the mix-up of the assignment operator and the equality operator in a logical expression can cause serious problems. For example, consider the following if statement:

```
if (drivingCode = 5)
...
```

In C++, the expression `drivingCode` = 5 returns the value 5. Because 5 is nonzero, the expression evaluates to `true`. So in C++, the expression evaluates to `true` and the value of the variable `drivingCode` is also changed. On the other hand, in Java, because the value 5 is not a `boolean` value, it cannot be typecasted to `true` or `false`. So the preceding statement in Java results in a compiler error, whereas in C++ it does not cause any syntax error.

Namespaces

When a header file, such as `iostream`, is included in a program, the global identifiers in the header file also become global identifiers in the program. Therefore, if a global identifier in a program has the same name as one of the global identifiers in the header file, the compiler generates a syntax error (such as "identifier redefined"). The same problem can occur if a program uses third-party libraries. To overcome this problem, third-party vendors begin their global identifier names with a special symbol. Moreover, compiler vendors begin their global identifier names with an underscore (_). Therefore, to avoid linking errors, you should not begin identifier names in your program with an underscore (_).

C++ tries to solve this problem of overlapping global identifier names with the `namespace` mechanism.

The general syntax of the statement `namespace` is as follows:

```
namespace namespaceName
{
    members
}
```

where a member is usually a named constant, variable declaration, function, or another `namespace`. Note that `namespaceName` is a C++ identifier.

In C++, `namespace` is a reserved word.

EXAMPLE G-2

The statement

```
namespace globalType
{
    const int n = 10;
    const double rate = 7.50;
    int count = 0;
    void printResult();
}
```

defines `globalType` to be a `namespace` with four members: named constants `n` and `rate`, the variable `count`, and the function `printResult`.

The scope of a `namespace` member is local to the `namespace`. You can usually access a `namespace` member outside the `namespace` in one of two ways, as described next.

The general syntax for accessing a `namespace` member is as follows:

```
namespaceName::identifier;
```

For example, to access the member `rate` of the `namespace globalType`, the following statement is required:

```
globalType::rate;
```

To access the member `printResult` (which is a function), the following statement is required:

```
globalType::printResult();
```

In C++, `::` is called the **scope resolution operator**. Thus, to access a member of a `namespace`, you use `namespaceName`, followed by the scope resolution operator, followed by the member name. That is, you attach the name of `namespaceName` and the scope resolution operator before the member name.

To simplify the accessing of a `namespace` member, C++ provides the use of the statement `using`. The syntax to use the statement `using` is as follows.

a.   To simplify the accessing of all `namespace` members:

```
using namespace namespaceName;
```

b.   To simplify the accessing of a specific `namespace` member:

```
using namespaceName::identifier;
```

For example, the `using` statement

```
using namespace globalType;
```

simplifies the accessing of all the members of the `namespace globalType`. The statement

```
using globalType::rate;
```

simplifies the accessing of the member `rate` of the `namespace globalType`.

In C++, `using` is a reserved word.

You typically put the `using` statement after the `namespace` declaration. For the `namespace globalType`, for example, you usually write the code as follows:

```
namespace globalType
{
    const int n = 10;
    const double rate = 7.50;
```

```
    int count = 0;
    void printResult();
}
```

```
using namespace globalType;
```

After the `using` statement, to access a `namespace` member, you do not have to put the `namespaceName` and the scope resolution operator before the `namespace` member. However, if a `namespace` member and a global identifier in a program have the same name, to access this `namespace` member in the program, the `namespaceName` and the scope resolution operator must precede the `namespace` member. Similarly, if a `namespace` member and an identifier in a block have the same name, to access this `namespace` member in the block, the `namespaceName` and the scope resolution operator must precede the `namespace` member.

 NOTE The identifiers in the system that provide the header files such as `iostream`, `cmath`, and `iomanip` are defined in the `namespace std`. For this reason, to simplify the accessing of identifiers from these header files, we use the following statement in the programs that we write:

```
using namespace std;
```

Functions and Parameters

Functions in Java are called methods. In C++, there are two types of functions—value-returning and `void`.

Value-Returning Functions

The syntax of a value-returning function is as follows:

```
functionType functionName(formal parameter list)
{
    statements
}
```

In this syntax template, `functionType` is the type of value that the function returns. This type is also called the data type of the value-returning function. Moreover, statements enclosed between curly braces form the body of the function.

SYNTAX: FORMAL PARAMETER LIST

The general syntax of the formal parameter list is as follows:

```
dataType identifier, dataType identifier,...
```

FUNCTION CALL

The syntax to call a value-returning function is as follows:

```
functionName(actual parameter list)
```

SYNTAX: ACTUAL PARAMETER LIST

The syntax of the actual parameter list is as follows:

```
expression or variable, expression or variable, ...
```

Thus, to call a value-returning function, you use its name, with the actual parameters (if any) in parentheses.

A function's formal parameter list can be empty. However, if the formal parameter list is empty, the parentheses are still needed.

A value-returning function returns its value via the `return` statement.

Void Functions

The definition of a `void` function has the following syntax:

```
void functionName(formal parameter list)
{
    statements
}
```

FORMAL PARAMETER LIST

The formal parameter list may be empty. If the formal parameter is nonempty, the formal parameter list has the following syntax:

```
dataType& variable, dataType& variable, ....
```

You must specify both the data type and the variable name in the formal parameter list. The symbol `&` after `dataType` has a special meaning; it is used only for certain formal parameters and is discussed later in this appendix.

FUNCTION CALL

The function call has the following syntax:

```
functionName(actual parameter list);
```

ACTUAL PARAMETER LIST

The actual parameter list has the following syntax:

```
expression or variable, expression or variable, ...
```

As with value-returning functions, in a function call the number of actual parameters, together with their data types, matches the formal parameters in the order given. Actual and formal parameters have a one-to-one correspondence. A function call causes the body of the called function to execute. (Functions with default parameters are discussed at the end of this appendix.)

EXAMPLE G-3

```
void funexp(int a, double b, char c, int& x)
{
    ...
}
```

The function `funexp` has four parameters.

In general, there are two types of formal parameters: **value parameters** and **reference parameters**.

Value parameter: A formal parameter that receives a copy of the content of the corresponding actual parameter.

Reference parameter: A formal parameter that receives the location (memory address) of the corresponding actual parameter.

When you attach & after the `dataType` in the formal parameter list of a function, the variable following that `dataType` becomes a reference parameter.

EXAMPLE G-4

```
void expfun(int one, int& two, char three, double& four);
```

The function `expfun` has four parameters: one, a value parameter of type int; two, a reference parameter of type int; three, a value parameter of type char; and four, a reference parameter of type double.

From the definition of value parameters, it follows that if a formal parameter is a value parameter, the value of the corresponding actual parameter is copied into the formal parameter. That is, the value parameter has its own copy of the data. Therefore, during program execution, the value parameter manipulates the data stored in its own memory space. After copying the data, the value parameter has no connection with the actual parameter.

On the other hand, if a formal parameter is a reference parameter, it receives the address of the corresponding actual parameter. That is, a reference parameter stores the address of the corresponding actual parameter. During program execution to manipulate the data, the address stored in the reference parameter directs it to the memory space of the corresponding actual parameter. In other words, during program execution, the reference parameter manipulates the data stored in the memory space of the corresponding actual parameter. Any changes that a reference parameter makes to its data immediately changes the value of the corresponding actual parameter.

A constant value cannot be passed to a reference parameter.

 NOTE In Java, parameters are passed by value only; that is, the formal parameter receives a copy of the actual parameter's data. Therefore, if a formal parameter is a variable of a primitive data type, it cannot pass its value outside the function. On the other hand, suppose that a formal parameter is a reference variable. Then both the formal and actual parameters point to the same object. Because the formal parameter contains the address of the object storing the data, the formal parameter *can* change the value of the actual object. Therefore, in Java, if a formal parameter is a reference variable, it works like a reference parameter in C++.

Reference Parameters and Value-Returning Functions

While describing the syntax of the formal parameter list of a value-returning function, we used only value parameters. You can also use reference parameters in a value-returning function, although this approach is not recommended. By definition, a value-returning function returns a single value; this value is returned via the `return` statement. If a function needs to return more than one value, you should change it to a `void` function and use the appropriate reference parameters to return the values.

Functions with Default Parameters

When a function is called, the number of actual and formal parameters must be the same. C++ relaxes this condition for functions with default parameters. You specify the value of a default parameter when the function name appears for the first time, such as in the prototype. In general, the following rules apply for functions with default parameters:

- If you do not specify the value of a default parameter, the default value is used for that parameter.
- All of the default parameters must be the rightmost parameters of the function.
- Suppose a function has more than one default parameter. In a function call, if a value to a default parameter is not specified, you must omit all of the arguments to its right.
- Default values can be constants, global variables, or function calls.
- The caller has the option of specifying a value other than the default for any default parameter.
- You cannot assign a constant value as a default value to a reference parameter.

Consider the following function prototype:

```
void funcExp(int x, int y, double t, char z = 'A', int u = 67,
             char v = 'G', double w = 78.34);
```

The function `funcExp` has seven parameters. The parameters z, u, v, and w are default parameters. If no values are specified for z, u, v, and w in a call to the function `funcExp`, their default values are used.

Suppose you have the following statements:

```
int a, b;
char ch;
double d;
```

The following function calls are legal:

1.   `funcExp(a, b, d);`
2.   `funcExp(a, 15, 34.6,'B', 87, ch);`
3.   `funcExp(b, a, 14.56,'D');`

In statement 1, the default values of z, u, v, and w are used. In statement 2, the default value of z is replaced by `'B'`, the default value of u is replaced by 87, the default value of v is replaced by the value of ch, and the default value of w is used. In statement 3, the default value of z is replaced by `'D'`, and the default values of u, v, and w are used.

The following function calls are illegal:

1.   `funcExp(a, 15, 34.6, 46.7);`
2.   `funcExp(b, 25, 48.76, 'D', 4567, 78.34);`

In statement 1, because the value of z is omitted, all the other default values must be omitted. In statement 2, because the value of v is omitted, the value of w should be omitted, too.

The following are illegal function prototypes with default parameters:

1.   `void funcOne(int x, double z = 23.45, char ch, int u = 45);`
2.   `int funcTwo(int length = 1, int width, int height = 1);`
3.   `void funcThree(int x, int& y = 16, double z = 34);`

In statement 1, because the second parameter z is a default parameter, all the other parameters after z must be default parameters. In statement 2, because the first parameter is a default parameter, all the parameters must be the default values. In statement 3, a constant value cannot be assigned to y because y is a reference parameter.

Arrays

Like Java, in C++, an **array** is a collection of a fixed number of components wherein all of the components are of the same data type. However, in C++ arrays are not objects and so need not be instantiated. In this section, we describe how one-dimensional arrays work in C++.

A **one-dimensional array** is an array in which the components are arranged in a list form. The general form of declaring a one-dimensional array is as follows:

```
dataType arrayName[intExp];
```

where `intExp` is any expression that evaluates to a positive integer. Also, `intExp` specifies the number of components in the array.

EXAMPLE G-5

The statement

```
int num[5];
```

declares an array `num` of five components. Each component is of type `int`. The components are `num[0]`, `num[1]`, `num[2]`, `num[3]`, and `num[4]`.

Accessing Array Components

In C++, array components are accessed just like in Java. The general form (syntax) used for accessing an array component is as follows:

```
arrayName[indexExp]
```

where `indexExp`, called the **index**, is any expression whose value is a nonnegative integer. The index value specifies the position of the component in the array. In C++, the array index starts at 0. Consider the following statement:

```
int list[10];
```

This statement declares an array `list` of 10 components. The components are `list[0]`, `list[1]`, ..., `list[9]`. The assignment statement

```
list[5] = 34;
```

stores 34 in `list[5]`, which is the sixth component of the array `list`.

Array Index Out of Bounds

Unfortunately, in C++, there is no guard against out-of-bounds indices. Thus, C++ does not check whether the index value is within range—that is, between 0 and `ArraySize - 1`. If the index goes out of bounds and the program tries to access the component specified by the index, then whatever memory location is indicated by the index is accessed. This situation can result in altering or accessing the data of a memory location that you never intended. Consequently, if during execution the index goes out of bounds, several strange things can happen. It is solely the programmer's responsibility to make sure that the index is within bounds. On some new compilers, if an array index goes out of bounds in a program, it is possible that the program terminates with an error message.

Arrays as Parameters to Functions

In C++, arrays are passed by reference only. Because arrays are passed by reference only, you do not use the symbol & when declaring an array as a formal parameter. When declaring a one-dimensional array as a formal parameter, the size of the array is usually omitted. If you specify the size of the one-dimensional array when it is declared as a formal parameter, it is ignored by the compiler. In Java, associated with each array is the variable `length`, which specifies the size of the array. However, no such variable is associated with C++ arrays. To pass the size of the array to a function, we use another parameter as in the following function:

```
void initialize(int list[], int size)
{
    for (int count = 0; count < size; count++)
        list[count] = 0;
}
```

The first parameter of the function `initialize` is an `int` array of any size. When the function `initialize` is called, the size of the actual array is passed as the second parameter of the function `initialize`.

When a formal parameter is a reference parameter, then whenever the formal parameter changes, the actual parameter changes as well. However, even though an array is always passed by reference, you can still prevent the function from changing the actual parameter. You do so by using the reserved word `const` in the declaration of the formal parameter. Consider the following function:

```
void example(int x[], const int y[], int sizeX, int sizeY)
{
    ...
}
```

Here, the function `example` can modify the array `x`, but not the array `y`. Any attempt to change `y` results in a compile-time error. It is a good programming practice to declare an array to be a constant as a formal parameter if you do not want the function to modify the array.

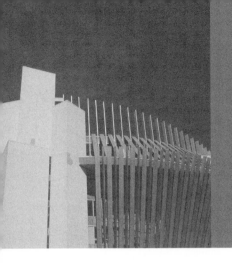

1. G. Booch, R.A. Maksimchuk, M.W. Engel, B.J. Young, J. Conallen, and K.A. Houston, *Object-Oriented Analysis and Design with Applications*, 3rd ed., Addison-Wesley, Reading, MA, 2007.

2. E. Horowitz, S. Sahni, and S. Rajasekaran, *Computer Algorithms C++*, Computer Science Press, New York, 1997.

3. N.M. Josuttis, *The C++ Standard Library: A Tutorial and Reference*, Addison-Wesley, Reading, MA, 1999.

4. D.E. Knuth, *The Art of Computer Programming, Volume 1: Fundamental Algorithms*, 3rd ed., Addison-Wesley, Reading, MA, 1997.

5. D.E. Knuth, *The Art of Computer Programming, Volume 2: Seminumerical Algorithms*, 3rd ed., Addison-Wesley, Reading, MA, 1998.

6. D.E. Knuth, *The Art of Computer Programming, Volume 3: Searching and Sorting*, 2nd ed., Addison-Wesley, Reading, MA, 1998.

7. S.B. Lippman and J. Lajoie, *C++ Primer*, 3rd ed., Addison-Wesley, Reading, MA, 1998.

8. D.S. Malik, *C++ Programming: From Problem Analysis to Program Design*, 4th ed., Course Technology, Boston, MA, 2009.

9. D. S. Malik and M.K. Sen, *Discrete Mathematical Structures, Theory and Applications*, Course Technology, Boston, MA, 2004.

10. E.M. Reingold and W. J. Hensen, *Data Structures in Pascal*, Little Brown and Company, Boston, MA, 1986.

11. R. Sedgewick, *Algorithms in C*, 3rd ed., Addison-Wesley, Boston, MA, Parts 1–4, 1998; Part 5, 2002.

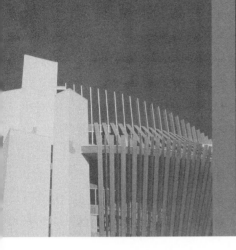

Chapter 1

1. a. true; b. false; c. false; d. false; e. false; f. true; g. false; h. false

3. The white box refers to testing the correctness of the program; that is, making sure that the program does what it is supposed to do. White-box testing relies on the internal structure and implementation of a function or algorithm. The objective is to ensure that every part of the function or algorithm is executed at least once.

5. a. $O(n^2)$

   b. $O(n^3)$

   c. $O(n^3)$

   d. $O(n)$

   e. $O(n)$

   f. $O(n\log_2 n)$

7. a. 43

   b. $4n + 3$

   c. $O(n)$

9. One possible answer is as follows:

```
int sumSquares(int n)
{
int sum = 0;

for (int j = 1; j <= n; j++)
    sum = sum + j * j;

return sum;
}
```

The function sumSquares is of the order $O(n)$.

11. The `for` loop has $2n - 4$ iterations. Each time through the loop a fixed number of statements execute. Hence, this algorithm is $O(n)$. Now each time through the loop there is one addition, one subtraction, and one multiplication. Thus, the numbers of additions is $2n - 4$, the number of subtractions is $2n - 4$, and the number of multiplications is $2n - 4$.

13. There are three nested `for` loops and each of these loops has n iterations. For each iteration of the outer loop, the middle loop has n iterations. Thus, the middle loop executes n times and has n^2 iterations. For each iteration of the middle loop, the innermost loop has n iterations. It follows that the innermost loop has n^3 iterations. Hence, this algorithm is $O(n^3)$.

15. a. 6

    b. 2

    c. 2

    d.
```
void xClass::func()
{
     u = 10;   v = 15.3;
}
```

    e.
```
void xClass::print()
{
     cout << u << " " << v << endl;
}
```

    f.
```
xClass::xClass()
{
     u = 0;
     v = 0;
}
```

    g. `x.print();`

    h. `xClass t(20, 35.0);`

17.
```
00:00:00
23:13:00
06:59:39
07:00:39
The two times are different.
```

19. a. `personType student("Buddy", "Arora");`

    b. `student.print();`

    c. `student.setName("Susan", "Miller");`

Chapter 2

1. a. true; b. true; c. true; d. false; e. false; f. true; g. true; h. false; i. false; j. true; k. false; l. true; m. false; n. false

3. Some of the data members that can be added to the `class employeeType` are department, `salary`, `employeeCategory` (such as supervisor and president), and `employeeID`. Some of the member functions are `setInfo`, `getSalary`, `getEmployeeCategory`, and `setSalary`.

5. a. The statement :

   ```
   class bClass public aClass
   ```

   should be:

   ```
   class bClass: public aClass
   ```

   b. Missing semicolon after }.

7. a.
   ```
   yClass::yClass()
   {
        a = 0;
        b = 0;
   }
   ```

   b.
   ```
   xClass::xClass()
   {
        z = 0;
   }
   ```

   c.
   ```
   void yClass::two(int u, int v)
   {
        a = u;
        b = v;
   }
   ```

9. a.
   ```
   void two::setData(int a, int b, int c)
   {
        one::setData(a, b);
        z = c;
   }
   ```

   b.
   ```
   void two::print() const
   {
        one::print();
        cout <<z << endl;
   }
   ```

11.
   ```
   In base: x = 7
   In derived: x = 3, y = 8, x + y = 11
   **** 7
   #### 11
   ```

13. Because the left operand of `<<` is a stream object, which is not of the type `mystery`.

15. a. `friend istream& operator>> (istream&, strange&);`

    b. `strange operator+ (const strange&) const;`

    c. `bool operator== (const strange&) const;`

    d. `strange operator++ (int);`

17. In Line 3, the word `operator` before `<=` is missing. The correct statement is as follows:

    ```
    bool mystery::operator<=(mystery rightObj)      //Line 3
    {

    }
    ```

19. In Line 2, the function `operator+` must have two parameters. The correct statement is as follows:

    ```
    friend operator+ (mystery, mystery);      //Line 2
    ```

21. One

23. Two

25. a. `strange<int> sObj;`

    b. `bool operator== (strange);`

    c.
    ```
    bool strange::operator==(strange right)
    {
          return(a == right.a && b = right.b);
    }
    ```

27. a. 21; b. `OneHow`

Chapter 3

1. a. false; b. false; c. false; d. true; e. true; f. true; g. false; h. false

3. 98 98

   98 98

5. b and c

7. 78 78

9. 4 4 5 7 10 14 19 25 32 40

11. In a shallow copy of data, two or more pointers points to the same memory space. In a deep copy of data, each pointer has its own copy of the data.

13. `Array p: 5 7 11 17 25`
`Array q: 25 17 11 7 5`

15. The copy constructor makes a copy of the actual parameter data.

17. Classes with pointer data members should include the destructor, overload the assignment operator, and explicitly provide the copy constructor by including it in the class definition and providing its definition.

19. `ClassA x: 4`

`ClassA x: 6`
`ClassB y: 5`

21. In compile-time binding, the compiler generates the necessary code to call a function. In run-time binding, the run-time system generates the necessary code to make the appropriate function call.

23. a. The statement creates the `arrayListType` object `intList` of size 100. The elements of `intList` are of the type `int`.

b. The statement creates the `arrayListType` object `stringList` of size 1000. The elements of `stringList` are of the type `string`.

c. The statement creates the `arrayListType` object `salesList` of size 100. The elements of `salesList` are of the type `double`.

Chapter 4

1. The three main components of the STL are containers, iterators, and algorithms.

3. `vector<double> doubleList(50);`

5. `ostream_iterator<int> screen(cout, " ");`

7. `0 2 4 6 8`

9. `3 7 9`

11. `50 75 100 200 95`

13. `vecList = {8, 23, 40, 6, 18, 9, 75, 9, 75}`

15. `70 76 34 45 23 5 35 210`

Chapter 5

1. a. false; b. false; c. false; d. false; e. true;

3. a. true; b. true; c. false; d. false; e. true

5. a. `A = A->link;`

b. `list = A->link->link;`

c. `B = B->link->link;`

d. `list = NULL;`

e. `B->link->info = 35;`

f.
```
newNode = new nodeType;
newNode->info = 10;
newNode->link = A->link;
A->link = newNode;
```

g.
```
p = A->link;
A->link = p->link;
delete p;
```

7. a. This is an invalid code. The statement `s->info = B;` is invalid because `B` is a pointer and `s->info` is an `int`.

   b. This is an invalid code. After the statement `s = s->link;` executes, `s` is `NULL` and so `s->info` does not exist.

9.
```
Item to be deleted is not in the list.
18 38 2 15 45 25
```

11.

```
doublyLinkedList<Type>
----------------------------------------
#count: int
#*first: nodeType<Type>
#*last: nodeType<Type>
----------------------------------------
+operator=(const doublyLinkedList<Type> &):
              const doublyLinkedList<Type>&
+initializeList(): void
+isEmptyList() const: bool
+destroy: void
+print() const: void
+reversePrint() const: void
+length() const: int
+front() const: Type
+back() const: Type
+search(const Type&) const: bool
+insert(const Type&): void
+deleteNode(const Type&): void
+doublyLinkedList()
+doublyLinkedList(const doublyLinkedList<Type>&)
+~doublyLinkedList()
-copyList(const doublyLinkedList<Type>&): void
```

FIGURE I-1 Chapter 5 Exercise 11

13. `intList = {5, 24, 16, 11, 60, 9, 3, 58, 78, 85, 6, 15, 93, 98, 25}`

15.

```
                              videoType
  -videoTitle: string
  -movieStar1: string
  -movieStar2: string
  -movieProducer: string
  -movieDirector: string
  -movieProductionCo: string
  -copiesInStock: int

  +operator<<(ostream&, const videoType&): friend ostream&
  +setVideoInfo(string, string, string, string,
                string, string, int): void
  +getNoOfCopiesInStock() const: int
  +checkOut(): void
  +checkIn(): void
  +printTitle() const: void
  +printInfo() const: void
  +checkTitle(string): bool
  +updateInStock(int): void
  +setCopiesInStock(int): void
  +getTitle() const: string
  +videoType(string = "", string = "", string = "",
             string = "", string = "", string = "",
             int = 0)
  +operator==(const videoType&) const: bool
  +operator!=(const videoType&) const: bool
```

FIGURE I-2 Chapter 5 Exercise 15

Chapter 6

1. a. true; b. true; c. false; d. false; e. false

3. The case in which the solution is defined in terms of smaller versions of itself.

5. A function that calls another function and eventually results in the original function call is said to be indirectly recursive.

7. a. The statements in Lines 3 and 4.

   b. The statements in Lines 5 and 6.

   c. Any nonnegative integer.

   d. It is a valid call. The value of mystery(0) is 0.

   e. It is a valid call. The value of mystery(5) is 15.

   f. It is an invalid call. It will result in an infinite recursion.

9. a. It does not produce any output.

b. 5 6 7 8 9

c. It does not produce any output.

d. It does not produce any output.

11. a. 2

b. 3

c. 5

d. 21

13.

$$multiply(m, n) = \begin{cases} 0 & if\, n = 0 \\ m & if\, n = 1 \\ m + multiply(m, n - 1) & otherwise \end{cases}$$

Chapter 7

1.
```
x = 3
y = 9
7
13
4
7
```

3. a. 26

b. 45

c. 8

d. 29

5. a. A * B + C

b. (A + B) * (C - D)

c. (A - B - C) * D

7. a. This is an invalid statement. Because stackADT is an abstract class, we cannot instantiate an object of this class.

b. Creates sales to be an object of the class stackType. The stack elements are of type double and the stack size is 100. (Note that because the value -10 is passed to the constructor with parameters, the definition of the constructor with parameters creates the stack of size 100.)

    c.   Creates names to be object of the `class stackType`. The stack elements are of type `string` and the stack size is 100.

    d.   This is an invalid statement. Because the `class linkedStackType` does not have a constructor with parameters, you cannot pass the value 50 to the default constructor.

9.   10
```
50 25 10
50
```

11.
```
template<class Type>
Type second(stackType<Type> stack)
{
    Type temp1, temp2;

    assert(!stack.isEmptyStack());
    temp1 = stack.top();
    stack.pop();
    assert(!stack.isEmptyStack());
    temp2 = stack.top();
    stack.push(temp1);

    return temp2;
}
```

13.
```
template<class type>
void clear(stack<type>& st)
{
    while (!st.empty())
        st.pop();
}
```

Chapter 8

1.   Queue Elements: 5 9 16 4 2

3.   The function `mystery` reverses the elements of a queue and also doubles the values of the queue elements.

5.   10
```
20 40 20 5 3
20 3
```

7.   a.   queueFront = 99; queueRear = 26

    b.   queueFront = 0; queueRear = 25

9.   a.   queueFront = 99; queueRear = 0

    b.   queueFront = 0; queueRear = 99

11. a.   `queueFront = 74; queueRear = 0`

     b.   `queueFront = 75; queueRear = 99`. The position of the removed element was 75.

13.
```
template<class Type>
int queueType<Type>::queueCount()
{
    return count;
}
```

15.

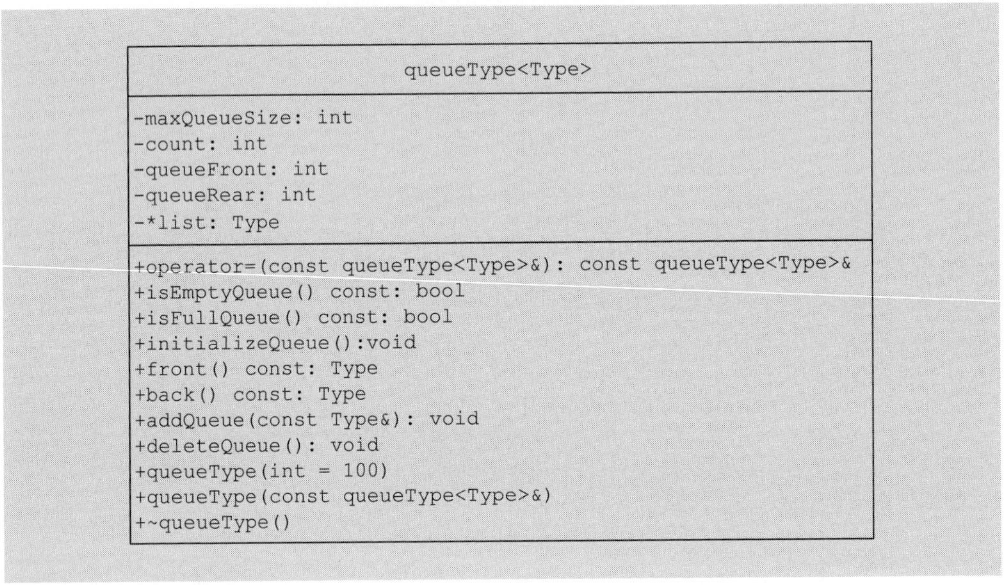

```
                        queueType<Type>
───────────────────────────────────────────────────────────
-maxQueueSize: int
-count: int
-queueFront: int
-queueRear: int
-*list: Type
───────────────────────────────────────────────────────────
+operator=(const queueType<Type>&): const queueType<Type>&
+isEmptyQueue() const: bool
+isFullQueue() const: bool
+initializeQueue():void
+front() const: Type
+back() const: Type
+addQueue(const Type&): void
+deleteQueue(): void
+queueType(int = 100)
+queueType(const queueType<Type>&)
+~queueType()
```

FIGURE I-3   Chapter 8 Exercise 15

Chapter 9

1.   a. false; b. true; c. false; d. false

3.
```
template<class elemType>
class orderedArrayListType: public arrayListType<elemType>
{
public:
    int binarySearch(const elemType& item);
    orderedArrayListType(int n = 100);
};
```

5.   There are 30 buckets in the hash table and each bucket can hold 5 items.

7.   Suppose that an item with key X is hashed at t, that is, $h(X) = t$, and $0 \leq t \leq$ $HTSize - 1$. Further suppose that position t is already occupied. In quadratic

probing, starting at position t, we linearly search the array at locations $(t + 1)$ % $HTSize$, $(t + 2^2)$ % $HTSize = (t + 4)$ % $HTSize$, $(t + 3^2)$ % $HTSize = (t + 9)$ % $HTSize, \ldots, (t + i^2)$ % $HTSize$. That is, the probe sequence is t, $(t + 1)$ % $HTSize$, $(t + 2^2)$ % $HTSize$, $(t+3^2)$ % $HTSize, \ldots, (t + i^2)$ % $HTSize$.

9. 30, 31, 34, 39, 46, and 55

11. 101

13. Let $k_1 = 2733$, $k_2 = 1409$, $k_3 = 2731$, $k_4 = 1541$, $k_5 = 2004$, $k_6 = 2101$, $k_7 = 2168$, $k_8 = 1863$. Suppose HT is of size 13 indexed $0,1,2,\ldots,12$. Define the function h: $\{k_1, k_2, k_3, k_4, k_5, k_6, k_7, k_8\} \rightarrow \{0,1,2,\ldots,12 \}$ by $h(k_i) = k_i$ %13.

Now, $h(k_1) = h(2733) = 2733$ % $13 = 3$. So the data of the student with ID 2733 is stored in $HT[3]$.

Also, 1409 % 13 = 5, 2731 % 13 = 1, 1541 % 13 = 7, 2004 % 13 = 2, 2101 % 13 = 8, 2168 % 13 = 10, and 1863 % 13 = 4. Hence, $h(1409) = 5$, $h(2731) = 1$, $h(1541) = 7$, $h(2004) = 2$, $h(2101) = 8$, $h(2168) = 10$, and $h(1863) = 4$.

Suppose $HT[b] \leftarrow a$ means "store the data of the student with ID a into $HT[b]$." Then

$HT[3] \leftarrow 2733$,	$HT[5] \leftarrow 1409$,	$HT[1] \leftarrow 2731$,
$HT[7] \leftarrow 1541$,	$HT[2] \leftarrow 2004$,	$HT[8] \leftarrow 2088$,
$HT[10] \leftarrow 2168$,	$HT[4] \leftarrow 1863$.	

15. Let $k_1 = 147$, $k_2 = 169$, $k_3 = 580$, $k_4 = 216$, $k_5 = 974$, $k_6 = 124$. Suppose HT is of size 13 indexed $0,1,2,\ldots,12$. Define the function h: $\{k_1, k_2, k_3, k_4, k_5, k_6\} \rightarrow \{0,1,2,\ldots,12 \}$ by

$h(k_i) = k_i$ %13.

Now $h(k_1) = h(147) = 147$ % $13 = 4$. So the data of the student with ID 147 is stored in $HT[4]$. We construct the following table that shows the array position where each student's data is stored.

ID	h(ID)	$(h$(ID)$ + 1)$ % 13	$(h$(ID)$ + 2)$ % 13
147	4		
169	0		
580	8		
216	8	9	
974	12		
124	7		

Now if $HT[b]\leftarrow a$ means "store the data of the student with ID a into $HT[b]$," then

HT[4]←147,	HT[0]←169,	HT[8]←580,
HT[9]←216,	HT[12]←974,	HT[7]←124.

17. Let $k_1 = 5701$, $k_2 = 9302$, $k_3 = 4210$, $k_4 = 9015$, $k_5 = 1553$, $k_6 = 9902$, $k_7 = 2104$.

Let $k = 5701$. Now 5701 % 19 = 1. Thus, $h(5701) = 1$. So the data of the student with ID 5701 is stored in $HT[1]$.

Next consider $k = 9302$. Now 9302 % 19 = 11. Thus, $h(9302) = 11$. Because $HT[11]$ is empty, we store the data of the student with ID 9302 in $HT[11]$.

Consider $k = 4210$. Now 4210 % 19 = 11. Therefore, $h(4210) = 11$. Because $HT[11]$ is already occupied, we compute $g(4210)$. Now $g(4210) = 1 + (4210 \% 17) = 1 + 11 = 12$. So the probe sequence for 4210 is 11, (11 + 12) % 19 = 23 % 19 = 4. Because $HT[4]$ is empty, we store the data of the student with ID 4210 in $HT[4]$.

We apply this process and find the array position to store the data of each student. If a collision occurs for an ID, the following table shows the probe sequence of that ID.

ID	h(ID)	g(ID)	Probe sequence	
5701	1			
9320	11			
4210	11	12	11, 4, 16, 9, 2, ...	$g(4210) = 1 + (4210 \% 17) = 1 + 11 = 12$
9015	9			
1553	14			
9902	3			
2104	14	14	14, 9, 4, 18, ...	$g(2104) = 1 + (2104 \% 17) = 1 + 13 = 14.$

Thus,

HT[1]←5701,	HT[11]←9320,	HT[4]←4210,	HT[9]←9015,
HT[14]←1553,	HT[3]←9902,	HT[18]←2104.	

19. In open hashing, the hash table, HT, is an array of pointers. (For each j, $0 \le j \le HTSize - 1$, $HT[j]$ is a pointer to a linked list.) Therefore, items are inserted into and deleted from a linked list, and so item insertion and deletion are simple and straightforward. If the hash function is efficient, few keys are hashed to the same home position. Thus, average linked list is short, which results in a shorter search length.

21. Suppose there are 1000 items and each item requires 10 words of storage. Further suppose that each pointer requires 1 word of storage. We then need 1000 words for the hash table, 10,000 words for the items, and 1000 words for the link in each node. A total of 12,000 words of storage space, therefore, is required to implement the chaining. On the other hand, if we use quadratic probing, if the hash table size is twice the number of items, we need 20,000 words of storage.

23. The load factor $\alpha = 750 / 1001 \approx .75$.

    a. $(1/2)\{1 + (1/(1- \alpha))\} \approx 2.49$.

    b. $(-\log_2 (1- \alpha)) / \alpha \approx 2.66$.

    c. $(1 + \alpha /2) = 1.38$.

Chapter 10

1. List before the first iteration: 26, 45, 17, 65, 33, 55, 12, 18

   List after the first iteration: 12, 45, 17, 65, 33, 55, 26, 18

   List after the second iteration: 12, 17, 45, 65, 33, 55, 26, 18

   List after the third iteration: 12, 17, 18, 65, 33, 55, 26, 45

   List after the fourth iteration: 12, 17, 18, 26, 33, 55, 65, 45

   List after the fifth iteration: 12, 17, 18, 26, 33, 55, 65, 45

   List after the sixth iteration: 12, 17, 18, 26, 33, 45, 65, 55

   List after the seventh iteration: 12, 17, 18, 26, 33, 45, 55, 65

3. 3

5. 10, 12, 18, 21, 25, 28, 30, 71, 32, 58, 15

7. In Shellsort, the elements of the list are viewed as sublists at a particular distance. Each sublist is sorted, so that elements that are far apart move closer to their final position.

9. In the quicksort, the list is partitioned according to an element, called `pivot`, of the list. After the partition, the elements in the first sublist are smaller than `pivot`, and in the second sublist are larger than `pivot`. The mergesort partitions the list by dividing it into two sublists of nearly equal size by breaking the list in the middle.

11. a. 35

    b.   18, 16, 40, 14, 17, 35, 57, 50, 37, 47, 72, 82, 64, 67

13. During the first pass, six key comparisons are made. After two passes of the heapsort algorithm, the list is as follows:

    85, 72, 82, 47, 65, 50, 76, 30, 20, 60, 28, 25, 45, 17, 35, 14, 94, 100

15. Suppose that the elements of L are indexed $0, 1, \ldots, n - 1$. Starting at firstOutOfOrder = 1, the for loop executes $n - 1$ times. Because L is sorted, for each iteration of the for loop, the expression in the if statement evaluates to false, so the body of the if statement never executes. Thus, it follows that for each iteration of the for loop, the number of comparisons is 1 and the number of item assignments is 0. Because the for loop executes $n - 1$ times, it follows that the total number of comparisons is $n - 1$ and the number of item assignments is 0.

17.
```
template<class Type>
class unorderedLinkedList: public linkedListType<Type>
{
public:
    bool search(const Type& searchItem) const;
    void insertFirst(const Type& newItem);
    void insertLast(const Type& newItem);
    void deleteNode(const Type& deleteItem);
    void linkedInsertionSort();
    void mergeSort();

private:
    void divideList(nodeType<elemType>* first1,
                    nodeType<elemType>* &first2);
    nodeType<elemType>* mergeList(nodeType<elemType>* first1,
                                  nodeType<elemType>* first2);
    void recMergeSort(nodeType<elemType>* &head);
};
```

Chapter 11

1. a. false; b. true; c. false; d. false

3. $L_A = \{B, C, D, E\}$

5. $R_B = \{E\}$

7. A B C D E F G

9. 80-55-58-70-79

11.

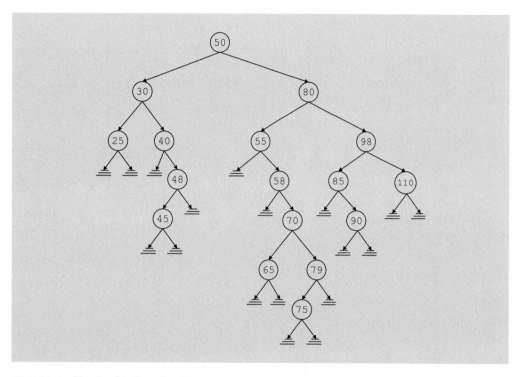

FIGURE I-4 Chapter 11 Exercise 11

13.

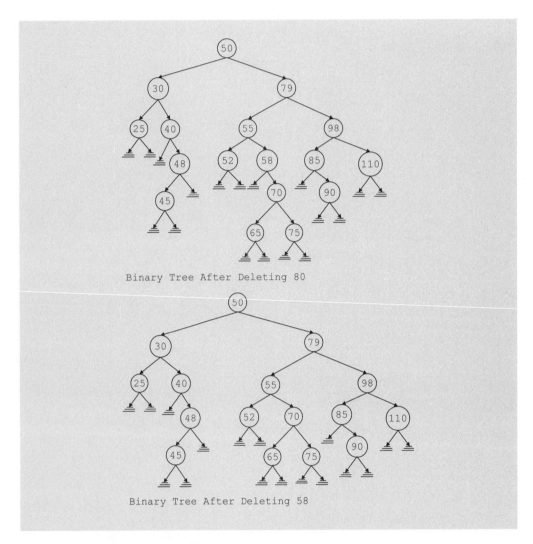

Binary Tree After Deleting 80

Binary Tree After Deleting 58

FIGURE I-5 Chapter 11 Exercise 13

15.

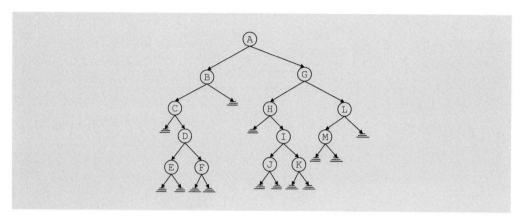

FIGURE I-6 Chapter 11 Exercise 15

17. The balance factor of the root node is 0.

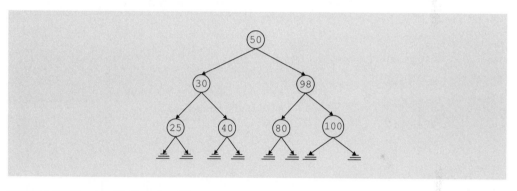

FIGURE I-7 Chapter 11 Exercise 17

19. The balance factor of the root node is 0.

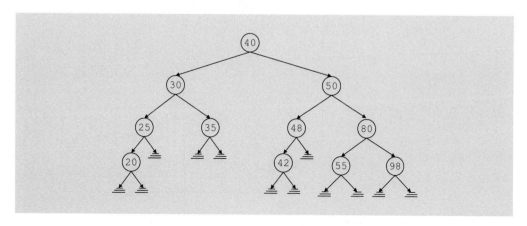

FIGURE I-8 Chapter 11 Exercise 19

21.

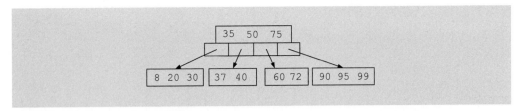

FIGURE I-9 Chapter 11 Exercise 21

23.

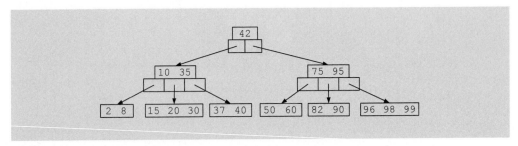

FIGURE I-10 Chapter 11 Exercise 23

25.

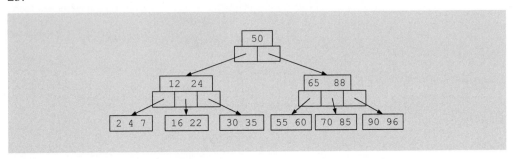

FIGURE I-11 Chapter 11 Exercise 25

27.

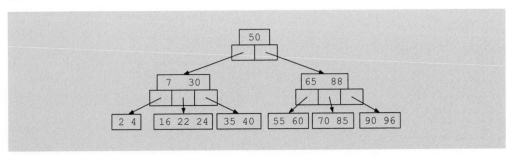

FIGURE I-12 Chapter 11 Exercise 27

Chapter 12

1.
$$\begin{bmatrix} 0 & 1 & 1 & 1 & 0 & 0 \\ 0 & 0 & 0 & 0 & 1 & 0 \\ 0 & 1 & 0 & 0 & 1 & 0 \\ 0 & 0 & 0 & 0 & 0 & 0 \\ 0 & 0 & 0 & 0 & 0 & 0 \\ 0 & 1 & 0 & 1 & 0 & 0 \end{bmatrix}$$

3. 0 1 4 2 3 5

5.
$$\begin{bmatrix} \infty & 10 & 6 & \infty & \infty & \infty & \infty \\ \infty & \infty & \infty & \infty & \infty & \infty & \infty \\ \infty & \infty & \infty & \infty & \infty & 4 & 8 \\ 3 & \infty & \infty & \infty & 11 & \infty & \infty \\ \infty & \infty & \infty & \infty & \infty & \infty & \infty \\ \infty & 6 & \infty & \infty & \infty & \infty & 10 \\ \infty & \infty & \infty & \infty & \infty & \infty & \infty \end{bmatrix}$$

7.

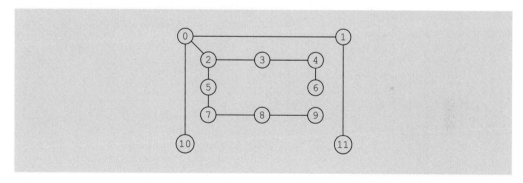

FIGURE I-13 Chapter 12 Exercise 7

9.

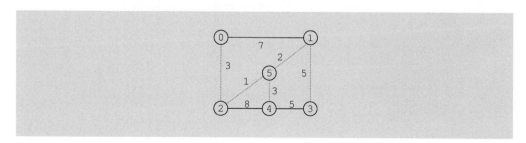

FIGURE I-14 Chapter 12 Exercise 9

```
Source Vertex: 0
Edges    Weight
(5, 1)     2
(0, 2)     3
(1, 3)     5
(5, 4)     3
(2, 5)     1

Minimal Spanning Tree Weight: 14
```

11. This graph has vertices of odd degree. For example, vertex 2 is of odd degree. Hence, this graph has no Euler circuit.

Chapter 13

1. A container is used to store data; an algorithm is used to manipulate the data stored in a container.

3. Duckey Donald

5. a. `map<string, string> stateDataMap;`

   b.
   ```
   stateDataMap.insert(make_pair("Nebraska", "Lincoln"));
   stateDataMap.insert(make_pair("New York", "Albany"));
   stateDataMap.insert(make_pair("Ohio", "Columbus"));
   stateDataMap.insert(make_pair("California", "Sacramento"));
   stateDataMap.insert(make_pair("Massachusetts", "Boston"));
   stateDataMap.insert(make_pair("Texas", "Austin"));
   ```

   c.
   ```
   map<string, string>::iterator mapItr;

   cout << left;
   cout << "The elements of stateDataMap:" << endl;
   for (mapItr = stateDataMap.begin();
        mapItr != stateDataMap.end(); mapItr++)
       cout << setw(15) << mapItr->first
            << setw(15) << mapItr->second << endl;
   cout << endl;
   ```

   d.
   ```
   map<string, string>::iterator mapItr;
   mapItr = stateDataMap.find("California");

   if (mapItr != stateDataMap.end())
       mapItr->second = "Los Angeles";
   ```

7. An STL function object contains a function that can be treated as a function using the function call operator.

9. 18 5 11 56 27 2

11. 0

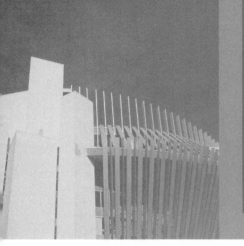

INDEX